THE
Expositor's
Bible
Commentary

with The New International Version

MATTHEW

CHAPTERS 1 THROUGH 12

THE
Expositor's Bible Commentary

with The New International Version

MATTHEW

CHAPTERS 1 THROUGH 12

D. A. Carson

ZondervanPublishingHouse

Grand Rapids, Michigan

A Division of HarperCollins*Publishers*

General Editor:

FRANK E. GAEBELEIN

Former Headmaster, Stony Brook School
Former Coeditor, *Christianity Today*

Associate Editors:

J. D. DOUGLAS

Editor, *The New International
Dictionary of the Christian Church*

RICHARD P. POLCYN

Matthew 1-12
Copyright © 1995 by D. A. Carson

Requests for information should be addressed to:
Zondervan Publishing House
Grand Rapids, Michigan 49530

Library of Congress Cataloging-in-Publication Data

The expositor's Bible commentary : with the New International Version of the Holy Bible /
Frank E. Gaebelein, general editor of series.
    p.   cm.
    Includes bibliographical references and index.
    Contents: v. 1-2. Matthew / D. A. Carson — Mark / Walter W. Wessel — Luke / Walter L.
Liefeld — John / Merrill C. Tenney — Acts / Richard N. Longenecker — Romans / Everett F.
Harrison — 1 and 2 Corinthians / W. Harold Mare and Murray J. Harris — Galatians and
Ephesians / James Montgomery Boice and A. Skevington Wood
    ISBN: 0-310-49961-5 (softcover : v. 1)
    1. Bible N.T. — Commentaries. I. Gaebelein, Frank Ely, 1899–1983.
BS2341.2.E96 1995
220.7-dc 00

94-47450
CIP

Printed in the United States of America

97 98 99 00 / ❖DH / 10 9 8 7 6 5 4 3

CONTENTS

Preface.. vii
Abbreviations.. ix
Transliterations.. xv
Matthew... 3

PREFACE

The title of this work defines its purpose. Written primarily by expositors for expositors, it aims to provide preachers, teachers, and students of the Bible with a new and comprehensive commentary on the books of the Old and New Testaments. Its stance is that of a scholarly evangelicalism committed to the divine inspiration, complete trustworthiness, and full authority of the Bible. Its seventy-eight contributors come from the United States, Canada, England, Scotland, Australia, New Zealand, and Switzerland, and from various religious groups, including Anglican, Baptist, Brethren, Free, Independent, Methodist, Nazarene, Presbyterian, and Reformed churches. Most of them teach at colleges, universities, or theological seminaries.

No book has been more closely studied over a longer period of time than the Bible. From the Midrashic commentaries going back to the period of Ezra, through parts of the Dead Sea Scrolls and the Patristic literature, and on to the present, the Scriptures have been expounded. Indeed, there have been times when, as in the Reformation and on occasions since then, exposition has been at the cutting edge of Christian advance. Luther was a powerful exegete, and Calvin is still called "the prince of expositors."

Their successors have been many. And now, when the outburst of new translations and their unparalleled circulation have expanded the readership of the Bible, the need for exposition takes on fresh urgency.

Not that God's Word can ever become captive to its expositors. Among all other books, it stands first in its combination of perspicuity and profundity. Though a child can be made "wise for salvation" by believing its witness to Christ, the greatest mind cannot plumb the depths of its truth (2 Tim. 3:15; Rom. 11:33). As Gregory the Great said, "Holy Scripture is a stream of running water, where alike the elephant may swim, and the lamb walk." So, because of the inexhaustible nature of Scripture, the task of opening up its meaning is still a perennial obligation of biblical scholarship.

How that task is done inevitably reflects the outlook of those engaged in it. Every biblical scholar has presuppositions. To this neither the editors of these volumes nor the contributors to them are exceptions. They share a common commitment to the supernatural Christianity set forth in the inspired Word. Their purpose is not to supplant the many valuable commentaries that have preceded this work and from which both the editors and contributors have learned. It is rather to draw on the resources of contemporary evangelical scholarship in producing a new reference work for understanding the Scriptures.

A commentary that will continue to be useful through the years should handle contemporary trends in biblical studies in such a way as to avoid becoming outdated when critical fashions change. Biblical criticism is not in itself inadmissible, as some have mistakenly thought. When scholars investigate the authorship, date, literary characteristics, and purpose of a biblical document, they are practicing biblical criticism. So also when, in order to ascertain as nearly as possible the original form of the text, they deal with variant readings, scribal errors, emendations, and other phenomena in the manuscripts. To do these things is essential to responsible exegesis and exposition. And always there is the need to distinguish hypothesis from fact, conjecture from truth.

The chief principle of interpretation followed in this commentary is the grammatico-historical one—namely, that the primary aim of the exegete is to make clear the meaning of the text at the time and in the circumstances of its writing. This endeavor to understand what in the first instance the inspired writers actually said must not be confused with an inflexible literalism. Scripture makes lavish use of symbols and figures of speech; great portions of it are poetical. Yet when it speaks in this way, it speaks no less truly than it does in its historical and doctrinal portions. To understand its message requires attention to matters of grammar and syntax, word meanings, idioms, and literary forms—all in relation to the historical and cultural setting of the text.

The contributors to this work necessarily reflect varying convictions. In certain controversial matters the policy is that of clear statement of the contributors' own views followed by fair presentation of other ones. The treatment of eschatology, though it reflects differences of interpretation, is consistent with a general premillennial position. (Not all contributors, however, are premillennial.) But prophecy is more than prediction, and so this commentary gives due recognition to the major lode of godly social concern in the prophetic writings.

THE EXPOSITOR'S BIBLE COMMENTARY is presented as a scholarly work, though not primarily one of technical criticism. In its main portion, the Exposition, and in Volume 1 (General and Special Articles), all Semitic and Greek words are transliterated and the English equivalents given. As for the Notes, here Semitic and Greek characters are used but always with transliterations and English meanings, so that this portion of the commentary will be as accessible as possible to readers unacquainted with the original languages.

It is the conviction of the general editor, shared by his colleagues in the Zondervan editorial department, that in writing about the Bible, lucidity is not incompatible with scholarship. They are therefore endeavoring to make this a clear and understandable work.

The translation used in it is the New International Version (North American Edition). To The International Bible Society thanks are due for permission to use this most recent of the major Bible translations. The editors and publisher have chosen it because of the clarity and beauty of its style and its faithfulness to the original texts.

Walter C. Kaiser, Jr. and Dr. Bruce K. Waltke for the Old Testament, and Dr. James Montgomery Boice and Dr. Merrill C. Tenney for the New Testament—the general editor expresses his gratitude for their unfailing cooperation and their generosity in advising him out of their expert scholarship. And to the many other contributors he is indebted for their invaluable part in this work. Finally, he owes a special debt of gratitude to Dr. Robert K. DeVries, publisher, The Zondervan Corporation; Richard P. Polcyn, manuscript editor; and Miss Elizabeth Brown, secretary, for their continual assistance and encouragement.

Whatever else it is—the greatest and most beautiful of books, the primary source of law and morality, the fountain of wisdom, and the infallible guide to life—the Bible is above all the inspired witness to Jesus Christ. May this work fulfill its function of expounding the Scriptures with grace and clarity, so that its users may find that both Old and New Testaments do indeed lead to our Lord Jesus Christ, who alone could say, "I have come that they may have life, and have it to the full" (John 10:10).

FRANK E. GAEBELEIN

ABBREVIATIONS

A. General Abbreviations

A	Codex Alexandrinus
Akkad.	Akkadian
ℵ	Codex Sinaiticus
Ap. Lit.	Apocalyptic Literature
Apoc.	Apocrypha
Aq.	Aquila's Greek Translation of the Old Testament
Arab.	Arabic
Aram.	Aramaic
b	Babylonian Gemara
B	Codex Vaticanus
C	Codex Ephraemi Syri
c.	*circa*, about
cf.	*confer*, compare
ch., chs.	chapter, chapters
cod., codd.	codex, codices
contra	in contrast to
D	Codex Bezae
DSS	Dead Sea Scrolls (see E.)
ed., edd.	edited, edition, editor; editions
e.g.	*exempli gratia*, for example
Egyp.	Egyptian
et al.	*et alii*, and others
EV	English Versions of the Bible
fem.	feminine
ff.	following (verses, pages, etc.)
fl.	flourished
ft.	foot, feet
gen.	genitive
Gr.	Greek
Heb.	Hebrew
Hitt.	Hittite
ibid.	*ibidem*, in the same place
id.	*idem*, the same
i.e.	*id est*, that is
impf.	imperfect
infra.	below
in loc.	*in loco*, in the place cited
j	Jerusalem or Palestinian Gemara
Lat.	Latin
LL.	Late Latin
LXX	Septuagint
M	Mishnah
masc.	masculine
mg.	margin
Mid	Midrash
MS(S)	manuscript(s)
MT	Masoretic text
n.	note
n.d.	no date
Nestle	Nestle (ed.) *Novum Testamentum Graece*
no.	number
NT	New Testament
obs.	obsolete
OL	Old Latin
OS	Old Syriac
OT	Old Testament
p., pp.	page, pages
par.	paragraph
Pers.	Persian
Pesh.	Peshitta
Phoen.	Phoenician
pl.	plural
Pseudep.	Pseudepigrapha
Q	Quelle ("Sayings" source in the Gospels)
qt.	quoted by
q.v.	*quod vide*, which see
R	Rabbah
rev.	revised, reviser, revision
Rom.	Roman
RVm	Revised Version margin
Samar.	Samaritan recension
SCM	Student Christian Movement Press
Sem.	Semitic
sing.	singular
SPCK	Society for the Promotion of Christian Knowledge
Sumer.	Sumerian
s.v.	*sub verbo*, under the word
Syr.	Syriac
Symm.	Symmachus
T	Talmud
Targ.	Targum
Theod.	Theodotion
TR	Textus Receptus
tr.	translation, translator, translated
UBS	Tha United Bible Societies Greek Text
Ugar.	Ugaritic
u.s.	*ut supra*, as above
v., vv.	verse, verses
viz.	*videlicet*, namely
vol.	volume
vs.	versus
Vul.	Vulgate
WH	Westcott and Hort, *The New Testament in Greek*

B. Abbreviations for Modern Translations and Paraphrases

AmT	Smith and Goodspeed, *The Complete Bible, An American Translation*	Mof	J. Moffatt, *A New Translation of the Bible*
ASV	American Standard Version, American Revised Version (1901)	NAB	The New American Bible
		NASB	New American Standard Bible
		NEB	The New English Bible
		NIV	The New International Version
Beck	Beck, *The New Testament in the Language of Today*	Ph	J. B. Phillips *The New Testament in Modern English*
BV	Berkeley Version (The Modern Language Bible)	RSV	Revised Standard Version
		RV	Revised Version — 1881–1885
JB	The Jerusalem Bible	TCNT	Twentieth Century New Testament
JPS	*Jewish Publication Society Version of the Old Testament*	TEV	Today's English Version
KJV	King James Version	Wey	*Weymouth's New Testament in Modern Speech*
Knox	R.G. Knox, *The Holy Bible: A Translation from the Latin Vulgate in the Light of the Hebrew and Greek Original*	Wms	C. B. Williams, *The New Testament: A Translation in the Language of the People*
LB	The Living Bible		

C. Abbreviations for Periodicals and Reference Works

AASOR	*Annual of the American Schools of Oriental Research*	BASOR	*Bulletin of the American Schools of Oriental Research*
AB	*Anchor Bible*	BC	Foakes-Jackson and Lake: *The Beginnings of Christianity*
AIs	de Vaux: *Ancient Israel*		
AJA	*American Journal of Archaeology*	BDB	Brown, Driver, and Briggs: *Hebrew-English Lexicon of the Old Testament*
AJSL	*American Journal of Semitic Languages and Literatures*	BDF	Blass, Debrunner, and Funk: *A Greek Grammar of the New Testament and Other Early Christian Literature*
AJT	*American Journal of Theology*		
Alf	Alford: *Greek Testament Commentary*	BDT	Harrison: *Baker's Dictionary of Theology*
ANEA	*Ancient Near Eastern Archaeology*	Beng.	Bengel's *Gnomon*
ANET	Pritchard: *Ancient Near Eastern Texts*	BETS	*Bulletin of the Evangelical Theological Society*
ANF	Roberts and Donaldson: *The Ante-Nicene Fathers*	BH	*Biblia Hebraica*
		BHS	*Biblia Hebraica Stuttgartensia*
ANT	M. R. James: *The Apocryphal New Testament*	BJRL	*Bulletin of the John Rylands Library*
A-S	Abbot-Smith: *Manual Greek Lexicon of the New Testament*	BS	*Bibliotheca Sacra*
		BT	*Babylonian Talmud*
AThR	*Anglican Theological Review*	BTh	*Biblical Theology*
BA	*Biblical Archaeologist*	BW	*Biblical World*
BAG	Bauer, Arndt, and Gingrich: *Greek-English Lexicon of the New Testament*	CAH	*Cambridge Ancient History*
		CanJTh	*Canadian Journal of Theology*
		CBQ	*Catholic Biblical Quarterly*
BAGD	Bauer, Arndt, Gingrich, and Danker: *Greek-English Lexicon of the New Testament* 2nd edition	CBSC	*Cambridge Bible for Schools and Colleges*
		CE	*Catholic Encyclopedia*
		CGT	*Cambridge Greek Testament*

CHS	Lange: *Commentary on the Holy Scriptures*	IDB	*The Interpreter's Dictionary of the Bible*
ChT	*Christianity Today*	IEJ	*Israel Exploration Journal*
DDB	*Davis' Dictionary of the Bible*	Int	*Interpretation*
Deiss BS	Deissmann: *Bible Studies*	INT	E. Harrison: *Introduction to the New Testament*
Deiss LAE	Deissmann: *Light From the Ancient East*	IOT	R. K. Harrison: *Introduction to the Old Testament*
DNTT	*Dictionary of New Testament Theology*	ISBE	*The International Standard Bible Encyclopedia*
EBC	*The Expositor's Bible Commentary*	ITQ	*Irish Theological Quarterly*
EBi	*Encyclopaedia Biblica*	JAAR	*Journal of American Academy of Religion*
EBr	*Encyclopaedia Britannica*	JAOS	*Journal of American Oriental Society*
EDB	*Encyclopedic Dictionary of the Bible*		
EGT	Nicoll: *Expositor's Greek Testament*	JBL	*Journal of Biblical Literature*
EQ	*Evangelical Quarterly*	JE	*Jewish Encyclopedia*
ET	*Evangelische Theologie*	JETS	*Journal of Evangelical Theological Society*
ExB	*The Expositor's Bible*		
Exp	*The Expositor*	JFB	Jamieson, Fausset, and Brown: *Commentary on the Old and New Testament*
ExpT	*The Expository Times*		
FLAP	Finegan: *Light From the Ancient Past*	JNES	*Journal of Near Eastern Studies*
GKC	Gesenius, Kautzsch, Cowley, *Hebrew Grammar,* 2nd Eng. ed.	Jos. Antiq.	Josephus: *The Antiquities of the Jews*
GR	*Gordon Review*	Jos. War	Josephus: *The Jewish War*
HBD	*Harper's Bible Dictionary*	JQR	*Jewish Quarterly Review*
HDAC	Hastings: *Dictionary of the Apostolic Church*	JR	*Journal of Religion*
		JSJ	*Journal for the Study of Judaism in the Persian, Hellenistic and Roman Periods*
HDB	Hastings: *Dictionary of the Bible*		
HDBrev.	Hastings: *Dictionary of the Bible,* one-vol. rev. by Grant and Rowley	JSOR	*Journal of the Society of Oriental Research*
		JSS	*Journal of Semitic Studies*
HDCG	Hastings: *Dictionary of Christ and the Gospels*	JT	*Jerusalem Talmud*
		JTS	*Journal of Theological Studies*
HERE	Hastings: *Encyclopedia of Religion and Ethics*	KAHL	Kenyon: *Archaeology in the Holy Land*
HGEOTP	Heidel: *The Gilgamesh Epic and Old Testament Parallels*	KB	Koehler-Baumgartner: *Lexicon in Veteris Testament Libros*
HJP	Schurer: *A History of the Jewish People in the Time of Christ*	KD	Keil and Delitzsch: *Commentary on the Old Testament*
HR	Hatch and Redpath: *Concordance to the Septuagint*	LSJ	Liddell, Scott, Jones: *Greek-English Lexicon*
		LTJM	Edersheim: *The Life and Times of Jesus the Messiah*
HTR	*Harvard Theological Review*		
HUCA	*Hebrew Union College Annual*	MM	Moulton and Milligan: *The Vocabulary of the Greek Testament*
IB	*The Interpreter's Bible*		
ICC	*International Critical Commentary*	MNT	Moffatt: *New Testament Commentary*

MST	McClintock and Strong: *Cyclopedia of Biblical, Theological, and Ecclesiastical Literature*	SJT	*Scottish Journal of Theology*
NBC	Davidson, Kevan, and Stibbs: *The New Bible Commentary*, 1st ed.	SOT	Girdlestone: *Synonyms of Old Testament*
		SOTI	Archer: *A Survey of Old Testament Introduction*
NBCrev.	Guthrie and Motyer: *The New Bible Commentary*, rev. ed.	ST	*Studia Theologica*
		TCERK	Loetscher: *The Twentieth Century Encyclopedia of Religious Knowledge*
NBD	J. D. Douglas: *The New Bible Dictionary*	TDNT	Kittel: *Theological Dictionary of the New Testament*
NCB	*New Century Bible*	TDOT	*Theological Dictionary of the Old Testament*
NCE	*New Catholic Encyclopedia*		
NIC	*New International Commentary*	THAT	*Theologisches Handbuch zum Alten Testament*
NIDCC	Douglas: *The New International Dictionary of the Christian Church*		
		ThT	*Theology Today*
NovTest	*Novum Testamentum*	TNTC	*Tyndale New Testament Commentaries*
NSI	Cooke: *Handbook of North Semitic Inscriptions*	Trench	Trench: *Synonyms of the New Testament*
NTS	*New Testament Studies*		
ODCC	*The Oxford Dictionary of the Christian Church*, rev. ed.	TWOT	*Theological Wordbook of the Old Testament*
		UBD	*Unger's Bible Dictionary*
Peake	Black and Rowley: *Peake's Commentary on the Bible*	UT	Gordon: *Ugaritic Textbook*
PEQ	*Palestine Exploration Quarterly*	VB	Allmen: *Vocabulary of the Bible*
PNF1	P. Schaff: *The Nicene and Post-Nicene Fathers* (1st series)		
		VetTest	*Vetus Testamentum*
		Vincent	Vincent: *Word-Pictures in the New Testament*
PNF2	P. Schaff and H. Wace: *The Nicene and Post-Nicene Fathers* (2nd series)	WBC	*Wycliffe Bible Commentary*
		WBE	*Wycliffe Bible Encyclopedia*
PTR	*Princeton Theological Review*	WC	*Westminster Commentaries*
RB	*Revue Biblique*	WesBC	*Wesleyan Bible Commentaries*
RHG	Robertson's *Grammar of the Greek New Testament in the Light of Historical Research*	WTJ	*Westminster Theological Journal*
		ZAW	*Zeitschrift für die alttestamentliche Wissenschaft*
		ZNW	*Zeitschrift für die neutestamentliche Wissenschaft*
RTWB	Richardson: *A Theological Wordbook of the Bible*		
SBK	Strack and Billerbeck: *Kommentar zum Neuen Testament aus Talmud und Midrasch*	ZPBD	*The Zondervan Pictorial Bible Dictionary*
		ZPEB	*The Zondervan Pictorial Encyclopedia of the Bible*
SHERK	*The New Schaff-Herzog Encyclopedia of Religious Knowledge*	ZWT	*Zeitschrift für wissenschaftliche Theologie*

D. Abbreviations for Books of the Bible, the Apocrypha, and the Pseudepigrapha

OLD TESTAMENT

				NEW TESTAMENT	
Gen	2 Chron	Dan		Matt	1 Tim
Exod	Ezra	Hos		Mark	2 Tim
Lev	Neh	Joel		Luke	Titus
Num	Esth	Amos		John	Philem
Deut	Job	Obad		Acts	Heb
Josh	Ps(Pss)	Jonah		Rom	James
Judg	Prov	Mic		1 Cor	1 Peter
Ruth	Eccl	Nah		2 Cor	2 Peter
1 Sam	S of Songs	Hab		Gal	1 John
2 Sam	Isa	Zeph		Eph	2 John
1 Kings	Jer	Hag		Phil	3 John
2 Kings	Lam	Zech		Col	Jude
1 Chron	Ezek	Mal		1 Thess	Rev
				2 Thess	

APOCRYPHA

1 Esd	1 Esdras	Ep Jer	Epistle of Jeremy
2 Esd	2 Esdras	S Th Ch	Song of the Three Children
Tobit	Tobit		(or Young Men)
Jud	Judith	Sus	Susanna
Add Esth	Additions to Esther	Bel	Bel and the Dragon
Wisd Sol	Wisdom of Solomon	Pr Man	Prayer of Manasseh
Ecclus	Ecclesiasticus (Wisdom of	1 Macc	1 Maccabees
	Jesus the Son of Sirach)	2 Macc	2 Maccabees
Baruch	Baruch		

PSEUDEPIGRAPHA

As Moses	Assumption of Moses	Pirke Aboth	Pirke Aboth
2 Baruch	Syriac Apocalypse of Baruch	Ps 151	Psalm 151
3 Baruch	Greek Apocalypse of Baruch	Pss Sol	Psalms of Solomon
1 Enoch	Ethiopic Book of Enoch	Sib Oracles	Sibylline Oracles
2 Enoch	Slavonic Book of Enoch	Story Ah	Story of Ahikar
3 Enoch	Hebrew Book of Enoch	T Abram	Testament of Abraham
4 Ezra	4 Ezra	T Adam	Testament of Adam
JA	Joseph and Asenath	T Benjamin	Testament of Benjamin
Jub	Book of Jubilees	T Dan	Testament of Dan
L Aristeas	Letter of Aristeas	T Gad	Testament of Gad
Life AE	Life of Adam and Eve	T Job	Testament of Job
Liv Proph	Lives of the Prophets	T Jos	Testament of Joseph
MA Isa	Martyrdom and Ascension	T Levi	Testament of Levi
	of Isaiah	T Naph	Testament of Naphtali
3 Macc	3 Maccabees	T 12 Pat	Testaments of the Twelve
4 Macc	4 Maccabees		Patriarchs
Odes Sol	Odes of Solomon	Zad Frag	Zadokite Fragments
P Jer	Paralipomena of Jeremiah		

E. Abbreviations of Names of Dead Sea Scrolls and Related Texts

CD	Cairo (Genizah text of the) Damascus (Document)	1QSa	Appendix A (Rule of the Congregation) to 1Qs
DSS	Dead Sea Scrolls	1QSb	Appendix B (Blessings) to 1QS
Hev	Nahal Hever texts	3Q15	Copper Scroll from Qumran Cave 3
Mas	Masada Texts	4QExod a	Exodus Scroll, exemplar "a" from Qumran Cave 4
Mird	Khirbet mird texts		
Mur	Wadi Murabba'at texts	4QFlor	Florilegium (or Eschatological Midrashim) from Qumran Cave 4
P	Pesher (commentary)		
Q	Qumran		
1Q, 2Q, etc.	Numbered caves of Qumran, yielding written material; followed by abbreviation of biblical or apocryphal book.	4Qmess ar	Aramaic "Messianic" text from Qumran Cave 4
		4QpNah	Pesher on portions of Nahum from Qumran Cave 4
QL	Qumran Literature		
1QapGen	Genesis Apocryphon of Qumran Cave 1	4QPrNab	Prayer of Nabonidus from Qumran Cave 4
1QH	*Hodayot* (Thanksgiving Hymns) from Qumran Cave 1	4QpPs37	Pesher on portions of Psalm 37 from Qumran Cave 4
1QIsa a,b	First or second copy of Isaiah from Qumran Cave 1	4QTest	Testimonia text from Qumran Cave 4
1QpHab	Pesher on Habakkuk from Qumran Cave 1	4QTLevi	Testament of Levi from Qumran Cave 4
1QM	*Milhamah* (War Scroll)	4QPhyl	Phylacteries from Qumran Cave 4
1QpMic	Pesher on portions of Micah from Qumran Cave 1	11QMelch	Melchizedek text from Qumran Cave 11
1QS	*Serek Hayyahad* (Rule of the Community, Manual of Discipline)	11QtgJob	Targum of Job from Qumran Cave 11

TRANSLITERATIONS

Hebrew

א	= '	ד	= $\underline{d}$	י	= y	ס	= s	ר	= r
ב	= b	ה	= h	כ	= k	ע	= '	שׂ	= $\acute{s}$
ב	= $\underline{b}$	ו	= w	ך כ	= $\underline{k}$	פ	= p	שׁ	= $\check{s}$
ג	= g	ז	= z	ל	= l	ף פ	= $\underline{p}$	ת	= t
ג	= $\underline{g}$	ח	= ḥ	ם מ	= m	ץ צ	= ṣ	ת	= $\underline{t}$
ד	= d	ט	= ṭ	ן נ	= n	ק	= q		

(ה) ָ	= $\hat{a}$ (h)	ָ	= $\bar{a}$	ַ	= a	ֲ	= ^{a}
ֵי	= $\hat{e}$	ֵ	= $\bar{e}$	ֶ	= e	ֱ	= ^{e}
ִי	= $\hat{i}$	ֹ	= $\bar{o}$	ִ	= i	ְ	= ^{e} (if vocal)
וֹ	= $\hat{o}$			ָ	= o	ֳ	= ^{o}
וּ	= $\hat{u}$			ֻ	= u		

Aramaic

' b g d h w z ḥ ṭ y k l m n s ' p ṣ q r ś š t

Arabic

' b t ṯ ǧ ḥ ḫ d ḏ r z s š ṣ ḍ ṭ ẓ ' ġ f q k l m n h w y

Ugaritic

' b g d ḏ h w z ḥ ḫ ṭ ẓ y k l m n s ś ' ġ ṗ ṣ q r š t ṯ

Greek

α	—	a	π	—	p	ai	—	ai
β	—	b	ρ	—	r	αὐ	—	au
γ	—	g	σ,ς	—	s	εἰ	—	ei
δ	—	d	τ	—	t	εὐ	—	eu
ε	—	e	υ	—	y	ηὐ	—	ēu
ζ	—	z	φ	—	ph	οἰ	—	oi
η	—	ē	χ	—	ch	οὐ	—	ou
θ	—	th	ψ	—	ps	υἰ	—	hui
ι	—	i	ω	—	ō			
κ	—	k				ῥ	—	rh
λ	—	l	γγ	—	ng	῾	—	h
μ	—	m	γκ	—	nk			
ν	—	n	γξ	—	nx	ᾳ	—	ā
ξ	—	x	γχ	—	nch	ῃ	—	ē
ο	—	o				ῳ	—	ō

MATTHEW

D.A. Carson

MATTHEW

Introduction

1. The Criticism of Matthew
2. History and Theology
3. The Synoptic Problem
4. Unity
5. Authorship
6. Date
7. Place of Composition and Destination
8. Occasion and Purpose
9. Canonicity
10. Text
11. Themes and Special Problems

    a. Christology
    b. Prophecy and fulfillment
    c. Law
    d. Church
    e. Eschatology
    f. The Jewish leaders
    g. Mission
    h. Miracles
    i. The disciples' understanding and faith

12. Literary Genre

    a. Gospel
    b. Midrash
    c. Miscellaneous

13. Bibliography

    a. Selected commentaries on Matthew
    b. Other selected works
    c. Selected articles
    d. Unpublished material

14. Structure and Outline
Maps

1. The Criticism of Matthew

The earliest church fathers to mention this Gospel concur that the author was the apostle Matthew. Papias's famous statement (cf. section 3) was interpreted to mean

"Matthew composed the *Logia* [Gospel?] in the Hebrew [Aramaic?] dialect and every one interpreted them as he was able." In other words the apostle first wrote his Gospel in Hebrew or Aramaic, and it was subsequently translated into Greek. Matthean priority was almost universally upheld; Mark was considered an abbreviation and therefore somewhat inferior. These factors—apostolic authorship (unlike Mark and Luke) and Matthean priority—along with the fact that Matthew preserves much of Jesus' teaching not found elsewhere, combined to give this first Gospel enormous influence and prestige in the church. With few exceptions these perspectives dominated Gospel study till after the Reformation.

The consensus could not last. An indication of its intrinsic frailty came in 1776 and 1778 when, in two posthumously published essays, A.E. Lessing insisted that the only way to account for the parallels and seeming discrepancies among the synoptic Gospels was to assume that they all derived independently from an Aramaic *Gospel of the Nazarenes*. Others (J.A. Eichorn, J.G. Herder) developed this idea; and the supposition of a Primal Gospel, whether oral or literary, began to gain influence. Meanwhile J.J. Griesbach (1745–1812) laid the foundations of the modern debate over the "synoptic problem" (cf. section 3) by arguing with some care for the priority of both Matthew and Luke over Mark, which was taken to be a condensation of the other two. In the middle of the nineteenth century, many in the Tübingen school adopted this view. As a result Matthew as an historical and theological source was elevated above the other Synoptics.

By the end of the nineteenth century, a new tide was running. Owing largely to the meticulous work of H.J. Holtzmann (1834–1910), the "two-source hypothesis" gained substantial acceptance (see EBC, 1:445–47, 510–14). By the beginning of the twentieth century, this theory was almost universally adopted; and subsequent developments were in reality mere modifications of this theory. B.H. Streeter,[1] advocating a "four-source hypothesis" that was essentially a detailed refinement of the two-source theory, argued that Luke's Gospel is made-up of a "Proto-Luke" that was filled out with Mark and Q. This raised the historical reliability of Proto-Luke to the same level as Mark. Streeter's hypothesis still has some followers, and today most scholars adopt some form of the two-source theory or the four-source theory. This consensus has recently been challenged (cf. section 3).

These predominantly literary questions combined with the substantial antisupernaturalism of some critics at the turn of the century to produce various reconstructions of Jesus' life and teaching (see EBC, 1:519–21). During the 1920s and 1930s, the source criticism implicit in these efforts was largely passed by in favor of form criticism (see EBC, 1:447–48). Philologists first applied this method to the "folk literature" of primitive civilizations, especially the Maoris. H. Gunkel and H. Gressmann then used it to classify OT materials according to their "form." New Testament scholars, especially K.L. Schmidt, M. Dibelius, and R. Bultmann (*Synoptic Tradition*), applied the method to the Gospels in an effort to explore the so-called tunnel period between Jesus and the earliest written sources. They began by isolating small sections of the Gospels that they took to be units of oral tradition, classifying them according to form (see EBC, 1:447). Only the passion narrative was taken as a connected account from the beginning. Oral transmission was thought to effect regular modifications common to all such literature (EBC, 1:444–45)—e.g.,

---

[1]*The Four Gospels* (London: Macmillan, 1924).

repetition engenders brevity in pronouncement stories and provides names in legends, rhythm and balance in didactic sayings, and multiple details in miracle stories. The form critics then assigned these forms to various *Sitze im Leben* ("life settings") in the church (see EBC, 1:511–13).

The historical value of any pericope was then assessed against a number of criteria. For instance, the "criterion of dissimilarity" was used to weed out statements attributed to Jesus that were similar to what Palestinian Judaism or early Christianity might have said. Only if a statement was "dissimilar" could it be ascribed with reasonable confidence to Jesus. The net result was a stifling historical skepticism with respect to the canonical Gospels. Many scholars used the same literary methods in a more conservative fashion (e.g., V. Taylor's great commentary on Mark); but the effect of form criticism was to increase the distance between our canonical Gospels and the historical Jesus, a distance increased yet further in Matthew's case because of the continued dominance of the two-source hypothesis. Few any longer believed that Matthew the apostle was the first evangelist.[2]

Following World War II a major change took place. Anticipated by Kilpatrick's study, which focused on the distinctives in Matthew's theology, the age of redaction criticism as applied to Matthew began with a 1948 essay by G. Bornkamm (printed in English as "The Stilling of the Storm in Matthew," *Tradition*, pp. 52–57). He presupposed Mark's priority and then in one pericope sought to explain every change between the two Gospels as a reflection of Matthew's theological interests and biases. Redaction criticism offered one great advantage over form criticism: it saw the evangelists, not as mere compilers of the church's oral traditions and organizers of stories preserved or created in various forms, but as theologians in their own right, shaping and adapting the material in order to make their own points. It became important to distinguish between "traditional" material and "redactional" material, i.e., between what came to the evangelist already formed and the changes and additions he made. In other words, while tradition may preserve authentic historical material, redactional material does not do so. It rather serves as the best way of discerning an evangelist's distinctive ideas. In his meticulous study of one pericope, Bornkamm sought to demonstrate a better method of understanding Matthew's theology—a method that could best be discerned by trying to understand how and why Matthew changed his sources (esp. Mark and Q).

Countless studies have poured forth in Bornkamm's wake, applying the same methods to virtually every pericope in Matthew. The translation of redaction-critical studies by G. Bornkamm, G. Barth, and H.J. Held (*Tradition*) has exercised profound influence in the world of New Testament scholarship; and in 1963 the first full-scale redaction-critical commentary on Matthew appeared (Bonnard). Bonnard handles his tools fairly conservatively. He frequently refuses to comment on historical questions and focuses on Matthew's theology and the reasons (based on reconstructed "life settings") for it. His work, which is immensely valuable, became the forerunner of several later English commentaries (notably Hill's).

Nevertheless a rather naive optimism regarding historical reconstruction has de-

---

[2]For a convenient history of the criticism of Matthew up to this point, see, in addition to some of the major introductions, W.G. Kümmel, *The New Testament: The History of the Investigation of Its Problems* (tr. S.McL. Gilmour and H.C. Kee [Nashville: Abingdon, 1972, and London: SCM, 1973]); Stephen Neill, *The Interpretation of the New Testament 1861–1961* (London and New York: Oxford University Press, 1964).

veloped. Virtually all recent writers on Matthew think they can read off from Matthew's redaction the theological beliefs either of Matthew's community or of the evangelist himself as he sought to correct or defend some part of his community. Kilpatrick argues that the book is catechetical, designed for the church of Matthew's time. Stendahl (*School of Matthew*) thinks the handling of the OT quotations reflects a "school" that stands behind the writing of this Gospel, a disciplined milieu of instruction. The major redaction-critical studies all attempt to define the historical context in which the evangelist writes, the community circumstances that call this Gospel into being (it is thought) between A.D. 80 and A.D. 100, and pay little useful attention to the historical context of Jesus. One need only think of such works as those of Trilling, Strecker (*Weg*), Cope (*Matthew*), Hare, Frankemölle, and the recent books by Thysman and Künzel, to name a few.[3]

Not all redaction critics interpret Matthew's reconstructed community the same way; indeed, the differences among them are often great. Moreover, several recent critics have argued that much more material in the Gospels (including Matthew's) is authentic than was recognized ten years ago.[4] Yet the wide diversity of opinion suggests at least some methodological and presuppositional disarray.

A modern commentary that aims primarily to explain the text must to some extent respond to current questions and the more so if it adopts a fairly independent stance.[5] For many of these questions greatly affect our understanding of what the text says.

2. History and Theology

Few problems are philosophically and theologically more complex than the possible relationships between history and theology. The broader issues in the tension between these two cannot be discussed here: e.g., How does a transcendent God manifest himself in space-time history? Can the study of history allow, in its reconstructions of the past, for authority and influence outside the space-time continuum? To what extent is the supernatural an essential part of Christianity, and what does it mean to approach such matters "historically"? What are the epistemological bases

---

[3]Raymond Thysman, *Communauté et directives ethiques. La catéchèse de Matthieu* (Gembloux: Duculot, 1974); G. Künzel, *Studien zum Gemeindeverständnis des Matthäus-Evangeliums* (Stuttgart: Calwer, 1978); and, for recent surveys of Matthean studies, R.P. Martin, *New Testament Foundations*, 2 vols. (Grand Rapids: Eerdmans, 1975–78), 1:224–43, and esp. the careful essay by Stanton ("Origin and Purpose").

[4]See, for instance, B.F. Meyer; R. Latourelle, *Finding Jesus Through the Gospels*, tr. A. Owen (New York: Alba, 1979); and the recent writings of such scholars as M. Hengel, J. Roloff, H. Schürmann, and P. Stuhlmacher.

[5]The various periods described are not completely sealed off from the other ones, and some did run against the tide of scholarly trends. From rather different perspectives, Schlatter and Stonehouse (*Witness of Matthew*) anticipated the more useful and reliable elements of redaction criticism, pointing out distinctive themes in Matthew's Gospel with deliberate caution and precision. On the other hand, when as recently as 1973 Hendriksen produced his large commentary on Matthew, he took relatively little note of recent developments; yet his work is doubtless of considerable help to pastors. Compare also the independent stances of Maier and of Albright and Mann.

for a system professing to be revealed religion?[6] Even the titles of recent books about Jesus show the chasm that separates scholar from scholar on these points.[7]

This section will therefore ask some preliminary methodological questions.[8] How appropriate and reliable are the various methods of studying the Gospels if we are to determine not only the theological distinctives of each evangelist but also something of the teaching and life of the historical Jesus? We must begin by avoiding many of the historical and theological disjunctions[9] notoriously common among NT scholars. An example is the recent essay by K. Tagama,[10] who arrives at his conclusion that the central theme of Matthew is "people and community" by insisting that all other important themes are mutually contradictory and therefore cancel one another out. But "contradiction" is a slippery category. As most commonly used in NT scholarship, it does not refer to logical contradiction but to situations, ideas, beliefs that on the basis of the modern scholar's reconstruction of early church history are judged to be mutually incompatible.[11]

Such judgments are only as convincing as the historical and theological reconstructions undergirding them; and too often historical reconstructions that in many cases have no other sources than the NT documents depend on illicit disjunctions. Did Jesus preach the nearness of the end of history and of the consummated kingdom? Then he could not have preached that the kingdom had already been inaugurated, and elements apparently denying this conclusion obviously spring from the church. Or did Jesus preach that the kingdom had already dawned? Then the apocalyptic element in the Gospels must be largely assigned to the later church. (On this particular problem, see comments at 3:2; 10:23; and ch. 24.) Was Jesus a proto-rabbi, steeped in OT law and Jewish tradition? Then Paul's emphasis on grace is entirely innovative. Or did Jesus break Jewish Halakah (rules of conduct based on traditional interpretations of the law)? Then clearly Matthew's emphasis on the law (e.g., 5:17-20; 23:1-26) reflects the stance of Matthew's church, or suggests that Matthew wishes to legislate for his church, without helping us come to grips with the historical Jesus. Better yet Matthew's Gospel may even be considered a Jewish-Christian reaction against "Paulinism."

All such disjunctive reconstructions are suspect. Historical "contradictions," as Fischer has shown, too often reside in the eye of the historian. Strange combina-

---

[6] On these and similar questions, see, in particular, E.E. Cairns, *God and Man in Time: A Christian Approach to Historiography* (Grand Rapids: Baker, 1979); G.H. Clark, *Historiography: Secular and Religious* (Nutley, N.J.: Craig, 1971); C.T. McIntyre, ed., *God, History and Historians: An Anthology of Modern Christian Views of History* (New York: Oxford University Press, 1977); J.A. Passmore, "The Objectivity of History," *Philosophical Analysis and History,* ed. W.H. Doty (New York: Harper and Row, 1966): 75–94; W.C. Smith, *Belief and History* (Charlottesville: University Press of Virginia, 1977); and A.C. Thiselton, *The Two Horizons* (Grand Rapids: Eerdmans, 1980).

[7] Contrast G. Vos, *The Self-Disclosure of Jesus: The Modern Debate About the Messianic Consciousness* (Grand Rapids: Eerdmans, 1954), and G. Vermes, *Jesus the Jew: A Historian's Reading of the Gospels* (London: Collins, 1973).

[8] Cf. H. Palmer, *The Logic of Gospel Criticism* (London: Macmillan, 1968), pp. 1ff.; B.F. Meyer, esp. pp. 76–110; Gundry, *Use of OT,* pp. 189ff.

[9] Cf. Fischer. A fine example is Schweizer's statement (*Matthew,* p. 11) that "the evangelist's intent . . . was theological rather than historical."

[10] "People and Community in the Gospel of Matthew," NTS 16 (1969–70): 149–62.

[11] This is dealt with at some length in Martin Hengel, *Acts and the History of Earliest Christianity* (London: SCM, 1979), pp. 35–68; Carson, "Historical Tradition," pp. 115–21.

tions of ideas may coexist side by side in one generation, even though a later generation cannot tolerate them and therefore breaks them up. So we need to be cautious
about pronouncing what ideas can be "historically" compatible. Acts and the early
Pauline Epistles show us considerable diversity in the fast-growing infant church, as
a number of NT studies attempt to explain.[12]

Reconstruction is a necessary part of historical inquiry; sometimes meticulous
reconstruction from a number of reliable documents shows that some further document is not what it purports to be. But as far as the Gospel of Matthew (or any of the
canonical Gospels) is concerned, we must frankly confess we have no access to the
alleged "Matthean [or Markan, Lukan, etc.] community" apart from the individual
Gospel itself. The numerous studies describing and analyzing Matthew's theology
against the background of Christianity and Judaism contemporary with Matthew's
"community" in A.D. 80–100 (cf. Stanton, "Origin and Purpose," ch.3) beg a host of
methodological questions. This is not to deny that Matthew's Gospel may have been
written within a community about A.D. 80, or may have addressed some such community; rather is it to argue the following points.

1. What Matthew aims to write is a Gospel telling us about Jesus, not a church
circular addressing an independently known problem.

2. There is substantial evidence that the early church was interested in the historical Jesus and wanted to know what he taught and why. Equally there is strong
evidence that the Gospels constitute, at least in part, an essential element of the
church's kerygmatic ministry, its evangelistic proclamation (Stanton, *Jesus of Nazareth*), each Gospel having been shaped for particular audiences.

3. It is therefore methodologically wrong to read off some theme attributed by
the evangelist to Jesus and conclude that what is actually being discussed is not the
teaching of Jesus but an issue of A.D. 80, unless the theme or saying can be shown
to be anachronistic.

4. Matthew's reasons for including or excluding this or that tradition, or for shaping his sources, must owe something to the circumstances he found himself in and
the concerns of his own theology. But it is notoriously difficult to reconstruct such
circumstances and commitments from a Gospel about Jesus of Nazareth.

5. Moreover, virtually all the themes isolated as reflections of A.D. 80 could in
fact reflect interests of any decade from A.D. 30 to 100. In the early thirties, for
instance, Stephen was martyred because he spoke against the law and the temple.
Similar concerns dominated the Jerusalem Council (A.D. 49) and demanded thought
both before and after the Jewish War (A.D. 66–70). The truth is that such themes as
law and temple, and even many christological formulations (see section 11), offer
very little help in identifying a "life-setting" for the church in Matthew's day. Although Matthean scholarship may advance by trying out new theories, no advance
that forces a Procrustean synthesis based on methodologically dubious deductions
constitutes genuine progress.

Today we are in a position to consider the proper if limited place of redaction
criticism. Since this method of study has been scrutinized elsewhere (cf. Carson,
"Redaction Criticism," and the literature cited there), only a few points need be
made here.

---

[12]Cf. D.A. Carson, "Unity and Diversity: On the Possibility of Systematic Theology," in Carson and
Woodbridge.

1. The "criteria of authenticity," as has often been pointed out,[13] are hopelessly inadequate. For instance, the "criterion of dissimilarity," viz., that only if a statement was "dissimilar" from what Palestinian Judaism or early Christianity might have said could it be ascribed with reasonable confidence to Jesus, can only cull out the distinctive or the eccentric, while leaving the characteristic untouched—unless one is prepared to argue that Jesus' teaching characteristically never resembled contemporary Judaism and was never adopted by the church.

2. The analysis of the descent of the tradition, though useful in itself, is marred by four major flaws. First, comparative studies in oral transmission have largely dealt with periods of hundreds of years, not decades. On any dating of the Gospels, some eyewitnesses were still alive when the evangelists published their books. Second, the work of several Scandinavian scholars[14] has drawn attention to the role of memory in Jewish education. Their work has been seriously criticized; but even their most perceptive critics[15] recognize that too little attention has been paid to the power of human memory before Guttenberg—a phenomenon attested in many third-world students today. More impressive yet, the detailed attack on form criticism by Güttgemanns[16] is so compelling that one wonders whether form criticism is of any value as a historical (as opposed to literary) tool. Oral traditions, especially religious oral traditions, are not conducive to tampering and falsification but are remarkably stable. Third, convincing reasons have been advanced for concluding that some written notes were taken even during Jesus' public ministry.[17] *Written* material, of course, necessarily fits into various "forms" or "genres"; but such genres must be considered quite separately from the "forms" of *oral* transmission and the shaping that takes place by this means. If traditions of Jesus' words and deeds were passed on by both oral and written forms, many of the historical conclusions of the form-critical model collapse. Fourth, classic form criticism is intrinsically incapable of dealing historically with several similar sayings of Jesus, since they all tend toward the same form.

3. More broadly, the fact that Jesus was an itinerant preacher (cf. comments at 4:23–25; 9:35–38; 11:21) is passed over too lightly. To attempt a tradition history of somewhat similar sayings, which the evangelists place in quite different contexts, overlooks the repetitive nature of itinerant ministry. Of course each case must be examined on its own merits and depends in some instances on source-critical considerations; but we shall observe how frequently this basic observation is ignored. See especially the introductory discussion on parables at 13:3a.

4. To deduce that all changes in Mark and Q (however Q be defined), including

---

[13]Cf. esp. R.T. France, "The Authenticity of the Sayings of Jesus," *History, Criticism and Faith*, ed. C. Brown (Downers Grove, Ill.: IVP, 1976), pp. 101–43; R.H. Stein, "The 'Criteria' for Authenticity," France and Wenham, 1:225–63; Hengel, *Acts and History*, esp. pp. 3–34.

[14]In particular, cf. H. Riesenfeld, "The Gospel Tradition and its Beginnings," *Studia Evangelica* 1 (1959): 43–65; B. Gerhardsson, *Memory and Manuscript: Oral Tradition and Written Transmission in Rabbinic Judaism and Early Christianity* (Lund: C.W.K. Gleerup, 1961).

[15]Viz., Davies, *Setting*, pp. 464ff.; Peter H. Davids, "The Gospels and Jewish Tradition: Twenty Years After Gerhardsson," France and Wenham, 1:75–99.

[16]E. Güttgemanns, *Candid Questions Concerning Gospel Form Criticism*, tr. W.H. Doty (Pittsburgh: Pickwick, 1979).

[17]Cf. esp. E.E. Ellis, "New Directions in Form Criticism," Strecker, *Jesus Christus*, pp. 299–315, basing itself in large part on the thought-provoking sociological analysis of H. Schürmann, "Die vorösterlichen Anfänge der Logientradition," *Traditionsgeschichtliche Untersuchungen zu den synoptischen Evangelien* (Düsseldorf: Patmos, 1968), pp. 39–65.

omissions and additions, are the result of exclusively theological motives fails to reckon with the extreme likelihood of a multiplicity both of reasons for introducing changes and of sources, oral and written, within the first few decades (cf. Luke 1:1–4) and with the possibility that the author was an apostle (cf. section 5). While apostolic authorship would not give the text more authority than nonapostolic authorship, it must affect our judgment of the role of oral and written sources in the making of this Gospel. These factors—multiplicity of sources and possible apostolic authorship—suggest that in most instances there is no compelling reason for thinking that material judged redactional is for that reason unhistorical.

5. Modern redaction criticism also suffers from dependency on a particular solution to the synoptic problem (cf. section 3).

6. Also, it fails to consider how many changes from Mark to Matthew (assuming Mark's priority) might owe something to stylistic predilections rather than theology. For example, F. Neirynck has clearly shown that Matthew's account of the feeding of the five thousand, often said to reflect more clearly than Mark the institution of the Eucharist, in reality turns out to be entirely consistent with the stylistic changes he introduces elsewhere.[18]

7. Too many redaction-critical studies develop an understanding of the theology of Matthew's Gospel solely on the basis of the changes, instead of giving adequate thought to the document as a whole. Surely what Matthew retains is as important to him as what he modifies. The possibility of distortion becomes acute when on the basis of changes Matthew's distinctive theology is outlined and then anything conflicting with this model is reckoned to be "unassimilated tradition" or the like. It is far wiser to check the "changes" again and determine whether they have been rightly understood and, avoiding a priori disjunctions, to seek to integrate them into all Matthew writes down.

Such considerations do not eliminate the need for redaction criticism. In God's providence we are able to compare the synoptic Gospels with one another, and such study helps us better understand each of them. Matthew's topical treatment of miracles (Matt 8–9), his chiastic arrangement of parables (Matt 13), the differences he exhibits when closely compared with Mark—these all help us identify his distinctives more precisely than would otherwise be possible. Thus no responsible modern commentary on the synoptic Gospels can avoid using redaction criticism. But redaction criticism, trimmed of its excesses and weaned from its radical heritage, throws only a little light on historical questions; and one must always guard against its dethroning what is essential by focusing on what is distinctive and idiosyncratic.

It is possible to approach the question of how much history is found in Matthew by examining the genre of literature—either of the Gospel as a whole or of some section of it. Perhaps a "Gospel" is not meant to convey historical information; perhaps certain stories in Matthew are "midrash" and, like parables, make theological points without pretending to be historical. Anticipating later discussion (section 12), we conclude that the evangelists, including Matthew, intended that their Gospels convey "historical" information. This does not mean they intended to write dispassionate, modern biographies. But advocacy does not necessarily affect truth telling: a Jewish writer on the Holocaust is not necessarily either more or less accurate because his family perished at Auschwitz. Nor is it proper in the study of

---

[18]"La rédaction Matthéenne et la structure du premier évangile," *De Jésus aux Évangiles*, ed. I. de la Potterie (Gembloux: Duculot, 1967), pp. 41–73, esp. p. 51.

any document professedly dealing with history to approach it with a neutral stance that demands proof of authenticity as well as proof of inauthenticity.[19] Goetz and Blomberg, in an adaptation of a Kantian argument, write:

> If the assumption was that no one ever wrote history for the sake of accuracy, then no fraudulent history could ever be written with the expectation that it would be believed. The process of deception is parasitic on the assumption that people normally write history with the intent of historical accuracy. People *must* (a) acknowledge the a priori truth that truth-telling is the logical backdrop to lying, and (b) *actually* assume that people tell the truth in order for a lie to be told with the expectation that it will be believed.[20]

So with any particular historian, including Matthew, the writer of history must be assumed reliable until shown to be otherwise. "The reader must make this a priori commitment if the practice of writing history is to be viable."[21] In other words, other things being equal, the burden of proof rests with the skeptic.

From this perspective harmonization, which currently has a very bad name in NT scholarship, retains a twofold importance: negatively, it is nothing more than one way of applying the coherence test for authenticity; and, positively, once we no longer insist that every Gospel distinctive is the result of theological commitment or that the only possible sources are Mark, Q, and a little undefined oral tradition, harmonization carefully handled may permit the illumination of one source by another, provided legitimate redaction-critical distinctions are not thereby obliterated.

This commentary endeavors to apply these observations and assessments to the Gospel of Matthew. Rigorous application would have trebled the length. Therefore certain sections and pericopes were singled out for more extensive treatment (cf., for instance, at 5:1; 6:9–13; 8:16–17; 13:3; 26:6, 17), in the hope that the positions outlined in this introduction could be grounded in the hard realities of the text. The aim must be to understand as closely as possible the Gospel of Matthew.

3. The Synoptic Problem

The recent return of the synoptic problem to center stage as the focus of much debate (see section 1) necessitates some assessment of the developments that impinge on questions of authorship, date, and interpretation of Matthew. One contributing factor to the debate is the quotation from Papias (c. A.D. 135) recorded by Eusebius (*Ecclesiastical History* 3.39.16). Several of Papias's expressions are ambiguous: "Matthew *synetaxeto* [composed? compiled? arranged?] the *logia* [sayings? Gospel?] in *hebraïdi dialektō* [in the Hebrew (Aramaic?) language? in the Hebrew (Aramaic?) style?]; and everyone *hērmēneusen* [interpreted? translated? transmitted?] them as he was able [contextually, who is 'interpreting' what?]." The early church understood the sentence to mean that the apostle Matthew first wrote his Gospel in Hebrew or Aramaic and then it was translated. But few today accept

---

[19]E.g., see Morna D. Hooker, "Christology and Methodology," NTS 17 (1970–71): 480–87.
[20]Stewart C. Goetz and Craig L. Blomberg, "The Burden of Proof," *Journal for the Study of the New Testament* 11 (1981): 39–63, esp. p. 52, emphasis theirs.
[21]Ibid.

this.[22] Although Matthew has Semitisms, much evidence suggests that it was first composed in Greek.

The most important attempts to understand this sentence from Papias include the following.[23]

1. Manson (*Sayings*, pp. 18ff.) has made popular the view that identifies the *logia* with sayings of Jesus found in Q. That would make Matthew the author of Q (a source or sources including approximately 250 verses common to Matthew and Luke), but not of this Gospel. Papias confused the two. This view falters on two facts. First, it cannot explain how an important apostolic source like the Q this theory requires could have so completely disappeared that there is no other mention of it, let alone a copy. Indeed, the entire Q hypothesis, however reasonable, is still only hypothesis. Second, Papias's two other instances of *logia* (recorded by Eusebius) suggest the word refers to both sayings and deeds of Jesus, while Q is made up almost exclusively of the former. From this perspective *logia* better fits the Gospel of Matthew than a source like Q.

2. This last criticism can also be leveled against the view that *logia* refers to OT "testimonia," a book of OT "proof-texts" compiled by Matthew from the Hebrew canon and now incorporated into the Gospel.[24] Furthermore, it is not certain that such "testimonia" ever existed as separate books; and in any case it would have been unnecessary to compile them in Hebrew and then translate them, since the LXX was already well established. Matthew demonstrably follows the LXX in passages where Mark has parallels (see section 11).

3. If by *logia* Papias meant our canonical Matthew,[25] then in the opinion of many scholars convinced that canonical Matthew was set down in Greek (e.g., Hill), Papias was plainly wrong. Either his testimony must be ignored as valueless or we must suppose that Papias was right as to the language but confused the Gospel with some other Semitic work, perhaps the apocryphal *Gospel According to the Hebrews*.

4. Kürzinger[26] offers a possible way out of the dilemma. He thinks *logia* refers to canonical Matthew but that *hebraïdi dialektō* refers, not to Hebrew or Aramaic language, but to Semitic style or literary form: Matthew arranged his Gospel in Semitic (i.e., Jewish-Christian) literary form dominated by Semitic themes and devices. In this view the last clause of Papias's statement cannot refer to translation, since language is no longer in view. Kürzinger points out that immediately before Papias's sentence about Matthew, he describes how Mark composed his Gospel by

---

[22]For general discussion of this difficult question, see the NT introductions and the literature cited below. For arguments against the view that canonical Matthew uses translation Greek, cf. also Nigel Turner, *Style* in J.H. Moulton, *A Grammar of New Testament Greek*, vol. 4 (Edinburgh: T. & T. Clark, 1976), pp. 37–38.

[23]For discussion, cf. Donald Guthrie, *New Testament Introduction*, 3d ed. (Downers Grove, Ill.: IVP, 1970), pp. 34–37.

[24]Cf. J.R. Harris, *Testimonies*, rev. ed., 2 vols. (Cambridge: University Press, 1920); F.C. Grant, *The Gospels: Their Origin and Their Growth* (New York: Harper, 1957), pp. 65, 144.

[25]So, among others, C.S. Petrie, "The Authorship of 'The Gospel According to Matthew': A Reconsideration of the External Evidence," NTS 14 (1967): 15–32.

[26]J. Kürzinger, "Das Papiaszeugnis und die Erstgestalt des Matthäusevangeliums," *Biblische Zeitschrift* 4 (1960): 19–38; id., "Irenäus und sein Zeugnis zur Sprache des Matthäusevangeliums," NTS 10 (1963): 108–15. The argument above diverges from Kürzinger at one or two minor points.

putting down Peter's testimony; and there Mark is called the *hērmēneutēs* of Peter. This cannot mean Mark was Peter's translator. It means he "interpreted" or "transmitted" (neither English word is ideal) what Peter said. If the same meaning is applied to the cognate verb in Papias's statement about Matthew, then it could be that everyone "passed on" or "interpreted" Matthew's Gospel to the world, as he was able.

It is difficult to decide which interpretation is correct. A few still argue that Matthew's entire Gospel was first written in Aramaic.[27] That view best explains the language of Papias, but it is not easy to reconcile with Matthew's Greek. Why, for instance, does he sometimes use a Greek source like the LXX? It cannot be argued that the alleged translator decided to use the LXX for all OT quotations in order to save himself some work, for only some of them are from the LXX. If this interpretation of Papias's statement does not stand, then Papias offers no support for Matthean priority.

The other two plausible interpretations of Papias are problematic. The view that Papias was referring to Q or some part of it offers the easiest rendering of *hebraïdi dialektō* ("in the Hebrew [Aramaic] language") but provides an implausible rendering for *logia*. Kürzinger's solution provides the most believable rendering of *logia* (viz., canonical Matthew) but a less likely interpretation of *hebraïdi dialektō* ("in the Semitic literary form"). Yet this rendering is possible (cf. LSJ, 1:401) and makes sense of the whole, even though Kürzinger's view has not been well received. The important point is that either of these last two views fits easily with a theory of Markan priority, which may also be hinted at in the fact that, as Eusebius preserves him, Papias discusses Mark at length before turning rather briefly to Matthew.

Quite apart from the testimony of Papias, the NT evidence itself demands some decisions, however tentative, regarding the synoptic problem. Its boundaries are well known. About 90 percent of Mark is found in Matthew, and very frequently Matthew agrees with Mark's ordering of pericopes as well as his wording (see esp. Matt 3–4; 12–28). Matthew's pericopes are often more condensed than Mark's but have a great deal of other material, much of it discourses. Of this material about 250 verses are common to Luke, and again the order is frequently (though by no means always) the same. In both instances the wording is often so similar throughout such lengthy passages that it is impossible to see oral fixation of the tradition as an adequate explanation. Some literary dependence is self-evident. It seems easiest to support the view that Matthew and Luke both depend on Mark rather than vice versa, largely because Matthew and Mark frequently agree against Luke, and Mark and Luke frequently agree against Matthew, but Matthew and Luke seldom agree against Mark. It is not the argument from order itself that is convincing, for all that proves is that Mark stands in the middle between the other two. What is more impressive is that close study finds it easier to explain changes from Mark to Matthew and Luke than the other way around.[28] The two-source hypothesis, despite its weaknesses—what, for instance, is the best explanation for the so-called minor

---

[27]Schlatter; P. Gaechter, both in his commentary, *Matthäus,* and in *Die literarische Kunst im Matthäusevangelium* (Stuttgart: Katholisches Bibelwerk, 1966); J.W. Wenham, "Gospel Origins," *Trinity Journal* 7 (1978): 112–34; and see n. 38, below.

[28]Cf. Christopher M. Tuckett, "The Argument from Order and the Synoptic Problem," *Theologische Zeitschrift* 36 (1980): 338–54.

agreements of Matthew and Luke against Mark if both Matthew and Luke depend on Mark?—is still more defensible than any of its competitors.[29]

Before pointing out a few of the historical and interpretive implications of this view, notice must be taken of the main alternatives.

1. By far the most common alternative is some form of the Griesbach hypothesis.[30] This argues for Matthean priority, dependence of Luke on Matthew (according to some), and Mark as an abbreviation of Matthew and Luke. Despite increasingly sophisticated defenses of this position, it remains implausible. It appears highly unlikely that any writer, let alone a first-century writer like Mark, would take two documents (in this case Matthew and Luke) and analyze them so carefully as to write a condensation virtually every word of which is in the sources—a condensation that is graphic, forceful, and not artificial (so Hill, *Matthew*, p. 28, citing E.A. Abbott's work in EBr 1879). The impressive list of literary analogies compiled by Frye,[31] who argues that Mark must be secondary because it is much shorter than Matthew and Luke and that literary parallels confirm that writers deeply dependent on written sources condense their sources, actually confounds his conclusion; for where he follows Mark, Matthew's account is almost always shorter. His greater total length—and even the occasional longer Matthean pericope—always comes from new material added to that from the Markan source. Frye therefore inadvertently supports the two-source hypothesis. Moreover the Griesbach hypothesis flies in the face of other evidence from Papias, who insists that Mark wrote his Gospel on the basis of material from Peter, not by condensing Matthew and Luke (Eusebius, *Ecclesiastical History* 3.39.15).

2. Gaboury and Léon-Dufour[32] argue that the pericopes preserving the same order in the triple tradition (i.e., in Matthew, Mark, and Luke) constitute a primary source on which all three synoptic Gospels have been built. But it is demonstrable that sometimes the evangelists chose topical arrangements quite different from their parallels (e.g., see at chs. 8–9); so why should it be assumed that all three synoptists conveniently chose to take over this alleged source without any change in topical arrangements?

3. Several British scholars adopt Markan priority but deny the existence of Q.[33]

---

[29]In addition to the standard NT introductions, cf. esp. Stonehouse, *Origins*, pp. 48–77, and the appendix by G.M. Styler in the forthcoming revised edition of Moule, *Birth of NT*.

[30]From the growing bibliography, particular mention may be made of W.R. Farmer, *The Synoptic Problem* (Dillsboro, N.C.: Western North Carolina Press, 1976); David L. Dungan, "Mark—The Abridgement of Matthew and Luke," *Jesus and Man's Hope* (Pittsburgh: Pittsburgh Theological Seminary, 1970), pp. 51–97; H.H. Stoldt, *Geschichte und Kritik des Markushypothese* (Göttingen: Vandenhoeck und Ruprecht, 1977); and several of the essays in *J.J. Griesbach: Synoptic and Text-Critical Studies 1776–1976*, edd. B. Orchard and Thomas R.W. Longstaff (Cambridge: University Press, 1978).

[31]Roland Mushat Frye, "The Synoptic Problems and Analogies in Other Literatures," *The Relationships Among the Gospels: An Interdisciplinary Dialogue*, ed. W.O. Walker, Jr. (San Antonio: Trinity University Press, 1978), pp. 261–302.

[32]A. Gaboury, *La structure des évangiles synoptiques* (SuppNovTest 22; Leiden: Brill, 1970); X. Léon-Dufour, "Redaktionsgeschichte of Matthew and Literary Criticism," *Jesus and Man's Hope* (Pittsburgh: Pittsburgh Theological Seminary, 1970), pp. 9–35.

[33]So Green; A.M. Farrer, "On Dispensing With Q," in Nineham, *Studies*, pp. 55–88; Goulder. This is quite different from B.C. Butler (*The Originality of St Matthew* [Cambridge: University Press, 1951]), who argued that Matthew was prior, Mark abridged Matthew, and Luke was dependent on Matthew for what we call Q material and on Mark for what Matthew and Mark had in common.

Parallels between Matthew and Luke are explained by saying that Luke read Matthew before composing his own Gospel. That is possible; but if so, he has hidden the fact extraordinarily well. Compare, for instance, Matthew 1–2 and Luke 1–2. Gundry (*Matthew*) holds to the existence of a somewhat expanded Q but argues as well that Luke used Matthew—and this explains the "minor agreements" between Matthew and Luke. But this view, though possible, is linked in Gundry's mind with his theory that sources shared by Matthew and Luke include even such matters as the Nativity story; and that is very doubtful.[34]

4. Rist[35] rejects both the two-source hypothesis and the Griesbach hypothesis and argues for the independence of Matthew and Mark. As many others have done, Rist focuses attention on 4:12–13:58, where there are numerous divergences in order between Matthew and Mark. He examines a short list of passages in the triple tradition where there is not only close verbal similarity but identical order and argues that in each case the order is either logical or the result of memory, not literary dependence. But Rist does not adequately weigh the impressive list of instances where Matthew agrees with Mark's order without close verbal similarity. Such order argues strongly for some kind of literary dependence, however the verbal dissimilarities be explained.

5. Others, in the hope of keeping Matthean priority alive, argue that his Gospel was first written in Aramaic; and this became a source for Mark, which in turn influenced the Greek rendering of Matthew.[36] This is possible, but we have already seen that Papias's testimony may not support a Semitic Matthew at all. And it remains linguistically improbable that the whole of Matthew was originally in Aramaic.

There are other proposed solutions to the synoptic problem, generally of much greater complexity.[37] But not only do they suffer from the improbability of some of their details, the theories as a whole are so complex as to be unprovable.

The two-source hypothesis remains the most attractive general solution. This does not mean that it can be proved with mathematical certainty or that all arguments advanced in its favor are convincing.[38] But some small details are very weighty. Gundry (*Use of OT*) has shown that the OT quotations and allusions Matthew and

---

[34]See at chs. 1–2, and D.A. Carson, "Gundry on Matthew: A Critical Review," *Trinity Journal* (1982): 71–91.

[35]J.M. Rist, *On the Independence of Matthew and Mark* (Cambridge: University Press, 1978).

[36]E.g., J.W. Wenham, n. 29; P. Benoit, *L'Evangile selon Saint Matthieu*, 4th ed. (Paris: du Cerf, 1972), pp. 27ff.; Pierson Parker, *The Gospel Before Mark* (Chicago: University of Chicago, 1953); L. Vaganay, *Le problème synoptique—une hypothèse de travail*. (Tournai: Desclée, 1954). Somewhat similar is the view of J.A.T. Robinson (*Redating the New Testament* [Philadelphia: Westminster, 1976], pp. 97–98). Others think the alleged Semitic original was written in Hebrew rather than Aramaic (e.g., Gaechter, *Matthäus*; Carmignac, pp. 33ff.). J. Munck ("Die Tradition über das Mt bei Papias," *Neotestamentica et Semitica* [SuppNovTest 6; Leiden: Brill, 1962], pp. 249ff.) disposes of the entire problem by supposing Papias was in error and that the early assumption of a Semitic source for Matthew developed in connection with the formation of the canon as a way to resolve the synoptic problem. Munck's proposal confuses content and purpose. Even if Papias and others were interested in explaining synoptic differences (a doubtful point), it does not follow that their "facts" are historically incorrect. It would be necessary to show they invented their "facts" in order to offer an explanation.

[37]E.g., J.C. O'Neill, "The Synoptic Problem," NTS 21 (1975): 273–85; P. Benoit, M.E. Boisward, and A. Lamouille, *Synopse des Quatre Evangiles en Français*, 3 vols. (Paris: du Cerf, 1977).

[38]D. Wenham, "Synoptic Problem" (pp. 8–17), exposes some of the weaker arguments—though not all his criticisms are equally telling.

Mark have in common are consistently from the LXX, whereas those found in Matthew alone are drawn from a variety of versions and textual traditions. It is singularly unlikely that Mark was condensing Matthew, for so consistent a collection of Matthew's OT quotations—only those from the LXX—seems too coincidental to be believed. The pattern is easy enough to understand if Matthew depended on Mark.[39]

Yet in itself the two-source hypothesis is almost certainly too simple. Source-critical questions are enormously complex;[40] many facets of the question demand tighter controls.[41] Moreover close study has convinced some careful scholars that the evidence does not warrant the degree of certainty with which many hold the two-source hypothesis.[42] Such uncertainty is unpopular; but it is scarcely more scientific to go beyond the evidence than to admit uncertainty where the evidence does not provide an adequate basis for anything more. Such hesitations are especially anathema to radical redaction critics, for every major redaction-critical study of Matthew rests on the two-source hypothesis. Their aim is to find out how Matthew changed Mark.

In view of the weaknesses inherent in a radical use of redaction criticism and the uncertainties surrounding the two-source hypothesis, this commentary adopts a cautious stance. The two-source hypothesis is sufficiently credible that we do not hesitate to speak of Matthew's changes of, additions to, and omissions from Mark. But such statements say little about historicity or about the relative antiquity of competing traditions (cf. B.F. Meyer, pp. 71–72). In some instances it is apparent that Matthew used not only Mark but Q (however Q is conceived), probably other sources, and perhaps his own memory as well. In some instances an excellent case can be made for Matthew's use of a source earlier than Mark. Any theory of literary dependence must also face subsidiary problems, such as the perplexing features of Luke's "central section" (see comments at Matt 19:1–2). Changes Matthew has introduced may sometimes be motivated by other than theological concerns; but in any case the total content of any pericope in Matthew's Gospel as a whole is a more reliable guide to determine distinct theological bent than the isolated change. As for dramatic diversity (see comments at 16:13–20; 19:16–30), the detailed differences must be treated and plausible reasons for the changes suggested. Rarely, however,

---

[39]Occasionally Gundry's judgment regarding textual affinities may be called in question, especially when he deals with brief allusions to the OT rather than explicit quotations, though the thrust of his argument is not lessened by these few points. D. Wenham ("Synoptic Problem," pp. 3–38) unsuccessfully attempts to reduce the cogency of Gundry's argument. Wenham points out that Mark almost always cites the OT on the lips of participants in his narrative, not in his own descriptions, and that Matthew normally uses the LXX when his participants cite the OT, even though his own use of the OT betrays a much broader array of textual affinities. Therefore it is possible, Wenham reasons, that Mark depended on Matthew; and Mark's consistent appeal to the LXX is explained by his decision to use OT (and therefore LXX) quotations primarily when they are on the lips of participants in his narratives. Wenham's critique, though clever, is not convincing. Not only are there exceptions to his observations, but, more importantly, Wenham deals only with explicit OT quotations, not with OT allusions that, though harder to handle, are more widely distributed.

[40]Cf. Palmer, *Gospel Criticism*, pp. 112–74.

[41]For instance, we speak of Q with little consensus of what is meant: cf. S. Schulz, *Q: Die Spruchquelle der Evangelisten* (Zürich: Theologischer Verlag, 1972); M. Devisch, "Le document Q source de Matthieu. Problematique actuelle," in Didier, pp. 71–97. Again, Fitzmyer (*Wandering Aramaen*, pp. 1ff., 85ff.) offers wise counsel on method in the search for Aramaic substrata underlying sayings of Jesus in the NT.

[42]See esp. E.P. Sanders, *The Tendencies of the Synoptic Tradition* (Cambridge: University Press, 1969).

are the solutions offered so dependent on the two-source hypothesis that a shift in scholarly opinion on the synoptic problem would irreparably damage them. The aim throughout has been to let Matthew speak as a theologian and historian independent of Mark, even if Mark has been one of his most important sources.

4. Unity

The question of the unity of Matthew's Gospel has little to do with source-critical questions. Instead it deals with how well the evangelist has integrated his material to form cohesive pericopes and a coherent whole. In sections very difficult to interpret (e.g., Matt 24), it is sometimes argued that the evangelist has sewn together diverse traditions that by nature are incapable of genuine coherence. Failing to understand the material, he simply passed it on without recognizing that some of his sources were mutually incompatible.

There are so many signs of high literary craftsmanship in this Gospel that such skepticism is unjustified. It is more likely, not to say more humble, to suppose that in some instances we may not understand enough of the first-century setting to be able to grasp exactly what the text says.

5. Authorship

Nowhere does the first Gospel name its author. The universal testimony of the early church is that the apostle Matthew wrote it, and our earliest textual witnesses attribute it to him (*KATA MATTHAION*). How much of that testimony depends on Papias is uncertain. We have already noted that many today think Papias is referring to some source of canonical Matthew rather than to the finished work or, alternatively, that Papias was wrong (cf. section 3). If Papias is right, the theory of Matthew's authorship may receive gentle support from passages like 10:3, where on this theory the apostle refers to himself in a self-deprecating way not found in Mark or Luke.

Modern literary criticism offers many reasons for rejecting Matthew's authorship. If the two-source hypothesis is correct, then (it is argued) it is unlikely that the eyewitness and apostle Matthew would depend so heavily on a document written by Mark, who was neither an apostle nor (for most events) an eyewitness. Moreover the reconstructions of canonical Matthew's life-setting, fostered by redaction criticism, converge on A.D. 80–100 in some kind of savage Jewish–Christian conflict. This is probably a trifle late to assume Matthew's authorship (though cf. traditions that say the apostle John composed his Gospel c. A.D. 90); and the details of the reconstructed settings discourage the notion. Kümmel (*Introduction*, p. 121) argues further than "the systematic and therefore nonbiographical form of the structure of Mt, the late-apostolic theological position and the Greek language of Mt make this proposal completely impossible." He concludes that the identity of the first evangelist is unknown to us but that he must have been a Greek-speaking Jewish Christian with some rabbinic knowledge, who depended on "a form of the Jesus tradition which potently accommodated the sayings of Jesus to Jewish viewpoints" (ibid.).

These reasons for rejecting Matthew's authorship are widely accepted today. So alternate proposals have sprung up. Kilpatrick (pp. 138–39) suggests that the early patristic tradition connecting the first Gospel with Matthew arose as a conscious community pseudonym by the church that wrote the Gospel, in order to gain acceptance and authority for it. Abel[43] argues that Matthew's extra material is so confused and contradictory that we must assume it represents the efforts of two separate individuals working independently of each other. Several redaction-critical studies have denied that the author was a Jew, feeling that the antipathy exhibited toward Jesus in this Gospel and the ignorance of Jewish life are so deep that the writer must have been a Gentile Christian.[44] Those who think Papias was referring to Q or to some other source used by Matthew are often prepared to say that the apostle composed the source if not the Gospel (e.g., Hill, *Matthew*). There are several other theories.

The objections are not so weighty as they at first seem. If what the modern world calls "plagiarism" (the wholesale takeover, without acknowledgment, of another document) was an acceptable literary practice in the ancient world, it is difficult to see why an apostle might not find it congenial. If Matthew thought Mark's account reliable and generally suited to his purposes (and he may also have known that Peter stood behind it), there can be no objection to the view that an apostle depended on a nonapostolic document. Kümmel's rejection of Matthew's authorship (*Introduction*, p. 121) on the grounds that this Gospel is "systematic and therefore nonbiographical" is a non sequitur because (1) a topically ordered account can yield biographical facts as easily as a strictly chronological account,[45] and (2) Kümmel wrongly supposes that apostolicity is for some reason incapable of choosing anything other than a chronological form. The alleged lateness of the theological position may be disputed at every point (see section 6 and this commentary).

Those who argue that the author could not have been a Jew, let alone an apostle, allege serious ignorance of Jewish life, including inability to distinguish between the doctrines of the Pharisees and the Sadducees (16:12) or, worse, thinking that the Sadducees were still an active force after A.D. 70 (22:23). But the second of these two passages has synoptic parallels (Mark 12:18; Luke 20:27; here Matthew has interpreted Mark's verb as a historical present); and neither Matthean passage denies that there are differences separating Pharisees and Sadducees—differences Matthew elsewhere highlights (22:23–33)—but merely insists that on some things the Pharisees and Sadducees could cooperate. This is scarcely surprising: after all, both groups sat in the same Sanhedrin. Politics and theology make strange bedfellows (see section 11.f). Other "glaring errors" (so Meier, *Vision*, pp. 17–23) prove equally ephemeral (e.g., Matthew's use of Zech 9:9; see comments at 21:4–5). Also Kilpatrick's suggestion of a conscious community pseudonym cannot offer any parallel.

The charge that the Greek of the first Gospel is too good to have come from a Galilean Jew overlooks the trilingual character of Galilee, the possibility that Matthew greatly improved his Greek as the church reached out to more and more Greek speakers (both Jews and Gentiles), and the discussion of Gundry (*Use of OT*, pp. 178–85), who argues that Matthew's training and vocation as a tax gatherer

---

[43]Ernest L. Abel, "Who Wrote Matthew?" NTS 17 (1970–71): 138–52.

[44]E.g., Meier, *Vision*, pp. 17–23; Poul Nepper-Christensen, *Das Matthäusevangelium: Ein judenchristliches Evangelium?* (Aarhus: Universitetsforlaget, 1958); Strecker, *Weg*, p. 34; van Tilborg, p. 171; R. Walker, p. 145.

[45]Not a few contemporary biographies treat certain parts of their subject's life in topical arrangements: e.g., A. Fraser, *Cromwell: Our Chief of Men* (St. Albans: Panther, 1975), esp. pp. 455ff.

(9:9–13; 10:3) would have uniquely equipped him not only with the languages of Galilee but with an orderly mind and the habit of jotting down notes, which may have played a large part in the transmission of the apostolic gospel tradition. Moule[46] wonders whether 13:52, which many take as an oblique self-reference by the evangelist, hides a use of *grammateus* that does not mean "teacher of the law" (NIV) but "clerk, secular scribe." "Is it not conceivable that the Lord really did say to that tax-collector Matthew: 'You have been a "writer" . . . ; you have had plenty to do with the commercial side of just the topics alluded to in the parables—farmer's stock, fields, treasure-trove, fishing revenues; now that you have become a disciple, you can bring all this out again—but with a difference.' "[47]

Moule proposes an apostle who was a secular scribe and note-taker and who wrote primarily in a Semitic language, leaving behind material that was arranged by another scribe, a Greek writer unknown to us. One may wonder if *grammateus*, used so often in the Jewish sense of "teacher of the law," can so easily be assigned a secular sense. But whatever its other merits or demerits, Moule's argument suggests that the link between this first Gospel and the apostle Matthew cannot be dismissed as easily as some have thought.

None of the arguments for Matthew's authorship is conclusive. Thus we cannot be entirely certain who the author of the first Gospel is. But there are solid reasons in support of the early church's unanimous ascription of this book to the apostle Matthew, and on close inspection the objections do not appear substantial. Though Matthew's authorship remains the most defensible position,[48] very little in this commentary depends on it. Where it may have a bearing on the discussion, a cautionary notice is inserted.

6. Date

During the first three centuries of the church, Matthew was the most highly revered and frequently quoted canonical Gospel.[49] The earliest extant documents referring to Matthew are the epistles of Ignatius (esp. *To the Smyrneans* 1.1 [cf. Matt. 3:15], c. A.D. 110–15). So the end of the first century or thereabouts is the latest date for the Gospel of Matthew to have been written.

The earliest possible date is much more difficult to nail down because it depends on so many other disputed points. If Luke depends on Matthew (which seems unlikely), then the date of Luke would establish a new *terminus ad quem* for Matthew; and the date of Luke is bound up with the date of Acts.[50] If the Griesbach hypothesis (cf. sections 1 and 3) is correct, then Matthew would have to be earlier

---

[46]C.F.D. Moule, "St. Matthew's Gospel: Some Neglected Features" *Studia Evangelica* 2 (1964): 91–99.

[47]Ibid., p. 98.

[48]Cf. Gaechter, *Matthäus;* E.J. Goodspeed, *Matthew, Apostle and Evangelist* (Philadelphia: Winston, 1959); Guthrie, *NT Introduction*, pp. 33–44; Maier; very cautiously, E.F. Harrison, *Introduction to the New Testament*, 2d ed. (Grand Rapids: Eerdmans, 1971), pp. 176–77; and esp. Gundry, *Matthew*, pp. 609–22; and Stonehouse, *Origins*, pp. 1–47.

[49]Cf. E. Masseaux, *Influence de l'Evangile de Saint Matthieu sur la littérature chrétienne avant Saint Irénée* (Louvain: Publications Universitaire de Louvain, 1950).

[50]Cf. esp. A.J. Mattill, Jr., "The Date and Purpose of Luke-Acts: Rackham Reconsidered," CBQ 40 (1978): 335–50.

than Mark. Conversely, if the two-source hypothesis is adopted, Matthew is later than Mark; and a *terminus a quo* is theoretically established. Even so there are two difficulties. First, we do not know when Mark was written, but most estimates fall between A.D. 50 and 65. Second, on this basis most critics think Matthew could not have been written till 75 or 80. But even if Mark is as late as 65, there is no reason based on literary dependence why Matthew could not be dated A.D. 66. As soon as a written source is circulated, it is available for copying.

Two other arguments are commonly advanced to support the view now in the ascendancy that Matthew was written between 80 and 100 (between which dates there is great diversity of opinion). First, many scholars detect numerous anachronistic details. Though many of these are discussed in the commentary, one frequently cited instance will serve as an example. It is often argued that Matthew transforms the parable of the great banquet (Luke 14:15–24) into the parable of the wedding banquet (Matt. 22:1–14); and the process of transformation includes an explicit reference to the destruction of Jerusalem in A.D. 70 (22:7). Therefore this Gospel must have been written after that. But the conclusion is much too hasty. Those who deny that Jesus could foretell the future concede that Mark predicts the Fall of Jerusalem (Mark 13:14; Matt 24:15), arguing that if Mark wrote about A.D. 65, he was so close to the events that he could see how political circumstances were shaping up. But on this reasoning Matthew could have done the same thing in 66.

More fundamentally it is at least doubtful that Matthew's parable (22:1–10) is a mere rewriting of Luke 14:15–24; more likely they are separate parables (cf. Stonehouse, *Origins*, pp. 35–42). And on what ground must we insist that Jesus could not foretell the future? That conclusion derives, not from the evidence, but from an antisupernatural presuppositionalism. Moreover the language of 22:7 derives from OT categories of judgment (cf. Reicke, "Synoptic Prophecies," p. 123), not from the description of an observer. One could almost say that the lack of more detailed description of the events of A.D. 70 argues for an earlier date. In any event, if it is legitimate to deduce from 22:7 a post-70 date, it must surely be no less legitimate to deduce from 5:23–24; 12:5–7; 23:16–22; and 26:60–61 a pre-70 date, when the temple was still standing. The absurdity of this contradictory conclusion must warn us against the dangers of basing the date of composition on passages that permit other interpretations.

Second, recent studies have tended to argue that the life-setting presupposed by the theological stance of the Gospel best fits the conditions of A.D. 80–100. It is more difficult to reconstruct a life-setting than is commonly recognized (cf. section 2). Many of the criteria for doing so are doubtful. Explicit references to "church" (16:18; 18:17–18) are taken to reflect an interest in later church order. But the authenticity of 16:18 has been ably defended by B.F. Meyer (see comments at 16:17–20). Moreover 18:17–18 says nothng about the details of order (e.g., elders or deacons are not mentioned) but only of broad principles appropriate to the earliest stages of Christianity. Persecution (24:9) and false prophets (24:11) are often taken to reflect circumstances of 80–100. Yet these circumstances appear as prophecies in Matthew and did not need to wait for 80, as Acts and the early Pauline Epistles make clear.

Though Matthew's Gospel seems to presuppose uneasy relations between church and synagogue, the Gospel is less anti-Jewish than anti-Jewish leaders and their position on Jesus (see section 11.f); and such a stance stretches all the way back to the days of Jesus' ministry. Significantly Matthew records more warnings against the

Sadducees than all other NT writers combined; and after A.D. 70 the Sadducees no longer existed as a center of authority. Other small touches seem to show a definite break with Judaism had not yet occurred;[51] and these agree with Reicke ("Synoptic Prophecies," p. 133), who says, "The situation presupposed by Matthew corresponds to what is known about Christianity in Palestine between A.D. 50 and *ca.* 64."

We must face the awkward fact that criteria such as Matthew's christology are not very reliable indices of Matthew's date (cf. section 11.a). They might easily allow a range from 40–100. Gundry (*Matthew*, pp. 599ff.) has an excellent discussion; because he believes Luke depends on Matthew and Luke-Acts was completed not later than 63, he argues that Matthew must be still earlier. Clearly this conclusion is only as valid as the hypothesis of Luke's dependence on Matthew, a hypothesis that does not seem well grounded. While surprisingly little in the Gospel conclusively points to a firm date, perhaps the sixties are the most likely decade for its composition.

7. Place of Composition and Destination

Most scholars take Antioch as the place of composition. Antioch was a Greek-speaking city with a substantial Jewish population; and the first clear evidence of anyone using the Gospel of Matthew comes from Ignatius, bishop of Antioch at the beginning of the second century. This is as good a guess as any. Yet we must remember that Ignatius depends more on John's Gospel and the Pauline Epistles than on Matthew. But this does not mean they were all written in Antioch.

Other centers proposed in recent years include Alexandria (van Tilborg, p. 172), Edessa,[52] the province of Syria,[53] and perhaps Tyre (Kilpatrick, pp. 130ff.) or Caesarea Maratima.[54] In each instance the grounds are inadequate (Stanton, "Origin and Purpose," ch. 5; Hill, *Matthew*). More plausible is Slingerland's proposal that Matthew 4:15; 19:1 show that the Gospel was written somewhere east of the Jordan (he specifies Pella, but this is an unnecessary and unprovable refinement); see commentary in loc. If he is right, then Antioch is ruled out.

Actually we cannot be sure of the first Gospel's place of composition. Still more uncertain is its destination. The usual assumption is that the evangelist wrote it to meet the needs of his own center—a not implausible view. But the evangelist may

---

[51]Cf. Robinson, *Redating the NT*, pp. 103–5, esp. p. 103: "Matthew's gospel shows all the signs of being produced for a community (and by a community) that needed to formulate, over against the main body of Pharisaic and Sadducaic Judaism, its own line on such issues as the interpretation of scripture and the place of the law, its attitude to the temple and its sacrifices, the sabbath, fasting, prayer, food laws and purification rites, its rules for admission to the community and the discipline of offenders, for marriage, divorce and celibacy, its policy toward Samaritans and Gentiles in a predominantly Jewish milieu, and so on. These problems reflect a period when the needs of co-existence force a clarification of what is the distinctively Christian line on a number of practical issues which previously could be taken for granted." (See further section 8.) This view differs from that of Hare, Walker et al., who think a decisive break had already come about by the time this Gospel was written.

[52]Bacon, *Studies in Matthew*, pp. 15, 36, 51; R.E. Osborne, "The Provenance of Matthew's Gospel," *Studies in Religion* 3 (1973): 22–25.

[53]E. Schweizer, *Matthäus und seine Gemeinde* (Stuttgart: KBW, 1974), pp. 138–39; Künzel, *Studien*, pp. 252ff.

[54]B.T. Viviano, "Where Was the Gospel According to Matthew Written?" CBQ 41 (1979): 533–46.

have been more itinerant than usually assumed; and out of such a ministry he may have written his Gospel to strengthen and inform a large number of followers and given them an evangelistic and apologetic tool. We do not know. The only reasonably certain conclusion is that the Gospel was written somewhere in the Roman province of Syria (so Bonnard, Filson, Hill, Kümmel [*Introduction*, pp. 119–20], and many others; for the area covered by the designation "Syria," see comment at 4:25).

8. Occasion and Purpose

Unlike many of Paul's epistles or even John's Gospel (20:30–31), Matthew tells his readers nothing about his purpose in writing or its occasion. To some extent the Gospel shows Matthew's purpose in the way it presents certain information about Jesus. But to go much beyond this and specify the kind of group(s) Matthew was addressing, the kind of problems they faced, and his own deep psychological and theological motivations, may verge on speculation. Three restraints are necessary.

1. It is unwise to specify too precise an occasion and purpose, because the possibility of error and distortion increases as one leaves hard evidence behind for supposition.

2. It is unwise to specify only one purpose; reductionism cannot do justice to the diversity of Matthew's themes.

3. Great caution is needed in reconstructing the situation in the church of Matthew's time from material that speaks of the historical Jesus (see sections 1–3). In one sense this may be legitimate, for in all probability Matthew did not compose his Gospel simply out of a dispassionate curiosity about history. He intended to address his contemporaries. But it does not necessarily follow that what he alleges occurred in Jesus' day is immediately transferable to his own day.

Nowhere are these restraints more important than in weighing recent discussion about the diverse emphases on evangelism in this Gospel. On the one hand, the disciples are forbidden to preach to others than Jews (10:5–6); on the other, they are commanded to preach to all nations (28:18–20). Because of this bifurcation, some scholars have suggested that Matthew is preserving the traditions of two distinct communities—one that remained narrowly Jewish and the other that was more outward looking. Others think Matthew had to walk a tightrope between conflicting perspectives within his own community and therefore preserves both viewpoints—a sort of committee report that satisfied neither side. Still others erect a more specific "occasion" for this tension, a conflict between the church and the synagogue over the place of Gentile mission, Matthew taking a mediating (not to say compromised) position whose aim was to avoid cleavage between the two groups.[55] Though such reconstructions cannot be ruled out, they suffer from a serious flaw. They fail to recognize that Matthew himself makes distinctions between what Jesus expects and

---

[55]There are many other reconstructions. For example, K.W. Clark ("The Gentile Bias in Matthew," JBL 66 [1947]: 165–72), followed by Nepper-Christensen (*Matthäusevangelium*) and Strecker (*Weg*, pp. 15–35), argues that the evangelist or final redactor must have been a Gentile addressing a Gentile Christian church. Schuyler Brown ("The Matthean Community and the Gentile Mission," NovTest 22 [1980]: 193–221) locates the Matthean church in a Greek-speaking area of Syria, after A.D. 70, when much Jewish Christianity was forced to move to Syria and therefore new crises in evangelism and conflicts with the Pharisees arose.

demands during his earthly ministry and what he expects and demands after his resurrection.

Matthew 10:5–6 tells us what Jesus required of his disciples in their first-recorded major assignment; it does not necessarily tell us anything about what was going on in Matthew's day. The reason Matthew includes 10:6 as well as 28:18–20, and all the texts akin to one passage or the other, may be to explain how Jesus began with his own people and moved outward from there. One might argue that Jesus' own example is the foundation of Paul's "first for the Jew, then for the Gentile" (Rom. 1:14–17). This change develops not merely on pragmatic grounds but as the outworking of a particular understanding of the OT (see comments at 1:1; 4:12–17; 8:5–13; 12:21; 13:11–17) and of the distinctive role of Jesus the Messiah in salvation history (see comments at 2:1–12; 3:2; 4:12–17; 5:17–20; 8:16–17; 10:16–20; 11:7–15, 20–24; 12:41–42; 13:36–43; 15:21–39; 21:1–11, 42–44; 24:14; 26:26–29, 64; 28:18–20). Matthew thus shows how from the nascent community during Jesus' ministry the present commission of the church developed.

If this is a responsible approach to the evidence, then we are not justified in postulating conflicting strands of tradition within the Matthean community. It may be that by this retelling of the changed perspective effected by Jesus' resurrection Matthew is encouraging Jewish Christians to evangelize beyond their own race. Or it may be that he is justifying before non-Christian Jews what he and his fellow Christian Jews are doing. Or it may be that he is explaining the origins of Christian mission to zealous Jewish-Christian personal evangelists who after the warmth of their initial experience want to learn about the historical developments and teaching of Jesus that made the Jewish remnant of his day the church of their own day. Or it may be that, though such questions have not yet arisen, Matthew forsees that they cannot be long delayed and, like a good pastor, decides to forestall the problem by clear teaching. Or it may be that Matthew has Gentile readers in mind. Or it may be that all these factors were at work because Matthew envisages an extensive and varied readership. Several other possibilities come to mind. But such precise reconstructions outstrip the evidence, fail to consider what other purposes Matthew may have had in mind, and frequently ignore the fact that he purports to talk about Jesus, not a Christian community in the sixth, eighth, or tenth decade of the first century.

Particularly unfortunate are several recent works that define the purpose of this Gospel in categories both reductionistic and improbable. Walker argues that this Gospel does not reflect specific church problems but that it was written as a piece of theological combat, designed to show that Israel has been totally rejected in the history of salvation and had been displaced by the church so completely that the Great Commission must be understood as a command to evangelize Gentiles only (see discussion at 28:18–20). The Jewish leaders are nothing but representative figures, and the Gospel as a whole has no interest in and little accurate information about the historical Jesus. Only rarely is Walker exegetically convincing; nowhere does he adequately struggle with the fact that all the disciples and early converts are Jews.

Frankemölle in his final chapter argues that Matthew's work is so different from Mark's—long discourses, careful structure, prologue, epilogue—that it is meaningless to say it is a "Gospel" in the same sense as Mark (see section 12). Instead, Matthew belongs to the literary *Gattung* (form or genre) to which Deuteronomy and Chronicles belong. Frankemölle (pp. 394ff.) cites several phrases (e.g., cf. Deut 31:1,

24; 32:44–45) used by Matthew to round off his own discourses; and from such evidence he concludes that Matthew's "Gospel" is in reality a "book of history," not of "salvation history" as normally understood, but of the community as it summarized its beliefs. Matthew, Frankmölle maintains, does not distinguish between the life and teaching of the historical Jesus and the present exalted Lord. In his "literary fiction" (p. 351), Matthew fuses the two. Thus Jesus becomes the idealized authority behind Matthew the theologian who here addresses his community. But Frankmölle overemphasizes formal differences between Mark and Matthew and neglects the substantial differences between Matthew and Deuteronomy or Chronicles. His investigation is far from even-handed.

Frankmölle's insistence that Matthew is a unified book is surely right. Yet a book may be theologically unified by appealing to prophecy-fulfillment and other salvation-historical categories. Theological unity does not entail ignoring historical data. Moreover neither Walker nor Frankemölle adequately recognizes that for most of his Gospel Matthew depends heavily on Mark and Q (however Q be understood). Matthew was creative, but not so creative as Walker and Frankemölle think.

Goulder offers a lectionary theory. Arguing somewhat along the lines of Carrington and Kilpatrick,[56] Goulder maintains that Matthew's purpose was to provide a liturgical book. He argues that the evangelist has taken the pattern of lections of the Jewish festal year as his base and developed a series of readings to be used in liturgical worship week by week. Mark, a lectionary book for a half-year cycle, has been expanded by Matthew (not the apostle) to a year-long lectionary; and Mark is Matthew's only source. Luke, dependent on Matthew, has also written a lectionary for a full year but has displaced the festal cycle followed by Matthew with the annual Sabbath cycle of readings. Q does not exist.

Despite Goulder's immense erudition, there is little to commend his thesis. We know very little of the patterns of worship in first-century Judaism.[57] At the end of the second century A.D., triennial cycles were used in some Jewish worship. But the annual cycles Goulder discerns behind Luke are almost certainly later than their triennial counterparts. As for Matthew, we have no evidence of a fixed "festal lectionary" in the first century; and even if it existed, it would have been connected with temple worship, with no evidence that it was ever connected with the synagogue worship Goulder's thesis requires (cf. Stanton, "Origin and Purpose," ch. 4). Not only is our knowledge of first-century *Jewish* liturgical custom very slender, our knowledge of *Christian* worship in the first century is even more slender. Thus we do not know whether Christian lectionary cycles—if they existed—developed out of Jewish lectionary cycles—if those cycles existed! Certainly by the time of Justin Martyr, the churches of which he had knowledge read the "memoirs of the apostles" (i.e., the Gospels) for "as long as time allowed" (*First Apology* 1.67), not according to some lectionary specification. Moreover, to make his pattern fit, Goulder must postulate lections in Matthew that vary enormously in length.[58] Goulder's thesis is unlikely to convince many.

---

[56]P. Carrington, *The Primitive Christian Calendar* (Cambridge: University Press, 1952); id., *According to Mark* (Cambridge: University Press, 1960); Kilpatrick, p. 100.

[57]Cf. Leon Morris, *The New Testament and the Jewish Lectionaries* (London: Tyndale, 1964).

[58]Cf. important critical reviews in Int 30 (1976): 91–94; JBL (1977): 453–55; and J.D.G. Dunn, *Unity and Diversity in the New Testament* (London: SCM, 1977), pp. 141–48.

Numerous studies characterized by more sober judgment have recently contributed to our understanding of Matthew's purposes. Many of these are referred to in the commentary. At the broadest level we may say that Matthew's purpose is to demonstrate (1) that Jesus is the promised Messiah, the Son of David, the Son of God, the Son of Man, Immanuel; (2) that many Jews, and especially the leaders, sinfully failed to perceive this during his ministry; (3) that the messianic kingdom has already dawned, inaugurated by the life, ministry, death, resurrection, and exaltation of Jesus; (4) that this messianic reign, characterized by obedience to Jesus and consummated by his return, is the fulfillment of OT prophetic hopes; (5) that the church, the community of those, both Jew and Gentile, who bow unqualifiedly to Jesus' authority, constitutes the true locus of the people of God and the witness to the world of the "gospel of the kingdom"; (6) that throughout this age Jesus' true disciples must overcome temptation, endure persecution from a hostile world, witness to the truth of the gospel, and live in deeply rooted submission to Jesus' ethical demands, even as they enjoy the new covenant, which is simultaneously the fulfillment of old covenant anticipation and the experience of forgiveness bestowed by the Messiah who came to save his people from their sins and who came to give his life a ransom for many.

Such a complex array of themes was doubtless designed to meet many needs: (1) to instruct and perhaps catechize (something facilitated by the careful arrangement of some topical sections; cf. Moule, *Birth*, p. 91); (2) to provide apologetic and evangelistic material, especially in winning Jews; (3) to encourage believers in their witness before a hostile world; and (4) to inspire deeper faith in Jesus the Messiah, along with a maturing understanding of his person, work, and unique place in the unfolding history of redemption.

9. Canonicity

As far as our sources go, the Gospel of Matthew was promptly and universally received as soon as it was published. It never suffered the debates that divided the Eastern church and the Western church over, for example, the Epistle to the Hebrews but was everywhere regarded as Scripture, at least from Ignatius (died 110) onward.

10. Text

Compared with that of Acts, the text of Matthew is fairly stable. Important variants do occur, however, and some of these are discussed. The most difficult textual questions in Matthew arise because it is a synoptic Gospel. This provides many opportunities for harmonization or disharmonization in the textual tradition (e.g., see comments at 12:47; 16:2–3; 18:10–11). Although harmonization is a secondary feature, this does not necessarily mean that every instance of possible harmonization must be understood as being secondary (e.g., see comments at 12:4, 47; 13:35). Certainly harmonization is more common in the sayings of Jesus than elsewhere. But much work remains to be done in this area, especially in examining the phenomenon of harmonization in conjunction with the synoptic problem (cf. section 3).[59]

11. Themes and Special Problems

We may consider Matthew's principal themes along with the special problems of this Gospel, because so many of Matthew's themes have turned into foci for strenuous debate. To avoid needless repetition, the following paragraphs do not so much summarize the nine themes selected as sketch in the debate and then provide references to the places in the commentary where these things are discussed.

a. Christology

Approaches to the distinctive elements of Matthew's christology usually run along one of three lines, and these are not mutually exclusive.

The first compares Matthew with Mark to detect what differences lie between the two wherever they run parallel. Perhaps the first important study along these lines was an essay by Styler.[60] He argues that Matthew's christology is frequently more explicit than Mark's (he compares, for instance, the two accounts of the Triumphal Entry, 21:1–11). This is surely right, at least in some instances. But it is much less certain that Matthew focuses more attention than Mark on ontology (see comments at 9:1–8; 19:16–17; cf. Hill, *Matthew*, pp. 64–66), at least in those pericopes treated by both evangelists.

The second approach examines the christological titles used in Matthew's Gospel. These are rich and diverse. "Son of David" appears in the first verse, identifying Jesus as the promised Davidic Messiah; and then the title recurs, often on the lips of the needy and the ill, who anticipate relief from him who will bring in the Messianic Age (see comment at 9:27). Matthew uses *kyrios* ("Lord") more often than Mark, and some have taken this to indicate anachronistic ascription of divinity to Jesus. But *kyrios* is a word with a broad semantic range. It often means no more than "sir" (e.g., 13:27). It seems fairer to say that Matthew frequently uses the word because it is vague. During Jesus' ministry before the Cross, it is very doubtful whether it was used as an unqualified confession of Deity. But because it is the most common LXX term for referring to God, the greater insight into Jesus' person and work afforded by the postresurrection perspective made the disciples see a deeper significance to their own use of *kyrios* than they could have intended at first. A somewhat similar but more complex ambiguity surrounds "Son of Man," which is discussed in the Excursus at 8:20. Other titles receive comment where they are used by the evangelist.

The third approach to Matthew's christology is the examination of broad themes, either in exclusively Matthean material (e.g., Nolan's study on Matt 1–2, which focuses on a christology shaped by the Davidic covenant), or throughout the Gospel (e.g., various studies linking messiahship to the Suffering Servant motif).[61] Some

---

[59]Cf. Fee, pp. 154–69; more broadly, cf. C.M. Martini, "La problématique générale du texte de Matthieu," in Didier, pp. 21–36.

[60]G.M. Styler, "Stages in Christology in the Synoptic Gospels," NTS 10 (1963–64): 398–409.

[61]E.g., B. Gerhardsson, "Gottes Sohn als Diener Gottes. Messias, *Agapē* and Himmelherrschaft nach dem Matthäusevangelium," ST 27 (1973): 73–106.

reference is made to these throughout the commentary. Doubtless it is best for these christological titles and themes to emerge from an inductive study of the text, for narrower approaches often issue in substantial distortion. For example, though Kingsbury (*Matthew*) ably demonstrates how important "Son of God" is in Matthew (see comments at 2:15; 3:17; 4:3; 8:29; 16:16; 17:5; 26:63), his insistence that it is the christological category under which, for Matthew's community, all the others are subsumed cannot be sustained.[62] Matthew offers his readers vignettes linked together in diverse ways; the resulting colorful mosaic is reduced to dull gray when we elevate one theme (a christological title or something else) to a preeminent place that suppresses others.

b. *Prophecy and fulfillment*

Untutored Christians are prone to think of prophecy and fulfillment as something not very different from straightforward propositional prediction and fulfillment. A close reading of the NT reveals that prophecy is more complex than that. The Epistle to the Hebrews, for instance, understands the Levitical sacrificial system to be prophetic of Christ's sacrifice, Melchizedek to point to Jesus as High Priest, and so on. In Matthew we are told that Jesus' return from Egypt fulfills the OT text that refers to the Exodus (2:15); the weeping of the mothers of Bethlehem fulfills Jeremiah's reference to Rachel weeping for her children in Rama; the priests' purchase of a field for thirty pieces of silver fulfills Scriptures describing actions performed by Jeremiah and Zechariah (27:9); and, in one remarkable instance, Jesus' move to Nazareth fulfills "what was said through the prophets" even though no specific text appears to be in mind (2:23). Add to this one other major peculiarity. A number (variously estimated between ten and fourteen) of Matthew's OT quotations are introduced by a fulfillment formula characterized by a passive form of *plēroō* ("to fulfill") and a text form rather more removed from the LXX than other OT quotations. These "formula quotations" are all asides of the evangelist, his own reflections (hence the widely used German word for them, *Reflexionszitate*). What explains these phenomena?

Such problems have been extensively studied with very little agreement.[63] When Matthew cites the OT, this commentary deals with many of these issues. In anticipation of these discussions, four observations may be helpful.

1. From very different perspectives, Gundry and Soarés Prabhu argue that Matthew is responsible for the formula quotations (the difference between them is that Gundry thinks the evangelist was the apostle Matthew, Soarés Prabhu does not). Wherever he follows Mark, Matthew uses the LXX; but he in no case clearly demonstrates a personal preference for the LXX by introducing closer assimilation. There is therefore no good a priori reason for denying that Matthew selected and sometimes translated the non-LXX formula quotations. Doubtless both Hebrew and

---

[62]Cf. the telling critique by D. Hill, "Son and Servant: An Essay on Matthean Christology," *Journal for the Study of the New Testament* 6 (1980): 2–16. Kingsbury maintains, for instance, that "Son of God" dominates the thought of one section of six chapters where the title does not once appear.

[63]See the bibliography in Doeve; Gundry, *Use of OT;* McConnell; Moo, "Use of OT," Rothfuchs; Soarés Prabhu; Stendahl, *School of Matthew;* Strecker, *Weg.* See also the helpful summaries and criticisms of F. Van Sebroeck, "Les citations d'accomplissement dans l'Evangile selon Matthieu d'après trois ouvrages récents," in Didier, pp. 107–30; cf. Longenecker, *Biblical Exegesis,* pp. 140–52; and Stanton, "Origin and Purpose," ch. 4.3.

Greek OT textual traditions were somewhat fluid during the first century (as the DSS attest); and so it is not always possible to tell where the evangelist is using a text form known in his day and where he is providing his own rendering. What does seem certain, however, is that there is no good reason to support the view that the fulfillment quotations arose from a Matthean "school" (Stendahl) or were taken over by the evangelist from a collection of testimonia (Strecker).

2. Though often affirmed, it does not seem very likely that the evangelists, Matthew included, invented their "history" in order to have stories corresponding to their favorite OT proof-texts. The question is most acute in Matthew 1–2 and 27:9 and is raised there. Several points, however, argue against a wholesale creation of traditions. The NT writers do not exploit much of the rich OT potential for messianic prediction.[64] The very difficulty of the links between story and OT text argues against the creation of the stories, because created stories would have eliminated the most embarrassing strains. The parallel of the DSS cannot be overlooked. Even when they treat the OT most tortuously, the Qumran covenanters do not invent "history" (cf. Gundry, Use of OT, pp. 193–204).

3. The ways the events surrounding Jesus are said to fulfill the OT varies enormously and cannot be reduced to a single label. Even the Jewish categories commonly applied need certain qualification (on "Midrash," cf. section 12).

Some of Matthew's fulfillment quotations are said to be examples of pesher exegesis (e.g., Stendahl, School of Matthew, p. 203; Longenecker, Biblical Exegesis, p. 143). Such rabbinical exegesis stresses revelation and authoritatively declares, "This event is the fulfillment of that prophecy" (e.g., Acts 2:16). But even here we must be careful. The clearest examples of pesher exegesis are found in 1QpHab. What is striking about its authoritative pronouncements is that the OT prophecy it refers to, Habakkuk, is interpreted exclusively in terms of the "fulfillments" it is related to, making its original context meaningless.[65] Even the most difficult passages in Matthew, such as 2:15, do not hint that the original OT meaning is void—in this case that the people of Israel were not called by God out of Egypt at the Exodus.

4. What must now be faced is a very difficult question: Even if Matthew does not deny the OT setting of the texts he insists are being fulfilled in Jesus, on what basis does he detect any relationship of prophecy to fulfillment? The verb pléroō ("to fulfill") is discussed in the commentary (see comments at 2:15 and esp. 5:17); but when it refers to fulfilling Scripture, it does not lose all teleological force except in rare and well-defined situations. But opinion varies as to exactly how these OT Scriptures point forward. Sometimes the OT passages cited are plainly or at least plausibly messianic. Often the relation between prophecy and fulfillment is typological: Jesus, it is understood, must in some ways recapitulate the experience of Israel or of David. Jesus must undergo wilderness testing and call out twelve sons of Israel as apostles. Even the kind of typology varies considerably. Yet the perception remains constant that the OT was preparing the way for Christ, anticipating him, pointing to him, leading up to him. When we ask how much of this forward-looking or "prophetic" aspect in what they wrote the OT writers themselves recognized, the answer must vary with the particular text. But tentative, nuanced judgments are

---

[64]Cf. C.H. Dodd, History and the Gospel (London: Nisbet, 1938), pp. 61–63.

[65]Cf. F.F. Bruce, Biblical Exegesis in the Qumran Texts (London: Tyndale; and Grand Rapids: Eerdmans, 1960), pp. 16–17.

possible even in the most difficult cases (e.g., see comments at 1:23; 2:15, 17–18, 23; 4:15–16; 5:17; 8:16–17; 11:10–11; 12:18–21; 13:13–15; 21:4–5, 16, 42; 22:44; 26:31; 27:9). Care in such formulations will help us perceive the deep ties that bind together the Old and New Testaments.

c. Law

Few topics in the study of Matthew's Gospel are more difficult than his attitude to the law. The major studies are discussed elsewhere (cf. esp. Stanton, "Origin and Purpose," ch. 4.4, and this commentary, esp. at 5:17–48); but we may summarize some aspects of the problem here.

The difficulties stem from several factors. First, several passages can be understood as staunch defenses of the law (e.g., 5:18–19; 8:4; 19:17–18) and even of the authority of the Pharisees and teachers of the law in interpreting it (23:2–3). Jesus' disciples are expected to fast, give alms (6:2–4), and pay the temple tax (17:24–27). Second, some passages can be seen as a softening of Mark's dismissal of certain parts of the law. The addition of the "except" clause in 19:9 and the omission of Mark 7:19b ("In saying this, Jesus declared all foods 'clean.' ") in Matthew's corresponding pericope (15:1–20) have convinced many that Matthew does not abrogate any OT command. Third, there are some passages where, formally at least, the letter of OT law is superseded (e.g., 5:33–37) or a revered OT institution appears to be depreciated and potentially superseded (e.g., 12:6). Fourth, there is one passage, 5:17–20, that is widely recognized to be programmatic of Matthew's view of the law. However, it embraces interpretive problems of extraordinary difficulty.

In light of these things, various theories have been proposed. Bacon (*Studies in Matthew*), followed by Kilpatrick (pp. 107–9), argues that the Gospel of Matthew presents a "new law" that is to the church what the Torah is to Judaism. The five discourses of Matthew (cf. section 14) became the new Pentateuch. Today few follow this theory; its thematic and formal links are just too tenuous. Some suggest that this Gospel reflects a Matthean church that has not yet broken away from Judaism, while others argue that the church has just broken free and now finds it necessary to define itself over against Judaism (cf. expressions such as "their teachers of the law," "their synagogues," or "your synagogues," when addressing certain Jews [e.g., 7:29; 9:35; 23:34]).

But such arguments are rather finespun. Does "their synagogue" imply a break with Judaism or distinctions within Judaism? The Qumran covenanters used the pronoun "their" of the Pharisees and mainline Judaism. Therefore could not Jesus himself have used such language to distinguish his position from that of his Jewish opponents without implying he was not a Jew? A liberal or high churchman in the Church of England may refer to their colleges, referring to Church of England training colleges reflecting evangelical tradition, without suggesting that any of the three principal groups does not belong to the Anglican communion. And if Jesus spoke in such terms and if Matthew reports this, then Matthew may also be consciously reflecting the circumstances of his own church. But if so, it still remains unclear whether his church (if it is in his mind at all) has actually broken free from Judaism (see further comments at 4:23; 7:29; 9:35; 10:17; 11:1; 12:9–10; 13:35 et al.).

Another example (8:4) is commonly taken to mean that the writer believes Jesus upholds even the ceremonial details of OT law, and that this reflects a conservative view of the continuing validity of the law in Matthew's community. This interpretation, though hard to prove, is logically possible. Alternatively one might also argue that 8:4 reflects a pre-A.D. 70 community, since after that offering temple sacrifices was impossible. Again, if Jesus said something like this, then Matthew's including it may not have been because of his community's conservatism but because it shows how Jesus used even ceremonial law to point to himself (see comment at 8:4).

It is very difficult to narrow down these various possibilities. Clearly they are also related to how one uses redaction criticism (cf. sections 1–3, 5, 7–8). Too frequently these methodological questions are not so much as raised, even when the most astounding conclusions are confidently put forward as established fact. Some argue that Matthew's church had so conservative a view of the OT law that the "evildoers" (lit., "workers of lawlessness") denounced in 7:23 are Pauline Christians (e.g., Bornkamm, *Tradition*, pp. 74–75). Quite apart from the authenticity of Jesus' saying and the danger of anachronism, this view misunderstands both Matthew and Paul. Matthew's attacks are primarily directed against Jewish leaders, especially the Pharisees, whose legal maneuvers blunt the power of the law and who fail to see the true direction in which the law pointed. They are, as the Qumran covenanters bitterly said, "expounders of smooth things" (CD 1:18).[66] As for Paul, doubtless many saw him as being antinomian. But he too spoke strongly about the kind of behavior necessary to enter the kingdom (Rom 8:14; 13:10; Gal 5:14).

Yet if Matthew attacks Pharisees, does this mean the Pharisees of Jesus' day, of Matthew's day, or of both? The least we can say is that Matthew chose to write a Gospel, not a letter. Since he chose to write about Jesus as the Messiah, the presumption must be that he intended to say something about Jesus' life and relationships. This leads us to ask whether some differences between Matthew and Paul are to be explained by the distinctive places in salvation history of their subject matter. Though he writes after Paul wrote Romans, Matthew writes about an earlier period. Undoubtedly he had certain readers and their needs in mind. Yet it is no help in understanding Matthew's treatment of the law to view the needs of his first readers from the viewpoint of his modern readers without first weighing the historical background of his book—viz., the life and teaching of Jesus.

Jesus' teaching about the law, whether gathered from Matthew or from all four Gospels, is not easy to define precisely. Sigal ("Halakah") has recently set forth an iconoclastic theory. He argues that the Pharisees of Jesus' day are not to be linked with the rabbis of the Mishnah (see section 11.f) but were a group of extremists wiped out by the events of A.D. 70. These extremists were opposed both by Jesus and by other teachers who occupied roles similar to his own. After all, ordination was unknown in Jesus' day, so there was no distinction between Jesus and other teachers. Jesus was himself a "proto-rabbi"—Sigal's term for the group that gave rise to the ordained rabbis of the post-Jamnian period (A.D. 85 on). All Jesus' legal decisions, Sigal says, fall within the range of what other proto-rabbis might say. Sigal tests this theory in Matthew's reports of Jesus' handling of the Sabbath (12:1–14) and divorce (19:1–12).

Sigal makes many telling points. His exegesis (cf. the fuller discussion in the commentary) of 5:17–20 and other test passages is not convincing, however, because he eliminates all christological claims (e.g., 12:8) as the church's interpolations into

---

[66]Several have pointed out the pun between $h^a l\bar{a}q\hat{o}t$ ("smooth things") and $h^a l\bar{a}\underline{k}\hat{o}t$ ("legal decisions affecting conduct"), the latter the aim of the Pharisees.

the narrative. He nowhere discusses, on literary or historical grounds, the authenticity of Jesus' christological claims but writes them off merely by referring to similar dismissals by other scholars. Yet the issue is crucial: if Jesus offered judgments concerning the law by making claims, implicit or explicit, concerning his messiahship, the function of the law in Jesus' teaching will certainly be presented differently from the way it would be if Jesus saw himself as no more than a "proto-rabbi." The commentary deals at length with this question (see on 5:17–20; 8:1–4, 16–17; 11:2–13; 12:1–14; 21; 13:35, 52; 15:1–20; 17:5–8; 19:3–12; 22:34–40; 27:51).

Doubtless we may link Matthew's treatment of the law with his handling of the OT (section 11.b). Matthew holds that Jesus taught that the law had a prophetic function pointing to himself. Its valid continuity lies in Jesus' own ministry, teaching, death, and resurrection. The unifying factor is Jesus himself, whose ministry and teaching stand with respect to the OT (including law) as fulfillment does to prophecy. To approach the problem of continuity and discontinuity—what remains unchanged from the Mosaic code—in any other terms is to import categories alien to Matthew's thought and his distinctive witness to Jesus (see esp. comments at 5:17–20; 11:7–15). Within this unifying framework, the problem passages mentioned at the beginning of this discussion can be most fairly explained; by it we may avoid the thesis that makes the double love commandment the sole hermeneutical key to Jesus' understanding of the OT (see comments at 22:34–40).

d. Church

The word *ekklēsia* ("church") occurs twice in Matthew (16:18; 18:17). Partly because it appears in no other Gospel, the "ecclesiasticism" of Matthew has often been overstressed.[67]

Certain things stand out. First, Matthew insists that Jesus predicted the continuation of his small group of disciples in a distinct community, a holy and messianic people, a "church" (see comment at 16:18). This motif rests on numerous passages, not just one or two texts of disputed authenticity. Second, Jesus insists that obeying the ethical demands of the kingdom, far from being optional to those who make up the church, must characterize their lives. Their allegiance proves false wherever they do not do what Jesus teaches (e.g., 7:21–23). Third, a certain discipline must be imposed on the community (see comments at 16:18–19; 18:15–18). But Matthew describes this discipline in principles rather than in details (there is no mention of deacons, elders, presbyteries, or the like), and therefore this discipline is not anachronistic provided we can accept the fact that Jesus foresaw the continuation of his community.

This third theme is much stronger in Matthew than in Mark or Luke. One might speculate on the pressures that prompted Matthew to include this material—apathy in the church, return to a kind of casuistical righteousness, infiltration by those not wholly committed to Jesus Messiah, the failure to discipline lax members. But this is speculation. The essential factor is that Matthew insists that the demand for a disciplined church goes back to Jesus himself.

---

[67]For a convenient summary of recent literature, cf. Stanton, "Origin and Purpose," ch. 4.2. Stanton neglects to mention the extraordinarily important work by B.F. Meyer (see comments at 16:17–19).

e. *Eschatology*

Matthew consistently distinguishes among four time periods: (1) the period of revelation and history previous to Jesus; (2) the inauguration of something new in his coming and ministry; (3) the period beginning with his exaltation, from which point on all of God's sovereignty is mediated through him, and his followers proclaim the gospel of the kingdom to all nations; (4) the consummation and beyond.

Many features of Matthew's eschatology are still being studied. The seven most important of these (the number may be eschatologically significant!) and the places where they are principally discussed in this commentary are (1) the meaning of peculiarly difficult verses (e.g., 10:23; 16:28); (2) the distinctive flavor of Matthew's dominant "kingdom of heaven" over against "kingdom of God" preferred by the rest of the NT writers (cf. comment at 3:2); (3) the extent to which the kingdom has already been inaugurated and the extent to which it is wholly future, awaiting the consummation (a recurring theme; cf. esp. ch. 13); (4) the bearing of the parables on eschatology (ch. 13, 25); (5) the relation between the kingdom and the church (another recurring theme; cf. esp. 13:37–39); (6) the sense in which Jesus saw the kingdom as imminent (see comments at ch. 24); (7) the Olivet Discourse (chs. 24–25).

f. *The Jewish leaders*

Two areas need clarification for understanding Matthew's treatment of the Jewish leaders. The first is the identification of the "Pharisees" at the time of Jesus. We may distinguish four viewpoints, each represented by able Jewish scholars.

1. The traditional approach is well defended by Guttmann,[68] who argues that the Pharisees were more effective leaders than the OT prophets. The prophets were uncompromising idealists; the Pharisees, whose views are largely reflected by their successors, the rabbis behind the Mishnah, were adaptable, adjusting the demands of Torah by a finely tuned exegetical procedure issuing in legal enactments designed to make life easier and clarify right conduct.

2. By contrast Neusner[69] insists that a chasm yawns between the rabbinic views reflected in Mishnah and pre-A.D. 70 Pharisaism. The Pharisees shaped the life of pre-70 Judaism by extending the purity rituals of the temple to the daily experience of every Jew.

3. Rivkin[70] argues that the Pharisees—a post-Maccabean and theologically revolutionary group—were men of considerable learning and persuasiveness. They developed the oral law, now largely codified in the Mishnah, and unwittingly departed radically from their OT roots. Rivkin denies that they had separatistic or ritualistic tendencies; their influence was broad and pervasive.

4. Sigal[71] argues for a complete disjunction between the Pharisees, whom he

---

[68]Alexander Guttmann, *Rabbinic Judaism in the Making: A Chapter in the History of the Halakah from Ezra to Judah I* (Detroit: Wayne State University, 1970).

[69]Jacob Neusner, *The Rabbinic Traditions of the Pharisees*, 3 vols. (Leiden: Brill, 1971). For a simplified treatment, cf. his *From Politics to Piety: The Emergence of Pharisaic Judaism* (Englewood Cliffs: Prentice-Hall, 1973).

[70]Ellis Rivkin, *A Hidden Revolution: The Pharisee's Search for the Kingdom Within* (Nashville: Abingdon, 1978).

[71]"Halakah"; id., *The Emergence of Contemporary Judaism*, vols. I.1; I.2, *The Foundations of Judaism*

identifies as the *perushim* ("separatists"), and the rabbis behind Mishnah. In Jesus' day the rabbis were not officially ordained: ordination had not yet been invented. That is why Jesus himself is addressed as "rabbi" in the Gospels (e.g., 26:49; Mark 9:5; 10:51; 11:21; John 1:38, 49; 3:2). He belonged to a class of "proto-rabbis," the forerunners of the ordained rabbis of the Mishnaic period. His opponents, the Pharisees, were extremists who died out after A.D. 70 and left virtually no literary trace.

The tentative assessment adopted in this commentary is that these competing interpretations of the evidence are largely right in what they affirm and wrong in what they deny. Sigal is almost certainly right in arguing that ordination was unknown in Jesus' day (cf. Westerholm, pp. 26–39), though there may have been informal procedures for recognizing a teacher of Scripture. There can be no simple equation of "Pharisee" and Mishnaic rabbi. But against Sigal, it is unlikely that the Pharisees were so separatistic that they did not embrace most if not all "proto-rabbis." The Gospels refer to every other major religious grouping—Sadducees, priests, scribes—and it is almost inconceivable that the evangelists should say almost nothing about the "proto-rabbis," the dominant group after A.D. 70, and vent so much criticism on a group (the Pharisees) so insignificant in Jesus' day that they disappeared from view after A.D. 70. The fairly rapid disappearance of the Sadducees after A.D. 70 is no parallel because much of their life and influence depended on the temple destroyed by the Romans; and in any case the evangelists do give us some description of their theological position.

As for Jesus, he cannot be reduced to a "proto-rabbi," training his followers to repeat his legal decisions. His messianic claims cannot so easily be dismissed. To onlookers he appeared as a prophet (21:11, 46).[72] Guttmann (n. 68) is right in saying that the Pharisees adapted the laws to the times and were effective leaders. The problem is that their minute regulations made ritual distinctions too difficult and morality too easy. The radical holiness demanded by the OT prophets became domesticated, preparing the way for Jesus' preaching that demanded a righteousness greater than that of the Pharisees (5:20). Though Neusner (n. 69) correctly detects the Pharisees' concern with ceremonial purity (cf. 15:1–12), his skepticism concerning the fixity of many oral traditions and the possibility of knowing more about the Pharisees is unwarranted. The evidence from Josephus cannot be so easily dismissed as Neusner would have us think. Even allowing for Josephus's own bias toward the Pharisees, his evidence so consistently demonstrates their wide influence in the nation, not to say their centrality during the Jewish War, that it is very difficult to think of them as a minor separatistic group (Sigal) or as exclusively concerned with ritual purity.

The Mishnah (c. A.D. 200) cannot be read back into A.D. 30 as if Judaism had not faced the growth of Christianity and the shattering destruction of temple and cultus. Nevertheless it preserves more traditional material than is sometimes thought. One suspects that the Pharisees of Jesus' day include the proto-rabbis, ideological forbears of the Mishnaic Tannaim (lit., "repeaters," i.e., the "rabbis" from roughly A.D. 70 to 200). In this view they included men every bit as learned and creative as the

---

from Biblical Origins to the Sixth Century A.D. (Pittsburgh: Pickwick, 1980). A somewhat similar dichotomy is adopted by John Bowker, *Jesus and the Pharisees* (Cambridge: University Press, 1973).

[72]Cf. B. Lindars, "Jesus and the Pharisees," *Donum Gentilicium*, edd. E. Bammel, C.K. Barrett, and W.D. Davies (Oxford: Clarendon, 1978), pp. 51–63, esp. pp. 62–63.

second-century rabbis. But they also included many lesser men, morally and intellectually, who were largely purged by the twin effects of the growth of Christianity and the devastation of A.D. 70. These events called forth a "counterreformation," whose legacy is Mishnah. Rivkin (n. 70) is undoubtedly right in seeing the Pharisees as learned scholars whose meticulous application and development of OT law massively influenced Judaism, though his identification of Pharisees with scribes and his handling of the development of oral law are simplistic.

We hold that the Pharisees were a nonpriestly group of uncertain origin, generally learned, committed to the oral law, and concerned with developing Halakah (rules of conduct based on deductions from the law). Most teachers of the law were Pharisees; and the Sanhedrin included men from their number as well (see comment at 21:23), though the leadership of the Sanhedrin belonged to the priestly Sadducees.

The second area needing clarification is the way Matthew refers to Jewish leaders. It is universally agreed that Matthew is quite strongly anti-Pharisaic. Recently, however, more and more scholars have argued that Matthew's picture of the Pharisees reflects the rabbis of the period A.D. 80–100, not the situation around A.D. 30. His grasp of the other Jewish parties, which largely fell away after A.D. 70, is shallow and sometimes wrong. Gaston thinks the depth of Matthew's ignorance, especially of the Sadducees, is "astonishing."[73]

The question is complex.[74] Certain observations, however, will qualify the charge of Matthew's ignorance.

1. If Matthew's sole target had been the rabbis of A.D. 80–100, designated "Pharisees," it is astonishing that they are virtually unmentioned during the Passion Week and the passion narrative when feeling against Jesus reached its height. What we discover is that the chief opponents are priests, elders, members of the Sanhedrin, which is just what we would expect in the vicinity of Jerusalem before A.D. 70. This demonstrates that Matthew is not entirely ignorant of historical distinctions regarding Jewish leaders; it calls in question the thesis that his opponents are exclusively Pharisees and urges caution in making similar judgments.

2. Matthew mentions the Sadducees more often than all the other evangelists combined. If Matthew was so ignorant of them, and if they were irrelevant to his alleged circumstances in A.D. 80–100, why did he multiply references to them?

3. Matthew demonstrates that he was aware of some of the Sadducees' doctrinal distinctives (see comment at 22:23–33). This should make us very cautious in evaluating the most difficult point—viz., that in five places Matthew uses the phrase "Pharisees and Sadducees" in a way that links them closely (3:7; 16:1, 6, 11, 11–12). This linking is peculiar to Matthew. The known antipathy between the two groups was sufficiently robust that many modern commentators have concluded this Gospel was written late enough and by someone far enough removed from the setting of A.D. 30 for this incongruity to slip into the text. But in addition to Matthew's historical awareness, two complementary explanations largely remove the difficulty.

First, the linking of Pharisees and Sadducees under one article in Matthew 3:7 may reflect, not their theological agreement, but their common mission. Just as the

---

[73]L. Gaston, "The Messiah of Israel as Teacher of the Gentiles," Int 29 (1975): 34.
[74]Cf. D.A. Carson, "Jewish Leaders in Matthew's Gospel: A Reappraisal," JETS 25 (1982): 161–74. For a concise presentation of the data, cf. Garland, pp. 218–21.

Sanhedrin raised questions about Jesus' authority, it is intrinsically likely they sent delegates to sound out John the Baptist. The Sanhedrin included both Pharisees and Sadducees (Acts 23:6); and their mutual distrust makes it likely that the delegation was made up of representatives from both parties. The fourth Gospel suggests this. The "Jews of Jerusalem" (who else but the Sanhedrin?) sent "priests and Levites" (John 1:19)—certainly Sadducees—to ask John who he was; but Pharisees were also sent (John 1:24). Matthew's language may therefore preserve accurate historical reminiscence. Something similar may be presupposed in 16:1. We must always remember that though the Pharisees and Sadducees could fight each other fiercely on certain issues, their political circumstances required that they work together at many levels.

Second, though the linking of the Pharisees and Sadducees in the remaining references (16:6, 11–12) appears to make their teaching common, the context demands restraint. In certain circumstances, a Baptist may warn against the "teaching of the Presbyterians and Anglicans," not because he is unaware of fundamental differences between them (or even among them!), but because he wishes to set their pedobaptism against his own views. Quite clearly in 16:5–12 Jesus cannot be denouncing everything the Pharisees and Sadducees teach, for some of what they teach he holds in common with them. The particular point of teaching in this context is their attitude toward Jesus and their desire to domesticate revelation and authenticate it—an attitude so blind it cannot recognize true revelation when it appears (see comment at 16:1–4). It is against this "yeast of the Pharisees and Sadducees" that Jesus warns his disciples; in his view both parties were guilty of the same error.

4. Categories for the Jewish leaders overlap in the Gospels, Matthew included. As far as we know, the Sanhedrin, for instance, was made up of Sadducees, Pharisees, and elders. The Sadducees were mostly priests. The elders were mostly lay nobility and probably primarily Pharisees. Thus "Pharisees" in the Sanhedrin were "laymen" in the sense that they were not priests; but many of them were scribes ("teachers of the law") and thus different from the elders. When 21:23 speaks of the chief priests and elders of the people coming to Jesus, it is probably referring to members of the Sanhedrin described in terms of their clerical status rather than their theological position. The ambiguities are considerable; but we must avoid indefensible disjunctions.

5. Our own ignorance of who the Pharisees were and of the distinctive beliefs of the Sadducees (we know them almost entirely through the writings of their opponents—"almost" because some scholars think that Sirach, for instance, is a proto-Sadducean document) should make us hesitate before ascribing "astonishing" ignorance to the evangelist. The astonishing ignorance may be our own. One suspects that in some instances Matthew's treatment of Jewish leaders is being pressed into a mold to suit a date of A.D. 80–100. The truth is that our knowledge of both Judaism and Christianity during that period has formidable gaps. Though Matthew may have been written then—though in my view this is unlikely—his treatment of Jewish leaders cannot be used to defend the late date view.

But is Matthew's polemic so harsh that he must be considered anti-Semitic (cf. the commentary at 23:1–36; 26:57–59)? The judgment of Légasse is sound.[75] Matthew's

---

[75]S. Légasse, "L' 'antijudaïsme' dans l'Evangile selon Matthieu," in Didier, pp. 417–28.

sternest denunciations are not racially motivated; they are prompted by the response of people to Jesus. These denunciations extend to professing believers whose lives betray the falseness of their profession (7:21–23; 22:11–14) as well as to Jews; the governing motives are concern for the perseverance of the Christian community and for the authoritative proclamation of the "gospel of the kingdom" to "all nations," Jew and Gentile alike (see comments at 28:18–20), to bring all to submission to Jesus Messiah.

g. Mission

It has long been recognized that the closing pericope (28:16–20) is fully intended to be the climax toward which the entire Gospel moves. By tying together some of Matthew's most dominant themes, these verses give them a new depth that reaches back and sheds light on the entire Gospel. For instance, the Great Commission is perceived to be the result of God's providential ordering of history (1:1–17) to bring to a fallen world a Messiah who would save his people from their sins (1:21); but the universal significance of Jesus' birth, hinted at in 1:1 and repeatedly raised in the flow of the narrative (e.g., see comments at 2:1–12; 4:14–16, 25; 8:5–13; 10:18; 13:36–52; 15:21–28; 24:9, 14) is now confirmed by the concluding lines.

We have already observed that the extent of the Great Commission has been limited by some—though on inadequate grounds—to Gentiles only (section 8; see comments at 28:18–20). Matthew does not trace the context of the people of God from a Jewish one to an exclusively Gentile one but from a Jewish context to a racially inclusive one. Unlike Luke (Luke 21:24) and Paul (Rom 11:25–27), Matthew raises no questions about Israel's future as a distinct people.

h. Miracles

The biblical writers do not see miracles as divine interventions in an ordered and closed universe. Rather, God as Lord of the universe and of history sustains everything that takes place under his sovereignty. Sometimes, however, he does extraordinary things; and then we in the modern world call them "miracles." Biblical writers preferred terms like "sign," "wonder," or "power." Parallels between Jesus and Hellenistic miracle workers are not so close as some form critics have thought (cf. Albright and Mann, pp. cxxiv–cxxxi). On the other hand, the value of miracles as proof of Jesus' deity is not so conclusive as some conservative expositors have thought.

Miracles in Matthew share certain characteristics with those in the other Synoptics, and these characteristics must be understood before Matthew's distinctives can be explored. Jesus' miracles are bound up with the inbreaking of the promised kingdom (8:16–17; 12:22–30; cf. Luke 11:14–23). They are part of his messianic work (4:23; 11:4–6) and therefore the dual evidence of the dawning of the kingdom and of the status of Jesus the King Messiah. This does not mean that Jesus did miracles on demand as a kind of spectacular attestation (see comments at 12:38–42; cf. John 4:48). Faith and obedience are not guaranteed by great miracles, though faith and God's mighty power working through Jesus are linked in several ways. Lack of faith may be an impediment to this power (e.g., 17:19–20), not because God's power is curtailed, but because real trust in him submits to his powerful reign and expects mercies from him (e.g., 15:28; cf. Mark 9:24).

"Nature miracles" (the stilling of the storm or the multiplication of loaves and fish) attest, not only the universal sweep of God's power, but may in some cases (calming the storm) provide the creation rebelling against God with a foretaste of restored order—an order to be climaxed by the consummation of the kingdom. In some cases (the multiplication of loaves and fish, the withered fig tree) miracles constitute a "prophetic symbolism" that promises unqualified fruition (the messianic banquet, the certainty of judgment) at the End.

Matthew's miracles are distinctive for the brevity with which they are reported. He condenses introductions and conclusions, omits secondary characters and the like (see comments at 8:1–4). Nevertheless it is too much to say, as Held does, "The miracles are not important for their own sakes, but by reason of the message they contain" (Bornkamm, *Tradition*, p. 210). This might almost suggest that the facticity of the miracles is of no consequence to Matthew provided their message is preserved. Matthew himself specifically disallows this (11:3–6). All the evangelists hold that miracles point beyond the mere factuality of wonderful events: in this Matthew is no different from the others. He simply shifts the balance of event and implication a little in order to stress the latter.

The particular themes most favored by Matthew in connection with Jesus' miracles are worked out in the commentary.

i. *The disciples' understanding and faith*

Ever since the work of G. Barth (in Bornkamm et al., *Tradition*, pp. 105ff.), many scholars have held that whereas in Mark the disciples do not understand what Jesus says till he explains it to them in secret, Matthew attributes large and instant understanding to the disciples. Indeed, this is what sets them apart from the crowd: the disciples understand, the outsiders do not. Where the disciples falter and must improve is not in their understanding but in their faith.

The thesis can be defended by a careful selection of the data, but it will not withstand close scrutiny. Apart from depending too much on the so-called messianic secret in Mark (see comments in this vol. at Mark 9:9), it does not adequately treat the disciples' request for private instruction (13:36), their failure to understand Jesus' teaching about his passion even after his explanations (e.g., 16:21–26; 17:23; 26:51–56), and the passages that deal with "stumbling" or "falling away." These are not peripheral matters; they are integral to what Jesus and Matthew say about discipleship.

The thesis also errs, not only for the two reasons mentioned above, but also for a third. Adopting a doctrinaire form of redaction criticism, it so stresses what the relevant passages reveal about Matthew's church that it blunts their real thrust. In particular the failure of the disciples to understand the significance of Jesus' passion and resurrection predictions is largely a function of the disciples' unique place in salvation history. They were unprepared before the events to accept the notion of a crucified and resurrected Messiah; not a few of Jesus' christological claims are sufficiently vague (cf. Carson, "Christological Ambiguities") that their full import could be grasped by those with a traditional Jewish mind-set only after Calvary and the empty tomb. To this extent the disciples' experience of coming to deeper understanding and faith was unique because it was locked into a phase of salvation history rendered forever obsolete by the triumph of Jesus' resurrection.

Matthew's readers, whether in the first century or today, may profit from studying the disciples' experience as he records it. But to try subjectively to imitate the disciples' coming to full faith and understanding following Jesus' resurrection is futile. Rather we should look back on this witness to the divine self-disclosure, observing God's wisdom and care as through his Son he progressively revealed himself and his purposes to redeem a fallen and rebellious race. Feeding our faith and understanding on the combined testimony of the earliest witnesses who tell how they arrived by a unique historical sequence at their faith and understanding, we shall learn to focus our attention, not on the disciples, but on their Lord. This is not to say that the disciples have nothing to teach us about personal growth; rather, it is to insist that we shall basically misunderstand this Gospel if we do not see that it deals with a unique coming to faith and understanding. This topic is so important that the commentary refers to it repeatedly (cf. 13:10–13, 23, 36, 43, 51–52; 14:15–17; 15:15–16; 16:21–28; 17:13, 23; 20:17–19, 22; 23:13–36; 24:1; 28:17). Elsewhere it has been comprehensively treated by Trotter.

12. Literary genre

The interpretation of any piece of literature is affected by an understanding of its genre. A sonnet, novel, parable, history, fable, free verse, or an aphorism must be read according to its literary form.

a. Gospel

What, then, is a Gospel? Many theories have been proposed and affinities discovered in other writings (e.g., apocalyptic literature, OT books, Graeco-Roman biographies, etc.). Recently Talbert[76] has argued that the Gospel belongs to the genre of Graeco-Roman biography. In a convincing rejoinder, Aune[77] has shown that Talbert has misunderstood not a few ancient sources and has arrived at his conclusions by adopting ambiguous categories that hide essential differences. Aune rightly insists that the Gospels belong in a class of their own. This does not mean that the Gospels have no relation to other genres. The truth is that " 'new' genres were constantly emerging during the Graeco-Roman period, if by 'new' we mean a recombination of earlier forms and genres into novel configurations."[78]

Thus our Gospels are made up of many pericopes, some belonging to recognized genres, others with close affinities to recognized genres. Each must be weighed, but the result is a flexible form that aims to give a selective account of Jesus, including his teaching and miracles and culminating in his death by crucifixion and his burial and resurrection. The selection includes certain key points in his career (his baptism, ministry, passion, and resurrection) and aims at a credible account of these historical events. At the same time the material is organized so as to stress certain subjects and motifs. The writing is not dispassionate but confessional—something the evangelists considered an advantage. Some of the material is organized along

---

[76]C.H. Talbert, *What is a Gospel? The Genre of the Canonical Gospels* (Philadelphia: Fortress, 1977).

[77]D.E. Aune, "The Problem of the Genre of the Gospels," France and Wenham, pp. 9–60; cf. R.H. Gundry, "Recent Investigations Into the Literary Genre 'Gospel,' " Longenecker and Tenney, pp. 97–114.

[78]Aune, "Problem of Genre," p. 48.

thematic lines, some according to a loose chronology; still other pericopes are linked by some combination of catchwords, themes, OT attestation, genre, and logical coherence. The result is not exactly a history, biography, theology, confession, catechism, tract, homage, or letter—though it is in some respects all these. It is a "Gospel," a presentation of the "good news" of Jesus the Messiah.

b. *Midrash*

Scholars have increasingly recognized the Jewishness of the NT and have therefore cultivated Jewish literary categories for understanding these documents. Among the most important of these categories is midrash. One application of this work, the lectionary theory of Goulder, has already been discussed (section 8). But the most recent development is the commentary by Gundry. He argues that Q is larger than is customarily recognized, embracing material normally designated "M" (cf. section 3), including the birth narratives in Matthew 1–2. What Matthew does, according to Gundry, is apply "midrashic techniques" to the tradition he takes over, adding nonhistorical touches to historical material, sometimes creating stories, designated "midrashim," to make theological points, even though the stories, like parables, have no historical referent.

Everything depends on definition. Etymologically "midrash" simply means "interpretation." But in this sense, every comment on another text is midrash—including this commentary. Such a definition provides no basis for saying that because Matthew relates midrashic stories in Matthew 1–2 they are not historically true. Most other definitions, however accurate, are not sufficient to yield Gundry's conclusion. Derrett (*NT Studies*, 2:205ff.), for instance, defines midrashic method in terms of its allusiveness to many sources, not in terms of historicity at all. Snodgrass defines midrash, not as a genre, but "as a process in which forms of tradition develop and enrich or intensify later adaptation of Old Testament texts."[79] Many other definitions have been offered.[80]

To compound the difficulty, the term seems to undergo a semantic shift within Jewish literature. By the time of the Babylonian Talmud (fourth century A.D.), midrash had developed a more specialized meaning akin to what Gundry clearly wants. Other Jewish commentaries, mainly the Qumran Pesharim,[81] were characterized by three things: (1) they attempted to deal systematically with every point in the text; (2) they limited themselves almost exclusively to the text; (3) they adopted a revelatory stance toward the text that identified virtually every point in the text with a point of fulfillment in the interpreter's day or later, without any sense of historical context. By contrast the midrashim worked through the text of Scripture more haphazardly, using Scripture as a sort of peg on which to hang discourse, stories, and other pieces to illuminate the theological meaning of the text. This was in conscious distinction from "peshat," the more "literal" meaning of the text. But in the first two centuries, it is very doubtful whether midrash had a

---

[79]Klyne R. Snodgrass, "Streams of Tradition Emerging From Isaiah 40:1–5 and Their Adaptation in the New Testament," *Journal for the Study of the New Testament* 8 (1980): 40.

[80]Cf. D.A. Carson, *Midrash and Matthew* (forthcoming).

[81]Cf. Maurya P. Horgan, *Pesharim: Qumran Interpretation of Biblical Books* (Washington: Catholic Biblical Assoc., 1979).

meaning even this specialized. It referred rather to "an interpretive exposition however derived and irrespective of the type of material under consideration" (Longenecker, *Biblical Exegesis*, p. 32).

In a wide-ranging chapter, Moo ("Use of OT," pp. 8ff.) discusses the various ways in which literature that treats the OT text may be analyzed. He distinguishes literary genre (form and general content), citation procedures (e.g., explicit quotation, allusion, conceptual influence, and the like), appropriation technique (the ways the OT text is applied to the contemporary setting), and the hermeneutical axioms implicitly adopted by the interpreter (e.g., that the Scripture was a closed entity needing to be ingeniously interpreted to elicit answers to questions about conduct not specifically treated in the text).

Now if "midrash" refers to genre, in the first century it is too wide a term to bear the weight Gundry places on it and is inadequate on other grounds (*Matthew*, pp. 63ff.). Attempts to define "midrash" in terms of appropriation techniques have not proved successful, because none of the techniques is restricted to midrash. Moo tentatively suggests that "midrash" be characterized "in terms of the hermeneutical axioms which guide the approach" ("Use of OT," p. 66). There is considerable merit in this; but of course this results in largely limiting midrash to rabbinic Judaism, since the operative hermeneutical axioms include a largely noneschatological perception of itself and a deep preoccupation with enunciating its identity and directing its conduct (corresponding roughly to the two forms haggadic midrash and Halakic midrash).[82] By contrast the stories of Matthew 1–2 are fundamentally eschatological: they are said to fulfill Scripture in the context of a book in which messianic fulfillment and the dawning of the eschatological kingdom constitute fundamental themes. Matthew 1–2 is little concerned with rules of conduct or the identity of the people of God. It bursts with christological concern and a teleological perspective.

When distinctions like these are borne in mind, the modern category "Midrash-Pesher," which some wish to apply to Matthew's treatment of the OT (cf. Moo, "Use of OT," p. 174), is seen as an inadequate label for the Qumran commentaries. Midrash and Pesher are alike in many of their techniques, but the hermeneutical axioms are profoundly different. But if the makeshift Midrash-Pesher is inappropriate for the commentaries of Qumran, it is equally inappropriate for Matthew. And in any case it is definitely not a genre recognized by Jewish readers of the first century.

These conclusions are inevitable:

1. Gundry cannot legitimately appeal to "midrash" as a well-defined and recognized genre of literature in the first century.

2. In particular, if "midrash" reflects genre, as opposed to hermeneutical axioms irrelevant to Matthew, it is being given a sense more or less well-defined only from the fourth century on. This raises the question of what we could expect Matthew's readers to have thought. Gundry argues that the reason the church has failed to recognize the "midrashic" (and therefore nonhistorical) nature of Matthew 1–2 is that this Gospel was quickly taken over by the Gentiles who had little appreciation for Jewish literary genres. This plausible argument is weakened by strong evidence that midrash in any specialized sense relevant to Gundry's thesis is too late in Jewish circles to be useful.

3. Even if we adopt this late narrowing of the term "midrash," it is still inappro-

---

[82]Cf. Daniel Patte, *Early Jewish Hermeneutic in Palestine* (Missoula: SBL, 1975), pp. 49ff.

priate as a description of Matthew's "M" material. Although the Jewish Midrashim are often only loosely connected with the texts they "expound," yet a line of continuity runs through those OT texts. By contrast Matthew's continuity in chapters 1–2, for instance, is established by the story line, not the OT texts, all of which could be removed without affecting the passage's cohesion.

4. Much of the force of Gundry's argument depends on his assessment of the tendencies in Matthew's editing of sources. Gundry feels that demonstrable tendencies in Matthew require appeal to midrashic technique as the only adequate explanation of material that diverges so radically from the sources. But another assessment of the same evidence is often possible. Few will be convinced by his postulation of a common source behind Matthew 1–2 and Luke 1–2. Moreover some of the "tendencies" he detects in Matthew—e.g., he follows the now popular line on the disciples' understanding (see section 11.i)—are better interpreted in other ways. These points depend on details of exegesis and emerge in this commentary. (See also the review of Gundry in Carson, "Gundry on Matthew.")

An important element in Gundry's argument is that the stories cannot be taken as history because, read that way, they include some demonstrable errors. For some of these matters, see the commentary in loc. Here it is sufficient to say that whoever uses "midrash" of any part of Matthew's Gospel should tell his readers precisely what the term means.

c. Miscellaneous

Several other important forms of literature make up the constituent parts of our canonical Gospels: wisdom sayings, genealogies, discourses, parables, and so forth. The most important receive brief treatment in the commentary, the most extensive note being devoted to parables (see at 13:3).

13. Bibliography

a. Selected Commentaries on Matthew

Albright, W.F., and Mann, C.S. *Matthew*. Garden City: Doubleday, 1971.

Alexander, J.A. *The Gospel According to Matthew*. New York: Scribner, 1860.

Allen, Willoughby C. *A Critical and Exegetical Commentary on the Gospel According to S. Matthew*. Edinburgh: T. & T. Clark, 1912.

Barnes, Albert. *Notes on the New Testament*. Grand Rapids: Kregel, repr. 1962.

Benoit, P. *L'Evangile selon Saint Matthieu*. 4th ed. Paris: du Cerf, 1972.

Bonnard, Pierre. *L'Evangile selon Saint Matthieu*. 2d ed. Neuchâtel: Delachaux et Niestlé, 1970.

Box, G. H. *St. Matthew*. Edinburgh: T.C. and E.C. Jack, n.d.

Broadus, John. *Commentary on the Gospel of Matthew*. Valley Forge: American Baptist Publication Society, 1886.

Calvin, John. *Calvin's New Testament Commentaries: Matthew, Mark, and Luke*. 3 vols. Translated by A.W. Morrison and T.H.L. Parker. Edited by D.W. Torrance and T.F. Torrance. Grand Rapids, 1972.

English, E.S. *Studies in the Gospel According to Matthew*. New York: Revell, 1935.

Erdman, Charles R. *The Gospel of Matthew: An Exposition*, 1920. Reprint. Philadelphia: Westminster, 1966.

Fenton, J.C. *Saint Matthew*. Harmondsworth: Penguin, 1963.

MATTHEW

Filson, Floyd V. *A Commentary on the Gospel According to St. Matthew*. New York: Harper, 1960.
Gaebelein, Arno C. *The Gospel of Matthew: An Exposition*. 2 vols. New York: Our Hope Publications, 1910.
Gaechter, Paul. *Das Matthäus Evangelium*. Innsbruck: Tyrolia-Verlag, 1963.
Gander, Georges. *L'Evangile de l'Eglise: Commentaire de l'Evangile selon Mattieu*. Aix-en-Provence: Faculte de Theologie Protestante, 1967.
Green, H. Benedict. *The Gospel According to Matthew*. Oxford: University Press, 1975.
Grosheide, F.W. *Het Heilig Evangelie Volgens Mattheus*. Kampen: Kok, 1954.
Grundmann, Walter. *Das Evangelium nach Matthäus*. 4th ed. Berlin: Evangelische Verlagsanstalt, 1975.
Gundry, Robert H. *Matthew: A Commentary on His Literary and Theological Art*. Grand Rapids: Eerdmans, 1981.
Hendriksen, William. *The Gospel of Matthew*. Grand Rapids: Baker, 1973.
Henry, Matthew. *A Commentary on the Holy Bible*. London: Marshall Bros., n.d.
Hill, David. *The Gospel of Matthew*. Grand Rapids: Eerdmans, 1972.
Kingsbury, Jack Dean. *Matthew*. Philadelphia: Fortress, 1977.
Klostermann, Erich. *Das Matthäus-Evangelium*. 2d ed. Tübingen: J.C.B. Mohr, 1927.
Lagrange, M.-J. *Évangile selon Saint Matthieu*. Paris: Lecoffre, 1948.
Lenski, R.C.H. *Interpretation of St. Matthew's Gospel*. Columbus, Ohio: Lutheran Book Concern, 1932.
Lohmeyer, Ernst. *Das Evangelium des Matthäus*. Edited by W. Schmauck. Göttingen: Vandenhoeck und Ruprecht, 1956.
Loisy, A. *Les évangiles synoptiques*. 2 vols. Ceffonds: n.p., 1907.
Luther, Martin. *Works*.
Maier, Gerhard. *Matthäus-Evangelium*. 2 vols. Neuhausen: Hänssler, 1979–.
McKenzie, John L. "The Gospel According to Matthew," *The Jerome Biblical Commentary*. Edited by R.E. Brown, J.A. Fitzmyer, and R.E. Murphy. Englewood Cliffs: Prentice-Hall, 1968.
McNeile, Alan Hugh. *The Gospel According to St. Matthew: The Greek Text with Introduction, Notes, and Indices*. London: Macmillan, 1915.
Merx, Adalbert. *Das Evangelium Matthaeus*. Berlin: Georg Reimer, 1902.
Meyer, Heinrich August Wilhelm. *Critical and Exegetical Commentary on the New Testament*. Part I. *The Gospel of Matthew*. 2 vols. Translated by W.P. Dickson and W. Stewart. Edinburgh: T. & T. Clark, 1877–79.
Micklem, Philip A. *St. Matthew*. London: Methuen and Co., 1917.
Morgan, G. Campbell. *The Gospel According to Matthew*. Old Tappan: Revell, 1929.
Morison, James. *A Practical Commentary on the Gospel According to St. Matthew*. London: Hodder and Stoughton, 1892.
Plummer, Alfred. *An Exegetical Commentary on the Gospel According to S. Matthew*. London: Robert Scott, 1915.
Plumptre, E.H. *The Gospel According to Matthew*. Reprint. Grand Rapids: Zondervan, 1957.
Ridderbos, H.N. *Het Evangelie naar Mattheus*. Kampen: Kok, 1952.
Rienecker, Fritz. *Das Evangelium des Matthäus*. Wuppertal: R. Brockhaus, 1953.
Robinson, Theodore H. *The Gospel of Matthew*. London: Hodder and Stoughton, 1928.
Sabourin, Leopold. *L'Evangile selon Saint Matthiew et ses principaux paralleles*. Rome: BIP, 1978.
Schlatter, Adolf. *Der Evangelist Matthäus: Seine Sprache, sein Ziel, seine Selbständigkeit*. 6th ed. Stuttgart: Calwer, 1963.
Schmid, Josef. *Das Evangelium nach Matthäus*. Regensburg: Friedrich Pustet, 1959.
Schniewind, Julius. *Das Evangelium nach Matthäus*. Göttingen: Vandenhoeck und Ruprecht, 1956.
Schweizer, Eduard. *The Good News According to Matthew*. Atlanta: John Knox, 1975.

Smith, B.T.D. *The Gospel According to S. Matthew*. Cambridge: University Press, 1927.
Spurgeon, C.H. *The Gospel of the Kingdom: A Popular Exposition of Matthew*. London: Passmore and Alabaster, 1893.
Tasker, R.V.G. *The Gospel According to St. Matthew: An Introduction and Commentary*. London: IVP, 1961.
Walvoord, John F. *Matthew: Thy Kingdom Come*. Chicago: Moody, 1974.
Weiss, Bernhard. *Das Matthäus-Evangelium*. Göttingen: Vandenhoeck und Ruprecht, 1898.
Wellhausen, J. *Das Evangelium Matthaei*. Berlin: Georg Reimer, 1904.
Zahn, Theodor. *Das Evangelium des Matthäus*. Leipzig: A. Deichert'sche Buchhandlung, 1903.

b. Other selected works

Arens, Eduardo. *The Ἦλθον-sayings in the Synoptic Tradition: A Historico-Critical Investigation*. Göttingen: Vandenhoeck und Ruprecht, 1976.
Bacon, Benjamin W. *Studies in Matthew*. London: Constable, 1930.
Bammel, E., ed. *The Trial of Jesus*. London: SCM, 1970.
Banks, Robert. *Jesus and the Law in the Synoptic Tradition*. Cambridge: University Press, 1975.
Beasley-Murray, G. R. *Baptism in the New Testament*. London: Macmillan, 1954.
Benoit, P. *Jesus and the Gospel*. New York: Herder and Herder, 1973.
Berger, K. *Die Gesetzesauslegung Jesu*. Neukirchen-Vluyn: Neukirchener Verlag, 1972.
Best, Ernest. *The Temptation and the Passion: The Markan Soteriology*. Cambridge: University Press, 1965.
_____, and Wilson, R. McL., edd. *Text and Interpretation*. Cambridge: University Press, 1979.
Beyer, Klaus. *Semitische Syntax im Neuen Testament*. Göttingen: Vandenhoeck und Ruprecht, 1968.
Black, Matthew. *An Aramaic Approach to the Gospels and Acts*. 3d ed. Oxford: Clarendon, 1967.
Blair, Edward P. *Jesus in the Gospel of Matthew*. New York: Abingdon, 1960.
Blinzler, Josef. *The Trial of Jesus*. Translated by F. McHugh. Cork: Mercier, 1959.
Bonhoeffer, Dietrich. *The Cost of Discipleship*. 6th ed. London: SCM, 1959.
Bornhäuser, Karl. *Die Bergpredigt: Versuch einer Zeitgenössischen Auslegung*. 2d ed. Gütersloh: C. Bertelsmann, 1927.
Bornkamm, Günther. *Jesus of Nazareth*. London: Hodder and Stoughton, 1960.
_____. *Geschichte und Glaube I*. München: Chr. Kaiser, 1968.
_____; Barth, G.; and Held, H.J. *Tradition and Interpretation in Matthew*. Translated by P. Scott. London: SCM, 1963.
Boucher, Madeleine. *The Mysterious Parable: A Literary Study*. Washington: Catholic Biblical Assoc., 1977.
Brown, Raymond E. *The Birth of the Messiah: A Commentary on the Infancy Narratives in Matthew and Luke*. Garden City: Doubleday, 1977.
_____; Donfried, Karl P.; and Reumann, John, edd. *Peter in the New Testament*. Minneapolis: Augsburg, 1973.
Bultmann, Rudolf. *Theology of the New Testament*. 2 vols. Translated by K. Grobel. London: SCM, 1952–55.
_____. *The History of the Synoptic Tradition*. Translated by J. Marsh. Oxford: Blackwells, 1963.
Burger, Christoph. *Jesus als Davidssohn: Eine traditionsgeschichtliche Untersuchung*. Göttingen: Vandenhoeck und Ruprecht, 1970.
Burton, E. de W. *Syntax of the Moods and Tenses in NT Greek*. Edinburgh: T. & T. Clark, 1894.
Carmignac, Jean. *Recherches sur le "Notre Père."* Paris: Letouzey et Aue, 1969.

43

Carson, D.A. *The Sermon on the Mount*. Grand Rapids: Baker, 1978.
_____. *The Farewell Discourse and Final Prayer of Jesus*. Grand Rapids: Baker, 1980.
_____. *Divine Sovereignty and Human Responsibility*. Atlanta: John Knox, 1981.
_____, ed. *From Sabbath to Lord's Day*. Grand Rapids: Zondervan, 1982.
_____, and Woodbridge, J.D., edd. *Scripture and Truth*. Grand Rapids: Zondervan, 1983.
Casey, Maurice. *Son of Man—The Interpretation and Influence of Daniel 7*. London: SPCK, 1980.
Catchpole, David R. *The Trial of Jesus: A Study in the Gospels and Jewish Historiography From 1770 to the Present Day*. Leiden: Brill, 1971.
Chilton, Bruce D. *God in Strength: Jesus' Announcement of the Kingdom*. Freistadt: F. Plöchl, 1977.
Cohn, Haim. *The Trial and Death of Jesus*. New York: Ktav, 1977.
Cope, O. Lamar. *Matthew: A Scribe Trained for the Kingdom of Heaven*. Washington: Catholic Biblical Assoc., 1976.
Cranfield, C.E.B. *The Gospel According to St. Mark*. Cambridge: University Press, 1972.
Cullmann, O. *The Christology of the New Testament*. Translated by Shirley C. Guthrie and Charles A. M. Hall. 2d ed. Philadelphia: Westminster, 1963.
Dahl, N.A. *Jesus in the Memory of the Early Church*. Minneapolis: Augsburg, 1976.
Dalman, A. *Jesus-Jeshua: Studies in the Gospels*. London: SPCK, 1929.
Daube, David. *The New Testament and Rabbinic Judaism*. London: Athlone, 1956.
Davies, W.D. *The Setting of the Sermon on the Mount*. Cambridge: University Press, 1963.
Derrett, J.D.M. *Law in the New Testament*. London: DLT, 1970.
_____. *Studies in the New Testament*. 2 vols. Leiden: Brill, 1977–78.
Didier, M., ed. *L'Evangile selon Matthieu: Rédaction et Théologie*. Gembloux: Duculot, 1972.
Dodd, C.H. *The Parables of the Kingdom*. London: Nisbet, 1936.
Doeve, J.W. *Jewish Hermeneutics in the Synoptic Gospels and Acts*. Assen: Van Gorcum, 1954.
Douglas, J.D., ed. *Illustrated Bible Dictionary*. 3 vols. Revised edition. Edited by N. Hillyer. Wheaton: Tyndale, 1980.
Dunn, J.D.G. *Jesus and the Spirit: A Study of the Religious and Charismatic Experience of Jesus and the First Christians as Reflected in the New Testament*. London: SCM, 1975.
_____. *Christology in the Making: An Inquiry into the Origins of the Doctrine of the Incarnation*. London: SCM, 1980.
Dupont, Jacques. *Mariage et divorce dans l'évangile, Matthieu 19, 3–12 et parallèles*. Bruges: Descleé de Brouwer, 1959.
Elliott, J.K., ed. *Studies in New Testament Language and Text*. SuppNovTest 44. Leiden: Brill, 1976.
Ellis, E. Earle, and Wilcox, Max, edd. *Neotestamentica et Semitica*. Edinburgh: T. & T. Clark, 1969.
_____, and Grässer, E., edd. *Jesus und Paulus*. Göttingen: Vandenhoeck und Ruprecht, 1975.
Fischer, David. *Historians' Fallacies: Toward a Logic of Historical Thought*. New York: Harper and Row, 1970.
Fitzmyer, Joseph A. *Essays on the Semitic Background of the New Testament*. London: Goeffrey Chapman, 1971.
_____. *A Wandering Aramaen: Collected Aramaic Essays*. Missoula: Scholars, 1978.
Flender, Helmut. *Die Botschaft Jesu von der Herr-schaft Gottes*. München: Chr. Kaiser, 1968.
France, R. T. *Jesus and the Old Testament: His Application of Old Testament Passages to Himself and His Mission*. London: Tyndale, 1971.
_____, and Wenham, D., edd. *Gospel Perspectives*. 2 vols. Sheffield: JSOT, 1980–81.
Frankemölle, Hubert. *Jahwebund und Kirche Christi: Studien zur Form- und Traditionsgeschichte des "Evangeliums" nach Matthäus*. Münster: Aschendorff, 1974.

Garland, David E. *The Intention of Matthew 23*. Leiden: Brill, 1979.

Gaston, Lloyd. *No Stone on Another: Studies in the Significance of the Fall of Jerusalem in the Synoptic Gospels*. Leiden: Brill, 1970.

Gerhardsson, Birgir. *The Mighty Acts of Jesus According to Matthew*. Lund: C.W.K. Gleerup, 1979.

Gnilka, J., ed. *Neues Testament und Kirche*. Freiburg: Herder, 1974.

Goppelt, Leonhard. *Theologie des Neuen Testaments*. Edited by Jürgen Roloff. Göttingen: Vandenhoeck und Ruprecht, 1976.

Goulder, M.D. *Midrash and Lection in Matthew*. London: SPCK, 1974.

Gundry, Robert H. *The Use of the Old Testament in St. Matthew's Gospel, with Special Reference to the Messianic Hope*. Leiden: Brill, 1975.

Guthrie, Donald. *New Testament Theology*. Downers Grove, Ill.: IVP, 1981.

Hare, Douglas R.A. *The Theme of Jewish Persecution of Christians in the Gospel According to St. Matthew*. Cambridge: University Press, 1967.

Haubeck, W., and Bachmann, M., edd. *Wort in der Zeit*. Leiden: Brill, 1980.

Hawthorne, G.F., ed. *Current Issues in Biblical and Patristic Interpretation*. Grand Rapids: Eerdmans, 1975.

Hennecke, E. *New Testament Apocrypha*. 2 vols. London: Lutterworth, 1965.

Hengstenberg, E.W. *Christology of the Old Testament*. Reprint. 2 vols. Florida: McDonald, n.d.

Hill, David. *Greek Words With Hebrew Meanings*. Cambridge: University Press, 1967.

Hoehner, Harold W. *Herod Antipas*. Cambridge: University Press, 1972.

_____. *Chronological Aspects of the Life of Christ*. Grand Rapids: Zondervan, 1977.

Hoekema, A.A. *The Bible and the Future*. Grand Rapids: Eerdmans, 1979.

Hoffmann, Paul et al., edd. *Orientierung an Jesus*. Freiburg: Herder, 1973.

Hooker, Morna D. *Jesus and the Servant*. London: SPCK, 1959.

_____. *The Son of Man in Mark*. London: SPCK, 1967.

Hull, John M. *Hellenistic Magic and the Synoptic Tradition*. London: SCM, 1974.

Hummel, Reinhardt. *Die Auseinandersetzung zwischen Kirche und Judentum im Matthäusevangelium*. München: Chr. Kaiser, 1966.

Isaksson, A. *Marriage and Ministry in the New Testament*. Lund: C.W.K. Gleerup, 1965.

Jeremias, J. *Jesus' Promise to the Nations*. Translated by John Bowden. London: SCM, 1958.

_____. *Jerusalem in the Time of Jesus*. Translated by F.H. and C.H. Cave. London: SCM, 1962.

_____. *The Parables of Jesus*. Translated by S.H. Hooke. London: SCM, 1963.

_____. *The Eucharistic Words of Jesus*. Translated by N. Perrin. 3d ed. London: SCM, 1966.

_____. *The Prayers of Jesus*. Translated by John Bowden and Christoph Burchard. London: SCM, 1967.

_____. *New Testament Theology*. Part I. *The Proclamation of Jesus*. Translated by John Bowden. London: SCM, 1971.

_____, and Zimmerli, W. *The Servant of the Lord*. London: SCM, 1965.

Johnson, Marshall D. *The Purpose of the Biblical Geneologies*. Cambridge: University Press, 1969.

Kilpatrick, G.D. *The Origins of the Gospel According to St. Matthew*. Oxford: Clarendon, 1946.

Kingsbury, Jack Dean. *The Parables of Jesus in Matthew 13: A Study in Redaction-Criticism*. London: SPCK, 1969.

_____. *Matthew: Structure, Christology, Kingdom*. Philadelphia: Fortress, 1975.

Kistemaker, Simon J. *The Parables of Jesus*. Grand Rapids: Baker, 1980.

Kümmel, W.G. *Jesus' Promise to the Nations*. Translated by S.H. Hooke. London: SCM, 1958.

_____. *Introduction to the New Testament*. Translated by Howard Clark Kee. Nashville: Abingdon, 1975.

Ladd, G.E. *The Presence of the Future: The Eschatology of Biblical Realism*. Grand Rapids: Eerdmans, 1974.

———. *A Theology of the New Testament*. Grand Rapids: Eerdmans, 1974.

Lane, William L. *The Gospel According to Mark*. Grand Rapids: Eerdmans, 1974.

Lindars, Barnabas. *New Testament Apologetic*. London: SCM, 1961.

Livingstone, E.A., ed. *Studia Biblica 1978*. 2 vols. Sheffield: JSOT, 1980.

Longenecker, Richard N. *The Christology of Early Jewish Christianity*. London: SCM, 1970.

———. *Biblical Exegesis in the Apostolic Period*. Grand Rapids: Eerdmans, 1975.

———, and Tenney, Merrill C., edd. *New Dimensions in New Testament Study*. Grand Rapids: Zondervan, 1974.

Machen, J. Gresham. *The Virgin Birth of Christ*. New York: Harper and Row, 1930.

Manson, T.W. *The Sayings of Jesus*. London: SCM, 1949.

Marshall, I. Howard. *The Gospel of Luke: A Commentary on the Greek Text*. Grand Rapids: Eerdmans, 1978.

———. *Last Supper and Lord's Supper*. Exeter: Paternoster, 1980.

———, ed. *New Testament Interpretation*. Exeter: Paternoster, 1977.

McConnell, Richard S. *Law and Prophecy in Matthew's Gospel*. Basel: Friedrich Reinhardt, 1969.

McHugh, John. *The Mother of Jesus in the New Testament*. Garden City: Doubleday, 1975.

McKay, J.R., and Miller, J.F., edd. *Biblical Studies*. London: Collins, 1976.

Meier, John P. *Law and History in Matthew's Gospel: A Redactional Study of Mt. 5:17–48*. Rome: BIP, 1976.

———. *The Vision of Matthew: Christ, Church, and Morality in the First Gospel*. New York: Paulist, 1979.

Metzger, Bruce M. *A Textual Commentary on the Greek New Testament*. London: UBS, 1971.

———. *New Testament Studies: Philological, Versional, and Patristic*. Leiden: Brill, 1980.

Meyer, Ben F. *The Aims of Jesus*. London: SCM, 1979.

Moore, G.F. *Judaism in the First Centuries of the Christian Era*. 3 vols. Cambridge: Harvard University Press, 1927–30.

Morris, Leon. *The Apostolic Preaching of the Cross*. Grand Rapids: Eerdmans, 1955.

———. *The Gospel According to John*. Grand Rapids: Eerdmans, 1971.

Moule, C.F.D. *An Idiom Book of New Testament Greek*. 2d ed. London: Cambridge University Press, 1959.

———. *The Birth of the New Testament*. London: A. and C. Black, 1962.

———. *The Origin of Christology*. Cambridge: University Press, 1977.

Moulton, James Hope. *A Grammar of New Testament Greek*. vol. 1. *Prolegomena*. Edinburgh: T. & T. Clark, 1908.

———. vol. 2. *Accidence and Word Formation*. Edited by W.F. Howard. Edinburgh: T. & T. Clark, 1920.

Nineham, D.E., ed. *Studies in the Gospels*. Oxford: Blackwell, 1955.

Nolan, Brian M. *The Royal Son of God: The Christology of Matthew 1–2 in the Setting of the Gospel*. Göttingen: Vandenhoeck und Ruprecht, 1979.

Parrot, Andre. *Golgotha and the Church of the Holy Sepulchre*. Translated by E. Hudson. London: SCM, 1957.

Piper, John. *Love Your Enemies*. Cambridge: University Press, 1979.

Przybylski, Benno. *Righteousness in Matthew and His World of Thought*. Cambridge: University Press, 1980.

Ridderbos, Herman. *The Coming of the Kingdom*. Translated by R. Zorn. Philadelphia: Presbyterian and Reformed, 1962.

Riesenfeld, H. *The Gospel Tradition*. Philadelphia: Fortress, 1970.

Robertson, A.T. *Word Pictures in the New Testament*. 6 vols. New York: Harper & Brothers, 1930.

Robinson, John A.T. *Twelve New Testament Studies*. London: SCM, 1962.

Rothfuchs, Wilhelm. *Die Erfüllungszitate des Matthäus-Evangeliums*. Stuttgart: W. Kohlhammer, 1969.

Sand, Alexander. *Das Gesetz und die Propheten: Untersuchungen zur Theologie des Evangeliums nach Matthäus*. Regensburg: Friedrich Pustet, 1976.

Schottroff, Luise et al. *Essays on the Love Commandment*. Philadelphia: Fortress, 1978.

Schweitzer, Albert. *The Quest of the Historical Jesus*. 2d ed. Translated by W. Montgomery. London: A. and C. Black, 1911.

Senior, Donald. *The Passion Narrative According to Matthew: A Redactional Study*. Leuven: Leuven University Press, 1975.

Sherwin-White, A.N. *Roman Society and Roman Law in the New Testament*. Oxford: Clarendon, 1963.

Soarés Prabhu, George M. *The Formula Quotations in the Infancy Narrative of Matthew*. Rome: BIP, 1976.

Stanton, Graham N. *Jesus of Nazareth in New Testament Preaching*. Cambridge: University Press, 1974.

Stendahl, Krister. *The School of St. Matthew and Its Use of the Old Testament*. 2d ed. Lund: C.W.K. Gleerup, n.d.

Stier, Rudolf. *The Words of the Lord Jesus*. Vol. 1. Translated by W.B. Pope. Edinburgh: T. & T. Clark, 1874.

Stonehouse, Ned B. *The Witness of Matthew and Mark to Christ*. Grand Rapids: Eerdmans, 1944.

———. *Origins of the Synoptic Gospels: Some Basic Questions*. Grand Rapids: Eerdmans, 1963.

Stott, John R.W. *Christian Counter-culture*. Downers Grove: IVP, 1978.

Strecker, Georg. *Der Weg der Gerechtigkeit*. Göttingen: Vandenhoeck und Ruprecht, 1962.

———, ed. *Jesus Christus in Historie und Theologie*. Tubingen: J.C.B. Mohr, 1975.

Suggs, M. Jack. *Wisdom, Christology, and Law in Matthew's Gospel*. Cambridge: Harvard University Press, 1970.

Taylor, Vincent. *The Gospel According to St. Mark*. 2d ed. London: Macmillan, 1966.

Thompson, William G. *Matthew's Advice to a Divided Community: Mt. 17, 22-18, 35*. Rome: BIP, 1970.

Thrall, Margaret E. *Greek Particles in the New Testament*. Leiden: Brill, 1962.

Trench, R.C. *Studies in the Gospels*. London: Macmillan, 1878.

Trilling, Wolfgang. *Das wahre Israel: Studien zur Theologie des Matthäus-Evangeliums*. München: Kösel, 1964.

Turner, Nigel. *Syntax*. Vol. 3 of J.H. Moulton. *A Grammar of New Testament Greek*. Edinburgh: T. & T. Clark, 1963.

———. *Grammatical Insights Into the New Testament*. Edinburgh: T. & T. Clark, 1965.

———. *Christian Words*. Edinburgh: T. & T. Clark, 1980.

Urbach, E.E. *The Sages: Their Concepts and Beliefs*. 2 vols. Translated by I. Abrahams. Jerusalem: Magnes, 1975.

van der Loos, H. *The Miracles of Jesus*. Leiden: Brill, 1965.

van Tilborg, Sjef. *The Jewish Leaders in Matthew*. Leiden: Brill, 1972.

Walker, Rolf. *Die Heilsgeschichte im ersten Evangelium*. Göttingen: Vandenhoeck und Ruprecht, 1967.

Warfield, Benjamin B. *Selected Shorter Writings*. 2 vols. Edited by John E. Meeter. Nutley, N.J.: Presbyterian and Reformed, 1970.

Westerholm, Stephen. *Jesus and Scribal Authority*. Lund: C.W.K. Gleerup, 1978.

Winter, Paul. *On the Trial of Jesus*. 2d ed. Berlin: de Gruyter, 1974.

Zerwick, M. *Biblical Greek*. Rome: Scripta Pontificii Instituti Biblici, 1963.

Zumstein, Jean. *La condition du croyant dans l'Evangile selon Matthieu*. Göttingen: Vandenhoeck und Ruprecht, 1977.

c. Selected articles

Berger, Klaus. "Die königlichen Messiastraditionen des Neuen Testaments." NTS 20 (1974): 1–44.

Blaising, Craig A. "Gethsemane: A Prayer of Faith." JETS 22 (1979): 333–43.

Brower, Kent. "Mark 9:1 Seeing the Kingdom in Power." *Journal for the Study of the New Testament* 6 (1980): 17–41.

Carson, D.A. "Historical Tradition in the Fourth Gospel—After Dodd, What?" France and Wenham, 2:83–145.

_____. "Jesus and the Sabbath in the Four Gospels." Id. *Sabbath*.

_____. "Jewish Leaders in Matthew's Gospel: A Reappraisal." JETS 25 (1982): 161–74.

_____. "Christological Ambiguities in the Gospel of Matthew." *Christ the Lord: Studies in Christology Presented to Donald Guthrie*. Edited by Harold Rowdon. Downers Grove, Ill.: IVP, 1982, pp. 97–114.

_____. "Redaction Criticism: On the Legitimacy and Illegitimacy of a Literary Tool." Carson and Woodbridge.

_____. "The ὅμοιος Word-Group as Introduction to Some Matthean Parables." NTS, in press.

Dodd, C.H. "New Testament Translation Problems I." *Bible Translator* 27 (1976): 301–11.

Dupont, J. "Le Point de vue de Matthieu dans le chapitre des paraboles." Didier, pp. 221–59.

Ellis, E.E. "New Directions in Form Criticism." Strecker, *Jesus Christus*, pp. 299–315.

Fee, G.D. "Modern Text Criticism and the Synoptic Problem." *J.J. Griesbach: Synoptic and Text-Critical Studies 1776–1976*. Edited by Bernard Orchard and Thomas R.W. Longstaff. Cambridge: University Press, 1978, pp. 154–69.

Fenton, J.C. "Matthew and the Divinity of Jesus: Three Questions Concerning Matthew 1:20–23." Livingston, 2:79–82.

France, R.T. "The Servant of the Lord in the Teaching of Jesus." *Tyndale Bulletin* 19 (1966): 26–52.

_____. "God and Mammon." EQ 51 (1979): 3–21.

_____. "Exegesis in Practice: Two Samples." Marshall, *New Testament Interpretation*, pp. 252–81.

_____. "The Formula Quotations of Matthew 2 and the Problem of Communications." NTS 27 (1980–81): 233–51.

_____. "Scripture, Tradition and History in the Infancy Narratives of Matthew." France and Wenham, 2:239–66.

Gooding, D.W. "Structure littéraire de Matthieu, XIII,53 à XVIII,35." RB 85 (1978): 227–52.

Hartman, L. "Scriptural Exegesis in the Gospel of St. Matthew and the Problem of Communication." Didier, pp. 131–52.

Heil, John Paul. "Significant Aspects of the Healing Miracles in Matthew." CBQ 41 (1979): 274–87.

Hill, David. "Son and Servant: An Essay on Matthean Christology." *Journal of Studies of the New Testament* 6 (1980): 2–16.

Huffmann, Norman A. "Atypical Features in the Parables of Jesus." JBL 97 (1978): 207–20.

Kaiser, W.C. "The Weightier and Lighter Matters of the Law." Hawthorne, pp. 176–92.

Lachs, S.T. "Some Textual Observations on the Sermon on the Mount." JQR 69 (1978): 98–111.

Liefeld, Walter L. "Theological Motifs in the Transfiguration Narrative." Longenecker and Tenney, pp. 162–79.

Neil, Willam. "Five Hard Sayings of Jesus." McKay and Miller, pp. 157–71.

O'Brien, P.T. "The Great Commission of Matthew 28:18–20." *Evangelical Review of Theology* 2 (1978): 254–67.

Ogawa, Akira. "Paraboles de l'Israel véritable? Réconsidération critique de Mt.xxi.28–xxii.14." NovTest 21 (1979): 121–49.

Pamment, Margaret. "The Kingdom of Heaven According to the First Gospel." NTS 27 (1980–81): 211–32.

Payne, Philip Barton. "The Authenticity of the Parable of the Sower and Its Interpretation." France and Wenham, 2:163–207.

Reicke, Bo. "Synoptic Prophecies on the Destruction of Jerusalem." *Studies in New Testament and Early Christian Literature*. Edited by D.E. Aune. Leiden: Brill, 1972, pp. 121–34.

Slingerland, H. Dixon. "The Transjordanian Origin of St. Matthew's Gospel." *Journal of the Study of the New Testament* 3 (1979): 18–28.

Stanton, Graham N. "The Origin and Purpose of Matthew's Gospel: Matthean Scholarship From 1945 to 1980." *Aufstieg und Niedergang der römischen Welt*. Berlin and New York: de Gruyter, 1982, 2:25/2.

Wenham, David. "The Synoptic Problem Revisited: Some New Suggestions About the Composition of Mark 4:1–34." *Tyndale Bulletin* 23 (1972): 3–38.

————. "The Resurrection Narratives in Matthew's Gospel." *Tyndale Bulletin* 24 (1973): 21–54.

————. "The Interpretation of the Parable of the Sower." NTS 20 (1974): 299–319.

————. "The 'Q' Tradition Behind Matthew X." NTS, in press.

d. Unpublished material

Blomberg, Craig. "The Tendencies of the Tradition in the Parables of the Gospel of Thomas." Master's thesis, Trinity Evangelical Divinity School, 1979.

————. "Tradition-History in the Parables Peculiar to Luke's Central Section." Ph.D. dissertation, University of Aberdeen, 1982.

Hulton, D. "The Resurrection of the Holy Ones (Matthew 27:51b–53). A Study of the Theology of the Matthean Passion Narrative." Ph.D. dissertation, Harvard University, 1970.

Martin, Brice L. "Matthew and Paul on Christ and the Law: Compatible or Incompatible Theologies?" Ph.D. dissertation, McMaster University, 1976.

Moo, Douglas J. "The Use of the Old Testament in the Passion Texts of the Gospels." Ph.D. dissertation, University of St. Andrews, 1979.

————. "Jesus Christ's Ethical Use of the Old Testament." Forthcoming in JSNT.

Sigal, Phillip. "The Halakah of Jesus of Nazareth according to the Gospel of Matthew." Ph.D. dissertation, University of Pittsburgh, 1979.

Trotter, Andrew H. "Understanding and Stumbling: A Study of the Disciples' Understanding of Jesus and His Teaching in the Gospel of Matthew." Ph.D. dissertation, Cambridge University, n.d.

14. Structure and Outline

Matthew was a skilled literary craftsman and gave his Gospel structure, form, and rhythm. Two of his larger chiasms are indicated in the outline below. But the structure of the Gospel as a whole is still disputed. With minor variations there are three main views.

First, some (e.g., McNeile) have detected a geographical framework. Matthew 1:1–2:23 is the prologue; 3:1–4:11 is Jesus' preparation for ministry; 4:12–13:58 finds Jesus in Galilee; 14:1–20:34 pictures him around Galilee and heading toward Jerusalem; and 21:1–28:20 finds him at Jerusalem. The divisions are neither precise nor helpful, for the result tells us nothing of Matthew's purposes.

Second, Kingsbury (*Structure*), taking a hint from Lohmeyer (*Matthäus*) and Stonehouse (*Witness of Matthew*, pp. 129–31), argues for three sections. The first he entitles "The Person of Jesus Messiah" (1:1–4:16), the second "The Proclamation of Jesus Messiah" (4:17–16:20), and the third "The Suffering, Death, and Resurrection of Jesus Messiah" (16:21–28:20). Immediately after the two breaks comes the phrase *apo tote* ("from that time on"). Kingsbury further notes that the last two sections each contain three "summary" passages, 4:23–25; 9:35; 11:1 and 16:21; 17:22–23; 20:17–19 respectively;[85] and he suggests that this outline does justice to the centrality of Matthew's christology.

Though this outline has gained adherents, it has serious weaknesses. It is not at all clear that *apo tote* is so redactionally important for Matthew: he also uses it in 26:18 without any suggestion of a break in his outline. One could argue that there are four passion summaries in the third section, not three (add 26:2). Kingsbury's outline not only breaks up the prime Peter passage in an unacceptable way (cf. comments at 16:13–16), but at both transitions Matthew may have been more influenced by the order of Mark than by "structural" considerations. The most important weakness, however, is the artificiality of the topical headings. The person of Jesus (section one) is still a focal point in sections two and three (e.g., 16:13–16; 22:41–46). Why the proclamation of Jesus should be restricted to section two when two of the discourses (chs. 18; 24–25) and several important exchanges (chs. 21–23) await the third section is not clear. The last heading, "The Suffering, Death, and Resurrection of Jesus Messiah," though it accurately summarizes the increasingly dominant theme of 16:21–28:20, seems an inadequate designation of much in those chapters (e.g., most of 18; 21–25).

The third scheme makes the book center on the five main discourses (see outline below). Each begins by placing Jesus in a specific context and ends with a formula found nowhere else in the Gospel (see comment at 7:28–29) and transitional pericope with links pointing forward and backward. Bacon[86] believed the five discourses correspond to the five books of the Pentateuch; but there is little in favor of this refinement (cf. Gundry, *Matthew*), since Moses typology is very weak in this Gospel and the links between the five discourses and the five books of Moses minimal.

Two frequently raised difficulties must be overcome.

1. Why restrict oneself to *five* discourses when chapter 11 could fall into that

---

[85]A slight modification of this scheme has been introduced by Tommy B. Slater, "Notes on Matthew's Structure," JBL 99(1980): 436.

[86]B.W. Bacon, "The 'Five Books' of Moses Against the Jews," Exp 15 (1918): 56–66. The idea is then worked out in detail in his *Studies in Matthew*.

category? This objection misses the mark. The fivefold sequence narrative-discourse does not assume that Jesus is not portrayed as speaking in the narrative sections. He may do so, even extensively (see also on ch. 21). The point is that the five discourses are sufficiently well-defined that it is hard to believe Matthew did not plan them as such.

2. Does this not relegate the birth narrative (chs. 1–2) and the Passion and Resurrection (chs. 26–28) to a sort of secondary status outside the central outline? There is little difficulty in seeing chapters 1–2 as a prologue anticipating the opening of the Gospel, a formal opening common to all the canonical Gospels (see comment at 1:1). But certainly Matthew 26–28 must not be dismissed as an epilogue; it is too much the point toward which the Gospel moves for that. On the other hand, Matthew 26–28 does not constitute an ordinary "conclusion"; for the final verses are purposely open-ended and anticipatory. It seems best to take 26:5–28:20 as constituting an exceptional sixth narrative section with the corresponding teaching section being laid on the shoulders of the disciples (28:18–20).

But no outline should be taken too seriously. The Gospels use vignettes—organized ones, doubtless, but vignettes nonetheless. The following outline organizes Matthew's Gospel and reflects some demonstrable structure. That structure is, however, a guide to its contents, not a comprehensive explanation.

I. Prologue: The Origin and Birth of Jesus the Christ (1:1–2:23)
  A. The Genealogy of Jesus (1:1–17)
  B. The Birth of Jesus (1:18–25)
  C. The Visit of the Magi (2:1–12)
  D. The Escape to Egypt (2:13–15)
  E. The Massacre of Bethlehem's Boys (2:16–18)
  F. The Return to Nazareth (2:19–23)

II. The Gospel of the Kingdom (3:1–7:29)
  A. Narrative (3:1–4:25)
    1. Foundational steps (3:1–4:11)
      a. The ministry of John the Baptist (3:1–12)
      b. The baptism of Jesus (3:13–17)
      c. The temptation of Jesus (4:1–11)
    2. Jesus' early Galilean ministry (4:12–25)
      a. The beginning (4:12–17)
      b. Calling the first disciples (4:18–22)
      c. Spreading the news of the kingdom (4:23–25)
  B. First Discourse: The Sermon on the Mount (5:1–7:29)
    1. Setting (5:1–2)
    2. The kingdom of heaven: its norms and witness (5:3–16)
      a. The norms of the kingdom (5:3–12)
        1) The Beatitudes (5:3–10)
        2) Expansion (5:11–12)
      b. The witness of the kingdom (5:13–16)
        1) Salt (5:13)
        2) Light (5:14–16)
    3. The kingdom of heaven: its demands in relation to the OT (5:17–48)
      a. Jesus and the kingdom as fulfillment of the OT (5:17–20)

   b. Application: the antitheses (5:21–48)
    1) Vilifying anger and reconciliation
     (5:21–26)
    2) Adultery and purity (5:27–30)
    3) Divorce and remarriage (5:31–32)
    4) Oaths and truthfulness (5:33–37)
    5) Personal injury and self-sacrifice (5:38–42)
    6) Hatred and love (5:43–47)
   c. Conclusion: the demand for perfection (5:48)
  4. Religious hypocrisy: its description and overthrow
   (6:1–18)
   a. The principle (6:1)
   b. Three examples (6:2–18)
    1) Alms (6:2–4)
    2) Prayer (6:5–15)
     a) Ostentatious prayer (6:5–6)
     b) Repetitious prayer (6:7–8)
     c) Model prayer (6:9–13)
     d) Forgiveness and prayer (6:14–15)
    3) Fasting (6:16–18)
  5. Kingdom perspectives (6:19–34)
   a. Metaphors for unswerving loyalty to kingdom values
    (6:19–24)
    1) Treasure (6:19–21)
    2) Light (6:22–23)
    3) Slavery (6:24)
   b. Uncompromised trust (6:25–34)
    1) The principle (6:25)
    2) The examples (6:26–30)
     a) Life and food (6:26–27)
     b) Body and clothes (6:28–30)
    3) Distinctive living (6:31–32)
    4) The heart of the matter (6:33)
    5) Abolishing worry (6:34)
  6. Balance and perfection (7:1–12)
   a. The danger of being judgmental (7:1–5)
    1) The principle (7:1)
    2) The theological justification (7:2)
    3) An example (7:3–5)
   b. The danger of being undiscerning (7:6)
   c. Source and means of power (7:7–11)
   d. Balance and perfection (7:12)
  7. Conclusion: call to decision and commitment
   (7:13–27)
   a. Two ways (7:13–14)
   b. Two trees (7:15–20)
   c. Two claims (7:21–23)
   d. Two builders (7:24–27)
  8. Transitional conclusion: Jesus' authority
   (7:28–29)

III. The Kingdom Extended Under Jesus' Authority (8:1–11:1)
   A. Narrative (8:1–10:4)
      1. Healing miracles (8:1–17)
         a. A leper (8:1–4)
         b. The centurion's servant (8:5–13)
         c. Peter's mother-in-law (8:14–15)
         d. Many at evening (8:16–17)
      2. The cost of following Jesus (8:18–22)
            Excursus: "The Son of Man" as a christological title
      3. Calming a storm (8:23–27)
      4. Further demonstration of Jesus' authority (8:28–9:8)
         a. Exorcising two men (8:28–34)
         b. Healing a paralytic and forgiving his sins (9:1–8)
      5. Calling Matthew (9:9)
      6. Eating with sinners (9:10–13)
      7. Fasting and the dawning of the messianic joy (9:14–17)
      8. A resurrection and more healings (9:18–34)
         a. Raising a girl and healing a woman (9:18–26)
         b. Healing two blind men (9:27–31)
         c. Exorcising a dumb man (9:32–34)
      9. Spreading the news of the kingdom (9:35–10:4)
         a. Praying for workers (9:35–38)
         b. Commissioning the Twelve (10:1–4)
   B. Second Discourse: Mission and Martyrdom (10:5–11:1)
      1. Setting (10:5a)
      2. The commission (10:5b–16)
      3. Warnings of future sufferings (10:17–25)
         a. The Spirit's help (10:17–20)
         b. Endurance (10:21–23)
         c. Inspiration (10:24–25)
      4. Prohibition of fear (10:26–31)
         a. The emergence of truth (10:26–27)
         b. The nonfinality of death (10:28)
         c. Continuing providence (10:29–31)
      5. Characteristics of discipleship (10:32–39)
         a. Acknowledging Jesus (10:32–33)
         b. Recognizing the gospel (10:34–36)
         c. Preferring Jesus (10:37–39)
      6. Encouragement: response to the disciples and to Jesus (10:40–42)
      7. Transitional conclusion: expanding ministry (11:1)

IV. Teaching and Preaching the Gospel of the Kingdom: Rising Opposition (11:2–13:53)
   A. Narrative (11:2–12:50)
      1. Jesus and John the Baptist (11:2–19)
         a. John's question and Jesus' response (11:2–6)
         b. Jesus' testimony to John (11:7–19)
            1) John in redemptive history (11:7–15)
            2) The unsatisfied generation (11:16–19)

2. The condemned and the accepted (11:20–30)
    a. The condemned: woes on unrepentant cities (11:20–24)
    b. The accepted (11:25–30)
        1) Because of the revelation of the Father (11:25–26)
        2) Because of the agency of the Son (11:27)
        3) Because of the Son's gentle invitation (11:28–30)
3. Sabbath conflicts (12:1–14)
    a. Picking heads of grain (12:1–8)
    b. Healing a man with a shriveled hand (12:9–14)
4. Jesus' as the prophesied Servant (12:15–21)
5. Confrontation with the Pharisees (12:22–37)
    a. The setting and accusation (12:22–24)
    b. Jesus' reply (12:25–37)
        1) The divided kingdom (12:25–28)
        2) The strong man's house (12:29)
        3) Blasphemy against the Spirit (12:30–32)
        4) Nature and fruit (12:33–37)
    c. Continued confrontation (12:38–42)
        1) Request for a sign (12:38)
        2) The sign of Jonah (12:39–42)
    d. The return of the evil spirit (12:43–45)
6. Doing the Father's will (12:46–50)
B. Third Discourse: The Parables of the Kingdom (13:1–53)
1. The setting (13:1–3a)
2. To the crowds (13:3b–33)
    a. The parable of the soils (13:3b–9)
    b. Interlude (13:10–23)
        1) On understanding parables (13:10–17)
        2) Interpretation of the parable of the soils (13:18–23)
    c. The parable of the weeds (13:24–30)
    d. The parable of the mustard seed (13:31–32)
    e. The parable of the yeast (13:33)
3. Pause (13:34–43)
    a. Parables as fulfillment of prophecy (13:34–35)
    b. Interpretation of the parable of the weeds (13:36–43)
4. To the disciples (13:44–52)
    a. The parable of the hidden treasure (13:44)
    b. The parable of the expensive pearl (13:45–46)
    c. The parable of the net (13:47–48)
    d. Interlude (13:49–51)
        1) Interpretation of the parable of the net (13:49–50)
        2) On understanding parables (13:51)
    e. The parable of the teacher of the law (13:52)
5. Transitional conclusion: movement toward further opposition (13:53)

V. The Glory and the Shadow: Progressive Polarization
(13:54–19:2)
  A. Narrative (13:54–17:27)
    1. Rejected at Nazareth (13:54–58)
    2. Herod and Jesus (14:1–12)
      a. Herod's understanding of Jesus (14:1–2)
      b. Background: Herod's execution of John the Baptist
        (14:3–12)
    3. The feeding of the five thousand (14:13–21)
    4. The walk on the water (14:22–33)
    5. Transitional summary of constant and unavoidable
      ministry (14:34–36)
    6. Jesus and the tradition of the elders (15:1–20)
    7. More healings (15:21–31)
      a. The Canaanite woman (15:21–28)
      b. The many (15:29–31)
    8. The feeding of the four thousand (15:32–39)
    9. Another demand for a sign (16:1–4)
    10. The yeast of the Pharisees and Sadducees (16:5–12)
    11. Peter's confession of Jesus and its aftermath (16:13–23)
      a. The confession (16:13–20)
      b. The first passion prediction (16:21–23)
    12. The way of discipleship (16:24–28)
    13. The Transfiguration (17:1–13)
      a. Jesus transfigured (17:1–8)
      b. The place of Elijah (17:9–13)
    14. The healing of an epileptic boy (17:14–20 [21])
    15. The second major passion prediction (17:22–23)
    16. The temple tax (17:24–27)
  B. Fourth Discourse: Life Under Kingdom Authority
    (18:1–19:2)
    1. Setting (18:1–2)
    2. Humility and greatness (18:3–4)
    3. The heinousness of causing believers to sin (18:5–9)
    4. The parable of the lost sheep (18:10–14)
    5. Treatment of a sinning brother (18:15–20)
    6. Forgiveness (18:21–35)
      a. Repeated forgiveness (18:21–22)
      b. The parable of the unmerciful servant (18:23–35)
    7. Transitional conclusion: introduction to the Judean
      ministry (19:1–2)

VI. Opposition and Eschatology: The Triumph of Grace
(19:3–26:5)
  A. Narrative (19:3–23:39)
    1. Marriage and divorce (19:3–12)
    2. Blessing little children (19:13–15)
    3. Wealth and the kingdom (19:16–30)
      a. The rich young man (19:16–22)
      b. Grace and reward in the kingdom (19:23–30)

4. The parable of the workers (20:1–16)
5. Third major passion prediction (20:17–19)
6. Suffering and service (20:20–28)
7. Healing two blind men (20:29–34)
8. Opening events of Passion Week (21:1–23:39)
   a. The Triumphal Entry (21:1–11)
   b. Jesus at the temple (21:12–17)
   c. The fig tree (21:18–22)
   d. Controversies in the temple court (21:23–22:46)
     1) The question of authority (21:23–27)
     2) The parable of the two sons (21:28–32)
     3) The parable of the tenants (21:33–46)
     4) The parable of the wedding banquet (22:1–14)
     5) Paying taxes to Caesar (22:15–22)
     6) Marriage at the resurrection (22:23–33)
     7) The greatest commandments (22:34–40)
     8) The son of David (22:41–46)
   e. Seven woes on the teachers of the law and the Pharisees (23:1–36)
     1) Warning the crowds and the disciples (23:1–12)
     2) The seven woes (23:13–36)
       a) First woe (23:13 [14])
       b) Second woe (23:15)
       c) Third woe (23:16–22)
       d) Fourth woe (23:23–24)
       e) Fifth woe (23:25–26)
       f) Sixth woe (23:27–28)
       g) Seventh woe (23:29–32)
     3) Conclusion (23:33–36)
   f. Lament over Jerusalem (23:37–39)
B. Fifth Discourse: The Olivet Discourse (24:1–25:46)
  1. Setting (24:1–3)
  2. The birth pains (24:4–28)
   a. General description of the birth pains (24:4–14)
   b. The sharp pain: the Fall of Jerusalem (24:15–21)
   c. Warnings against false messiahs during the birth pains (24:22–28)
  3. The coming of the Son of Man (24:29–31)
  4. The significance of the birth pains (24:32–35)
  5. The day and hour unknown: the need to be prepared (24:36–41)
   a. The principle (24:36)
   b. Analogy of the days of Noah (24:37–39)
   c. Two in the field; two with a mill (24:40–41)
  6. Parabolic teaching: variations on watchfulness (24:21–25:46)
   a. The homeowner and the thief (24:42–44)
   b. The two servants (24:45–51)
   c. The ten virgins (25:1–13)

        d. The talents (25:14–30)

        e. The sheep and the goats (25:31–46)

     7. Transitional conclusion: fourth major passion prediction and the plot against Jesus (26:1–5)

VII. The Passion and Resurrection of Jesus (26:6–28:20)

    A. The Passion (26:6–27:66)

       1. Anointed at Bethany (26:6–13)

       2. Judas's betrayal agreement (26:14–16)

          Excursus: Chronological considerations

       3. The Lord's Supper (26:17–30)

          a. Preparations for the Passover (26:17–19)

          b. Prediction of the betrayal (26:20–25)

          c. The words of institution (26:26–30)

       4. Prediction of abandonment and denial (26:31–35)

       5. Gethsemane (26:36–46)

       6. The arrest (26:47–56)

       7. Jesus before the Sanhedrin (26:57–68)

       8. Peter's denial of Jesus (26:69–75)

       9. Formal decision of the Sanhedrin (27:1–2)

      10. The death of Judas (27:3–10)

      11. Jesus before Pilate (27:11–26)

      12. The soldiers' treatment of Jesus (27:27–31)

      13. The Crucifixion and mocking (27:32–44)

      14. The death of Jesus (27:45–50)

      15. Immediate impact of the death (27:51–56)

      16. The burial of Jesus (27:57–61)

      17. The guard at the tomb (27:62–66)

    B. The Resurrection (28:1–15)

       1. The empty tomb (28:1–7)

       2. First encounter with the risen Christ (28:8–10)

       3. First fraudulent denials of Jesus' resurrection (28:11–15)

    C. The Risen Messiah and His Disciples (28:16–20)

       1. Jesus in Galilee (28:16–17)

       2. The Great Commission (28:18–20)

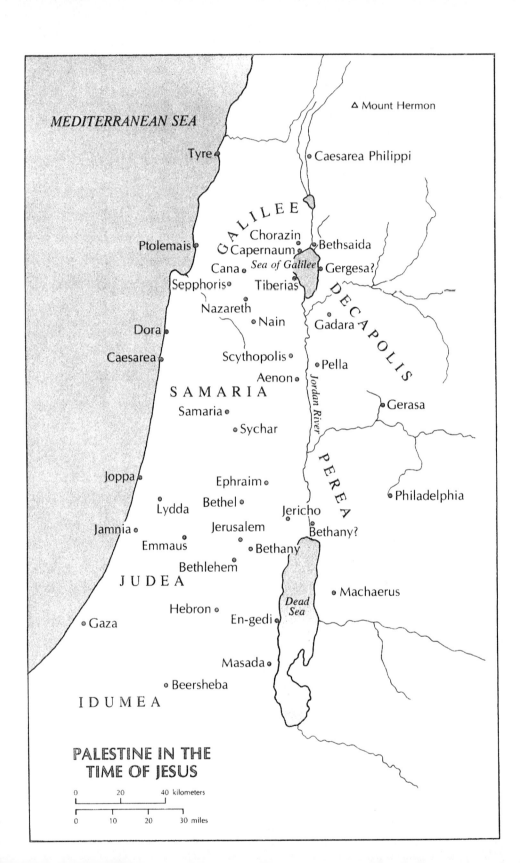

MEDITERRANEAN SEA

△ Mount Hermon

Tyre •

• Caesarea Philippi

G A L I L E E

Chorazin

Ptolemais •

Capernaum • • Bethsaida

Cana •   *Sea of Galilee* • Gergesa?

Sepphoris •

Tiberias

D E C A P O L I S

Nazareth •

• Nain

Gadara •

Dora •

Caesarea •

Scythopolis •

• Pella

Aenon •

Jordan River

S A M A R I A

Samaria •

• Gerasa

• Sychar

P E R E A

Joppa •

Ephraim •

Lydda •

Bethel •

Jericho •

• Philadelphia

Jamnia •

Jerusalem

Bethany?

Emmaus •

• Bethany

Bethlehem •

J U D E A

Dead Sea

• Machaerus

Hebron •

En-gedi •

• Gaza

Masada •

• Beersheba

I D U M E A

**PALESTINE IN THE
TIME OF JESUS**

0   20   40 kilometers

0   10   20   30 miles

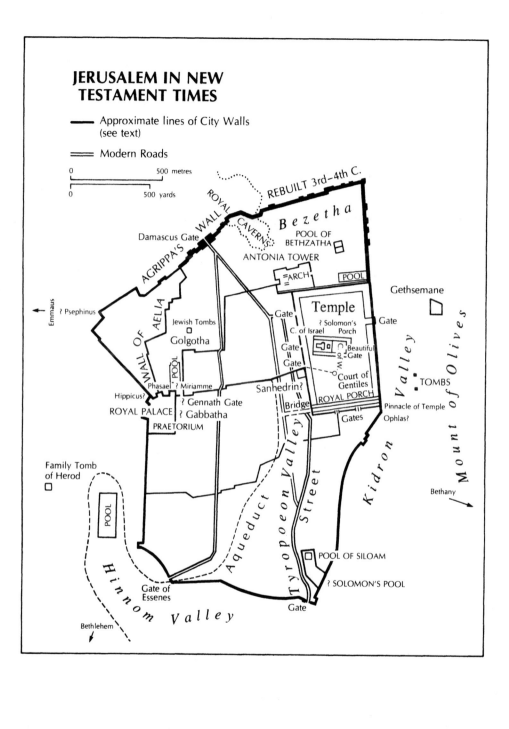

JERUSALEM IN NEW TESTAMENT TIMES

━━━ Approximate lines of City Walls
(see text)

═══ Modern Roads

0 ———————— 500 metres
0 ———————— 500 yards

REBUILT 3rd–4th C.

ROYAL CAVERNS

AGRIPPA'S WALL

Damascus Gate

Bezetha

POOL OF BETHZATHA

ANTONIA TOWER

ARCH

POOL

Gethsemane

Emmaus

? Psephinus

WALL OF AELIA

Jewish Tombs

Golgotha

Gate

Temple

? Solomon's Porch

C. of Israel

Gate

Beautiful Gate

C. of W.

Gate

Gate

POOL

Phasael ? Miriamme

Court of Gentiles

Sanhedrin?

ROYAL PORCH

TOMBS

Kidron Valley

Mount of Olives

Hippicus?

ROYAL PALACE

? Gennath Gate

? Gabbatha

PRAETORIUM

Bridge

Gates

Pinnacle of Temple

Ophlas?

Bethany

Family Tomb of Herod

POOL

Aqueduct

Tyropoeon Valley

Street

POOL OF SILOAM

? SOLOMON'S POOL

Hinnom Valley

Gate of Essenes

Gate

Bethlehem

Text and Exposition

I. Prologue: The Origin and Birth of Jesus the Christ (1:1–2:23)

A. *The Genealogy of Jesus*

1:1–17

A record of the genealogy of Jesus Christ the son of David, the son of Abraham:

²Abraham was the father of Isaac,
  Isaac the father of Jacob,
  Jacob the father of Judah and his brothers,
  ³Judah the father of Perez and Zerah, whose mother was Tamar,
  Perez the father of Hezron,
  Hezron the father of Ram,
  ⁴Ram the father of Amminadab,
  Amminadab the father of Nahshon,
  Nahshon the father of Salmon,
  ⁵Salmon the father of Boaz, whose mother was Rahab,
  Boaz the father of Obed, whose mother was Ruth,
  Obed the father of Jesse,
  ⁶and Jesse the father of King David.

David was the father of Solomon, whose mother had been Uriah's wife,
  ⁷Solomon the father of Rehoboam,
  Rehoboam the father of Abijah,
  Abijah the father of Asa,
  ⁸Asa the father of Jehoshaphat,
  Jehoshaphat the father of Jehoram,
  Jehoram the father of Uzziah,
  ⁹Uzziah the father of Jotham,
  Jotham the father of Ahaz,
  Ahaz the father of Hezekiah,
  ¹⁰Hezekiah the father of Manasseh,
  Manasseh the father of Amon,
  Amon the father of Josiah,
  ¹¹and Josiah the father of Jeconiah and his brothers at the time of the exile to Babylon.

¹²After the exile to Babylon:
  Jeconiah was the father of Shealtiel,
  Shealtiel the father of Zerubbabel,
  ¹³Zerubbabel the father of Abiud,
  Abiud the father of Eliakim,
  Eliakim the father of Azor,
  ¹⁴Azor the father of Zadok,
  Zadok the father of Akim,
  Akim the father of Eliud,
  ¹⁵Eliud the father of Eleazar,
  Eleazar the father of Matthan,
  Matthan the father of Jacob,
  ¹⁶and Jacob the father of Joseph, the husband of Mary, of whom was born Jesus, who is called Christ.

¹⁷Thus there were fourteen generations in all from Abraham to David, fourteen from David to the exile to Babylon, and fourteen from the exile to the Christ.

In each Gospel Jesus' earthly ministry is preceded by an account of John the Baptist's ministry. This formal similarity does not extend to the introductions to the

Gospels. Mark (1:1) opens with a simple statement. Luke begins with a first-person preface in which he explains his purpose and methods, followed by a detailed and often poetic account of the miraculous births of John and Jesus (1:5–2:20) and brief mention of Jesus' boyhood trip to the temple (2:21–52). Luke reserves Jesus' genealogy for chapter 3. John's prologue (1:1–18) traces Jesus' beginnings to eternity and presents the Incarnation without referring to his conception and birth. In each Gospel the introduction anticipates major themes and emphases. In Matthew the prologue (1:1–2:23) introduces such themes as the son of David, the fulfillment of prophecy, the supernatural origin of Jesus the Messiah, and the Father's sovereign protection of his Son in order to bring him to Nazareth and accomplish the divine plan of salvation from sin (cf. esp. Stonehouse, *Witness of Matthew*, pp. 123–28).

1 The first two words of Matthew, *biblos geneseōs*, may be translated "record of the genealogy" (NIV), "record of the origins," or "record of the history." NIV limits this title to the genealogy (1:1–17), the second could serve as a heading for the prologue (1:1–2:23), and the third as a heading for the entire Gospel. The expression is found only twice in the LXX: in Genesis 2:4 it refers to the creation account (Gen 2:4–25) and in Genesis 5:1 to the ensuing genealogy. From the latter it appears possible to follow NIV (so also Hendriksen; Lohmeyer, *Matthäus*; McNeile); but because the noun *genesis* (NIV, "birth") reappears in 1:18 (one of only four NT occurrences), it seems likely that the heading in 1:1 extends beyond the genealogy. No occurrence of the expression as a heading for a book-length document has come to light. Therefore we must discount the increasingly popular view (Davies, *Setting*; Gaechter, *Matthäus*; Hill, *Matthew*; Maier; Zahn) that Matthew means to refer to his entire Gospel, "A record of the history of Jesus Christ." Matthew rather intends his first two chapters to be a coherent and unified "record of the origins of Jesus Christ."

The designation "Jesus Christ the son of David, the son of Abraham" resonates with biblical nuances. (For comments regarding "Jesus," see on 1:21.) "Christ" is roughly the Greek equivalent to "Messiah" or "Anointed." In the OT the term could refer to a variety of people "anointed" for some special function: priests (Lev 4:3; 6:22), kings (1 Sam 16:13; 24:10; 2 Sam 19:21; Lam 4:20), and, metaphorically, the patriarchs (Ps 105:15) and the pagan king Cyrus (Isa 45:1). Already in Hannah's prayer "Messiah" parallels "king": the Lord "will give strength to his king and exalt the horn of his anointed" (1 Sam 2:10). With the rising number of OT prophecies concerning King David's line (e.g., 2 Sam 7:12–16; cf. Ps 2:2; 105:15), "Messiah," or "Christ," became the designation of a figure representing the people of God and bringing in the promised eschatological reign.

In Jesus' day Palestine was rife with messianic expectation. Not all of it was coherent, and many Jews expected two different "Messiahs." But Matthew's linking of "Christ" and "son of David" leaves no doubt of what he is claiming for Jesus.

In the Gospels "Christ" is relatively rare (as compared with Paul's epistles). More important it almost always appears as a title, strictly equivalent to "the Messiah" (see esp. 16:16). But it was natural for Christians after the Resurrection to use "Christ" as a name not less than as a title; increasingly they spoke of "Jesus Christ" or "Christ Jesus" or simply "Christ." Paul normally treats "Christ," at least in part, as a name; but it is doubtful whether the titular force ever entirely disappears (cf. N.T. Wright, "The Messiah and the People of God: A Study in Pauline Theology with Particular Reference to the Argument of the Epistle to the Romans" [Ph.D.

diss., Oxford University, 1980], p. 19). Of Matthew's approximately eighteen occurrences, all are exclusively titular except this one (1:1), probably 1:16, certainly 1:18, and possibly the variant at 16:21. The three uses of "Christ" in the prologue reflect the confessional stance from which Matthew writes; he is a committed Christian who has long since become familiar with the common way of using the word as both title and name. At the same time it is a mark of Matthew's concern for historical accuracy that Jesus is not so designated by his contemporaries.

"Son of David" is an important designation in Matthew. Not only does David become a turning point in the genealogy (1:6, 17), but the title recurs throughout the Gospel (9:27; 12:23; 15:22; 20:30-31; 21:9, 15; 22:42, 45). God swore covenant love to David (Ps 89:29) and promised that one of his immediate descendants would establish the kingdom—even more, that David's kingdom and throne would endure forever (2 Sam 7:12-16). Isaiah foresaw that a "son" would be given, a son with the most extravagant titles: Wonderful Counselor, Mighty God, Everlasting Father, Prince of Peace: "Of the increase of his government and peace there will be no end. He will reign on David's throne and over his kingdom, establishing and upholding it with justice and righteousness from that time on and forever. The zeal of the LORD Almighty will accomplish this" (Isa 9:6-7).

In Jesus' day at least some branches of popular Judaism understood "son of David" to be messianic (cf. Pss Sol 17:21; for a summary of the complex intertestamental evidence, cf. Berger, "Die königlichen Messiastraditionen," esp. pp. 3-9). The theme was important in early Christianity (cf. Luke 1:32, 69; John 7:42; Acts 13:23; Rom 1:3; Rev 22:16). God's promises, though long delayed, had not been forgotten; Jesus and his ministry were perceived as God's fulfillment of covenantal promises now centuries old. The tree of David, hacked off so that only a stump remained, was sprouting a new branch (Isa 11:1).

Jesus is also "son of Abraham." It could not be otherwise, granted that he is son of David. Yet Abraham is mentioned for several important reasons. "Son of Abraham" may have been a recognized messianic title in some branches of Judaism (cf. T Levi 8:15). The covenant with the Jewish people had first been made with Abraham (Gen 12:1-3; 17:7; 22:18), a connection Paul sees as basic to Christianity (Gal 3:16). More important, Genesis 22:18 had promised that through Abraham's offspring "all nations" (*panta ta ethnē*, LXX) would be blessed; so with this allusion to Abraham, Matthew is preparing his readers for the final words of this offspring from Abraham—the commission to make disciples of "all nations" (28:19, *panta ta ethnē*). Jesus the Messiah came in fulfillment of the kingdom promises to David and of the Gentile-blessings promises to Abraham (cf. also Matt 3:9; 8:11).

2-17 Study has shown that genealogies in the Ancient Near East could serve widely diverse functions: economic, tribal, political, domestic (to show family or geographical relationships), and others (see Johnson; also Robert R. Wilson, *Genealogy and History in the Biblical World* [New Haven: Yale University Press, 1977]; R.E. Brown, *Birth of Messiah*, pp. 64-66). The danger in such study is that Matthew's intentions may be overridden by colorful backgrounds of doubtful relevance to the text itself. Johnson sees Matthew's genealogy as a response to Jewish slander. H.V. Wickings ("The Nativity Stories and Docetism," NTS 23 [1977]: 457-60) sees it as an answer to late first-century Docetism that denied the essential humanity of Jesus. One wonders whether a virgin birth would have been the best way to go about correcting the Docetists.

D.E. Nineham ("The Genealogy in St. Matthew's Gospel and Its Significance for the Study of the Gospels," BJRL 58 [1976]: 421–44) finds in this genealogy the assurance that God is in sovereign control. Yet it is unclear how he reconciles this assurance with his conviction that the genealogy is of little historical worth. If Matthew made much of it up, then we may admire his faith that God was in control. But since Matthew's basis was (according to Nineham) faulty, it gives the reader little incentive to share the same faith.

Actually, Matthew's chief aims in including the genealogy are hinted at in the first verse—viz., to show that Jesus Messiah is truly in the kingly line of David, heir to the messianic promises, the one who brings divine blessings to all nations. Therefore the genealogy focuses on King David (1:6) on the one hand, yet on the other hand includes Gentile women (see below). Many entries would touch the hearts and stir the memories of biblically literate readers, though the principal thrust of the genealogy ties together promise and fulfillment. "Christ and the new covenant are securely linked to the age of the old covenant. Marcion, who wished to sever all the links binding Christianity to the Old Testament, knew what he was about when he cut the genealogy out of his edition of Luke" (F.F. Bruce, NBD, p. 459).

For many, whatever its aims, the historical value of Matthew's genealogy is nil. R.E. Brown (*Birth of Messiah*, pp. 505–12) bucks the tide when he cautiously affirms that Jesus sprang from the house of David. Many ancient genealogies are discounted as being of little historical value because they evidently intend to impart more than historical information (cf. esp. Wilson, *Genealogy and History*). To do this, however, is to fall into a false historical disjunction; for many genealogies intend to make more than historical points by referring to historical lines.

Part of the historical evaluation of Matthew 1:2–17 rests on the reliability of Matthew's sources: the names in the first two-thirds of the genealogy are taken from the LXX (1 Chron 1–3, esp. 2:1–15; 3:5–24; Ruth 4:12–22). After Zerubbabel, Matthew relies on extrabiblical sources of which we know nothing. But there is good evidence that records were kept at least till the end of the first century. Josephus (Life 6 [1]) refers to the "public registers" from which he extracts his genealogical information (cf. also Jos. *Contra Apion* I, 28–56 [6–10]). According to Genesis R 98:8, Rabbi Hillel was proved to be a descendant of David because a genealogical scroll was found in Jerusalem. Eusebius (*Ecclesiastical History* 3.19–20) cites Hegesippus to the effect that Emperor Domitian (A.D. 81–96) ordered all descendants of David slain. Nevertheless two of them when summoned, though admitting their Davidic descent, showed their calloused hands to prove they were but poor farmers. So they were let go. But the account shows that genealogical information was still available.

While no twentieth-century Jew could prove he was from the tribe of Judah, let alone from the house of David, that does not appear to have been a problem in the first century, when lineage was important in gaining access to temple worship. Whether Matthew had access to the records himself or gleaned his information from intermediate sources, we cannot know from this distance; but in any case we "have no good reason to doubt that this genealogy was transmitted in good faith" (Albright and Mann).

More difficult is the question of the relation of Matthew's genealogy to Luke's, in particular the part from David on (cf. Luke 3:23–31). There are basic differences between the two: Matthew begins with Abraham and moves forward; Luke begins with Jesus and moves backward to Adam. Matthew traces the line through Jeconiah, Shealtiel, and Zerubbabel; Luke through Neri, Shealtiel, and Zerubbabel. More important, Luke (3:31) traces the line through David's son Nathan (cf. 2 Sam 5:14), and Matthew through the kingly line of Solomon. It is often said that no reconciliation between the two genealogies is possible (e.g., E.L. Abel, "The Genealogies of Jesus Ο ΧΡΙΣΤΟΣ," NTS 20 [1974]: 203-10). Nevertheless two theories are worth weighing.

1. Some have argued that Luke gives Mary's genealogy but substitutes Joseph's name (Luke 3:23) to avoid mentioning a woman. And there is some evidence to support the notion that Mary herself was a descendant of David (cf. Luke 1:32). That Mary was related to Elizabeth, who was married to the Levite Zechariah (Luke 1:5-36), is no problem, since intermarriage between tribes was not uncommon. Indeed, Aaron's wife may well have sprung from Judah (cf. Exod 6:23; Num 2:3) (so Beng., CHS, Luther). H.A.W. Meyer rearranges the punctuation in Luke 3:23 to read "being the son (of Joseph as was supposed) of Heli [i.e., Mary's father], of Matthat." But this is painfully artificial and could not easily be deduced by a reader with a text without punctuation marks or brackets, which is how our NT Greek MSS were first written. Few would guess simply by reading Luke that he is giving Mary's genealogy. The theory stems, not from the text of Luke, but from the need to harmonize the two genealogies. On the face of it, both Matthew and Luke aim to give Joseph's genealogy.

2. Others have argued, more plausibly, that Luke provides Joseph's real genealogy and Matthew the throne succession—a succession that finally jumps to Joseph's line by default. Hill (Matthew) offers independent Jewish evidence for a possible double line (Targ. Zech 12:12). This hypothesis has various forms. The oldest goes back to Julius Africanus (c. A.D. 225; cf. Eusebius Ecclesiastical History 1.7), who argued that Matthew provides the natural genealogy and Luke the royal—the reverse of the modern theory (so Alf, Farrer, Hill, Taylor, Westcott, Zahn). In its modern form the theory seems reasonable enough: where the purpose is to provide Joseph's actual descent back to David, this could best be done by tracing the family tradition through his real father Heli, to his father Matthat, and thus back to Nathan and David (so Luke); and where the purpose is to provide the throne succession, it is natural to begin with David and work down.

As most frequently presented, this theory has a serious problem (cf. R.E. Brown, Birth of Messiah, pp. 503-4). It is normally argued that Joseph's father in Matthew 1:16, Jacob, was a full brother of Joseph's father mentioned in Luke 3:23, Heli; that Jacob, the royal heir, died without offspring; and that Heli married Jacob's widow according to the laws of levirate marriage (Deut 25:5-10). (Though levirate marriages may not have been common in the first century, it is unlikely that they were completely unknown. Otherwise the question of the Sadducees [22:24-28] was phrased in irrelevant terms.) But if Jacob and Heli are to be reckoned as full brothers, then Matthan (Matt) and Matthat (Luke) must be the same man—even though their fathers, Eleazar (Matt) and Levi (Luke) respectively, are different. It seems artificial to appeal to a second levirate marriage. Some have therefore argued that Jacob and Heli were only half-brothers, which entails a further coincidence—viz., that their mother married two men, Matthan and Matthat, with remarkably similar names. We do not know whether levirate marriage was practiced in the case of half-brothers. Moreover since the whole purpose of levirate marriage was to raise up a child in the deceased father's name, why does Luke provide the name of the actual father?

R.E. Brown judges the problems insurmountable but fails to consider the elegant solution suggested by Machen (pp. 207–9) fifty years ago. If we assume that Matthat and Matthan are *not* the same person, there is no need to appeal to levirate marriage. The difficulty regarding the father of Matthat and the father of Matthan disappears; yet their respective sons Levi and Jacob may have been so closely related (e.g., if Levi was an heirless only son whose sister married Jacob or Joseph) that if Levi died, Jacob's son Joseph became his heir. Alternatively, if Matthan and Matthat *are* the same person (presupposing a levirate marriage one generation earlier), we "need only to suppose that Jacob [Joseph's father according to Matthew] died without issue, so that his nephew, the son of his brother Heli [Joseph's father according to Luke] would become his heir" (p. 208).

Other differences between Matthew and Luke are more amenable to obvious solutions. As for the omissions from Matthew's genealogy and the structure of three series of fourteen, see on 1:17.

2 Of the twelve sons of Jacob, Judah is singled out, as his tribe bears the scepter (Gen 49:10; cf. Heb 7:14). The words "and his brothers" are not "an addition which indicates that of the several possible ancestors of the royal line Judah alone was chosen" (Hill, *Matthew*), since that restriction was already achieved by stipulating Judah; and in no other entry (except 1:11; see comment) are the words "and his brothers" added. The point is that, though he comes from the royal line of Judah and David, Messiah emerges within the matrix of the covenant people (cf. the reference to Judah's brothers). Neither the half-siblings of Isaac nor the descendants of Jacob's brother, Esau, qualify as the covenant people in the OT. This allusive mention of the Twelve Tribes as the locus of the people of God becomes important later (cf. 8:11 with 19:28). Even the fact that there were twelve apostles is relevant.

3–5 Probably Perez and Zerah (v.3) are both mentioned because they are twins (Gen 38:27; cf. 1 Chron 2:4); Judah's other sons receive no mention. Ruth 4:12, 18–22 traces the messianic line from Perez to David. There is some evidence that "son of Perez" was a rabbinic designation of Messiah (SBK, 1:18), but the dating of the sources is uncertain.

Tamar, wife of Judah's son Er, is the first of four women mentioned in the genealogy (for comment, see on 1:6). Little is known of Hezron (Gen 46:12; 1 Chron 2:5), Ram (1 Chron 2:9), Amminadab (v.4; Exod 6:23; Num 1:7; 1 Chron 2:10), Nahshon (Num 2:3; 7:12; "the leader of the people of Judah," 1 Chron 2:10), and Salmon (v.5; Ruth 4:18–21; 1 Chron 2:11). Amminadab is associated with the desert wanderings in the time of Moses (Num 1:7). Therefore approximately four hundred years (Gen 15:13; Exod 12:40) are covered by the four generations from Perez to Amminadab. Doubtless several names have been omitted: the Greek verb translated "was the father of" (*gennaō*) does not require immediate relationship but often means something like "was the ancestor of" or "became the progenitor of."

Similarly, the line between Amminadab and David is short: more names may have been omitted. Whether such names properly fit before Boaz, so that Rahab was not the immediate mother of Boaz (just as Eve was not immediately "the mother of all the living," Gen 3:20), or after Boaz, or both, one cannot be sure. It is almost certain, however, that the Rahab mentioned is the prostitute of Joshua 2 and 5 (see further on 1:6). Boaz (1 Chron 2:11–12), who figures so prominently in the Book of Ruth, married the Moabitess (see on 1:6) and sired Obed, who became the father of Jesse (Ruth 4:22; 1 Chron 2:12).

6 The word "King" with "David" would evoke profound nostalgia and arouse eschatological hope in first-century Jews. Matthew thus makes the royal theme explicit: King Messiah has appeared. David's royal authority, lost at the Exile, has now been regained and surpassed by "great David's greater son" (so James Montgomery's hymn "Hail to the Lord's Anointed"; cf Box; Hill, *Matthew*; also cf. 2 Sam 7:12-16; Ps 89:19-29, 35-37; 132:11). David became the father of Solomon; but Solomon's mother "had been Uriah's wife" (cf. 2 Sam 11:27; 12:4). Bathsheba thus becomes the fourth woman to be mentioned in this genealogy.

Inclusion of these four women in the Messiah's genealogy instead of an all-male listing (which was customary)—or at least the names of such great matriarchs as Sarah, Rebekah, and Leah—shows that Matthew is conveying more than merely genealogical data. Tamar enticed her father-in-law into an incestuous relationship (Gen 38). The prostitute Rahab saved the spies and joined the Israelites (Josh 2, 5); Hebrews 11:31 and James 2:25 encourage us to think she abandoned her former way of life. She is certainly prominent in Jewish tradition, some of it fantastic (cf. A.T. Hanson, "Rahab the Harlot in Early Christian Tradition," *Journal for the Study of the New Testament* 1 [1978]: 53–60). Ruth, Tamar, and Rahab were aliens. Bathsheba was taken into an adulterous union with David, who committed murder to cover it up. Matthew's peculiar way of referring to her, "Uriah's wife," may be an attempt to focus on the fact that Uriah was not an Israelite but a Hittite (2 Sam 11:3; 23:39). Bathsheba herself was apparently the daughter of an Israelite (1 Chron 3:5 [variant reading]); but her marriage to Uriah probably led to her being regarded as a Hittite.

Several reasons have been suggested to explain the inclusion of these women. Some have pointed out that three were Gentiles and the fourth probably regarded as such (Lohmeyer, *Matthäus;* Maier; Schweizer, *Matthew*). This goes well with the reference to Abraham (cf. on 1:1); the Jewish Messiah extends his blessings beyond Israel, even as Gentiles are included in his line. Others have noted that three of the four were involved in gross sexual sin; but it is highly doubtful that this charge can be legitimately applied to Ruth. As a Moabitess, however, she had her origins in incest (Gen 19:30-37); and Deuteronomy 23:3 banned the offspring of Moabites from the assembly of the Lord to the tenth generation. R.E. Brown (*Birth of Messiah*, pp. 71–72) discounts this interpretation of the role of the four women, because in first-century Jewish piety they were largely whitewashed and revered. Yet it is not at all certain that Matthew follows his contemporaries in all this. It is important that in this same chapter Matthew introduces Jesus as the one who "will save his people from their sins" (1:21), and this verse may imply a backward glance at some of the better-known sins of his own progenitors.

A third interpretation (favored by Allen, R.E. Brown, Filson, Fenton, Green, Hill, Klostermann, Lohmeyer, Peake) holds that all four reveal something of the strange and unexpected workings of Providence in preparation for the Messiah and that as such they point to Mary's unexpected but providential conception of Jesus.

There is no reason to rule out any of the above interpretations. Matthew, Jew that he is, knows how to write with an allusive touch; and readers steeped in the OT would naturally call to mind a plethora of images associated with many names in this selective genealogy.

7–10 The names in these verses seem to have been taken from 1 Chronicles 3:10–14. Behind "Asa" (v.7) lurks a difficult textual decision (cf. Notes). There is no obvious pattern: wicked Rehoboam was the father of wicked Abijah, the father of the good king Asa. Asa was the father of the good king Jehoshaphat (v.8), who sired the wicked king Joram. Good or evil, they were part of Messiah's line; for though grace does not run in the blood, God's providence cannot be deceived or outmaneuvered.

Three names have been omitted between Joram and Uzziah: Ahaziah, Joash, and Amaziah (2 Kings 8:24; 1 Chron 3:11; 2 Chron 22:1, 11; 24:27). "Uzziah" (vv.8–9) is equivalent to Azariah (1 Chron 3:11; cf. 2 Kings 15:13, 30 with 2 Kings 15:1). The three omissions not only secure fourteen generations in this part of the genealogy (see on 1:17) but are dropped because of their connection with Ahab and Jezebel, renowned for wickedness (2 Kings 8:27), and because of their connection with wicked Athaliah (2 Kings 8:26), the usurper (2 Kings 11:1–20). Two of the three were notoriously evil; all three died violently.

R.E. Brown (*Birth of Messiah*, p. 82) points out that Manasseh was even more wicked, and he is included. Therefore (with Schweizer, *Matthew*), Brown prefers an explanation of the omissions based on a text-critical confusion between "Azariah" and "Uzziah." This conjecture is plausible; but if it is correct, it would have to be pre-Matthean, because Matthew's "fourteens" (see on 1:17) would require this omission or an equivalent. But there is no textual evidence to support the conjecture. Also, Manasseh (v.10), though notoriously evil, repented, unlike the other three.

11 Another name has been dropped: Josiah was the father of Jehoiakim (609–597 B.C.), who was deposed in favor of his son Jehoiachin (some MSS in both OT and NT have "Jeconiah" for the latter). He was deposed after a reign of only three months; and his brother Zedekiah reigned in his stead till the final deportation and destruction of the city in 587 B.C. (cf. 2 Kings 23:34; 24:6, 14–15; 1 Chron 3:16; Jer 27:20; 28:1). The words "and his brothers" are probably added in this instance because one of them, Zedekiah, maintained a caretaker reign until the tragedy of 587 B.C.; but Zedekiah is not mentioned because the royal line does not flow through him but through Jeconiah. The Exile to Babylon marked the end of the reign of David's line, a momentous event in OT history. Alternatively "and his brothers" may refer, not to the royal brothers, but to all the Jews who went into captivity with Jeconiah (Gundry, *Matthew*). The locus of the people of God is thus traced from the patriarchs ("and his brothers," 1:2) to the shame of the Exile, a theme to be developed later (see on 2:16–18).

12 The final list of "fourteen" (see on 1:17) begins with a further mention of the Exile. First Chronicles 3:17 records that Jeconiah (Jehoiachin) was the father of Shealtiel. Matthew goes on to present Shealtiel as the father of Zerubbabel, in accord with Ezra 3:2; 5:2; Nehemiah 12:1; Haggai 1:1; 2:2, 23. The difficulty lies in 1 Chronicles 3:19, which presents Zerubbabel as the son of Pedaiah, a brother of Shealtiel.

Several solutions have been offered, most not very convincing (cf. Machen, pp. 206–7). Some Greek MSS omit Pedaiah in 1 Chronicles 3:19. But the best suggestion is a levirate marriage (Deut 25:5–10; cf. Gen 38:8–9), scarcely an embarrassment to those who have adopted the explanation above (cf. on vv.2–17) and find no other levirate marriage in the genealogy. If Shealtiel were the older brother and died childless, Pedaiah might well have married the widow to "build up his brother's family line" (Deut 25:9). In any case Zerubbabel himself becomes a messianic model (cf. Hag 2:20–23).

13–15 The nine names from Abiud to Jacob are not otherwise known to us today. Possibly names have been omitted from this genealogical section also, but then one wonders why this third section of the genealogy appears to lack one entry (see on 1:17). Gundry's explanations (*Matthew*) of these names is tortured: certain names from Luke's list "catch the evangelist's [Matthew's] eye," as do names from the priestly (nonroyal) list in 1 Chronicles 6:3–14—names that then need abbreviating or changing to mask their priestly connection.

16 The wording in the best reading (cf. Notes), reflected in NIV, is precise. Joseph's royal line has been traced; Joseph is the husband of Mary; Mary is the mother of Jesus. The relation between Joseph and Jesus is so far unstated. But this peculiar form of expression cries out for the explanation provided in the ensuing verses. Legally Jesus stands in line to the throne of David; physically he is born of a woman "found to be with child through the Holy Spirit" (1:18). Her son is Jesus, "who is called Christ." The Greek does not make it clear whether "Christ" is titular or not; but name or title, Jesus' messiahship is affirmed.

17 It was customary among Jewish writers to arrange genealogies according to some convenient scheme, possibly for mnemonic reasons. Strictly speaking the Greek text speaks of "all the generations from Abraham to David . . . to Christ" (cf. KJV, NASB); but since the omissions are obvious to both Matthew and his readers, the expression must mean "all the generations . . . included in this table." So it becomes a hint that the fourteens, here so strongly brought to the reader's attention, are symbolic.

Various arrangements of the three fourteens have been proposed. In one the first set of fourteen runs from Abraham to David, the second from Solomon to Jeconiah, and the third attains fourteen by repeating Jeconiah and running to Jesus. Hendriksen (pp. 125–26) suggests Matthew purposely counts Jeconiah twice: first he presents Jeconiah as cursed, childless, deported (2 Kings 24:8–12; Jer 22:30); the second time he reminds the reader that Jeconiah was subsequently released from prison and restored and became the father of many (2 Kings 25:27–30; 1 Chron 3:17–18; Jer 52:31–34)—a new man as it were. But Matthew does not mention these themes, which do not clearly fit into the main concerns of this chapter. Schweizer prefers to count from Abraham to David. Then, because David is mentioned twice, he passes from David to Josiah, the last free king; and then Jeconiah to Jesus provides a third set of fourteen, at the expense of making the central set one member short and of ignoring the small but distinct literary pause at the end of 1:11. McNeile postulates a possible loss of one name between Jeconiah and Shealtiel owing to homoeoteleuton (identical endings), but there is no textual evidence for it. Gundry (*Matthew*) thinks that Mary as well as Joseph counts for one, pointing to the two kinds of generation, legal (Joseph's) and physical (Mary's). No solution so far proposed seems entirely convincing, and it is difficult to rule any out.

The symbolic value of the fourteens is of more significance than their precise breakdown. Herman C. Waetjen ("The Genealogy as the Key to the Gospel According to Matthew," JBL 95 [1976]: 205–30; cf. Johnson, pp. 193–94) tries to solve both problems by appealing to 2 Baruch 53–74 (usually dated c. A.D. 50–70). This apocalyptic book divides history into a scheme of 12 + 2 = 14 units. Matthew, Waetjen argues, holds that just as David and Jeconiah are transitional figures in the genealogy, so also is Jesus. He is the end of the third period and simultaneously the beginning of the fourth, the inaugurated kingdom. Jesus is therefore the thirteenth and the fourteenth entries, the former a period of gloom in 2 Baruch (corresponding to the Passion in Matthew) and the fourteenth opening into the new age.

But this analysis will not do. Two objections are crucial: (1) it is not at all clear that one may legitimately jump from schematized time periods in apocalyptic literature to names in a genealogy (Is anything less apocalyptic than a genealogy?) just because of a common number; (2) Waetjen has "corrected" the omission in the third set of fourteen by listing Jesus twice, even though the second reference to Jesus, in his scheme, properly belongs to the inaugurated kingdom and not to the third set, which remains deficient.

Schemes like those of Hendriksen and Goodspeed that reduce the 3 × 14 pattern to 6 × 7 and then picture Jesus' coming to inaugurate the seventh seven—the sign of perfection, the dawning of the Messianic Age (cf. 1 Enoch 91:12–17; 93:1–10)— stumble over the fact that Matthew has not presented his genealogy as six sevens but as three fourteens (cf. R.E. Brown, *Birth of Messiah*, p. 75). Other suggestions include those of Johnson (pp. 189–208) and Goulder (pp. 228–33).

The simplest explanation—the one that best fits the context—observes that the numerical value of "David" in Hebrew is fourteen (cf. Notes). By this symbolism Matthew points out that the promised "son of David" (1:1), the Messiah, has come. And if the third set of fourteen is short one member, perhaps it will suggest to some readers that just as God cuts short the time of distress for the sake of his elect (24:22), so also he mercifully shortens the period from the Exile to Jesus the Messiah.

Notes

1 For a broader grasp of the place of the Messiah in the OT, cf. Ladd, *NT Theology*, pp. 136ff.; Douglas, *Bible Dictionary*, 2:987–95.

3 Older EV (e.g., KJV) have the names Tamar and Hezron in the OT and Thamar and Esrom in the NT. Because English OT names are roughly transliterated from the Hebrew and English NT names are roughly transliterated from the Greek, which for many names transliterates from the Hebrew, we have these variations. NIV rightly smooths them out.

7–8 In these verses the best textual evidence supports Ἀσάφ (*Asaph*), not Ἀσά (*Asa*). It is transcriptionally more probable that *Asaph* would be changed to *Asa* than vice versa (for the opposite view, cf. Lagrange). Julius Schniewind (*Das Evangelium nach Matthäus* [Göttingen: Vandenhoeck und Ruprecht, 1965]) and Gundry (*Matthew*) suggest *Asaph* is a deliberate change by Matthew to call up images of the psalmist (Pss 50, 73–83), as "Amos" (cf. note on v.10) calls to mind the prophet. This is too cryptic to be believable. Orthography was not so consistent in the ancient world as it is today. Josephus (Antiq. VIII, 290–315 [xii. 1–6]), for instance, uses Ἄσανος (*Asanos*); but in the ancient Latin translation *Asaph* is presupposed. "Mary" varies in the NT between Μαρία (*Maria*) and Μαριάμ (*Mariam*). In 1 Chron 3:10 LXX most MSS read (*Asa*, but one offers Ἀσάβ

(*Asab;* cf. Metzger, *Textual Commentary,* p. 1, n. 1). In short Matthew could well be following a MS with *Asaph* even though *Asa* is quite clearly the person meant.

10 The textual evidence for Ἀμώς (*Amōs*) and Ἀμών (*Amōn*) breaks down much as in vv.7–8. In this case, however, there is greater diversity in the readings of LXX MSS for 1 Chron 3:14, on which Matt 1:10 depends.

11 The term μετοικεσία (*metoikesia,* "exile") occurs but three times in the NT, all in this chapter (vv.11–12, 17); but it refers (in LXX) to the Babylonian exile in 2 Kings 24:16; 1 Chron 5:22; Ezek 12:11. Βαβυλῶνος (*Babylōnos,* "Babylon") is a genitive "of direction and purpose" (cf. BDF, par. 166).

Schweizer's suggestion (*Matthew*) that Jehoiakim and his son Jehoiachin have been fused into a single figure because in 2 Kings 24:6 (LXX) they are both called "Jehoiakim" explains little, since Matthew betrays a deep knowledge of the OT not likely to be confused by one versional mistransliteration; and in any case Matthew's term is "Jeconiah."

16 The best textual variant, supported by a spread of text types in Greek and versional witnesses and by all but one uncial, stands behind NIV. Several Caesarean and OL witnesses prefer "Joseph, to whom was betrothed the virgin Mary who begot Jesus who is called Christ." This is transcriptionally less likely than the first alternative, in which "the husband" of Mary might well have been thought misleading. No Greek MS supports syr[s] in its reading: "Joseph, to whom was betrothed Mary the virgin, begot Jesus who is called the Christ." At first glance it seems to deny the Virgin Birth by ascribing paternity to Joseph; but the "begot" may have merely legal significance, since Mary is still referred to as "the virgin." In any case this last reading is not well attested. The enormously complex problems of textual criticism in this verse are competently treated by Metzger, *NT Studies,* pp. 105–13; Machen, pp. 176–87; R.E. Brown, *Birth of Messiah,* pp. 62–64, 139; and A. Globe, "Some Doctrinal Variants in Matthew 1 and Luke 2, and the Authority of the Neutral Text," CBQ 42 (1980): 55–72, esp. pp. 63–65.

17 In the ancient world letters served not only as the building blocks of words but also as symbols of numbers. Hence any word had a numerical value; and the use of such symbolism is known as gematria. In Hebrew "David" is דָּוִד (*dāwiḏ*); and d = 4, w = 6 (the vowels, a later addition to the text, don't count). Therefore "David" = *dwd* = 4 + 6 + 4 = 14. (This would not work in the DSS, where, with one exception [CD 7:16], the consonantal spelling of "David" is *dwyd* = דּוּיד.)

B. *The Birth of Jesus*

1:18–25

18This is how the birth of Jesus Christ came about: His mother Mary was pledged to be married to Joseph, but before they came together, she was found to be with child through the Holy Spirit. 19Because Joseph her husband was a righteous man and did not want to expose her to public disgrace, he had in mind to divorce her quietly.

20But after he had considered this, an angel of the Lord appeared to him in a dream and said, "Joseph son of David, do not be afraid to take Mary home as your wife, because what is conceived in her is from the Holy Spirit. 21She will give birth to a son, and you are to give him the name Jesus, because he will save his people from their sins."

22All this took place to fulfill what the Lord had said through the prophet: 23"The virgin will be with child and will give birth to a son, and they will call him Immanuel"—which means, "God with us."

24When Joseph woke up, he did what the angel of the Lord had commanded him and took Mary home as his wife. 25But he had no union with her until she gave birth to a son. And he gave him the name Jesus.

Two matters call for brief remarks: the historicity of the Virgin Birth (more properly, virginal conception), and the theological emphases surrounding this theme in Matthew 1–2 and its relation to the NT.

First, the historicity of the Virgin Birth is questioned for many reasons.

1. The accounts in Matthew and Luke are apparently independent and highly divergent. This argues for creative forces in the church making up all or parts of the stories in order to explain the person of Jesus. But the stories have long been shown to be compatible (Machen), even mutually complementary. Moreover literary independence of Matthew and Luke at this point does not demand the conclusion that the two evangelists were ignorant of the other's content. Yet if they were, their differences suggest to some the strength of mutual compatibility without collusion. Matthew focuses largely on Joseph, Luke on Mary. R.E. Brown (*Birth of Messiah*, p. 35) does not accept this because he finds it inconceivable that Joseph could have told his story without mentioning the Annunciation or that Mary could have passed on her story without mentioning the flight to Egypt. True enough, though it does not follow that the evangelists were bound to include all they knew. It is hard to imagine how the Annunciation would have fit in very well with Matthew's themes. Moreover we have already observed that Matthew was prepared to omit things he knew in order to present his chosen themes coherently and concisely.

2. Some simply discount the supernatural. Goulder (p. 33) says Matthew made the stories up; Schweizer (*Matthew*) contrasts the ancient world in which virgin birth was (allegedly) an accepted notion with modern scientific limitations on what is possible. But the antithesis is greatly exaggerated: thoroughgoing rationalists were not uncommon in the first century (e.g., Lucretius); and millions of modern Christians, scientifically aware, find little difficulty in believing in the Virgin Birth or in a God who is capable of intervening miraculously in what is, after all, his own creation. More important, Matthew's point in these chapters is surely that the Virgin Birth and attendant circumstances were most extraordinary. Only here does he mention Magi; and dreams and visions as a means of guidance are by no means common in the NT (though even here one wonders whether Western Christianity could learn something from Third-World Christianity). Certainly Matthew's account is infinitely more sober than the wildly speculative stories preserved in the apocryphal gospels (e.g., *Protevangelium of James* 12:3–20:4; cf. Hennecke, 1:381–85). R.E. Brown (*Birth of Messiah*) accepts the historicity of the Virgin Birth but discounts the historicity of the visit of the Magi and related events. But if he can swallow the Virgin Birth, it is difficult to see why he strains out the Magi. (See the useful book of Manuel Miguens, *The Virgin Birth: An Evaluation of Scriptual Evidence* [Westminster, Md.: Christian Classics, 1975].)

3. Many point to artificialities in the narrative: e.g., the structure of the genealogy or the delay in mentioning Bethlehem as the place of birth (Hill, *Matthew*). We have noted, however, that though Matthew's arrangement of the genealogy gives us more than a mere table of names and dates, it does not tell us less. More than any of the synoptists, Matthew delights in topical arrangements. But that does not make his accounts less than historical. We are not shut up to the extreme choice historical chronicles or theological invention! Matthew does not mention Bethlehem in 1:18–25 because it does not suit any of his themes. In chapter 2, however, as Tatum has shown (W.B. Tatum, Jr., "The Matthean Infancy Narratives: Their Form, Structure, and Relation to the Theology of the First Evangelist" [Ph.D. dissertation,

Duke University, 1967]), one of the themes unifying Matthew's narrative is Jesus' "geographical origins"; and therefore Bethlehem is introduced.

4. It has become increasingly common to identify the literary genre in Matthew 1–2 as "midrash" or "midrashic haggadah" and to conclude that these stories are not intended to be taken literally (e.g., with widely differing perspectives, Gundry, *Matthew;* Goulder; Davies, *Setting*, pp. 66–67). There is nothing fundamentally objectionable in the suggestion that some stories in the Bible are not meant to be taken as fact; parables are such stories. The problem is the slipperiness of the categories (cf. Introduction, section 12.b; and cf. further on 2:16–18). If the genre has unambiguous formal characteristics, there should be little problem in recognizing them. But this is far from being so; the frequently cited parallels boast as many formal differences (compared with Matt 1–2) as similarities. To cite one obvious example: Jewish Midrashim (in the technical, fourth-century sense) present stories as illustrative material by way of comment on a running OT text. By contrast Matthew 1–2 offers no running OT text: the continuity of the text depends on the story-line; and the OT quotations, taken from a variety of OT books, could be removed without affecting that continuity (cf. esp. M.J. Down, "The Matthean Birth Narratives," ExpT 90 [1978–79]: 51–52; and France, *Jesus;* see on 2:16–18).

R.E. Brown (*Birth of Messiah*, pp. 557–63) argues convincingly that Matthew 1–2 is not midrash. Yet he thinks the sort of person who could invent stories to explain OT texts (midrash) could also invent stories to explain Jesus. Matthew 1–2, though not itself midrash, is at least midrashic. That may be so. Unfortunately, not only does the statement fall short of proof, but the appeal to a known and recognizable literary genre is thus lost. So we have no objective basis for arguing that Matthew's first readers would readily detect his midrashic methods. Of course, if "midrashic" means that Matthew intends to present a panorama of OT allusions and themes, these chapters are certainly midrashic: in that sense the studies of Goulder, Gundry, Davies, and others have served us well, by warning us against a too-rigid pattern of linear thought. But used in this sense, it is not at all clear that "midrashic material" is necessarily unhistorical.

5. A related objection insists that these stories "are not primarily didactic but kerygmatic" (Davies, *Setting* p. 67), that they are intended as proclamations about the truth of the person of Jesus but not as factual information. The rigid dichotomy between proclamation and teaching is not as defensible as when C.H. Dodd first proposed it (see on 3:1). More important, we may ask just what the proclamation intended to proclaim. If the stories express the appreciation of the first Christians for Jesus, precisely what did they appreciate? On the face of it, Matthew in chapters 1–2 is not saying something vague, such as, "Jesus was so wonderful there must be a touch of the divine about him," but rather, "Jesus is the promised Messiah of the line of David, and he is 'Emmanuel,' 'God with us,' because his birth was the result of God's supernatural intervention, making Jesus God's very Son; and his early months were stamped with strange occurrences which, in the light of subsequent events, weave a coherent pattern of theological truths and historical attestation to divine providence in the matter."

6. Some argue that the (to us) artificial way these chapters cite the OT shows a small concern for historicity. The reverse argument is surely more impressive: If the events of Matthew 1–2 do not relate easily to the OT texts, this attests their historical credibility; for no one in his right mind would invent "fulfillment" episodes problematic to the texts being fulfilled. The fulfillment texts, though difficult, do fit

into a coherent pattern (cf. Introduction, section 11.b, and below on 1.22–23). More importantly, their presence shows that Matthew sees Jesus as one who fulfills the OT. This not only sets the stage for some of Matthew's most important themes; it also means that Matthew is working from a perspective on salvation history that depends on before and after, prophecy and fulfillment, type and antitype, relative ignorance and progressive revelation. This has an important bearing on our discussion of midrash, because whatever else Jewish midrash may be, it is not related to salvation history or fulfillment schemes. Add to the foregoing considerations the fact that, wherever in chapters 1–2 he can be tested against the known background of Herod the Great, Matthew proves reliable (some details below). There is a good case for treating chapters 1–2 as both history and theology.

Second, the following theological considerations require mention.

1. Often it is argued, or even assumed (e.g., Dunn, *Christology*, pp. 49–50), that the concepts "virginal conception" and "preexistence" applied to the one person Jesus are mutually exclusive. Certainly it is difficult to see how a divine being could become genuinely human by means of an ordinary birth. Nevertheless there is no logical or theological reason to think that virginal conception and preexistence preclude each other.

2. Related to this is the theory of R.E. Brown (*Birth of Messiah*, pp. 140–41), who proposes a retrojected Christology. The early Christians, he argues, first focused attention on Jesus' resurrection, which they perceived as the moment of his installation into his messianic role. Then with further reflection they pushed back the time of his installation to his baptism, then to his birth, and finally to a theory regarding his preexistence. There may be some truth to the scheme. Just as the first Christians did not come to an instant grasp of the relationship between law and gospel (as the Book of Acts amply demonstrates), so their understanding of Jesus doubtless matured and deepened with time and further revelation. But the theory often depends on a rigid and false reconstruction of early church history (cf. Introduction, section 2) and dates the documents, against other evidence, on the basis of this reconstruction. Worse, in the hands of some it transforms the understanding of the disciples into historical reality: that is, Jesus had no preexistence and was not virgin born, but these things were progressively predicated of him by his followers. Gospel evidence for Jesus' self-perception as preexistent is then facilely dismissed as late and inauthentic. The method is of doubtful worth.

Matthew, despite his strong insistence on Jesus' virginal conception, includes several veiled allusions to Jesus' preexistence; and there is no reason to think he found the two concepts incompatible. Moreover R.H. Fuller ("The Conception/Birth of Jesus as a Christological Moment," *Journal for the Study of the New Testament* 1 [1978]: 37–52) has shown that the virginal conception-birth motif in the NT is not infrequently connected with the "sending of the Son" motif, which (contra Fuller) in many places already presupposes the preexistence of the Son.

3. We are dealing in these chapters with King Messiah who comes to his people in covenant relationship. The point is well established, if occasionally exaggerated, by Nolan, who speaks of the "Royal Covenant Christology."

4. It is remarkable that the title "Son of God," important later in Matthew, is not found in Matthew 1–2. It may lurk behind 2:15. Still it would be false to argue that Matthew does not connect the Virgin Birth with the title "Son of God." Matthew 1–2 serves as a finely wrought prologue for every major theme in the Gospel. We must therefore understand Matthew to be telling us that if Jesus is physically Mary's

son and legally Joseph's son, at an even more fundamental level he is God's Son; and in this Matthew agrees with Luke's statement (Luke 1:35). The dual paternity, one legal and one divine, is unambiguous (cf. Cyrus H. Gordon, "Paternity at Two Levels," JBL 96 [1977]: 101).

18 The word translated "birth" is, in the best MSS (cf. Notes), the word translated "genealogy" in 1:1. Maier prefers "history" of Jesus Christ, taking the phrase to refer to the rest of the Gospel. Yet it is best to take the word to mean "birth" or "origins" in the sense of the beginnings of Jesus Messiah. Even a well-developed christology would not want to read the man "Jesus" and his name back into a preexistent state (cf. on 1:1). The pledge to be married was legally binding. Only a divorce writ could break it, and infidelity at that stage was considered adultery (cf. Deut 22:23-24; Moore, *Judaism*, 2:121-22). The marriage itself took place when the groom (already called "husband," 1:19) ceremoniously took the bride home (see on 25:1-13). Mary is here introduced unobtrusively. Though comparing the Gospel accounts gives us a picture of her, she does not figure largely in Matthew.

"Before they came together" (*prin ē synelthein autous*) occasionally refers in classical Greek to sexual intercourse (LSJ, p. 1712); in the other thirty instances of *synerchomai* in the NT, there is, however, no sexual overtone. But here sexual union is included, occurring at the formal marriage when the "wife" moved in with her "husband." Only then was sexual intercourse proper. The phrase affirms that Mary's pregnancy was discovered while she was still betrothed, and the context presupposes that both Mary and Joseph had been chaste (cf. McHugh, pp. 157-63; and for the customs of the day, M *Kiddushin* ["Betrothals"] and M *Ketuboth* ["Marriage Deeds"]).

That Mary was "found" to be with child does not suggest a surreptitious attempt at concealment ("found out") but only that her pregnancy became obvious. This pregnancy came about through the Holy Spirit (even more prominent in Luke's birth narratives). There is no hint of pagan deity-human coupling in crassly physical terms. Instead, the power of the Lord, manifest in the Holy Spirit who was expected to be active in the Messianic Age, miraculously brought about the conception.

19 The peculiar Greek expression in this verse allows several interpretations. There are three important ones.

1. Because Joseph, knowing about the virginal conception, was a just man and had no desire to bring the matter out in the open (i.e., to divulge this miraculous conception), he felt unworthy to continue his plans to marry one so highly favored and planned to withdraw (so Gundry, *Matthew*; McHugh, pp. 164-72; Schlatter). This assumes that Mary told Joseph about the conception. Nevertheless the natural way to read vv.18-19 is that Joseph learned of his betrothed's condition when it became unmistakable, not when she told him. Moreover the angel's reason for Joseph to proceed with the marriage (v.20) assumes (contra Zerwick, par. 477) that Joseph did not know about the virginal conception.

2. Because Joseph was a just man, and because he did not want to expose Mary to public disgrace, he proposed a quiet divorce. The problem with this is that "just" (NIV, "righteous") is not defined according to OT law but is taken in the sense of "merciful," "not given to passionate vengeance," or even "nice" (cf. 1 Sam 24:17). But this is not its normal sense. Strictly speaking justice conceived in Mosaic prescriptions demanded some sort of action.

3. Because he was a righteous man, Joseph therefore could not in conscience marry Mary who was now thought to be unfaithful. And because such a marriage would have been a tacit admission of his own guilt, and also because he was unwilling to expose her to the disgrace of public divorce, Joseph therefore chose a quieter way, permitted by the law itself. The full rigor of the law might have led to Mary's stoning, though that was rarely carried out in the first century. Still, a public divorce was possible, though Joseph was apparently unwilling to expose Mary to such shame. The law also allowed for private divorce before two witnesses (Num 5:11–31, interpreted as in M *Sotah* 1:1–5; cf. David Hill, "A Note on Matthew i. 19," ExpT 76 [1964–65]: 133–34; rather similar, A. Tosato, "Joseph, Being a Just Man (Matt 1:19)," CBQ 41 [1979]: 547–51). That was what Joseph purposed. It would leave both his righteousness (his conformity to the law) and his compassion intact.

20 Joseph tried to solve his dilemma in what seemed to him the best way possible. Only then did God intervene with a dream. Dreams as means of divine communication in the NT are concentrated in Matthew's prologue (1:20; 2:2, 13, 19, 22; elsewhere, possibly 27:19; Acts 2:17). An "angel of the Lord" (four times in the prologue: 1:20, 24; 2:13, 19) calls to mind divine messengers in past ages (e.g., Gen 16:7–14; 22:11–18; Exod 3:2–4:16), in which it was not always clear whether the heavenly "messenger" (the meaning of *angelos*) was a manifestation of Yahweh. They most commonly appeared as men. We must not read medieval paintings into the word "angel" or the stylized cherubim of Revelation 4:6–8. The focus is on God's gracious intervention and the messenger's private communication, not on the details of angelology and their panoramic sweeps of history common in Jewish apocalyptic literature (Bonnard).

The angel's opening words, "Joseph son of David," ties this pericope to the preceding genealogy, maintains interest in the theme of the Davidic Messiah, and, from Joseph's perspective, alerts him to the significance of the role he is to play. The prohibition, "Do not be afraid," confirms that Joseph had already decided on his course when God intervened. He was to "take" Mary home as his wife—an expression primarily reflecting marriage customs of the day but not excluding sexual intercourse (cf. TDNT, 4:11–14, for other uses of the verb)—because Mary's pregnancy was the direct action of the Holy Spirit (a reason that makes nonsense of the attempt by James Lagrand ["How Was the Virgin Mary 'like a man'. . .? A Note on Mt i 18b and Related Syriac Christian Texts," NovTest 22 (1980): 97–107] to make the reference to the Holy Spirit in 1:18, *ek pneumatos hagiou* ["through the Holy Spirit"], mean that Mary brought forth, "as a man, by will").

21 It was no doubt divine grace that solicited Mary's cooperation before the conception and Joseph's cooperation only after it. Here Joseph is drawn into the mystery of the Incarnation. In patriarchal times either a mother (Gen 4:25) or a father (Gen 4:26; 5:3; cf. R.E. Brown, *Birth of Messiah*, p. 130) could name a child. According to Luke 1:31, Mary was told Jesus' name; but Joseph was told both name and reason for it. The Greek is literally "you will call his name Jesus," strange in both English and Greek. This is not only a Semitism (BDF, par. 157 [2]—the expression recurs in 1:23, 25; Luke 1:13, 31) but also uses the future indicative (*kaleseis*, lit., "you will call") with imperatival force—hence NIV, "You are to give him the name Jesus." This construction is very rare in the NT, except where the LXX is being cited; the effect is to give the verse a strong OT nuance.

"Jesus" (*Iēsous*) is the Greek form of "Joshua" (cf. Gr. of Acts 7:45; Heb 4:8), which, whether in the long form *yᵉhôšuaʿ* ("Yahweh is salvation," Exod 24:13) or in one of the short forms, e.g., *yēšûaʿ* ("Yahweh saves," Neh 7:7), identifies Mary's Son as the one who brings Yahweh's promised eschatological salvation. There are several Joshuas in the OT, at least two of them not very significant (1 Sam 6:14; 2 Kings 23:8). Two others, however, are used in the NT as types of Christ: Joshua, successor to Moses and the one who led the people into the Promised Land (and a type of Christ in Heb 3–4), and Joshua the high priest, contemporary of Zerubbabel (Ezra 2:2; 3:2–9; Neh 7:7), "the Branch" who builds the temple of the Lord (Zech 6:11–13). But instead of referring to either of these, the angel explains the significance of the name by referring to Psalm 130:8: "He [Yahweh] himself will redeem Israel from all their sins" (cf. Gundry, *Use of OT*, pp. 127–28).

There was much Jewish expectation of a Messiah who would "redeem" Israel from Roman tyranny and even purify his people, whether by fiat or appeal to law (e.g., Pss Sol 17). But there was no expectation that the Davidic Messiah would give his own life as a ransom (20:28) to save his people from their sins. The verb "save" can refer to deliverance from physical danger (8:25), disease (9:21–22), or even death (24:22); in the NT it commonly refers to the comprehensive salvation inaugurated by Jesus that will be consummated at his return. Here it focuses on what is central, viz., salvation from sins; for in the biblical perspective sin is the basic (if not always the immediate) cause of all other calamities. This verse therefore orients the reader to the fundamental purpose of Jesus' coming and the essential nature of the reign he inaugurates as King Messiah, heir of David's throne (cf. Ridderbos, pp. 193ff.).

Though to Joseph "his people" would be the Jews, even Joseph would understand from the OT that some Jews fell under God's judgment, while others became a godly remnant. In any event, it is not long before Matthew says that both John the Baptist (3:9) and Jesus (8:11) picture Gentiles joining with the godly remnant to become disciples of the Messiah and members of "his people" (see on 16:18; cf. Gen 49:10; Titus 2:13–14; Rev 14:4). The words "his people" are therefore full of meaning that is progressively unpacked as the Gospel unfolds. They refer to "Messiah's people."

22 Although most EV conclude the angel's remarks at the end of v.21, there is good reason to think that they continue to the end of v.23, or at least to the end of the word "Immanuel." This particular fulfillment formula occurs only three times in Matthew: here; 21:4; 26:56. In the last it is natural to take it as part of Jesus' reported speech (cf. 26:55); and this is possible, though less likely, in 21:4. Matthew's patterns are fairly consistent. So it is not unnatural to extend the quotation to the end of 1:23 as well. (JB recognizes Matthew's consistency by ending Jesus' words in 26:55, making 26:56 Matthew's remark!) This is more convincing when we recall that only these three fulfillment formulas use the perfect *gegonen* (NIV, "took place") instead of the expected aorist. Some take the verb as an instance of a perfect standing for an aorist (so BDF, par. 343, but this is a disputed classification). Others think it means that the event "stands recorded" in the abiding Christian tradition (McNeile; Moule, *Idiom Book*, p. 15); still others take it as a stylistic indicator that Matthew himself introduced the fulfillment passage (Rothfuchs, pp. 33–36). But if we hold that Matthew presents the angel as saying the words, then the perfect may enjoy its normal force: "all this has taken place" (cf. esp. Fenton; cf. also Stendahl, Peake; B. Weiss, *Das Matthäus-Evangelium* [Göttingen: Vandenhoeck und Ruprecht, 1898]; Zahn).

R.E. Brown (*Birth of Messiah*, p. 144, n. 31) objects that nowhere in Scripture does an angel cite Scripture in this fashion; but, equally, nowhere in Scripture is there a virgin birth in this fashion. Matthew knew that Satan can cite Scripture (4:6–7); he may not have thought it strange if an angel does. Broadus's objection, that the angel would in that case be anticipating an event that has not yet occurred, and this is strange when cast in fulfillment language, lacks weight; for the conception has occurred, and the pregnancy has become well advanced, even if the birth has not yet taken place. Joseph needs to know at this stage that "all this took place" to fulfill what the Lord had said through the prophet. The weightiest argument is the perfect tense.

The last clause is phrased with exquisite care, literally, "the word spoken by [hypo] the Lord through [dia] the prophet." The prepositions make a distinction between the mediate and the intermediate agent (RHG, p. 636), presupposing a view of Scripture like that in 2 Peter 1:21. Matthew uses the verb "to fulfill" (*plēroō*) primarily in his own fulfillment formulas (1:22; 2:15, 17, 23; 4:14; 8:17; 12:17; 13:35; 21:4; 26:56; 27:9; cf. 26:54) but also in a few other contexts (3:15; 5:17; 13:48; 23:32). (On Matthew's understanding of fulfillment and on the origins of his fulfillment texts, cf. 5:17–20 and Introduction, section 11.b.)

Here two observations are in order. First, most of Matthew's OT quotations are easy enough to understand, but the difficult exceptions have sometimes tended to increase the difficulty of the easier ones. Hard cases make bad theology as well as bad law. Second, Matthew is not simply ripping texts out of OT contexts because he needs to find a prophecy in order to generate a fulfillment. Discernible principles govern his choices, the most important being that he finds in the OT not only isolated predictions regarding the Messiah but also OT history and people as paradigms that, to those with eyes to see, point forward to the Messiah (e.g., see on 2:15).

23 This verse, on which the literature is legion, is reasonably clear in its context here in Matthew. Mary is the virgin; Jesus is her son, Immanuel. But because it is a quotation from Isaiah 7:14, complex issues are raised concerning Matthew's use of the OT.

The linguistic evidence is not as determinative as some think. The Hebrew word 'almāh is not precisely equivalent to the English word "virgin" (NIV), in which all the focus is on the lack of sexual experience; nor is it precisely equivalent to "young woman," in which the focus is on age without reference to sexual experience. Many prefer the translation "young woman of marriageable age." Yet most of the few OT occurrences refer to a young woman of marriageable age who is also a virgin. The most disputed passage is Proverbs 30:19: "The way of a man with a *maiden*." Here the focus of the word is certainly not on virginity. Some claim that here the maiden cannot possibly be a virgin; others (see esp. E.J. Young, *Studies in Isaiah* [London: Tyndale, 1954], pp. 143–98; Richard Niessen, "The Virginity of the עַלְמָה in Isaiah 7:14," BS 137 [1980]: 133–50) insist that Proverbs 30:19 refers to a young man wooing and winning a maiden still a virgin.

Although it is fair to say that most OT occurrences presuppose that the 'almāh is a virgin, because of Proverbs 30:19, one cannot be certain the word necessarily means that. Linguistics has shown that the etymological arguments (reviewed by Niessen) have little force. Young argues that 'almāh is chosen by Isaiah because the most likely alternative (*bᵉtûlāh*) can refer to a married woman (Joel 1:8 is commonly cited; Young is supported by Gordon J. Wenham, "*Bethulah*, 'A Girl of

Marriageable Age,'" VetTest 22 [1972]: 326–29). Again, however, the linguistic argument is not as clear-cut as we might like. Tom Wadsworth ("Is There a Hebrew Word for Virgin? *Bethulah* in the Old Testament," *Restoration Quarterly* 23 [1980]: 161–71) insists that every occurrence of *bᵉṭûlāh* in the OT does refer to a virgin: the woman in Joel 1:8, for instance, is betrothed. Again the evidence is a trifle ambiguous. In short there is a presumption in favor of rendering *ʿalmāh* by "young virgin" or the like in Isaiah 7:14. Nevertheless other evidence must be given a hearing.

The LXX renders the word by *parthenos*, which almost always means "virgin." Yet even with this word there are exceptions: Genesis 34:4 refers to Dinah as a *parthenos* even though the previous verse makes it clear she is no longer a virgin. This sort of datum prompts C.H. Dodd ("New Testament Translation Problems I," *The Bible Translator* 27 [1976]: 301–5, published posthumously) to suggest that *parthenos* means "young woman" even in Matthew 1:23 and Luke 1:27. This will not do; the overwhelming majority of the occurrences of *parthenos* in both biblical and profane Greek require the rendering "virgin"; and the unambiguous context of Matthew 1 (cf. vv.16, 18, 20, 25) puts Matthew's intent beyond dispute, as Jean Carmignac ("The Meaning of *parthenos* in Luke 1.27: A reply to C.H. Dodd," *The Bible Translator* 28 [1977]: 327–30) was quick to point out. If, unlike the LXX, the later (second century A.D.) Greek renderings of the Hebrew text of Isaiah 7:14 prefer *neanis* ("young woman") to *parthenos* (so Aq., Symm., Theod.), we may legitimately suspect a conscious effort by the Jewish translators to avoid the Christian interpretation of Isaiah 7:14.

The crucial question is how we are to understand Isaiah 7:14 in its relationship to Matthew 1:23. Of the many suggestions, five deserve mention.

1. Hill, J.B. Taylor (Douglas, *Bible Dictionary*, 3:1625), and others support W.C. van Unnik's argument ("Dominus Vobiscum," *New Testament Essays*, ed. A.J.B. Higgins [Manchester: University Press, 1959], pp. 270–305), who claimed Isaiah meant that a young woman named her child Immanuel as a tribute to God's presence and deliverance and that the passage applies to Jesus because Immanuel fits his mission. This does not take the "sign" (Isa 7:11, 14) seriously; v.11 expects something spectacular. Nor does it adequately consider the time lapse (vv.15–17). Moreover, it assumes a very casual link between Isaiah and Matthew.

2. Many others take Isaiah as saying that a young woman—a virgin at the time of the prophecy (Broadus)—would bear a son and that before he reaches the age of discretion (perhaps less than two years from the time of the prophecy), Ahaz will be delivered from his enemies. Matthew, being an inspired writer, sees a later fulfillment in Jesus; and we must accept it on Matthew's authority. W.S. LaSor thinks this provides canonical support for a *sensus plenior* ("fuller sense") approach to Scripture ("The *Sensus Plenior* and Biblical Interpretation," *Scripture, Tradition, and Interpretation*, edd. W. Ward Gasque and William S. LaSor [Grand Rapids: Eerdmans, 1978], pp. 271–72). In addition to several deficiencies in interpreting Isaiah 7:14–17 (e.g., the supernaturalness of the sign in 7:11 is not continued in 7:14), this position is intrinsically unstable, seeking either a deeper connection between Isaiah and Matthew or less reliance on Matthew's authority. Hendriksen (p. 140) holds that the destruction of Pekah and Rezin was a clear sign that the line of the Messiah was being protected. But this is to postulate, without textual warrant, two signs—the sign of the child and the sign of the deliverance—and it presupposes that Ahaz possessed remarkable theological acumen in recognizing the latter sign.

3. Many (esp. older) commentators (e.g., Alexander, Hengstenberg, Young) reject any notion of double fulfillment and say that Isaiah 7:14 refers exclusively to Jesus Christ. This does justice to the expectation of a miraculous sign, the significance of "Immanuel," and the most likely meaning of 'almāh and parthenos. But it puts more strain on the relation of a sign to Ahaz. It seems weak to say that before a period of time equivalent to the length of time between Jesus' (Immanuel's) conception and his reaching an age of discretion Ahaz's enemies will be destroyed. Most commentators in this group insist on a miraculous element in "sign" (v.11). But though Immanuel's birth is miraculous, how is the "sign" given Ahaz miraculous?

4. A few have argued, most recently Gene Rice ("A Neglected Interpretation of the Immanuel Prophecy," ZAW 90 [1978]: 220–27), that in Isaiah 7:14–17 Immanuel represents the righteous remnant—God is "with them"—and that the mother is Zion. This may be fairly applied to Jesus and Mary in Matthew 1:23, since Jesus' personal history seems to recapitulate something of the Jews' national history (cf. 2:15; 4:1–4). Yet this sounds contrived. Would Ahaz have understood the words so metaphorically? And though Jesus sometimes appears to recapitulate Israel, it is doubtful that NT writers ever thought Mary recapitulates Zion.

5. The most plausible view is that of J.A. Motyer ("Context and Content in the Interpretation of Isaiah 7:14," *Tyndale Bulletin* 21 [1970]: 118–25). It is a modified form of the third interpretation and depends in part on recognizing a crucial feature in Isaiah. Signs in the OT may function as a "present persuader" (e.g., Exod 4:8–9) or as "future confirmation" (e.g., Exod 3:12). Isaiah 7:14 falls in the latter case because Immanuel's birth comes too late to be a "present persuader." The "sign" (v.11) points primarily to threat and foreboding. Ahaz has rejected the Lord's gracious offer (vv.10–12), and Isaiah responds in wrath (v.13). The "curds and honey" Immanuel will eat (v.15) represent the only food left in the land on the day of wrath (vv.18–22). Even the promise of Ephraim's destruction (v.8) must be understood to embrace a warning (v.9b; Motyer, "Isaiah 7:14," pp.121–22). Isaiah sees a threat, not simply to Ahaz, but to the "house of David" (vv.2, 13) caught up in faithlessness. To this faithless house Isaiah utters his prophecy. Therefore Immanuel's birth follows the coming events (it is a "future confirmation") and will take place when the Davidic dynasty has lost the throne.

Motyer shows the close parallels between the prophetic word to Judah (7:1–9:7) and the prophetic word to Ephraim (9:8–11:16). To both there come the moment of decision as the Lord's word threatens wrath (7:1–17; 9:8–10:4), the time of judgment mediated by the Assyrian invasion (7:18–8:8; 10:5–15), the destruction of God's foes but the salvation of a remnant (8:9–22; 10:16–34), and the promise of a glorious hope as the Davidic monarch reigns and brings prosperity to his people (9:1–7; 11:1–16). The twofold structure argues for the cohesive unity between the prophecy of Judah and that to Ephraim. If this is correct, Isaiah 7:1–9:7 must be read as a unit—i.e., 7:14 must not be treated in isolation. The promised Immanuel (7:14) will possess the land (8:8), thwart all opponents (8:10), appear in Galilee of the Gentiles (9:1) as a great light to those in the land of the shadow of death (9:2). He is the Child and Son called "Wonderful Counselor, Mighty God, Everlasting Father, Prince of Peace" in 9:6, whose government and peace will never end as he reigns on David's throne forever (9:7).

Much of Motyer's work is confirmed by a recent article by Joseph Jensen ("The Age of Immanuel," CBQ 41 [1979]: 220–39; he does not refer to Motyer), who extends the plausibility of this structure by showing that Isaiah 7:15 should be taken in a final sense; i.e., Immanuel will eat the bread of affliction in order to learn (unlike Ahaz!) the lesson of obedience. There is no reference to "age of discretion." Further, Jensen believes that 7:16–25 points to Immanuel's coming only after the destruction of the land (6:9–13 suggests the destruction extends to Judah as well as to Israel); that Immanuel and Maher-Shalal-Hash-Baz, Isaiah's son (8:1), are not the same; and that only Isaiah's son sets a time limit relevant to Ahaz.

The foregoing discussion was unavoidable. For if Motyer's view fairly represents Isaiah's thought, and if Matthew understood him in this way, then much light is shed on the first Gospel. The Immanuel figure of Isaiah 7:14 is a messianic figure, a point Matthew has rightly grasped. Moreover this interpretation turns on an understanding of the place of the Exile in Isaiah 6–12, and Matthew has divided up his genealogy (1:11–12, 17) precisely in order to draw attention to the Exile. In 2:17–18 the theme of the Exile returns. A little later, as Jesus begins his ministry (4:12–16), Matthew quotes Isaiah 9:1–2, which, if the interpretation adopted here is correct, properly belongs to the Immanuel prophecies of Isaiah 7:14, 9:6. Small wonder that after such comments by Matthew, Jesus' next words announced the kingdom (4:17; cf. Isa 9:7). Isaiah's reference to Immanuel's affliction for the sake of learning obedience (cf. on Isa 7:15 above) anticipates Jesus' humiliation, suffering, and obedient sonship, a recurring theme in this Gospel.

This interpretation also partially explains Matthew's interest in the Davidic lineage; and it strengthens a strong interpretation of "Immanuel." Most scholars (e.g., Bonnard) suppose that this name in Isaiah reflects a hope that God would make himself present with his people ("Immanuel" derives from ʿ *imnānû* ʾēl, "God with us"); and they apply the name to Jesus in a similar way, to mean that God is with us, and for us, because of Jesus. But if Immanuel in Isaiah is a messianic figure whose titles include "Mighty God," there is reason to think that "Immanuel" refers to Jesus himself, that he is "God with us." Matthew's use of the preposition "with" at the end of 1:23 favors this (cf. Fenton, "Matthew 1:20–23," p. 81). Though "Immanuel" is not a name in the sense that "Jesus" is Messiah's name (1:21), in the OT Solomon was named "Jedidiah" ("Beloved of Yahweh," 2 Sam 12:25), even though he apparently was not called that. Similarly Immanuel is a "name" in the sense of title or description.

No greater blessing can be conceived than for God to dwell with his people (Isa 60:18–20); Ezek 48:35; Rev 21:23). Jesus is the one called "God with us": the designation evokes John 1:14, 18. As if that were not enough, Jesus promises just before his ascension to be with us to the end of the age (28:20; cf. also 18:20), when he will return to share his messianic banquet with his people (25:10).

If "Immanuel" is rightly interpreted in this sense, then the question must be raised whether "Jesus" (1:21) should receive the same treatment. Does "Jesus" ("Yahweh saves") mean Mary's Son merely brings Yahweh's salvation, or is he himself in some sense the Yahweh who saves? If "Immanuel" entails the higher christology, it is not implausible that Matthew sees the same in "Jesus." The least we can say is that Matthew does not hesitate to apply OT passages descriptive of Yahweh directly to Jesus (cf. on 3:3).

Matthew's quotation of Isaiah 7:14 is very close to the LXX; but he changes "you will call" to "they will call." This may reflect a rendering of the original Hebrew, if 1QIsaᵃ is pointed appropriately (cf. Gundry, *Use of OT*, p. 90). But there is more here: The people whose sins Jesus forgives (1:21) are the ones who will gladly call him "God with us" (cf. Frankemölle, pp. 17–19).

24–25. When Joseph woke up (from his sleep, not his dream), he "took Mary home as his wife" (v.24; same expression as in 1:20). Throughout Matthew 1–2 the pattern of God's sovereign intervention followed by Joseph's or the Magi's response is repeated. While the story is told simply, Joseph's obedience and submission under these circumstances is scarcely less remarkable than Mary's (Luke 1:38).

Matthew wants to make Jesus' virginal conception quite unambiguous, for he adds that Joseph had no sexual union with Mary (lit., he did not "know" her, an OT euphemism) until she gave birth to Jesus (v.25). The "until" clause most naturally means that Mary and Joseph enjoyed normal conjugal relations after Jesus' birth (cf. further on 12:46; 13:55). Contrary to McHugh (p. 204), the imperfect *eginōsken* ("did not know [her]") does not hint at continued celibacy after Jesus' birth but stresses the faithfulness of the celibacy till Jesus' birth.

So the virgin-conceived Immanuel was born. And eight days later, when the time came for him to be circumcised (Luke 2:21), Joseph named him "Jesus."

Notes

18 Some MSS have γέννησις (gennēsis, "birth") instead of γένεσις (genesis, "birth," "origin," or "history"): the two words are easily confused both orthographically and, in early pronunciation systems, phonetically. The former word is common in the Fathers to refer to the Nativity and is cognate with γεννάω (gennaō, "I beget"); so it is transcriptionally less likely to be original.

The δέ (de, "but") beginning the verse is doubtless a mild adversative. All the preceding generations have been listed, "but" the birth of Jesus comes into a class of its own.

Οὕτως (houtōs, "thus") with the verb ἦν (ēn, "was") is rare and is here equivalent to τοιαύτη (toiautē, "in this way"; cf. BDF, par. 434 [2]).

"Holy Spirit" is anarthrous, which is not uncommon in the Gospels; and in that case the word order is always πνεῦμα ἅγιον (pneuma hagion). When the article is used, there is an approximately even distribution between τὸ ἅγιον πνεῦμα (to hagion pneuma, "the Holy Spirit") and τὸ πνεῦμα τὸ ἅγιον (to pneuma to hagion, "the Spirit the Holy"); cf. Moule, *Idiom Book*, p. 113.

19 In δίκαιος ὢν καὶ μὴ θέλων (dikaios ōn kai mē thelōn, lit., "being just and not willing"; NIV, "a righteous man and did not want"), it does not seem possible to take the first participle concessively (i.e., "although a righteous man") because of the kai; the two participles should be taken as coordinate.

20 Ἰδού (idou, "behold") appears for the first of sixty-two times in Matthew. It often introduces surprising action (Schlatter), or serves to arouse interest (Hendriksen); but it is so common it seems sometimes to have no force at all (cf. Moulton, *Prolegomena*, p. 11; E.J. Pryke, "ΙΔΕ and ΙΔΟΥ," NTS 14 [1968]: 418–24).

21 The noun ἁμαρτία (hamartia, "sin") occurs at 3:6; 9:2, 5–6; 12:31; 26:38; ἁμαρτάνω (hamartanō, "I sin") is found at 18:15, 21; 27:4; and ἁμαρτωλός (hamartōlos, "sinner") at 9:10–11, 13; 11:19; 26:45.

22 Contrary to Moule (*Idiom Book*, p. 142), the ἵνα (hina, "in order to" or "with the result that") clause is not ecbatic (consecutive). Although in NT Greek hina is not always telic, yet the very idea of fulfillment presupposes an overarching plan; and if there be such a

plan, it is difficult to imagine Matthew saying no more than that such and such took place with the result that the Scriptures were fulfilled, unless the Mind behind the plan has no power to effect it—which is clearly contrary to Matthew's thought. See further on 5:17.

C. The Visit of the Magi

2:1–12

[1]After Jesus was born in Bethlehem in Judea, during the time of King Herod, Magi from the east came to Jerusalem [2]and asked, "Where is the one who has been born king of the Jews? We saw his star in the east and have come to worship him."

[3]When King Herod heard this he was disturbed, and all Jerusalem with him. [4]When he had called together all the people's chief priests and teachers of the law, he asked them where the Christ was to be born. [5]"In Bethlehem in Judea," they replied, "for this is what the prophet has written:

[6] 'But you, Bethlehem, in the land of Judah,
are by no means least among the rulers of Judah;
for out of you will come a ruler
who will be the shepherd of my people Israel.' "

[7]Then Herod called the Magi secretly and found out from them the exact time the star had appeared. [8]He sent them to Bethlehem and said, "Go and make a careful search for the child. As soon as you find him, report to me, so that I too may go and worship him."

[9]After they had heard the king, they went on their way, and the star they had seen in the east went ahead of them until it stopped over the place where the child was. [10]When they saw the star, they were overjoyed. [11]On coming to the house, they saw the child with his mother Mary, and they bowed down and worshiped him. Then they opened their treasures and presented him with gifts of gold and of incense and of myrrh. [12]And having been warned in a dream not to go back to Herod, they returned to their country by another route.

Few passages have received more diverse interpretations than this one (cf. W.A. Schulze, "Zur Geschichte der Auslegung von Matth. 2,1–12," *Theologische Zeitschrift* 31 [1975]: 150–60: M. Hengel and H. Merkel, "Die Magier aus dem Osten und die Flucht nach Ägypten (Mt 2) im Rahmen der antiken Religionsgeschichte und der Theologie des Matthäus," in Hoffmann et al., pp. 139–69). During the last hundred years or so, such diversity has sometimes sprung from a reluctance to accept either the supernatural details or the entire story as historically true. Thus it becomes necessary to find theological motive for creating the pericope. E. Nellessen (*Das Kind und seine Mutter* [Stuttgart: KBW, 1969]), though acute in his theological observations, maintains the evangelist has fused and improved two Palestinian (and probably Galilean) legends (similarly Soarés Prabhu, pp. 261–93).

Many (e.g., Gundry, Hill, Schweizer) suppose that the OT quotations constituted a collection of testimonia to Jesus in their own right, before Matthew (or the church from which he sprang) embellished them with midrashic stories to produce our Matthew 2. The stories have doubtful ties with history. Their real point is theological, to show that the Messiah was born in Bethlehem as predicted, that his appearance provoked Jewish hostility but won Gentile acceptance (the Magi), and above all to set up a contrast between Moses and Jesus.

Jewish tradition is steeped in stories about Pharaoh's astrologers knowing that the mother of Israel's future deliverer was pregnant, that there was a slaughter (by drowning) of all Jewish and Egyptian infants for the next nine months, that the entire house in which Moses was born was filled with great light, etc. Matthew, therefore, may have been trying to show Jesus' significance by ascribing to his birth similar and perhaps greater effects. Full-blown, these stories about Moses are preserved in Midrash Rabbah on Exodus 1, an eighth century A.D. compilation. Their roots, however, stretch at least as far back as the first century (Jos. Antiq. II, 205–7, 15–16[ix.2–3]; cf. also Targ. j on Exod 1:15; and Davies, *Setting*, pp. 78–82, for other veiled hints to Moses in Matt. 1–2).

This reconstruction has numerous weaknesses. The independent existence of collected testimonia is not certain. There is no evidence of Midrashim written on such a diverse collection of texts (if the collection itself ever existed). The presupposed antithesis between theology and history is false; on the face of it, Matthew records history so as to bring out its theological significance and its relation to Scripture. Matthew writes at so early a time that if Jesus had not been born in Bethlehem this claim would have been challenged. We are dealing with decades, not the millennium and a half separating Moses from Josephus.

First-century stories about astrological deductions connected with Augustus Caesar's birth (Suetonius *De Vita Caesarum* 94), about Parthian visits to Nero (Cicero *De Divinatione* 1.47), or about Moses' birth (above) may suggest that Matthew 2:1–12 was fabricated; but they may equally attest the prevalence of astrology and the fact that some such visits undoubtedly occurred in the ancient world. Thus they would establish the verisimilitude of the passage. More important, the stories about Moses' birth (e.g., in Jos.) were almost certainly regarded by most readers as factually true; and there can be little doubt (contra Gundry) that Matthew intends his stories about Jesus to be read the same way. If so, we may conceivably argue that Matthew was himself deceived or else wished to deceive. What we cannot do is to argue that he wrote in a fashion recognized by its form to be divorced from historical reality. In any case, the suggested backdrop—stories about Moses' birth—is not very apt; close study shows the theological matrix of the prologue centering on Jesus as the Davidic King and Son of God (cf. esp. Nolan; Kingsbury, *Matthew*), not on him as the new Moses, to whom the allusions are few and inexplicit.

Of course Matthew did not just chronicle meaningless events. He wrote to develop his theme of fulfillment of Scripture (Had not God promised that nations would be drawn to Messiah's light [Isa 60:3]?); to establish God's providential and supernatural care of this virgin-born Son; to anticipate the hostilities, resentment, and suffering he would face; and to hint at the fact that Gentiles would be drawn into his reign (cf. Isa 60:3; Nellessen, *Das Kind*, p. 120, acutely compares 8:11–12; cf. 28:16–20). The Magi will be like the men of Nineveh who will rise up in judgment and condemn those who, despite their privilege of much greater light, did not receive the promised Messiah and bow to his reign (12:41–42).

1 Bethlehem, the place near which Jacob buried his Rachel (Gen 35:19) and Ruth met Boaz (Ruth 1:22–2:6), was preeminently the town where David was born and reared. For Christians it has become the place where angel hosts broke the silence and announced Messiah's birth (Luke 2). It is distinguished from the Bethlehem in Zebulun (Josh 19:15) by the words "in Judea." Scholars have seen in these two words a preparation for v.6: "Bethlehem, in the land of Judah" (though there the Hebrew form "Judah" is used rather than the Greek "Judea"), or for v.2: "king of

the Jews." But "Bethlehem in Judea" may be not much more than a stereotyped phrase (cf. Judg 17:7, 9; 19:1–20; Ruth 1:1–2; 1 Sam 17:12; Matt 2:5). Luke 2:39 makes no mention of an extended stay in Bethlehem and a trip to Egypt before the return to Nazareth; if he knew of these events, Luke found them irrelevant to his purpose.

Unlike Luke, Matthew offers no description of Jesus' birth or the shepherd's visit; he specifies the time of Jesus' birth as having occurred during King Herod's reign (so also Luke 1:5). Herod the Great, as he is now called, was born in 73 B.C. and was named king of Judea by the Roman Senate in 40 B.C. By 37 B.C. he had crushed, with the help of Roman forces, all opposition to his rule. Son of the Idumean Antipater, he was wealthy, politically gifted, intensely loyal, an excellent administrator, and clever enough to remain in the good graces of successive Roman emperors. His famine relief was superb and his building projects (including the temple, begun 20 B.C.) admired even by his foes. But he loved power, inflicted incredibly heavy taxes on the people, and resented the fact that many Jews considered him a usurper. In his last years, suffering an illness that compounded his paranoia, he turned to cruelty and in fits of rage and jealousy killed close associates, his wife Mariamne (of Jewish descent from the Maccabeans), and at least two of his sons (cf. Jos. Antiq. XIV–XVIII; S. Perowne, *The Life and Times of Herod the Great* [London: Hodder and Stoughton, 1956]; and esp. Abraham Schalit, *König Herodes: Der Mann und sein Werk* [Berlin: de Gruyter, 1969]).

Traditionally some have argued that Herod died in 4 B.C.; so Jesus must have been born before that. Josephus (Antiq. XVII, 167[vi.4]) mentions an eclipse of the moon shortly before Herod's death, and this has normally been identified as having occurred on 12–13 March 4 B.C. After Herod's death there was a Passover celebration (Jos. Wars II, 10[i.3]; Antiq. XVII, 213[ix.3]), presumably 11 April 4 B.C.; so the date of his death at first glance seems secure. Recently, however, Ernest L. Martin (*The Birth of Christ Recalculated!* [Pasadena: FBR, 1978], pp. 22–49) has advanced solid reasons for thinking the eclipse occurred 10 January 1 B.C.; and, integrating this information with his interpretation of other relevant data, Martin proposes a birth date for Jesus in September, 2 B.C. (His detailed pinpointing of 1 Sept., based on his understanding of Rev 12:1–5, is too speculative to be considered.) Several lines of evidence stand against this thesis: Josephus dates the length of Herod's reign as thirty-seven years from his accession or thirty-four from the time of his effective reign (Antiq. XVII, 191[viii.1]; Wars I, 665[xxxiii.8]), and these favor a death date in 4 B.C. Coins dated at the time of 4 B.C., minted under the reign of Herod's sons, support the traditional date.

Martin answers these objections by supposing that Herod's successors antedated their reigns to 4 B.C. in honor of Herod's sons Alexander and Aristobulus whom he had killed in that year and by arguing that between 4 B.C. and 1 B.C. there was some form of joint rule shared by Herod and his son Antipater. In that case Josephus's figures relating to the length of Herod's rule refer to his unshared reign. This is psychologically unconvincing; the man who murdered two of his sons out of paranoia and jealousy and arranged to have hundreds of Jewish leaders executed on the day of his death was not likely to share his authority, even in a merely formal way. The question remains unresolved. For a more traditional dating of Jesus' birth in late 5 B.C. or early 4 B.C., see Hoehner, *Chronological Aspects*, pp. 11–27 (written before Martin's work).

The "Magi" (*magoi*) are not easily identified with precision. Several centuries earlier the term was used for a priestly caste of Medes who enjoyed special power to interpret dreams. Daniel (1:20; 2:2; 4:7; 5:7) refers to *magoi* in the Babylonian Empire. In later centuries down to NT times, the term loosely covered a wide variety of men interested in dreams, astrology, magic, books thought to contain mysterious references to the future, and the like. Some Magi honestly inquired after truth; many were rogues and charlatans (e.g., Acts 8:9; 13:6, 8; cf. R.E. Brown, *Birth of Messiah*, pp. 167–68, 197–200; TDNT, 4:356–59). Apparently these men came to Bethlehem spurred on by astrological calculations. But they had probably built up their expectation of a kingly figure by working through assorted Jewish books (cf. W.M. Ramsey, *The Bearing of Recent Discovery on the Trustworthiness of the New Testament*, 4th ed. [London: Hodder and Stoughton, 1920], pp. 140–49).

The tradition that the Magi were kings can be traced as far back as Tertullian (died c. 225). It probably developed under the influence of OT passages that say kings will come and worship Messiah (cf. Pss 68:29, 31; 72:10–11; Isa 49:7; 60:1–6). The theory that there were *three* "wise men" is probably a deduction from the *three* gifts (2:11). By the end of the sixth century, the wise men were named: Melkon (later Melchior), Balthasar, and Gasper. Matthew gives no names. His *magoi* come to Jerusalem (which, like Bethlehem, has strong Davidic connections [2 Sam 5:5–9]), arriving, apparently (cf. Note 5), from the east—possibly from Babylon, where a sizable Jewish settlement wielded considerable influence, but possibly from Persia or from the Arabian desert. The more distant Babylon may be supported by the travel time apparently required (see on 2:16).

2 The Magi saw a star "when it rose" (NIV mg.; cf. note at 2:1). What they saw remains uncertain.

1. Kepler (died 1630) pointed out that in the Roman year A.U.C. 747 (7 B.C.), there occurred a conjunction of the planets Jupiter and Saturn in the zodiacal constellation of Pisces, a sign sometimes connected in ancient astrology with the Hebrews. Many details can be fitted to this suggestion (Alf; R.E. Brown, *Birth of Messiah*, pp. 172–73; DNTT, 3:735; Maier), not least that medieval Jews saw messianic significance in the same planetary conjunction. Moreover the conjunction occurred in May, October, and November of 7 B.C.; and one of the latter two appearances could account for 2:9. But there is no solid evidence that the ancients referred to such conjunctions as "stars"; and even at their closest proximity, Jupiter and Saturn would have been about one degree apart—a perceived distance about twice the diameter of the moon—and therefore never fused into one image.

2. Kepler himself preferred the suggestion that this was a supernova—a faint star that violently explodes and gives off enormous amounts of light for a few weeks or months. The suggestion is no more than guess: there is no confirming evidence, and it is difficult on this theory to account for 2:9.

3. Others have suggested comets, what some older writers refer to as "variable stars." The most likely is Halley's Comet (cf. Lagrange), which passed overhead in 12 B.C.; but this seems impossibly early.

4. Martin opts for a number of planetary conjunctions and massings in 3/2 B.C. This suggestion depends on his entire reconstruction and late date for Herod's death (see on 2:1), which is no more than a possibility. The theory also shares some of the difficulties of 1.

5. In the light of 2:9, many commentators insist that astronomical considerations are a waste of time: Matthew presents the "star" as strictly supernatural. This too is possible and obviously impossible to falsify, but 2:9 is not as determinative as is often suggested (cf. on 2:9). The evidence is inconclusive.

Matthew uses language almost certainly alluding to Numbers 24:17: "A star will come out of Jacob; a scepter will rise out of Israel." This oracle, spoken by Balaam, who came "from the eastern mountains" (Num 23:7), was widely regarded as messianic (Targ. Jonathan and Onkelos; CD 7:19–20; 1QM 11:6; 1QSb 5:27; 4QTest 12–13; T Judah 24:1). Both Matthew and Numbers deal with the king of Israel (cf. Num 24:7), though Matthew does not resort to the uncontrolled allegorizing on "star" frequently found in early postapostolic Christian writings (cf. Jean Daniélou, *The Theology of Jewish Christianity* [London: Darton, Longman & Todd, 1964], pp. 214–24).

Granting Matthew's informed devotion to the OT, he surely knew that the OT mocks astrologers (Isa 47:13–15; Dan 1:20; 2:27; 4:7; 5:7) and forbids astrology (Jer 10:1–2). Nevertheless it was widely practiced in the first century, even among Jews (cf. Albright and Mann). Matthew neither condemns nor sanctions it; instead, he contrasts the eagerness of the Magi to worship Jesus, despite their limited knowledge, with the apathy of the Jewish leaders and the hostility of Herod's court—all of whom had the Scriptures to inform them. Formal knowledge of the Scriptures, Matthew implies, does not in itself lead to knowing who Jesus is; just as God sovereignly worked through Caesar's decree that a census be taken (Luke 2:1) to ensure Jesus' birth in Bethlehem to fulfill prophecy, so God sovereignly used the Magi's calculations to bring about the situation this pericope describes.

The question the Magi asked does not tell how their astrology led them to seek a "king of the Jews" and what made them think this particular star was "his." The widely held idea that the ancient world was looking for a Jewish leader of renown (based largely on Jos. War VI, 312–13[v.4]; Suetonius *Vespasian* 4; Tacitus *Histories* v.13; Virgil *Eclogue* 4) cannot stand close scrutiny. The Josephus passage refers to Jewish expectations of Messiah, and the others probably borrowed from Josephus. The Magi may have linked the star to "the king of the Jews" through studying the OT and other Jewish writings—a possibility made plausible by the presence of the large Jewish community in Babylon.

We must not think that the Magi's question meant, Where is the one born to become king of the Jews? but, Where is the one born king of the Jews? (cf. Notes). His kingly status was not conferred on him later on; it was his from birth. Jesus' participation in the Davidic dynasty has already been established by the genealogy. The same title the Magi gave him found its place over the cross (27:37).

"Worship" (cf. Notes) need not imply that the Magi recognized Jesus' divinity; it may simply mean "do homage" (Broadus). Their own statement suggests homage paid royalty rather than the worship of Deity. But Matthew, having already told of the virginal conception, doubtless expected his readers to discern something more —viz., that the Magi "worshiped" better than they knew.

3 In contrast with (*de*, a mild adversative; NIV, "when") the Magi's desire to worship the King of the Jews, Herod is deeply troubled. In this "all Jerusalem" joins him, not because most of the people would have been sorry to see Herod replaced or because they were reluctant to see the coming of King Messiah, but because they well knew that any question like the Magi's would result in more cruelty from the ailing Herod, whose paranoia had led him to murder his favorite wife and two sons.

4 Here "all" modifies "chief priests and teachers of the law," not "the people," and refers to those who were living in Jerusalem and could be quickly consulted. "Chief priests" refers to the hierarchy, made up of the current high priest and any who had formerly occupied this post (since Herod, contrary to the law, made fairly frequent changes in the high priesthood) and a substantial number of other leading priests (cf. Jos. Antiq. XX, 180[viii.8]; War IV, 159–60[iii.9]; the same Greek word is used for "high priests" and "chief priests"). The "teachers of the law," or "scribes" as other EV call them, were experts in the OT and in its copious oral tradition. Their work was not so much copying out OT MSS (as the word "scribes" suggests) as teaching the OT. Because much civil law was based on the OT and the interpretations of the OT fostered by the leaders, the "scribes" were also "lawyers" (cf. 22:35: "an expert in the law").

The vast majority of the scribes were Pharisees; the priests were Sadducees. The two groups barely got along, and therefore Schweizer (*Matthew*) judges this verse "historically almost inconceivable." But Matthew does not say the two groups came together at the same time; Herod, unloved by either group, may well have called both to guard against being tricked. If the Pharisees and Sadducees barely spoke to one another, there was less likelihood of collusion. "He asked them" (*epynthaneto*, the imperfect tense sometimes connotes tentative requests: Herod may have expected the rebuff of silence; cf. Turner, *Insights*, p. 27) where the Christ (here a title: see on 1:1) would be born, understanding that "the Christ" and "the king of the Jews" (2:2) were titles of the same expected person. (See 26:63; 27:37 for the same equivalence.)

5 The Jewish leaders answered the question by referring to what stands written, which is the force of the perfect passive verb *gegraptai* (NIV, "has written"), suggesting the authoritative and regulative force of the document referred to (Deiss BS, pp. 112–14, 249–50). NIV misses the preposition *dia* (lit., "what stands written *through* the prophet"), which implies that the prophet is not the ultimate source of what stands written (cf. on 1:22). Both in 1:22 and here, some textual witnesses insert the name of the prophet (e.g., Micah or even Isaiah). "Bethlehem in Judea" was introduced into the narrative in 2:1.

6 While expectation that the Messiah must come from Bethlehem occurs elsewhere (e.g., John 7:42; cf. Targ. on Mic 5:1: "Out of you shall come forth before me the Messiah"), here it rests on Micah 5:2(1 MT), to which are appended some words from 2 Samuel 5:2 (1 Chron 11:2). Matthew follows neither the MT nor the LXX, and his changes have provoked considerable speculation.

1. "Bethlehem Ephrathah" (LXX, "house of Ephrathah") becomes "Bethlehem, in the land of Judah." Hill (*Matthew*) says this change was made to exclude "any other Judean city like Jerusalem." But this reads too much into what is a normal LXX way of referring to Bethlehem (cf. Gundry, *Use of OT*, p. 91). "Ephrathah" is archaic and even in the MT primarily restricted to poetical sections like Micah 5:2.

2. The strong negative "by no means" (*oudamōs*) is added in Matthew and formally contradicts Micah 5:2. It is often argued that this change has been made to highlight Bethlehem as the birthplace of the Messiah. Indeed, Gundry's commentary uses this change as an example of Matthew's midrashic use of the OT, a use so free that he does not fear outright contradiction. There are better explanations. Even the MT of Micah implies Bethlehem's greatness: "though you are small among the clans [or rulers, who personify the cities; KJV's 'thousands' is pedantically cor-

rect, but 'thousands' was a way of referring to the great clans into which the tribes were subdivided; cf. Judg 6:15; 1 Sam 10:19; 23:23; Isa 60:22] of Judah" sets the stage for the greatness that follows. Equally, Matthew's formulation assumes that, apart from being Messiah's birthplace, Bethlehem is indeed of little importance (cf. Hengstenberg, 1:475–76, noted by Gundry, *Use of OT*, pp. 91–92). To put it another way, though the second line of Micah 5:2 formally contradicts the second line of Matthew 2:6, a wholistic reading of the verses shows the contradiction to be merely formal. Matthew 2:6 has perhaps slightly greater emphasis on the one factor that makes Bethlehem great.

3. Matthew adds the shepherd language of 2 Samuel 5:2, making it plain that the ruler in Micah 5:2 is none other than the one who fulfills the promises to David.

It is tempting to think that Matthew sees a pair of contrasts (1) between the false shepherds of Israel who have provided sound answers but no leadership (cf. 23:2–7) and Jesus who is the true Shepherd of his people Israel and (2) between a ruler like Herod and the one born to rule. The words "my people Israel" are included, not simply because they are found in 2 Samuel 5:2, but because Matthew, like Paul, faithfully records both the esssential Jewish focus of the OT promises and the OT expectation of broader application to the Gentiles (cf. on 1:1, 5, 21). Jesus is not only the promised Davidic king but also the promised hope of blessing to all the nations, the one who will claim their obeisance (cf. Ps 68:28–35; Isa 18:1–3, 7; 45:14; 60:6; Zeph 3:10). That same duality makes the desires of the Gentile Magi to worship the Messiah stand out against the apathy of the leaders who did not, apparently, take the trouble to go to Bethlehem. Of course, the Jewish leaders may have seen the arrival of the Magi in Jerusalem as one more false alarm.

As far as we can tell, the Sadducees (and therefore the chief priests) had no interest in the question of when the Messiah would come; the Pharisees (and therefore most teachers of the law) expected him to come only somewhat later. The Essenes alone, who were not consulted by Herod, expected the Messiah imminently (cf. R.T. Beckwith, "The Significance of the Calendar for Interpreting Essene Chronology and Eschatology," *Revue de Qumran* 38 [1980]: 167–202). But Matthew plainly says that, though Jesus was the Messiah, born in David's line and certain to be Shepherd and Ruler of Israel, it was the Gentiles who came to worship him.

7–10 The reason Herod wanted to learn, at his secret meeting with the Magi (v.7), the exact time the star appeared was that he had already schemed to kill the small boys of Bethlehem (cf. v.16). The entire story hangs together (see on v.16). Herod's hypocritical humility—"so that I may go and worship him" (v.8)—deceived the Magi. Conscious of his success, Herod sent no escort with them. This was not "absurdly trusting" (Schweizer, *Matthew*), since the deception depended on winning the Magi's confidence. Herod could scarcely have been expected to foresee God's intervention (v.12).

Matthew does not say that the rising star the Magi had seen (cf. on 2:2) led them to Jerusalem. They went first to the capital city because they thought it the natural place for the King of the Jews to be born. But now the star reappeared ahead of them (v.9) as they made their way to Bethlehem (it was not uncommon to travel at night). Taking this as confirming their purposes, the Magi were overjoyed (v.10). The Greek text does not imply that the star pointed out the house where Jesus was; it may simply have hovered over Bethlehem as the Magi approached it. They would then have found the exact house through discreet inquiry since (Luke 2:17–18) the shepherds who came to worship the newborn Jesus did not keep silent about what they saw.

11 This verse plainly alludes to Psalm 72:10-11 and Isaiah 60:6, passages that reinforce the emphasis on the Gentiles (cf. on v.6). Nolan's suggestion (pp. 206-9) that the closest parallel is Isaiah 39:1-2 is linguistically attractive but contextually weak. The evidence that Hezekiah served as an eschatological figure is poor and fails to explain why he should be opening up his treasure store to his visitors. Some time had elapsed since Jesus' birth (vv.7, 16), and the family was settled in a house. While the Magi saw both the child and his mother, their worship (cf. on v.2) was for him alone.

Bringing gifts was particularly important in the ancient East when approaching a superior (cf. Gen 43:11; 1 Sam 9:7-8; 1 Kings 10:2). Usually such gifts were reciprocated (Derrett, *NT Studies*, 2:28). That is not mentioned here, but a first-century reader might have assumed it and seen the Great Commission (28:18-20) as leading to its abundant fruition. Frankincense is a glittering, odorous gum obtained by making incisions in the bark of several trees; myrrh exudes from a tree found in Arabia and a few other places and was a much-valued spice and perfume (Ps 45:8; S of Songs 3:6) used in embalming (John 19:39). Commentators, ancient (Origen, *Contra Celsum* 1.60) and modern (Hendriksen), have found symbolic value in the three gifts—gold suggesting royalty, incense divinity, and myrrh the Passion and burial. This interpretation demands too much insight from the Magi. The three gifts were simply expensive and not uncommon presents and may have helped finance the trip to Egypt. The word "treasures" probably means "coffers" or "treasure-boxes" in this context.

12 This second dream (cf. 1:20) mentions no angel. Perhaps Joseph and the Magi compared notes and saw their danger (cf. P. Gaechter, "Die Magierperikope," *Zeitschrift für Katholische Theologie* 90 [1968]: 257-95); amid their fear and uncertainty, the dreams led them (vv.12-13) to flee. Which way the Magi went is unclear; they might have gone around the north end of the Dead Sea, avoiding Jerusalem, or they might have gone around the south end of the sea.

Notes

1-2 The word ἀνατολή (*anatolē*) can mean "rising" or "east." In v.1 ἀπὸ ἀνατολῶν (*apo anatolōn*, "from the east") is rightly translated by NIV, since the noun normally indicates the point of the compass when it is plural and anarthrous (cf. BDF, 253[5]). By the same token ἐν τῇ ἀνατολῇ (*en tē anatolē*) in vv.2, 9 is less likely to be "in the East" than "at its rising" (the article can have mild possessive force). Other suggestions—e.g., that the expression refers to a particular land in the east or to Anatolia in the west—seem less convincing; but the question is extraordinarily complex (cf. Turner, *Insights*, pp. 25-26; R.E. Brown, *Birth of Messiah*, p. 173).

2 The participle in the construction ὁ τεχθεὶς βασιλεύς (*ho techtheis basileus*, lit., "the born king") is adjectival, not substantival, and is used attributively. Moreover there is no suggestion of "newborn" (cf. C. Burchard, "Fussnoten zum neutestamentlichen Griechisch II," ZNW 29 [1978]: 143-57), which is already ruled out by chronological notes (vv.7, 16).

The verb προσκυνέω (proskyneō, "worship") occurs three times in this pericope (cf. vv.8, 11) and ten other times in Matthew. In the NT the object of this "worship" is almost always God or Jesus, except where someone is acting ignorantly and is rebuked (Acts 10:25-26; Rev 19:10; 22:8-9). But Rev 3:9 is an important exception (NIV, "fall down at your feet"). Secular Greek used the verb for a wide variety of levels of obeisance, and it is precarious to build too much christology on the use of the term in the Gospels.

3 The words πᾶσα Ἱεροσόλυμα (pasa Hierosolyma, "all Jerusalem") betray breach of concord, since pasa is feminine, but this form of "Jerusalem," unlike the alternative Ἱερουσαλήμ (Ierousalēm), is not feminine but neuter plural. Possibly pasa is a precursor of modern Greek's indeclinable pasa (so BDF, par. 56[4]); but it is marginally more likely that the noun is being treated as feminine singular since there are other instances where it is construed as feminine singular even though no pasa is present.

5-6 Matthew uses the singular προφήτου (prophētou, "prophet") even though two different passages, from the latter and former prophets respectively, are cited. Yet it seems a common practice to refer to one author, perhaps the principal one, when citing two or three (cf. 27:9; Mark 1:2-3).

7 Τότε (tote, "then") is very common in Matthew, occurring ninety times as compared with Mark's six and Luke's fourteen; but in Matthean usage only sometimes does it have temporal force (as here), serving more frequently as a loose connective.

10 The words "they were overjoyed" render a cognate accusative, ἐχάρησαν χαράν (echarēsan charan, lit., "they rejoiced with joy"), probably under Semitic influence (cf. Moule, Idiom Book, p. 32; BDF, par. 153[1]).

D. The Escape to Egypt

2:13-15

13When they had gone, an angel of the Lord appeared to Joseph in a dream. "Get up," he said, "take the child and his mother and escape to Egypt. Stay there until I tell you, for Herod is going to search for the child to kill him."
14So he got up, took the child and his mother during the night and left for Egypt, 15where he stayed until the death of Herod. And so was fulfilled what the Lord had said through the prophet: "Out of Egypt I called my son."

Many commentators think this account has been created to flesh out the OT text said to be "fulfilled" (v.15). On the broader critical questions, see introductory comments at 1:18-25 and 2:1-12. Granted what we know of Herod's final years, there is nothing historically improbable about this account; and precisely because the fulfillment text is difficult, one may assume that the story called forth reflection on the OT text rather than vice versa.

13-14 The verb "had gone" (v.13) is the same as "returned" in the preceding verse, tying the two accounts together. This is the third dream in these two chapters, and for the second time an angel of the Lord is mentioned (cf. 1:20; 2:12). The point is that God took sovereign action to preserve his Messiah, his Son—something well understood by Jesus himself, and a major theme in the Gospel of John. Egypt was a natural place to which to flee. It was nearby, a well-ordered Roman province outside Herod's jurisdiction; and, according to Philo (writing c. A.D. 40), its population included about a million Jews. Earlier generations of Israelites fleeing their homeland (1 Kings 11:40; Jer 26:21-23; 43:7) had sought refuge in Egypt. But if Matthew was thinking of any particular OT parallel, probably Jacob and his family

(Gen 46) fleeing the famine in Canaan was in his mind, since that is the trip that set the stage for the Exodus (cf. 2:15).

The angel's command was explicit. Joseph, Mary, and the Child must remain in Egypt, not only till Herod's death, but till given leave to return (cf. vv. 19-20). The command was also urgent. Joseph left at once, setting out by night to begin the seventy-five mile journey to the border. The focus on God's protection of "the child" is unmistakable. Herod was going to try to kill him (v. 13), and Joseph took "the child and his mother" (v. 14—not the normal order) to Egypt.

15 The death of Herod brought relief to many. Only then, for instance, did the Qumran covenanters return to their center, destroyed in 31 B.C., and rebuild it. In Egypt, Herod's death made possible the return of the Child, Mary, and Joseph, who awaited a word from the Lord. The Greek could be rendered "And so was fulfilled" (NIV) or "[This came about] in order that the word of the Lord . . . might be fulfilled." Either way the notion of fulfillment preserves some telic force in the sentence: Jesus' exodus from Egypt fulfilled Scripture written long before.

The OT quotation (v. 15) almost certainly (cf. Notes) comes from Hosea 11:1 and exactly renders the Hebrew, not the LXX, which has "his children," not "my son." (In this Matthew agrees with Aq., Symm., and Theod., but only because all four rely on the Hebrew.) Some commentators (e.g., Beng.; Gundry, *Use of OT*, pp. 93–94) argue that the preposition *ek* ("out of," NIV) should be taken temporally, i.e., "since Egypt" or, better, "from the time [he dwelt] in Egypt." The preposition can have that force; and it is argued that v. 15 means God "called" Jesus, in the sense that he specially acknowledged and preserved him, from the time of his Egyptian sojourn on, protecting him against Herod. After all, the exodus itself is not mentioned till vv. 21-22.

Some commentators interpret the calling of Israel in Hosea 11:1 in a similar way. But there are convincing arguments against this. The context of Hosea 11:1 mentions Israel's *return* to Egypt (11:5), which presupposes that 11:1 refers to the Exodus. To preserve the temporal force of *ek* in Matthew 2:15, Gundry is reduced to the unconvincing assertion that the preposition in Hosea is both temporal and locative. In support of this view, it is pointed out that Jesus' actual departure *out of* Egypt is not mentioned until v. 21. But, although this is so, it is nevertheless implied by vv. 13-14. The reason Matthew has introduced the Hosea quotation at this point, instead of after v. 21, is probably because he wishes to use the return journey itself to set up the reference to the destination, Nazareth (v. 23), rather than the starting-point, Egypt (R.E. Brown, *Birth of Messiah*, p. 220).

If Hosea 11:1 refers to Israel's Exodus from Egypt, in what sense can Matthew mean that Jesus' return to the land of Israel "fulfilled" this text? Four observations clarify the issue.

1. Many have noticed that Jesus is often presented in the NT as the antitype of Israel or, better, the typological recapitulation of Israel. Jesus' temptation after forty days of fasting recapitulated the forty years' trial of Israel (see on 4:1-11). Elsewhere, if Israel is the vine that does not bring forth the expected fruit, Jesus, by contrast, is the True Vine (Isa 5; John 15). The reason Pharaoh must let the people of Israel go is that Israel is the Lord's son (Exod 4:22-23), a theme picked up by Jeremiah (31:9) as well as Hosea (cf. also Ps 2:6, 12). The "son" theme in Matthew (cf. esp. T. de Kruijf, *Der Sohn des lebendigen Gottes: Ein Beitrag zur Christologie des Matthäusevangeliums* [Rome: BIP, 1962], pp. 56-58, 109), already present since

Jesus is messianic "son of David" and, by the virginal conception, Son of God, becomes extraordinarily prominent in Matthew (see on 3:17): "This is my Son, whom I love."

2. The verb "to fulfill" has broader significance than mere one-to-one prediction (cf. Introduction, section 11.b; and comments on 5:17). Not only in Matthew but elsewhere in the NT, the history and laws of the OT are perceived to have prophetic significance (cf. on 5:17-20). The Epistle to the Hebrews argues that the laws regarding the tabernacle and the sacrificial system were from the beginning designed to point toward the only Sacrifice that could really remove sin and the only Priest who could serve once and for all as the effective Mediator between God and man. Likewise Paul insists that the Messiah sums up his people in himself. When David was anointed king, the tribes acknowledged him as their bone and flesh (2 Sam 5:1), i.e., David as anointed king summed up Israel, with the result that his sin brought disaster on the people (2 Sam 12, 24). Just as Israel is God's son, so the promised Davidic Son is also Son of God (2 Sam 7:13-14; cf. N.T. Wright, "The Paul of History," *Tyndale Bulletin* 29 [1978]: esp. 66-67). "Fulfillment" must be understood against the background of these interlocking themes and their typological connections.

3. It follows, therefore, that the NT writers do not think they are reading back into the OT things that are not already there germinally. This does not mean that Hosea had the Messiah in mind when he penned Hosea 11:1. This admission prompts W.L. LaSor ("Prophecy, Inspiration, and *Sensus Plenior*," *Tyndale Bulletin* 29 [1978]: 49-60) to see in Matthew's use of Hosea 11:1 an example of *sensus plenior*, by which he means a "fuller sense" than what was in Hosea's mind, but something nevertheless in the mind of God. But so blunt an appeal to what God has absolutely hidden seems a strange background for Matthew's insisting that Jesus' exodus from Egypt in any sense fulfills the Hosea passage. This observation is not trivial; Matthew is reasoning with Jews who could say, "You are not playing fair with the text!" A mediating position is therefore necessary.

Hosea 11 pictures God's love for Israel. Although God threatens judgment and disaster, yet because he is God and not man (11:9), he looks to a time when in compassion he will roar like a lion and his children will return to him (11:10-11). In short Hosea himself looks forward to a saving visitation by the Lord. Therefore his prophecy fits into the larger pattern of OT revelation up to that point, revelation that both explicitly and implicitly points to the Seed of the woman, the Elect Son of Abraham, the Prophet like Moses, the Davidic King, the Messiah. The "son" language is part of this messianic matrix (cf. Willis J. Beecher, *The Prophets and the Promise* [New York: Thomas Y. Crowell, 1905], pp. 331-35); insofar as that matrix points to Jesus the Messiah and insofar as Israel's history looks forward to one who sums it up, then so far also Hosea 11:1 looks forward. To ask whether Hosea thought of Messiah is to ask the wrong question, akin to using a hacksaw when a scalpel is needed. It is better to say that Hosea, building on existing revelation, grasped the messianic nuances of the "son" language already applied to Israel and David's promised heir in previous revelation so that had he been able to see Matthew's use of 11:1, he would not have disapproved, even if messianic nuances were not in his mind when he wrote that verse. He provided one small part of the revelation unfolded during salvation history; but that part he himself understood to be a pictorial representative of divine, redeeming love.

The NT writers insist that the OT can be rightly interpreted only if the entire revelation is kept in perspective as it is historically unfolded (e.g., Gal 3:6–14). Hermeneutically this is not an innovation. OT writers drew lessons out of earlier salvation history, lessons difficult to perceive while that history was being lived, but lessons that retrospect would clarify (e.g., Asaph in Ps 78; cf. on Matt 13:35). Matthew does the same in the context of the fulfillment of OT hopes in Jesus Christ. We may therefore legitimately speak of a "fuller meaning" than any one text provides. But the appeal should be made, not to some hidden divine knowledge, but to the pattern of revelation up to that time—a pattern not yet adequately discerned. The new revelation may therefore be truly new, yet at the same time capable of being checked against the old.

4. If this interpretation of Matthew 2:15 is correct, it follows that for Matthew Jesus himself is the locus of true Israel. This does not necessarily mean that God has no further purpose for racial Israel; but it does mean that the position of God's people in the Messianic Age is determined by reference to Jesus, not race.

Notes

13 The historical present φαίνεται (*phainetai*, lit., "appears") adds a vivid touch.

15 Because "out of Egypt" occurs in Num 23:22; 24:8, some have suggested a connection between Matt 2:15 and Num 24:7–8 (e.g., Lindars, Hill, Schweizer). In its strongest form this argument depends on the LXX, which reads, "A man shall come forth from his seed," instead of, "Water will flow from their buckets" (Num 24:7), and "him" instead of "them" (Num 24:8). This transforms Num 24:28 into a reference to God bringing Messiah out of Egypt. Apart from the textual question, it must be noted that (1) Matt 2:15 corresponds exactly with MT Hos 11:1 but only approximately with LXX Num 24:8; (2) the LXX rendering makes Num 24 rather incoherent.

E. *The Massacre of Bethlehem's Boys*

2:16–18

> [16]When Herod realized that he had been outwitted by the Magi, he was furious, and he gave orders to kill all the boys in Bethlehem and its vicinity who were two years old and under, in accordance with the time he had learned from the Magi. [17]Then what was said through the prophet Jeremiah was fulfilled:
>
> > [18]"A voice is heard in Ramah,
> > weeping and great mourning,
> > Rachel weeping for her children
> > and refusing to be comforted,
> > because they are no more."

Few sections of Matthew 1–2 have been as widely criticized as this one. Most modern scholars think Matthew made the story up (e.g., Goulder, p. 33; E.M. Smallwood, *The Jews Under Roman Rule* [Leiden: Brill, 1976], pp. 103–4), spinning it out of Jeremiah 31:15, cited in Matthew 2:18 (so C.T. Davis, "Tradition and Redaction in Matthew 1:18–2:23," JBL 90 [1971]: 419). In this view, perhaps Matthew invented the tale to draw an analogy between Jesus and Moses or between Jesus and late Jewish traditions about Abraham or Jacob or out of an apologetic need to construct an initial sign of the impending judgment on Israel for rejecting her Messiah (Kingsbury, *Structure*, p. 48). But v.16 cannot be excised from the chapter without rewriting it all.

The OT citation in v.18, like other such citations in Matthew 1–2, is itself not strictly necessary to the narrative. These citations illumine the narrative and show its relation to OT Scripture, but they do not create it (cf. on 1:18–25; 2:1–12). It is difficult to see a real parallel with Moses, since Pharaoh's edict was general and before Moses' birth, whereas Herod's edict is specifically for Bethlehem and came after Jesus' birth. At best the parallel is tenuous. Furthermore vv.16–18 offer a poor sign of the destruction to befall Israel—not least because Jesus escapes rather than suffers, and the children have done Jesus no harm.

Actually, the story is in perfect harmony with what we know of Herod's character in his last years (Schalit, p. 648). That there is no extra-Christian confirmation is not surprising; the same can be said of Jesus' crucifixion. The death of a few children (perhaps a dozen or so; Bethlehem's total population was not large) would hardly have been recorded in such violent times. (See the excellent treatment by R.T. France, "Herod and the Children of Bethlehem," NovTest 21 [1979]: 98–120; id., "The Massacre of the Innocents," Livingstone, pp. 83–94.) "Matthew is not simply meditating on Old Testament texts, but claiming that in what has happened they find fulfillment. If the events are legendary, the argument is futile" (France, "Herod," p. 120).

16 It probably did not take long to carry out Herod's barbarous order. Bethlehem is only five miles from Jerusalem. The Magi set out in the same evening (v.9) and may have left that same night after their dream (v.12); the same would be true of Joseph with Jesus and Mary (vv.13–15). By the next evening Herod's patience would have been exhausted. The two-years age limit was to prevent Jesus' escape; at the time he was between six and twenty months old. Herod, aiming to eliminate a potential king, restricted the massacre to boys. Furious at being deceived (a better translation than "outwitted"), he raged against the Lord and his Anointed One (Ps 2:2). Yet this was no narrow escape. The One enthroned in heaven laughs and scoffs at the Herods of this world (Ps 2:4).

17–18 Jeremiah is named three times in Matthew (cf. 16:14; 27:9) and nowhere else in the NT. The text form of this OT citation in these verses is complex but is probably Matthew's rendering of the Hebrew (cf. Gundry, *Use of OT*, pp. 94–97; R.E. Brown, *Birth of Messiah*, pp. 221–23).

It is uncertain whether Jeremiah 31:15 refers to the deportation of the northern tribes by Assyria in 722–721 B.C. or to the deportation of Judah and Benjamin in 587–586 B.C. (cf. R.E. Brown, *Birth of Messiah*, pp. 205–6). The latter is more likely. Nebuzaradan, commander of Nebuchadnezzar's imperial guard, gathered the captives at Ramah before taking them into exile in Babylon (Jer 40:1–2). Ramah lay north of Jerusalem on the way to Bethel; Rachel's tomb was at Zelzah in the same vicinity (1 Sam 10:2). Jeremiah 31:15 depicts mourning at the prospect of exile; Rachel is seen as crying out from her tomb because her "children," her descendants (Rachel is the idealized mother of the Jews, though Leah gave birth to more tribes than Rachel) "are no more"—i.e., they are being removed from the land and are no longer a nation. But elsewhere we are told that Rachel was buried on the way to Ephrathah, identified as Bethlehem (Gen 35:19; 48:7). Some see a confusion of traditions here and assume that the clan of Ephrathah later settled in Bethlehem and gave it its name, thus starting a false connection Matthew follows. The problem, however, is artificial. Genesis 35:16 makes it clear that Jacob was some distance from Bethlehem-Ephrathah when Rachel died—viz., somewhere between Bethel and Bethlehem (only 1 Sam 10:2 says more exactly where he was). Moreover Matthew does not say Rachel was buried at Bethlehem; the connection between the prophecy and its "fulfillment" is more subtle than that.

Why does Matthew refer to this OT passage? Some think the connection results from word association: the children were killed at Bethlehem, Bethlehem = Ephrathah, Ephrathah is connected with Rachel's death, and Rachel figures in the oracle. Rothfuchs (p. 64) sees a parallel between the condemnation to exile as a result of sin (Jer) and the judgment on Israel as a result of rejecting the Messiah (an interpretation that sees the slaughter at Bethlehem as a sign of the latter). More believable is the observation (Gundry, Use of OT, p. 210; Tasker) that Jeremiah 31:15 occurs in a setting of hope. Despite the tears, God says, the exiles will return; and now Matthew, referring to Jeremiah 31:15, likewise says that, despite the tears of the Bethlehem mothers, there is hope because Messiah has escaped Herod and will ultimately reign. The further suggestion that the deep grief in Bethlehem reflected the belief that the Messiah had been massacred and news of his escape should assuage that grief (cf. Broadus) is fanciful.

But there may be a further reason why Matthew quotes this OT passage, a reason discernible once the differences between Matthew and the OT are spelled out. Here Jesus does not, as in v.15, recapitulate an event from Israel's history. The Exile sent Israel into captivity and thereby called forth tears. But here the tears are not for him who goes into "exile" but because of the children who stay behind and are slaughtered. Why, then, refer to the Exile at all? Help comes from observing the broader context of both Jeremiah and Matthew. Jeremiah 31:9, 20 refers to Israel = Ephraim as God's dear son and also introduces the new covenant (31:31–34) the Lord will make with his people. Therefore the tears associated with Exile (31:15) will end. Matthew has already made the Exile a turning point in his thought (1:11–12), for at that time the Davidic line was dethroned. The tears of the Exile are now being "fulfilled"—i.e., the tears begun in Jeremiah's day are climaxed and ended by the tears of the mothers of Bethlehem. The heir to David's throne has come, the Exile is over, the true Son of God has arrived, and he will introduce the new covenant (26:28) promised by Jeremiah.

Notes

16 "He gave orders to kill" is an excellent rendering of the "graphic participle" in ἀποστείλας ἀνεῖλεν (aposteilas aneilen, lit., "having sent, he killed"; cf. Zerwick, par. 363).

17 Only here and in 27:9 is the fulfillment formula devoid of a ἵνα (hina) or a ὅπως (hopōs), both of which normally have telic force ("in order that"), though consecutive force is not uncommon in NT Greek (cf. on 2:15). This is probably because in these two passages the action that is fulfilling Scripture is so horrible that there is an instinctive reluctance to use phraseology that might be (mis)-understood to ascribe enormous wickedness to God (cf. Broadus; Rothfuchs, pp. 36–39).

18 The longer reading, reflected in KJV ("lamentation and weeping and great mourning") is most likely an assimilation to some LXX witnesses.

F. The Return to Nazareth

2:19–23

19After Herod died, an angel of the Lord appeared in a dream to Joseph in Egypt 20and said, "Get up, take the child and his mother and go to the land of Israel, for those who were trying to take the child's life are dead."
21So he got up, took the child and his mother and went to the land of Israel. 22But when he heard that Archelaus was reigning in Judea in place of his father Herod, he was afraid to go there. Having been warned in a dream, he withdrew to the district of Galilee, 23and he went and lived in a town called Nazareth. So was fulfilled what was said through the prophets. "He will be called a Nazarene."

19–21 This fourth dream and third mention of the angel of the Lord (v.19) continues the divine initiative in preserving and guiding the Child, who is again made prominent ("the child and his mother," v.20). On the date of Herod's death, see on 2:1. (Josephus, Antiq. XVII, 168–69[vi.5], gives a shocking account of Herod's final illness.) The plural ("those who were trying to take the child's life") may owe something to Exodus 4:19 (so Hill, Matthew, following Davies, Setting). If so, Jesus is being compared with Moses. But that motif is at best weak in Matthew 1–2, and the plural may be accounted for in other ways. H.A.W. Meyer suggests that Herod's father, Antipater, who died a few days before him, may have been associated with Herod in the massacre. More probably the plural is a generalizing or categorical plural (cf. Turner, Syntax, pp. 25–26; BDF, par. 141). "Land of Israel" occurs only in vv.20–21 (cf. "cities of Israel," 10:23). Although the whole land was before him and he apparently hoped to settle in Judea (perhaps in Bethlehem, the city of David), Joseph was forced to retire to despised Galilee.

22 Probably Joseph had expected Herod Antipas to reign over the entire kingdom; but Herod the Great made a late change in his will, dividing his kingdom into three parts. Archelaus, known for his ruthlessness, was given Judea, Samaria, and Idumea (see map, p. 58.). Augustus Caesar agreed and gave him the title "ethnarch" (more honorable than "tetrarch") and promised the title "king" if it was earned. But Archelaus proved to be a poor ruler and was banished for misgovernment in A.D. 6. Rome ruled the south through a procurator. But by that time Joseph had settled the family in Galilee. Herod Antipas, who reappears in Matthew 14:1–10, was given the title "tetrarch" and ruled in Galilee and in Perea. Herod Philip (not to be confused with Herodias's first husband, who was not a king) became tetrarch of Iturea, Trachonitis, and some other territories. He was the best of Herod the Great's children; Jesus frequently retired into his territory (14:13; 15:29; 16:13) away from the weak but cruel Antipas. Joseph, guided by the fifth and final dream, settled the family in Galilee.

23 The town Joseph chose was Nazareth, which, according to Luke 1:26–27; 2:39, was his former home and that of Mary (cf. 13:53–58). This final quotation formula,

like that of v.15, should probably be construed as telic: this took place "in order to fulfill." But the formula is unique in two respects: only here does Matthew use the plural "prophets"; and only here does he omit the Greek equivalent of "saying" and replace it with the conjunction *hoti*, which can introduce a direct quotation (NIV), but more probably should be rendered "that," making the quotation indirect: "in order to fulfill what was said through the prophets, that he would be called a Nazarene" (cf. W. Barnes Tatum, Jr., "Matthew 2.23," *The Bible Translator* 27 [1976]: 135–37; contra Hartman, "Scriptural Exegesis," pp. 149–50). This suggests that Matthew had no specific OT quotation in mind; indeed, these words are found nowhere in the OT.

The interpretation of this verse has such a long history (for older works, cf. Broadus; for recent studies, cf. Gundry, *Use of OT*, pp. 97–104; R.E. Brown, *Birth of Messiah*, pp. 207–13) that it is not possible to list here all the major options. We may exclude those that see some word-play connection with an OT Hebrew word but have no obvious connection with Nazareth. This eliminates the popular interpretation that makes Jesus a Nazirite or second Samson (cf. esp. Judg 13:5, 7; 16:17, where LXX has *Naziraios* as opposed to Matthew's *Nazōraios*; cf. Luke 1:15). Defenders include Calvin, Loisy, Stendahl, Schweizer, and, more recently, Ernst Zuckschwerdt ("Nazōraîos in Matth.2,23," *Theologische Zeitschrift* 31 [1975]: 65–77). Also to be eliminated are interpretations that try to find in Matthew's term a reference to some kind of pre-Christian sect. But the evidence for this is feeble (cf. Soarés Prabhu, pp. 197–201) and the connection with Nazareth merely verbal. E. Earle Ellis ("How the New Testament Uses the Old," Marshall, *NT Interpretation*, p. 202) sees a pun here as an "implicit midrash," but significantly he then has to put the word "fulfillment" in quotation marks.

Matthew certainly used *Nazōraios* as an adjectival form of *apo Nazaret* ("from Nazareth" or "Nazarene"), even though the more acceptable adjective is *Nazarēnos* (cf. Bonnard, Brown, Albright and Mann, Soarés Prabhu). Possibly *Nazōraios* derives from a Galilean Aramaic form. Nazareth was a despised place (John 7:42, 52), even to other Galileans (cf. John 1:46). Here Jesus grew up, not as "Jesus the Bethlehemite," with its Davidic overtones, but as "Jesus the Nazarene," with all the opprobrium of the sneer. When Christians were referred to in Acts as the "Nazarene sect" (24:5), the expression was meant to hurt. First-century Christian readers of Matthew, who had tasted their share of scorn, would have quickly caught Matthew's point. He is not saying that a particular OT prophet foretold that the Messiah would live in Nazareth; he is saying that the OT prophets foretold that the Messiah would be despised (cf. Pss 22:6–8, 13; 69:8, 20–21; Isa 11:1; 49:7; 53:2–3, 8; Dan 9:26). The theme is repeatedly picked up by Matthew (e.g., 8:20; 11:16–19; 15:7–8). In other words Matthew gives us the substance of several OT passages, not a direct quotation (so also Ezra 9:10–12; cf. SBK, 1:92–93).

It is possible that at the same time there is a discreet allusion to the *neser* ("branch") of Isaiah 11:1, which received a messianic interpretation in the Targums, rabbinic literature, and DSS (cf. Gundry, *Use of OT*, p. 104); for here too it is affirmed that David's son would emerge from humble obscurity and low state. Jesus is King Messiah, Son of God, Son of David; but he was a branch from a royal line hacked down to a stump and reared in surroundings guaranteed to win him scorn. Jesus the Messiah, Matthew is telling us, did not introduce his kingdom with outward show or present himself with the pomp of an earthly monarch. In accord with prophecy he came as the despised Servant of the Lord.

Notes

20 The participle οἱ ζητοῦντες (hoi zētountes, lit., "those seeking"; NIV, "those who were trying"), quite apart from its being plural, does not because it is present tense signify antecedent action but rather continued, persistent action; the context determines that temporally it is virtually an imperfect (cf. Turner, *Syntax*, pp. 80–81; Moule, *Idiom Book*, p. 206; rightly, NIV).

22 It is uncertain whether the verb χρηματίζω (chrēmatizō, "I warn") includes the specification of Nazareth as Joseph's proper destination, or whether he was merely "warned" not to remain in Judea, leaving the choice of town with him.

II. The Gospel of the Kingdom (3:1–7:29)

A. Narrative (3:1–4:25)

1. Foundational steps (3:1–4:11)

a. The ministry of John the Baptist

3:1–12

> [1]In those days John the Baptist came, preaching in the Desert of Judea [2]and saying, "Repent, for the kingdom of heaven is near." [3]This is he who was spoken of through the prophet Isaiah:
>
> > "A voice of one calling in the desert,
> > 'Prepare the way for the Lord,
> >   make straight paths for him.' "
>
> [4]John's clothes were made of camel's hair, and he had a leather belt around his waist. His food was locusts and wild honey. [5]People went out to him from Jerusalem and all Judea and the whole region of the Jordan. [6]Confessing their sins, they were baptized by him in the Jordan River.
> [7]But when he saw many of the Pharisees and Sadducees coming to where he was baptizing, he said to them: "You brood of vipers! Who warned you to flee from the coming wrath? [8]Produce fruit in keeping with repentance. [9]And do not think you can say to yourselves, 'We have Abraham as our father.' I tell you that out of these stones God can raise up children for Abraham. [10]The ax is already at the root of the trees, and every tree that does not produce good fruit will be cut down and thrown into the fire.
> [11]"I baptize you with water for repentance. But after me will come one who is more powerful than I, whose sandals I am not fit to carry. He will baptize you with the Holy Spirit and with fire. [12]His winnowing fork is in his hand, and he will clear his threshing floor, gathering the wheat into the barn and burning up the chaff with unquenchable fire."

For the first time Matthew parallels Mark (1:1–11), Luke (3:1–22), and, more loosely, John (1:19–34). Whatever diversity there is among prologues, the four Gospels unanimously preface the ministry of Jesus with that of John the Baptist. Matthew omits any mention of Jesus' youth (Luke 2:41–52) or of John's birth and background (Luke 1:5–25, 39–45; 57–80). This may imply that Matthew's readers were already familiar with that background (Tasker) or that Matthew wants to plunge dramatically into his account. After four hundred silent years, God was speaking through a new prophet who called people to repentance and promised someone greater to come.

In addition to the implications of this commentary's outline of Matthew, the gospel has many substructures pointing to a writer of great literary skill. Gooding (p. 234) points out interesting parallels between chapters 1-2 and 3-4, too lengthy to be detailed here (cf. also 13:3-53).

1 Matthew's temporal note, "In those days," is vague and reflects a similarly loose expression in the OT (e.g., Gen 38:1; Exod 2:11, 23; Isa 38:1). His phrase may mean "in those crucial days" (Hill, *Matthew*) or even "in the days in which Jesus and his family lived at Nazareth" (Broadus; cf. 4:13). More likely, however, it is a general term that reveals little chronologically but insists that the account is historical (Bonnard). Luke 3:1 offers more chronological help, but its significance is disputed (cf. Hoehner, *Chronological Aspects*, pp. 29-44). The year was A.D. 27, 28, or 29 (less likely 26).

"John," or "Johanan," had been a popular name among the Jews from the time of John Hyrcanus (died 106 B.C.). Four or five "Johns" are mentioned in the NT. The John in Matthew 3:1 was soon designated "the Baptist" (cf. Notes) because baptism was so prominent in his ministry. He began his preaching in the "Desert of Judea," a vaguely defined area including the lower Jordan Valley north of the Dead Sea and the country immediately west of the Dead Sea. It is hot and, apart from the Jordan itself, largely arid, though not unpopulated. It was used for pasturage (Ps 65:12; Joel 2:22; Luke 15:4) and had Essene communities. "Desert" had long had prophetic overtones (the Law was given in the "wilderness"). The Zealots used the desert as a hiding place (cf. Matt 24:26; Acts 21:38; Jos. Antiq. XX, 97-98 [v.1]). Therefore some commentators see more theological than geographical force in Matthew 3:1 (e.g., Bonnard, Maier). The modifying phrase "of Judea" makes the antithesis between geography and theology false. The desert was a particular area (cf. R. Funk, "The Wilderness," JBL 78 [1959]: 205-14) but may also have had prophetic implications for first-century readers.

2 John's preaching had two elements. The first was a call to repent. Though the verb *metanoeō* is often explained etymologically as "to change one's mind," or popularly as "to be sorry for something," neither rendering is adequate. In classical Greek the verb could refer to a purely intellectual change of mind. But the NT usage has been influenced by the Hebrew verbs *nāham* ("to be sorry for one's actions") and *šûb* ("to turn around to new actions"). The latter is common in the prophets' call to the people to return to the covenant with Yahweh (cf. DNTT, 1:357-59; Turner, *Christian Words*, pp. 374-77). What is meant is not a merely intellectual change of mind or mere grief, still less doing penance (cf. Notes), but a radical transformation of the entire person, a fundamental turnaround involving mind and action and including overtones of grief, which results in "fruit in keeping with repentance." Of course, all this assumes that man's actions are fundamentally off course and need radical change. John applies this repentance to the religious leaders of his day (3:7-8) with particular vehemence. (On the differences between biblical and rabbinic emphases on repentance, cf. Lane, *Mark*, pp. 593-600.)

The second element in John's preaching was the nearness of the kingdom of heaven, and this is given as the ground for repentance. Throughout the OT there was a rising expectation of a divine visitation that would establish justice, crush opposition, and renew the very universe. This hope was couched in many categories: it was presented as the fulfillment of promises to David's heir, as the Day of the Lord (which often had dark overtones of judgment, though there were bright exceptions, e.g., Zeph 3:14–20), as a new heaven and a new earth, as a time of regathering of Israel, as the inauguration of a new and transforming covenant (2 Sam 7:13–14; Isa 1:24–28; 9:6–7; 11:1–10; 64–66; Jer 23:5–6; 31:31–34; Ezek 37:24; Dan 2:44; 7:13–14; cf. esp. Ridderbos, pp. 3–17; Ladd, *Presence*, pp. 45–75).

The predominant meaning of "kingdom" in the OT (Heb. *malkût*; Aram. *malkûta*) is "reign": the term has dynamic force. Similarly in the NT, though *basileia* ("kingdom") can refer to a territory (4:8), the overwhelming majority of instances use the term with dynamic force. This stands over against the prevailing rabbinic terminology in which "kingdom" was increasingly spiritualized or planted in men's hearts (e.g., b *Berakoth* 4a). Contrary to counterclaims (Alva J. McClain, *The Greatness of the Kingdom* [Grand Rapids: Zondervan, 1959], pp. 274ff), in the first century there was little agreement among Jews as to what the messianic kingdom would be like. One very popular assumption was that the Roman yoke would be shattered and there would be political peace and mounting prosperity.

Except at 12:28; 19:24; 21:31, 43, and in some MSS of 6:33, Matthew always uses "kingdom of heaven" instead of "kingdom of God" (this reckoning excludes references to "my kingdom" and the like), whereas Mark and Luke prefer "kingdom of God." Matthew's preferred expression certainly does not restrict God's reign to the heavens. The biblical goal is the manifest exercise of God's sovereignty, his "reign" on earth and among men. There are enough parallels among the Synoptics to imply that "kingdom of God" and "kingdom of heaven" denote the same thing (e.g., Matt 19:23–24 = Mark 10:23–25); the connotative distinction is less certain.

Dispensationalists (e.g., A.C. Gaebelein, Walvoord) hold that "kingdom of God" is a distinctively spiritual kingdom, a narrower category embracing only true believers, whereas "kingdom of heaven" is the kingdom of millennial splendor, a broader category including (as in the parable, 13:47–50) both good and bad fish. The distinction is unfortunate: it comes perilously close to confusing kingdom and church (see further on ch. 13; 16:17–19), fails to account for passages where the Matthean category is no less restrictive than "kingdom of God" in the other evangelists, and fundamentally misapprehends the dynamic nature of the kingdom. Equally unconvincing is the suggestion of Pamment that "kingdom of heaven" always refers to the future reign following the consummation, whereas in Matthew "kingdom of God" refers to the present manifestation. To arrive at this absolute dichotomy, Pamment must resort to very unlikely interpretations of numerous passages (e.g., 11:12; parables in ch. 13). Many other proposals (e.g., J. Julius Scott, EBC, 1:508) are stated firmly but cannot withstand close scrutiny.

The most common explanation is that Matthew avoided "kingdom of God" to remove unnecessary offense to Jews who often used circumlocutions like "heaven" to refer to God (e.g., Dan 4:26; 1 Macc 3:50, 60; 4:55; Luke 15:18, 21). The suggestion has merit. Yet Matthew is a subtle and allusive writer, and two other factors may also be involved: (1) "kingdom of heaven" may anticipate the extent of Christ's postresurrection authority: God's sovereignty *in heaven* and on earth is now mediated through him (28:18); and (2) "kingdom of God" makes God the King, and though this does not prevent the other Synoptics from ascribing the kingship to Jesus (cf. Luke 22:16, 18, 29–30), there is less room to maneuver. Matthew's "kingdom of heaven" assumes it is God's kingdom and occasionally assigns it specifically to the Father (26:29), though leaving room to ascribe it frequently to Jesus (16:28; 25:31, 34, 40; 27:42; probably 5:35); for Jesus is King Messiah. This inevitably has christological implications. The kingdom of heaven is simultaneously the kingdom of the Father and the kingdom of the Son of Man.

This kingdom, John preached, "is near" (*ēngiken*, lit., "has drawn near"). Jews spoke of the Messiah as "the coming one" (11:3) and the Messianic Age as "the coming age" (Heb 6:5): John says it has now drawn "near," the same message preached by Jesus (4:17) and his disciples (10:7). It is possible, but not certain, that the verb has the same force as *ephthasen* in 12:28. There Jesus unambiguously affirms that the kingdom "has come." That passage makes it clear that it is the exercise of God's saving sovereignty or reign that has dawned. The ambiguous "is near" (3:2; 4:17), coupled with the dynamic sense of "kingdom," prepares us for a constant theme: The kingdom came with Jesus and his preaching and miracles, it came with his death and resurrection, and it will come at the end of the age.

Matthew has already established that Jesus was born King (2:2). Later Jesus declared that his work testified the kingdom had come (12:28), even though he frequently spoke of the kingdom as something to be inherited when the Son of Man comes in his glory. It is false to say that "kingdom" undergoes a radical shift with the mention of "mystery" ("secrets," NIV; see on 13:11). Already in the Sermon on the Mount, entering the kingdom (5:3, 10; 7:21) is equivalent to entering into life (7:13–14; cf. 19:14, 16; and see Mark 9:45, 47).

These and related themes become clearer as the Gospel progresses (cf. esp. Ladd, *NT Theology*, pp. 57–90). But two observations cannot be delayed. First, the Baptist's terminology, though veiled, necessarily roused enormous excitement (3:5). But assorted apocalyptic and political expectations would have brought about a profound misunderstanding of the kingdom being preached. Therefore Jesus himself purposely used veiled terminology when treating themes like this. This becomes increasingly obvious in the Gospel. The second observation relates to the first. Just as the angel's announcement to Joseph declared Jesus' primary purpose to be to save his people from their sins (1:21), so the first announcement of the kingdom is associated with repentance and confession of sin (3:6). These themes are constantly intertwined in Matthew (cf. Goppelt, *Theologie*, pp. 128–88).

3 If the *gar* ("for") has its full force, then NIV should read, "For this is he"; and v.3 becomes the ground for the Baptist's preaching in v.2. This is the one OT citation of Matthew's own eleven direct OT quotations that is not introduced by a fulfillment formula (cf. Introduction, section 11.b). It goes too far, however (contra Gundry), to say that the omission of fulfillment language means that for Matthew, John the Baptist does not fulfill Scripture but serves merely as a "protypical Christian preacher." If Matthew had wanted to say so little, he would have been better off eliminating the OT passage. Instead he introduces it with a Pesher formula (e.g., Acts 2:16; cf. Introduction, section 11.b) that can only be understood as identifying the Baptist in an eschatological, prophecy-and-fulfillment framework with the one of whom Isaiah (40:3) spoke.

The Baptist's role is minimally exemplary. According to John 1:23, the Baptist once applied this passage to himself. Here Matthew does it for him. In the MT the words "in the desert" modify "prepare": "In the desert prepare the way of the LORD." But all three Synoptics here follow the LXX. The immediate effect is to locate in the desert the one who is calling. Some have thought this a deliberate attempt to make the fulfillment extend to geographical details. But Mark consistently follows the LXX, and Matthew often follows Mark. So we must not read too much into the change. There may be an error in the Hebrew accents, which associate "in the desert" with "prepare" (Gundry, *Use of OT*, p. 10). In any case, if one shouts a command in the desert, his intent is that it be spread everywhere; so there is little difference in meaning (Alexander).

In Isaiah 40:3 the way of Yahweh is being "made straight" (a metaphor using road building to refer to repentance); in Matthew 3:3 it is the way of Jesus. This sort of identification of Jesus with Yahweh is common in the NT (e.g., Exod 13:21 and 1 Cor 10:4; Isa 6:1 and John 12:41; Ps 68:18 and Eph 4:8; Ps 102:25–27 and Heb 1:10–12) and confirms the kingdom as being equally the kingdom of God and the kingdom of Jesus. While the deity of Christ is only implicit in such texts, it certainly goes beyond Jesus' being merely a royal envoy. The Qumran covenanters cited the same passage to foster study of the law in preparation for the eschaton (1QS 8:12ff.; 9:19; cf. Fitzmyer, *Semitic Background*, pp. 34–36); but Matthew identifies the Baptist as the voice and the eschatological age as already dawning in Jesus' coming.

4–5 Clothes of camel's hair and a leather belt (v.4, the latter to bind up the loose outer garment) were not only the clothes of poor people but establish links with Elijah (2 Kings 1:8; cf. Mal 4:5). "Locusts" (*akrides*) are large grasshoppers, still eaten in the East, not the fruit of the "locust tree" (BAGD, s.v.). Wild honey is what it purports to be, not gum from a tree (cf. Judg 14:8–9; 1 Sam 14:25–29; Ps 81:16). Both suggest a poor man used to wilderness living, and this suggests a connection with the prophets (cf. 3:1; 11:8–9)—so much so that in Zechariah's day (13:4) some false prophets dressed like prophets to deceive people. Both Elijah and John had stern ministries in which austere garb and diet confirmed their message and condemned the idolatry of physical and spiritual softness. "Even the food and dress of John preached" (Beng.). John's impact was enormous (v.5), and his crowds came from a wide area. In Greek, the places are personified (as in 2:3).

6 Confession of sin was commanded in the law, not only as part of a priest's duties (Lev 16:21), but as an individual responsibility for wrongs done (Lev 5:5; 26:40; Num 5:6–7; Prov 28:13). In Israel's better days this was carried out (Neh. 9:2–3; Ps 32:5). In the NT (cf. Acts 19:18; 1 John 1:9) confession is scarcely less important. Because Matthew does not include "for the forgiveness of sins" (Mark 1:4), some have deduced that he wants to avoid suggesting any possibility of forgiveness until Jesus' death (Matt 26:28). This is too subtle. A first-century reader would hardly hold that sins were not forgiven after being honestly confessed. And since Matthew regularly abbreviates Mark where he uses him, we must be cautious in drawing theological conclusions from such omissions.

The Greek does not make clear whether the confession was individual or corporate, simultaneous with baptism or antecedent to it. Josephus (Antiq. XVIII, 116–17 [v.2] says that John, "surnamed the Baptist," required righteous conduct as a "necessary preliminary if baptism was to be acceptable to God." Since John was urging people to prepare for Messiah's coming by repenting and being baptized, we may surmise that open renunciation of sin was a precondition of his baptism, which was therefore both a confirmation of confession and an eschatological sign.

Since the discovery of the DSS, many have tried to link John's baptism with that of the Qumran covenanters. But their washings, though related to confession, were probably regarded as purifying and were repeated (cf. 1QS 1:24ff.; 5:13–25) to remove ritual uncleanness. John's baptism, probably a once-only rite (contra Albright and Mann), was unrelated to ceremonial impurity. The rabbis used baptism to induct proselytes but never Jews (SBK, 1:102–12). As far as we know, though baptism itself was not uncommon, the pointed but limited associations placed on John's baptism stem from the Baptist himself—not unlike circumcision, which predates Abraham but lacked covenantal significance before his time.

The Jordan River is fast flowing. No doubt John stationed himself at one of the fords, and prepared the way for the Lord.

7 Many have raised the question of the probability of individuals from groups so mutually hostile as Pharisees and Sadducees (cf. Introduction, section 11.f) presenting themselves together (one article governs both nouns) for baptism. But the Greek text need not be taken to mean that they came to be baptized. It may only mean that they were "coming to where he was baptizing" (cf. Notes). If so, it might suggest that representatives of the Sanhedrin (composed of both parties with elders) came to examine what John was doing (cf. John 1:19, 24, which mentions not only priests and Levites [Sadducees] but also Pharisees). Or many Pharisees and Sadducees may have come for baptism with the ostentation that characterized their other religious activities (e.g., 6:2, 5, 16)—i.e., they were showing the world how ready they were for Messiah, though they had not truly repented. Matthew lumps them together because they were leaders; elsewhere he distinguishes them (22:34). The question with which the Baptist confronted them has this sense: "Who suggested to you that you would escape the coming wrath?" Thus John's rhetorical question takes on a sarcastic nuance: "Who warned you to flee the coming wrath and come for baptism—when in fact you show no signs of repentance?" Though the question is the same in Luke 3:7, there Luke relates it to the crowd, whereas Matthew relates it to the Jewish leaders.

John the Baptist stands squarely in the prophetic tradition—a tradition in which the Day of the Lord points much more to darkness than to light for those who think they have no sin (Amos 2:4–8; 6:1–7). "You brood of vipers!" also belongs to the prophetic tradition (cf. Isa 14:29; 30:6; cf. CD 19:22); in Matthew 12:34, Jesus uses these terms to excoriate the Pharisees.

8–9 The coming of God's reign either demands repentance (v.2) or brings judgment. Repentance must be genuine: if we wish to escape the coming wrath (v.7), then our entire lifestyle must be in harmony with our oral repentance (v.8). Mere descent from Abraham is not enough (v.9). In the OT God repeatedly cut off many Israelites and saved a remnant. Yet in the intertestamental period the general use of descent from Abraham, in the context of a rising merit theology, supported the notion that Israel was chosen because it was choice and that the merits of the patriarchs would suffice for their descendants (cf. Carson, *Divine Sovereignty*, pp. 39ff.). But not only may God narrow Israel down to a remnant, he may also raise up authentic children of Israel from "these stones" (perhaps stones lying in the river bed—both Hebrew and Aramaic have a pun on "children" and "stones"). Ordinary stones will suffice; there is no need for the "rocks" of the patriarchs and their merits (cf. S. Schechter, *Some Aspects of Rabbinic Theology* [London: Black, 1903], p. 173; cf. also Rom 4). Verse 9 not only rebukes the self-righteousness of the leaders but implies that participation in the kingdom results from grace and extends the borders of God's people beyond racial frontiers (cf. 8:11).

10 The ax is "already" (emphatic) at the root of the trees (for the idiom, cf. Isa 10:33–34; Jer 46:22). "Not only is there a coming Messianic wrath, but already there is a beginning Messianic discrimination among the descendants of Abraham" (Broadus). Just as the kingdom is dawning already (v.2), so also is the judgment; the two are inseparable. To preach the kingdom is to preach repentance; any tree (not "every tree," NIV; cf. Turner, *Syntax*, p. 199), regardless of its roots, that does not bring forth good fruit will be destroyed.

11 Compare vv.11–12 with Luke 3:15–18 (Q?). Because only Matthew says, "I baptize you with water *for repentance*" (emphasis mine), Hill detects a conscious effort to subordinate John to Jesus. John baptizes as preparation "for repentance"; Jesus baptizes for fulfillment "with the Holy Spirit and fire." But both Mark (1:4) and Luke (3:3) have spoken of John's baptism as one of repentance. And when Jesus begins to preach, he too demands repentance (4:17). If there is an antithesis here between John and Jesus, it is in all three synoptic Gospels. Matthew may be stressing the difference between the baptisms of John and Jesus in order to make a point about eschatology (see below and on 11:7–13).

The phrase "for repentance" (*eis metanoian*) is difficult: *eis* plus the accusative frequently suggests purpose ("I baptize you in order that you will repent"). Contextually (v.6) this is unlikely, even in the peculiar telic sense suggested by Broadus: "I baptize you with a view to continued repentance." But causal *eis*, or something very close to it, is not unknown in the NT (cf. Turner, *Syntax*, pp. 266–67): "I baptize you because of your repentance." The force may, however, be weaker—i.e., "I baptize you with reference to or in connection with repentance." In any case John wants to contrast his baptism with that of the one who comes after him (any allusion here to the messianic title "the one who comes" is doubtful; cf. Arens, pp. 288–90). That one is "more powerful" than John: the same term (*ischyros*) is applied to God in the OT (LXX Jer 32:18; Dan 9:4; cf. also Isa 40:10) and the cognate noun to the Messiah in Psalms of Solomon 17. This is not the normal order: usually the one who follows is the disciple, the lesser one (cf. Matt 16:24; John 13:16; 15:20). But because John's particular ministry is to announce the eschatological figure, he cannot do other than precede him.

Though John was the most sought-after preacher in Israel for centuries, he protested that he was not fit to "carry" (Mark and Luke have "untie") the sandals of the Coming One. Many scholars have argued that this saying must be a late invention of Christians determined to keep the Baptist in his place and exalt Jesus. In fact, such humility as John's is in Christian ethics a virtue, not a weakness. Moreover if he saw his role as that of forerunner to the Messiah, John could not well have set himself on a par with the one to whom he pointed (cf. also John 3:28–31). No doubt the church readily used John's self-depreciation in later conflicts with his followers. But there is no evidence they invented it.

It follows that just as John's purpose was to prepare a way for the Lord by calling people to repentance, so his baptism pointed to the one who would bring the eschatological baptism in spirit and fire. John's baptism was "essentially preparatory" (cf. J.D.G. Dunn, *Baptism in the Holy Spirit* [London: SCM, 1970], pp. 14–17; Bonnard; F. Lang, "Erwägungen zur eschatologischen Verkündigung Johannes des

Täufers," in Strecker, *Jesus Christus*, pp. 459–73); Jesus' baptism inaugurated the Messianic Age.

"Baptism in the Holy Spirit" is not a specialized term in the NT. Its OT background includes Ezekiel 36:25–27; 39:29; Joel 2:28. We need not think that John the Baptist could not have mentioned the Holy Spirit, not least because of somewhat similar references in the literature at Qumran (1QS 3:7–9; 4:21; 1QH 16:12; cf. Dunn, *Baptism*, pp. 8–10). But Matthew and Luke add "and fire." Many see this as a double baptism, one in the Holy Spirit for the righteous and one in fire for the unrepentant (cf. the wheat and chaff in v.12). Fire (Mal 4:1) destroys and consumes.

There are good reasons, however, for taking "fire" as a purifying agent along with the Holy Spirit. The people John is addressing are being baptized by him; presumably they have repented. More important the preposition *en* ("with") is not repeated before fire: the one preposition governs both "Holy Spirit" and "fire," and this normally suggests a unified concept, Spirit-fire or the like (cf. M.J. Harris, DNTT, 3:1178; Dunn, *Baptism*, pp. 10–13). Fire often has a purifying, not destructive, connotation in the OT (e.g., Isa 1:25; Zech 13:9; Mal 3:2–3). John's water baptism relates to repentance; but the one whose way he is preparing will administer a Spirit-fire baptism that will purify and refine. In a time when many Jews felt the Holy Spirit had been withdrawn till the Messianic Age, this announcement could only have been greeted with excited anticipation.

12 Messiah's coming will separate grain from chaff. A winnowing fork tossed both into the air. The wind blew the chaff away, and the heavier grain fell to be gathered up from the ground. The scattered chaff was swept up and burned and the threshing floor cleared (cf. Ps 1:4; Isa 5:24; Dan 2:35; Hos 13:3). The "unquenchable fire" signifies eschatological judgment (cf. Isa 34:10; 66:24; Jer 7:20), hell (cf. 5:29). "Unquenchable fire" is not just metaphor: fearful reality underlies Messiah's separation of grain from chaff. The "nearness" of the kingdom therefore calls for repentance (v.2).

Notes

1 Matthew has ὁ βαπτιστής (*ho baptistēs*, "the baptist"); Mark (1:4) uses the participle [ὁ] βαπτίζων ([*ho*] *baptizōn*, lit., "the baptizer"). It is doubtful whether any distinction is intended since "Baptist" has no sectarian or denominational flavor. It is too much to say with Gundry (*Matthew*) that Matthew consistently uses "the Baptist" instead of "the baptizer" to divert attention from John's practice of baptism to his role as preacher; for the latter is not stressed, and Matthew includes the specific statement of v.6: "they were baptized by" John.

"Preaching" (verb κηρύσσω [*kēryssō*], noun κήρυγμα [*kērygma*]) has often, during the past fifty years, been distinguished from "teaching" (διδαχή [*didachē*]) in such a way that the so-called kerygmatic elements were often robbed of content; and virtually everything in the NT was confidently assigned to one category or the other. More recent study has demonstrated how grossly oversimplified such an antithesis is (J.I.H. McDonald, *Kerygma and Didache* [Cambridge: University Press, 1980]) and has suggested other equally important and sometimes overlapping categories (e.g., A.A. Trites, *The New Testament Concept of Witness* [Cambridge: University Press, 1977]).

2 The verb μετανοέω (*metanoeō*, "I repent") was rendered in Latin *poenitentiam agere* ("to exercise penitence"), the word "penitence" suggesting grief, distress, pain, but not necessarily change. Eventually *poenitentiam agite* ("to do penitence") was preferred; and the contraction to "do penance" completed the slide to a pernicious concept quite alien to the NT.

7 The expression ἐπὶ τὸ βάπτισμα αὐτοῦ (*epi to baptisma autou*) is peculiar (lit., coming "to his baptism"); it could either mean "coming to be baptized" or "coming to the place where he was baptizing" (so NIV).

10 Moule (*Idiom Book*, p. 53) sees πρός (*pros*) plus the accusative here combining linear motion with punctiliar rest on arrival: the ax has taken its first chop, as it were. But it is possible that the verb κεῖται (*keitai*, lit., "lies"; NIV, "is") suggests the ax is merely lying at the root of the tree, ready for action.

---

b. The baptism of Jesus

3:13–17

> ¹³Then Jesus came from Galilee to the Jordan to be baptized by John. ¹⁴But John tried to deter him, saying, "I need to be baptized by you, and do you come to me?"
> ¹⁵Jesus replied, "Let it be so now; it is proper for us to do this to fulfill all righteousness." Then John consented.
> ¹⁶As soon as Jesus was baptized, he went up out of the water. At that moment heaven was opened, and he saw the Spirit of God descending like a dove and lighting on him. ¹⁷And a voice from heaven said, "This is my Son, whom I love; with him I am well pleased."

Comparing the three synoptic accounts of Jesus' baptism (cf. Mark 1:9–11; Luke 3:21–22) reveals distinctive features (e.g., only Matthew has 3:14–15). But it is easy to exaggerate differences. As is often pointed out, Luke does not say John baptized Jesus; but in view of Luke 3:1–21, there is no doubt of this. As will be shown, some alleged distinctions among the evangelists are artificial; others highlight valuable theological emphases.

13 "Then" (*tote*) is vague in Matthew (see on 2:7); each use needs separate handling. Here *tote* implies that during the time John the Baptist was preaching to the crowds and baptizing them, "then" Jesus came—i.e., it is equivalent to Luke's "When all the people were being baptized, Jesus was baptized too" (3:21). If so, to say that in Luke baptism is a public testimony to Jesus but a private one in Matthew is artificial. This conclusion is especially important to Kingsbury (*Structure*, pp. 13–15) because he wants to avoid any public recognition of Jesus till 4:17. Jeremias (*NT Theology*, p. 51) thinks Luke is closer to historical reality and supposes that Jesus immersed himself along with others in John's presence. Both refinements are too finespun. Any interpretation demanding either privacy or crowds at Jesus' baptism as Matthew or Luke report it reads too much into the texts and probably misses the evangelists' chief points. Jesus came from Galilee (Mark specifies Nazareth) to be baptized by John (though Matthew makes this aim explicit, in Mark and Luke it is implicit), and as a result the Father testified to his Son. This much is common to all three accounts, and it matters little whether only John heard this heavenly witness or whether the crowds heard it as well.

14 Matthew 3:14–15 is peculiar to this Gospel. John tried to deter Jesus (imperfect of attempted action) from his baptism, insisting (the pronouns are emphatic) that he stood in need of baptism by Jesus. Earlier John had difficulty baptizing the Pharisees and Sadducees because they were not worthy of his baptism. Now he has trouble baptizing Jesus because his baptism is not worthy of Jesus.

There are two possible ways of understanding John's reluctance:

1. John recognizes Jesus as the Messiah and wants to receive Jesus' Spirit-and-fire baptism. Despite the rising popularity of this view, it entails serious difficulties. The Spirit theme is not important in Matthew; righteousness is, and it is central to Jesus' response (v.15). Matthew does not present Jesus as bestowing his Spirit-and-fire baptism on anyone: the Cross and Resurrection are focal for him; and, writing after Pentecost (Acts 2), Matthew doubtless believes Jesus' baptism was bestowed on his people later than the time he is writing about. In view of the Baptist's statements about his relation to the Messiah (v.11), if he had recognized Jesus as the Messiah it is doubtful whether Jesus' rebuttal would have convinced him (v.15). Moreover this view brings Matthew into needless conflict with the fourth Gospel (John 1:31–34), which says the Baptist did not "know" Jesus—i.e., recognize him as the Messiah—till after his baptism.

2. But John's baptism did not have purely eschatological significance. It also signified repentance and confession of sin. Whether John knew Jesus well, we do not know. It is, however, inconceivable that his parents had not told him of Mary's visit to Elizabeth some three decades earlier (Luke 1:39–45). At the very least John must have recognized that Jesus, to whom he was related, whose birth was more marvelous than his own, and whose knowledge of Scripture was prodigious even as a child (Luke 2:41–52), outstripped him. John the Baptist was a humble man; conscious of his own sin, he could detect no sin Jesus needed to repent of and confess. So John thought that Jesus should baptize him. Matthew does not tell us when John also perceived that Jesus was the Messiah (though that may be implied by vv.16–17); Matthew focuses on Jesus' sinlessness and the Father's testimony, not on John's testimony (unlike the fourth Gospel, where the Baptist's witness to Jesus is very important).

15 John's consent was won because Jesus told him, "It is proper for us to fulfill all righteousness." Here interpretations are legion. They may be summed up as follows:

1. By undergoing baptism Jesus anticipates his own baptism of death, by which he secures "righteousness" for all. This reads in the Suffering Servant of Isaiah 53:11 ("by his knowledge my righteous servant will justify many"). This view, espoused by many, is well defended by O. Cullmann (*Baptism in the New Testament* [London: SCM, 1950], pp. 15ff.). It presupposes that the significance of Christian baptism should be read back into John's baptism and takes no account of its salvation-historical location. Worse, Cullmann reads Paul's use of "righteousness" back into Matthew, who in fact never uses the term that way but always as meaning "conformity to God's will" or the like (cf. Bonnard's discussion and notes, and esp. Przybylski, pp. 91–94). Moreover the "us" is not a royal "us"; both Jesus *and* John must "fulfill all righteousness," which renders doubtful any theory that ties the righteousness too closely to Jesus' death. G. Barth (Bornkamm, *Tradition*, pp. 140ff.) rejects Cullmann's view but falls into the same weaknesses, holding that Jesus fulfills all right-

eousness by humbly entering the ranks of sinners and acting for them. The same objections apply.

2. Others suggest that Jesus must obey ("fulfill") every divine command ("all righteousness"), and baptism is one such command. Put so crassly this view forgets that the baptism relates to repentance and confession of sins, not to righteousness itself. A slight modification of it says that by being baptized Jesus is acknowledging as valid the righteous life preached by John and demanded of those who accept John's baptism, for Jesus acknowledges (21:32) that John came to show the way of righteousness. But this view forces "fulfill" to become "acknowledge" and neglects the fact that John's baptism relates, not to the standards of righteousness John preached, but to repentance.

3. The strengths of the alternative views may be integrated in a better synthesis. John's baptism, it will be remembered, had two foci: repentance and its eschatological significance. Jesus affirms, in effect, that it is God's will ("all righteousness") that John baptize him; and *both* John *and* Jesus "fulfill" that will, that righteousness, by going through with it ("it is proper for *us*"). The aftermath, as Matthew immediately notes (vv. 16-17), shows that this baptism really did point to Jesus. Within this framework we may recognize other themes. In particular Jesus is indeed seen as the Suffering Servant (Isa 42:1; cf. on 3:17). But the Servant's first mark is obeying God: he "fulfills all righteousness" since he suffers and dies to accomplish redemption in obedience to the will of God. By his baptism Jesus affirms his determination to do his assigned work. Thus the "now" may be significant: Jesus is saying that John's objection (v. 14) is in principle valid. Yet he must "now," at this point in salvation history, baptize Jesus; for at this point Jesus must demonstrate his willingness to take on his servant role, entailing his identification with the people. Contrary to Gundry, "now" does not serve to tell Christian converts they must not delay "this first step on the way of righteousness."

This interpretation assumes that Jesus knew of his Suffering-Servant role from the beginning of his ministry; cf. further at v. 17. This role was hinted at in 2:23; here it makes its first veiled appearance in Jesus' actions. The immediately following temptation narrative confirms it (4:1-11). There Jesus rejects the devil's temptation to pursue messianic glory and power, choosing instead the servant role of obeying every word that comes from the mouth of God.

16 "As soon as" not only suggests that Jesus left the water immediately after his baptism but that the Spirit's witness was equally prompt. Jesus' baptism and its attestation are of a piece and must be interpreted together. "He saw" most naturally refers to Jesus (cf. Mark 1:10), not John, not so much because Matthew excludes John as because he is not the focus of interest. The presence of John (and possibly others) is probably implied by the third-person address "This is my Son" (v. 17), displacing Mark's "You are my Son" (1:11).

"Heaven . . . opened" calls to mind OT visions (e.g., Isa 64:1; Ezek 1:1; cf. Acts 7:56; Rev 4:1; 19:11). "The Spirit of God descending like a dove" simile could mean either that the manner of the Spirit's descent was like a dove's or that the Spirit appeared in a dove's form. Whether or not the latter is visionary, Luke 3:22 specifies it. Because no clear pre-Christian reference links dove and Holy Spirit, some have advanced complex theories: e.g., Mark collected two stories, one mentioning the Holy Spirit's descent and the other the dove's descent, and fused them together (S. Gero, "The Spirit as a Dove at the Baptism of Jesus," NovTest 18 [1976]: 17-35).

But to exclude any new metaphor from the Christian revelation is surely rash. The Spirit's descent cannot be adequately considered apart from v.17; and so resolution of its meaning awaits comment on v.17.

17 Some see in the "voice from heaven" the *bat̲-k̲ôl* (lit., "daughter of a voice"), the category used by rabbinic and other writers to refer to divine communication echoing the Spirit of God after the Spirit and the prophets through whom he spoke had been withdrawn. The point, however, is stronger than that. This voice is God's ("from heaven") and testifies that God himself has broken silence and is again revealing himself to men—a clear sign of the dawning of the Messianic Age (cf. 17:5 and John 12:28). What Heaven says in Mark and Luke is "You are my Son"; here it is "This is my Son." The change not only shows Matthew's concern only for the *ipsissima vox* (not generally the *ipsissima verba*; cf. Notes) but also assumes someone besides Jesus heard heaven's witness. There may have been a crowd; if so, that does not interest Matthew. But John needed to hear the Voice confirm his decision (v.15).

Despite arguments to the contrary (e.g., Hooker, *Jesus and the Servant*, pp. 70ff.), the utterance reflects Isaiah 42:1: "Here is my servant, whom I uphold, my chosen one in whom I delight; I will put my Spirit upon him"; and this has been modified by Psalm 2:7: "You are my Son" (cf. Gundry, *Use of OT*, pp. 29–32; and esp. Moo, "Use of OT," pp. 112ff.). The results are extraordinarily important.

1. These words from heaven link Jesus with the Suffering Servant at the very beginning of his ministry and confirm our interpretation of v.15.

2. God here refers to Jesus as "my Son"; implicitly the title "Son of God" is introduced and picked up immediately in the next chapter (4:3, 6). Psalm 2 is Davidic: though it was not regarded in the first century as messianic, the link with David recalls other "son" passages where David or his heir is seen as God's son (e.g., 2 Sam 7:13–14; Ps. 89:26–29).

3. Jesus has already been set forth as the true Israel to which actual Israel was pointing and as such God's Son (see on 2:15); now the heavenly witness confirms the link.

4. At the same time the virginal conception suggests a more than titular or functional sonship: in this context there is the hint of an ontological sonship, made most explicit in the Gospel of John.

5. Jesus is the "beloved" (*agapētos*) Son: the term may mean not only affection but also election, reinforced by the aorist tense that follows (lit., "with him I was well pleased"), suggesting a pretemporal election of the Messiah (cf. John 1:34 [Gr. mg.]).

6. These things are linked in the one utterance: at the very beginning of Jesus' public ministry, his Father presented him, in a veiled way, as at once Davidic Messiah, very Son of God, representative of the people, and Suffering Servant. Matthew has already introduced all these themes and will develop them further. Indeed he definitely cites Isaiah 42:1–4 in 12:18–21, which ends with the assertion (already made clear) that the nations will trust in this Servant.

"Son of God" has particularly rich associations. Therefore it is hard to nail down its precise force at every occurrence. As it is wrong to see ontological sonship in every use, so is it wrong to exclude it prematurely. (For more adequate discussion, see, in addition to the standard dictionaries, Blair, pp. 60ff.; Cullman, *Christology*, pp. 270–305; Kingsbury, *Structure*, pp. 40–83 [though he exaggerates the importance of the theme in Matthew: cf. Hill, "Son and Servant," pp. 2–16]; Ladd, *NT Theology*, pp. 159–72; and Moule, *Christology*, pp. 22ff.)

The Spirit's descent in v.16 needs to be understood in the light of v.17. The Spirit is poured out on the servant in Isaiah 42:1–4, to which v.17 alludes. This outpouring does not change Jesus' status (he was the Son before this) or assign him new rights. Rather it identifies him as the Promised Servant and Son and marks the beginning of his public ministry and direct confrontation with Satan (4:1), the dawning of the Messianic Age (12:28).

Notes

14 The καί (*kai*, "and") has adversative force—"and yet" (cf. Zerwick, par. 455; Turner, *Syntax*, p. 334). This may reflect the beginning of an Aramaic apodosis (Lagrange, p. xci).

16 If αὐτῷ (*autō*) is the correct reading, the text says the heavens opened "to him," i.e., to Jesus. But this need not mean that no one else experienced anything (see comment on "This is" in v.17) but only that, in addition to the more public voice, Jesus alone perceived heaven opening. In the NT period the preposition ἀπό (*apo*, "out of") cannot always be distinguished in meaning from ἐκ (*ek*), used in Mark 1:10 (cf. Zerwick, par. 87; Turner, *Syntax*, p. 259).

17 The Latin *vox* simply means "voice" and *verba* "words." *Ipsissima*, from the Latin *ipse* ("self"), basically means "all by oneself" or the like. *Ipsissima vox* and *ipsissima verba* in NT study usually refer to "[Jesus'] own voice" and "[Jesus'] own words" respectively. The first implies that Jesus' teaching is accurately preserved but in the evangelist's own words, style, etc., whereas the latter refers to those places where Jesus' actual words are preserved. In the narrowest sense, however, *ipsissima verba*, since Jesus primarily spoke Aramaic, would be restricted to words like *abba, talitha cum*, etc. Others understand the term to include words of Jesus that are given in precise translation into Greek; but this, too, would be a destructive category to use as the only acceptable reflection of what Jesus taught. In this verse, of course, the words are not those of Jesus but of the Voice from heaven. Even so, Matthew preserves only the general sense, the *ipsissima vox*. For further discussion, see EBC, 1:13–20.

c. *The temptation of Jesus*

4:1–11

¹Then Jesus was led by the Spirit into the desert to be tempted by the devil. ²After fasting forty days and forty nights, he was hungry. ³The tempter came to him and said, "If you are the Son of God, tell these stones to become bread." ⁴Jesus answered, "It is written: 'Man does not live on bread alone, but on every word that comes from the mouth of God.' " ⁵Then the devil took him to the holy city and had him stand on the highest point of the temple. ⁶"If you are the Son of God," he said, "throw yourself down. For it is written:

" 'He will command his angels concerning you,
    and they will lift you up in their hands,
  so that you will not strike your foot against a stone.' "

⁷Jesus answered him, "It is also written: 'Do not put the Lord your God to the test.' "

8Again, the devil took him to a very high mountain and showed him all the kingdoms of the world and their splendor. 9"All this I will give you," he said, "if you will bow down and worship me."
10Jesus said to him, "Away from me, Satan! For it is written: 'Worship the Lord your God, and serve him only.'"
11Then the devil left him, and angels came and attended him.

In the past many scholars took this pericope and its parallel (Luke 4:1–13) as imaginative embellishments of Mark's much briefer account. But J. Dupont ("L'Arrière-fond Biblique du Récit des Tentations de Jésus," NTS 3 [1956–57]: 287–304) has argued persuasively that Mark's brevity and the ambiguity of such statements as "he was with the wild animals" (Mark 1:13) implies that Mark's readers were familiar with a larger account to which Mark makes brief reference. The account could only have come from Jesus, given to his disciples perhaps after Caesarea Philippi (Dupont). Therefore it gives an important glimpse into Jesus' self-perception as the Son of God (3:17; 4:3, 6), and, judging by the Scripture he quotes, the way he perceived his own relation to Israel (cf. France, *Jesus*, pp. 50–53).

Both Matthew and Mark tie the temptations to Jesus' baptism (see on 4:1). Luke, however, inserts his genealogy between the two, suggesting a contrast between Adam, who though tested in the bliss of Eden yet fell, and Jesus, who was tested in the hardships of the wilderness yet triumphed. Jesus' responses to Satan (all taken from Deut 6–8; i.e., 6:13, 16; 8:3) have led some to argue that this account is a haggadic midrash—i.e., explanatory but minimally historical stories—on the OT text (cf. esp. B. Gerhardsson, *The Testing of God's Son* [Lund: CWK Gleerup, 1966]). But the story line stands independent of the OT background; there are more themes allusively hidden in Matthew's account than first meet the eye (e.g., possible "new Moses" motifs: Davies, *Setting*, pp. 45–48; cf. Bonnard; Petr Pokorny, "The Temptation Stories and Their Intention," NTS 20 [1974]: 115–27); and the repeated reference to Deuteronomy 6–8 is better explained in terms of Israel-Christ typology.

Luke reverses the order of the last two temptations for topographical reasons. Matthew's order is almost certainly original (Schweizer; Walvoord).

It is difficult to be certain exactly what happened or in what form Satan came to Jesus. Standing on a high mountain (v.8) would not itself provide a glimpse of "all the kingdoms of the world"; some supernatural vision is presupposed. Moreover a forty-day fast is scarcely the ideal background for a trek to three separate and rugged sites. When we remember that Paul was not always sure whether his visions were "in the body or out of the body" (2 Cor 12:2), we may be cautious about dogmatizing here. But there is no reason to think the framework of the story is purely symbolic as opposed to visionary, representing Jesus' inward struggles; if the demons could address him directly (e.g., 8:29, 31), it is difficult to say Satan wouldn't or couldn't do this.

1 Jesus' three temptations tie into his baptism, not only by the references to sonship and the Spirit, but by the opening "Then" (*tote*). Jesus' attestation as the Son (3:17) furnishes "the natural occasion for such special temptations as are here depicted" (Broadus). The same Spirit who engendered Jesus (1:20) and attested the Father's acknowledgment of his sonship (3:16–17) now leads him into the desert to be tempted by the devil. The "desert" (cf. on 3:1) is not only the place associated

with demonic activity (Isa 13:21; 34:14; Matt 12:43; Rev 18:2; Trench, pp. 7–8) but, in a context abounding with references to Deuteronomy 6–8, the place where Israel experienced her greatest early testings.

The devil must not be reduced to impersonal "forces" behind racism and pogroms (Schweizer). The Greek word *diabolos* strictly means "slanderer"; but the term is the regular LXX rendering of "Satan" (e.g., 1 Chron 21:1; Job 1:6–13; 2:1–7; Zech 3:1–2), the chief opposer of God, the archenemy who leads all the spiritual hosts of darkness (cf. Gen 3; 2 Sam 19:23; John 8:37–40; 1 Cor 11:10; 2 Cor 11:3; 12:7; Rev 12:3–9; 20:1–4; 7–10; Maier). In a day of rising occultism and open Satanism, it is easier to believe the Bible's plain witness to him than twenty years ago.

That Jesus should be led "by the Spirit" to be tempted "by the devil" is no stranger than Job 1:6–2:7 or 2 Samuel 24:1 (1 Chron 21:1). Recognizing that "to tempt" (*peirazō*) also means "to test" in a good or bad sense somewhat eases the problem. In Scripture "tempting" or "testing" can reveal or develop character (Gen 22:1; Exod 20:20; John 6:6; 2 Cor 13:5; Rev 2:2) as well as solicit to evil (1 Cor 7:5; 1 Thess 3:5). For us to "tempt" or "test" God is wrong because it reflects unbelief or attempted bribery (Exod 17:2, 7 [Ps 95:9]; Deut 6:16 [Matt 4:7]; Isa 7:12; Acts 5:9; 15:10). Moreover God uses means and may bring good out of his agents' evil motives—see Joseph's experience (Gen 50:19–20). In Jesus' "temptations" God clearly purposed to test him just as Israel was tested, and Jesus' responses prove that he understood.

2 The parallels with historic Israel continue. Jesus' fast (doubtless total abstention from food but not from drink; cf. Luke 4:2) of forty days and nights reflected Israel's forty-year wandering (Deut 8:2). Both Israel's and Jesus' hunger taught a lesson (Deut 8:3); both spent time in the desert preparatory to their respective tasks. Other parallels have been noticed (cf. Dupont). The main point is that both "sons" were tested by God's design (Deut 8:3, 5; cf. Exod 4:22; Gerhardsson, *Testing God's Son*, pp. 19–35), the one after being redeemed from Egypt and the other after his baptism, to prove their obedience and loyalty in preparation for their appointed work. The one "son" failed but pointed to the "Son" who would never fail (cf. on 2:15). In this sense the temptations legitimized Jesus as God's true Son (cf. Berger, "Die königlichen Messiastraditionen," pp. 15–18).

At the same time Jesus' hunger introduces us to a number of ironies to which Matthew more or less explicitly alludes: Jesus is hungry (v.2) but feeds others (14:13–21; 15:29–39); he grows weary (8:24) but offers others rest (11:28); he is the King Messiah but pays tribute (17:24–27); he is called the devil but casts out demons (12:22–32); he dies the death of a sinner but comes to save his people from their sins (1:21); he is sold for thirty pieces of silver but gives his life a ransom for many (20:28); he will not turn stones to bread for himself (4:3–4) but gives his own body as bread for people (26:26).

3–4 The tempter came to Jesus—we cannot say in what form—and referred to Jesus' sonship (v.3). The form of the "if" clause in Greek (*ei* + indicative) does not so much challenge his sonship as assume it to build a doubtful imperative. Satan was not inviting Jesus to doubt his sonship but to reflect on its meaning. Sonship of the living God, he suggested, surely means Jesus has the power and right to satisfy his own needs.

Jesus' response is based solely on Scripture: "It is written" (v.4). The Scripture is Deuteronomy 8:3, following the LXX, which reads "every word" instead of a more ambiguous Hebrew expression (unless the non-LXX reading of D be adopted: cf. Gundry, *Use of OT*, p. 67); and it applies initially to Israel. But the statement itself is an aphorism. Even though "man" (*ho anthrōpos*) can specify old Israel (e.g., Ps 80:17), yet it is always true that everyone must recognize his utter dependence on God's word. Jesus' food is to do the will of his Father who sent him (John 4:34).

The point of each temptation must be determined by closely examining both the temptation and Jesus' response. This clearly shows that this first temptation was no simple incitement to use improper means of making bread (Morison), or an attempt to use a miracle to prove to himself that he was really God's Son (J.A.T. Robinson, pp. 55–56) or to act alone without thought of others (Riesenfeld, pp. 87–88); it was a temptation to use his sonship in a way inconsistent with his God-ordained mission. The same taunt, "If you are the Son of God," is hurled at him in 27:40, when for him to have left the cross would have annulled the purpose of his coming. Similarly, though Jesus could have gained the aid of legions of angels, how then could the Scriptures that say Jesus had to suffer and die have been fulfilled (26:53–54)? Israel's hunger had been intended to show them that hearing and obeying the word of God is the most important thing in life (Deut 8:2–3). Likewise Jesus learned obedience through suffering as a son in God's house (Heb 3:5–6; 5:7–8). More necessary than bread for Jesus was obedience to God's Word.

In the light of these parallels, we must conclude that Satan's aim was to entice Jesus to use powers rightly his but which he had voluntarily abandoned to carry out the Father's mission. Reclaiming them for himself would deny the self-abasement implicit in his mission and in the Father's will. Israel demanded its bread but died in the wilderness; Jesus denied himself bread, retained his righteousness, and lived by faithful submission to God's Word. (There may be an allusion to Hab 2:4; cf. J. Andrew Kirk, "The Messianic Role of Jesus and the Temptation Narrative," EQ 44 [1972]: 11–29, 91–102.)

5–7 The second temptation (Luke's third) is set in the "holy city" (v.5), Jerusalem (cf. Neh 11:1; Isa 48:2; Dan 9:24; Matt 21:10; 27:53), on the highest point of the temple complex (*hieron* probably refers to the entire complex, not the sanctuary itself, which Jesus, not being a Levite, would not have approached; but see on 27:5). Josephus (Antiq. XV, 412[xi.v]) testifies to the enormous height from the structure's top to the ravine's bottom. Late Jewish midrash says that Messiah would prove himself by leaping from the temple pinnacle; but apart from its lateness, it mentions no spectators. So it is unlikely that this was a temptation for Jesus to prove himself to the people as a new "David" who will again rid Jerusalem of the "Jebusites" (i.e., Romans—contra Kirk, "Messianic Role," pp. 91–95).

Satan quoted Psalm 91:11–12 (v.6) from the LXX, omitting the words "to guard you in all your ways." The omission itself does not prove he handled the Scriptures deceitfully (contra Walvoord), since the quotation is well within the range of common NT citation patterns. Satan's deceit lay in misapplying his quotation into a temptation that easily traps the devout mind by apparently warranting what might otherwise be thought sinful. Psalm 91:11–12 refers to anyone who trusts God and thus preeminently to Jesus. The angels will lift such a person up in their hands like a nurse a baby (cf. Num 11:12; Deut 1:31; Isa 49:22; Heb 1:14). At the temple, the place where God has particularly manifested himself, Jesus is tempted to test his sonship ("If you are the Son of God") against God's pledge to protect his own. Deuteronomy 6:16 was Jesus' reply.

Jesus' hesitation came, not from wondering whether he or his Father could command the normal forces of nature (cf. 8:26; 14:31), but because Scripture forbids putting God to the test (v.7). The reference alludes to Exodus 17:2–7 (cf. Num 20:1–13), where the Israelites "put the Lord to the test" by demanding water. So Jesus was tempted by Satan to test God; but Jesus recognized Satan's testing as a sort of manipulative bribery expressly forbidden in the Scriptures (cf. esp. J.A.T. Robinson, *Twelve*, pp. 54–56). For both Israel and Jesus, demanding miraculous protection as proof of God's care was wrong; the appropriate attitude is trust and obedience (Deut 6:17). We see then, something of Jesus' handling of Scripture: his "also" shows that he would not allow any interpretation that generates what he knew would contradict some other passage.

8–10 The "very high mountain" (v.8) does not seem much more than a prop for the vision of the world's kingdoms (cf. introduction to this pericope). It is doubtful that there is a conscious reference to Moses' looking at the Promised Land (Deut 34:1–4; contra Dupont, Hill); the parallels are not close. No condition Moses could have met at that point would have let him enter the land.

Satan offers the kingdoms of the world and their "splendor" without showing their sin. Jesus, however, came to remove sin. Here was a temptation "to achieve power by worship of God's rival" (France, *Jesus*, p. 52), a shortcut to fullest messianic authority. Satan was offering an interpretation of the theocratic ideal that sidestepped the Cross and introduced idolatry. At Jesus' baptism the Voice spoke words that united Davidic messiahship and suffering servanthood (cf. on 3:17); here was enticement to enjoy the former without the latter. Small wonder Jesus would later turn on Peter so sharply when the apostle made a similar suggestion (16:23).

Jesus recognized that Satan's suggestion entailed depriving God of his exclusive claim to worship: neither God's "son" Israel nor God's "Son" Jesus may swerve from undivided allegiance to God himself (v.10; cf. Exod 23:20–33; Deut 6:13; cf. esp. McNeile, Bonnard). So Jesus responded with a third "it is written" and banished Satan from his presence. The time would come when Jesus' expanding kingdom would progressively destroy the kingdom Satan had to offer (12:25–28; cf. Luke 10:18). The day still lies ahead when King Messiah's last enemy is destroyed (1 Cor 15:25–26). But Jesus achieves it all without compromising his filial submission to the Father.

In other words Jesus had in mind from the very beginning of his earthly ministry the combination of royal kingship and suffering servanthood attested at his baptism and essential to his mission. Moreover the twin themes of kingly authority and filial submission, developed so clearly in the fourth Gospel (cf. Carson, *Divine Sovereignty*, pp. 146–62), are already present as the complementary poles of the life and self-revelation of Immanuel: "God with us."

11 The devil left Jesus "until an opportune time" (Luke 4:13); and Matthew's present tense (*aphiēsin*) may suggest the same thing (Hill, *Matthew*). Though the conflict has barely begun, the pattern of obedience and trust has been established. He has learned to resist the devil (cf. James 4:7). The angelic help is not some passing blessing but a sustained one (the imperfect tense is probably significant). Jesus had refused to relieve his hunger by miraculously turning stones to bread;

now he is fed supernaturally (*diēkonoun*, "attended," is often used in connection with food; e.g., 8:15; 25:44; 27:55; Acts 6:2; cf. Elijah in 1 Kings 19:6–7). He had refused to throw himself off the temple heights in the hope of angelic help; now angels feed him. He had refused to take a shortcut to inherit the kingdom of the world; now he fulfills Scripture by beginning his ministry and announcing the kingdom in Galilee of the Gentiles (vv. 12–17).

Notes

1–11 The question of the impeccability of Christ is much discussed in older literature but is of doubtful concern to Matthew in this pericope. The problem is partly definitional: to say Christ could not sin does not resolve the nature of the impossibility, and many writers have said he could not sin because he would not (cf. Trench, pp. 25–30). But at a deeper level, the problem concerns the truth of the Incarnation and how to formulate it. The NT documents affirm both Jesus' deity and his humanity, and neither of these affirmations may be permitted to deny the complementary truth. One might argue that Christ's impeccability is a function of his deity but must not be taken to mitigate his humanity, and Christ's temptability is a function of his humanity but must not be taken to mitigate his deity.

2 The aorist participle νηστεύσας (*nēsteusas*, "after fasting") does not prove the hunger began only after the forty days were over, since an aorist participle sometimes indicates action coordinate with the main verb. Luke's more explicit statement has been pushed too hard by some scholars: Luke is saying that Jesus' hunger was caused by the forty-day fast, not that the hunger began then. There is little exegetical warrant for appealing to the supernatural here.

2. *Jesus' early Galilean ministry* (4:12–25)

a. *The beginning*

4:12–17

> [12]When Jesus heard that John had been put in prison, he returned to Galilee. [13]Leaving Nazareth, he went and lived in Capernaum, which was by the lake in the area of Zebulun and Naphtali— [14]to fulfill what was said through the prophet Isaiah:
>
> > [15]"Land of Zebulun and land of Naphtali,
> > the way to the sea, along the Jordan,
> > Galilee of the Gentiles—
> > [16]the people living in darkness
> > have seen a great light;
> > on those living in the land of the shadow of death
> > a light has dawned."
>
> [17]From that time on Jesus began to preach, "Repent, for the kingdom of heaven is near."

12 John the Baptist's imprisonment appears to have prompted Jesus to return (cf. Notes) to Galilee. Though Mark 1:14–15 likewise links the two events, it is saying too much to conclude that Matthew has so strengthened the language to make John's imprisonment the cause of Jesus' withdrawal (*akousas* more likely means "when he heard" than "because he heard"). Equally important is the fact that the language suggests that Jesus remained for some time in Judea—unless we suppose the Baptist's arrest immediately followed Jesus' baptism. The Synoptics make no mention of Jesus' early Judean ministry but imply that his ministry began in Galilee. By contrast the fourth Gospel seems to presuppose an earlier Galilean ministry (John 1:19–2:12), a Judean ministry that overlapped with that of the Baptist (John 2:13–3:21), and then a return to the north via Samaria (John 3:22–4:42). The Johannine chronology has often been dismissed as of little historical worth. Yet there are hints even in the synoptic Gospels that presuppose an early Judean ministry (e.g., Luke 10:38), one such hint being the delay implicit in this verse.

If this approach is valid, we must ask why the synoptists eliminate Jesus' earliest months of ministry. Several reasons are possible.

1. With the Baptist's removal from the scene, Jesus' ministry entered a new phase. The function of the forerunner was over; the one to whom he pointed had come. This transfer might be neatly indicated by beginning the account of Jesus' ministry from the time of John's imprisonment. (Compare years of intercalation among OT kings and their varied treatment by OT writers.)

2. By contrast, when the fourth Gospel was written, the explicit connection between the Baptist and Jesus may have been of more urgent interest if the writer was responding to organized groups of the Baptist's followers (cf. Acts 19:1–4). The synoptists do not seem to be under such pressure.

3. In Matthew, Galilee is of profound significance because it heralds the fulfillment of prophecy (vv. 14–16) and points to the gospel's extension to "all nations" (28:19).

According to 1 Maccabees 5:23, the Jewish population in Galilee in 164 B.C. was so small it could be transported to Judea for protection. By Jesus' day, however, though the large population was mixed, owing to both the proximity of Gentile peoples in surrounding areas and the importation of colonists during the Maccabean conquest, the Jewish population was substantial. The many theories concerning the influence of this region on Jesus and thence on Christianity have been neatly summarized and criticized by L. Goppelt (*Christentum und Judentum* [Gütersloh: Bertelsmann, 1954] pp. 32–41). "Galilee" as referring to some part of the northern district has long roots (cf. Josh 20:7; 1 Kings 9:11; 2 Kings 15:29).

13 In Luke, Jesus' move from Nazareth to Capernaum (4:31) follows the violent reaction of the Nazareth townspeople (vv. 16–30); and it is uncertain whether Matthew's account (13:54–58) reports the same incident or another one. Capernaum ("village of Nahum"?) lay a little north of the plain of Gennesaret (14:34), on the northwest shore of Lake Galilee. Tell Hum marks the site today, its synagogue ruins dating from the second century. The village enjoyed a fishing industry that probably demanded the presence of a tax collector's booth (9:9). Here, too, was Peter's house (8:14; cf. Mark 1:29; 2:1). But Matthew is interested in pointing out Capernaum's location with reference to the ancient tribal allotments of Zebulun and Naphtali as showing the minute correspondence with the prophecy cited in vv. 15–16.

14–16 Jesus' move fulfilled (v. 14; cf. Notes) Isaiah 9:1–2. This prophecy is part of a large structure looking to Immanuel's coming (see on 1:23). It is extraordinarily difficult to identify the text form; either this is an independent translation of the Hebrew (Gundry, *Use of OT*, pp. 105–8) or else a modification of divergent LXX MSS (Chilton, *God in Strength*, p. 111). NIV's "the way to the sea" (v. 15) is better translated "seawards," i.e., lying by the Sea of Galilee; and "along the Jordan," though convenient, has little lexical warrant and should be replaced by "beyond the Jordan" (cf. Notes).

The point of the quotation is clear enough. In despised Galilee, the place where people live in darkness (i.e., without the religious and cultic advantages of Jerusalem and Judea), the land of the shadow of death (i.e., where the darkness is most dense; cf. Job 10:21; Ps 107:10; Jer 13:16; Amos 5:8), here the light has dawned (v. 16). "Dawned" (*aneteilen*) suggests that the light first shone brilliantly here, not that it was shining brightly elsewhere and then moved here (Lindars, *Apologetic*, p. 198). This was God's prophesied plan. Matthew is not interested in the mere fact that some prophecy was fulfilled in Galilee but in this particular prophecy: from of old the Messiah was promised to "Galilee of the Gentiles" (*tōn ethnōn*), a foreshadowing of the commission to "all nations" (*panta ta ethnē*, 28:19). Moreover, if the messianic light dawns on the darkest places, then Messiah's salvation can only be a bestowal of grace—namely, that Jesus came to call, not the righteous, but sinners (9:13).

17 Several have argued that the words "from that time on" (*apo tote*), found only here and in 16:21; 26:16, mark major turning points in this Gospel (Stonehouse, *Witness of Matthew*, pp. 129–31; Kingsbury, *Structure*). In its strong form, this theory divides Matthew into three sections (1:1–4:16; 4:17–16:20; 16:21–28:20) with important interpretive implications. Though there are good reasons for rejecting this structure (cf. Introduction, section 14), the phrase "from that time on" nevertheless marks an important turning point because it ties something new to what has just preceded it.

We best see this when we examine the content of Jesus' preaching. Assuming the soundness of the text preserved in the NIV (cf. Notes), the burden of Jesus' preaching so far is, in itself, identical to that of John the Baptist: "Repent, for the kingdom of heaven is near" (v. 17; cf. 3:2). Matthew often shows ties between Jesus and John the Baptist (Klostermann; Chilton, *God in Strength*, p. 117). But when John the Baptist says these words, they are placed in an OT context that highlights his function as the forerunner who looks forward to the Messiah and his kingdom (3:2–12); when Jesus says the same words, they are linked (by "from that time") with an OT context that insists Jesus fulfills the promises of a light rising to shine on the Gentiles (Schweizer).

The longstanding debate that largely discounted C.H. Dodd's theory (that "is near" [3:2; 4:17] equals "has come" [12:28]) rather misses the mark. Neither Dodd nor his critics are subtle enough. The kingdom (see on 3:2) is still future. But the separate contexts of the announcements made by John and by Jesus (3:2; 4:17) show that with Jesus the kingdom has drawn so near that it has actually dawned. Therefore Jesus' hearers must repent—a demand made not only by the Baptist but by Jesus. The structure of the book thus sets up an implicit parallelism: Jesus is not so much a new Moses as a new Joshua (on their names, cf. 1:21); for as Moses did not enter the Promised Land but was succeeded by Joshua who did, so John the Baptist announces the kingdom and is followed by Jesus (Joshua) who leads his people into it (cf. Albright and Mann).

Notes

12 The verb ἀνεχώρησεν (anechōrēsen, "he returned") is characteristic of Matthew (2:12, 13, 14, 22; 4:12, 24; 12:15; 14:13; 15:21; 27:5). Only in 9:24 does Jesus use it; elsewhere in the NT it occurs only in Mark 3:7; John 6:15; Acts 23:19; 26:31. On the basis of Matthew's usage, Hill (Matthew), following Fenton, suggests the verb means Jesus withdrew strategically—i.e., that the rejection of God's word in one place (here in John's ministry) leads to its proclamation in another place (in Jesus' ministry). But this meaning is possible only in 12:15; 14:13; 15:21; it is impossible in most of the other occurrences in Matthew. More commonly Jesus "withdraws" because of threats or plots. That he then preaches elsewhere is a consequence of his withdrawal for safety's sake, not a sign of judgment on a people who will not hear.

14 The dash separating v.13 and v.14 (NIV) rightly interprets the ἵνα (hina, "in order to") as referring to Jesus' move rather than Jesus' motive. In other words, judging by his usage elsewhere (e.g., 1:22; 2:15), Matthew is not saying that Jesus moved in order to fulfill Scripture but that his move fulfilled Scripture.

15 The words ὁδὸν θαλάσσης (hodon thalassēs, "the way to the sea") are in LXX Isa 8:23 and may well be a literal rendering of the Hebrew דֶּרֶךְ יָם (derek yām), "seawards"; i.e. "by the sea" (cf. "by the way of the sea," NIV, Isa 9:1) rather than the "way to the sea" (cf. Turner, Syntax, p. 247). The translation "along the Jordan" for πέραν τοῦ Ἰορδάνου (peran tou Iordanou) reflects the fact that Zebulun and Naphtali do not extend east of the Jordan. But linguistically the phrase must mean "beyond the Jordan." Normally "beyond the Jordan" refers to the east bank, but the vantage of the speaker must be borne in mind, and sometimes it refers to the west bank (e.g., Num 32:19; Deut 11:30; Josh 5:1; 22:7). The Hebrew is more naturally translated "beyond Jordan." Most likely Isaiah sees the Assyrians coming from the northeast; as they progressively inflict judgment on the nation, they proceed "beyond the Jordan" to the west bank. So Matthew's rendering may simply preserve the same stance—in which case, is there a further reference to the "exile" now ended by Messiah's coming (see on 2:17–18)? The LXX inserts a καί (kai, "and") before "beyond the Jordan," eliminating the problem by making two regions. Yet if Matthew is reflecting his own stance, it is possible he is writing from the east bank (so Slingerland), perhaps from the Decapolis. It is hard to be sure of this because of uncertainties in the text form of the quotation and in the meaning of the Hebrew. See further on 19:1.

16 Αὐτοῖς (autois, "on them") is redundant after τοῖς καθημένοις (tois kathēmenois, lit., "on those sitting [NIV, 'living']"); but, though not unknown in classical Greek, it is common in Hebrew (cf. BDF, par. 466[4]).

17 The reading omitting μετανοεῖτε (metanoeite, "repent") and γάρ (gar, "for") is not well attested but is treated seriously because of the possibility of assimilation to 3:2. Nevertheless the longer text stands (cf. esp. Chilton, God in Strength, pp. 302–10; Fee, pp. 164f.).

b. Calling the first disciples

4:18–22

18As Jesus was walking beside the Sea of Galilee, he saw two brothers, Simon called Peter and his brother Andrew. They were casting a net into the lake, for they were fishermen. 19"Come, follow me," Jesus said, "and I will make you fishers of men." 20At once they left their nets and followed him.

21Going on from there, he saw two other brothers, James son of Zebedee and his brother John. They were in a boat with their father Zebedee, preparing their nets. Jesus called them, 22and immediately they left the boat and their father and followed him.

Since no temporal expression links this pericope with the last one, there may have been some time lapse. Bultmann's skepticism (*Synoptic Tradition*, p. 28) about the historical worth of these verses is unwarranted (cf. Hill, *Matthew*).

The relation of the various "callings" of the disciples in the Gospel records is obscure. If we take John 1:35–51 as historical, Simon, Andrew, Philip, and Nathaniel first followed Jesus at an earlier date. On returning to Galilee, they again took up their normal work. This is inherently plausible. The disciples' commitment and understanding advanced by degrees; even after the Resurrection, they returned once more to their fishing (John 21). Here (4:20) an earlier commitment may explain their haste in following Jesus. If the miracle of Luke 5:1–11 occurred the night before Matthew 4:18–22 (Mark 1:16–20), that would be another reason for their immediate response to Jesus. In this connection the meaning of *katartizontas* ("preparing," v.21; cf. below) is significant. See further 9:9–13; 10:1–4.

18 In Hebrew "sea," like the German *See*, can refer to lakes. Classical Greek prefers not to use *thalassa* (or *thalatta*—"sea") for lakes; and Luke follows the same pattern by using *limnē* ("lake"), though Matthew, Mark, and John prefer "sea." The Sea of Galilee (named from the district), otherwise known as the "Lake of Gennesaret" (the name "Kinnereth" [Num 34:11; Josh 12:3] comes from a plain on its northwest shore; cf. Matt 14:34), or the "Sea of Tiberias" (a city Herod built on the southwest shore: John 6:1; 21:1), is 12¼ by 8¾ miles at the longest and broadest points respectively. Its surface is 682 feet below sea level. It is subject to violent squalls. In Jesus' day it supported flourishing fisheries; on its west shore were nine towns, and "Bethsaida" may be freely translated "Fishtown." Simon and his brother Andrew came from Bethsaida (John 1:44), though Capernaum was now their home (Mark 1:21, 29).

Simon, Matthew says, was "called Peter"; but he does not tell us how Peter received this name (cf. 10:2; 16:18; Mark 3:16; Luke 6:14). While uncertainties remain, what is quite certain is that *kêpā'* ("rock," "stone"), the Aramaic equivalent of "Peter," was already an accepted name in Jesus' day (cf. Joseph A. Fitzmyer, "Aramaic Kepha' and Peter's Name in the New Testament," in Best and Wilson, pp. 121–32)—a fact that has an important bearing on the interpretation of 16:17–18.

Simon and Andrew were casting a "net" (*amphiblestron*, a NT *hapax legomenon* [found only once], with a cognate at Mark 1:16). It refers to a circular "casting-net" and is not to be confused with the more generic term *diktua* in 4:20.

19–20 Greek has several expressions for "follow me" (v.19; cf. at 10:38; Luke 9:23; 14:27), but they all presuppose a physical "following" during Jesus' ministry. His "followers" were not just "hearers"; they actually followed their Master around (as students then did) and became, as it were, trainees. The metaphor "fishers of men" glances back to the work of the two being called. It may also be reminiscent of Jeremiah 16:16. There Yahweh sends "fishermen" to gather his people for the Exile; here Jesus sends "fishermen" to announce the end of the Exile (cf. on 1:11–12; 2:17–18) and the beginning of the messianic reign. But this allusion is uncertain; the danger of "parallelomania" (coined by S. Sandmel, "Parallelomania," JBL 81 [1962]: 2–13) is evident when E.C.B. MacLaurin ("The Divine Fishermen," *St. Mark's Review* 94 [1978]: 26–28) works out many parallels and then opts for Ugaritic mythology a millennium and a half old. In any case there is a straight line from this

119

commission to the Great Commission (28:18-20). Jesus' followers are indeed to catch men.

On the prompt obedience of Simon and Andrew (v.20), see the comments at the introduction to this section. Peter later used this obedience almost as a bartering point (19:27).

21-22 This second pair of brothers were "preparing their nets" (v.21), which sounds as if they were just setting out. The verb *katartizō*, however, connotes "mend" or "restore to a former condition." So James and John may have been making repairs after a night's fishing (cf. Luke 5:1-11 and its possible place in the chronology). Fenton notes that Paul uses *katartizo* for perfecting the church (1 Cor 1:10; 2 Cor 13:11) and sees here an allusion to pastoral ministry. But this is fanciful because the verb is not a technical term. The boat (*ploion* was used of all kinds of boats) was big enough for several men (Mark 1.20). Mark's remark that hired men were left with Zebedee when his sons followed Jesus reminds us that we must not exaggerate the ignorance and poverty of Jesus' first followers. While they were not trained scribes or rabbis, they were not illiterate, stupid, or destitute. Indeed, Peter's protest in 19:27 implies that many or all of the Twelve had given up much to follow Jesus.

Jesus took the initiative and "called" James and John. In the Synoptics, unlike Paul's epistles, Jesus' call is not necessarily effectual. But in this instance it was immediately obeyed.

c. Spreading the news of the kingdom

4:23-25

> 23Jesus went throughout Galilee, teaching in their synagogues, preaching the good news of the kingdom, and healing every disease and sickness among the people. 24News about him spread all over Syria, and people brought to him all who were ill with various diseases, those suffering severe pain, the demon-possessed, those having seizures, and the paralyzed, and he healed them. 25Large crowds from Galilee, the Decapolis, Jerusalem, Judea and the region across the Jordan followed him.

Summaries are common to narrative literature; but the one before us, with its parallel in 9:35-38, has distinctive features.

1. It does not just summarize what has gone before but shows the geographical extent and varied activity of Jesus' ministry.

2. It therefore sets the stage for the particular discourses and stories that follow and implies that the material presented is but a representative sampling of what was available.

3. It is not a mere chronicle but conveys theological substance. Thus it is easy to detect different emphases between this summary and 9:35-38 (see comments in loc.).

Older commentators see in vv.23-25 a first circuit of Galilee and in 9:35-38 a second one. This is possible, but both pericopes may refer to the constant ministry of Jesus rather than to tightly defined circuits.

23 Jesus' ministry included teaching, preaching, and healing. Galilee, the district covered, is small (approximately seventy by forty miles); but according to Josephus (Life 235[45]; War III, 41-43[iii.2]), writing one generation later, Galilee had 204 cities and villages, each with no fewer than fifteen thousand persons. Even if this figure refers only to the walled cities and not to the villages (which is not what Josephus says), a most conservative estimate points to a large population, even if less than Josephus's three million. At the rate of two villages or towns per day, three months would be required to visit all of them, with no time off for the Sabbath. Jesus "went around doing good" (Acts 10:38; cf. Mark 1:39; 6:6). The sheer physical drain must have been enormous. Above all we must recognize that Jesus was an itinerant preacher and teacher who necessarily repeated approximately the same material again and again and faced the same problems, illnesses, and needs again and again.

The connection between "teaching" and "synagogue" recurs at 9:35; 13:54. A visiting Jew might well be asked to teach in the local synagogue (on which cf. Moore, *Judaism*, 1:281–307; Douglas, *Illustrated Dictionary*, 3:1499–503) as part of regular worship (e.g., Luke 4:16). The word "their" may indicate a time when the synagogue and the church had divided. On the other hand, it may simply indicate that the author and his readers viewed these events from outside Galilee (see further on 7:29; 9:35 et al.).

The message Jesus preaches is the "good news [*euangelion*, "gospel"] of the kingdom." The term recurs in 9:35; 24:14, and becomes "this gospel" in 26:13. "Of the kingdom" is an objective genitive: the "good news" concerns the kingdom (cf. Notes), whose "nearness" has already been announced (3:2; 4:17) and which is the central subject of the Sermon on the Mount (5–7). Mark prefers "the gospel" or "the gospel of Christ" or "the gospel of God" (Mark 1:1, 14; 8:35; 10:29; 13:10); but the difference between these expressions and "gospel of the kingdom" is purely linguistic, since the "good news" concerns God and the inbreaking of his saving reign in the person of his Son the Messiah.

The healings of various diseases among the people further attest the kingdom's presence and advance (cf. 11:2–6; Isa 35:5–6). Walvoord (p. 39) relegates these "kingdom blessings . . . due for fulfillment in the future kingdom" to the status of mere "credentials of the King"; but if the kingdom blessings are present, then the kingdom too must have broken in, even if not yet in the splendor of its consummation (cf. Rev 21:3–5).

24 The geographical extent of "Syria" is uncertain. From the perspective of Jesus in Galilee, Syria was to the north. From the Roman viewpoint Syria was a Roman province embracing all Palestine (cf. Luke 2:2; Acts 15:23, 41; Gal 1:21), Galilee excepted, since it was under the independent administration of Herod Antipas at this time. The term "Syria" reflects the extent of the excitement aroused by Jesus' ministry; if the Roman use of the term is here presumed, it shows his effect on people far beyond the borders of Israel. Those "ill with various diseases" and "those suffering severe" pain are divided into three overlapping categories: (1) the demon possessed (cf. 8:28–34; 12:22–29); (2) those having seizures—viz., any kind of insanity or irrational behavior whether or not related to demon possession (17:14–18; on *selēniazomenous* ["epileptics"], which etymologically refers to the "moonstruck" [i.e., "lunatic"], cf. DNTT, 3:734; J.M. Ross, "Epileptic or Moonstruck?" BTh 29 [1978]: 126–28)—and (3) the paralyzed, whose condition also had various causes.

In the NT sickness may result directly from a particular sin (e.g., John 5:14; 1 Cor 11:30) or may not (e.g., John 9:2–3). But both Scripture and Jewish tradition take sickness as resulting directly or indirectly from living in a fallen world (cf. on 8:17).

The Messianic Age would end such grief (Isa 11:1–5; 35:5–6). Therefore Jesus' miracles, dealing with every kind of ailment, not only herald the kingdom but show that God has pledged himself to deal with sin at a basic level (cf. 1:21; 8:17).

25 Jesus' reputation at this point extended far beyond Galilee, even though that is where the light "dawned" (v.16). Two of the named areas, the region across the Jordan (east bank? see on v.15) and the Decapolis, were mostly made up of Gentiles, a fact already emphasized (see on 1:3–5; 2:1–12, 22–23; 3:9; 4:8, 15–16). The Decapolis (lit., "Ten Cities") refers to a region east of Galilee extending from Damascus in the north to Philadelphia in the south, ten cities (under varied ,reckonings) making up the count (cf. S. Thomas Parker, "The Decapolis Reviewed," JBL 94 [1975]: 437–41). People from all these areas "followed" Jesus. Despite contrary arguments "follow" does not necessarily indicate solid discipleship. It may, as here, refer to those who at some particular time followed Jesus around in his itinerant ministry and thus were loosely considered his disciples.

Notes

---

23 Further evidence that "preaching the good news of the kingdom" requires taking "of the kingdom" as an objective genitive is suggested by comparing the Greek κηρύσσων τὸ εὐαγγέλιον τῆς βασιλείας (kēryssōn to euangelion tēs basileias, "preaching the good news of the kingdom") with the expression found in Luke 8:1: εὐαγγελιζόμενος τὴν βασιλείαν (euangelizomenos tēn basileian, "proclaiming the good news of the kingdom"), in which "kingdom" is the direct object.

24 The strange expression τοὺς κακῶς ἔχοντας (tous kakōs echontas; NIV, "[those] ill") is idiomatic: elsewhere in the NT, only at 8:16; 9:12; 14:35; Mark 1:32; 2:17; 6:55; Luke 5:31. The only other strictly comparable constructions in the NT are in Acts 24:25; 1 Tim 5:25; 1 Peter 4:5.

B. *First Discourse: The Sermon on the Mount*

5:1–7:29

The Sermon on the Mount is the first of five major discourses in the Gospel of Matthew. All five follow blocks of narrative material; all five end with the same formula (see on 7:28–29; and Introduction, section 14). Not only because it is first and longest of the five, and therefore helps determine the critical approach toward all of them, but also because it deals with ethical issues of fundamental importance in every age, this "sermon" has called forth thousands of books and articles. Some orientation is necessary.

A useful starting point is Warren S. Kissinger's *The Sermon on the Mount: A History of Interpretation and Bibliography* (Metuchen, N.J.: Scarecrow, 1975). K. Beyschlag ("Zur Geschichte der Bergpredigt in der Alten Kirche," *Zeitschrift für Theologie und Kirche* 74 [1977]: 291–322) and Robert M. Grant ("The Sermon on the Mount in Early Christianity," *Semeia* 12 [1978]: 215–31) unfold the treatment of these chapters in the earliest centuries of Christianity. For clarification of the varied treatment of the sermon during the present century, we are now indebted to Ursula Berner (*Die Bergpredigt: Rezeption und Auslegung im 20. Jahrhundert* [Göttingen:

Vandenhoeck und Ruprecht, 1979]). Popular, recent expositions of use to the working preacher include James M. Boice, *The Sermon on the Mount* (Grand Rapids: Zondervan, 1972); Carson, *Sermon on the Mount;* D. Martyn Lloyd-Jones, *Studies in the Sermon on the Mount,* 2 vols. (London: IVP, 1959–60); F.B. Meyer, *The Sermon on the Mount* (reprint ed., Grand Rapids: Baker, 1959); Stott.

Four introductory matters demand comment:

1. *Unity and authenticity of the discourse.* Since the work of Hans Windisch (*The Meaning of the Sermon on the Mount,* tr. S.M. Gilmour [1929; reprint ed., Philadelphia: Fortress, 1951]), few have regarded Matthew 5–7 as thoroughly authentic. The most common proposal today is that these chapters preserve some authentic teaching of Jesus, originally presented at various occasions and collected and shaped by oral tradition. To this the evangelist has added church teaching, taught, perhaps, by an inspired prophet speaking for the exalted Christ; and the discourse has then been further molded by catechetical and liturgical considerations (so, for instance, J. Jeremias, *The Sermon on the Mount* [Philadelphia: Fortress, 1963], and the magisterial study by Davies, *Setting*). According to these critics, at best the so-called Sermon on the Mount preserves no more than isolated sayings of Jesus.

Much of one's judgment in these matters depends on conclusions as to source, form, and redaction criticism (cf. Introduction, sections 1–3). For instance, if one insists that every saying elsewhere in the Gospels similar to any saying in Matthew 5–7 must be traced back to one utterance only (thus ignoring Jesus' role as an itinerant preacher), one may develop a more or less plausible theory of the growth of oral tradition in each case (so, e.g., H.-T. Wrege, *Die Überlieferungsgeschichte der Bergpredigt* [WUNT 9; Tübingen: J.C.B. Mohr, 1968]). This can be done precisely because so many sayings in these chapters do occur elsewhere, either in roughly similar or in identical language (see on 5:13, 15, 18, 25, 29, 32; 6:9, 22, 24–25; 7:2, 7, 17, 23). Moreover, where parallels exist, Matthew's forms are often more stylized or structured.

There is no need to repeat introductory remarks about authenticity. Several observations will, however, focus the approach adopted here.

a. We cannot make much out of Matthew's clear tendency to treat his material topically. Nor can we conclude from his grouping of miracles that he has composed his discourses out of grouped but independent sayings. In the former case Matthew does not pretend to do otherwise, whereas in all his discourses he gives the impression, especially in his concluding formulas (7:28–29; 11:1; 13:53; 19:1; 26:1), that the material is not only authentic but delivered on one occasion.

b. We dare not claim too much on the basis of the unity or its lack in the discourses. Even if the Sermon on the Mount represents material Jesus delivered on one occasion, perhaps over several days, its extreme compression, necessary selection, and problems of translation from Aramaic to Greek (assuming Jesus preached in Aramaic) might all unite to break the flow. If the unity of the discourse be defended (e.g., by A. Farrar, *St Matthew and St Mark* [London: Dacre/A. and C. Black, 1954, 1966], but cf. Davies, *Setting*, pp. 9–13), that unity might be nothing more than the evangelist's editing. He must have seen some coherence in these chapters to leave them in this form. Thus neither unity nor disunity are sufficient criteria for the authenticity of a brief account of extensive discourse.

c. We must suppose that Jesus preached the same thing repeatedly (see on 4:23–25); he was an extremely busy itinerant preacher. The pithier the saying, the more likely it was to be repeated word-perfect. The more common the natural phenomenon behind a metaphor or aphorism, the more likely Jesus repeated it in new situations. Any experienced itinerant preacher will confirm the inescapability of these tendencies. More important, if one distances oneself from the more radical presuppositions of form and tradition criticism, the NT documents themselves confirm this approach (cf. 11:15 with 13:9; 18:3 with 19:14, and cf. 20:26 [and Luke 12:24–31; John 13:13–17]; Matt 17:20 with 21:21; 10:32 with Luke 9:26 and 12:8; 10:24 with Luke 6:40 and John 13:16 and 15:20; 10:38–39 with 16:24–25 and Luke 17:33 and John 12:25). Even longer sections like Jesus' model prayer (6:9–13; see discussion below) are susceptible of such treatment, if for different reasons.

d. Jesus himself was a master teacher. In his sayings, whose authenticity is not greatly disputed, there is evidence of structure, contrast, and assonance. So when some scholars tell us that Matthew's account has more structure (perhaps from catechetical influence) than the other Synoptics, is this a sign of greater nearness to or distance from Jesus? What criteria are there for distinguishing the two possibilities? Surely if we do not pretend to be able to retrieve all the *ipsissima verba* of Jesus but only his *ipsissima vox*, most of the common criteria for testing authenticity evaporate.

e. The assumptions of some form critics make their work more questionable than they think. For if a certain kind of saying tends to take on a certain form in oral tradition, and if the period of oral transmission is long enough to develop that form, then the repetition of the saying on half-a-dozen different occasions in slightly different words would ultimately lead to one common form of the saying. Thus, far from enabling the critic to trace a precise development, form criticism obliterates the richness of the tradition attested by the evangelists themselves.

f. As Matthew's Gospel stands, we must weigh two disparate pieces of evidence: (1) that all five of Matthew's discourses are bracketed by introductory and concluding remarks that cannot fail to give the impression that he presents his discourses as not only authentic but delivered by Jesus on the specified occasions and (2) that many individual bits of each discourse find synoptic parallels in other settings. Many think the second point to be so strong that they conclude that Matthew himself composed the discourses. Conservative writers in this camp say that all of Jesus' sayings are authentic but that Matthew brought them together in their present form. Therefore the first piece of evidence has to be reinterpreted; i.e., the introductory and concluding notes framing each of Matthew's discourses are seen as artistic, compositional devices.

A more subtle approach is to say that Jesus actually did deliver a discourse on each of the five occasions specified but that not all the material Matthew records was from that occasion. In other words the evangelist has added certain "footnotes" of his own, at a time when orthography was much more flexible and there were no convenient ways to indicate what he was doing. While either of these reconstructions is possible, each faces two steep hurdles: (1) the introductory and concluding brackets around the five discourses do not belong to any clear first-century pattern or genre that would show the reader that they are merely artistic devices and not the real settings they manifestly claim to be; and (2) it is remarkable that each conclusion sweeps together all the sayings of the preceding discourse under some such rubric as "when Jesus had finished saying these things" (a possible exception is 11:1). That the introductory and concluding formulas were not recognizable as artistic devices is confirmed by the fact that for the first millennium and a half or so of its existence, the church recognized them as concrete settings. (This is not a surreptitious appeal to return to precritical thinking but a note on the recognizability of a literary genre.)

In view of the above, it seems the wiser course to believe Matthew intended to present real, historical settings for his discourses; and the parallels found elsewhere, though they must be considered individually, do not seem to present insurmountable problems. While many sayings in the Gospels appear in "loose" or in "floating" settings, where an evangelist ostensibly specifies the context, the authenticity of that context must be assumed. This is particularly easy to maintain in Matthew if the date and authorship are as stated in the Introduction (sections 5–6). Thus this commentary takes Matthew's settings seriously. Not that it takes all the discourses as verbatim accounts or unedited reports of Jesus' teaching, it rather assumes that they are condensed notes, largely in Matthew's idiom, selected and presented in accord with his own concerns. But behind them stand the voice and authority of Jesus.

2. *Relation to the Sermon on the Plain (Luke 6:20–49).* Augustine claimed that Matthew 5–7 and the passage in Luke are two separate discourses, and almost all writers agreed with him till the Reformation. Even after it some scholars followed Augustine (e.g., Alexander, Plumptre), and today some are returning to Augustine's view.

Origen, Chrysostom, Calvin, and the majority of recent scholars, however, defend the view (often with appropriate theorizing about Q) that the two accounts represent the same discourse. This has much to commend it. The two sermons begin with beatitudes and end with the same simile. Nearly everything in the Sermon on the Plain is in some form in the Sermon on the Mount and often in identical order. Both are immediately followed by the same events—viz., entrance into Capernaum and healing the centurion's servant. (The point is valid even if it indicates nothing more than a common link in the tradition.) Luke's sermon is much shorter and has its own thematic emphases (e.g., humility); and much of the extra material in Matthew is scattered elsewhere in Luke, especially in his "travel narrative" (Luke 9:51–18:14; discussed at 19:1–2). Moreover Matthew speaks of a mountain, Luke a plain; and Luke's discourse follows the choosing of the Twelve, which does not take place in Matthew till chapter 10.

But these problems can be readily solved.

a. Much of what Luke omits, mostly in Matthew 5:17–37; 6:1–18, is exactly the sort of material that would interest Matthew's Jewish readers more than Luke's readers. Luke has also omitted some material from his "Sermon on the Plain" that he has placed elsewhere (Matt 6:25–34; Luke 12:22–31). It is possible that Jesus gave the sermon more than once. Alternatively, Luke's context is so loose that he may have been responsible for the topical rearrangement. In any case to insist that a writer must include everything he knows or everything in his sources is poor methodology. In the other Matthean discourses, Matthew includes much and Luke includes less; in the Sermon on the Mount, though Matthew's account is much longer than Luke's, in certain places Luke preserves a little more than Matthew (compare Matt 5:12 with Luke 6:23–26; Matt 5:47 with Luke 6:33–35).

b. Of the several solutions to the mountain or plain, the most convincing one takes Matthew's "on a mountainside" to mean "up in the hills" and Luke's "plain" as being some kind of plateau. The linguistic evidence is convincing (see on 5:1–2).

c. Luke's order, placing the sermon after the choosing of the Twelve, is historically believable. But Matthew is clearly topical in his order. Connectives at 5:1; 8:1; 9:35; 11:2; 12:1; 14:1 et al. are loose; his favorite word "then" is general in meaning (see on 2:7). It is unlikely that Matthew intends his readers to think that the Sermon on the Mount succeeded Jesus' circuit (4:23–25). Rather, this sermon was preached during that circuit. Moreover some of Matthew's reasons for placing it here instead of after 10:1–4 are apparent (see below under 4). It seems best, then, to take Matthew 5–7 and Luke 6:20–49 as separate reports of the same occasion, each dependent on some shared tradition (Q?), but not exclusively so. Space limitations prevent tracing all the likely connections; but some attention will be given selected critical problems within this overall approach.

3. *Theological structure and affinities.* Whatever its sources and manner of compilation, the inclusion of the Sermon on the Mount in Matthew must be significant. Some have noted its similarities to Jewish thought. G. Friedlander's classic work, *The Jewish Sources of the Sermon on the Mount* (New York: Ktav, 1911), shows that virtually all the statements in Matthew 5–7 can be paralleled in the Talmud or other Jewish sources. Of course this is right, but it is a little like saying that the parts of a fine automobile can be found in a vast warehouse. Read any fifty pages of the Babylonian Talmud and compare them with Matthew 5–7, and it becomes obvious that they are not saying the same things. Sigal ("Halakhah") argues that the forms of argument in Matthew 5–7 fit into well-accepted patterns of the early rabbis ("proto-rabbis"); Gary A. Tuttle ("The Sermon on the Mount: Its Wisdom Affinities and Their Relation to Its Structure," JETS 20 [1977]: 213–30) draws attention to connections with the forms of argument in wisdom literature. Both are too restrictive: rabbinic and wisdom argumentation overlap much more than is commonly acknowledged, and Jesus (and Matthew) echo both and more—yet they must be interpreted first of all in their own right.

The attempt to do that has not produced consistent results. Schweizer lists seven major interpretive approaches to the Sermon on the Mount; Harvey K. McArthur (*Understanding the Sermon on the Mount* [New York: Harper and Row, 1960], pp. 105–48) lists twelve. Some of the most important are as follows:

a. Lutheran orthodoxy often understands the Sermon on the Mount as an exposition of law designed to drive men to cry for grace. This is Pauline (Rom 3–4; Gal 3), and grace is certainly presupposed in the sermon (e.g., see on 5:3). But though one of Jesus' purposes may have been to puncture self-righteous approaches to God, the sermon cannot be reduced to this. The righteousness envisaged (see on 5:20) is not imputed righteousness. Moreover, Paul himself insists that personal righteousness must characterize one who inherits the kingdom (Gal 5:19–24). Above all, this view fails to grasp the flow of salvation history (see below).

b. Some have argued that Jesus' eschatology is so "realized" that the ethic of the Sermon on the Mount is a sort of moral road map toward social progress. Classic liberalism has been invalidated by two world wars, the Great Depression and repeated recessions, the threat of nuclear holocaust, and post-Watergate, post-Vietnam, post-OPEC malaise. Nor can it be integrated with apocalyptic elements in Jesus' teaching (e.g., Matt 24) or with the vision of a suffering and witnessing community (Matt 10).

c. Today the sermon is commonly interpreted as a set of moral standards used catechetically within Matthew's community. While that may be so if there was a Matthean community, this view is reductionistic. It fails to wrestle with salvation history. The entire Book of Matthew presents itself as *Jesus'* teaching and ministry before the church was called into existence in the full, post-Pentecost sense. This Gospel does not present itself as the catechesis of a church but as a theological portrayal of the one who fulfilled Scripture and introduced the end times.

d. The Anabaptist–Mennonite tradition interprets the ethical demands to apply to all believers in every age and every circumstance. The resulting philosophy of pacifism in the context of a power-loving world demands the conclusion that Christians should not seek to be involved in affairs of state. This tradition rightly perceives the separate status of the believing community, which must not be confused with the world (e.g., 7:13–14, 21–23). But it is insensitive to the place of this sermon in the progress of redemption and absolutizes some of its teaching in a way incompatible with its context and with other Scripture (see on 5:38–42; 6:5–8).

e. Existential interpretation finds in these chapters a summons to personal decision and authentic faith but jettisons the personal and infinite God who makes the summons. Also, by denying the uniqueness of the Jesus who delivers the sermon, it fails to cope with its fulfillment theme and its implications.

f. Still others claim that Jesus is advocating an "interim ethic" to remain in force till the soon-expected consummation. But Jesus, they assume, erred as to the timing of this event; so the "interim ethic" must be toned down accordingly. All this rests on a view of Jesus derived from other passages (not least Matt 24–25 and parallels).

g. It is common among evangelicals and others to interpret the Sermon on the Mount as an intensifying or radicalizing of OT moral law. But this depends largely on a doubtful interpretation of 5:17–20 (cf. below).

h. Classic dispensationalism interprets the Sermon on the Mount as law for the millennial kingdom first offered by Jesus to the Jews. This has faced so many objections (e.g., Can any age be justly described as "millennial" that requires "laws" to govern face slapping?) that the approach has been qualified. J. Dwight Pentecost ("The Purpose of the Sermon on the Mount," BS 115 [1958]: 128ff., 212ff., 313ff.) and Walvoord take the ethical content of the sermon to be binding on any age but continue to drive a wedge between these chapters and the Christian gospel by pointing out that they do not mention the cross, justification by faith, new birth, etc. On that basis the Epistle of James is also non-Christian! Moreover they misinterpret Matthew's fulfillment motif and impose a theological structure on this Gospel demanding improbable exegesis of numerous passages (occasionally identified in this commentary). The disjunction between Matthew 5–7 and the Christian gospel is theologically and historically artificial.

This sketch overlooks many variations of the principal interpretations of the Sermon on the Mount. Recently several scholars have narrowed the focus: C. Burchard ("The Theme of the Sermon on the Mount," in Schottroff, Command, pp. 57–75) understands chapters 5–7 to provide rules of conduct for the Matthean church in the light of opposition to its witness; G. Bornkamm ("Der Aufbau der Bergpredigt," NTS 24 [1977–78]: 419–32) interprets the sermon around the Lord's Prayer (6:9–13). Though these perspectives highlight neglected themes, they overlook both the thrust of the sermon as a whole and its place in Matthew.

The unifying theme of the sermon is the kingdom of heaven. This is established, not by counting how many times the expression occurs, but by noting where it occurs. It envelopes the Beatitudes (5:3, 10) and appears in 5:17–20, which details the relation between the OT and the kingdom, a subject that leads to another literary envelope around the body of the sermon (5:17; 7:12). It returns at the heart of the Lord's Prayer (6:10), climaxes the section on kingdom perspectives (6:33), and is presented as what must finally be entered (7:21–23). Matthew places the sermon immediately after two verses insisting that the primary content of Jesus' preaching was the gospel of the kingdom (4:17, 23). It provides ethical guidelines for life in the kingdom, but does so within an explanation of the place of the contemporary setting within redemption history and Jesus' relation to the OT (5:17–20). The community forming around him, his "disciples," is not yet so cohesive and committed a group that exhortations to "enter" (7:13–14) are irrelevant. The glimpse of kingdom life (horizontally and vertically) in these chapters anticipates not only the love commandments (22:34–40) but also grace (5:3; 6:12; 7:7–11; cf. 21:28–46).

4. *Location in Matthew*. Unlike Luke, Matthew does not place the sermon after the calling of the Twelve (10:1–4); for there he puts a second discourse, one concerning mission. This links the call with the commission, a theme of great importance to Matthew (see on 11:11–12; 28:16–20). Not less important is the location of the Sermon on the Mount so early in the Gospel, before any sign of controversies between Jesus and the Jewish leaders as to the law's meaning. This means that, despite the antitheses in 5:17–48 ("You have heard . . . but I tell"), these should not be read as tokens of confrontation but in the light of the fulfillment themes richly set out in chapters 1–4 and made again explicit in 5:17–20: Jesus comes "to fulfill" the Law and the Prophets (i.e., the OT Scriptures). Therefore his announcements concerning the kingdom must be read against that background, not with reference to debates over Halakic details. This framework is Matthew's; by it he tells us that whatever controversies occupied Jesus' attention, the burden of his kingdom proclamation always made the kingdom the goal of the Scriptures, the long-expected messianic reign foretold by the Law and the Prophets alike.

1. *Setting*

5:1–2

> [1]Now when he saw the crowds, he went up on a mountainside and sat down. His disciples came to him, [2]and he began to teach them, saying:

1 The "crowds" are those referred to in 4:23–25. Here Jesus stands at the height of his popularity. Although his ministry touched the masses, he saw the need to teach his "disciples" (*mathētai*) closely. The word "disciple" must not be restricted to the Twelve, whom Matthew has yet to mention (10:1–4). Nor is it a special word for full-fledged believers, since it can also describe John the Baptist's followers (11:2). In the Lukan parallel we are told of a "large crowd of his disciples" as well as "a great number of people" (6:17). This goes well with Matthew 4:25, which says large crowds "followed" Jesus. Those who especially wanted to attach themselves to him, Jesus takes aside to instruct; but it is anachronistic to suppose that all are fully committed in the later "Christian" sense of Acts 11:26 (cf. Matt 7:13–14, 21–23). Matthew sees the disciples as paradigms for believers in his own day but never loses sight, as we shall repeatedly notice, of the unique, historical place of the first followers (contra U. Luz, "Die Jünger im Matthäusevangelium," ZNW 62 [1971]: 141–71 —though Luz wisely avoids reducing Matthew's disciples to the Twelve. On the importance of the theme of discipleship in this Gospel, cf. Martin H. Franzmann, *Follow Me: Discipleship According to Saint Matthew* [St. Louis: Concordia, 1961]).

At this point in his ministry, Jesus could not escape the mounting crowds; and by the end of his sermon (7:28–29), he was surrounded by yet larger crowds. This suggests that his teaching covered several days, not just an hour or two (cf. the three-day meeting, 15:29–39). The place of retreat Jesus chose was in the hill country (cf. Notes), not "on a mountainside." He "sat down" to teach. Sitting was the accepted posture of synagogue or school teachers (Luke 4:20; cf. Matt 13:2; 23:2; 24:3; cf. DNTT, 3:588–89). The attempt of Lachs (pp. 99–101) to find an anachronism here fails because his sources refer to the position of one who is *learning* Torah, not teaching it. Luke has Jesus standing (6:17) but ministering to the larger crowd from which he could not escape (6:17–19).

2 NIV masks the idiom "he opened his mouth and taught them," found elsewhere in the NT (13:35; Acts 8:35; 10:34; 18:14) and reflecting OT roots (Job 3:1; 33:2; Dan 10:16). It is used in solemn or revelatory contexts. "To teach" (*edidasken*) is imperfect and inceptive: "He began to teach them." Contrary to Davies (*Setting*, pp. 7–8), one must not draw too sharp a distinction between preaching (*kēryssō*, 4:17) and teaching (*didaskō*, 5:2): see on 3:1 and the linking of these categories in 4:23; 9:35. SBK (1:189) notes that teaching was not uncommonly done outdoors as well as in synagogues.

Notes

1 NIV's "on a mountainside" renders εἰς τὸ ὄρος (*eis to oros*). The article does not suggest some well-known mountain (Hendriksen; Turner, *Syntax*, p. 173), still less the mountain where Moses received the law (Loisy). Even Davies (*Setting*, p. 93), after exploring all possibilities, concedes Matthew could have more explicitly delineated a "new Moses" theme. In fact, *to oros* (lit., "the mountain") and the corresponding Hebrew and Aramaic may mean nothing more than "the mountain region" or "the hill country," a point rightly recognized by NIV when it renders *eis to oros* elsewhere in Matthew "into the hills" (14:23; 15:29) or, in the plural, "to the mountains" (24:16). Jesus withdrew to the hill country west of Lake Galilee: the text requires nothing more. Attempts to discern profound symbolic significance (e.g., Gundry; J.B. Livio, "La signification théologique de la 'montagne' dans le premier évangile," *BullCentreProtd'Etud* 30 [1978]: 13–20) are here misguided. Moreover πεδινός (*pedinos*, "plain" or "a level place") in Luke 6:17, a NT *hapax legomenon*, should not conjure up images of American prairie but a relatively flat place in rough, rocky, or hilly terrain—perhaps "plateau" (cf. usage in Jer 21:13 LXX ["rocky plateau" in NIV], or in Isa 13:2 LXX—ἐπ ὄρους πεδινοῦ [*ep' orous pedinou*, lit., "on a level (flat) mountain"; NIV, "on a bare hilltop"]). There is little difference between Matthew's "mountain" and Luke's "plain."

2. *The kingdom of heaven: its norms and witness* (5:3–16)

a. *The norms of the kingdom* (5:3–12)

1) *The Beatitudes*

5:3–10

³"Blessed are the poor in spirit,
  for theirs is the kingdom of heaven.
⁴Blessed are those who mourn,
  for they will be comforted.

⁵Blessed are the meek,
  for they will inherit the earth.
⁶Blessed are those who hunger and thirst for righteousness,
  for they will be filled.
⁷Blessed are the merciful,
  for they will be shown mercy.
⁸Blessed are the pure in heart,
  for they will see God.
⁹Blessed are the peacemakers,
  for they will be called sons of God.
¹⁰Blessed are those who are persecuted because
    of righteousness
  for theirs is the kingdom of heaven.

The Beatitudes (Lat. *beatus,* "blessed"), otherwise called macarisms (from Gr. *makarios,* "blessed"), have been the subject of many valuable studies, the most detailed being J. Dupont's *Les Béatitudes,* 3 vols., 2d ed. (Paris: Gabalda, 1969). As to form beatitudes find their roots in wisdom literature and especially the Psalms (for the best discussion of the OT background, cf. W. Zimmerli, "Die Seligpreisungen der Bergpredigt und das Alte Testament," *Donum Gentilicium,* ed. E. Bammel et al. [Oxford: Clarendon, 1978], pp. 8–26; cf. Pss 1:1; 31:1–2; 144:15; Prov 3:13; Dan 12:12). OT beatitudes never bunch more than two together (e.g., Ps 84:4–5; elsewhere, cf. Ecclus 25:7–9).

Comparison of 5:3–12 with Luke 6:20–26 shows that, along with smaller differences, the four Lukan beatitudes stand beside four woes—all in the second person. But Matthew mentions no woes, and his eight beatitudes (vv. 3–10) are in the third person, followed by an expansion of the last one in the second person (vv. 11–12). Pre-NT beatitudes are only rarely in the second person (e.g., 1 Enoch 58:2) and occur with woes only in the Greek text of Ecclesiasticus 10:16–17; so on formal grounds there is no reason to see Matthew's beatitudes as late adaptations.

No doubt both Matthew and Luke selected and shaped their material. But though this results in differences in the thrust of the two sets of beatitudes, such differences are often overstated (e.g., C.H. Dodd, *More New Testament Studies* [Manchester: University Press, 1968], pp. 7–8). Dupont (*Les Béatitudes*) and Marshall (*Luke*) argue that Luke describes what disciples actually are, Matthew what they ought to be; Luke, the social implications of Jesus' teaching and reversals at the consummation, Matthew, the standards of Christian righteousness to be pursued now for entrance into the kingdom. Similarly, G. Strecker ("Les macarismes du discours sur la montagne," in Didier, pp. 185–208) insists that in Matthew's beatitudes ethics has displaced eschatology: the Beatitudes become ethical entrance requirements rather than eschatological blessings associated with the Messianic Age.

A more nuanced interpretation is presented by R.A. Guelich ("The Matthean Beatitudes: 'Entrance-Requirements' or Eschatological Blessings?" JBL 95 [1973]: 415–34). He notes that Matthew 5:3–5 contains planned echoes of Isaiah 61:1–3, which is certainly eschatological in orientation. Moreover both Isaiah 61:1–3 and the Matthean beatitudes are formally declarative but implicitly hortatory: one must not overlook function for form. The Beatitudes "are but an expression of the fulfillment of Isaiah 61, the OT promise of the *Heilszeit* ['time of salvation'], in the person and proclamation of Jesus. This handling of the Beatitudes is certainly in keeping with Matthew's emphasis throughout the Gospel that Jesus comes in light of the OT promise" (ibid., p. 433). The implicit demands of the Beatitudes are therefore comprehensible only because of the new state of affairs the proclamation of the kingdom initiates (4:17, 23), the insistence that Jesus has come to fulfill the Law and the Prophets (5:17).

3 Two words and their cognates stand behind "blessed" and "blessing" in the NT. The word used in vv.3–11 is *makarios*, which usually corresponds in the LXX to *'ašrê*, a Hebrew term used almost as an interjection: "Oh the blessednesses [pl.] of." Usually *makarios* describes the man who is singularly favored by God and therefore in some sense "happy"; but the word can apply to God (1 Tim 1:11; 6:15). The other word is *eulogētos*, found in the LXX primarily for Hebrew *berākāh*, and used chiefly in connection with God in both OT and NT (e.g., Mark 14:61; Luke 1:68; Rom 1:25; 2 Cor 1:3). *Eulogētos* does not occur in Matthew; but the cognate verb appears five times (14:19; 21:9; 23:39; 25:34; 26:26), in one of which it applies to man (25:34), not God or Christ. Attempts to make *makarios* mean "happy" and *eulogētos* "blessed" (Broadus) are therefore futile; though both appear many times, both can apply to either God or man. It is difficult not to conclude that their common factor is approval: man "blesses" God, approving and praising him; God "blesses" man, approving him in gracious condescension. Applied to man the OT words are certainly synonymous (cf. *Theologisches Handwörterbuch zum Alten Testament*, 1:356).

As for "happy" (TEV), it will not do for the Beatitudes, having been devalued in modern usage. The Greek "describes a state not of inner feeling on the part of those to whom it is applied, but of blessedness from an ideal point of view in the judgment of others" (Allen). In the eschatological setting of Matthew, "blessed" can only promise eschatological blessing (cf. DNTT, 1:216–17; TDNT, 4:367–70); and each particular blessing is specified by the second clause of each beatitude.

The "poor in spirit" are the ones who are "blessed." Since Luke speaks simply of "the poor," many have concluded that he preserves the true teaching of the historical Jesus—concern for the economically destitute—while Matthew has "spiritualized" it by adding "in spirit." The issue is not so simple. Already in the OT, "the poor" has religious overtones. The word *ptōchos* ("poor"—in classical Gr., "beggar") has a different force in the LXX and NT. It translates several Hebrew words, most importantly (in the pl.) *'anāwîm* ("the poor"), i.e., those who because of sustained economic privation and social distress have confidence only in God (e.g., Pss 37:14; 40:17; 69:28–29, 32–33; Prov 16:19 [NIV, "the oppressed"; NASB, "the lowly"]; 29:23; Isa 61:1; cf. Pss Sol 5:2, 11; 10:7). Thus it joins with passages affirming God's favor on the lowly and contrite in spirit (e.g., Isa 57:15; 66:2). This does not mean there is lack of concern for the materially poor but that poverty itself is not the chief thing (cf. the Prodigal Son's "self-made" poverty). Far from conferring spiritual advantage, wealth and privilege entail great spiritual peril (see on 6:24; 19:23–24). Yet, though poverty is neither a blessing nor a guarantee of spiritual rewards, it can be turned to advantage if it fosters humility before God.

That this is the way to interpret v.3 is confirmed by similar expressions in the DSS (esp. IQM 11:9; 14:6–7; IQS 4:3; IQH 5:22). "Poor" and "righteous" become almost equivalent in Ecclesiasticus 13:17–21; CD 19:9; 4QpPs (37)2:8–11 (cf. Schweizer; Bonnard; Dodd, "Translation Problems," pp. 307–10). These parallels do not prove literary dependence, but they do show that Matthew's "poor in spirit" rightly interprets Luke's "poor" (cf. Gundry, *Use of OT*, pp. 69–71). In rabbinic circles, too, meekness and poverty of spirit were highly praised (cf. Felix Böhl, "Die Demut als höchste der Tugenden," *Biblische Zeitschrift* 20 [1976]: 217–23).

Yet biblical balance is easy to prostitute. The emperor Julian the Apostate (332–63) is reputed to have said with vicious irony that he wanted to confiscate Christians' property so that they might all become poor and enter the kingdom of heaven. On the other hand, the wealthy too easily dismiss Jesus' teaching about poverty here and elsewhere (see on 6:24) as merely attitudinal and confuse their hoarding with good stewardship. France's "God and Mammon" (pp. 3–21) presents a fine balance in these matters.

To be poor in spirit is not to lack courage but to acknowledge spiritual bankruptcy. It confesses one's unworthiness before God and utter dependence on him. Therefore those who interpret the Sermon on the Mount as law and not gospel—whether by H. Windisch's historical reconstructions or by classical dispensationalism (cf. Carson, *Sermon on the Mount*, pp. 155–57), which calls the sermon "pure law" (though it concedes that its principles have a "beautiful moral application" for the Christian)—stumble at the first sentence (cf. Stott, pp. 36–38). The kingdom of heaven is not given on the basis of race (cf. 3:9), earned merits, the military zeal and prowess of Zealots, or the wealth of a Zacchaeus. It is given to the poor, the despised publicans, the prostitutes, those who are so "poor" they know they can offer nothing and do not try. They cry for mercy and they alone are heard. These themes recur repeatedly in Matthew and present the sermon's ethical demands in a setting that does not treat the resulting conduct as conditions for entrance to the kingdom that people themselves can achieve. All must begin by confessing that by themselves they can achieve nothing. Fuller disclosures of the gospel in the years beyond Jesus' earthly ministry do not change this; in the last book of the canon, an established church must likewise recognize its precarious position when it claims to be rich and fails to see its own poverty (Rev 3:14–22).

The kingdom of heaven (see on 3:2; 4:17) belongs to the poor in spirit; it is they who enjoy Messiah's reign and the blessings he brings. They joyfully accept his rule and participate in the life of the kingdom (7:14). The reward in the last beatitude is the same as in the first; the literary structure, an "inclusio" or envelope, establishes that everything included within it concerns the kingdom: i.e., the blessings of the intervening beatitudes are kingdom blessings, and the beatitudes themselves are kingdom norms.

While the rewards of vv.4–9 are future ("they will be comforted," "will inherit," etc.), the first and last are present ("for theirs is the kingdom of heaven"). Yet one must not make too much of this, for the present tense can function as a future; and the future tense can emphasize certainty, not mere futurity (Tasker). There is little doubt that here the kingdom sense is primarily future, postconsummation, made explicit in v.12. But the present tense "envelope" (vv.3, 10) should not be written off as insignificant or as masking an Aramaic original that did not specify present or future; for Matthew must have meant something when he chose *estin* ("is") instead of *estai* ("will be"). The natural conclusion is that, though the full blessedness of those described in these beatitudes awaits the consummated kingdom, they already share in the kingdom's blessedness so far as it has been inaugurated (see on 4:17; 8:29; 12:28; 19:29).

4 Black (*Aramaic Approach,* p. 157) notes how the Matthean and Lukan (6:21b, 25b) forms of this beatitude could each have been part of a larger parallelism—an observation that goes nicely with the hypothesis that the Sermon on the Mount and the Sermon on the Plain are reports of one discourse, relying somewhat on common sources (cf. introductory comments).

Some commentators deny that this mourning is for sin (e.g., Bonnard). Others (e.g., Schweizer) understand it to be mourning for any kind of misery. The reality is subtler. The godly remnant of Jesus' day weeps because of the humiliation of Israel, but they understand that it comes from personal and corporate sins. The psalmist testified, "Streams of tears flow from my eyes, for your law is not obeyed" (Ps 119:136; cf. Ezek 9:4). When Jesus preached, "The kingdom of heaven is near," he, like John the Baptist before him, expected not jubilation but contrite tears. It is not enough to acknowledge personal spiritual bankruptcy (v.3) with a cold heart. Weeping for sins can be deeply poignant (Ezra 10:6; Ps 51:4; Dan 9:19–20) and can cover a global as well as personal view of sin and our participation in it. Paul understands these matters well (cf. Rom 7:24; 1 Cor 5:2; 2 Cor 12:21; Phil 3:18).

"Comfort, comfort my people" (Isa 40:1) is God's response. These first two beatitudes deliberately allude to the messianic blessing of Isaiah 61:1–3 (cf. also Luke 4:16–19; France, *Jesus*, pp. 134–35), confirming them as eschatological and messianic. The Messiah comes to bestow "the oil of gladness instead of mourning, and a garment of praise instead of a spirit of despair" (Isa 61:3). But these blessings, already realized partially but fully only at the consummation (Rev 7:17), depend on a Messiah who comes to save his people from their sins (1:21; cf. also 11:28–30). Those who claim to experience all its joys without tears mistake the nature of the kingdom. In Charles Wesley's words:

> He speaks, and listening to his voice
> New life the dead receive,
> The mournful, broken hearts rejoice,
> The humble poor believe.

5 This beatitude and those in vv.7–10 have no parallel in Luke. It would be wrong to suppose that Matthew's beatitudes are for different groups of people, or that we have the right to half the blessings if we determine to pursue four out of the eight. They are a unity and describe the norm for Messiah's people.

The word "meek" (*praus*) is hard to define. It can signify absence of pretension (1 Peter 3:4, 14–15) but generally suggests gentleness (cf. 11:29; James 3:13) and the self-control it entails. The Greeks extolled humility in wise men and rulers, but such humility smacked of condescension. In general the Greeks considered meekness a vice because they failed to distinguish it from servility. To be meek toward others implies freedom from malice and a vengeful spirit. Jesus best exemplifies it (11:29; 21:5). Lloyd-Jones (*Sermon on the Mount*, 1:65–69) rightly applies meekness to our attitudes toward others. We may acknowledge our own bankruptcy (v.3) and mourn (v.4). But to respond with meekness when others tell us of our bankruptcy is far harder (cf. also Stott, pp. 43–44). Meekness therefore requires such a true view about ourselves as will express itself even in our attitude toward others.

And the meek—not the strong, aggressive, harsh, tyrannical—will inherit the earth. The verb "inherit" often relates to entrance into the Promised Land (e.g., Deut 4:1; 16:20; cf. Isa 57:13; 60:21). But the specific OT allusion here is Psalm 37:9, 11, 29, a psalm recognized as messianic in Jesus' day (4QpPs 37). There is no need to interpret the land metaphorically, as having no reference to geography or space;

nor is there need to restrict the meaning to "land of Israel" (cf. Notes). Entrance into the Promised Land ultimately became a pointer toward entrance into the new heaven *and the new earth* ("earth" is the same word as "land"; cf. Isa 66:22; Rev 21:1), the consummation of the messianic kingdom. While in Pauline terms believers may now possess all things in principle (2 Cor 6:10) since they belong to Christ, Matthew directs our attention yet further to the "renewal of all things" (19:28).

6 "Hunger and thirst" vividly express desire. The sons of Korah cried, "My soul thirsts for God, for the living God" (Ps 42:2; cf. 63:1) for the deepest spiritual famine is hunger for the word of God (Amos 8:11–14).

The precise nature of the righteousness for which the blessed hunger and thirst is disputed. Some argue that it is the imputed righteousness of God—eschatological salvation or, more narrowly, justification. the blessed hunger for it and receive it (e.g., Grundmann; Lohmeyer; McNeile, Schniewind, Schrenk [TDNT, 2:198], Zahn; Bornkamm, *Tradition* [pp. 123–24]; Bultmann [*Theology*, 1:273]). This is certainly plausible, since the immediate context does arouse hopes for God's eschatological action, and hungering suggests that the righteousness that satisfies will be given as a gift.

The chief objection is that *dikaiosynē* ("righteousness") in Matthew does not have that sense anywhere else (Przybylski, pp. 96–98). So it is better to take this righteousness as simultaneously personal righteousness (cf. Hill, *Greek Words*, pp. 127f.; Strecker, *Weg*, pp. 156–58) and justice in the broadest sense (cf. esp. Ridderbos, pp. 190f.). These people hunger and thirst, not only that they may be righteous (i.e., that they may wholly do God's will from the heart), but that justice may be done everywhere. All unrighteousness grieves them and makes them homesick for the new heaven and earth—the home of righteousness (2 Peter 3:13). Satisfied with neither personal righteousness alone nor social justice alone, they cry for both: in short, they long for the advent of the messianic kingdom. What they taste now whets their appetites for more. Ultimately they will be satisfied (same verb as in 14:20; Phil 4:12; Rev 19:21) without qualification only when the kingdom is consummated (cf. discussion in Gundry, *Matthew*).

7 This beatitude is akin to Psalm 18:25 (reading "merciful" [ASV] instead of "faithful" [NIV]; following MT [v.26], not LXX [17:26]; cf. Prov 14:21). Mercy embraces both forgiveness for the guilty and compassion for the suffering and needy. No particular object of the demanded mercy is specified, because mercy is to be a function of Jesus' disciples, not of the particular situation that calls it forth. The theme is common in Matthew (6:12–15; 9:13; 12:7; 18:33–34). The reward is not mercy shown by others but by God (cf. the saying preserved in 1 Clement 13:2). This does not mean that our mercy is the causal ground of God's mercy but its occasional ground (see on 6:14–15). This beatitude, too, is tied to the context. "It is 'the meek' who are also 'the merciful'. For to be meek is to acknowledge to others that *we* are sinners; to be merciful is to have compassion on others, for they are sinners too" (Stott, p. 48, emphasis his).

8 Commentators are divided on "pure in heart."

1. Some take it to mean inner moral purity as opposed to merely external piety or ceremonial cleanness. This is an important theme in Matthew and elsewhere in the

Scriptures (e.g., Deut 10:16; 30:6; 1 Sam 15:22; Pss 24:3–4 [to which there is direct allusion here]; 51:6, 10; Isa 1:10–17; Jer 4:4; 7:3–7; 9:25–26; Rom 2:9; 1 Tim 1:5; 2 Tim 2:22; cf. Matt 23:25–28).

2. Others take it to mean singlemindedness, a heart "free from the tyranny of a divided self" (Tasker; cf. Bonnard). Several of the passages just cited focus on freedom from deceit (Pss 24:4; 51:4–17; cf. also Gen 50:5–6; Prov 22:11). This interpretation also prepares the way for 6:22. The "pure in heart" are thus "the utterly sincere" (Ph).

The dichotomy between these two options is a false one; it is impossible to have one without the other. The one who is singleminded in commitment to the kingdom and its righteousness (6:33) will also be inwardly pure. Inward sham, deceit, and moral filth cannot coexist with sincere devotion to Christ. Either way this beatitude excoriates hypocrisy (cf. on 6:1–18). The pure in heart will see God—now with the eyes of faith and finally in the dazzling brilliance of the beatific vision in whose light no deceit can exist (cf. Heb 12:14; 1 John 3:1–3; Rev 21:22–27).

9 Jesus' concern in this beatitude is not with the peaceful but with the peacemakers. Peace is of constant concern in both testaments (e.g., Prov 15:1; Isa 52:7; Luke 24:36; Rom 10:15; 12:18; 1 Cor 7:15; Eph 2:11–22; Heb 12:14; 1 Peter 3:11). But as some of these and other passages show, the making of peace can itself have messianic overtones. The Promised Son is called the "Prince of Peace" (Isa 9:6–7); and Isaiah 52:7—"How beautiful on the mountains are the feet of those who bring good news, who proclaim peace, who bring good tidings, who proclaim salvation, who say to Zion, 'Your God reigns!' "—linking as it does peace, salvation, and God's reign, was interpreted messianically in the Judaism of Jesus' day.

Jesus does not limit the peacemaking to only one kind, and neither will his disciples. In the light of the gospel, Jesus himself is the supreme peacemaker, making peace between God and man, and man and man. Our peacemaking will include the promulgation of that gospel. It must also extend to seeking all kinds of reconciliation. Instead of delighting in division, bitterness, strife, or some petty "divide-and-conquer" mentality, disciples of Jesus delight to make peace wherever possible. Making peace is not appeasement: the true model is God's costly peacemaking (Eph 2:15–17; Col 1:20). Those who undertake this work are acknowledged as God's "sons." In the OT, Israel has the title "sons" (Deut 14:1; Hos 1:10; cf. Pss Sol 17:30; Wisd Sol 2:13–18). Now it belongs to the heirs of the kingdom who, meek and poor in spirit, loving righteousness yet merciful, are especially equipped for peacemaking and so reflect something of their heavenly Father's character. "There is no more godlike work to be done in this world than peacemaking" (Broadus). This beatitude must have been shocking to Zealots when Jesus preached it, when political passions were inflamed (Morison).

10 It is no accident that Jesus should pass from peacemaking to persecution, for the world enjoys its cherished hates and prejudices so much that the peacemaker is not always welcome. Opposition is a normal mark of being a disciple of Jesus, as normal as hungering for righteousness or being merciful (cf. also John 15:18–25; Acts 14:22; 2 Tim 3:12; 1 Peter 4:13–14; cf. the woe in Luke 6:26). Lachs (pp. 101–3) cannot believe Christians were ever persecuted because of righteousness; so he repoints an alleged underlying Hebrew text to read "because of the Righteous One"—a reference to Jesus. But he underestimates how offensive genuine righteousness, "proper

conduct before God" (Przybylski, p. 99), really is (cf. Isa 51:7). The reward of these persecuted people is the same as the reward of the poor in spirit—viz., the kingdom of heaven, which terminates the inclusion (see on 5:3).

Notes

3 Most scholars interpret τῷ πνεύματι (*tō pneumati*, "in spirit") as a dative of respect (e.g., Zerwick, par. 53). Moule (*Idiom Book*, p. 46) wonders whether it might not border on an instrumental usage, which can often best be rendered by an English adverb: i.e., οἱ πτωχοὶ τῷ πνεύματι (*hoi ptōchoi tō pneumati*) = "the poor used in its spiritual [i.e., religious] sense," over against "the literally [i.e., materially] poor" of James 2:5. But he acknowledges that Ps 34:18 points in another direction.

5 The word γῆ (*gē*, "land") occurs forty-three times in Matthew: once for the land of Judah (2:6); twice for the land of Israel (2:20–21); several times for some region (e.g., 4:15; 9:26, 31; 11:24; and possibly 27:45); several times in the expression "heaven and earth" or something similar (5:18, 35; 11:25; 24:35; 28:18); several times to distinguish earth from heaven (6:10; 9:6; 16:19; 18:18 [*bis*], 19; 23:9); once to refer to the place where sinful people live (5:13); several times to refer to "ground" (e.g., 10:29; 15:35; 25:18, 25; 27:51), "soil" (13:5, 8, 23), or "shore" (14:24); and several times to refer to the whole earth without any of the above connotations (12:40, 42; 17:25; 23:35; 24:30). In Matthew, therefore, *gē* is used to refer to a specified region or nation (Israel, Judah, Zebulon, Naphtali et al.) only if that region's name is given. The possible exception is 27:45. The most natural way to render this noun in 5:5 is therefore "earth," not "land [of Israel]."

9 Although "son of" can have ontological force, it often means "one who reflects the character of" or the like. Hence a "son of Belial" (= "son of worthlessness") refers to a worthless person, someone of worthless conduct. Similarly, "son of God" may have ontological or purely functional force, depending on the context.

10 The perfect passive participle οἱ δεδιωγμένοι (*hoi dediōgmenoi*, "those who are persecuted") is rather awkward if the perfect force is retained: "those who have been persecuted." Many see this as a sign of anachronism: persecution had broken out by the time Matthew wrote (e.g., Hill, *Matthew*). Some older commentators treat it as a more or less Hebraizing "prophetic" perfect; and Broadus adds that the perfect accords "with the fact that the chief rewards of such sufferers do not so much attend on the persecution as follow it." But then we may ask why a future perfect isn't used, or why the same rule isn't applied to those who mourn (5:4). The question must at least be raised whether the perfect occasionally begins to take on aoristic force in the NT and the perfect participle a merely adjectival force (cf. discussion in Burton, par. 88; Moule, *Idiom Book*, p. 14).

2) *Expansion*

5:11–12

> 11"Blessed are you when people insult you, persecute you and falsely say all kinds of evil against you because of me. 12Rejoice and be glad, because great is your reward in heaven, for in the same way they persecuted the prophets who were before you.

11–12 These two verses (cf. Luke 6:22–23, 26), switching from third person to second, apply the force of the last beatitude (v. 10), not to the church (which would be anachronistic), but to Jesus' disciples. Doubtless Matthew and his contemporaries also applied it to themselves. Verse 11 extends the persecution of v.10 to include insult, persecution, and slander (Luke 6:22–23 adds hate). The reason for the persecution in v.10 is "because of righteousness"; now, Jesus says, it is "because of me." "This confirms that the righteousness of life that is in view is in imitation of Jesus. Simultaneously, it so identifies the disciple of Jesus with the practice of Jesus' righteousness that there is no place for professed allegiance to Jesus that is not full of righteousness" (Carson, *Sermon on the Mount*, p. 28). Moreover, it is an implicit christological claim, for the prophets to whom the disciples are likened were persecuted for their faithfulness to God and the disciples for faithfulness to Jesus. Not Jesus but the disciples are likened to the prophets. Jesus places himself on a par with God. The change from "the Son of Man" (Luke) to "me" is probably Matthew's clarification (see excursus at 8:20).

The appropriate response of the disciple is rejoicing. The second verb, *agalliasthe* ("be glad"), Hill (*Matthew*) takes to be "something of a technical term for joy in persecution and martyrdom" (cf. 1 Peter 1:6, 8; 4:13; Rev 19:7). Yet its range of associations seems broader (Luke 1:47; 10:21; John 5:35; 8:56; Acts 2:26; 16:34). The disciples of Jesus are to rejoice under persecution because their heavenly reward (cf. Notes) will be great at the consummation of the kingdom (v.12). Opposition is sure, for the disciples are aligning themselves with the OT prophets who were persecuted before them (e.g., 2 Chron 24:21; Neh 9:26; Jer 20:2; cf. Matt 21:35; 23:32–37; Acts 7:52; 1 Thess 2:15). This biblical perspective was doubtless part of the historical basis on which Jesus built his own implied prediction that his followers would be persecuted. Treated seriously, it makes ineffective the ground on which some treat the prediction as anachronistic (e.g., Hare, pp. 114–21). Stendahl's suggestion (Peake, par. 678k) that Matthew here refers to Christian prophets is not only needlessly anachronistic but out of step with both Matthew's use of "prophet" and his link between the murder of "prophets" and the sin of the "forefathers" (23:30–32), which shows that the prophets belong to the OT period.

These verses neither encourage seeking persecution nor permit retreating from it, sulking, or retaliation. From the perspective of both redemptive history ("the prophets") and eternity ("reward in heaven"), these verses constitute the reasonable response of faith, one which the early Christians readily understood (cf. Acts 5:41; 2 Cor 4:17; 1 Peter 1:6–9; cf. Dan 3:24–25). "Discipleship means allegiance to the suffering Christ, and it is therefore not at all surprising that Christians should be called upon to suffer. In fact it is a joy and a token of his grace" (Bonhoeffer, pp. 80–81). But in reassuring his disciples that their sufferings are "neither new, nor accidental, nor absurd" (Bonnard), Jesus spoke of principles that will appear again (esp. chs. 10, 24).

Notes

11 Matthew's "falsely say all kinds of evil against you" (cf. Acts 28:21) is an explanation of a Hebrew or Aramaic idiom still preserved in Luke's "reject your name as evil" (6:22; cf. Deut 22:14, 19). The word ψευδόμενοι (*pseudomenoi*, "falsely"), given a D in UBS (3d ed.), is implied whether original or not. External evidence strongly favors inclusion; the internal evidence is equivocal.

12 Morton Smith, *Tannaitic Parallels to the Gospels* (Philadelphia: SBL, 1951), pp. 46–77,

161–84, represents those who hold that the concept of reward in the synoptic Gospels does not differ materially from the concept of reward in early rabbinic literature. His work is essentially a word study and overlooks the substantial conceptual differences (cf. D.A. Carson, "Predestination and Responsibility: Some Elements of Tension Theology Against Jewish Background" [Ph.D. diss., Cambridge University, 1975], pp. 268f.); nor does he mention the balanced treatment of A. Marmorstein, *The Doctrine of Merits in the Old Rabbinical Literature* (London: Jesus' College, 1920). The recent book by E.P. Sanders (*Paul and Palestinian Judaism* [London: SCM, 1977]) rightly warns against reading very late Jewish traditions, steeped in merit theology, back into the NT period; but he seriously oversteps the evidence when he sees no difference at all, on the grace-merit front, between Paul and the "covenantal nomism" of Judaism (cf. Carson, *Divine Sovereignty*, ch. 8). C.S. Lewis (*They Asked For a Paper* [London: Geoffrey Bles, 1962], p. 198; cited in Stott, pp. 131–32) rightly distinguishes various kinds of rewards. A man who marries a woman for her money is "rewarded" by her money, but he is rightly judged mercenary because the reward is not naturally linked with love. On the other hand, marriage is the proper reward of an honest and true lover; and he is not mercenary for desiring it because love and marriage are naturally linked. "The proper rewards are not simply tacked on to the activity for which they are given, but are the activity itself in consummation" (ibid.). The rewards of the NT belong largely to this second category. Life lived under kingdom norms is naturally linked with the bliss of life in the consummated kingdom. Talk of "merit" or of "earning" the reward betrays lack of understanding of Jesus' meaning (cf. further on 11:25; 19:16–26; 20:1–16; 25:31–46).

---

b. *The witness of the kingdom* (5:13–16)

1) *Salt*

5:13

13"You are the salt of the earth. But if the salt loses its saltiness, how can it be made salty again? It is no longer good for anything, except to be thrown out and trampled by men.

13 Salt and light are such common substances (cf. Pliny, *Natural History* 31.102: "Nothing is more useful than salt and sunshine") that they doubtless generated many sayings. Therefore it is improper to attempt a tradition history of all Gospel references as if one original stood behind the lot (cf. Mark 4:21; 9:50; Luke 8:16; 11:33; 14:34–35). Salt was used in the ancient world to flavor foods and even in small doses as a fertilizer (cf. Eugene P. Deatrick, "Salt, Soil, Savor," BA 25 [1962]: 44–45, who wants *tēs gēs* to read "for the soil," not "of the earth"; but notice the parallel "of the world" in v.14). Above all, salt was used as a preservative. Rubbed into meat, a little salt would slow decay. Strictly speaking salt cannot lose its saltiness; sodium chloride is a stable compound. But most salt in the ancient world derived from salt marshes or the like, rather than by evaporation of salt water, and therefore contained many impurities. The actual salt, being more soluble than the impurities, could be leached out, leaving a residue so dilute it was of little worth.

In modern Israel savorless salt is still said to be scattered on the soil of flat roofs. This helps harden the soil and prevent leaks; and since the roofs serve as playgrounds and places for public gathering, the salt is still being trodden under foot (Deatrick, "Salt," p. 47). This explanation negates the attempt by some (e.g., Lenski, Schniewind, Grosheide) to suppose that, precisely because pure salt cannot lose its savor, Jesus is saying that true disciples cannot lose their effectiveness. The question "How can it be made salty again?" is not meant to have an answer, as Schweizer rightly says. The rabbinic remark that what makes salt salty is "the after-birth of a mule" (mules are sterile) rather misses the point (cf. Schweizer, *Matthew*). The point is that, if Jesus' disciples are to act as a preservative in the world by conforming to kingdom norms, if they are "called to be a moral disinfectant in a world where moral standards are low, constantly changing, or non-existent . . . they can discharge this function only if they themselves retain their virtue" (Tasker).

Notes

---

13 The verb μωρανθῇ (*mōranthē*, "loses its saltiness") is used four times in the NT. In Luke 14:34 it again relates to salt, but in Rom 1:22 and 1 Cor 1:20 it has its more common meaning "to make or become foolish" (cf. cognate μωρέ [*mōre*, "fool"] in 5:22). It is hard not to conclude that disciples who lose their savor are in fact making fools of themselves. The Greek may hide an Aramaic pun: תפל (*tāpēl*, "foolish") and תבל (*tabel*, "salted") (Black, *Aramaic Approach*, pp. 166–67).

---

2) Light

5:14–16

> 14"You are the light of the world. A city on a hill cannot be hidden. 15Neither do people light a lamp and put it under a bowl. Instead they put it on its stand, and it gives light to everyone in the house. 16In the same way, let your light shine before men, that they may see your good deeds and praise your Father in heaven.

14–15 As in v.13, "you" is emphatic—viz., You, my followers and none others, are the light of the world (v.14). Though the Jews saw themselves as the light of the world (Rom 2:19), the true light is the Suffering Servant (Isa 42:6; 49:6), fulfilled in Jesus himself (Matt 4:16; cf. John 8:12; 9:5; 12:35; 1 John 1:7). Derivatively his disciples constitute the new light (cf. Eph 5:8–9; Phil 2:15). Light is a universal religious symbol. In the OT as in the NT, it most frequently symbolizes purity as opposed to filth, truth or knowledge as opposed to error or ignorance, and divine revelation and presence as opposed to reprobation and abandonment by God.

The reference to the "city on a hill" is at one level fairly obvious. Often built of white limestone, ancient towns gleamed in the sun and could not easily be hidden. At night the inhabitants' oil lamps would shed some glow over the surrounding area (cf. Bonnard). As such cities could not be hidden, so also it is unthinkable to light a lamp and hide it under a peck-measure (v.15, NIV, "bowl"). A lamp is put on a lampstand to illuminate all. Attempts to identify "everyone in the house" as a refer-ence to all Jews in contrast with Luke 11:33, referring to Gentiles (so Manson, *Sayings*, p. 93) are probably guilty of making the metaphor run on all fours, espe-cially in view of the Gentile theme so strongly present in Matthew.

But the "city on a hill" saying may also refer to OT prophecies about the time when Jerusalem or the mountain of the Lord's house, or Zion, would be lifted up before the world, the nations streaming to it (e.g., Isa 2:2–5; cf. chs. 42, 49, 54, 60). This allusion has recently been defended by Grundmann, Trilling (p. 142), and especially K.M. Campbell ("The New Jerusalem in Matthew 5.14," SJT 31 [1978]: 335–63). It is not a certain allusion, and the absence of definite articles tells against it; if valid it insists that Jesus' disciples constitute the true locus of the people of God, the outpost of the consummated kingdom, and the means of witness to the world—all themes central to Matthew's thought.

16 Jesus drives the metaphor home. What his disciples must show is their "good works," i.e., all righteousness, everything they are and do that reflects the mind and will of God. And men must see this light. It may provoke persecution (vv.10–12), but that is no reason for hiding the light others may see and by which they may come to glorify the Father—the disciples' only motive (cf. 2 Cor 4:6; 1 Peter 2:12). Witness includes not just words but deeds, as Stier remarks, "The good word without the good walk is of no avail."

Thus the kingdom norms (vv.3–12) so work out in the lives of the kingdom's heirs as to produce the kingdom witness (vv.13–16). If salt (v.13) exercises the negative function of delaying decay and warns disciples of the danger of compromise and conformity to the world, then light (vv.14–16) speaks positively of illuminating a sin-darkened world and warns against a withdrawal from the world that does not lead others to glorify the Father in heaven. "Flight into the invisible is a denial of the call. A community of Jesus which seeks to hide itself has ceased to follow him" (Bonhoeffer, p. 106).

Notes

15 There are several probable Semitisms in this verse (Hill, *Matthew*). The μόδιος (*modios*, "bowl") is a wooden grain measure, usually given as 8¾ liters, i.e., almost exactly one peck (cf. further on 13:33). It is doubtful whether the vessel was used for hiding light, despite various suggestions. A different word is used in Josephus (Antiq. V, 223[vi.5]), and in any case Jesus' point turns on what is *not* done.

3. *The kingdom of heaven: its demands in relation to the OT* (5:17–48)

a. *Jesus and the kingdom as fulfillment of the OT*

5:17–20

[17]"Do not think that I have come to abolish the Law or the Prophets; I have not come to abolish them but to fulfill them. [18]I tell you the truth, until heaven and earth disappear, not the smallest letter, not the least stroke of a pen, will by any means disappear from the Law until everything is accomplished. [19]Anyone who breaks one of the least of these commandments and teaches others to do the same will be called least in the kingdom of heaven, but whoever practices and teaches these commands will be called great in the kingdom of heaven. [20]For I tell you that unless your righteousness surpasses that of the Pharisees and the teachers of the law, you will certainly not enter the kingdom of heaven.

Three important debates bear on the interpretation of these complex yet programmatic verses.

1. Apart from parallels to v.18 in Mark 13:31 and Luke 16:17, these verses have no synoptic parallel. Partly because of this, many have argued that these four verses represent four separate sayings from different and even conflicting churches or strata, heavily edited by Matthew (for discussion and recent examples, cf. R.G. Hamerton-Kelly, "Attitudes to the Law in Matthew's Gospel," *Biblical Research* 17 [1972]: 19–32; Arens, pp. 91–116). G. Barth, for instance, insists that the leap from v.19 to v.20 is so great that both could not have come from Matthew (Bornkamm, *Tradition*, p. 66). A better synthesis is possible. Yet even if the leap between these verses were as great as Barth imagines, what possessed Matthew (or the "final redactor") to put them together? He must have thought they meant something. And then how does one distinguish methodologically between weak links discerned by a redactor and weak links written up by an author? We shall focus primary attention on the meaning of the text as it stands.

2. The theological and canonical ramifications of one's exegetical conclusions on this pericope are so numerous that discussion becomes freighted with the intricacies of biblical theology. At stake are the relation between the testaments, the place of law in the context of gospel, and the relation of this pericope to other NT passages that unambiguously affirm that certain parts of the law have been abrogated as obsolete (e.g., Mark 7:19; Acts 10–11; Heb 7:1–9:10). Only glancing attention may be given to these issues here.

3. It is often argued that the setting of the pericope is debate in the church, especially among Palestinian Jewish Christians, about the continuation of law. There is no inherent implausibility in this hypothesis if by setting we refer to the circle in which these teachings were preserved because of their immediate relevance. But it must be remembered that Matthew presents these sayings as the teaching of the historical Jesus, not the creation of the church; and we detect no implausibility in his claim.

17 The formula "Do not think that" (or "Never think that," Turner, *Syntax*, p. 77) is repeated by Jesus in 10:34 (cf. 3:9). Jesus' two sayings were designed to set aside potential misunderstandings as to the nature of the kingdom; but neither demonstrably flows out of open confrontation on the issue at stake. Matthew has not yet recorded any charge that Jesus was breaking the law. (On the relation between these verses and the preceding pericopes, cf. W.J. Dumbull, "The Logic of the Role of the Law in Matthew v 1–20," NovTest 23 [1981]: 1–21).

Some have argued that many Jews in Jesus' day believed that law would be set aside and a new law introduced at Messiah's coming (cf. esp. Davies, *Setting*, pp. 109ff., 446ff.). But this view has been decisively qualified by R. Banks ("The Eschatological Role of Law," *Pre- and Post-Christian Jewish Thought*, ed. R. Banks [Exeter: Paternoster, 1982], pp. 173–85; id. *Jesus*, pp. 65ff.), who presents a more nuanced treatment.

The upshot of the debate is that the introductory words "Do not think that" must be understood, not as the refutation of some well-entrenched and clearly defined position, but as a teaching device Jesus used to clarify certain aspects of the kingdom and of his own mission and to remove potential misunderstandings. Moreover, comparison with 10:34 shows that the antithesis may not be absolute. Few would want to argue that there is *no* sense in which Jesus came to bring peace (cf. on 5:9). Why then argue that there is *no* sense in which Jesus abolishes the law?

The words "I have come" do not necessarily prove Jesus' consciousness of his preexistence, for "coming" language can be used of prophets and indeed is used of the Baptist (11:18–19). But it can also speak of coming into the world (common in John; cf. also 1 Tim 1:15) and in the light of Matthew's prologue is probably meant to attest Jesus' divine origins. At very least it shows Jesus was sent on a mission (cf. Maier).

Jesus' mission was not to abolish (a term more frequently connected with the destruction of buildings [24:2; 26:61; 27:40], but not exclusively so [e.g., 2 Macc 2:22]) "the law or the prophets." By these words Matthew forms a new "inclusio" (5:17–7:12), which marks out the body of the sermon and shows that Jesus is taking pains to relate his teaching and place in the history of redemption to the OT Scriptures. For that is what "Law or the Prophets" here means: the Scriptures. The disjunctive "or" makes it clear that neither is to be abolished. The Jews of Jesus' day could refer to the Scriptures as "the Law and the Prophets" (7:12; 11:13; 22:40; Luke 16:16; John 1:45; Acts 13:15; 28:23; Rom 3:21); "the Law. . . , the Prophets, and the Psalms" (Luke 24:44); or just "Law" (5:18; John 10:34; 12:34; 15:25; 1 Cor 14:21); the divisions were not yet stereotyped. Thus even if "or the Prophets" is redactional (Dalman, p. 62, and many after him), the referent does not change when only law is mentioned in v.18, but it may be a small hint that law, too, has a prophetic function (cf. 11:13, and discussion). Yet it is certainly illegitimate to see in "Law and Prophets" some vague reference to the will of God (so G.S. Sloyan, *Is Christ the End of the Law?* [Philadelphia: Westminster, 1978], pp. 49f.; Sand, p. 186; K. Berger, *Die Gesetzesauslegung Jesu* [Neukirchen-Vluyn: Neukirchener Verlag, 1972], p. 224) and not to Scripture, especially in the light of v.18.

The nub of the problem lies in the verb "to fulfill" (*plēroō*). N.J. McEleney ("The Principles of the Sermon on the Mount," JBL 41 [1979]; 552–70) finds the verb so difficult in a context (vv.17–48) dealing with law that he judges it a late addition to the tradition. Not a few writers, especially Jewish scholars, take the verb to reflect the Aramaic verb *qûm* ("establish," "validate," or "confirm" the law). Jesus did not come to abolish the law but to confirm it and establish it (e.g., Dalman, pp. 56–58; Daube, *New Testament*, pp. 60f.; Schlatter, pp. 153f.; and esp. Sigal, "Halakah," pp. 23ff.)

There are several objections.

1. The focus of Matthew 5 is the relation between the OT and Jesus' teaching, not his actions. So any interpretation that says Jesus fulfills the law by doing it misses the point.

2. If it is argued that Jesus confirms the law, even its jot and tittle, by both his life and his teaching (e.g., Hill; Ridderbos, pp. 292ff.; Maier)—the latter understood as setting out his own *Halakah* (rules of conduct) within the framework of the law (Sigal)—one marvels that the early church, as the other NT documents testify, misunderstood Jesus so badly on this point; and even the first Gospel, as we shall see, is rendered inconsistent.

3. The LXX never uses *plēroō* ("fulfill") to render *qûm* or cognates (which prefer *histanai* or *bebaioun* ["establish" or "confirm"]). The verb *plēroō* renders *mālē'* and means "to fulfill." In OT usage this characteristically refers to the "filling up" of volume or time, meanings that also appear in the NT (e.g., Acts 24:27; Rom 15:19). But though the NT uses *plēroō* in a number of ways, we are primarily concerned

with what is meant by "fulfilling" the Scriptures. Included under this head are specific predictions, typological fulfillments, and even the entire eschatological hope epitomized in the OT by God's covenant with his people (cf. C.F.D. Moule, "Fulfilment Words in the New Testament: Use and Abuse," NTS 14 [1967-68]: 293-320; see on 2:15).

The lack of background for *plēroō* ("fulfill") as far as it applies to Scripture requires cautious induction from the NT evidence. In a very few cases, notably James 2:23, the NT writers detect no demonstrable predictive force in the OT passage introduced. Rather, the OT text (in this case Gen 15:6) in some sense remains "empty" until Abraham's action "fulfills" it. But Genesis 15:6 does not predict the action. Most NT uses of *plēroō* in connection with Scripture, however, require some teleological force (see note on 1:22); and even the ambiguous uses presuppose a typology that in its broadest dimensions is teleological, even if not in every detail (see discussion on 2:15). In any case the interchange of *mālē'* ("fulfill") and *qûm* ("establish") in the Targumim is not of sufficient importance to overturn the LXX evidence, not least owing to problems of dating the Targumim (cf. Meier, *Law*, p. 74; Banks, *Jesus*, pp. 208f.).

Other views are not much more convincing. Many argue that Jesus is here referring only to moral law: the civil and ceremonial law are indeed abolished, but Jesus confirms the moral law (e.g., Hendriksen; D. Wenham, "Jesus and the Law: an Exegesis on Matthew 5:17-20," *Themelios* 4 [1979]: 92-96). Although this tripartite distinction is old, its use as a basis for explaining the relationship between the testaments is not demonstrably derived from the NT and probably does not antedate Aquinas (cf. the work of R.J. Bauckham in Carson, *Sabbath*; and Carson, "Jesus"). Also, the interpretation is invalidated by the all-inclusive "not the smallest letter, not the least stroke of a pen" (v.18).

Others understand the verb *plēroō* to mean that Jesus "fills up" the law by providing its full, intended meaning (e.g., Lenski), understood perhaps in terms of the double command to love (so O. Hanssen, "Zum Verständnis der Bergpredigt," *Der Ruf Jesu und die Antwort der Gemeinde*, ed. Edward Lohse [Göttingen: Vandenhoeck und Ruprecht, 1970], pp. 94-111). This, however, requires an extraordinary meaning for *plēroō*, ignores the "jot and tittle" of v.18, and misinterprets 22:34-40.

Still others, in various ways, argue that Jesus "fills up" the OT law by extending its demands to some better or transcendent righteousness (v.20), again possibly understood in terms of the command to love (e.g., Bornhäuser; Lagrange; A. Feuillet, "Morale Ancienne et Morale Chrétienne d'après Mt 5.17-20; Comparaison avec la Doctrine de l'Épître aux Romains," NTS 17 [1970-71]: 123-37, esp. p. 124; Grundmann; Trilling, pp. 174-79). Thus the reference to prophets (v.17) becomes obscure, and the entire structure is shaky in view of the fact that mere extension of law will not abolish any of its stringencies—yet in both Matthew and other NT documents some abolition is everywhere assumed. H. Ljungmann (*Das Gesetz erfüllen: Matth.5, 17ff. und 3, 15 untersucht* [Lund: C.W.K. Gleerup, 1954]) takes the "fulfillment" to refer to the fulfillment of Scripture in the self-surrender of the Messiah, which in turn brings forgiveness of sins and the new righteousness the disciples are both to receive and do. But in addition to weaknesses of detail, it is hard to see how all this can be derived from vv.17-20.

The best interpretation of these difficult verses says that Jesus fulfills the Law and the Prophets in that they point to him, and he is their fulfillment. The antithesis is not between "abolish" and "keep" but between "abolish" and "fulfill." "For Matthew, then, it is not the question of Jesus' relation to the Law that is in doubt but rather its relation to him!" (Robert Banks, "Matthew's Understanding of the Law: Authenticity and Interpretation in Matthew 5:17–20," JBL 93 [1974]: 226–42). Therefore we give *plēroō* ("fulfill") exactly the same meaning as in the formula quotations, which in the prologue (Matt 1–2) have already laid great stress on the prophetic nature of the OT and the way it points to Jesus. Even OT events have this prophetic significance (see on 2:15). A little later Jesus insists that "all the Prophets and the Law prophesied" (11:13).

The manner of the prophetic foreshadowing varies. The Exodus, Matthew argues (2:15), foreshadows the calling out of Egypt of God's "son." The writer to the Hebrews argues that many cultic regulations of the OT pointed to Jesus and are now obsolete. In the light of the antitheses (vv.21–48), the passage before us insists that just as Jesus fulfilled OT prophecies by his person and actions, so he fulfilled OT law by his teaching. In no case does this "abolish" the OT as canon, any more than the obsolescence of the Levitical sacrificial system abolishes tabernacle ritual as canon. Instead, the OT's real and abiding authority must be understood through the person and teaching of him to whom it points and who so richly fulfills it.

As in Luke 16:16–17, Jesus is not announcing the termination of the OT's relevance and authority (else Luke 16:17 would be incomprehensible), but that "the period during which men were related to God under its terms ceased with John" (Moo, "Jesus," p. 1); and the nature of its valid continuity is established only with reference to Jesus and the kingdom. The general structure of this interpretation has been well set forth by Banks (*Jesus*), Meier (*Law*), Moo ("Jesus"), Carson ("Jesus"; at a popular level, *Sermon on the Mount*, pp. 33ff.). For a somewhat similar approach, see Zumstein (pp. 119f.) and McConnell (pp. 96–97), who points out that Jesus' implicit authority is also found in the closing verses of the sermon (7:21–23) where as eschatological Judge he exercises the authority of God alone.

The chief objection to this view is that the use of "to fulfill" in the fulfillment quotations is in the passive voice, whereas here the voice is active. But it is doubtful whether much can be made out of this distinction (Meier, *Law*, pp. 80f.).

Three theological conclusions are inevitable.

1. If the antitheses (vv.21–48) are understood in the light of this interpretation of vv.17–20, then Jesus is not primarily engaged there in extending, annulling, or intensifying OT law, but in showing the direction in which it points, on the basis of his own authority (to which, again, the OT points). This may work out in any particular case to have the same practical effect as "intensifying" the law or "annulling" some element; but the reasons for that conclusion are quite different. On the ethical implications of this interpretation, see the competent essay by Moo ("Jesus").

2. If vv.17–20 are essentially authentic (see esp. W.D. Davies, "Matthew 5:17, 18," *Christian Origins and Judaism* [London: DLT, 1962], pp. 31–66; and Banks, "Matthew's Understanding") and the above interpretation is sound, the christological implications are important. Here Jesus presents himself as the eschatological goal of the OT, and thereby its sole authoritative interpreter, the one through whom alone the OT finds its valid continuity and significance.

3. This approach eliminates the need to pit Matthew against Paul, or Palestinian Jewish Christians against Pauline Gentile believers, the first lot adhering to Mosaic stipulations and the second abandoning them. Nor do we need the solution of Brice Martin, who argues that Matthew's approach to law and Paul's approach are non-

complementary but noncontradictory: they simply employ different categories. This fails to wrestle with Matthew's positioning of Jesus within the history of redemption; and Paul well understood that the Law and the Prophets pointed beyond themselves (e.g., Rom 3:21; Gal 3–4; cf. Rom 8:4). The focus returns to Jesus, which is where, on the face of it, both Paul and Matthew intend it to be. The groundwork is laid out in the Gospels for an understanding of Jesus as the one who established the essentially christological and eschatological approach to the OT employed by Paul. But this is made clearer in v.18.

18 "I tell you the truth" signals that the statement to follow is of the utmost importance (cf. Notes). In Greek it is connected to the preceding verse by an explanatory "for" (*gar*): v.18 further explains and confirms the truth of v.17. The "jot" (KJV) has become "the smallest letter" (NIV): this is almost certainly correct, for it refers to the letter ' (*yôd*), the smallest letter of the Hebrew alphabet. The "tittle" (*keraia*) has been variously interpreted: it is the Hebrew letter ו (*wāw*) (so G. Schwarz, "ἰῶτα ἓν ἢ μία κεραία [Matthaus 5₁₈]," ZNW 66 [1975]: 268–69); or the small stroke that distinguishes several pairs of Hebrew letters (ב/כ; ר/ד; ד/ר) (so Filson, Lenski, Allen, Zahn); or a purely ornamental stroke, a "crown" (Tasker, Schniewind, Schweizer; but cf. DNTT, 3:182); or it forms a hendiadys with "jot," referring to the smallest part of the smallest letter (Lachs, pp. 106–8). In any event Jesus here upholds the authority of the OT Scriptures right down to the "least stroke of a pen." His is the highest possible view of the OT.

But vv.17–18 do not wrestle abstractly with OT authority but with the nature, extent, and duration of its validity and continuity. The nature of these has been set forth in v.17. The reference to "jot and tittle" establishes its extent: it will not do to reduce the reference to moral law, or the law as a whole but not necessarily its parts, or to God's will in some general sense. "Law" almost certainly refers to the entire OT Scriptures, not just the Pentateuch or moral law (note the parallel in v.17).

That leaves the duration of the OT's authority. The two "until" clauses answer this. The first—"until heaven and earth disappear"—simply means "until the end of the age": i.e., not quite "never" (contra Meier, *Law*, p. 61), but "never, as long as the present world order persists." The second—"until everything is accomplished" —is more difficult. Some take it to be equivalent to the first (cf. Sand, pp. 36–39). But it is more subtle than that. The word *panta* ("all things" or "everything" has no antecedent. Contrary to Sand (p. 38), Hill, Bultmann (*Synoptic Tradition*, pp. 138, 405), Grundmann, and Zahn, the word cannot very easily refer to all the demands of the law that must be "accomplished," because (1) the word "law" almost certainly refers here to all Scripture and not just its commands—but even if that were not so, v.17 has shown that even imperatival law is prophetic; (2) the word *genētai* ("is accomplished") must here be rendered "happen," "come to pass" (i.e., "accomplished" in that sense, not in the sense of obeying a law; cf. Meier, *Law*, pp. 53f.; Banks, *Jesus*, pp. 215ff.).

Hence *panta* ("everything") is best understood to refer to everything in the law, considered under the law's prophetic function—viz., until all these things have taken place as prophesied. This is not simply pointing to the Cross (Davies, "Matthew 5:17, 18," pp. 60ff.; Schlatter), nor simply to the end of the age (Schniewind). The parallel with 24:34–35 is not that close, since in the latter case the events are

145

specified. Verse 18d simply means the entire divine purpose prophesied in Scripture must take place; not one jot or tittle will fail of its fulfillment. A similar point is made in 11:13. Thus the first "until" clause focuses strictly on the duration of OT authority but the second returns to considering its nature; it reveals God's redemptive purposes and points to their fulfillment, their "accomplishment," in Jesus and the eschatological kingdom he is now introducing and will one day consummate.

Meier (*Law*) ably establishes the centrality of the death and resurrection of Jesus as the pivotal event in Matthew's presentation of salvation history. Before it Jesus' disciples are restricted to Israel (10:5–6); after it they are to go everywhere. Similarly, the precise form of the Mosaic law may change with the crucial redemptive events to which it points. For that which prophesies is in some sense taken up in and transcended by the fulfillment of the prophecy. Meier has grasped and explained this redemptive-historical structure better than most commentators. He may, however, have gone too far in interpreting v. 18d too narrowly as a reference to the Cross and the Resurrection.

19 The contrast between the least and the greatest in the kingdom probably supports gradation within kingdom ranks (as in 11:11, though the word for "least" is different there; cf. 18:1–4). It is probably not a Semitic way of referring to the exclusion-inclusion duality (contra Bonnard). The one who breaks "one of the least of these commandments" is not excluded from the kingdom—the linguistic usage is against this interpretation (see Meier, *Law*, pp. 92–95)—but is very small or very unimportant in the kingdom (taking *elachistos* in the elative sense). The idea of gradations of privilege or dishonor in the kingdom occurs elsewhere in the synoptic Gospels (20:20–28; cf. Luke 12:47–48). Distinctions are made not only according to the measure by which one keeps "the least of these commandments" but also according to the faithfulness with which one teaches them.

But what are "these commandments"? It is hard to justify restriction of these words to Jesus' teachings (so Banks, *Jesus*, pp. 221–23), even though the verb cognate to "commands" (*entolōn*) is used of Jesus' teachings in 28:20 (*entellomai*); for the noun in Matthew never refers to Jesus' words, and the context argues against it. Restriction to the Ten Commandments (TDNT, 2:548) is equally alien to the concerns of the context. Nor can we say "these commandments" refers to the antitheses that follow, for in Matthew *houtos* ("this," pl. "these") never points forward. It appears, then, that the expression must refer to the commandments of the OT Scriptures. The entire Law and the Prophets are not scrapped by Jesus' coming but fulfilled. Therefore the commandments of these Scriptures—even the least of them (on distinctions in the law, see on 22:36; 23:23)—must be practiced. But the nature of the practicing has already been affected by vv. 17–18. The law pointed forward to Jesus and his teaching; so it is properly obeyed by conforming to his word. As it points to him, so he, in fulfilling it, establishes what continuity it has, the true direction to which it points and the way it is to be obeyed. Thus ranking in the kingdom turns on the degree of conformity to Jesus' teaching as that teaching fulfills OT revelation. His teaching, toward which the OT pointed, must be obeyed.

20 And that teaching, far from being more lenient, is nothing less than perfection (see on 5:48). The Pharisees and teachers of the law (see on 2:4; 3:7; and Introduction, section 11.f) were among the most punctilious in the land. Jesus' criticism is "not that they were not good, but that they were not good enough" (Hill, *Matthew*). While their multiplicity of regulations could engender a "good" society, it domesticated the law and lost the radical demand for absolute holiness demanded by the Scriptures.

What Jesus demanded is the righteousness to which the law truly points, exemplified in the antitheses that follow (vv.21-48). Contrary to Flender (pp. 45f.), v.3 (poverty of spirit) and v.20 (demand for radical righteousness) do not stand opposite each other in flat contradiction. Verse 20 does not establish how the righteousness is to be gained, developed, or empowered; it simply lays out the demand. Messiah will develop a people who will be called "oaks of righteousness . . . for the display of [Yahweh's] splendor" (Isa 61:3). The verb "surpasses" suggests that the new righteousness outstrips the old both qualitatively and quantitatively (Bonnard) (see on 25:31-46). Anything less does not enter the kingdom.

Notes

18 "I tell you the truth" is NIV's rendering of two expressions merged together: (1) ἀμήν (*amēn*)—a Greek transliteration of a Hebrew word meaning "faithful," "reliable," often used in the OT as an adverb, "surely," "truly," often at the end of a sentence endorsing or wishing that the sentence is true or may prove true (cf. "Amen" in English at the end of prayers); it also begins some sentences (Jer 28:6; Rev 7:12; 19:4; 22:20) or develops into a response (1 Cor 14:16; Rev 5:14; cf. Deut 27:15-26; cf. also Daube, *New Testament*, pp. 388-93; Jeremias, *Prayers*, pp. 112-15)—and (2) γὰρ λέγω ὑμῖν (*gar legō hymin*, "for I tell you"), which of course would take the order λέγω γὰρ ὑμῖν if it stood on its own.

b. Application: the antitheses (5:21-48)

1) Vilifying anger and reconciliation

5:21-26

21"You have heard that it was said to the people long ago, 'Do not murder, and anyone who murders will be subject to judgment,' 22But I tell you that anyone who is angry with his brother will be subject to judgment. Again, anyone who says to his brother, 'Raca,' is answerable to the Sanhedrin. But anyone who says, 'You fool!' will be in danger of the fire of hell.

23"Therefore, if you are offering your gift at the altar and there remember that your brother has something against you, 24leave your gift there in front of the altar. First go and be reconciled to your brother; then come and offer your gift.

25"Settle matters quickly with your adversary who is taking you to court. Do it while you are still with him on the way, or he may hand you over to the judge, and the judge may hand you over to the officer, and you may be thrown into prison. 26I tell you the truth, you will not get out until you have paid the last penny.

Verses 21-48 are often called the six antitheses because all six sections begin with some variation of "you have heard it said . . . but I say." Daube (*New Testament*, pp. 55-62) offers a number of much-cited rabbinic parallels, some of which, in the first part, raise an interpretation as a theoretical possibility only to reject it, and others of which raise a literal interpretation only to circumscribe it with broader consider-ations. Daube rightly points out that the first part of Matthew's formulas means something like "you have understood" or "you have literally understood." That is, Jesus is not criticizing the OT but the understanding of the OT many of his hearers adopted. This is especially true of vv.22, 43, where part of what was "heard" cer-tainly does not come from the OT.

Beginning with this point, many (e.g., Stendahl [Peake], Hill) hold that Jesus nowhere abrogates the law but merely intensifies it or shows its ultimate meaning. Others (e.g., McConnell) point out that, formally speaking, some OT laws are in-deed contravened (e.g., laws on oaths, vv. 33–37). R.A. Guelich ("The Antitheses of Matthew v.21–48: Traditional or Redactional?" NTS 22 [1975–76]: 444–57), in the course of arguing that the first, second, and fourth are traditional, and the third, fifth, and sixth redactional, suggests that the former transcend the law's demands, whereas the latter annul the law—a point contested by G. Strecker ("Die Anti-thesen der Bergpredigt," ZNW 69 [1978]: 36–72). Apart from the fact that the traditional-redactional bifurcation is not an entirely happy one (cf. Introduction, sections 1–3), a unifying approach to the antitheses is possible in the light of our exegesis of vv.17–20.

The contrast between what the people had heard and what Jesus taught is not based on distinctions like casuistry versus love, outer legalism versus inner commit-ment, or even false interpretation versus true interpretation, though all of them impinge collaterally on the text. Rather, in every case Jesus contrasts the people's misunderstanding of the law with the true direction in which the law points, accord-ing to his own authority as the law's "fulfiller" (in the sense established in v.17). He makes no attempt to fence in the law (contra Przybylski, pp. 80–87) but declares unambiguously the true direction to which it points. Thus if certain antitheses revoke at least the letter of the law (and they do: cf. Meier, *Law*, pp. 125ff.), they do so, not because they are thereby affirming the law's true spirit, but because Jesus insists that his teaching on these matters is the direction in which the laws actually point.

Likewise Jesus' "you have heard . . . but I say" is not quite analogous to corre-sponding rabbinic formulas; Jesus is not simply a proto-rabbi (contra Daube, Sigal). The Sermon on the Mount is not set in a context of scholarly dispute over *halakic* details but in a context of messianic and eschatological fulfillment. Jesus' authority bursts the borders of the relatively "narrow context of legal interpretation and inno-vation which the rabbis circumscribed for themselves" (Banks, *Jesus*, p. 85). It is for this reason that the crowds were amazed at his authority (7:28–29).

21–22 Jesus' contemporaries had heard that the law given their forefathers (cf. Notes) forbade murder (not the taking of all life, which could, for instance, be a judicial mandate: cf. Gen 9:6) and that the murderer must be brought to "judgment" (*krisis*, which here refers to legal proceedings, perhaps the court set up in every town [Deut 16:18; 2 Chron 19:5; cf. Jos. Antiq. IV, 214(vii.14); War II, 570–71 (xx.5)]; or the council of twenty-three persons set up to deal with criminal matters, SBK, 1:275). But Jesus insists—the "I" is emphatic in each of the six antitheses—that the law really points to his own teaching: the root of murder is anger, and anger is murderous in principle (v.22). One has not conformed to the better righteousness of the kingdom simply by refraining from homicide. The angry person will be sub-ject to *krisis* ("judgment"), but it is presupposed this is God's judgment, "since no human court is competent to try a case of inward anger" (Stott). To stoop to insult exposes one not merely to (God's) council (*synedrion* can mean either "Sanhedrin" [NIV] or simply "council") but to the "fire of hell."

The expression "fire of hell" (*geenna tou pyros*, lit., "gehenna of fire") comes from the Hebrew *gê-hinnōm* ("Valley of Hinnom," a ravine south of Jerusalem once associated with the pagan god Moloch and his disgusting rites [2 Kings 23:10; 2 Chron 28:3; 33:6; Jer 7:31; Ezek 16:20; 23:37], prohibited by God [Lev 18:21; 20:2-5]). When Josiah abolished the practices, he defiled the valley by making it a, dumping ground for filth and the corpses of criminals (2 Kings 23:10). Late traditions suggest that in the first century it may still have been used as a rubbish pit, complete with smoldering fires. The valley came to symbolize the place of eschatological punishment (cf. 1 Enoch 54:12; 2 Bar 85:13; cf. Matt 10:28; 23:15, 33; and 18:9 for the longer expression "gehenna of fire"). Gehenna and Hades (11:23 [NIV mg.]; 16:18) are often thought to refer, respectively, to eternal hell and the abode of the dead in the intermediate state. But the distinction can be maintained in few passages. More commonly the two terms are synonymous and mean "hell" (cf. W.J.P. Boyd, "Gehenna—According to J. Jeremias," in Livingstone, 2:9-12).

"Brother" (*adelphos*) cannot in this case be limited to male siblings. Matthew's Gospel uses the word extensively. Whenever it clearly refers to people beyond physical brothers, it is on the lips of Jesus; and its narrow usage is almost always Matthean. This suggests that the Christian habit of calling one another "brother" goes back to Jesus' instruction, possibly part and parcel of his training them to address God as Father (6:9). Among Christian brothers, anger is to be eliminated.

The passage does not suggest a gradation and climax of punishments (Hendriksen, pp. 297-99), for this would require a similar gradation of offense. There is no clear distinction between the person with seething anger, the one who insultingly calls his brother a fool, and the one who prefers, as his term of abuse, "Raca" (transliteration for Aram. *rēkā'*, "imbecile," "fool," "blockhead"). To a Greek, *mōros* would suggest foolishness, senselessness; but to a speaker of Hebrew, the Greek word might call to mind the Hebrew *mōreh*, which has overtones of moral apostasy, rebellion, and wickedness (cf. Ps 78:8[77:8 LXX]; Jer 5:23).

Many Jewish maxims warn against anger (examples in Bonnard), but this is not just another maxim. Here Jesus offers not just advice but insists that the sixth commandment points prophetically to the kingdom's condemnation of hate.

Jesus' anger, expressed in diverse circumstances (21:12-19; 23:17; Mark 3:1-5), is no personal inconsistency.

1. Jesus is a preacher who gets down to essentials on every point he makes. Thus for a clear understanding of his thought on a particular issue, one must examine the balance of his teaching. Compare, for instance, 6:2-4 with Luke 18:1-8. Similarly, to learn all Jesus says about anger, it is necessary to integrate this passage with others such as 21:12-13 without absolutizing any one text.

2. When suffering, Jesus is proverbial for his gentleness and forbearance (Luke 23:34; 1 Peter 2:23). But if he comes as Suffering Servant, he comes equally as Judge and King. His anger erupts not out of personal pique but out of outrage at injustice, sin, unbelief, and exploitation of others. Unfortunately his followers are more likely to be angered at personal affronts (cf. Carson, *Sermon on the Mount*, pp. 41f.).

23-24 Jesus gives two illustrations exposing the seriousness of anger, the first in a setting of temple worship (vv.23-24, which implies a pre-70 setting), and the second in a judicial setting (vv.25-26). The first concerns a brother (see on v.22); the second an adversary. Remarkably neither illustration deals with "your" anger but with "your" offense that has prompted the brother's or the adversary's rancor. Some take this as a sign that vv.23-26 represent displaced, independent logia. Yet the connection with vv.21-22 is very powerful. We are more likely to remember when we have something against others than when we have done something to offend others. And if we are truly concerned about our anger and hate, we shall be no less concerned when we engender them in others.

The "altar" (v.23) is the one in the inner court. There amid solemn worship, recollection of a brother with something against one (on the expression, cf. Mark 11:25) should in Christ's disciples prompt immediate efforts to be reconciled (v.24). Only then is formal worship acceptable.

25-26 Compare Luke 12:57-59, where the contextual application warns impenitent Israel to be reconciled to God before it is too late. Many conclude that Matthew has "ethicized" an originally eschatological saying. But the language of the two pericopes is not close, and it is more realistic to postulate two stories from one itinerant preacher. Explanations for one or two of the changes (e.g., McNeile) are not convincing unless they fit a pattern that justifies all the changes.

Jesus again urges haste (v.25). Settle matters with the offended adversary while still "with him on the way" to court, not on "the road to life" (Bonnard). In the ancient world debtors were jailed till the debts were paid. Thus v.26 is part of the narrative fabric and gives no justification for purgatory, universal restoration, or urgent reconciliation to God. It simply insists on immediate action: malicious anger is so evil—and God's judgment so certain (v.22)—that we must do all in our power to end it (cf. Eph 4:26-27).

Notes

21 The word ἀρχαίοις (archaiois, "to the people long ago") is translated as an instrumental dative in KJV: "by them of old time," following Beza. The reading is also found in some OL copies: ab antiquis (it[a.b.c]) instead of antiquis (it[d.f.ff.]), which is as ambiguous as the Greek (similarly in v.33). NIV is almost certainly right: (1) the normal way of expressing agency in Greek is with ὑπό (hypo, "by") plus the genitive (though there are exceptional datives, e.g., 6:1; 23:5); and (2) Jesus' point is not to correct "the people long ago" but the misunderstandings of his contemporaries, for which the NIV rendering is more suitable.

The verb οὐ φονεύσεις (ou phoneuseis, "Do not murder") is future, a not uncommon way for the LXX to express an imperative. Most examples in the NT are in quotations from the LXX (e.g., 5:33, 43, 48). But the construction is not unknown in secular Greek, and some non-LXX instances occur in the NT (e.g., 6:5; 20:26; 21:3, 13; cf. Turner, Syntax p. 86).

22 The words "without cause" (NIV mg.) probably reflect an early and widespread softening of Jesus' strong teaching. Their absence does not itself prove there is no exception: see commentary.

23 The change from plural to singular occurs again at 5:29, 36, 39; 6:5, and may reflect the style of a preacher who knows how to bring his lesson home by making it personal.

2) *Adultery and purity*

5:27-30

> 27"You have heard that it was said, 'Do not commit adultery.' 28But I tell you that anyone who looks at a woman lustfully has already committed adultery with her in his heart. 29If your right eye causes you to sin, gouge it out and throw it away. It is better for you to lose one part of your body than for your whole body to be thrown into hell. 30And if your right hand causes you to sin, cut it off and throw it away. It is better for you to lose one part of your body than for your whole body to go into hell.

27-28 The OT command not to commit adultery (Exod 20:14; Deut 5:18) is often treated in Jewish sources not so much as a function of purity as of theft: it was to steal another's wife (references in Bonnard). Jesus insisted that the seventh commandment points in another direction—toward purity that refuses to lust (v.28). The tenth commandment had already explicitly made the point; and *gynē* here more likely means "woman" than "wife." "To interpret the law on the side of stringency is not to annul the Law, but to change it in accordance with its own intention" (Davies, *Setting*, p. 102; cf. Job 31:1; Prov 6:25; 2 Peter 2:14).

Klaus Haacker ("Der Rechtsatz Jesu zum Thema Ehebruch," *Biblische Zeitschrift* 21 [1977]: 113-16) has convincingly argued that the second *autēn* ("[committed adultery] with her") is contrary to the common interpretation of this verse. In Greek it is unnecessary, especially if the sin is entirely the man's. But it is explainable if *pros to epithymēsai autēn*, commonly understood to mean "with a view to lusting for her," is translated "so as to get her to lust." The evidence for this interpretation is strong (cf. Notes). The man is therefore looking at the woman with a view to enticing her to lust. Thus, so far as his intention goes, he is committing adultery *with her*, he makes her an adulteress. This does not weaken the force of Jesus' teaching; the heart of the matter is still lust and intent.

29-30 The radical treatment of parts of the body that cause one to sin (cf. Notes) has led some (notoriously Origen) to castrate themselves. But that is not radical enough, since lust is not thereby removed. The "eye" (v.29) is the member of the body most commonly blamed for leading us astray, especially in sexual sins (cf. Num 15:39; Prov 21:4; Ezek 6:9; 18:12; 20:8; cf. Eccl 11:9); the "right eye" refers to one's best eye. But why the "right hand" (v.30) in a context dealing with lust? This may be merely illustrative or a way of saying that even lust is a kind of theft. More likely it is a euphemism for the male sexual organ (cf. *yād*, "hand," most likely used in this way in Isa 57:8 [cf. BDB, s.v., 4.g]; see Lachs, pp. 108f.).

Cutting off or gouging out the offending part is a way of saying that Jesus' disciples must deal radically with sin. Imagination is a God-given gift; but if it is fed dirt by the eye, it will be dirty. All sin, not least sexual sin, begins with the imagination. Therefore what feeds the imagination is of maximum importance in the pursuit of kingdom righteousness (compare Phil 4:8). Not everyone reacts the same way to all objects. But if (vv.28-29) your eye is causing you to sin, gouge it out; cr at very least, don't look (cf. the sane exposition of Stott, pp. 88-91)! The alternative is sin and hell, sin's reward. The point is so fundamental that Jesus doubtless repeated it on numerous occasions (cf. 18:8-9).

Notes

28 The verb ἐπιθυμέω (*epithymeō*, "I lust") can have positive force ("I desire"), but more commonly it has a bad sense. It is used explicitly in connection with sexual lust in Rom 1:24.

The expression πρὸς τὸ ἐπιθυμῆσαι αὐτήν (*pros to epithymēsai autēn*) could mean "so as to lust after her," whether with telic or ecbatic force (cf. BDF, par. 402 [5]), here presumably the former. If so, it is the only place where this kind of verb uses the accusative: *autēs* (gen.) rather than *autēn* is expected (cf. BDF, par. 171 [1]. The accusative *autēn* more probably therefore functions as the accusative of reference (i.e., the quasi-subject) of the infinitive (as in the equivalent construction in Luke 18:1) to generate the translation "so that she lusts."

29 The verb σκανδαλίζω (*skandalizō*) can mean (1) "I cause to stumble," "I cause to sin" (as here, 18:6–9; Luke 17:2; Rom 14:21; 1 Cor 8:13; 2 Cor 11:29); (2) "I obstruct another's path," and, hence, "I cause [someone] to disbelieve, reject, forsake" (Matt 11:6; 13:21, 57; 15:12; 24:10; 26:31, 33; John 16:1); (3) "I offend" (Matt 17:27; John 6:61). The cognate noun σκάνδαλον (*skandalon*), originally referring to the trigger of a trap (cf. Rom 11:9), comes to mean, in a similar breakdown, (1) "stumbling block," i.e., "causing another to fall into sin" (Matt 13:41; 18:7; Luke 17:1; Rom 14:13; 1 John 2:10; Rev 2:14); (2) "an obstruction," and, hence, "an occasion of disbelief" (Rom 9:32–33; 16:17; 1 Cor 1:23; 1 Peter 2:8); (3) an object one strikes and which hurts or repels one; hence, "an offense" (Matt 16:23; Gal 5:11). Some texts may appeal to more than one meaning (cf. Broadus; DNTT, 2:707–10).

3) *Divorce and remarriage*

5:31–32

> 31"It has been said, 'Anyone who divorces his wife must give her a certificate of divorce.' 32But I tell you that anyone who divorces his wife, except for marital unfaithfulness, causes her to become an adulteress, and anyone who marries the divorced woman commits adultery.

31–32 The introductory formula "It has been said" is shorter than all the others in this chapter and is linked to the preceding by a connective *de* ("and"). Therefore, though these two verses are innately antithetical, they carry further the argument of the preceding pericope. The OT not only points toward insisting that lust is the moral equivalent of adultery (vv. 27–30) but that divorce is as well. This arises out of the fact that the divorced woman will in most circumstances remarry (esp. in first-century Palestine, where this would probably be her means of support). That new marriage, whether from the perspective of the divorcee or the one marrying her, is adulterous.

The OT passage to which Jesus refers (v.31) is Deuteronomy 24:1–4, whose thrust is that if a man divorces his wife because of "something indecent" (not further defined) in her, he must give her a certificate of divorce, and if she then becomes another man's wife and is divorced again, the first man cannot remarry her. This double restriction—the certificate and the prohibition of remarriage—discouraged hasty divorces. Here Jesus does not go into the force of "something indecent." Instead he insists that the law was pointing to the sanctity of marriage.

The natural way to take the "except" clause is that divorce is wrong because it generates adultery *except* in the case of fornication. In that case, where sexual sin has already been committed, nothing is laid down, though it appears that divorce is then implicitly permitted, even if not mandated (cf. the paraphrase in Stonehouse, *Witness of Matthew*, p. 203).

The numerous points for exegetical dispute (e.g., the meaning of *porneia* ["fornication," or, in NIV, "marital unfaithfulness"], the force of the "except" clause, and the tradition history behind these verses and their relationship to 19:3–9; Mark 10:11–12; Luke 16:18) are treated more fully at 19:3–12. The one theory that must be rejected here (because it has no counterpart in 19:3–12) is that which takes the words "makes her an adulteress" to mean "stigmatizes her as an adulteress (even though it is not so)" (B. Ward Powers, "Divorce and the Bible," *Interchange* 23 [1938]: 159). The Greek uses the verb, not the noun (cf. NIV's "causes her to become an adulteress"). The verbal construction disallows Powers's paraphrase.

4) *Oaths and truthfulness*

5:33–37

> [33]"Again, you have heard that it was said to the people long ago, 'Do not break your oath, but keep the oaths you have made to the Lord.' [34]But I tell you, Do not swear at all: either by heaven, for it is God's throne; [35]or by the earth, for it is his footstool; or by Jerusalem, for it is the city of the Great King. [36]And do not swear by your head, for you cannot make even one hair white or black. [37]Simply let your 'Yes' be 'Yes,' and your 'No,' 'No'; anything beyond this comes from the evil one.

33 "Again" probably confirms 5:31–32 as an excursus to the preceding antithesis rather than a new one. Matthew now reports an antithesis on a new theme. What the people have heard is not given as direct OT quotation but as a summary statement accurately condensing the burden of Exodus 20:7; Leviticus 19:12; Numbers 30:2; and Deuteronomy 5:11; 6:3; 22:21–23. The Mosaic law forbade irreverent oaths, light use of the Lord's name, broken vows. Once Yahweh's name was invoked, the vow to which it was attached became a debt that had to be paid to the Lord.

A sophisticated casuistry judged how binding an oath really was by examining how closely it was related to Yahweh's name. Incredible distinctions proliferate under such an approach. Swearing by heaven and earth was not binding, nor was swearing *by* Jerusalem, though swearing *toward* Jerusalem was. That an entire mishnaic tract (M *Shebuoth*) is given over to the subject (cf. also M *Sanhedrin* 3.2; *Tosephta Nedarim* 1; SBK, 1:321–36) shows that such distinctions became important and were widely discussed. Matthew returns to the topic with marvelous examples in the polemical setting of 23:16–22. The context is not overtly polemical here but simply explains how Jesus relates the kingdom and its righteousness to the OT.

34–36 If oaths designed to encourage truthfulness become occasions for clever lies and casuistical deceit, Jesus will abolish oaths (v.34). For the direction in which the OT points is the fundamental importance of thorough and consistent truthfulness. If one does not swear at all, one does not swear falsely. Not dissimilar reasoning was found among the Essenes, who avoided taking oaths, "regarding it as worse than perjury, for they say that one who is not believed without an appeal to God stands condemned already" (Jos. War II, 135[viii.6])—though they did require "tremendous oaths" of neophytes joining the community (ibid., 139[viii.7]; cf. 1QS 5:7-11; CD 15:5).

Jesus insists that whatever a man swears by is related to God in some way, and therefore every oath is implicitly in God's name—heaven, earth, Jerusalem, even the hairs of the head are all under God's sway and ownership (v.36). (There may be allusions here to Ps 48:2; Isa 66:1.) Significantly, Matthew breaks the flow to say (in Gr.) "toward Jerusalem" rather than "by Jerusalem" (on the distinction, cf. on v.33). The "Great King" (v.35) may well be God, but see on 25:34.

37 The Greek might more plausibly be translated "But let your word be, 'Yes, Yes; No, No.'" The doubling has raised questions: according to some rabbinic opinion, a doubled "yes" or "no" constitutes an oath; and Broadus suggests this is an appropriate way to strengthen an assertion. This sounds like casuistry every bit as tortuous as that which Jesus condemns. The doubling is probably no more than preacher's rhetoric, the point made clear by NIV (cf. James 5:12). *Tou ponērou* could be rendered either "of evil" or "of the evil one" ("the father of lies," John 8:44). The same ambiguity recurs at 5:39; 6:13; 13:38.

Many groups (e.g., Anabaptists, Jehovah's Witnesses) have understood these verses absolutely literally and have therefore refused even to take court oaths. Their zeal to conform to Scripture is commendable, but they have probably not interpreted the text very well.

1. The contextual purpose of this passage is to stress the true direction in which the OT points—viz., the importance of truthfulness. Where oaths are not being used evasively and truthfulness is not being threatened, it is not immediately obvious that they require such unqualified abolition.

2. In the Scriptures God himself "swears" (e.g., Gen 9:9-11; Luke 1:68, 73; cf. Ps 16:10 and Acts 2:27-31), not because he sometimes lies, but in order to help men believe (Heb 6:17). The earliest Christians still took oaths, if we may judge from Paul's example (Rom 1:9; 2 Cor 1:23; 1 Thess 2:5, 10; cf. Phil 1:8), for much the same reason. Jesus himself testified under oath (26:63-64).

3. Again we need to remember the antithetical nature of Jesus' preaching (see on 5:27-30; 6:5-8).

It must be frankly admitted that here Jesus formally contravenes OT law: what it permits or commands (Deut 6:13), he forbids. But if his interpretation of the direction in which the law points is authoritative, then his teaching fulfills it.

Notes

34 Ὀμνύναι ἐν or εἰς (*omnynai en* or *eis*, "to swear by" or "by-toward" [Gr. is not entirely unambiguous]) is Hebraic (cf. Moulton, *Accidence*, pp. 463-64); only with "Jerusalem" is *eis* used in the NT. Turner (*Insights*, p. 31) argues that the present prohibition in James 5:12 means "stop swearing," whereas the aorist prohibition here presupposes that the disciples have stopped and now forbids them from starting. This classic distinction based on tenses in prohibitions usually holds but can be too finely spun (cf. Moule, *Idiom Book*,

p. 21). In the strictest sense the aorist is timeless; and linked in v.34 with $\mu\grave{\eta}$ . . . $\ddot{o}\lambda\omega\varsigma$ (*mē* . . . *holōs*, "not . . . at all") it probably simply generates an unconditional negative: "Do not swear at all" (NIV: cf. Schlatter).

---

5) *Personal injury and self-sacrifice*

5:38-42

> [38]"You have heard that it was said, 'Eye for eye, and tooth for tooth.' [39]But I tell you, Do not resist an evil person. If someone strikes you on the right cheek, turn to him the other also. [40]And if someone wants to sue you and take your tunic, let him have your cloak as well. [41]If someone forces you to go one mile, go with him two miles. [42]Give to the one who asks you, and do not turn away from the one who wants to borrow from you.

The order of the last two antitheses (vv.38–48) is reversed in Luke 6:27–36. While the reasons for this are debatable, if both evangelists are recording the same sermon, the reversal shows that rearranging the order of the materials (preserved in Q and/or other notes) was thought acceptable. Bonnard rightly criticizes the tradition history of Wrege. Parallels repudiating vengeance and vindictiveness are not unknown (T Benjamin 4:1–5:5; 1QS 10:18; CD 8:5–6). The distinctive element in Jesus' teaching is the way he sets it over against the *lex talionis* (the principle of retribution) and the reasons he does this.

38 The OT prescription (Exod 21:24; Lev 24:19–20; Deut 19:21) was not given to foster vengeance; the law explicitly forbade that (Lev 19:18). Rather, it was given, as the OT context shows, to provide the nation's judicial system with a ready formula of punishment, not least because it would decisively terminate vendettas. On occasion payment in money or some other commodity was exacted instead (e.g., Exod 21:26–27); and in Jesus' day the courts seldom imposed *lex talionis*. The trouble is that a law designed to limit retaliation and punish fairly could be appealed to as justification for vindictiveness. But it will not do to argue that Jesus is doing nothing more than combatting a personal as opposed to a judicial use of the *lex talionis*, since in that case the examples would necessarily run differently: e.g., if someone strikes you, don't strike back but let the judiciary administer the just return slap. The argument runs in deeper channels.

39 Jesus' disciple is not to resist "an evil person" (*tō ponērō* could not easily be taken to refer here to the Devil or to evil in the abstract). In the context of the *lex talionis*, the most natural way of understanding the resistance is "do not resist in a court of law." This interpretation is required in the second example (v.40). As in vv.33–37, therefore, Jesus' teaching formally contradicts the OT law. But in the context of vv.17–20, what Jesus is saying is reasonably clear: the OT, including the *lex talionis*, points forward to Jesus and his teaching. But like the OT laws permitting divorce, enacted because of the hardness of men's hearts (19:3–12), the *lex talionis* was instituted to curb evil because of the hardness of men's hearts. "God gives by concession a legal regulation as a dam against the river of violence which flows from man's evil heart" (Piper, p. 90).

As this legal principle is overtaken by that toward which it points, so also is this hardness of heart. The OT prophets foretold a time when there would be a change of heart among God's people, living under a new covenant (Jer 31:31–34; 32:37–41; Ezek 36:26). Not only would the sins of the people be forgiven (Jer 31:34; Ezek 36:25), but obedience to God would spring from the heart (Jer 31:33; Ezek 36:27) as the eschatological age dawned. Thus Jesus' instruction on these matters is grounded in eschatology. In Jesus and the kingdom, fulfillment (even if partial) of the OT promises, the eschatological age that the Law and Prophets had prophesied (11:13) arrives; and the prophecies that curbed evil while pointing forward to the eschaton are now superseded by the new age and the new hearts it brings (cf. Piper, pp. 89–91).

Four illustrations clarify Jesus' point and drive it home. In the first, a man strikes another on the cheek—not only a painful blow, but a gross insult (cf. 2 Cor 11:20). If a right-handed person strikes someone's right cheek, presumably it is a slap by the back of the hand, probably considered more insulting than a slap by the open palm (cf. M *Baba Kamma* 8:6). The verb "strikes" (*rhapizei*) probably refers to a sharp slap. Many commentators contrast Luke's *typtō* ("strikes," Luke 6:29), arguing the latter refers to blows with a rod—i.e., Luke deals not with insult but with pain and damage. The contrast is false; the semantic overlap between the two verbs is substantial, and *typtō* can refer to a slap (e.g., Acts 23:3). But instead of seeking recompense at law under the *lex talionis*, Jesus' disciples will gladly endure the insult again. (There are overtones of Isa 50:6 here, applied in Matt 26:67 to Jesus; cf. Gundry, *Use of OT*, pp. 72–73.)

40 Although under Mosaic law the outer cloak was an inalienable possession (Exod 22:26; Deut 24:13), Jesus' disciples, if sued for their tunics (an inner garment like our suit but worn next to the skin), far from seeking satisfaction, will gladly part with what they may legally keep. Luke 6:29 says nothing about legal action but mentions the garments in reverse order. This has led some to think that Luke had violent robbery in mind because then the outer garment would be snatched off first. But perhaps the order is simply that in which the garments would normally be removed.

41 The third example refers to the Roman practice of commandeering civilians to carry the luggage of military personnel a prescribed distance, one Roman "mile." (On the verb *angareuō*, "I commandeer," cf. W. Hatch, *Essays in Biblical Greek* [Oxford: Clarendon, 1889], pp. 37–38.) Impressment, like a lawsuit, evokes outrage; but the attitude of Jesus' disciples under such circumstances must not be spiteful or vengeful but helpful—willing to go a second mile (exemplars of the Western text say "two more [miles]," making a total of three!). This illustration is also implicitly anti-Zealot.

42 The final illustration requires not only interest-free loans (Exod 22:25; Lev 25:37; Deut 23:19) but a generous spirit (cf. Deut 15:7–11; Pss 37:26; 112:5). The parallel form of this verse (Luke 6:30) does not imply two requests but only one; the repetition reinforces the point. These last two illustrations confirm our interpretation of vv.38–39. The entire pericope deals with the heart's attitude, the better righteousness. For there is actually no legal recourse to the oppression in the third illustration, and in the fourth no harm that might lead to retaliation has been done.

While these four vignettes have powerful shock value, they were not meant to be new legal prescriptions. Verse 42 does not commit Jesus' disciples to giving endless amounts of money to every one who seeks a "soft touch" (cf. Prov 11:15; 17:18;

22:26). Verse 40 is clearly hyperbolic: no first-century Jew would go home wearing only a loin cloth. Nor does this pericope deal with the validity of a state police force. Yet the illustrations must not be diluted by endless equivocations; the only limit to the believer's response in these situations is what love and the Scriptures impose. Paul could "resist" (same Gr. word) Peter to his face (Gal 2) because love demanded it in light of the damage being done to the gospel and to fellow believers. (On the practical outworking of this antithesis, cf. Neil, pp. 160–63; Piper, pp. 92–99; Stott, pp. 104–14.)

6) *Hatred and love*

5:43–47

> 43"You have heard that it was said, 'Love your neighbor and hate your enemy.' 44But I tell you: Love your enemies and pray for those who persecute you, 45that you may be sons of your Father in heaven. He causes his sun to rise on the evil and the good, and sends rain on the righteous and the unrighteous. 46If you love those who love you, what reward will you get? Are not even the tax collectors doing that? 47And if you greet only your brothers, what are you doing more than others? Do not even pagans do that?

43 The command "Love your neighbor" is found in Leviticus 19:18, but no OT Scripture adds "and hate your enemies." Rabbinic literature as it was later preserved does not usually leap to so bold and negative a conclusion. Thus some commentators have taken this passage as a later Christian mockery of Jewish values. But other considerations question this.

1. The Qumran covenanters explicitly commanded love for those within the community ("those whom God has elected") and hatred for the outsider (cf. 1QS 1:4, 10; 2:4–9; 1QM 4:1–2; 15:6; 1QH 5:4), and they doubtless represent other groups with similar positions. This love-hate antithesis may be mitigated by the covenanters' conviction that they alone were the faithful remnant; at least some of the language anticipates divine eschatological language. But not all of it can be dismissed so easily (cf. Davies, *Setting*, pp. 245ff.).

2. Quite apart from the problems in dating rabbinic literature, we must remember that such literature represents scholarly debate, not common thought. For example, Carl F.H. Henry writes learned tomes read by a few thousand; Hal Lindsey writes popular material read by millions. In a hundred years, if the world lasts that long, some of Henry's work may still be in print, but few will remember Lindsey. Yet today Lindsey is read by far more church people than Henry; and the wise preacher will not forget it. Likewise the popular perversion of Leviticus 19:18 presupposed by Matthew 5:43 was doubtless far more widespread than the rabbinic literature intimates.

The quotation also omits "as yourself," words included in 19:19; 22:39; and the attitude reflected ignores the fact that Leviticus 19:33–34 also commands love of the same depth for the sojourner, the resident alien in the land. The popular reasoning seems to have been that if God commands love for "neighbor," then hatred for "enemies" is implicitly conceded and perhaps even authorized. Luke 10:25–37 shows how far the "neighbor" category extends.

44–47 Jesus allowed no casuistry. The real direction indicated by the law is love, rich and costly, and extended even to enemies. Many take the verb "love" (agapaō) and the noun (agapē) as always signifying self-giving regardless of emotion. For instance, Hill (Matthew) comments on this passage. "The love which is inculcated is not a matter of sentiment and emotion, but, as always in the OT and NT, of concrete action." If this were so, 1 Corinthians 13:3 could not disavow "love" that gives everything to the poor and suffers even to martyrdom; for these are "concrete actions." The same verb is used when Amnon incestuously loves his half-sister Tamar (2 Sam 13:1 LXX); when Demas, because he loves this world (2 Tim 4:10), forsakes Paul; and when tax collectors love those who love them (Matt 5:46).

The rise of this word group in Greek is well traced by Robert Joly, Ἀγαπᾶν et Φιλεῖν: Le vocabulaire chrétien de l'amour, est-il original? (Bruxelles: Presses Universitaires, 1968). Christians doubtless took over the word group and largely filled it with their own content; but the content of that love is not based on a presupposed definition but on Jesus' teaching and example. To love one's enemies, though it must result in doing them good (Luke 6:32–33) and praying for them (Matt 5:44), cannot justly be restricted to activities devoid of any concern, sentiment, or emotion. Like the English verb "to love," agapaō ranges widely from debased and selfish actions to generous, warm, costly self-sacrifice for another's good. There is no reason to think the verb here in Matthew does not include emotion as well as action.

Much recent scholarship identifies the "enemies" with the persecutors of Matthew's church. Verses 44–47 are then seen as Matthew's transformation of Luke's more general exhortation (6:32–35) into encouragement for believers in Matthew's day to submit graciously to their persecutors. If Matthew's first readers were being persecuted for their faith, that was doubtless one application they made, though it is unlikely that Matthew himself intends to be quite so restrictive and anachronistic. The words "those who persecute you" introduce one important kind of "enemy" but do not exclude other kinds. Jesus himself repeatedly warns his disciples of impending persecution (e.g., vv. 10–12; 10:16–23; 24:9–13); so there is little need to doubt the authenticity of the warning here.

One manifestation of love for enemies will be in prayer; praying for an enemy and loving him will prove mutually reinforcing. The more love, the more prayer; the more prayer, the more love.

> Jesus seems to have prayed for his tormentors actually while the iron spikes were being driven through his hands and feet; indeed the imperfect tense suggests that he kept praying, kept repeating his entreaty, "Father, forgive them; for they know not what they do" (Luke 23:34). If the cruel torture of crucifixion could not silence our Lord's prayer for his enemies, what pain, pride, prejudice or sloth could justify the silencing of ours? (Stott, p. 119).

Jesus' disciples have as their example God himself, who loves so indiscriminately that he sends sun and rain (they are his to bestow) on both the righteous and the unrighteous (cf. Seneca De Beneficiis 4.26; b Taanith 7b). Yet we must not conclude that God's love toward men is in all respects without distinction, and that therefore all must be saved in the end. The same Jesus teaches otherwise—e.g., in 25:31–46 —and the NT shows that some aspects of God's love are indeed related to his moral character and demands for obedience (e.g., John 15:9–11; Jude 21). Theologians since Calvin have related God's love in vv. 44–45 to his "common grace" (i.e., the gracious favor God bestows "commonly," without distinction, on all men). He could with justice condemn all; instead he shows repeated and prolonged favor on all. That is the point here established for our emulation, not that God's love is amoral or without any distinctions whatsoever.

It is equally unsound to conclude that the OT requires harsh terms for an enemy, but that the NT overcomes this dark portrait with new demands for unqualified love. Counter evidence refutes this notion: the OT often mandates love for others (e.g., Exod 23:4–5; Lev 19:18, 33–34; 1 Sam 24:5; Job 31:29; Ps 7:4; Prov 24:17, 29; 25:21–22 [cf. Rom 12:20], and the NT speaks against the reprobate (e.g., Luke 18:7; 1 Cor 16:22; 2 Thess 1:6–10; 2 Tim 4:18; Rev 6:10). Rather, vv.44–45 insist that the OT law cited (v.43) points to the wealth of love exercised by the heirs of the kingdom, a love qualitatively different from that experienced by other people (see on vv.46–47).

God's example provides the incentive for Jesus' disciples to be (*genēsthe*, more likely, "become") sons of their Father (v.45). Ultimately this clause does not mean that the disciples act in a loving way to show what they already are (contra Schniewind, Zahn) but to become what they not yet are (Bonnard, Lagrange)—sons of the Father, in the sense established in v.9. The point of the passage is not to state the means of becoming sons but the necessity of pursuing a certain kind of sonship patterned after the Father's character. "To be persecuted because of righteousness is to align oneself with the prophets (5:12); but to bless and pray for those who persecute us is to align oneself with the character of God" (Carson, *Sermon on the Mount*, p. 53). "To return evil for good is devilish; to return good for good is human; to return good for evil is divine" (Plummer). Both these verses show that Jesus' disciples must live and love in a way superior to the patterns around them. Luke 6:32 uses *charis* ("grace"; NIV, "credit") rather than *misthos* ("reward"), a distinction that has fostered various complex theories concerning the relationship between the two passages. But in the same context, Luke also speaks of *misthos* ("reward," 6:35); and his use of *charis* means no more than thanks or gratitude: "What thanks have you?" (cf. BAGD, p. 878b; hence "credit" in NIV). The two passages are therefore very close, and neither construes "reward" in purely meritorious categories (see on v.12). But the Scriptures do appeal to the hopes and fears of men (e.g., Heb 11:2, 26; cf. Matt 5:12; 6:1) and to greater and lesser felicity in heaven and punishment in hell (Luke 12:47–48; cf. 1 Cor 9:16–18). The verb *echete* ("you have"; NIV, "you get") may be a literal present; but more likely it is future along the line of 6:19–21: i.e., a man "stores up" and therefore "has" various treasure awaiting him in heaven.

The tax collectors in the Synoptics are not the senior holders of the tax-farming contracts (Lat. *publicani*), usually foreigners, but local subordinate collectors (Lat. *portitores*) working under them (BAGD). The latter were despised, not only because the tax-farming scheme encouraged corruption on a massive scale, but also because strict Jews would perceive them as both traitorous (raising taxes for the enslaving power) and potentially unclean (owing to possible contamination from association with Gentiles—a danger for at least the senior ranks of *portitores*, who necessarily had dealings with their Gentile overlords). They are often associated with harlots and other public sinners (cf. Notes). But even these people love those who love them—at least their mothers and other tax collectors!

Proper salutation was a mark of courtesy and respect; but if Jesus' disciples tender such greeting only to their "brothers"—i.e., other like-minded disciples (see on vv.23–24), they do not rise above the standards of *ethnikoi* (strictly speaking, "Gentiles"; but since most Gentiles were pagans, the word came to have more than racial overtones). "In loving his friends a man may in a certain sense be loving only himself—a kind of expanded selfishness" (Broadus). Jesus will not condone this. "The life of the old (fallen) humanity is based on rough justice, avenging injuries and returning favours. The life of the new (redeemed) humanity is based on divine love, refusing to take revenge but overcoming evil with good" (Stott, p. 123).

Notes

43 Zerwick, Par. 279 argues that the future μισήσεις (*miseseis*) may here be used modally: "You shall love your neighbor but you *may hate* your enemy." This is unlikely because (1) the only parallel, 7:4, renders a question; and (2) the command to love in the same sentence is also in the future form (ἀγαπήσεις [*agapeseis*, "you shall love"—see on v.21]). It is therefore best to see the second verb as imperatival, as in NIV.

44 The extra words in KJV are assimilations to Luke 6:27–28. They are not only absent from some early representatives of Alexandrian, Western, and Caesarean texts but also "the divergence of reading among the added clauses likewise speaks against their originality" (Metzger, *Textual Commentary*, p. 14).

46 William O. Walker, Jr. ("Jesus and the Tax Collectors," JBL 97 [1978]: 221–38) has recently argued that passages like this and others unflattering to tax collectors suggest that Jesus did not have so warm a relationship with such men as has generally been supposed and that therefore passages supporting the latter (esp. 9:10–13; 11:19; and parallels) must not be accepted as authentic too readily. But Walker creates a false historical disjunction: either this or that, when all the evidence demands both–and. Jesus denounces all sin but befriends both tax collectors and Pharisees (see on 9:9–13).

c. *Conclusion: the demand for perfection*

5:48

⁴⁸Be perfect, therefore, as your heavenly Father is perfect.

48 Some interpret this verse as the conclusion of the last antithesis (vv.43–47; e.g., Allen, Hendriksen). In that case the perfection advocated is perfection in love. But "perfection" has far broader associations, and it is better to understand v.48 as the conclusion to the antitheses.

The word *teleios* ("perfect") usually reflects *tamim* ("perfect") in the OT. It can refer to the soundness of sacrificial animals (Exod 12:5) or to thorough commitment to the Lord and therefore uprightness (Gen 6:9; Deut 18:13; 2 Sam 22:26). The Greek word can be rendered "mature" or "full-grown" (1 Cor 14:20; Eph 4:13; Heb 5:14; 6:1). Many judge its force to be nonmoral in v.48, which becomes an exhortation to total commitment to God (e.g., Bonnard; B. Rigaux, "Révélation des Mystères et Perfection à Qumrân et dans le Nouveau Testament," NTS 4 [1957–58]: 237–62). But this makes for a fairly flat conclusion of the antitheses.

A better understanding of the verse does justice to the word *teleios* but also notes that the form of the verse is exactly like Leviticus 19:2, with "holy" displaced by "perfect," possibly due to the influence of Deuteronomy 18:13 (where NIV renders *teleios* by "blameless"; cf. Gundry, *Use of OT*, pp. 73f.). Nowhere is God directly and absolutely called "perfect" in the OT: he is perfect in knowledge (Job 37:16) or in his way (Ps 18:30), and a man's name may be "Yahweh is perfect" (so *yōtām* [Jotham], Judg 9:5; 2 Kings 15:32). But here for the first time perfection is predicated of God (cf. L. Sabourin, "Why Is God Called 'Perfect' in Mt 5, 48?" *Biblische Zeitschrift* 24 [1980]: 266–68).

In the light of the preceding verses (17–47), Jesus is saying that the true direction in which the law has always pointed is not toward mere judicial restraints, concessions arising out of the hardness of men's hearts, still less casuistical perversions, nor even to the "law of love" (contra C. Dietzfelbinger, "Die Antithesen der Bergpredigt im Verständnis des Matthäus," ZNW 70 [1979]: 1–15; cf. further on 22:34–35). No, it pointed rather to all the perfection of God, exemplified by the authoritative interpretation of the law bound up in the preceding antitheses. This perfection Jesus' disciples must emulate if they are truly followers of him who fulfills the Law and the Prophets (v.17).

The Qumran community understood perfection in terms of perfect obedience, as measured exclusively by the teachings of their community (1QS 1:8–9, 13; 2:1–2; 4:22–23; 8:9–10). Jesus has transposed this to a higher key, not by reducing the obedience, but by making the standard the perfect heavenly Father. Ronald A. Ward (*Royal Theology* [London: MMS, 1964], pp. 117–20) points out that in classical and Hellenistic usage *teleios* can have a static and a dynamic force, "the one appropriate to One Who does not develop, and the other suitable for men who can *grow* in grace" (p. 119, emphasis his): "Be perfect, therefore, as your heavenly Father is perfect."

The Gospel writers refer to God as Father only in contexts pertaining to the Messiah or to believers. He is not the Father of all men but the Father of Jesus and the Father of Jesus' disciples (cf. H.F.D. Sparks, "The Doctrine of the Fatherhood of God in the Gospels," in Nineham, *Studies*, pp. 241–62). Just as in the OT it was the distinctive mark of Israel that they were set apart for God to reflect his character (Lev 19:2; cf. 11:44–45; 20:7, 26), so the messianic community carries on this distinctiveness (cf. 1 Peter 1:16) as the true locus of the people of God (cf. France, *Jesus*, pp. 61–62). This must not encourage us to conclude that Jesus teaches that unqualified perfection is already possible for his disciples. He teaches them to acknowledge spiritual bankruptcy (v.3) and to pray "Forgive us our debts" (6:12). But the perfection of the Father, the true eschatological goal of the law, is what all disciples of Jesus pursue.

Notes

48 The future ἔσεσθε (*esesthe*, lit., "you will be") is imperatival as in Lev 19:2 (cf. on 5:21).

Many commentators compare Luke 6:36 ("Be merciful, just as your Father is merciful") and discuss which form of the saying is closer to the original. For instance, Hill (*Matthew*) notes (1) that "merciful" eminently suits Luke's context; (2) Matthew's τέλειοι (*teleioi*, "perfect") may render the Aramaic שְׁלִים (*šᵉlîm*, "perfect"), which could have been part of a pun with שְׁלָם (*šᵉlam*, "greetings") in the greetings of v.47; and (3) concludes that Matthew's version is probably more original. But a good case could be made for the position that there were two sayings:

1. Not only does Matthew have "perfect" and Luke "merciful," the verb is different in the two cases: ἔσεσθε (esesthe, "Be") and γίνεσθε, (ginesthe, "Be") respectively. Luke also omits "heavenly." In other words, the two sayings have little in common except the comparison between the believer and the Father.

2. Luke's verse indeed fits its context admirably, but so does Matthew's.

3. Matthew may have omitted any reference to mercy in his sixth beatitude because he has already dealt with the theme in v.7 (absent from Luke; and there the word for "mercy" is different).

4. The Aramaic pun is possible (though another Semitic term more commonly stands behind τέλειος [teleios, "perfect"]). Strictly speaking, however, such evidence supports the authenticity of v.48 but does not render Luke 6:36 secondary unless it is already assumed they came from the same source—which is the very point in dispute.

---

4. Religious hypocrisy: its description and overthrow (6:1–18)

a. The principle

6:1

> ¹"Be careful not to do your 'acts of righteousness' before men, to be seen by them. If you do, you will have no reward from your Father in heaven.

1 If the text behind NIV is correct (cf. Notes), Jesus, having told his disciples of the superior righteousness expected of them, now warns them of the danger of religious hypocrisy. "Your righteousness," first occurring in 5:20, recurs here, though the focus has changed from "righteousness" in a purely positive sense to "righteousness" in a formal, external sense. Modern translations try to show the distinction by various means: NIV renders the word "acts of righteousness" (in quotation marks); RSV offers "Beware of practicing your piety before men," and NEB, "Be careful not to make a show of your religion before men." Unfortunately they are overstepping the evidence.

"To do righteousness" is an expression found elsewhere (Ps 106:3; Isa 58:2; 1 John 2:29; 3:7, 10). In 1 John 2:29, for instance, it is rendered by NIV "to do what is right"; and that could suffice in Matthew 6:1 as well. Jesus is not so much dealing with a different kind of righteousness or with mere acts of righteousness as with the motives behind righteous living. To attempt to live in accord with the righteousness spelled out in the preceding verses but out of motives eager for men's applause is to prostitute that righteousness. For this there will be no reward (see on 5:12) from the heavenly Father. There is no contradiction with 5:14–16, where disciples are told to let their light shine before men so that they may see their good deeds; there the motive is for men to praise the heavenly Father. Righteous conduct under kingdom norms must be visible so that God may be glorified. Yet it must never be visible in order to win man's acclaim. Better by far to hide any righteous deed that may lead to ostentation. To trade the goal of pleasing the Father for the trivial and idolatrous goal of pleasing man will never do.

This verse introduces the three chief acts of Jewish piety (cf. vv.2–18)—almsgiving, prayer, fasting (C.G. Montefiore and H. Loewe, A Rabbinic Anthology [London: Macmillan, 1938], pp. 412–39; Moore, Judaism, 2:162–79). In each act the logical structure is the same: (1) a warning not to do the act to be praised by men, (2) a guarantee that those who ignore this warning will get what they want but no more, (3) instruction on how to perform the act of piety secretly, and (4) the assurance that the Father who sees in secret will reward openly (for details of the logical structure, cf. H.D. Betz, "Eine judenchristliche Kult-Didache in Matthäus 6:1–18," in Strecker, *Jesus Christus*, pp. 445–57).

Notes

1 Two variants are of interest.

Ἐλεημοσύνην (*eleēmosynēn*, "alms") was probably an early marginal gloss on δικαιο σύνην (*dikaiosynēn*, "righteousness"), since in the LXX "righteousness" in Hebrew was often rendered "alms." The gloss was then inserted into the text by a copyist. If "alms" were in fact original, then v.1 should be read with vv.2–4, not as the introduction to vv.2–18; and this would break the carefully wrought structure (discussed above). Moreover the external evidence strongly supports *dikaiosynēn*.

The evidence in favor of the connective δέ (*de*, "but") is evenly divided (brackets, UBS; untranslated, NIV). An adversative *de* fits the context very well and therefore may have been inserted.

On εἰ δέ μή γε (*ei de mē ge*, "otherwise," or "If you do" [NIV]), cf. Thrall, pp. 9–10.

b. *Three examples* (6:2–18)

1) *Alms*

6:2–4

2"So when you give to the needy, do not announce it with trumpets, as the hypocrites do in the synagogues and on the streets, to be honored by men. I tell you the truth, they have received their reward in full. 3But when you give to the needy, do not let your left hand know what your right hand is doing, 4so that your giving may be in secret. Then your Father, who sees what is done in secret, will reward you.

Although 6:1–6 has no parallel in the synoptic Gospels, its authenticity is supported by the numerous word plays in Aramaic reconstructions (cf. Black, *Aramaic Approach*, pp. 176–78).

2 The "you" is singular (see on 5:28). While some in Jesus' day believed almsgiving earned merit (Tobit 12:8–9; Ecclus 3:30; 29:11–12; cf. SBK in loc.), ostentation, not merit theology, is the point here. Jesus assumes his disciples will give alms: "*When* you give to the needy," he says, not "*If* you give to the needy" (cf. 10:42; 25:35–45; 2 Cor 9:6–7; Phil 4:18–19; 1 Tim 6:18–19; James 1:27). Rabbinic writers also warn against ostentation in almsgiving (cf. SBK, 1:391ff.): the frequency of the warnings attests the commonness of the practice.

The reference to trumpet announcements is difficult. Many commentators still say this refers to "the practice of blowing trumpets at the time of collecting alms in the Temple for the relief of some signal need" (Hill, *Matthew*, following Bonnard); but no Jewish sources confirm this, and the idea seems to stem only from early Christian expositors who assumed its correctness. Likewise there is no evidence (contra Calvin) that the almsgivers themselves really blew trumpets on their way to the temple. Alfred Edersheim (*The Temple: Its Ministry and Services* [London: Religious Tract Society, n.d.], p. 26), followed by Jeremias (*Jerusalem*, p. 170, n. 73), suggests this is a reference to horn-shaped collection boxes used at the temple to discourage pilfering. Lachs (*Textual Observations*, pp. 103–5), without mentioning Edersheim, has followed up on that idea by postulating a mistranslation from an underlying Semitic source. But unless the trumpet is a metaphorical caricature (like "tooting your own horn")—a poorly attested suggestion—the solution of A. Büchler ("St. Matthew vi 1–6 and Other Allied Passages," JTS 10 [1909]: 266–70) still seems best: public fasts were proclaimed by the sounding of trumpets. At such times prayers for rain were recited in the streets (cf. v.5), and it was widely thought that alms-giving insured the efficacy of the fasts and prayers (e.g., b *Sanhedrin* 35a; P. *Tannith* 2:6; *Leviticus* R 34:14). But these occasions afforded golden opportunities for ostentation.

Lachs objects that this interpretation makes the givers pompous but not hypocrites. In older Greek a *hypokritēs* ("hypocrite") was an actor, but by the first century the term came to be used for those who play roles and see the world as their stage. What Lachs overlooks is that there are different kinds of hypocrisy. In one the hypocrite feigns goodness but is actually evil and knows he is being deceptive (e.g., 22:15–18). In another the hypocrite is carried away by his own acting and deceives himself. Such pious hypocrites (as in 7:1–5), though unaware of their own deceit, do not fool most onlookers; and this *may* be the meaning here. A third kind of hypocrite deceives himself into thinking he is acting for the best interests of God and man and also deceives onlookers. The needy are unlikely to complain when they receive large gifts, and their gratitude may flatter and thus bolster the giver's self-delusion (cf. D.A. Spieler, "Hypocrisy: An Exploration of a Third Type," *Andrews University Seminary Studies* 13 [1975]: 273–79). Perhaps it is best to identify the hypocrisy in 6:2 with this third type.

The Pharisees' great weakness was that they loved men's praise more than God's praise (cf. John 5:44; 12:43). Those who give out of this attitude receive their reward in full (such is the force of *apechousin;* cf. Deiss LAE, pp. 110–11). They win human plaudits, and that is all they get (cf. Ps 17:14).

3–4 The way to avoid hypocrisy is not to cease giving but to do so with such secrecy that we scarcely know what we have given. Jesus' disciples must themselves be so given to God (cf. 2 Cor 8:5) that their giving is prompted by obeying God and having compassion on men. Then their Father, who sees what is done in secret (Heb 4:13), will reward them. The verb "to reward" (*apodidomai*), with God as subject, here and in vv.6, 18, is different from that used in v.2. Bonnard rightly notes it has a sense of "pay back," and this is compatible with "reward" (see on 5:12). "Openly" (KJV), here and in vv.6, 18, is a late gloss designed to complete the antithetic parallelism with "secretly" or "in secret." Jesus does not discuss the locale and nature of the reward; but we will not be far from the NT evidence if we understand it to be "both in time and in eternity, both in character and in felicity" (Broadus).

2) *Prayer* (6:5–15)

a) *Ostentatious prayer*

6:5–6

> [5]"And when you pray, do not be like the hypocrites, for they love to pray stand-ing in the synagogues and on the street corners to be seen by men. I tell you the truth, they have received their reward in full. [6]But when you pray, go into your room, close the door and pray to your Father, who is unseen. Then your Father, who sees what is done in secret, will reward you.

5 Again Jesus assumes that his disciples will pray, but he forbids the prayers of "hypocrites" (see on v.2). Prayer had a prominent place in Jewish life and led to countless rabbinic decisions (cf. M *Berakoth*). In synagogue worship someone from the congregation might be asked to pray publicly, standing in front of the ark. And at certain times prayers could be offered in the streets (M *Taanith* 2:1–2; see on v.2). But the location was not the critical factor. Neither is the "standing" posture in itself significant. In the Bible people pray prostrate (Num 16:22; Josh 5:14; Dan 8:17; Matt 26:39; Rev 11:16), kneeling (2 Chron 6:13; Dan 6:10; Luke 22:41; Acts 7:60; 9:40; 20:36; 21:5), sitting (2 Sam 7:18), and standing (1 Sam 1:26; Mark 11:25; Luke 18:11, 13). Again it is the motive that is crucial: "to be seen by men." And again there is the same reward (cf. v.2 and v.5).

6 If Jesus were forbidding all public prayer, then clearly the early church did not understand him (e.g., 18:19–20; Acts 1:24; 3:1; 4:24–30). The public versus private antithesis is a good test of one's motives; the person who prays more in public than in private reveals that he is less interested in God's approval than in human praise. Not piety but a reputation for piety is his concern. Far better to deal radically with this hypocrisy (cf. 5:29–30) and pray in a private "room"; the word *tameion* can refer to a storeroom (Luke 12:24), some other inner room (Matt 12:26; 24:26; Luke 12:3, 24), or even a bedroom (Isa 26:20 LXX, with which this verse has several common elements; cf. also 2 Kings 4:33). The Father, who sees in secret, will reward the disciple who prays in secret (see on v.4).

Notes

5 UBS and Nestle follow the plural reading, Nestle-Kilpatrick the singular. The former is marginally more probable on external grounds, and many argue that corruption to the singular occurred because of assimilation to the singular in v.4 and v.6. But copyists might equally have noted the recurring pattern of plural to singular changes in these verses (v.1—vv.2–4; v.16—vv.17–18). See on 5:23.

The use of the future οὐκ ἔσεσθε (*ouk esesthe*, "do not be") with imperatival force usually reflects legal language from the OT (BDF, par. 362). But here and in 20:26 it is found in words ascribed to Jesus with no unambiguous OT precedent (Zerwick, par. 443).

On the idiom φιλοῦσιν . . . προσεύχεσθαι (*philousin . . . proseuchesthai*, "they love . . . to pray"), cf. Turner, *Syntax*, p. 226.

b) *Repetitious prayer*

6:7–8

> ⁷And when you pray, do not keep on babbling like pagans, for they think they will be heard because of their many words. ⁸Do not be like them, for your Father knows what you need before you ask him.

7–8 Matthew 6:7–15 digresses from the three chief acts of Jewish piety. Yet the content of these verses is certainly relevant to the second of these, which is prayer. Prayer is central to a believer's life. So Jesus gives further warnings and a positive example.

Many argue that whereas vv.5–6 warn against the prayer practices of Jews, vv.7–8 warn against those of Gentiles (pagans; see on 5:47), partly because the parallel in Luke 11:2 (MS D) has "the rest of men." But the distinction is not quite so cut and dried. Every religious group harbors some who pray repetitiously. So with the Jews of Jesus' day. He labeled all such praying—even that of his own people—as pagan! "Pagans" (cf. 1 Kings 18:26) are not so much the target as the negative example of all who pray repetitiously.

The verb *battalogeō* ("keep on babbling") is very rare, apart from writings dependent on the NT (BAGD, p. 137b). It may derive from the Aramaic *baṭṭal* ("idle," "useless") or some other Semitic word; or it may be onomatopoetic: if so, "babble" is a fine English equivalent. Jesus is not condemning prayer any more than he is condemning almsgiving (v.2) or fasting (v.16). Nor is he forbidding all long prayers or all repetition. He himself prayed at length (Luke 6:12), repeated himself in prayer (Matt 26:44; unlike Ecclus 7:14!), and told a parable to show his disciples that "they should always pray and not give up" (Luke 18:1). His point is that his disciples should avoid meaningless, repetitive prayers offered under the misconception that mere length will make prayers efficacious. Such thoughtless babble can occur in liturgical and extemporaneous prayers alike. Essentially it is thoroughly pagan, for pagan gods allegedly thrive on incantation and repetition. But the personal Father God to whom believers pray does not require information about our needs (v.8). "As a father knows the needs of his family, yet teaches them to ask in confidence and trust, so does God treat his children" (Hill, *Matthew*).

c) *Model prayer*

6:9–13

> ⁹"This, then, is how you should pray:
>
>> " 'Our Father in heaven,
>> hallowed be your name,
>> ¹⁰your kingdom come,
>> your will be done
>> on earth as it is in heaven.
>> ¹¹Give us today our daily bread.
>> ¹²Forgive us our debts,
>> as we also have forgiven our debtors.
>> ¹³And lead us not into temptation,
>> but deliver us from the evil one.'

"The Lord's Prayer," as it is commonly called, is not so much his own prayer

(John 17 is just that) as the model he gave his disciples. Much of the literature has focused on the complex question of the relation between 6:9–13 and Luke 11:2–4. The newer EVs reveal the many differences. KJV does not show the differences so clearly because it preserves the numerous assimilations to Matthew in late MSS of Luke (cf. Metzger, *Textual Commentary*, pp. 154–56). Various theories attempt to account for the differences.

1. Formerly some argued that Matthew's form is the original and Luke's a simplified version of it. This view is no longer popular, largely because of the difficulty of believing that Luke, who was highly interested in Jesus' prayer life, would omit words and clauses from one of his prayers if they were already in a source.

2. Others have argued strongly that Luke's account is original and that Matthew has added to it according to his own theology and linguistic habit (so Jeremias, *Prayers*, pp. 85ff., and Hill). Several reasons for this theory follow.

a) All Luke's content is found in Matthew 6:9–13. But this could support condensation by Luke as easily as expansion by Matthew. More important, mere expansion-condensation theories do not account for the linguistic differences (e.g., tense in the fourth petition, vocabulary and tense in the fifth); and the theory is further weakened when it is argued (e.g., by Hill, *Matthew*) that in the fourth petition the priorities are reversed and Matthew's form is probably more original than Luke's.

b) Matthew's more rhythmical, liturgical formulation may reflect the desire to construct an ecclesiastical equivalent, for Jewish Christians, of the synagogue's main prayer, the *Eighteen Benedictions* (Davies, *Setting*, pp. 310ff.), to which the Lord's Prayer structurally and formally corresponds. But these correspondences have been greatly exaggerated. They are no closer than those found in fine extemporaneous prayers prayed in evangelical churches every Wednesday night (on the differences, cf. Bornkamm, *Jesus*, pp. 136f.). Moreover, Jesus was far removed from innovation for its own sake. Why should he not have expressed himself in current forms of piety?

c) Hill (*Matthew*) argues that the Matthean introduction (v.9) suggests that the prayer is a standardized liturgical form. On the contrary, the text reads "this is *how* [houtōs] you should pray," not "this is *what* you should pray." The emphasis is on paradigm or model, not liturgical form.

d) Hill (*Matthew*) also argues that the emphatic "you" (v.9) "sets off the new Christian community from the synagogue (and Gentile usage) whose piety is being contrasted with Christian worship in the surrounding context." But not only is this needlessly anachronistic, it also ignores the constant stress on "you" designating Jesus' disciples as the exclusive messianic community in Jesus' day (see on 6:2).

3. Ernst Lohmeyer (*The Lord's Prayer* [London: Collins, 1965], p. 293) argues that the two prayers do not spring from one source (Q?) but from two separate traditions. In Matthew the prayer reflects the liturgical tradition of the Galilean Christian community and emphasizes a certain eschatological outlook, whereas in Luke the prayer reflects the liturgical tradition of the Jerusalem church and focuses more on daily life. He refuses to be drawn out on what stands behind these two traditions. Lohmeyer's geographical speculations are not convincing, but his emphasis on two separate traditions of the Lord's Prayer is worth careful consideration. Evidence from the *Didache* and the demonstrable tendency for local churches to think of themselves as Christian synagogues (e.g., in the letters of Ignatius) and to adopt some synagogal liturgical patterns combine to suggest that the Lord's Prayer was used in corporate worship from a very early date. If (and this is a big "if") such

167

church liturgies stretch back to the time when Matthew and Luke were written, it seems unlikely that the evangelists would disregard the liturgical habits of their own communities, unless for overwhelming historical or theological reasons (e.g., correction of heresy within the accepted liturgy). But none such is evident. This reinforces the theory of two separate liturgical traditions. On the other hand, if fixed liturgical patterns had not yet included any form of the Lord's Prayer by the time the evangelists wrote, the differences between the two are not easily explained by a common source.

4. These complexities have generated several mediating theories. To give but one, Marshall (*Luke*, p. 455) suggests that Luke either drew his form of the prayer from Q or from a recension of Q different from that of Matthew, whereas Matthew drew his either from separate tradition and substituted it for what he found in Q (if his recension of Q was the same as Luke's) or else from a separate recension. This is little more than an elegant way of saying that Lohmeyer's two-traditions theory is basically correct. It may be too elegant: many suspect that Q is not a single document (Introduction, section 3), and to speak thus of recensions of Q when our knowledge of Q is so uncertain makes one wonder how to distinguish methodologically between recensions of Q and entirely separate accounts of two historical occasions within Jesus' ministry. Resolving the unknown by appealing to the more unknown is of dubious merit.

5. Though the evidence for two traditions is strong, equally significant is the fact that there are two entirely different historical settings of the prayer. Unless one is prepared to say that one or the other is made up, the reasonable explanation is that Jesus taught this sort of prayer often during his itinerant ministry and that Matthew records one occasion and Luke another. Matthew's setting is not so historically specific as that of Luke only if one interprets the introduction and the conclusion of the entire discourse loosely or if one postulates Matthew's freedom to add "footnotes" to the material he provides (see prefatory remarks for 5:1–7:29). The former is exegetically doubtful, the latter without convincing literary controls; and even in these instances the evidence for two separate traditions for the Lord's Prayer is so strong that the simplest comprehensive explanation is that Jesus himself taught this form of prayer on more than one occasion.

Few have doubted that the prayer is in some form authentic. Goulder (pp. 296–301) argues that Matthew composed it from fragments, most of which were authentic but uttered on other and separate occasions, and that Luke copied and adapted Matthew's work. His theory is unconvincing because it does no more than show parallels between elements of this prayer and other things Jesus said or prayed. The same evidence could equally be read as supporting the prayer's authenticity. It is well worth noting that there is no anachronism in the prayer—no mention of Jesus as high priestly Mediator, no allusion to themes developed only after the Resurrection.

There are signs of Semitic background, whether Aramaic (e.g., Black, *Aramaic Approach*, pp. 203–8) or Hebrew (Carmignac, pp. 29–52). Scholars debate whether Matthew's version has six petitions (Chrysostom, Calvin, and Reformed theologians) or seven, interpreting v.13 as two (Augustine, Luther, most Lutheran theologians). The issue affects the meaning but little. More important, as Bengel remarks, is the division of the petitions: the first three are cast in terms of God's glory ("your . . . your . . . your"); the others in terms of our good ("us . . . us . . . us").

9 By contrast with ostentatious prayer (vv.5–6) or thoughtless prayer (vv.7–8), Jesus gives his disciples a model. But it is only a model: "This is how [not what] you should pray."

The fatherhood of God is not a central theme in the OT. Where "father" does occur with respect to God, it is commonly by way of analogy, not direct address (Deut 32:6; Ps 103:13; Isa 63:16; Mal 2:10). One can also find occasional references to God as father in the Apocrypha and pseudepigrapha (Tobit 13:4; Ecclus 23:1; 51:10; Wisd Sol 2:16; 14:3; Jub 1:24–25, 28; T Levi 18:6; T Judah 24:2—though some of these may be Christian interpolations). There is but one instance in the DSS (1QS 9:35); the assorted rabbinic references are relatively rare and few unambiguously antedate Jesus (b. *Taanith* 25b; the fifth and sixth petitions of the *Eighteen Benedictions*). Pagans likewise on occasion addressed their gods as father: e.g., *Zeu pater* ("Zeus, Father"; Lat. *Jupiter*). But not till Jesus is it characteristic to address God as "Father" (Jeremias, *Prayers*, pp. 11ff.). This can only be understood against the background of customary patterns for addressing God.

The overwhelming tendency in Jewish circles was to multiply titles ascribing sovereignty, lordship, glory, grace, and the like to God (cf. Carson, *Divine Sovereignty*, pp. 45ff.). Against such a background, Jesus' habit of addressing God as his own Father (Mark 14:36) and teaching his disciples to do the same could only appear familiar and presumptuous to opponents, personal and gracious to followers. Unfortunately, many modern Christians find it very difficult to delight in the privilege of addressing the Sovereign of the universe as "Father" because they have lost the heritage that emphasizes God's transcendence.

Jesus' use of *Abba* ("Father" or "my Father"; Mark 14:36; cf. Matt 11:25; 26:39, 42; Luke 23:34; John 11:41; 12:27; 17:1–26) was adopted by early Christians (Rom 8:15; Gal 4:6); and there is no evidence of anyone before Jesus using this term to address God (cf. DNTT, 1:614–15). Throughout the prayer the reference is plural: "Our Father" (which in Aram. would have been *'abînû*, not *'abba*). In other words this is an example of a prayer to be prayed in fellowship with other disciples (cf. 18:19), not in isolation (cf. John 20:17). Very striking is Jesus' use of pronouns with "Father." When forgiveness of sins is discussed, Jesus speaks of "your Father" (6: 14–15) and excludes himself. When he speaks of his unique sonship and authority, he speaks of "my Father" (e.g., 11:27) and exludes others. The "our Father" at the beginning of this model prayer is plural but does not include Jesus, since it is part of his instruction regarding what his disciples should pray.

This opening designation establishes the kind of God to whom prayer is offered: He is personal (no mere "ground of being") and caring (a Father, not a tyrant or an ogre, but the one who establishes the real nature of fatherhood; cf. Eph 3:14–15). That he is "our Father" establishes the relationship that exists between Jesus' disciples and God. In this sense he is not the Father of all men indiscriminately (see on 5:45). The early church was right to forbid non-Christians from reciting this prayer as vigorously as they forbade them from joining with believers at the Lord's Table. But that he is "our Father in heaven" (the designation occurs twenty times in Matthew, once in Mark [11:25], never in Luke, and in some instances may be a Matthean formulation) reminds us of his transcendence and sovereignty, while preparing us for v.10b. The entire formula is less concerned with the proper protocol in approaching Deity than with the truth of who he is, to establish within the believer the right frame of mind (Stott, p. 146).

God's "name" is a reflection of who he is (cf. DNTT, 2:648ff.). God's "name" is God himself as he is and has revealed himself, and so his name is already holy. Holiness, often thought of as "separateness," is less an attribute than what he is. It has to do with the very godhood of God. Therefore to pray that God's "name" be "hallowed" (the verbal form of "holy," recurring in Matt only at 23:17, 19 [NIV, "makes sacred"]) is not to pray that God may become holy but that he may be treated as holy (cf. Exod 20:8; Lev 19:2, 32; Ezek 36:23; 1 Peter 1:15), that his name should not be despised (Mal 1:6) by the thoughts and conduct of those who have been created in his image.

10 As God is eternally holy, so he eternally reigns in absolute sovereignty. Yet it is appropriate to pray not only "hallowed be your name" but also "your kingdom come." God's "kingdom" or "reign," as we have seen (see on 3:2; 4:17, 23), can refer to that aspect of God's sovereignty under which there is life. That kingdom is breaking in under Christ's ministry, but it is not consummated till the end of the age (28:20). To pray "your kingdom come" is therefore simultaneously to ask that God's saving, royal rule be extended now as people bow in submission to him and already taste the eschatological blessing of salvation and to cry for the consummation of the kingdom (cf. 1 Cor 16:22; Rev 11:17; 22:20). Godly Jews were waiting for the kingdom (Mark 15:43), "the consolation of Israel" (Luke 2:25). They recited "Qaddish" ("Sanctification"), an ancient Aramaic prayer, at the close of each synagogue service. In its oldest extant form, it runs, "Exalted and *hallowed* be his great name in the world which he created according to his will. *May he let his kingdom rule* in your lifetime and in your days and in the lifetime of the whole house of Israel, speedily and soon. And to this, say: amen" (Jeremias, *Prayers,* p. 98, emphasis his). But the Jew looked forward to the kingdom, whereas the reader of Matthew's Gospel, while looking forward to its consummation, perceives that the kingdom has already broken in and prays for its extension as well as for its unqualified manifestation.

To pray that God's will, which is "good, pleasing and perfect" (Rom 12:2), be done on earth as in heaven is to use language broad enough to embrace three requests.

1. The first request is that God's will be done now on earth as it is now accomplished in heaven. The word *thelēma* ("will") includes both God's righteous demands (7:21; 12:50; cf. Ps 40:8) and his determination to bring about certain events in salvation history (18:14; 26:42; cf. Acts 21:14). So for that will to be "done" includes both moral obedience and the bringing to pass of certain events, such as the Cross. This prayer corresponds to asking for the present extension of the messianic kingdom.

2. The second request is that God's will may ultimately be as *fully accomplished* on earth as it is now accomplished in heaven. "Will" has the same range of meanings as before; and this prayer corresponds to asking for the consummation of the messianic kingdom.

3. The third request is that God's will may ultimately be done on the earth *in the same way* as it is now accomplished in heaven. In the consummated kingdom it will not be necessary to discuss superior righteousness (5:20–48) as antithetical to lust, hate, retaliatory face-slapping, divorce, and the like; for then God's will, construed now as his demands for righteousness, will be done as it is now done in heaven: freely, openly, spontaneously, and without the need to set it over against evil (Carson, *Sermon on the Mount,* pp. 66f.).

These first three petitions, though they focus on God's name, God's kingdom, and

God's will, are nevertheless prayers that he may act in such a way that his people will hallow his name, submit to his reign, and do his will. It is therefore impossible to pray this prayer in sincerity without humbly committing oneself to such a course.

11 The last petitions explicitly request things for ourselves. The first is "bread," a term used to cover all food (cf. Prov 30:8; Mark 3:20; Acts 6:1; 2 Thess 3:12; James 2:15). Many early fathers thought it inappropriate to talk about physical food here and interpreted "bread" as a reference to the Lord's Supper or to the Word of God. This depended in part on Jerome's Latin rendering of *epiousios* ("daily," NIV) as *superstantialem:* Give us today our "supersubstantial" bread—a rendering that may have depended in part on the influence of Marius Victorinus (cf. F.F. Bruce, "The Gospel Text of Marius Victorinus," in Best and Wilson, p. 70). There is no linguistic justification for this translation. The bread is real food, and it may further suggest all that we need in the physical realm (Luther).

That does not mean that *epiousios* ("daily") is easy to translate. The term appears only here and in Luke's prayer (11:3); and the two possible extrabiblical references, which could support "daily," have had grave doubt cast on them by B.M. Metzger ("How Many Times Does ἐπιούσιος Occur Outside the Lord's Prayer?" Exp 69 [1957–58]: 52–54). P. Grelot has recently attempted to support the same translation ("daily") by reconstructing an Aramaic original ("La quatrième demande du 'Pater' et son arrièreplan sémitique," NTS 25 [1978–79]: 299–314). But his article deals inadequately with the Greek text, and other Aramaic reconstructions are possible (e.g., Black, *Aramaic Approach,* pp. 203–7).

The prayer is for our needs, not our greeds. It is for one day at a time ("today"), reflecting the precarious lifestyle of many first-century workers who were paid one day at a time and for whom a few days' illness could spell tragedy. Many have suggested a derivation from *epi tēn ousan* [viz., *hēmeran*] ("for today") or *hē epiousa hēmera* ("for the coming day"), referring in the morning to the same day and at night to the next. This meaning is almost certainly right; but it is better supported by deriving the word from the fem. participle *epiousa,* already well established, with the sense of "immediately following," by the time the NT was written (cf. the forthcoming article by C.J. Hemer in JSNT). Whatever the etymological problems, this makes sense of Luke 11:3, where "each day" is part of the text: "Give us each day our bread for the coming day." Equally it makes sense in Matthew, where "today" displaces "each day": "Give us today our bread for the coming day." This may sound redundant to Western readers, but it is a precious and urgent petition to those who live from hand to mouth.

Some derive *epiousios* ("daily") from the verb *epienai,* referring not to the future, still less to the food of the messianic banquet (contra Jeremias, *Prayers,* pp. 100–102), but to the bread that belongs to it, i.e., that is necessary and sufficient for it (cf. R. Ten Kate, "Geef ons heden ons 'dagelijks' brood," *Nederlands Theologisch Tijdschrift* 32 [1978]: 125–39; with similar conclusions but by a different route, H. Bourgoin, "Ἐπιούσιος expliqué par la notion de préfixe vide," *Biblica* 60 [1979]: 91–96; and for literature, BAGD, pp. 296–97; Gundry, *Use of OT,* pp. 74–75). This has the considerable merit of meshing well with both "today" and "each day" (Matthew and Luke respectively), and in Matthew's case it may be loosely rendered "Give us today the food we need." But the derivation is linguistically artificial (cf. C.J. Hemer).

The idea of God "giving" the food in no way diminishes responsibility to work (see further on vv. 25–34) but presupposes not only that Jesus' disciples live one day at a time (cf. v. 34) but that all good things, even our ability to work and earn our food, come from God's hand (cf. Deut 8:18; 1 Cor 4:7; James 1:17). It is a lesson easily forgotten when wealth multiplies and absolute self-sufficiency is portrayed as a virtue.

12 The first three petitions stand independently from one another. The last three, however, are linked in Greek by "ands," almost as if to say that life sustained by food is not enough. We also need forgiveness of sin and deliverance from temptation.

In Matthew what we ask to be forgiven for is *ta opheilēmata hēmōn* ("our debts"); in Luke, it is our "sins." Hill (*Matthew*) notes that the crucial word *to opheilēma* ("debt") "means a literal 'debt' in the LXX and *NT*, except at this point." And on this basis S. T. Lachs ("On Matthew vi. 12," NovTest 17 [1975]: 6–8) argues that in Matthew this petition of the Lord's Prayer is not really dealing with sins but with loans in the sixth year, one year before the Jubilee. But the linguistic evidence can be read differently. The word *opheilēma* is rather rare in biblical Greek. It occurs only four times in the LXX (Deut 24:10 [*bis*]; 1 Esd 3:20; 1 Macc 15:8); and in Deuteronomy 24:10, where it occurs twice, it renders two different Hebrew words. In the NT it appears only here and in Romans 4:4. On this basis it would be as accurate to say the word always means "sin" in the NT except at Romans 4:4, as to say it always means "debt" except at Matthew 6:12.

More important, the Aramaic word *ḥôḇā* ("debt") is often used (e.g., in the Targums) to mean "sin" or "transgression." Deiss BS (p. 225) notes an instance of the cognate verb *hamartian opheilō* (lit., "I owe sin"). Probably Matthew has provided a literal rendering of the Aramaic Jesus probably most commonly used in preaching; and even Luke (11:4) uses the cognate participle in the second line, *panti opheilonti hēmin* ("everyone who sins against us"). There is therefore no reason to take "debts" to mean anything other than "sins," here conceived as something owed God (whether sins of commission or of omission).

Some have taken the second clause to mean that our forgiveness is the real cause of God's forgiveness, i.e., that God's forgiveness must be earned by our own. The problem is often judged more serious in Matthew than Luke, because the latter has the present "we forgive," the former the aorist (not perfect, as many commentators assume) *aphēkamen* ("we have forgiven"). Many follow the suggestion of Jeremias (*Prayers*, pp. 92–93), who says that Matthew has awkwardly rendered an Aramaic *perfectum praesens* (a "present perfect"): he renders the clause "as we also herewith forgive our debtors."

The real solution is best expounded by C. F. D. Moule ("'. . . As we forgive . . .': a Note on the Distinction between Deserts and Capacity in the Understanding of Forgiveness," *Donum Gentilicium*, edd. E. Bammel et al. [Oxford: Clarendon, 1978], pp. 68–77), who, in addition to detailing the most important relevant Jewish literature, rightly insists on distinguishing "between, on the one hand, earning or meriting forgiveness, and, on the other hand, adopting an attitude which makes forgiveness possible—the distinction, that is, between deserts and capacity. . . . Real repentance, as contrasted with a merely self-regarding remorse, is certainly a *sine qua non* of receiving forgiveness—an indispensable condition" (pp. 71–72). "Once our eyes have been opened to see the enormity of our offence against God, the injuries which others have done to us appear by comparison extremely trifling.

If, on the other hand, we have an exaggerated view of the offences of others, it proves that we have minimized our own" (Stott, pp. 149-50; see on 5:5, 7; 18: 23-35).

13 The word *peirasmos* ("temptation") and its cognate noun rarely if ever before the NT mean "temptation" in the sense of "enticement to sin" (whether from inward lust or outward circumstances) but rather "testing" (cf. also on 4:1-12). But testing can have various purposes (e.g., refinement, ascertaining the strength of character, enticement to sin) and diverse results (greater purity, self-confidence, growth in faith, sin); and as a result the word can slide over into the entirely negative sense of "temptation." See comments on the cognate verb in 4:1. The word sustains the unambiguous meaning in James 1:13-14, which assures us that "God cannot be tempted by evil, nor does he tempt anyone [i.e., with evil]" (cf. also Matt 4:1, 3; 1 Cor 7:5; 1 Thess 3:5; Rev 2:10). In this light *peirasmos* cannot easily mean "temptation" in Matthew 6:13; for that would be to pray God would not do what in fact he cannot do, akin to praying that God would not sin.

But if *peirasmos* in v.13 means "testing," we face another problem. The NT everywhere insists that believers will face testings or trials of many kinds but that they should be faced with joy (James 1:2; cf. 1 Cor 10:13). If this be so, to pray for grace and endurance in trial is understandable; but to pray not to be brought to testings is strange. For detailed probing of the problem and interaction with the sources, see C.F.D. Moule, "An Unsolved Problem in the Temptation-Clause in the Lord's Prayer," *Reformed Theological Review* 33 (1974): 65-75.

Some have argued that the testing is the eschatological tribulation, the period of messianic woes (e.g., Jeremias, *Prayers*, pp. 104-7) characterized by apostasy. The petition becomes a plea to be secured from that final apostasy and is reflected in NEB's "do not bring us to the test." But not only is *peirasmos* ("temptation") never used for this tribulation unless carefully qualified (and therefore Rev 3:10 is no exception, regardless of its interpretation), but one would at least expect to find the article in the Matthean clause. Carmignac (pp. 396, 445) so reconstructs the alleged Hebrew original that he distinguishes "*to* testing" from "*into* testing," interpreting the latter to mean actually succumbing. The prayer then asks to be spared, not from testing, but from failing. Unfortunately his linguistic arguments are not convincing.

Many cite b *Berakoth* 60b as a parallel: "Bring me not into sin, or into iniquity, or into temptation, or into contempt." It is possible that the causative form of the Lord's Prayer is, similarly, not meant to be unmediated but has a permissive nuance: "Let us not be brought into temptation [i.e., by the devil]." This interpretation is greatly strengthened if the word "temptation" can be taken to mean "trial or temptation that results in fall"; and this appears to be required in two NT passages (Mark 14:38; Gal 6:1; cf. J.V. Dahms, "Lead Us Not Into Temptation," JETS 17 [1974]: 229). It also may be that we are forcing this sixth petition into too rigid a mold. The NT tells us that this age will be characterized by wars and rumors of wars (see on 24:6) but does not find it incongruous to urge us to pray for those in authority so "that we may live peaceful and quiet lives" (1 Tim 2:2). While Jesus told his disciples to rejoice when persecuted (5:10-12) he nevertheless exhorted them to flee from it (10:23) and even to pray that their flight should not be too severe (24:20). Similarly, a prayer requesting to be spared testings may not be incongruous when placed beside exhortations to consider such testings, when they come, as pure joy.

"Deliver us" could mean either, on the one hand, "spare us from," "preserve us against" or, on the other hand, "deliver us out of," "save us from" (BAGD, p. 737, s.v. *rhyomai*). Both are spiritually relevant, and which way the verb is taken largely depends on how the preceding clause is understood. The words *tou ponērou* ("the evil one") could be either neuter ("evil"; cf. Luke 6:45; Rom 12:9; 1 Thess 5:22) or masculine ("the evil one," referring to Satan: 13:19, 38; Eph 6:16; 1 John 2:13-14; 3:12; 5:19). In some cases the Greek does not distinguish the gender (see on 5:37). However, a reference to Satan is far more likely here for two reasons: (1) "deliver us" can take either the preposition *ek* ("from") or *apo* ("from"), the former always introducing things from which to be delivered, the latter being used predominantly of persons (cf. J.-B. Bauer, "Libera nos a malo," *Verbum Domini* 34 [1965]: 12-15; Zerwick, par. 89); and (2) Matthew's first mention of temptation (4:1-11) is unambiguously connected with the Devil. Thus the Lord's model prayer ends with a petition that, while implicitly recognizing our own helplessness before the Devil whom Jesus alone could vanquish (4:1-11), delights to trust the heavenly Father for deliverance from the Devil's strength and wiles.

The doxology—"for yours is the kingdom and the power and the glory forever. Amen"—is found in various forms in many MSS. The diversity of what parts are attested is itself suspicious (for full discussion, cf. Metzger, *Textual Commentary*, pp. 16-17; cf. Hendriksen, pp. 337f.); and the MS evidence is overwhelmingly in favor of omission—a point conceded by Davies (*Setting*, pp. 451-53), whose liturgical arguments for inclusion are not convincing. The doxology itself, of course, is theologically profound and contextually suitable and was no doubt judged especially suitable by those who saw in the last three petitions a veiled allusion to the Trinity: the Father's creation and providence provides our bread, the Son's atonement secures our forgiveness, and the Spirit's indwelling power assures our safety and triumph. But "surely it is more important to know what the Bible really contains and really means, than to cling to something not really in the Bible, merely because it gratifies our taste, or even because it has for us some precious associations" (Broadus).

Notes

11 Matthew's aorist δὸς ἡμῖν σήμερον (*dos hēmin sēmeron*, "give us today") and Luke's (11:3) present δίδου ἡμῖν τὸ καθ᾽ ἡμέραν (*didou hēmin to kath᾽ hēmeran*, "give us each day") are both contextually appropriate.
12 KJV has the present "we forgive" in both Matthew and Luke and is widely supported. The aorist is attested by ℵ* B Z 1 22 124mg 1365 1582, five MSS of the Latin Vulgate, and several MSS of the Syriac and Coptic versions. This represents a fair spread of text type. But the convincing arguments are the likelihood of assimilation to Luke and the converse implausibility of a copyist changing the present to an aorist.

d) *Forgiveness and prayer*

6:14-15

14For if you forgive men when they sin against you, your heavenly Father will also forgive you. 15But if you do not forgive men their sins, your Father will not forgive your sins.

14–15 These verses reinforce the thought of the fifth petition (see on v.12). The repetition serves to stress the deep importance for the community of disciples to be a forgiving community if its prayers are to be effective (cf. Ps 66:18). The thought is repeated elsewhere (18:23–35; Mark 11:25). (On the possible literary relation with Mark 11:25, see Lane, pp. 410–11.)

3) Fasting

6:16–18

> [16]"When you fast, do not look somber as the hypocrites do, for they disfigure their faces to show men they are fasting. I tell you the truth, they have received their reward in full. [17]But when you fast, put oil on your head and wash your face, [18]so that it will not be obvious to men that you are fasting, but only to your Father, who is unseen; and your Father, who sees what is done in secret, will reward you.

16 Under Mosaic legislation, fasting was commanded only on the Day of Atonement (Lev 16:29–31; 23:27–32; Num 29:7); but during the Exile regular fasts of remembrance were instituted (Zech 7:3–5; 8:19). In addition to these national fasts, both OT and NT describe personal or group fasts with a variety of purposes, especially to indicate and foster self-humiliation before God, often in connection with the confession of sins (e.g., Neh 9:1–2; Ps 35:13; Isa 58:3, 5; Dan 9:2–20; 10:2–3; Jonah 3:5; Acts 9:9) or to lay some special petition before the Lord, sometimes out of anguish, danger, or desperation (Exod 24:18; Judg 20:26; 2 Sam 1:12; 2 Chron 20:3; Ezra 8:21–23; Esth 4:16; Matt 4:1–2; Acts 13:1–3; 14:23). It may belong to the realm of normal Christian self-discipline (1 Cor 9:24–27; cf. Phil 3:19; 1 Peter 4:3); but already in the OT it is bitterly excoriated when it is purely formal and largely hypocritical (Isa 58:3–7; Jer 14:12; Zech 7:5–6)—when, for instance, men fasted but did not share their food with the hungry (Isa 58:1–7).

In Jesus' day the Pharisees fasted twice a week (Luke 18:12; cf. SBK, 2:242ff.), probably Monday and Thursday (M *Taanith* 1:4–7). Some devout people, like Anna, fasted often (Luke 2:37). But such voluntary fasts provided marvelous opportunities for religious showmanship to gain a reputation for piety. One could adopt an air that was "somber" (or "downcast," Luke 24:17, the only other place in the NT where the word *skythrōpos* is used) and disfigure oneself, perhaps by not washing and shaving, by sprinkling ashes on one's head to signify deep contrition or self-abnegation, or by omitting normal use of oil to signify deep distress (cf. 2 Sam 14:2; Dan 10:3). The point is not that there was no genuine contrition but that these hypocrites were purposely drawing attention to themselves. They wanted the plaudits of men and got them. And that's all they got.

17–18 Yet Jesus, far from banning fasting, assumes his disciples will fast, even as he assumes they will give alms and pray (vv.3, 6). His disciples may not fast at the moment, for the messianic bridegroom is with them; and it is the time for joy (9:14–17). But the time will come when they will fast (9:15). (Observe in passing that here Jesus assumes the continued existence of his disciples after his departure.) What he condemns is ostentation in fasting. Moreover he forbids any sign at all that a fast has been undertaken, because the human heart is so mixed in its motives that the desire to seek God will be diluted by the desire for human praise, thus vitiating the fast.

Washing and anointing with oil (v.17) were merely normal steps in hygiene. Oil does not here symbolize extravagant joy but normal body care (cf. Ruth 3:3; 2 Sam 12:20; Pss 23:5; 104:15; 133:2; Eccl 9:8; Luke 7:46; cf. DNTT, 1:120). The point of v.18 is not to draw attention to oneself, whether by somber mien or extravagant joy. Jesus desires reticence, not deception. And the Father, who sees in secret, will provide the reward (see on v.4).

The three principal acts of Jewish piety (vv.1–18) are only examples of many practices susceptible of religious hypocrisy. Early in the second century, the Christian document *Didache*, while polemicizing against the Monday and Thursday "fasts of the hypocrites," enjoins Christians to fast on Wednesday and Friday (8:1). Christian copyists added "fasting" glosses at several points in the NT (Matt 17:21; Mark 9:29; Acts 10:30; 1 Cor 7:5). Hypocrisy is not the sole preserve of Pharisees. The solution is not to abolish fasting (cf. Alexander's remark that mortification of the flesh "can be better attained by habitual temperance than by occasional abstinence") but to set it within a biblical framework (references on v.16) and sincerely to covet God's blessing. For if the form of vv.1–18 is negative, the point is positive—viz., to seek first God's kingdom and righteousness (cf. v.33).

5. *Kingdom perspectives* (6:19–34)

Many argue that these verses are made up of four blocks of material that originally had independent settings: (1) Matthew 6:19–21 = Luke 12:33–34; (2) Matthew 6:22–23 = Luke 11:34–36; (3) Matthew 6:24 = Luke 16:13; (4) Matthew 6:25–34 = Luke 12:22–31. But the first pair are very different and should be treated as separate traditions of separate sayings; the third pair are very close (only a one-word difference) and both Matthew and Luke assign it to the same sermon; the second and fourth pairs are fairly close, but exegesis of Luke suggests his settings are topical. The context Matthew establishes should be accepted at face value. Certainly the flow is coherent: having excoriated religious piety that is little more than ostentation, Jesus warns against the opposite sins of greed, materialism, and worry that stem from misplaced and worldly priorities. Instead, he demands unswerving loyalty to kingdom values (vv.19–24) and uncompromised trust (vv.25–34).

a. *Metaphors for unswerving loyalty to kingdom values* (6:19–24)

1) *Treasure*

6:19–21

> [19]"Do not store up for yourselves treasures on earth, where moth and rust destroy, and where thieves break in and steal. [20]But store up for yourselves treasures in heaven, where moth and rust do not destroy, and where thieves do not break in and steal. [21]For where your treasure is, there your heart will be also.

Black (*Aramaic Approach*, pp. 178–79) shows the poetical character of vv.19–21, v.19 warning against the wrong way, v.20 prescribing the right way, and v.21 rounding it off with a memorable aphorism. "Such rhythm and balance suggest that these verses contain original dominical teaching" (Hill, *Matthew*). The assessment is fair; one wonders, however, why similar structure and rhythm should elsewhere be judged liturgical, catechetical, and inauthentic (see on 5:1–12).

19 The present tense prohibition *mē thēsaurizete* could well be rendered "Stop storing up treasures" (Turner, *Syntax*, p. 76) rather than "Do not store up"; the time for a decisive break has come (similarly at v.25).

The love of wealth is a great evil (1 Tim 6:10), calling forth frequent warnings. For heirs of the kingdom to hoard riches in the last days (James 5:2–3) is particularly shortsighted. Yet as with many of Jesus' prohibitions in this sermon, it would be foolhardy so to absolutize this one that wealth itself becomes an evil (cf. Luke 14:12; John 4:21; 1 Peter 3:3–4; for other statements that cannot properly be absolutized). Elsewhere the Scriptures require a man to provide for his relatives (1 Tim 5:8), commend work and provision for the future (Prov 6:6–8), and encourage us to enjoy the good things the Creator has given us (1 Tim 4:3–4; 6:17). Jesus is concerned about selfishness in misplaced values. His disciples must not lay up treasure *for themselves;* they must honestly ask where their heart is (vv.20–21).

This verse does not prohibit "being provident (making sensible provision for the future) but being covetous (like misers who hoard and materialists who always want more)" (Stott, p. 155). But it is folly to put oneself in the former category while acting and thinking in the latter (cf. France, "God and Mammon").

The "treasures on earth" might be clothing that could be attacked by moths. Fashions changed little, and garments could be passed on. They could also deteriorate. "Rust" (*brōsis*) refers not only to the corrosion of metals but to the destruction effected by rats, mildew, and the like. Older commentaries often picture a farm being devoured by mice and other vermin. Less corruptible treasures could be stolen: thieves could break in (*dioryssousin,* "dig through," referring to the mudbrick walls of most first-century Palestinian homes) and steal.

20–21 By contrast, the treasures in heaven are forever exempt from decay and theft (v.20; cf. Luke 12:33). The words "treasures in heaven" go back to Jewish literature (M *Peah* 1:1; T Levi 13:5; Pss Sol 9:9). Here it refers to whatever is of good and eternal significance that comes out of what is done on earth. Doing righteous deeds, suffering for Christ's sake, forgiving one another—all these have the promise of "reward" (see on 5:12; cf. 5:30, 46; 6:6, 15; 2 Cor 4:17). Other deeds of kindness also store up treasure in heaven (Matt 10:42; 25:40), including willingness to share (1 Tim 6:13–19).

In the best MSS the final aphorism (v.21) reverts to second person singular (cf. vv.2, 6, 17; see on 5:23). The point is that the things most highly treasured occupy the "heart," the center of the personality, embracing mind, emotions, and will (cf. DNTT, 2:180–84); and thus the most cherished treasure subtly but infallibly controls the whole person's direction and values. "If honour is rated the highest good, then ambition must take complete charge of a man; if money, then forthwith greed takes over the kingdom; if pleasure, then men will certainly degenerate into sheer self-indulgence" (Calvin). Conversely, those who set their minds on things above (Col 3:1–2), determining to live under kingdom norms, discover at last that their deeds follow them (Rev 14:13).

2) *Light*

6:22–23

²²"The eye is the lamp of the body. If your eyes are good, your whole body will be full of light. ²³But if your eyes are bad, your whole body will be full of darkness. If then the light within you is darkness, how great is that darkness!

22–23 "The eye is the lamp of the body" (v.22) in the sense that through the eye the body finds its way. The eye lets in light, and so the whole body is illuminated. But bad eyes let in no light, and the body is in darkness (v.23). The "light within you" seems ironic; those with bad eyes, who walk in darkness, think they have light, but this light is in reality darkness. The darkness is all the more terrible for failure to recognize it for what it is (cf. John 9:41).

This fairly straightforward description has metaphorical implications. The "eye" can be equivalent to the "heart." The heart set on God so as to hold to his commands (Ps 119:10) is equivalent to the eye fastened on God's law (Ps 119:18, 148; cf. 119:36–37). Similarly Jesus moves from "heart" (v.21) to "eye" (vv.22–23). Moreover the text moves between physical description and metaphor by the words chosen for "good" and "bad." *Haplous* ("good," v.22) and its cognates can mean either "single" (vs. *diplous*, "double," 1 Tim 5:17) in the sense of "single, undivided loyalty" (cf. 1 Chron 29:17) or in cognate forms "generous," "liberal" (cf. Rom 12:8; James 1:5). Likewise, *poneros* ("bad," v.23) can mean "evil" (e.g., Rom 12:9) or in the Jewish idiomatic expression "the evil eye" can refer to miserliness and selfishness (cf. Prov 28:22). Jesus is therefore saying either (1) that the man who "divides his interest and tries to focus on both God and possessions . . . has no clear vision, and will live without clear orientation or direction" (Filson)—an interpretation nicely compatible with v.24; or (2) that the man who is stingy and selfish cannot really see where he is going; he is morally and spiritually blind—an interpretation compatible with vv.19–21. Either way, the early crossover to metaphor may account for the difficult language of v.22.

At the physical level the "whole body" is just that, a body, of which the eye is the part that provides "light" (cf. R. Gundry, *Soma* [Cambridge: University Press, 1976], pp. 24–25). At the metaphorical level it represents the entire person who is plunged into moral darkness. The "light within you" is therefore the vision that the eye with divided loyalties provides, or the attitude characterized by selfishness; in both cases it is darkness indeed. This approach, which depends on the OT and Jewish usage, is much to be preferred to the one that goes to Hellenistic literature and interprets "the light within you" in a neoplatonic sense (e.g., H.D. Betz, "Matthew vi.22f and ancient Greek theories of vision," in Best and Wilson, pp. 43–56).

3) *Slavery*

6:24

> [24]"No one can serve two masters. Either he will hate the one and love the other, or he will be devoted to the one and despise the other. You cannot serve both God and Money.

24 "Jesus now explains that behind the choice between two treasures (where we lay them up) and two visions (where we fix our eyes) there lies the still more basic choice between two masters (whom we are going to serve)" (Stott, p. 158). "Money" renders Greek *mamona* ("mammon"), itself a transliteration of Aramaic *māmônā'* (in the emphatic state; "wealth," "property"). The root in both Aramaic and Hebrew (*'mn*) indicates that in which one has confidence; and the connection with money and wealth, well attested in Jewish literature (e.g., *Peah* 1:1; b *Berakoth* 61b; M *Aboth* 2:7; and not always in a negative sense), is painfully obvious. Here it is personified. Both God and Money are portrayed, not as employers, but as slave-owners. A man may work for two employers; but since "single ownership and full-time service are of the essence of slavery" (Tasker), he cannot serve two slave-owners. Either God is served with a single-eyed devotion, or he is not served at all. Attempts at divided loyalty betray, not partial commitment to discipleship, but deep-seated commitment to idolatry.

b. Uncompromised trust (6:25–34)

1) The principle

6:25

> 25"Therefore I tell you, do not worry about your life, what you will eat or drink; or about your body, what you will wear. Is not life more important than food, and the body more important than clothes?

25 "Therefore," in the light of the alternatives set out (vv.19–24) and assuming his disciples will make the right choices, Jesus goes on to prohibit worry. KJV's "Take no thought" is deceptive in modern English, for Jesus himself demands that we think even about birds and flowers (vv.26–30). "Do not worry" can be falsely absolutized by neglecting the limitations the context imposes and the curses on careless-ness, apathy, indifference, laziness, and self-indulgence expressed elsewhere (cf. Carson, *Sermon on the Mount*, pp. 82–86; Stott, pp. 165–68). The point here is not to worry about the physical necessities, let alone the luxuries implied in the preced-ing verses, because such fretting suggests that our entire existence focuses on and is limited to such things. The argument is *a fortiori* ("how much more") but not (contra Hill, *Matthew*) *a minori ad maius* ("from the lesser to the greater") but the reverse: if God has given us life and a body, both admittedly more important than food and clothing, will he not also give us the latter? Therefore fretting about such things betrays the loss of faith and the perversion of more valuable commitments (cf. Luke 10:41–42; Heb 13:5–6).

Notes

25 Because the subjunctives τί φάγητε ἤ τί πίητε (*ti phagēte ē ti piēte*, "what you will eat or drink") are in indirect discourse, they should be taken as deliberative subjunctives retained with the shift in discourse (cf. the subjunctives in v.31).

2) The examples (6:26–30)

a) Life and food

6:26–27

> 26Look at the birds of the air; they do not sow or reap or store away in barns, and yet your heavenly Father feeds them. Are you not much more valuable than they? 27Who of you by worrying can add a single hour to his life?

26 To worry about food and drink is to have learned nothing from the natural creation. If the created order testifies to God's "eternal power and divine nature" (Rom 1:20), it testifies equally to his providence. The point is not that disciples need not work—birds do not simply wait for God to drop food into their beaks—but that they need not fret. Disciples may further strengthen their faith when they remember that God is in a special sense their Father (not the birds' Father), and that they are worth far more than birds ("you" is emphatic). Here the argument is from the lesser to the greater.

This argument presupposes a biblical cosmology without which faith makes no sense. God is so sovereign over the universe that even the feeding of a wren falls within his concern. Because he normally does things in regular ways, there are "scientific laws" to be discovered; but the believer with eyes to see simultaneously discovers something about God and his activity (cf. Carson, *Sermon on the Mount,* pp. 87–90).

27 The word *hēlikia* ("life") can also be rendered "stature" (cf. Luke 19:3); and *pēchys* ("hour") means either "cubit" (about eighteen inches) or "age" (Heb 11:11). No combination fits easily; no one would be tempted to think worrying could add eighteen inches to his stature (KJV), and a linear measure (eighteen inches) does not fit easily with "life." This disparity accounts for the diversity of translations. Most likely the linear measure is being used in a metaphorical sense (cf. "add one cubit to his span of life" [RSV]), akin to "passing a milepost" at one's birthday. Worry is more likely to shorten life than prolong it, and ultimately such matters are in God's hands (cf. Luke 12:13–21). To trust him is enough.

Notes

---

26 Τὰ πατεινὰ τοῦ οὐρανοῦ (*ta pateina tou ouranou,* lit., "the birds of the heaven") is rightly rendered "birds of the air" (NIV) because "heaven" can refer to the atmosphere around us (cf. Gen 1:26; Matt 8:20; 13:32).

---

b) *Body and clothes*

6:28–30

> [28]"And why do you worry about clothes? See how the lilies of the field grow. They do not labor or spin. [29]Yet I tell you that not even Solomon in all his splendor was dressed like one of these. [30]If that is how God clothes the grass of the field, which is here today and tomorrow is thrown into the fire, will he not much more clothe you, O you of little faith?

28–30 "Lilies of the field" (v.28) may be any of the wild flowers so abundant in Galilee, and these "flowers of the field" correspond to "birds of the air." The point is a little different from the first illustration, where birds work but do not worry. The flowers neither toil nor spin (cf. Notes). The point is not that Jesus' disciples may opt for laziness but that God's providence and care are so rich that he clothes the grass with wild flowers that are neither productive nor enduring (v.30). Even Solomon, the richest and most extravagant of Israel's monarchs, "in all his splendor" (v.29) was not arrayed like one of these fields. Small wonder that Jesus gently chastises his disciples as *oligopistoi* ("people of little faith"; cf. 8:26; 14:31; 16:8; and the abstract noun at 17:20). The root of anxiety is unbelief.

Notes

28 On the nest of variants, cf. Metzger (*Textual Commentary*, p. 18) and the literature he cites, to which may be added K. Brunner, "Textkritisches zu Mt 6.28: *ou xainousin* statt *auxainousin* vorgeschlagen," *Zeitschrift für Katholische Theologie* 100 (1978): 251–56.

30 The κλίβανος (*klibanos*, "oven") was a pottery oven often fired by burning grass inside, the ashes falling through a hole, and the flat cakes distributed both inside and on top. The term was used metaphorically to refer to the Day of Judgment as early as Hos 7:4 LXX.

3) *Distinctive living*

6:31–32

> ³¹So do not worry, saying, 'What shall we eat?' or 'What shall we drink?' or 'What shall we wear?' ³²For the pagans run after all these things, and your heavenly Father knows that you need them.

31–32 In the light of God's bountiful care ("So"), the questions posed in v.31 (cf. v.25) are unanswerable; and the underlying attitudes are thoughtless and an affront to God who knows the needs of his people (cf. v.8). Worse, they are essentially pagan (v.32); for pagans "run after" (*epizētousin*, a strengthened form of "seek") these things, not God's kingdom and righteousness (v.33). Jesus' disciples must live lives qualitatively different from those of people who have no trust in God's fatherly care and no fundamental goals beyond material things.

4) *The heart of the matter*

6:33

> ³³But seek first his kingdom and his righteousness, and all these things will be given to you as well.

33 In view of vv.31–32, this verse makes it clear that Jesus' disciples are not simply to *refrain* from the *pursuit* of temporal things as their primary goal in order to differentiate themselves from pagans. Instead, they are to *replace* such pursuits with goals of far greater significance. To seek first the kingdom ("of God" in some MSS) is to desire above all to enter into, submit to, and participate in spreading the news of the saving reign of God, the messianic kingdom already inaugurated by Jesus, and to live so as to store up treasures in heaven in the prospect of the kingdom's consummation. It is to pursue the things already prayed for in the first three petitions of the Lord's Prayer (6:9–10).

To seek God's righteousness is not, in this context, to seek justification (contra Filson, McNeile). "Righteousness" must be interpreted as in 5:6, 10, 20; 6:1. It is to pursue righteousness of life in full submission to the will of God, as prescribed by Jesus throughout this discourse (cf. Przybylski, pp. 89–91). Such righteousness will lead to persecution by some (5:10), but others will themselves become disciples and praise the Father in heaven (5:16). Such goals alone are worthy of one's wholehearted allegiance. For any other concern to dominate one's mind is to stoop to pagan fretting. "In the end, just as there are only two kinds of piety, the self-centered and the God-centered, so there are only two kinds of ambition: one can be ambitious either for oneself or for God. There is no third alternative" (Stott, p. 172). Within such a framework of commitment, Jesus' disciples are assured that all the necessary things will be given them by their heavenly Father (see on 5:45; 6:9), who demonstrates his faithfulness by his care even for the birds and his concern even for the grass.

5) *Abolishing worry*

6:34

34Therefore do not worry about tomorrow, for tomorrow will worry about itself. Each day has enough trouble of its own.

34 In view of God's solemn promise to meet the needs of those committed to his kingdom and righteousness (v.33), "therefore" do not worry about tomorrow. Today has enough *kakia* ("trouble," NIV; what is evil from man's point of view; once applied to crop damage caused by hail [MM]; and frequently translates Heb. *rā'āh* ["evil," "misfortune," "trouble"] in LXX: Eccl 7:14; 12:1; Amos 3:6) of its own. Worry over tomorrow's misfortunes is nonsensical, because today has enough to occupy our attention and because tomorrow's feared misfortunes may never happen (cf. b *Sanhedrin* 100b; b *Berakoth* 9a). It is almost as if Jesus, aware that his disciples are still unsettled and immature, ends his argument by setting the highest ideals and motives aside for a moment and, in a whimsical sally, appeals to common sense. At the same time, he is implicitly teaching that even for his disciples today's grace is sufficient only for today and should not be wasted on tomorrow. If tomorrow does bring new trouble, there will be new grace to meet it.

6. *Balance and perfection* (7:1–12)

Many argue that these verses have (1) no connection with what precedes, (2) little internal cohesion, and (3) probably find their original context in Luke 6:37–38, 41–42. Only the third assertion is believable.

1. The lack of Greek connectives at vv.1, 7 is not inherently problematic; similar omissions (e.g., 6:19, 24) do not disturb the flow of thought so much as indicate a new "paragraph" or set off an aphorism. The connection with what precedes is internal. The demand for the superior righteousness of the kingdom, in fulfillment of the OT (5:17–20), has called forth warnings against hypocrisy (6:1–18) and the formulation of kingdom perspectives (6:19–34). But there are other dangers. Demands for perfection can breed judgmentalism (vv.1–5), while demands for love can cause chronic shortage of discernment (v.6).

2. Thus the internal connection is in part established by dealing with opposing evils. But such great demands on Jesus' followers must force them to recognize their personal inadequacy and so drive them to prayer (vv. 7–11). The Golden Rule (v. 12) summarizes the body of the sermon (5:17–7:12).

3. The relationship between 7:1–12 and Luke 6:37–38, 41–42 (part of Luke's "sermon") is difficult to assess. After his beatitudes and woes (Luke 6:20–26), Luke adds material (6:27–30) akin to Matthew 5:38–48. He then adds the Golden Rule (Luke 6:31), some material akin to Matthew 5, and then the parallel to Matthew 7:1–5. Thus he omits all of Matthew 6, while Matthew 7:1–5 omits part of what Luke keeps in 6:37–42. One or both of the evangelists have rearranged the order of the material. Both make such good sense in their own context that it seems impossible to decide in favor of either. Though a saying as aphoristic as the Golden Rule may well have been repeated during the course of several days' teaching, there is no sure way of demonstrating this was or was not the case.

a. The danger of being judgmental (7:1–5)

1) The principle

7:1

> ¹"Do not judge, or you too will be judged.

1 The verb *krinō* ("judge") has a wide semantic range: "judge" (judicially), "condemn," "discern." It cannot here refer to the law courts, any more than 5:33–37 forbids judicial oaths. Still less does this verse forbid all judging of any kind, for the moral distinctions drawn in the Sermon on the Mount require that decisive judgments be made. Jesus himself goes on to speak of some people as dogs and pigs (v. 6) and to warn against false prophets (vv. 15–20). Elsewhere he demands that people "make a right judgment" (John 7:24; cf. 1 Cor 5:5; Gal 1:8–9; Phil 3:2; 1 John 4:1). All this presupposes that some kinds of "judging" are not only legitimate but mandated.

Jesus' demand here is for his disciples not to be judgmental and censorious. The verb *krinō* has the same force in Romans 14:10–13 (cf. James 4:11–12). The rigor of the disciples' commitment to God's kingdom and the righteousness demanded of them do not authorize them to adopt a judgmental attitude. Those who "judge" like this will in turn be "judged," not by men (which would be of little consequence), but by God (which fits the solemn tone of the discourse). The disciple who takes it on himself to be the judge of what another does usurps the place of God (Rom 14:10) and therefore becomes answerable to him. The *hina mē* ("in order that . . . not"; NIV, "or") should therefore be given full telic force: "Do not assume the place of God by deciding you have the right to stand in judgment over all—do not do it, I say, in order to avoid being called to account by the God whose place you usurp" (cf. b *Shabbath* 127b; M *Sotah* 1:7; b *Baba Metzia* 59b).

2) The theological justification

7:2

> ²For in the same way you judge others, you will be judged, and with the measure you use, it will be measured to you.

183

2 The strong play on words in Greek suggests that this is a proverbial saying. Formally it is very close to M *Sotah* 1:7; but the use made of it is in each case rather distinctive (cf. Dalman, pp. 223f.). Indeed, precisely because it is a proverb, Jesus himself elsewhere turns it to another use (cf. Mark 4:24). The point is akin to that already established (5:7; 6:12, 14–15): the judgmental person by not being forgiving and loving testifies to his own arrogance and impenitence, by which he shuts himself out from God's forgiveness (cf. Manson, *Sayings*, p. 56).

According to some rabbis, God has two "measures"—mercy and justice (Lev R 29.3). Possibly Jesus used this language, adapting it to his own ends. He who poses as a judge cannot plead ignorance of the law (Rom 2:1; cf. James 3:1); he who insists on unalloyed justice for others is scarcely open to mercy himself (James 2:13; 4:12). The problem returns in 18:23–35; here "the command to *judge not* is not a requirement to be blind, but rather a plea to be generous. Jesus does not tell us to cease to be men (by suspending our critical powers which help to distinguish us from animals) but to renounce the presumptuous ambition to be God (by setting ourselves up as judges)" (Stott, p. 177, emphasis his).

3) An example

7:3–5

> **3**"Why do you look at the speck of sawdust in your brother's eye and pay no attention to the plank in your own eye? **4**How can you say to your brother, 'Let me take the speck out of your eye,' when all the time there is a plank in your own eye? **5**You hypocrite, first take the plank out of your own eye, and then you will see clearly to remove the speck from your brother's eye.

3–5 The *karphos* ("speck of sawdust") could be any bit of foreign matter (v.3). The *dokos* ("plank" or "log") is obviously colorful hyperbole. Jesus does not say it is wrong to help your brother (for "brother," see on 5:22; Jesus is apparently referring to the community of his disciples) remove the speck of dust in his eye, but it is wrong for a person with a "plank" in his eye to offer help. That is sheer hypocrisy of the second sort (see on 6:2). Second Samuel 12:1–12 is a dramatic OT example (cf. also Luke 18:9). It will not do to say that Jesus' words in this pericope are "meant to exclude all condemnation of others" (Hill, *Matthew*), for to do that requires not taking v.5 seriously and excluding what v.6 says. In the brotherhood of Jesus' disciples, censorious critics are unhelpful. But when a brother in a meek and self-judging spirit (cf. 1 Cor 11:31; Gal 6:1) removes the log in his own eye, he still has the responsibility of helping his brother remove his speck (cf. 18:15–20).

Notes

4 The future πῶς ἐρεῖς (*pōs ereis*, lit., "how will you say") is an instance in which, under Semitic influence, this tense is sometimes used modally to describe what may be (Zerwick, par. 279). See Luke 6:42: πῶς δύνασαι λέγειν (*pōs dynasai legein*, "how can you say").

b. The danger of being undiscerning

7:6

> 6"Do not give dogs what is sacred; do not throw your pearls to pigs. If you do, they may trample them under their feet, and then turn and tear you to pieces.

6 Though used later to exclude unbaptized persons from the Eucharist (*Didache* 9.5), that is not the purpose of this saying. Nor is it connected with the previous verses by dealing now with persons who, though properly confronted about their "specks," refuse to deal with them, as in 18:12–20 (so Schlatter). Rather, it warns against the converse danger. Disciples exhorted to love their enemies (5:43–47) and not to judge (v. 1) might fail to consider the subtleties of the argument and become undiscerning simpletons. This verse guards against such a possibility.

The "pigs" are not only unclean animals but wild and vicious, capable of savage action against a person. "Dogs" must not be thought of as household pets: in the Scriptures they are normally wild, associated with what is unclean, despised (e.g., 1 Sam 17:43; 24:14; 1 Kings 14:11; 21:19; 2 Kings 8:13; Job 30:1; Prov 26:11; Eccl 9:4; Isa 66:3; Matt 15:27; Phil 3:2; Rev 22:15). The two animals serve together as a picture of what is vicious, unclean, and abominable (cf. 2 Peter 2:22). The four lines of v. 6 are an ABBA chiasmus (Turner, *Syntax*, pp. 346–47). The pigs trample the pearls under foot (perhaps out of animal disappointment that they are not morsels of food), and the dogs are so disgusted with "what is sacred" that they turn on the giver.

The problem lies in *to hagion* ("what is sacred"). How is this parallel to "pearls," and what reality is envisaged to make the story "work"?

1. Some suggest *to hagion* refers to "holy food" offered in connection with the temple services (cf. Exod 22:31; Lev 22:14; Jer 11:15; Hag 2:12). But this is a strange way to refer to it, and it is not obvious why the dogs would spurn it.

2. Another suggestion is that *to hagion* is a mistranslation of the Aramaic *qᵉdaša* (Heb. *nezem*, "ring"), referring to Proverbs 11:22 (cf. Black, *Aramaic Approach*, pp. 200ff.). But appeals to mistranslation should not be the first line of approach; and here the parallelism of pearls and pigs, pearls obviously being mistaken for food, is destroyed.

3. P.G. Maxwell-Stuart ("'Do not give what is holy to the dogs.' [Mt 7⁶]," ExpT 90 [1978–79]: 341) offers a textual emendation.

4. However, it seems wiser to recognize that, as in 6:22–23, the interpretation of the metaphor is already hinted at in the metaphor itself. "What is sacred" in Matthew is the gospel of the kingdom; so the aphorism forbids proclaiming the gospel to certain persons designated as dogs and pigs. Instead of trampling the gospel under foot, everything must be "sold" in pursuit of it (13:45–46).

Verse 6 is not a directive against evangelizing the Gentiles, especially in a book full of various supports for this, not least 28:18–20 (10:5, properly understood, is no exception). "Dogs" and "pigs" cannot refer to all Gentiles but, as Calvin rightly perceived, only to persons of any race who have given clear evidences of rejecting the gospel with vicious scorn and hardened contempt. The disciples are later given a similar lesson (10:14; 15:14), and the postresurrection Christians learned it well (cf. Acts 13:44–51; 18:5–6; 28:17–28; Titus 3:10–11). So when taken together vv. 1–5 and v. 6 become something of a Gospel analogue to the proverb "Do not rebuke a mocker or he will hate you; rebuke a wise man and he will love you" (Prov 9:8).

c. *Source and means of power*

7:7–11

7"Ask and it will be given to you; seek and you will find; knock and the door will be opened to you. 8For everyone who asks receives; he who seeks finds; and to him who knocks, the door will be opened.

9"Which of you, if his son asks for bread, will give him a stone? 10Or if he asks for a fish, will give him a snake? 11If you, then, though you are evil, know how to give good gifts to your children, how much more will your Father in heaven give good gifts to those who ask him!

7–8 Zahn tries to establish a connection between these verses and the preceding ones by saying that Jesus now teaches that it is best to ask God to remove the speck in the other person's eye. Stott understands vv.1–11 in terms of relationships: to believers (vv.1–5), to "pigs" and "dogs" (v.6), and to God (vv.7–11). Bonnard best exemplifies those who say there is no connection at all between vv.7–11 and the preceding verses. Yet there are in fact deep thematic connections. Schlatter perceives one of them when he remarks that Jesus, having told his disciples the difficulties, now exhorts them to prayer. Moreover one of the most pervasive features of Jesus' teaching on prayer is the assurance it will be heard (cf. H.F. von Campenhausen, "Gebetserhörung in den überlieferten Jesusworten und in den Reflexion des Johannes," *Kerygma und Dogma* 23 [1977]: 157–71). But such praying is not for selfish ends but always for the glory of God according to kingdom concerns. So here: the Sermon on the Mount lays down the righteousness, sincerity, humility, purity, and love expected of Jesus' followers; and now it assures them such gifts are theirs if sought through prayer.

The sermon has begun with acknowledgment of personal bankruptcy (5:3) and has already provided a model prayer (6:9–13). Now (v.7) in three imperatives (ask, seek, knock) symmetrically repeated (v.8) and in the present tense to stress the persistence and sincerity required (cf. Jer 29:13), Jesus assures his followers that, far from demanding the impossible, he is providing the means for the otherwise impossible. "One may be a truly industrious man, and yet poor in temporal things; but one cannot be a truly praying man, and yet poor in spiritual things" (Broadus). Far too often Christians do not have the marks of richly textured discipleship because they do not ask, or they ask with selfish motives (James 4:2–3). But the best gifts, those advocated by the Sermon on the Mount, are available to "everyone" (v.8) who persistently asks, seeks, and knocks.

Jesus' disciples will pray ("ask") with earnest sincerity ("seek") and active, diligent pursuit of God's way ("knock"). Like a human father, the heavenly Father uses these means to teach his children courtesy, persistence, and diligence. If the child prevails with a thoughtful father, it is because the father has molded the child to his way. If Jacob prevails with God, it is Jacob who is wounded (Gen 32:22–32).

9–11 Another *a fortiori* argument (see on 6:25) is introduced. In Greek both v.9 and v.10 begin with *ē* ("or"), probably meaning "or to put the matter another way, which of you, etc." No parent would deceive a child asking for bread or fish by giving him a similar looking but inedible stone or a dangerous snake. The point at issue is not merely the parents' willingness to give but their willingness to give good gifts—even though they themselves are evil. Jesus presupposes the sinfulness (v.11) of human nature (himself exempted; "you," he says, not "we") but implicitly acknowledges that does not mean all human beings are as bad as they could be or utterly evil in all they do. People are evil; they are self-centered, not God-centered. This taints all they do. Nevertheless they can give good gifts to their children. How much more, then, will the heavenly Father, who is pure goodness without alloy, give good gifts to those who ask?

Four observations will tie up some loose ends.

1. Lachs ("Textual Observations," pp. 109f.) insists that the "concept that man is evil from birth, born in sin, and similar pronouncements, is a later theological development" and therefore proposes to emend the text of an alleged Semitic original. While it is true that rabbinic literature does not normally portray man as inherently evil, it is false to say that the idea arose only after Jesus, presumably with Paul (cf. Pss 14:1–3; 51; 53:1–3; Eccl 7:20). Jesus regularly assumes the sinfulness of humanity (cf. TDNT, 6:554–55). Therefore the rabbinic parallels to vv.7–11 are of limited value: they stress the analogy of the caring parent, but not on the supposition that the human parent is evil.

2. The fatherhood-of-God language is reserved for God's relationship with Jesus' disciples (see on 5:45). The blessings promised as a result of these prayers are not the blessings of common grace (cf. 5:45) but of the kingdom. And though we must ask for them, it is not because God must be informed (6:8) but because this is the Father's way of training his family.

3. What is fundamentally at stake is man's picture of God. God must not be thought of as a reluctant stranger who can be cajoled or bullied into bestowing his gifts (6:7–8), as a malicious tyrant who takes vicious glee in the tricks he plays (vv.9–10), or even as an indulgent grandfather who provides everything requested of him. He is the heavenly Father, the God of the kingdom, who graciously and willingly bestows the good gifts of the kingdom in answer to prayer.

4. On the "good gifts" as spiritual gifts (cf. Rom 3:8; 10:15; Heb 9:11; 10:1) and the parallel reference to the Holy Spirit (Luke 11:13), see Marshall, *Luke*, pp. 469f.

d. *Balance and perfection*

7:12

> 12So in everything, do to others what you would have them do to you, for this sums up the Law and the Prophets.

12 The Golden Rule was not invented by Jesus; it is found in many forms in highly diverse settings. About A.D. 20, Rabbi Hillel, challenged by a Gentile to summarize the law in the short time the Gentile could stand on one leg, reportedly responded, "What is hateful to you, do not do to anyone else. This is the whole law; all the rest is commentary. Go and learn it" (b *Shabbath* 31a). Apparently only Jesus phrased the rule positively. Thus stated it is certainly more telling than its negative counterpart, for it speaks against sins of omission as well as sins of commission. The goats in 25:31–46 would be acquitted under the negative form of the rule, but not under the form attributed to Jesus.

The *oun* ("therefore") might refer to vv.7–11 (i.e., because God gives good gifts, therefore Jesus' disciples should live by this rule as a function of gratitude) or to vv. 1–6 (i.e., instead of judging others, we should treat them as we ourselves would want to be treated). But more probably it refers to the entire body of the sermon (5:17–7:12), for here there is a second reference to "the Law and the Prophets"; and this appears to form an envelope with 5:17–20. "Therefore," in the light of all I have taught about the true direction in which the OT law points, obey the Golden Rule; for this is (*estin;* NIV, "sums up") the Law and the Prophets (cf. Rom 13:9). This way of putting it provides a powerful yet flexible maxim that helps us decide moral issues in a thousand cases without the need for multiplied case law. The rule is not arbitrary, without rational support, as in radical humanism; in Jesus' mind its rationale ("for") lies in its connection with revealed truth recorded in "the Law and the Prophets." The rule embraces quantity ("in everything") and quality (*houtōs kai,* "[do] even so"). And in the context of fulfilling the Scriptures, the rule provides a handy summary of the righteousness to be displayed in the kingdom.

Above all this verse is not to be understood as a utilitarian maxim like "Honesty pays." We are to do to others what we would have them do to us, not just because we expect the same in return, but because such conduct is the goal of the Law and the Prophets. The verb *estin* (NIV, "sums up") might properly be translated "fulfill," as in Acts 2:16. In the deepest sense, therefore, the rule *is* the Law and the Prophets in the same way the kingdom is the fulfillment of all that the Law and the Prophets foretold.

7. Conclusion: call to decision and commitment (7:13–27)

a. Two ways

7:13–14

> ¹³"Enter through the narrow gate. For wide is the gate and broad is the road that leads to destruction, and many enter through it. ¹⁴But small is the gate and narrow the road that leads to life, and only a few find it.

The Sermon on the Mount ends with four warnings, each offering paired contrasts: two ways (vv. 13–14), two trees (vv. 15–20), two claims (vv. 21–23), and two builders (vv. 24–27). They focus on eschatological judgment and so make it plain that the theme is still the kingdom of heaven. But if some will not enter it (vv. 13–14, 21–23), the sole basis for such a tragedy is present response to Jesus' words. At the close of the sermon, the messianic claim is implicit and only thinly veiled.

13–14 "Two ways" language is common in Jewish literature, both canonical and extracanonical (e.g., Deut 30:19; Ps 1; Jer 21:8; Ecclus 21:11–14; 2 Esd 7:6–14; T Asher 1:3, 5; 1QS 3:20ff.). The general picture is clear enough: there are two gates, two roads, two crowds, two destinations. The "narrow" gate (KJV's "strait" is from Lat. *strictum,* "narrow"; nothing is said about gate or road being "straight," despite the modern phrase "straight and narrow") is clearly restrictive and does not permit entrance to what Jesus prohibits. The "wide" gate seems far more inviting. The "broad" road (not "easy," RSV) is spacious and accommodates the crowd and their baggage; the other road is "narrow"—but two different words are used: *stenē* ("narrow," v. 13) and *tethlimmenē* (v. 14), the latter being cognate with *thlipsis* ("tribulation"), which almost always refers to persecution. So this text says that the way of discipleship is "narrow," restricting, because it is the way of persecution and opposition—a major theme in Matthew (see on 5:10–12, 44; 10:16–39; 11:11–12; 24:4–13; cf. esp. A.J. Mattill, Jr., "'The Way of Tribulation,'" JBL 98 [1979]: 531–46). Compare Acts 14:22: "We must go through many hardships [*dia pollōn thlipseōn*, 'through much persecution'] to enter the kingdom of God."

But the two roads are not ends in themselves. The narrow road leads to life, i.e., to the consummated kingdom (cf. vv.21–23; John's Gospel); but the broad road leads to *apōleia* ("destruction")—"definitive destruction, not merely in the sense of the extinction of physical existence, but rather of an eternal plunge into Hades and a hopeless destiny of death" (A. Opeke, TDNT, 1:396); cf. 25:34, 46; John 17:12; Rom 9:22; Phil 1:28; 3:19; 1 Tim 6:9; Heb 10:39; 2 Peter 2:1, 3; 3:16; Rev 17:8, 11). (On the relative numbers ["many . . . few"], see 22:14; Luke 13:22–30; Rev 7:9.) Democratic decisions do not determine truth and righteousness in the kingdom. That there are only two ways is the inevitable result of the fact that the one that leads to life is exclusively by revelation. But if truth in such matters must not be sought by appealing to majority opinion (Exod 23:2), neither can it be found by each person doing what is right in his own eyes (Prov 14:12; cf. Judg 21:25). God must be true and every man a liar (Rom 3:4).

There remains an important metaphorical difficulty. Granted the correctness of the text (cf. Metzger, *Textual Commentary*, p. 19), are we to think of roads heading up to the gate, so that once through the gate the traveler has arrived at his destination, whether destruction or the consummated kingdom? Or is the gate something entered *in this life*, with the roads, broad and narrow, stretching out before the pilgrim? Tasker and Jeremias (TDNT, 6:922–23) adopt the former alternative, Jeremias appealing to Luke 13:23–24, where a door, not a road, is mentioned. He argues that Jesus originally said something about entering a door or gate and that Matthew's form is a popular *hysteron-proteron* ("later-earlier") way of saying things with the real order reversed (like "thunder and lightning").

Not only is Luke 13:23–24 so far removed from the language of Matthew 7:13–14 (even "door," not "gate") that one may question whether the two spring from the same saying, but even in Luke entrance through the door is not merely eschatological since there comes a time when the door is shut and no more may enter. This suggests that it is the shutting of the door that eliminates further opportunity for entrance, while the entrance itself takes place now—a form of realized eschatology. This conceptual parallel with Matthew, plus the order of gate-road, suggests, not that the gate marks entrance into the consummated kingdom, nor that the gate and road are a hendiadys (Ridderbos), but that entrance through the gate into the narrow way of persecution begins *now* but issues in the consummated kingdom at the other end of that way (Grosheide, Hendriksen). The narrow gate is not thereby rendered superfluous; instead, it confirms that even the beginning of this path to life is restrictive. Here is no funnel that progressively narrows down but a decisive break.

This exegesis entails two conclusions.

1. Jesus is not encouraging committed disciples, "Christians," to press on along the narrow way and be rewarded in the end. He is rather commanding his disciples to enter the way marked by persecution and rewarded in the end. Jesus' "disciples" (see on 5:1) are therefore not full-fledged Christians in the post-Pentecost sense. Jesus is dealing with people more or less committed to him but who have not yet really entered on the "Christian" way. How could they have entered on it? Only

now was it being introduced into the stream of redemptive history as the fulfillment of what had come before. That Matthew should preserve such fine distinctions speaks well of his ability to follow the development of salvation history and thus avoid historical anachronism. Theologian though he is, Matthew is a responsible historian.

2. Implicitly, entrance into the kingdom—or, to preserve the language Matthew uses here but not always elsewhere (e.g., 12:28), entrance into the way to the kingdom—begins here and now in coming through the small gate, onto the narrow way of persecution, and under the authority of Jesus Christ (cf. vv.21, 26).

Notes

13 The phrase δι' αὐτῆς (di' autēs, "through it") could in Greek refer to either the gate or the road (cf. 8:28); but the main lines of exegesis (above) are not affected.

14 Probably τί (ti, normally "what?" or "why?"; "for," KJV; "but," NIV) is the correct reading, carrying the same force as מָה (māh, "how"—e.g., Ps 139:17) in Hebrew (cf. Black, *Aramaic Approach*, p. 123; BDF, Par. 299[4]; Metzger, *Textual Commentary*, p. 19).

b. Two trees

7:15-20

15"Watch out for false prophets. They come to you in sheep's clothing, but inwardly they are ferocious wolves. 16By their fruit you will recognize them. Do people pick grapes from thornbushes, or figs from thistles? 17Likewise every good tree bears good fruit, but a bad tree bears bad fruit. 18A good tree cannot bear bad fruit, and a bad tree cannot bear good fruit. 19Every tree that does not bear good fruit is cut down and thrown into the fire. 20Thus, by their fruit you will recognize them.

Much recent debate has focused attention on the identity of these false prophets in the Matthean church. The argument turns in large part on identifying v.15 as Matthew's creation and on attempting to discuss the tradition history of vv.16–20; 12:33–35; Luke 6:43–45. The same evidence is better interpreted to support the thesis that Jesus in his itinerant preaching uses similar metaphors in a wide variety of ways. Verse 15 has no synoptic parallel; but the thought is certainly not foreign to Jesus' other warnings (e.g., 24:4–5, 11, 23–24; Mark 13:22), and Matthew's language is small evidence for inauthenticity (cf. Introduction, section 2). The very diversity of the identifications—the false prophets are Zealots, Gnostics, scribes, antinomians, anti-Paulinists (for a recent survey, cf. D. Hill, "False Prophets and Charismatics: Structure and Interpretation in Matthew 7, 15–23," *Biblica* 57 [1976]: 327–48)—argues that Jesus gave a warning with rather broad limits susceptible to diverse applications. Hill himself sees Pharisees of the A.D. 80 period in vv.15–20 (Were rabbis of A.D. 80 ever called Pharisees?) and Charismatics in vv.21–23. E. Cothenet ("Les prophètes chrétiens dans l'Evangile selon Saint Matthieu," Didier, pp. 281–308) thinks Jesus in vv.15–23 is condemning Zealots, but Matthew reapplies his words to condemn antinomians. And Paul S. Minear ("False Prophecy and Hypocrisy in the Gospel of Matthew," Gnilka, *Neues Testament*, pp. 76–93) criticizes theories that center on antinomians and Pharisees and understands the pericope to warn against hypocrisy and false prophecy entirely within the Christian community.

There is nothing intrinsically unlikely about the notion that Jesus warned against false prophets, provided he foresaw the continued existence of his newly formed community for a sustained period. He was doubtless steeped in the OT reports of earlier false prophets (Jer 6:13–15; 8:8–12; Ezek 13; 22:27; Zeph 3:4). Certainly the first Christians faced the false prophets (cf. v.15) Jesus had predicted (Acts 20:29; 2 Cor 11:11–15; 2 Peter 2:1–3, 17–22; cf. 1 John 2:18, 22; 4:1–6). In view of Matthew's care in preserving historical distinctions (see on 7:13–14), there is little reason to doubt that he is here dealing with the teaching of the historical Jesus. Of course this presupposes that Jesus saw himself as true prophet (cf. 21:11, 46).

15 Warnings against false prophets are necessarily based on the conviction that not all prophets are true, that truth can be violated, and that the gospel's enemies usually conceal their hostility and try to pass themselves off as fellow believers. At first glance they use orthodox language, show biblical piety, and are indistinguishable from true prophets (cf. 10:41). Thus it is vital to know how to distinguish sheep from wolves in sheep's clothing. Jesus does not explicitly say who will have the discernment to protect the community but implies that the community itself, by whatever agency, must somehow protect itself from the wolves.

Neither the damage these false prophets do nor their brand of false teaching is stated; but the flow of the Sermon on the Mount as well as its OT background suggest that they neither acknowledge nor teach the narrow way to life subject to persecution (vv.13–14; cf. Jer 8:11; Ezek 13, where prophets cry "Peace!" when there is no peace). They have never really come under kingdom authority (vv.21–23); and since the only alternative to life is destruction (vv.13–14), they imperil their followers.

16–20 From a distance the little black berries on the buckthorn could be mistaken for grapes, and the flowers on certain thistles might deceive one into thinking figs were growing (v.16). But no one would be long deceived. So with people! One's "fruit"—not just what one does, but all one says and does—will ultimately reveal what one is (cf. James 3:12). The Semitic way of expression (i.e., both positive and negative—viz., every good tree bears good fruit, no good tree bears bad fruit, etc.) makes the test certain, but not necessarily easy or quick. Living according to kingdom norms can be feigned for a time; but what one is will eventually reveal itself in what one does. However guarded one's words, they will finally betray him (cf. 12:33–37; Luke 6:45). Ultimately false prophets tear down faith (2 Tim 2:18) and promote divisiveness, bitterness (e.g., 1 Tim 6:4–5; 2 Tim 2:23), and various kinds of ungodliness (2 Tim 2:16). Meek discernment and understanding the dire consequences of the false prophets' teachings are needed. But at the same time censoriousness over minutiae must be avoided.

The common wording between 3:10 (spoken by the Baptist) and 7:19 may suggest that v.19 was proverbial or that during the time Jesus and the Baptist were both ministering, various expressions became standard (cf. 3:2; 4:17). Verse 19 is an important example of this, for here we have independent evidence that Jesus preached in this vein (cf. Mark 1:15) so that there is no need to suppose Matthew has transferred a saying of the Baptist to the lips of Jesus.

c. Two claims

7:21-23

> 21"Not everyone who says to me, 'Lord, Lord,' will enter the kingdom of heaven, but only he who does the will of my Father who is in heaven. 22Many will say to me on that day, 'Lord, Lord, did we not prophesy in your name, and in your name drive out demons and perform many miracles?' 23Then I will tell them plainly, 'I never knew you. Away from me, you evildoers!'

21-23 If vv.15-20 deal with false prophets, vv.21-23 deal with false followers. Perhaps some became false because of the false prophets. Their cry of "Lord, Lord" (v.21) reflects fervency. In Jesus' day it is doubtful whether "Lord" when used to address him meant more than "teacher" or "sir." But in the postresurrection period, it becomes an appellation of worship and a confession of Jesus' deity. Therefore some suspect an anachronism here. Two factors support authenticity: (1) the parallel in Luke 6:46 (cf. also John 13:12-16); (2) the fact that throughout Jesus' ministry he referred to himself in relatively veiled categories whose full significance could only be grasped after the Resurrection. The latter point is central to understanding the "Son of Man" title (see on 8:20), recurs in various forms throughout all the Gospels, and is especially focal in John (cf. Carson, "Christological Ambiguities"; id., "Understanding Misunderstandings in the Fourth Gospel," *Tyndale Bulletin* [1982]: 59-91).

On the background of *kyrios* ("Lord") as a christological title, see Fitzmyer, *Wandering Aramaen*, pp. 115-32. Here Jesus' point is made during his ministry, if at that time his disciples understood "Lord" to mean "teacher." But implicitly Jesus is claiming more, since his "name" becomes the focus of kingdom activity; and he alone decrees who does or does not enter the kingdom (vv.22-23). Thus the warning and rebuke would take on added force when early Christians read the passage from their postresurrection perspective.

Indeed, the tables may be turned. Far from providing evidence that virtually every use of *kyrios* ("Lord") in this Gospel is anachronistic because it presupposes a high christology (e.g., Kingsbury, *Matthew*), these verses suggest that Matthew is painfully aware that the title may mean nothing. This explains, for instance, the deep irony of Peter's "Never, Lord" (16:22). Jesus himself is preparing his followers to put the deepest content in the title. For finally obedience, not titles, is decisive.

The determinative factor regarding who enters the kingdom is obedience to the Father's will (v.19; cf. 12:50). This is the first use of "my Father" in Matthew (cf. Luke 2:49; John 2:16); as such it may support the truth, taught throughout the sermon, that Jesus alone claims to be the authoritative Revealer of his Father's will (v.21). It quite misses the point to say that the Father's will is simply the OT law, mildly touched up by Jesus, and that therefore the Matthean church "seems to have been unaware of or uninfluenced by Pauline Christianity" (Hill, *Matthew*), for:

1. If the preceding exegesis of the Sermon on the Mount is correct, Matthew is not saying that Jesus is simply taking over the law but that Jesus *fulfills* the law and thus determines the nature of its continuity.

2. Within this framework Matthew presents Jesus as standing at a different (i.e., earlier) point in salvation-history than any church in Matthew's day, for Jesus is the one who brings about the new dispensation.

3. Paul's alleged antinomian tendencies are implicitly exaggerated by Hill's reconstruction, for it is difficult to think of one thing in the sermon Paul does not say in other words. The differences between Matthew and Paul—and there are major ones—have more to do with differences in interest and in their relative place in the stream of redemptive history. Moreover, Matthew, as we shall see, strongly stresses grace; therefore it is legitimate to wonder whether he is presenting obedience to the will of the Father as the ground or as the requirement for entrance to the kingdom. Paul would deny only the former and insist on the latter no less than Matthew would.

"That day" is the Day of Judgment (cf. Mal 3:17–18; 1 Enoch 45:3; cf. Matt 25:31–46; Luke 10:12; 2 Thess 1:7–10; 2 Tim 1:12; 4:8; Rev 16:14). The false claimants have prophesied in Jesus' name and by that name exorcised demons and performed miracles. There is no reason to judge their claims false; their claims are not false but insufficient. Significantly the miracles Jesus specifies were all done by his disciples during his ministry (cf. 10:1–4): he does not mention a later gift, such as tongues.

Verse 23 presupposes an implicit christology of the highest order. Jesus himself not only decides who enters the kingdom on the last day but also who will be banished from his presence. That he never knew these false claimants strikes a common biblical note, viz., how close to spiritual reality one may come while knowing nothing of its fundamental reality (e.g., Balaam; Judas Iscariot; Mark 9:38–39; 1 Cor 13:2; Heb 3:14; 1 John 2:19). "But not everyone who speaks in a spirit is a prophet, except he have the behavior of the Lord" (*Didache* 11.8).

Two final observations can be made. First, although "I have nothing to do with you" is the mildest of rabbinic bans (SBK, 4:293), the words used here are clearly final and eschatological in a solemn context of "that day" and entrance into the kingdom. Second, "Away from me, you evildoers" is quoted from Psalm 6:8 (cf. Luke 13:27). In the psalm the sufferer, vindicated by Yahweh, tells the evildoers to depart. Again it is difficult to avoid the conclusion that Jesus himself links the authority of the messianic King with the righteous Sufferer, however veiled the allusion may be (see on 3:17).

d. *Two builders*

7:24–27

> [24]"Therefore everyone who hears these words of mine and puts them into practice is like a wise man who built his house on the rock. [25]The rain came down, the streams rose, and the winds blew and beat against that house; yet it did not fall, because it had its foundation on the rock. [26]But everyone who hears these words of mine and does not put them into practice is like a foolish man who built his house on sand. [27]The rain came down, the streams rose, and the winds blew and beat against that house, and it fell with a great crash."

24–27 Luke's sermon ends on the same note (Luke 6:47–49). Probably the evangelists adapted the parable to the situation of their readers. Verses 21–23 contrast "saying" and "doing"; these verses contrast "hearing" and "doing" (Stott, p. 208), not unlike James 1:22–25; 2:14–20 (cf. Ezek 33:31–32). Moreover the will of the Father (v.21) becomes definitive in what Jesus calls "these words of mine" (v.24): *his* teaching is definitive (see on 5:17–20; 28:18–20).

In the light of the radical choice of vv. 21–23, "therefore" (v. 24) the two positions can be likened to two builders and their houses. Each house looks secure in good weather. But Palestine is known for torrential rains that can turn dry wadis into raging torrents. Only storms reveal the quality of the work of the two builders. The thought reminds us of the parable of the sower in which the seed sown on rocky ground lasts only a short time, until "trouble or persecution comes because of the word" (13:21). The greatest storm is eschatological (cf. Isa 28:16–17; Ezek 13:10–13; cf. Prov 12:7). But Jesus' words about the two houses need not be thus restricted. The point is that the wise man (a repeated term in Matthew; cf. 10:16; 24:45; 25:2, 4, 8–9) builds to withstand anything.

What wisdom (phronimos; the term is absent from Mark and occurs twice in Luke [12:42; 16:8]) consists of is clear. A wise person represents those who put Jesus' words into practice; they too are building to withstand anything. Those who pretend to have faith, who have a merely intellectual commitment, or who enjoy Jesus in small doses are foolish builders. When the storms of life come, their structures fool no one, above all not God (cf. Ezek 13:10–16).

The sermon ends with what has been implicit throughout it—the demand for radical submission to the exclusive lordship of Jesus, who fulfills the Law and the Prophets and warns the disobedient that the alternative to total obedience, true righteousness, and life in the kingdom is rebellion, self-centeredness, and eternal damnation.

Notes

---

24 The future passive reading ὁμοιωθήσεται (homoiōthēsetai, lit., "will become like") is more probable than the active ὁμοιώσω αὐτόν (homoiōsō auton, lit., "I will liken him to"), not only on textual grounds, but also because of the possibility of assimilation to the active in Luke 6:47–48: ὑποδείξω ὑμῖν . . . ὅμοιος (hypodeixō hymin . . . homoios, "I will show you what he is like"). The future tense is significant: the one who puts Jesus' words into practice will become like the man who, etc.: i.e., on Judgment Day, when the great storm comes, he will stand fast because of his good foundation. See on 13:24.

24–26 The words ἀκούει μου τοὺς λόγους τούτους (akouei mou tous logous toutous, "hears these words of mine") could be rendered "hears me, in respect of these sayings"; and Davies (Setting, p. 94) argues that "in this sense, the ethical teaching is not detached from the life of him who uttered it and with whom it is congruous." But the verb ἀκούω (akouō, "I hear") only once takes the genitive in Matthew, and then it is not a pronoun. The emphatic μου (mou, "of mine") is best understood as a way of forcefully identifying Jesus' teaching with the will of his Father (v. 21), an important point in light of the exegesis of 5:17–20.

---

8. Transitional conclusion: Jesus' authority

7:28–29

28When Jesus had finished saying these things, the crowds were amazed at his teaching, 29because he taught as one who had authority, and not as their teachers of the law.

28–29 This is the first of the five formulaic conclusions that terminate the discourses in this Gospel. All five begin with *kai egeneto* (lit., "and it happened") plus a finite verb (7:28; 11:1; 13:53; 19:1; 26:1), a construction common in the LXX (classical Greek preferred *egeneto* plus the infinitive; cf. Zerwick, par. 388; Beyer, pp. 41–60). The only other occurrence in Matthew is of the rather different "Hebrew" construction *kai egeneto . . . kai* (lit., "and it happened . . . and") plus finite verb, which appears once (9:10). Matthew's formula is therefore a self-conscious stylistic device that establishes a structural turning point. (It is not necessary to adopt Bacon's theory of parallelism to the Five Books of Moses; cf. Introduction, section 14.) Moreover, in each case the conclusion is transitional and prepares for the next section. Here (as we shall see below) mention of Jesus' authority leads into his authority in other spheres (8:1–17). In 11:1 Jesus' activity sets the scene for John the Baptist's question (11:2–3). And 13:53 anticipates rejection of Jesus in his hometown, while 19:1–2 points forward to his Judean ministry with new crowds and renewed controversies. Finally, 26:1–5 looks to the Cross, now looming very near.

The crowds—probably a larger group than his disciples—again pressing in on him (see on 5:1–2), are amazed (v.28). Because this is the only conclusion to a discourse that mentions the crowds' amazement, Hill (*Matthew*) suggests that Matthew is returning to Mark 1:22 (Luke 4:32) as his source. This is very tenuous: (1) a closer Matthean parallel is 13:54; (2) the next pericope in Matthew (8:1–4) is paralleled in Mark by 1:40–45, too far on for us to believe Matthew has "returned to his source" at 1:22.

The word *didachē* ("teaching," v.29) can refer to both content and manner (see also on 3:1); and no doubt the crowds were astonished at both. Their astonishment says nothing about their own heart commitment. The cause of their astonishment was Jesus' *exousia* ("authority"). The term embraces power as well as authority, and the theme becomes central (cf. 8:9; 9:6, 8; 10:1; 21:23–24, 27; 28:18). In his authority Jesus differs from the "teachers of the law" (see on 2:4). Many of them limited their teaching to the authorities they cited, and a great part of their training centered on memorizing the received traditions. They spoke by the authority of others; Jesus spoke with his own authority. Yet many teachers of the law did indeed offer new rulings and interpretations; so some have tried to interpret vv.28–29 along other lines.

Daube (pp. 205–16), in arguing that Jesus' lack of official rabbinic authority was an early issue in his ministry, says that some of the crowds' response in Galilee was because they did not often hear ordained rabbis so far north. Sigal ("Halakah"), dating the sources a little differently, insists (probably rightly) that there was no official ordination of rabbis till after Jesus' death. He argues that Jesus himself was not essentially different in his authority from other proto-rabbis. Both these reconstructions miss the central point, which transcends Halakic applications of the law, the formulas used, and the latitude of interpretation permitted.

The central point is this: Jesus' entire approach in the Sermon on the Mount is not only ethical but messianic—i.e., christological and eschatological. Jesus is not an ordinary prophet who says, "Thus says the Lord!" Rather, he speaks in the first person and claims that his teaching fulfills the OT; that he determines who enters the messianic kingdom; that as the Divine Judge he pronounces banishment; that the true heirs of the kingdom would be persecuted for their allegiance to him; and that he alone fully knows the will of his Father. It is methodologically indefensible for Sigal to complain that all such themes are later Christian additions and therefore to focus exclusively on points of Halakic interpretation. Jesus' authority is unique (see on 5:21–48), and the crowds recognized it even if they did not always understand it. This same authority is now to be revealed in powerful, liberating miracles, signs of the kingdom's advance (chs. 8–9; cf. 11:2–5).

Notes

29 The word "their" may indicate a distinction between "Christian" teachers and those of the synagogues. Hummel (pp. 28ff.) and others, following Kilpatrick (*Origins*, p. 40), make much of Matthew's "their" (4:23; 9:35; 10:17; 12:9; 13:54; 23:34) to support a theory that Matthew's life-setting is *just before* the division between church and synagogue (since 6:2, 5; 23:6 make no allusion to Christian synagogues). But "their" may be quite innocuous. It may reflect the geographical stance of a writer not in Galilee (see on 4:23). Better yet, where Jesus' authority is emphasized, "their" may subtly remind the reader that Jesus himself, though a Jew of the line of David (1:1), has his ultimate origin beyond the Jewish race (1:18–25) and so cannot be classed with *their* teachers of the law. Moreover, in two places Matthew is merely following Mark (Mark 1:23, 29) and seems to use "their" in still other, highly unusual places (e.g., 11:1), which caution the reader against reading too much into the word. And some of the preceding debate (e.g., as to the relevance of 6:2, 5; 23:6) is relevant only if anachronism is already assumed, since these references make perfectly good sense under the obvious assumption that the Gospel really is about Jesus. Yet there may well be theological significance in some of the "their" passages (see on 10:17), which gets transferred by association to other occurrences of the pronoun.

III. The Kingdom Extended Under Jesus' Authority (8:1–11:1)

A. *Narrative* (8:1–10:4)

1. *Healing miracles* (8:1–17)

a. *A leper*

8:1–4

> [1]When he came down from the mountainside, large crowds followed him. [2]A man with leprosy came and knelt before him and said, "Lord, if you are willing, you can make me clean."
> [3]Jesus reached out his hand and touched the man. "I am willing," he said. "Be clean!" Immediately he was cured of his leprosy. [4]Then Jesus said to him, "See that you don't tell anyone. But go, show yourself to the priest and offer the gift Moses commanded, as a testimony to them."

Matthew's arrangement of the pericopes in chapters 8–9 is demonstrably topical, not chronological. All these pericopes except 8:5–13, 18–22; 9:32–34 are paralleled in Mark, but not in the same order, and these three are paralleled in Luke. Mark 1:40–2:22 appears to provide the basic framework with numerous exceptions. The events in Matthew 8:18–22 originally occurred not only after the Sermon on the Mount but apparently after the "day of parables" (ch. 13; cf. Luke 8:22–56). On the other hand, 8:2–4; 8:14–17; 9:2–13 almost certainly took place before the Sermon on the Mount (cf. Mark 1:29–34, 40–45; Luke 4:38–41; Hendriksen). Matthew does not purport to follow anything other than a topical arrangement, and most of his "time" indicators are very loose.

This does not mean that Matthew's arrangement is entirely haphazard but that it is governed by themes. Linkage from pericope to pericope is provided by ideas, catchwords, dominant motifs (cf. K. Gatzweiler, "Les récits de miracles dans l'Evangile selon saint Matthieu," in Didier, pp. 209–20). However, it does not follow that all the outlines suggested by various scholars to explain this topical design are equally convincing. Klostermann, for instance, notes the central place of the ten plagues in Jewish thought (e.g., *Pirke Aboth* 5:5, 8) and suggests that the ten miracles in these chapters are planned to picture Jesus as the new Moses or the church as a new Exodus (cf. Grundmann; Davies, *Setting*, pp. 86–93). But this is not convincing: Matthew lays no stress on the number ten, his miracles are not individually parallel to the plagues, and his main themes run on other lines.

J.D. Kingsbury ("Observations on the 'Miracle Chapters' of Matthew 8–9," CBQ 40 [1978]: 559–73) ably discusses and rejects outlines proposed by Burger, Schniewind, Thompson, and others, and opts for a modification of Burger's fourfold division: (1) 8:1–17 treats christology; (2) 8:18–34 concerns discipleship; (3) 9:1–17 focuses on questions pertaining to the separation of Jesus and his followers from Israel; (4) 9:18–34 centers on faith; and over all the "Son of God" christology predominates. But it is hard to avoid the feeling that this outline, like the others, is too simplistic. Christology extends beyond 8:1–17; a new title appears in 8:20 and reappears in 9:6; and Jesus' godlike authority to forgive sins does not appear till chapter 9. Why discipleship should be restricted to 8:18–34 when Matthew is called in 9:9–13 and the distinctive habits of Jesus' disciples are discussed in 9:14–17 is unclear. The distinctions between Jesus' followers and racial Israel can scarcely be said to await 9:1–17 in the light of 8:10, 28–34. Faith, far from awaiting the fourth division, is already central in 8:5–13. And we have already seen that Kingsbury tends to emphasize the Son-of-God theme while minimizing other equally strong christological emphases (see on 3:17).

These chapters cannot legitimately be broken down so simplistically. Though Matthew's pericopes cohere nicely, he intertwines his themes, keeping several going at once like a literary juggler. Thus these chapters are best approached inductively; and one can trace emphases on faith, discipleship, the Gentile mission, a diverse christological pattern, and more. At the same time these chapters prove that Jesus, whose mission in part was to preach, teach, and heal (4:23; 9:35), fulfilled the whole of it. Matthew has shown Jesus preaching the gospel of the kingdom (4:17, 23) and teaching (chs. 5–7). Now he records some examples of his healing ministry.

The first miracle, the healing of a leper, is much shorter in Matthew (vv. 1–4) than in Mark (1:40–45). The omission of Mark 1:41a, 45 and several other bits prompts some to think Matthew is here independent of Mark (Lohmeyer, Schlatter), others to think oral tradition is still having its influence (Bonnard, Hill), still others to offer some theological explanation, e.g, that Matthew suppressed any reference to Jesus' compassion because it did not fit the image the Matthean church members had formed of Christ (e.g., Leopold Sabourin, *L'Evangile selon Saint Matthieu et ses principaux parallèles* [Rome: BIP, 1978], in loc.; cf. Hull, pp. 133f.). But when Matthew follows Mark, he condenses controversy stories by about 20 percent, stories that prove Jesus is the Christ by about 10 percent, actual sayings of Jesus scarcely at all, and miracle stories by about 50 percent (cf. Schweizer).

Matthew, though allusive, is a highly disciplined writer, rigorously eliminating everything unrelated to his immediate concerns. So we must take it as a rule of thumb that Matthew's theology cannot be accurately discovered by studying what he omits—which cannot show more than what is not his immediate concern, and even then some of his omissions are purely stylistic—but primarily by what he includes. This is especially significant in the miracles where Matthew leaves out so much. In the leper's healing, Sabourin's suggestion is especially implausible since Matthew stresses elsewhere Jesus' compassion and draws theological meaning from it (9:35–38).

1 Jesus came down out of the hills (see on 5:1), where the Sermon on the Mount had been delivered; and still the great crowds (4:23–25; 7:28–29) pursued him.

2–3 The introductory *kai idou* (lit , "and behold"; also in Luke, absent from Mark, untranslated in NIV) does not require that this healing immediately follow the sermon. In Matthew *kai idou* has a broad range, sometimes serving as a loose connective, sometimes introducing a startling thought or event, and sometimes, as here, marking the beginning of a new pericope. Whether NT leprosy was actual leprosy ("Hansen's disease"; cf. DNTT, 2:463–66) or a broader category of skin ailments including leprosy is uncertain. But the Jews abhorred it, not only because of the illness itself, but because it rendered the sufferer and all with whom he came in direct contact ceremonially unclean. To be a leper was interpreted as being cursed by God (cf. Num 12:10, 12; Job 18:13). Healings were rare (cf. Num 12:10–15; 2 Kings 5:9–14) and considered as difficult as raising the dead (2 Kings 5:7, 14; cf. SBK, 4:745ff.). In the Messianic Age there would be no leprosy (cf. 11:5).

The man *prosekynei* ("knelt") before Jesus, but the verb can also mean "worshiped." Clearly the former is meant in this historical setting. Yet as with the title "Lord" (see on 7:22–23), Christian readers of Matthew could not help concluding that this leper spoke and acted better than he knew. "If you are willing" reflects the leper's great faith, prompted by Jesus' healing activity throughout the district (4:24): he had no question about Jesus' healing power but feared only that he would be passed by. In affirming his willingness to heal, Jesus proved that his will is decisive. He already had the authority and power and only needed to decide and act. J.D. Kingsbury ("Retelling the 'Old, Old Story,'" *Currents in Theology and Missions* 4 [1976]: 346) suggests that "reached out his hand" symbolizes the exercise of authority (cf. Exod 7:5; 14:21; 15:6; 1 Kings 8:42); but Matthew's use of the same Greek expression elsewhere (12:13 [*bis*], 49; 14:31; 26:51) shows that Kingsbury's interpretation is fanciful. More probably Jesus had to reach to touch the leper because the leper did not dare come close to him.

By touching an unclean leper, Jesus would become ceremonially defiled himself (cf. Lev 13–14). But at Jesus' touch nothing remains defiled. Far from becoming unclean, Jesus makes the unclean clean. Both Jesus' word and touch (8:15; 9:20–21, 29; 14:36) are effective, possibly implying that authority is vested in his message as well as in his person.

4 Despite Held's view (Bornkamm, *Tradition,* p. 256), this verse is not the "entire goal of this story." That is reductionistic and ignores the intertwined themes (cf. comments on 8:1–4; Heil, "Healing Miracles," p. 280, n. 25). While prohibitions against telling of cures and exorcisms are more common in Mark than Matthew,

they are not unknown in the latter (8:4; 9:30; 12:16; cf. 16:20; 17:9). They have nothing to do with the so-called messianic secret proposed by Wrede and defended by Bultmann (as Hill rightly holds). Nor does this particular prohibition enjoin silence only till the cured leper has been to Jerusalem to be cleared by the priest (Lenski, Barnes). The synoptic parallels (Mark 1:45; Luke 5:15) as well as other similar occurrences in Matthew demonstrate that these commands to be silent have other functions—to show that Jesus is not presenting himself as a mere wonder-worker (Stonehouse, *Witness of Matthew*, p. 62; Maier) who can be pressured into messiahship by crowds whose messianic views are materialistic and political. Jesus' authority derives from God alone, not the acclaim of men (Bonnard); he came to die, not to trounce the Romans. The people who disobeyed Jesus' injunctions to silence only made his mission more difficult.

Jesus commanded the cured man to follow the Mosaic prescriptions for lepers who claimed healing (cf. Lev 14). This, he said, was *eis martyrion autois* ("as a testimony to them"). Much debate surrounds *autois*. Is the testimony positive, "for them" (Trilling, pp. 128f.), as proof of the healing, or negative, "against them" (Hummel, pp. 81f.), as a sort of denunciation of their unbelief? Such conflicting categories are not helpful. Of the other places where the Synoptics use *eis martyrion* ("for a witness"; 10:18; 24:14; Mark 1:44; 6:11; 13:9; Luke 5:14; 9:5; 21:13), only two require "witness against" (contra Frankmölle, p. 120, n. 193, who insists 10:18 and 24:14 are also negative). Most of the rest are "neutral" and imply division around the "witness" presented.

Better progress can be made by asking why, in this setting, Jesus commands obedience. It cannot be simply to prove that Jesus remains faithful to the law (Calvin) and so encourages Matthew's Jewish Christians to be similarly faithful (Hill, Schniewind, Schweizer). Formally speaking, Jesus has already transcended the law by touching the leper without being defiled, a confirmation of our exegesis of 5:17–20. Furthermore, if around A.D. 85 (when Hill thinks the first Gospel was written) Matthew were simply trying to get his community to adhere (unlike Pauline communities) to the details of OT law, he chose a singularly ill-suited story to make his point, because by that date the destruction of the temple had effectively abolished priests and offerings. It is far easier to deduce from the setting that this material is authentic.

In one sense Jesus does submit to the law. He puts himself under its ordinances. But the result is startling: the law achieves new relevance by pointing to Jesus. In conforming to the law, the cured leper becomes the occasion for the law to confirm Jesus' authority as the healer who needs but to will the deed for it to be done. Thus the supreme function of the "gift" Moses commanded is not as a guilt offering (Lev 14:10–18) but as a witness to men concerning Jesus. In this context "to them" is relatively incidental: it might refer to the priests or the people, but in either case it points to Jesus Christ (see on 5:17–20).

b. The centurion's servant

8:5–13

⁵When Jesus had entered Capernaum, a centurion came to him, asking for help. ⁶"Lord," he said, "my servant lies at home paralyzed and in terrible suffering."
⁷Jesus said to him, "I will go and heal him."
⁸The centurion replied, "Lord, I do not deserve to have you come under my

roof. But just say the word, and my servant will be healed. [9]For I myself am a man under authority, with soldiers under me. I tell this one, 'Go,' and he goes; and that one, 'Come,' and he comes. I say to my servant, 'Do this,' and he does it."

[10]When Jesus heard this, he was astonished and said to those following him, "I tell you the truth, I have not found anyone in Israel with such great faith. [11]I say to you that many will come from the east and the west, and will take their places at the feast with Abraham, Isaac and Jacob in the kingdom of heaven. [12]But the subjects of the kingdom will be thrown outside, into the darkness, where there will be weeping and gnashing of teeth."

[13]Then Jesus said to the centurion, "Go! It will be done just as you believed it would." And his servant was healed at that very hour.

If this story (cf. Luke 7:1–10) comes from Q, then at least in this instance Q contains more than short sayings of Jesus; or, better, this is evidence against a unitary Q. It is uncertain whether this account is the same as the one in John 4:46–53. The many differences argue against this, though admittedly some of these are overemphasized. In John, Jesus rebukes the centurion and the onlookers for their love of signs; but though there is no mention of that here, Matthew treats that theme elsewhere (12:38–39; 16:1–4). Most modern scholars, unlike those of earlier generations, simply assume that there is but one incident. However, the matter is ably discussed by Edward F. Siegman, "St. John's Use of Synoptic Material," CBQ 30 (1968): 182–98. (On the distinctive theological emphases of Matthew and Luke, cf. R.P. Martin, "The Pericope of the Healing of the 'Centurion's' Servant/Son [Matt 8:5–13 par. Luke 7:1–10]: Some Exegetical Notes," *Unity and Diversity in the New Testament,* ed. R.A. Guelich [Grand Rapids: Eerdmans, 1978], pp. 14–22.)

Form critics find the purpose of the story in the dialogue to which the miracle leads and call it a "pronouncement story" or "apophthegm" rather than a "miracle story." One wonders why it can't be both (cf. Stephen H. Travis, "Form Criticism," Marshall, *NT Interpretation,* esp. pp. 157–60). The chief difference, apart from theological emphases, between vv.5–13 and Luke 7:1–10 is the use of intermediaries in the latter. Probably Matthew, following his tendency to condense, makes no mention of the servants in order to lay the greater emphasis on faith according to the principle *qui facit per alium facit per se* ("he who acts by another acts himself")—a principle the centurion's argument implies (vv.8–9).

5 This is Matthew's second mention of Capernaum (cf. 4:13). In Jesus' day it was an important garrison town. No Roman legions were posted in Palestine, but there were auxiliaries under Herod Antipas, who had the right to levy troops. These were non-Jews, probably recruited from outside Galilee, perhaps from Lebanon and Syria. Centurions were the military backbone throughout the empire, maintaining discipline and executing orders. Luke stresses this centurion's Jewish sympathies and his humility, Matthew his faith and race (vv.10–11). Indeed, one reason Matthew says nothing of the intermediaries may be because they were Jews, and he does not want to blur the racial distinction.

6–7 On "Lord," see on 7:21–23. The word *pais* (v.6) can mean "servant" or "son." Luke's word (*doulos*) means "servant," and many (e.g., Bultmann, *Synoptic Tradition,* p. 38, n. 4) insist Matthew's *pais* means "son." But fair examination of NT usage (cf. France, "Exegesis," p. 256) reveals that only one of twenty-four NT occurrences requires "son," viz., John 4:51. This further supports the view that John 4 records a different healing on a separate occasion. Conceivably it was the earlier healing of an official's son (John 4) that strengthened the centurion's faith in this instance. Though paralysis coupled with severe pain is attested elsewhere (e.g., 1 Macc 9:55–56), the nature of the servant's malady is unknown. Derrett's psychosomatic speculations (*NT Studies*, 1:156–57, 166–68) are fanciful.

Jewish rabbis, like ministers today, were often invited to pray for the sick (cf. SBK, 1:475); but the parallels are not close, for the centurion is implicitly asking for healing, not prayers. Many (Zahn; Klostermann; Turner [*Insights*, pp. 50f.]; Held [Bornkamm, *Tradition*, p. 194]) interpret Jesus' response (v.7) as a question: "Shall I [*egō*, emphatic; i.e., I, a Jew] come and heal him?" This is probably right. The parallel with the Canaanite woman (15:21–28) is compelling, and otherwise it is difficult to explain the emphatic "I." Jesus' response was not based on fears of ritual defilement—vv.1–4 set that to rest—or even on his general restriction of his ministry to Israel (see on 10:5–6; 15:24; but even in Matthew there are significant exceptions, e.g., 8:28–34). It was based on a desire to find out exactly what the centurion was after and what degree of faith stood behind his ambiguous request (v.6).

8–9 Both here and in the story of the Canaanite woman (15:21–28), faith triumphs over the obstacle Jesus erects. Luke records neither Jesus' question (see on v.7) nor the story of the Canaanite woman; his treatment of faith is not quite so pointed. The centurion's reply opens with "Lord" (v.8), implying tenacity and deference (cf. v.6; 7:21–23). As John the Baptist felt unworthy to baptize Jesus, so this centurion felt unworthy to entertain him in his home. The feeling of unworthiness did not arise from an awareness that the centurion might render Jesus ceremonially defiled (contra Bonnard); race had nothing to do with it. *Hikanos* ("sufficient," "worthy") here as elsewhere (3:11; 1 Cor 15:9; 2 Cor 2:16) reveals the man's sense of unworthiness (NIV, "do not deserve") in the face of Jesus' authority (cf. TDNT, 3:294; France. "Exegesis," p. 258). "Here was one who was in the state described in the first clauses of the 'Beatitudes,' and to whom came the promise of the second clauses; because Christ *is* the connecting link between the two" (LTJM 1:549; emphasis his).

The centurion believed that Jesus' word was sufficient to heal his servant. It is significant that we have no recorded evidence that up to this point Jesus had performed a healing miracle at a distance and by word alone (unless John 4:46–53 is an exception). The centurion's thinking (v.9) is profound. There is no need to take the first clause as implying that the *only* parallel between his authority and that of Jesus was in their ability to order things to be done: "I, although I am a man under orders, can effect things by my word" (Hill, *Matthew*). That is a barely possible rendering of the opening *kai gar egō;* the more natural translation is that of NIV ("for I myself"), which applies the words to the entire verse. This means that the centurion's words presuppose an understanding of the Roman military system. All "authority" (*exousia*, as in 7:29) belonged to the emperor and was delegated. Therefore, because he was under the emperor's authority, when the centurion spoke, he spoke with the emperor's authority, and so his command was obeyed. A footsoldier who disobeyed would not be defying a mere centurion but the emperor, Rome itself, with all its imperial majesty and might (cf. Derrett, *NT Studies*, 1:159f.). This self-understanding the centurion applied to Jesus. Precisely because Jesus was under God's authority, he was vested with God's authority, so that when Jesus spoke, God spoke. To defy Jesus was to defy God; and Jesus' word must therefore be vested with God's authority that is able to heal sickness. This analogy, though not perfect, reveals an astonishing faith that recognizes that Jesus needed neither ritual, magic, nor any other help; his authority was God's authority, and his word was effective because it was God's word.

10 In Mark 6:6 Jesus is astonished at deeply rooted unbelief. Here he is astonished (same verb) at the faith of the centurion. "Though amazement is not appropriate for God, seeing it must arise from new and unexpected happenings, yet it could occur in Christ, inasmuch as he had taken on our human emotions, along with our flesh" (Calvin). Jesus spoke to those following him (not necessarily his disciples; cf. 4:25; 8:1) with the prefatory notice ("I tell you"; cf. on 5:22) that warns of the solemn remark to follow.

Jesus commended the man's faith (cf. also v.13). The greatness of his faith did not rest in the mere fact that he believed Jesus could heal from a distance but in the degree to which he had penetrated the secret of Jesus' authority. That faith was the more surprising since the centurion was a Gentile and lacked the heritage of OT revelation to help him understand Jesus. But this Gentile penetrated more deeply into the nature of Jesus' person and authority than any Jew of his time. Matthew's words stress even more than Luke's the uniqueness of the centurion's faith and underline the movement of the gospel from the Jews to the Gentiles, or rather from the Jews to all people regardless of race—a movement prophesied in the OT, developed in Jesus' ministry (see on 1:1, 3–5; 2:1–12; 3:9–10; 4:15–16), and commanded by the Great Commission (28:18–20). "This incident is a preview of the great insight which came later through another centurion's faith, 'Then to the Gentiles God has granted repentance unto life' (Acts 11:18)" (France, "Exegesis," p. 260).

11–12 Again "I say to you" (v.11) solemnizes what follows (cf. v.10). Most interpreters assume that Matthew has added these two verses (not in Luke) to the narrative, taking them from an entirely different setting (viz., Luke 13:28–29; e.g., Chilton, *God in Strength*, pp. 179–201). But this is problematic apart from clear criteria distinguishing it from the obvious alternative—that Jesus said similar things more than once. The words of the saying are not very close in the two passages; but the imagery is so colorful that an itinerant preacher could have used it repeatedly, especially if warnings to the Jews and the prospect of Gentile admission to the fellowship of God's people were two of his major themes.

The picture is that of the "messianic banquet," derived from such OT passages as Isaiah 25:6–9 (cf. 65:13–14) and embellished in later Judaism (cf. TDNT, 2:34–35). These embellishments did not usually anticipate the presence of Gentiles at the banquet, which symbolized the consummation of the messianic kingdom (cf. 22:1–14; 25:10; 26:29). But Jesus here insists that many will come from the four points of the compass and join the patriarchs at the banquet. These "many" can only be Gentiles, contrasted as they are (v.12) with "subjects of the kingdom" (*hoi huioi tēs basileias*, lit., "the sons of the kingdom").

"Son of" or "sons of" can mean "belonging to" or "destined for" (cf. "sons of the bridal chamber" [9:15; NIV, "guests of the bridegroom"] and "son of hell" [23:15; cf. SBK, 1:476–78; 1QS 17:3; and comments on 5:9]). So the "subjects of the kingdom" are the Jews, who see themselves as sons of Abraham (cf. 3:9–10), belonging to the kingdom by right. Some Jews (e.g., those at Qumran) restricted the elect to a smaller group of the pious within Israel. But Jesus reverses roles (cf. 21:43); and the sons of the kingdom are thrown aside, left out of the future messianic banquet, consigned to darkness where there are tears and gnashing of teeth—elements common to descriptions of gehenna, hell (cf. 4 Ezra 7:93; 1 Enoch 63:10; Pss Sol 14:9; 15:10; Wisd Sol 17:21; cf. Matt 22:13; comments on 5:29).

The definite articles with "weeping" and "gnashing" (cf. Gr.) emphasize the horror of the scene: *the* weeping and *the* gnashing (Turner, *Syntax*, p. 173). Weeping suggests suffering and gnashing of teeth despair (McNeile). The reversal is not absolute. The patriarchs themselves are Jews, as were the earliest disciples (Rom 11:1–5). But these verses affirm, in a way that could only shock Jesus' hearers, that the locus of the people of God would not always be the Jewish race. If these verses do not quite authorize the Gentile mission, they open the door to it and prepare for the Great Commission (28:18–20) and Ephesians 3.

There may be a still deeper implication in these words of Jesus. OT passages that may be reflected in vv. 11–12 can be divided into three groups: (1) those that desribe a gathering of Israel from all quarters of the earth (Ps 107:3; Isa 43:5–6; 49:12); (2) those that predict the worship of God by Gentiles in all parts of the earth (Isa 45:6; 59:19; Mal 1:11); (3) those that predict the coming of Gentiles to Jerusalem (Isa 2:2–3; 60:3–4; Mic 4:1–2; Zech 8:20–23). The closest literary parallels lie between vv. 11–12 and the first group (cf. Gundry, *Use of OT*, pp. 76f.); and on this basis France (*Jesus*, p. 63; id., "Exegesis," pp. 261–63) proposes that a typology is assumed—the true "Israel" is now being gathered from the four corners of the earth, i.e., from the Gentiles. This is possible, for we have already seen several ways Matthew treats OT history as prophetic. But because he is not using fulfillment language here, Jesus may be using OT language without affirming that the relationship between OT and NT at this point is typological.

13 The *hōs* ("just as," NIV) must be rightly understood: Jesus performed a miracle, not *in proportion to* the centurion's faith, nor *because of* the centurion's faith, but in content what was *expected by* the centurion's faith (cf. 15:28, where the emphasis is also on faith).

Notes

9 The three commands are aorist, present, and aorist respectively. Sometimes "the tense appears to be determined more by the meaning of the verb or by some obscure habit than by the 'rules' of *Aktionsart*" (Moule, *Idiom Book*, p. 135).

11 The verb ἀνακλιθήσονται (*anaklithēsontai*, lit., "will recline") describes the normal posture when eating; people lay on low couches or pallets (cf. John 13:23; 21:20). In the NT reclining is not restricted to banquets (e.g., Mark 6:39; Luke 7:36), and there is no theological or symbolic significance in the act itself (contra Schlatter; Lohmeyer, *Matthäus*). Hence NIV's paraphrastic "take their places."

12 Stonehouse (*Witness of Matthew*, pp. 231f.), to avoid saying that the "subjects of the kingdom" are such only in appearance and self-estimation, understands "kingdom" to refer to the "theocratic kingdom" as opposed to the "kingdom of heaven." But strictly speaking the theocratic kingdom was no longer in existence; and it is difficult to see how "kingdom" in the phrase "subjects of the kingdom" may properly be taken as anything other than the kingdom just mentioned (v. 11).

c. Peter's mother-in-law

8:14-15

> 14When Jesus came into Peter's house, he saw Peter's mother-in-law lying in bed with a fever. 15He touched her hand and the fever left her, and she got up and began to wait on him.

14-15 In Mark 1:29-31; Luke 4:38-39, this incident follows the casting out of a demon on a Sabbath from a man in the synagogue at Capernaum. Presumably this healing takes place on that same Sabbath. Matthew, however, condenses the account by omitting what does not bear on his immediate theme—Jesus' authority.

Peter was married (1 Cor 9:5) and had moved with his brother Andrew from their home in Bethsaida (John 1:44) to Capernaum, possibly to remain near Jesus (Matt 4:13). His mother-in-law's fever (v. 14) may have been malarial; fever itself was considered a disease, not a symptom, at that time (cf. John 4:52; Acts 28:8). Jewish Halakah forbade touching persons with many kinds of fever (SBK, 1:479f.). But Jesus healed with a touch (v. 15). As in v. 3, the touch did not defile the healer but healed the defiled. The imperfect *diēkonei* is best taken as conative: "began to serve," almost certainly a reference to waiting on him. Matthew mentions her service, not to tell his readers that those touched by Jesus become his servants (contra P. Lamarche, "La guérison de la belle-mère de Pierre et le genre littéraire des évangiles," *Nouvelle Revue Théologique* 87 [1965]: 515-26), but to make it clear that the miracle was effective and instantaneous (cf. v. 26, where the result of Jesus' stilling the storm is complete calm). Jesus' authority instantly accomplishes what he wills.

d. Many at evening

8:16-17

> 16When evening came, many who were demon-possessed were brought to him, and he drove out the spirits with a word and healed all the sick. 17This was to fulfill what was spoken through the prophet Isaiah:
>
> > "He took up our infirmities
> > and carried our diseases."

16 Because the context is still the Sabbath in Mark 1:32-34; Luke 4:40-41, mention of the evening there suggests that the people waited till Sabbath was over at sundown before again flocking to Jesus with their sick. Here in Matthew, where there is no indication this is a Sabbath, mention of the evening simply shows the pace of Jesus' ministry (cf. also other summaries—4:23-24; 9:35; 11:4-5; 12:15; 14:35; 15:30; 19:2).

With the exception of the quotation from Isaiah 53 (v. 17), most of Matthew's other changes are not very significant. The addition of "a word" is neither typical (vv. 3, 8) nor atypical (v. 15) of Matthew's healing reports. The change from "many" (Mark) to "all" (Matthew) is less significant than is often claimed, for Mark does not say Jesus healed many but not all the sick; rather, when "the whole town gathered at the door," he healed "many" of the people (Mark 1:33-34). Matthew does not say that Jesus forbade the demons to tell who he was; he prefers to focus attention on Jesus' power and on the Scripture witness to his person and ministry. Other differences are even more minor. (Omission of Luke 4:41 may tell against Kingsbury's view of the centrality of the "Son of God" theme.)

Jesus drives out *ta pneumata* ("the spirits" ["demons" in Mark and Luke]), often recognized in intertestamental literature as agents of disease. They are normally qualified by the adjective "evil" in the NT. On the idiom for "the sick," see on 4:24.

17 (On the fulfillment formulas, see on 1:23; 2:5, 15, 23; 4:14; Introduction, section 11.b.) This quotation is Isaiah 53:4. Matthew's rendering does not follow LXX or Targum, both of which spiritualize the Hebrew. Most likely v.17 is Matthew's own translation of the Hebrew (Stendahl, *School*, pp. 106f.). Because Isaiah 52:13–53:12, the fourth "Servant Song," pictures the Servant suffering vicariously for others, whereas, on the face of it, Matthew renders the Hebrew in such a way as to speak of "taking" and "carrying" physical infirmities and physical diseases but not in terms of suffering vicariously for sin, many detect in this passage strong evidence that Matthew cites the OT in an indefensible and idiosyncratic fashion. McConnell (p. 120) sees this as another instance of Matthew's using an OT passage out of context for his own ends (cf. also Rothfuchs, pp. 70–72). McNeile suggests Isaiah 53:4 had already become detached from its context when Matthew used it.

There are, however, better ways of interpreting this passage:

1. It is generally understood since the work of C.H. Dodd (*According to the Scriptures* [London: Nisbet, 1952]) that when the NT quotes a brief OT passage, it often refers implicitly to the entire context of the quotation. This is very likely here, for Matthew has a profound understanding of the OT. Moreover, Isaiah 53:7 is probably alluded to in Matthew 27:12, Isaiah 53:9 in Matthew 27:57, and Isaiah 53:10–12 in Matthew 20:28, the latter in a context affirming vicarious atonement theology. Any interpretation of v.17 that does not take into account the thrust of the entire Servant Song is therefore dubious.

2. Both Scripture and Jewish tradition understand that all sickness is caused, directly or indirectly, by sin (see on 4:24; cf. Gundry, *Use of OT*, pp. 230f.). This encourages us to look for a deeper connection between v.17 and Isaiah 53:4.

3. Isaiah is thinking of the servant's "taking the diseases of others upon himself through his suffering and death for their sin" (Gundry, *Use of OT*, p. 230). The two verbs he uses are *nāśā'*("took up [our infirmities]") and *sᵉbālām* ("carried [our sorrows]"), which do not themselves necessarily have the force of substitution, though they can be interpreted that way. The LXX spiritualizes "infirmities" to "sins"; and in this sense the verse is referred to in 1 Peter 2:24 in defense of substitutionary atonement. That interpretation of the verse is legitimate because the flow of the Servant Song supports it. But strictly speaking Isaiah 53:4 simply speaks of the Servant's bearing infirmities and carrying sicknesses; and it is only the context, plus the connection between sickness and sin, that shows that the *way* he bears the sickness of others is through his suffering and death.

4. Isaiah 53, as we have seen, is important among NT writers for understanding the significance of Jesus' death (e.g., Acts 8:32–33; 1 Peter 2:24); but when Matthew here cites Isaiah 53:4, at first glance he applies it only to Jesus' healing ministry, not to his death. But in the light of the three preceding points, the discrepancy is resolved if Matthew holds that *Jesus' healing ministry is itself a function of his substitutionary death,* by which he lays the foundation for destroying sickness. Matthew's two verbs, contrary to some opinion, exactly render the Hebrew: the Servant "took up" (*elaben*) our infirmities and "carried" (*ebastasen*) our diseases (Gundry,

Use of OT, pp. 109, 111). Matthew could not have used the LXX and still referred to physical disease. Yet his own rendering of the Hebrew, far from wrenching Isaiah 53:4 out of context, indicates his profound grasp of the theological connection between Jesus' healing ministry and the Cross.

5. That connection is supported by various collateral arguments. The prologue insists Jesus came to save his people from their sin, and this within the context of the coming of the kingdom. When Jesus began his ministry, he not only proclaimed the kingdom but healed the sick (see on 4:24). Healing and forgiveness are tied together, not only in a pericope like 9:1-8, but by the fact that the consummated kingdom, in which there is no sickness, is made possible by Jesus' death and the new covenant that his death enacted (26:27-29). Thus the healings during Jesus' ministry can be understood not only as the foretaste of the kingdom but also as the fruit of Jesus' death. It could be that Matthew also judges Isaiah 53:4 appropriate because it seems to form a transition from the Servant's being despised to his suffering and death. Certainly at least some rabbinic tradition understood Isaiah 53:4 to refer to physical disease (cf. SBK, 1:481-82).

6. This means that for Matthew, Jesus' healing miracles pointed beyond themselves to the Cross. In this he is like the evangelist John, whose "signs" similarly point beyond themselves.

7. But even here there is a deeper connection than first meets the eye. These miracles (ch. 8) have been framed to emphasize Jesus' authority. This authority was never used to satisfy himself (cf. 4:1-10). He healed the despised leper (vv.1-4), a Gentile centurion's servant who was hopelessly ill (vv.5-13), other sick (vv.14-15), no matter how many (vv.16-17). Thus when he gave his life a ransom for many (20:28), it was nothing less than an extension of the same authority directed toward the good of others (cf. Hill, "Son and Servant," pp. 9, 11, who also points out how reductionistic Kingsbury's "Son of God" christology is in light of such intertwining themes). Jesus' death reflected the intermingling of authority and servanthood already noted (e.g., 3:17) and now progressively developed. After all, following the momentous miracles of vv.1-17, the Son of Man had nowhere to lay his head (v.20).

Despite the stupendous signs of kingdom advance, the royal King and Suffering Servant faced increasingly bitter opposition. The Father had committed everything to him, but he was gentle and humble in heart (11:27, 29). This moving theme needs to be traced out inductively (cf. B. Gerhardsson, "Gottes Sohn als Diener Gottes: Messias, *Agapē* und Himmelherrschaft nach dem Matthäus-evangelium," ST 27 [1973]: 73-106). If the Davidic Messiah of Jewish expectation (Pss Sol 17:6) purifies his people by annihilating sinners, Matthew's Davidic Messiah–Suffering Servant purifies his people with his death, takes on himself their diseases, and opens fellowship to sinners (cf. Hummel, pp. 124-25).

This discussion does not resolve two related questions.

1. Did Jews in Jesus' day understand Isaiah 53 messianically? Most scholars say no. Jeremias answers more cautiously—viz., many Jews did so interpret Isaiah's "Servant" but ignored references to his suffering (cf. Jeremias and Zimmerli).

2. Did Jesus interpret his own ministry in terms of the Suffering Servant? Matthew 8:17 does not help us because it gives us no more than Matthew's understanding of the significance of Jesus' healing miracles. (See further on 20:28; cf. Hooker, *Jesus and the Servant*; T.W. Manson, *The Servant Messiah* [Cambridge: University Press, 1953], pp. 57-58, 73.)

It should be stated that this discussion cannot be used to justify healing on demand. This text and others clearly teach that there is healing in the Atonement; but similarly there is the promise of a resurrection body in the Atonement, even if believers do not inherit it until the Parousia. From the perspective of the NT writers, the Cross is the basis for all the benefits that accrue to believers; but this does not mean that all such benefits can be secured at the present time on demand, any more than we have the right and power to demand our resurrection bodies. The availability of any specific blessing can be determined only by appealing to the overall teaching of Scripture. Modern Christians should avoid the principal danger of Corinth, viz., an over-realized eschatology (cf. A.C. Thistleton, "Realized Eschatology at Corinth," NTS 24 [1977]: 510–26), which demands blessings that may not be ours till the end of the age.

2. The cost of following Jesus

8:18–22

> [18]When Jesus saw the crowd around him, he gave orders to cross to the other side of the lake. [19]Then a teacher of the law came to him and said, "Teacher, I will follow you wherever you go."
> [20]Jesus replied, "Foxes have holes and birds of the air have nests, but the Son of Man has no place to lay his head."
> [21]Another disciple said to him, "Lord, first let me go and bury my father."
> [22]But Jesus told him, "Follow me, and let the dead bury their own dead."

Compare Luke 9:57–62, in a later but detached setting, with three inquirers, not two. The stilling-of-the-storm incident (vv.23–27; Mark 4:35–41), following the "day of parables," shows that Matthew 8:18 parallels Mark 4:35. Matthew does not specify the time of this pericope (vv.18–22) beyond saying that it was one of many occasions when crowds pressed Jesus. Apparently Matthew chose to insert these two vignettes here because they help show the nature of Jesus' ministry and the disciples he was seeking. Hengel's attempt to limit to a few selected individuals Jesus' call to discipleship (M. Hengel, *Nachfolge und Charisma* [Berlin: Töpelmann, 1968], pp. 68–70) is insensitive to Jesus' place in the history of redemption and the ambiguity of what it meant at that time to be his disciple (see further, below).

18–19 Perhaps Jesus' imminent departure to the east side of the lake (v.18) prompted certain people to beg him to include them in the circle of disciples going with him. Discipleship in the strict sense required close attachment to the master's person. The fact that the first candidate was "a [*heis*, "one," can have the force of *tis*, "a certain," in NT Gr.: cf. Zerwick, par. 155; Moule, *Idiom Book*, p. 125] teacher of the law" (see on 2:4) has led to no little controversy; for it is often argued that the opponents in Matthew are Pharisees and scribes ("teachers of the law"), yet here a scribe appears as a candidate for discipleship. R. Walker (pp. 26–27) and others therefore say Jesus rejected this teacher of the law (v.19). By comparison with the next inquirer, he is neither called a disciple nor told to follow Jesus (vv.21–22). But this reasoning will not stand up.

1. "Disciple" does not necessarily refer to a fully committed follower and cannot have that force in v.21 (see on 5:1). Albright and Mann dislike this fact so much that they are reduced to emending the text. It is difficult to see why a wedge should be drawn between the two inquirers, both "disciples" in this loose sense.

2. Verse 21 does not say, "Another man, one of his disciples" (NIV), but, "Another of his disciples," implying that the teacher of the law was also a disciple in this loose sense. Moreover *heteros* ("another," sometimes "another of a different kind") cannot normally be distinguished in the NT from *allos* ("another," sometimes "another of the same kind"), and certainly not in Matthew (cf. BAGD, p. 315).

3. Judged by their respective approaches to Jesus, if either of the two approaches Jesus with no hesitation, it is the teacher of the law, not the "other disciple." Significantly, the scribe, a teacher of the law, addressed Jesus as "teacher" and simply promised to follow him anywhere.

4. In this light Jesus' response to the second man—"Follow me"—does not mean he is preferred but is necessary precisely because the inquirer was not at this time planning to follow Jesus.

Scholars who reject the reconstruction of Walker and others argue that Matthew, far from being opposed to teachers of the law, has positive things to say about them (v.19; 13:52; 23:8–10, 34), some of which even suggest that Matthew's church had leaders who called themselves "teachers of the law" (cf. Grundmann; Hummel, p. 27; Kilpatrick, pp. 110ff.).

But this reverse argument is too strong. What other categories could Jesus have used for his church's future leaders than those already established (13:52; 23:34)? A great deal of the reconstructed Matthean church hangs by the thread of overdrawn exegesis. But they have correctly pointed out that vv.19–20 and similar passages show that Matthew is not in principle antiscribe or anti-anyone else: rather, in Matthew's view, all people, scribes or not, divide around the absolute claims of Jesus and must be weighed according to their response to him (cf. van Tilborg, pp. 128–31). This is the fruit, not of anti-Semitism (see further on 26:57–68), but of claims to truth and, like other matters judged offensive by both Jews and Gentiles (1 Cor 1:21–23), cannot be eliminated without relativizing truth and him who is the truth.

20 Jesus' response shows that he identifies the scribe's request as less the commitment of an Ittai (2 Sam 15:21) than the overconfidence of a Peter (Luke 22:33). "Nothing has done more harm to Christianity than the practice of filling the ranks of Christ's army with every volunteer who is willing to make a little profession, and talk fluently of experience" (Ryle). "Nothing was less aimed at by our Lord than to have *followers*, unless they were genuine and sound; he is as far from desiring this as it would have been easy to attain it" (Stier, emphasis his). Jesus' reply says nothing about the inquirer's response. Strictly speaking it was neither invitation nor rebuke but a pointed way of saying that true discipleship to the "Son of Man" (see excursus, below) is not comfortable and should not be undertaken without counting the cost (cf. Luke 14:25–33). In the immediate context of Jesus' ministry, the saying does not mean that Jesus was penniless but homeless; the nature of his mission kept him on the move (cf. 4:23–25; 9:35–38) and would keep his followers on the move.

21–22 For the significance of the reference to "disciples," see on vv.19–20. If the scribe was too quick in promising, this "disciple" was too slow in performing (v.21). Palestinian piety, basing itself on the fifth commandment (Exod 20:12; cf. Deut 27:16), expected sons to attend to the burial of their parents (cf. Tobit 4:3; 14:10–11; M Berakoth 3:1; cf. Gen 25:9; 35:29; 50:13). Jesus' reply used paradoxical language (as in 16:25): Let the (spiritually) dead bury the (physically) dead (cf. Notes). Yet the response seems harsh to many interpreters; so they understand the inquirer to be requesting a delay to wait for an aged parent to die rather than a delay to bury a father who has died. Hebrew or Aramaic could mean that, Greek only with difficulty; and it is difficult to see how it makes Jesus' answer (v.22) more compassionate. Though in the OT certain people were not permitted to come in contact with corpses (Lev 21:1–12; Num 6:7), it is doubtful that Jesus saw his followers as priests or Nazirites needing special ceremonial safeguards (contra Trench, *Studies*, p. 169). More likely vv.21–22 are a powerful way of expressing the thought in 10:37—even closest family ties must not be set above allegiance to Jesus and the proclamation of the kingdom (Luke 9:60).

In actuality we may well question whether Jesus was really forbidding attendance at the father's funeral, any more than he was really advocating self-castration in 5:27–30. In this inquirer he detected insincerity, a qualified acceptance of Jesus' lordship. And that was not good enough. Commitment to Jesus must be without reservation. Such is the importance Jesus himself attached to his own person and mission.

Excursus: "The Son of Man" as a christological title

During the last twenty-five years, more than a dozen books and scores of important articles on the Son of Man have appeared. This excursus on the Son of Man as a christological title will provide some of the evidence and its interpretation in the recent debate and will sketch in the approach adopted for the commentary. Good summaries of earlier treatments are found in the work of A.J.B. Higgins (*Jesus and the Son of Man* [London: Lutterworth, 1964]), J. Neville Birdsall ("Who Is This Son of Man?" EQ 42 [1970]: 7–17), and I. Howard Marshall ("The Son of Man in Contemporary Debate," EQ 42 [1970]: 67–87). More recent treatments of the term and its major theological implications may be found in the works and bibliographies of C. Colpe (TDNT, 8:400–477), C.F.D. Moule (*Christology*, pp. 11–22), I. Howard Marshall (*The Origins of Christology* [Downers Grove, Ill.: IVP, 1976], pp. 63–82), the essays edited by R. Pesch and R. Schnackenburg (*Jesus und der Menschensohn* [Freiburg: Herder, 1975]), Goppelt (*NT Theologie*, pp. 226–53), Ladd (*NT Theology*, pp. 145–58), Dunn (*Christology*, pp. 65–97), Guthrie (*NT Theology*, pp. 270–82), Matthew Black ("Jesus and the Son of Man," *Journal for the Study of the New Testament* 1 [1978]: 4–18), and Stanton (*Jesus of Nazareth*, pp. 156ff.). To this can be added the recent work by Maurice Casey and that of A.J.B. Higgins (*The Son of Man in the Teaching of Jesus* [Cambridge: University Press, 1980]).

The expression Son of Man occurs eighty-one times in the Gospels, sixty-nine in the Synoptics. In every instance it is found either on Jesus' lips or, in two instances, on the lips of those quoting Jesus (viz., Luke 24:7; John 12:34). Outside the Gospels it is found in the NT as a christological title only in Acts 7:56; Revelation 1:13; 14:14 (Heb 2:6–8 is not relevant). The Gospel occurrences are usually classified according to the themes associated with the title: (1) the apocalyptic Son of Man who comes at the end of the age; (2) the suffering and dying Son of Man; and (3) the earthly Son of Man, engaged in a number of present ministries (in this context the title many serve as a circumlocution for "I"). Ladd (*NT Theology*, pp. 149–51) offers a typical breakdown of all the passages. There is some overlap of these categories and room for differences of interpretation. But of the thirty occurrences of "Son of Man" in Matthew, approximately thirteen belong to the first category (13:41; 16:27; 19:28; 24:27, 30 [bis], 37, 44; 25:31; 26:64; probably 24:39; and possibly 10:23; 16:28), ten to the second (12:40; 17:9, 12, 22; 20:18, 28; 26:2, 24 [bis], 45), and seven to the third (8:20; 9:6; 11:19; 12:8, 32; 13:37; probably 16:13; cf. also the variant at 18:11).

The meaning of any term or title depends at least in part on the way it has been used before. Much of the debate surrounding the precise significance of "Son of Man" in the Gospels turns on the influence ascribed to one or the other of the following backgrounds.

1. Daniel 7:13–14 pictures "one like a son of man" who approaches the Ancient of Days and is given "authority, glory and sovereign power" and "an everlasting dominion that will not pass away" in which "all peoples, nations and men of every language" worship him.

2. In Psalm 8:4 it is used generically for man.

3. In Ezekiel it appears repeatedly in the vocative as God's favorite way of addressing the prophet.

4. Psalm 80:17 places "son of man" in the context of vine imagery in such a way that it clearly refers to the nation Israel.

5. In 1QapGen 21:13 it appears as a Semitism for man generically ("I will make your descendants as the dust of the earth, which no son of man can number"). According to Vermes, "son of man" or "the son of man" in Aramaic was used in Jesus' day to refer generically to man or as a circumlocution by which a speaker might refer to himself (cf. G. Vermes in Black, *Aramaic Approach*, Appendix E; id., "The 'Son of Man' Debate," *Journal for the Study of the New Testament* [1978]: 19–32). But some of his claims must be tempered by the more sober dating and philology of Joseph A. Fitzmyer ("Another View of the 'Son of Man' Debate," *Journal for the Study of the New Testament* 4 [1979]: 58–68).

6. Many detect a background in the Similitudes of Enoch (1 Enoch 37–71) or other apocalyptic literature. Some have raised grave doubts that such literature is pre-Christian, based largely on the fact that the Similitudes are not found in the DSS copy of 1 Enoch; and if they are right, clearly the use of "Son of Man" in 1 Enoch 37–71 cannot have influenced Jesus' use of the term (cf. Longenecker, *Christology*, pp. 82–88; Dunn, *Christology*, pp. 67–82). The consensus among specialists of 1 Enoch, however, is that the Similitudes were in fact written before Christ's ministry, but that the "Son of Man" in these writings unambiguously refers to Enoch. The famous but unsupported emendation by R. H. Charles ("This is the Son of Man who was born unto Righteousness," 1 Enoch 71:14) is without warrant: the text reads "Thou, O Enoch, art the Son of Man" (cf. further James H. Charlesworth, *The Pseudepigrapha and the New Testament* [Cambridge: University Press, forthcoming]). We thus reach an ironic conclusion: the similitudes are pre-Christian and therefore must be considered a possible influence on Jesus' usage of "the Son of Man"; but they narrowly identify the figure with Enoch, and so whatever influence they exercised cannot be more than that of model or pattern, if that.

Against such diverse backgrounds, then, how are we to understand "the Son of Man" in the NT? Numerous proposals have been made, many of which fail to explain the evidence. The following are the most important.

1. Bultmann (*NT Theology*, 1:29–31, 49) made popular the view, later espoused by P. Vielhauer, H. Conzelmann, and H.M. Teeple, that Jesus never used the title "Son of Man" of himself but only of another figure coming in the future; and this future figure was based in Jesus' mind on the apocalyptic redeemer figure in 1 Enoch. This idea has been developed by other scholars who say that Jesus originally justified his authority by referring to a future apocalyptic figure who would come and vindicate him but that the church connected that

figure with Jesus himself. This will not do, for even if the Similitudes are not a late addition to 1 Enoch, the "Son of Man" figure there *may* not be an apocalyptic figure (cf. Casey, pp. 99–112) and in any case refers primarily to Enoch. Moreover the NT evidence connects Jesus with the Son of Man (e.g., Mark 14:62 and parallels); and, more important yet, any interpretation is called in question that flies in the face of the fact that the Gospel writers never use the term to describe Jesus but always report it as being on Jesus' lips. On the face of it, this shows that it was Jesus' favorite self-designation and that the early church respected this, even when it did not always know what to make of it (cf. further Jeremias, *NT Theology*, pp. 267f.).

2. Jeremias (*NT Theology*, pp. 257–76) has argued that some of the Son-of-Man sayings in all three classifications are authentic; but where in synoptic parallels one Gospel includes the reference to the Son of Man and another omits it (e.g., Matt 24:39–Luke 17:27; Matt 10:32–Luke 12:8), the latter is authentic. On the last point, some have argued just the reverse (e.g., F.H. Borsch, *The Son of Man in Myth and History* [London: SCM, 1967]). The weakness of Jeremias's view lies primarily in the consistency with which the expression occurs on Jesus' lips alone: if evangelists were adding the title to displace "I," it is at least strange they never use the title to refer to Jesus in contexts where there is no synoptic parallel. Here it seems best to side with Borsch, though we cannot be sure. Moreover Jeremias's chosen background runs from Daniel 7:13–14 in a straight line through the Similitudes of Enoch to the NT. Thus he depends on an established apocalyptic Son-of-Man figure that the sources do not support.

3. By appealing to Aramaic background, Vermes (Black, *Aramaic Approach*, Appendix E) argues that only those passages are authentic in which "Son of Man" is no more than a circumlocution for "I," by which the speaker refers to himself obliquely out of modesty or humility; the other uses in the Gospels are the creation of an apocalyptically minded church. Somewhat similar stances are adopted by Casey, who deems authentic the sayings that refer to mankind generally, and Barnabas Lindars ("Jesus as Advocate: A Contribution to the Christology Debate," BJRL 62 [1980]: 476–97; id., "The New Look on the Son of Man," BJRL 63 [1981]: 437–62), who argues that the use of the article (*ho*) in Greek, making the expression "*that* Son of Man" or "the [known] Son of Man" or "the [expected] Son of Man," shows that it was the translation of the tradition from Aramaic to Greek that gave messianic or Danielic meaning to the term. Therefore usages reflecting such meaning cannot be authentic. Quite apart from problems surrounding the dating of the linguistic evidence (cf. Fitzmyer, above), this theory postulates a creative church and a comparatively dull Jesus even though the evangelists consistently restrict the creative use of "Son of Man" to Jesus. The more it is argued that the church exercised a creative role in the theological development of this title, the stranger it is that the evangelists themselves do not apply the term to Jesus.

4. In his most recent book (*Son of Man*), Higgins reiterates and polishes his thesis that the "kernel" (i.e., authentic) sayings are all from Q and refer without exception to some of the future activities of the Son of Man, but not to his "coming" or "coming in glory," based on the "reasonable assumption of the existence of a Son of man concept in Judaism" (p. 124), and on a strange appeal to multiple attestation even though all his "kernel" sayings originally spring from Q (p. 125). Higgins says Jesus does not so much identify himself as the Son of Man (counterevidence, such as Mark 14:62, he ascribes to the church) as confine the term "to Jesus' clothing of his message of his anticipated judicial function in the judgment in symbolic imagery" (ibid.). The theory therefore falls under the strictures raised against 1 and 2.

5. C.F.D. Moule ("Neglected Features in the Problem of 'the Son of Man,' " in Gnilka, *Neues Testament*, pp. 413ff.; id., *Christology*, pp. 11–22), in contrast to Vermes, insists that the definite article (used everywhere except John 5:27) proves the designation to be titular, and thus whatever Semitic construction lay behind it, it must have referred to a particular, known "Son of Man." The only candidate is the figure in Daniel 7:13–14, possibly expounded in Judaism. This figure was understood to refer in a corporate way to "the saints of the Most High" (Dan 7:18); and, applied to Jesus, the title simultaneously affirms that he represents those saints and is a part of them. "Son of Man" is less a title than "a symbol of a vocation to be utterly loyal, even to death, in the confidence of ultimate vindication in the heavenly court. . . . Jesus is thus referring to the authority (whether in heaven or on earth) of true Israel, and so, of authentic Man, obedient, through thick and thin, to God's design" (*Christology*, p. 14).

Despite attractive features of this reconstruction, some reservations must be voiced. There appears to be more titular (indeed, messianic) force in some passages than Moule allows (e.g., Matt 16:13–20; 26:63–64); yet ironically he may be overemphasizing the significance of the definite article, since there is evidence in the Gospels that the people of Jesus' day did not always understand the designation to refer to the "well-known" Son of Man (e.g., Matt 16:13–30; John 12:34).

The best explanation attempts to avoid the reductionism that is implicit in most of the previous approaches, which too quickly rules out certain kinds of evidence or takes them as late creations of the church. Apart from the fact that in the Gospels "Son of Man" is always found on Jesus' lips, the authenticity of the Son-of-Man sayings stands up well under the criteria of redaction criticism (R.N. Longenecker, " 'Son of Man' Imagery," JETS 18 [1975]:8–9).

But what did Jesus mean by the expression? The simplest answer is that he used the term precisely because it was ambiguous: it could conceal as well as reveal (cf. E. Schweizer, "The Son of Man," JBL 79 [1960]: 128; Longenecker, " 'Son of Man' Imagery," pp. 10–12; Hendriksen; Marshall, *Origins*, pp. 76–78). When Jesus vested the term with its full messianic significance, it could only refer to Daniel 7:13–14. He did this most often toward the end of his ministry, when alone with his disciples and talking about eschatological events (esp. 24:27, 30 and parallels), or when under oath at his trial (26:63–64). Despite the fact that the Danielic figure is often said to be a symbol for the saints of the Most High (Dan 7:18), this is not certain. A good case can be made for the hypothesis that "one like a son of man" is not a symbol for the saints (7:18, 27). *He* is in the presence of the Ancient of Days; *they* are on earth during the time of the "little horn" (v.21). Perhaps "one like a son of man" secures the everlasting kingdom for the saints of the Most High (cf. W.J. Dumbrell, "Daniel 7 and the Function of Old Testament Apocalyptic," *Reformed Theological Review* 34 [1975]: 16ff.; and esp. Christopher Rowland, "The Influence of the First Chapter of Ezekiel on Jewish and Early Christian Literature," [Ph.D. dissertation, Cambridge University, 1974], p. 95). One "like a son of man" is a representative figure, not a corporate one; and the use of the symbol of the cloud rider favors a personal rather than a corporate interpretation.

Be that as it may, the messianic import of the title in some NT passages can scarcely be doubted. But Daniel 7:13–14 did not wield such large influence on first-century Judaism that simple reference to "the Son of Man," even with the article, would be instantly taken to refer to the Messiah. John Bowker ("The Son of Man," JTS 28 [1977]: 19–48) has decisively shown how many Semitic passages —in Ezekiel, Psalm 8, the Targums—use the term to contrast the chasm between frail, mortal man and God himself. This admirably suits a host of NT references, not only the suffering and passion texts, but others like Matthew

8:20. Jesus combined the two, Danielic Messiah and frail mortal, precisely because his own understanding of messiahship was laced with both themes.

We have already detected in Matthew the intermingling of Davidic Messiah and Suffering Servant. While "Son of Man" captures both authority and suffering, it is ambiguous enough that people who did not think of the Messiah in this dual way would have been mystified till after the Cross. It may well have been an acceptable way for a speaker to refer to himself, in which case the titular usage could only have been discerned from the context. Moreover it would have been extremely difficult for Jews expecting a purely political and glorious Messiah to know what the title meant, because just when they thought they had discerned its messianic significance, Jesus inserted something about the Son of Man's sufferings. That explains the perplexed question, "Who is this 'Son of Man'?" (John 12:34; cf. Luke 22:69–70). Even the disciples who had at some level begun to recognize Jesus the Son of Man as Messiah (Matt 16:13–16) could not accept or comprehend Jesus' repeated assertions that the Son of Man was destined to suffer and die (Matt 16:21–23; 17:9–12, 22, and parallels). Only when under oath and when it no longer mattered whether his enemies heard his clear claim to messiahship did Jesus reveal without any ambiguity at all that he, the Son of Man, was the messianic figure of Daniel 7:13–14 (Matt 26:63–64 and parallels); and then his opponents did not realize that an essential part of his messiahship was suffering and death. In Jesus' ministry "Son of Man" both reveals and conceals. Therefore he chose it as the ideal expression for progressively, and to some extent retrospectively, revealing the nature of his person and work.

After the Passion, Jesus' disciples could not help but find in his frequent earlier use of the term a messianic claim. Indeed, it is a mark of their fidelity to the separate historical stages of the unfolding history of redemption that in describing Jesus' prepassion ministry they confine the designation to the lips of Jesus alone. Thus no reader of Matthew who through the prologue knows that Jesus though a man is more than a man and through 16:13–20; 26:63–64 knows that the Son of Man is the Messiah could fail to see irony in 9:1–8. Jesus forgives sins and performs a miracle so that the onlookers may know that the "Son of Man" has authority on earth to forgive sins; but the people praise God because he has given such authority "to men." They are right (Jesus, the Son of Man, is mortal, a man born of woman, and heading for suffering and death), and they are wrong (they do not yet recognize him as more than a man, virgin born, and the messianic figure who appeared "as a son of man"—i.e., in human form—in one of Daniel's visions). So the interpretation that prevailed from the second century on—that "Son of Man" designates Jesus' humanity and "Son of God" his divinity —is not so much wrong as simplistic.

In Matthew 8:20, "the Son of Man" could easily be replaced by "I." Moreover it occurs in a setting that stresses Jesus' humanity and may foreshadow his sufferings. For postpassion Christian readers, it could only speak of the Messiah's wonderful self-humiliation. For the teacher of the law (vv.18–19), it was a great challenge—just how great a one could only be known after the Resurrection.

Notes

22 Black (*Aramaic Approach*, pp. 207–8) suggests that the original Aramaic may have read, "Let the מְתַנְיִין [*mᵉtiniyn*, 'waverers'] bury their מִיתִיהוֹן [*miṭihûn*, 'dead']"—and the first of the two Aramaic words has been mistakenly translated as if it were from מִיתִין (*mîtin*,

"corpses"). But like many of Black's suggestions, though philologically plausible, these hardly help explain the text and are hampered by the implausible thesis that Matthew (or some unknown person in the process of the oral tradition) was rather incompetent in Hebrew and Aramaic.

3. *Calming a storm*

8:23–27

23Then he got into the boat and his disciples followed him. 24Without warning, a furious storm came up on the lake, so that the waves swept over the boat. But Jesus was sleeping. 25The disciples went and woke him, saying, "Lord, save us! We're going to drown!"

26He replied, "You of little faith, why are you so afraid?" Then he got up and rebuked the winds and the waves, and it was completely calm.

27The men were amazed and asked, "What kind of man is this? Even the winds and the waves obey him!"

Jesus' authority over nature is now displayed. He may have less shelter than the beasts and birds of nature (v.20); yet he is nature's master (cf. parallels in Mark 4:35–41; Luke 8:22–25). Cope's attempt (*Matthew*, pp. 96–98) to argue that the pericope, at a pre-Matthean level, has been structured on Jonah is far from convincing. His parallels are either painfully forced ("a miraculous stilling related to the main character") or so general that it is difficult to conceive of any miraculous stilling-of-the-sea story that would not fit in his list of parallels.

23–25 The narrative moves forward from v.18; the order to cross the lake to escape the crowd is now carried out. A *ploion* ("boat") was a vessel of almost any size and description (v.23). Here it is doubtless a fishing boat, big enough for a dozen or more men and a good catch of fish, but not large, and without sails.

Bornkamm's insight—viz., that this pericope faces Matthew's readers with the demand for greater faith (v.26) in a setting requiring total discipleship (vv.18–22; cf. Bornkamm, *Tradition*, pp. 52–57)—has been distorted to make discipleship the exclusive concern. Because the disciples "followed" Jesus into the boat, Matthew, it is alleged (e.g., Bonnard, Hill), is using a characteristic theme, almost a technical term, to describe discipleship: those who follow Jesus need not fear, for they will be safe in any storm. But in Matthew *akoloutheō* ("to follow"), though it can refer to true followers (e.g., 4:20, 22; 9:9), often describes the action of the crowd as opposed to the disciples (e.g., 4:25; 8:1, 10; 12:15). When someone is physically following another, it is risky to invest the term with deep notions of discipleship; in 9:19 Jesus and his disciples "follow" (Gr.) the ruler but were certainly not his disciples! And if "follow" is so crucial a category for Matthew, why in 8:28–34 does he omit the parallel reference to following Jesus (Mark 5:18–20)?

Tertullian (*De Baptismo* 12) saw in the boat a picture of the church. Therefore some conclude that the storm "is a threat to the boat, rather than to the disciples" because it stands for the church, "and, in particular, the Church facing the upheaval of persecution (perhaps under Domitian, A.D. 81–96)" (Hill, *Mathew*; cf. Bonnard). But aside from the anachronistic nature of this appeal to Domitian, it is historically very doubtful whether there was widespread persecution under his reign (cf. John

Sweet, *Revelation* [London: SCM, 1979], esp. pp. 25–27). And is Matthew's story greatly helped by seeing danger for the boat but not the disciples? One wonders what would happen to them if the boat were destroyed.

While Matthew may have seen some kind of valid application of the principles in this pericope to his own situation, the story was for him primarily a miracle story with christological implications (see on vv.26–27). Some redaction critics, in their desire to interpret the Gospels exclusively in terms of reconstructed church life-settings instead of hearing the church's thoughtful witness to the historical Jesus, come close to undisciplined allegorizing.

It is well known that violent squalls (the term *seismos* can refer to an earthquake or a sea storm) develop quickly on Lake Galilee (v.24). The surface is more than six hundred feet below sea level, and the rapidly rising hot air draws from the south-eastern tablelands violent winds whose cold air churns up the water. Those among Jesus' contemporaries who really knew the OT would remember that in it God is presented as the one who controls and stills the seas (cf. Job 38:8–11; Pss 29:3–4, 10–11; 65:5–7; 89:9; 107:23–32).

The form of the cry, *Kyrie, sōson* (lit., "Lord, save!" v.25), is often thought to reflect liturgical influence (cf. Mark 4:38; Luke 8:24). But it is doubtful that the disciples all used the same words; and the verbal differences among the Synoptics may reflect, not theological motivation, but historical recollection of various cries (esp. if Matthew was present). This event almost certainly occurs later chronologically than Matthew's call (9:9–13; cf. Luke 5:27–32). The words of later liturgy took on this form. Yet we know almost nothing about first-century liturgy, and it is more likely that the Bible influenced the shape of liturgy than vice versa. Significantly, later textual tradition adds "us" (cf. Metzger, *Textual Commentary*, p. 22). The verb *akoloutheō* ("follow") does not require a direct object, though it is difficult to see why "us" should have been eliminated if it had been there originally. The later liturgical form prefers to abandon the "us." If that form was not strong enough to control the textual tradition, is it likely that it was strong enough (let alone early enough) to control the shape of the cry in the transfer from Mark to Matthew?

26–27 "He does not chide them for disturbing him with their prayers, but for disturbing themselves with their fears" (Matthew Henry). The word *oligopistoi* ("you of little faith," v.26) occurs five times in the NT (6:30; here; 14:31; 16:8; Luke 12:28; cf. the cognate noun at Matt 17:20) and always with reference to disciples. Lack of faith among those for whom faith must be central is especially disappointing. Mark (4:40) has "Do you still have no faith?" and Matthew's "little faith" is therefore taken by many as a conscious toning down of the rebuke, perhaps because he cannot envisage discipleship apart from *some* faith (Gundry, *Matthew*). But there are reasons for thinking this conclusion is somewhat hasty.

1. It may be pushing Mark's question too hard to understand it as meaning that the disciples were utterly without faith. An exasperated preacher might well berate those he regards as believing disciples with words like those in Mark precisely because he believes their conduct in the face of some crisis belies their profession of faith. The large change in meaning ascribed to Matthew may therefore rest on too pedantic an understanding of Mark. This is confirmed by Mark's not developing the notion of "disciples" who have no faith.

2. *Both* Matthew (17:17) *and* Mark (9:19) preserve sayings about the unbelieving generation that must in context be applied to Jesus' disciples.

3. The word *oligopistoi* ("you of little faith") probably does not refer merely to quantity of faith but to its poor quality (see on 17:20). If so, Matthew may be credited with a little more theological precision than Mark but scarcely a radically new meaning. The change from a question (Mark) to the one word epithet *oligopistoi* (Matthew) is quite within the range of reportage in the Gospels. What Jesus' exact words were, we cannot know; nor can we be certain that Matthew's only access to the event was Mark's report.

4. If Matthew were so eager to insist that true discipleship involves *some* faith and changes Mark's expression for this reason, it is strange that he would insert a verse like 17:20 (contrast Mark 9:29). It is more likely that Matthew favors *oligopistoi* as part of his working vocabulary, but without heavy, theological implications; the demonstrable redactional tendencies of an author do not necessarily bear on questions of authenticity (cf. Introduction, section 2).

5. What is clear is that both Mark and Matthew set faith over against fear. Faith chases out fear, or fear chases out faith.

That the disciples could cry to Jesus for help reveals that they believed, or hoped, he could do something. More than others they had witnessed his miracles and apparently believed he could rescue them. Jesus' rebuke is therefore not against skepticism of his ability, nor against the fear that the disciples like others might drown. Rather they failed to see that the one so obviously raised up by God to accomplish the messianic work could not possibly have died in a storm while that work remained undone. They lacked faith, not so much in his ability to save them, as in Jesus as Messiah, whose life could not be lost in a storm, as if the elements were out of control and Jesus himself the pawn of chance. This aspect of their unbelief is hinted at in Mark and Luke; in Matthew it is rendered more explicit with the disciples' cry to save them, for here they cannot be thought to be awakening Jesus because of pique at his still being asleep. Jesus' sleep stems not only from his exhaustion (see on v.16) or from the Son of Man having nowhere to lay his head (v.20) but from his confidence that, to use John's language, his hour had not yet come.

The disciples' response to the miracle (v.27) does not weaken this interpretation, as if their surprise shows they were not expecting Jesus to intervene. Just as a crowd expects a magician to do his trick, yet marvels when it is done, so the disciples turn to Jesus for help, yet are amazed when he stills the storm so that there is complete calm. What kind of man is this? Readers of this Gospel know the answer—he is the virgin-born Messiah who has come to redeem his people from their sins and whose mission is to fulfill God's redemptive purposes. But the disciples did not yet understand these things. They saw that his authority extended over nature and were thus helped in their faith. Yet they did not grasp the profundity of his rebuke. Indeed, wherever *oligopistos* is used in Matthew, a root cause of the "little faith" is the failure to see beyond the mere surface of things. Thus the pericope is deeply christological: themes of faith and discipleship are of secondary importance and point to the "kind of man" (cf. BDF, par. 298[3]) Jesus is.

It may also be that Matthew is again juxtaposing Jesus with man's limitations and Jesus with God's authority, a device he so effectively uses in this Gospel. As Jesus is tempted but rebukes Satan (4:1-11), as he is called the devil but casts out demons (12:22-32); so he sleeps from weariness but muzzles nature (see further at 4:2).

4. Further demonstration of Jesus' authority (8:28–9:8)

a. Exorcising two men

8:28–34

> 28When he arrived at the other side in the region of the Gadarenes, two dem-on-possessed men coming from the tombs met him. They were so violent that no one could pass that way. 29"What do you want with us, Son of God?" they shouted. "Have you come here to torture us before the appointed time?"
>
> 30Some distance from them a large herd of pigs was feeding. 31The ·demons begged Jesus, "If you drive us out, send us into the herd of pigs."
>
> 32He said to them, "Go!" So they came out and went into the pigs, and the whole herd rushed down the steep bank into the lake and died in the water. 33Those tending the pigs ran off, went into the town and reported all this, including what had happened to the demon-possessed men. 34Then the whole town went out to meet Jesus. And when they saw him, they pleaded with him to leave their region.

All three synoptists (cf. Mark 5:1–20; Luke 8:26–39) place this event after the boat landed, after the storm had been stilled. Matthew's account is much shorter than the other two; and he does not refer to "Legion," or to the desire of the liberated men to follow Jesus. The central motif, Jesus' authority over the evil spirits, is accented and only lightly interwoven with other themes.

28 The locale seems to have been in the district controlled by the town of Gadara, near the village of Gerasa (cf. Notes), which lay about midpoint on the lake's eastern shore. On the adjacent hillside are ancient tombs. Probably small antechambers or caves provided some protection from the weather; and a graveyard would, apparently, prove a congenial environment for demons and render the man ceremonially defiled. This region lay in the predominantly Gentile territory of the Decapolis (see on 4:25); the presence of the pigs (v.30), inconceivable in a Jewish milieu, points to its Gentile background. Jesus has withdrawn here, not for ministry, but to avoid the crowds (v.18). Yet there can be no rest as long as the hosts of darkness oppose him.

On differences between Jewish and NT views of demon possession, see Eder-sheim (LTJM, Appendix XVI; cf. SBK, 1:491–92). Matthew mentions two men; Mark and Luke only one. This pattern occurs elsewhere (20:30), making it very unlikely that Matthew changed the number because he saw an implication of more than one man in Mark's "Legion" (applied to the demons). It is even less likely that Matthew introduced the extra person to make up the legally acceptable minimum of two witnesses, since not only is the witness theme not found in either of the two Matthean pericopes (vv.28–34; 20:29–34), but here Matthew has eliminated the witness theme (cf. Mark 5:18–20). While the disciples could have served as witnesses, the best explanation is that Matthew had independent knowledge of the second man. Mention of only one by the other Gospel writers is not problematic. Not only was one sufficient for the purpose at hand, but where one person is more remarkable or prominent, it is not uncommon for the Gospels to mention only that one (cf. "I saw John Smith in town today. I hadn't seen him in years"—even though both John and Mary Smith were in fact seen).

The violence of these demoniacs is more fully described by Mark and Luke.

29 "While the men in the boat are doubting what manner of man this is, that even the winds and the sea obey him, the demons come to tell them" (Theophylact, cited in Broadus). They knew who Jesus was and yet remained demons; to know Jesus yet hate him is demonic. The question the demoniacs hurled at Jesus could be either harsh or gentle, depending on context (2 Sam 16:10; Mark 1:24; John 2:4). Here it is hateful and tinged with fear. The title "Son of God" is probably to be taken in its richest sense: Jesus was recognized, not solely in terms of his power but in terms of his person. He was the Messiah, God's Son (see on 3:17). Even if Jesus had already begun to confront them when they reacted so venomously (cf. Mark 5:7–8), there was nothing in Jesus' command in itself to betray his identity. We must suppose that the demons enjoyed some independent knowledge of Jesus' identity (cf. Acts 19:15; Ladd, *NT Theology*, p. 165).

The second question shows that there will be a time for demonic hosts to be tortured and rejected forever (cf. Jude 6; Rev 20:10; cf. 1 Enoch 16:1; Jub 10:8–9; T Levi 18:12; 1QS 3:24–25; 4:18–20). As the question is phrased, it recognizes that Jesus is the one who will discharge that judicial function at the "appointed time"; therefore it confirms the fullest meaning of "Son of God." That Jesus was in any sense circumscribing their activity before the appointed time (Matthew only) already shows that Jesus' casting out of demons was an eschatological function, a sign that the kingdom was dawning (cf. 12:28).

The significance of "here" is disputed. It can mean either (1) "here in this Gentile territory," reflecting "the difficulty of the Church's mission in those regions of Palestine" (Hill, *Matthew*)—but surely demon possession was not restricted to Gentile territory (cf. 10:5, 8; 12:22–24), and "the appointed time" makes little sense in such an interpretation—or (2) "here on earth, here where we have been given some freedom to trouble men before the end." This obvious sense of the text presupposes that Jesus has come to the earth before the End. It is difficult to avoid the conclusion that Jesus' preexistence is presupposed.

30–31 Mark (5:13) puts the number of the herd at two thousand and says it was "there." Matthew says it was "some distance from them" (v.30), the sort of detail an eyewitness might well remember. This detail also weakens the suggestion that the pigs stampeded because of the men's convulsions. J.D.M. Derrett's proposed reconstruction ("Legend and Event: The Gerasene Demoniac: An Inquest into History and Liturgical Projection," in Livingstone, 2:63–73), based on the Romans' sacrificing of pigs and on Jewish myths connecting Gentiles with bestiality, has no textual support. There are other reasons why the demons may have pled (v.31) to be sent into the herd of pigs: (1) desire for a bodily "home"; (2) hatred of God's creatures; (3) desire to stir up animosity against Jesus. The first does not seem likely because the first thing the demons do is precipitate the death of their new "home." The second and third are more plausible, because the Gospels elsewhere show that exorcized evil spirits sometimes expressed their rage by visible acts of violence or mischief (e.g., 17:14–20 = Mark 9:14–32; cf. Jos Antiq. VIII, 48[ii.5], often cited, but of doubtful relevance because the exorcist there commands the demon to manifest himself).

Gundry (*Matthew*) observes that the herd rushes down the slope but that in Matthew "they" (pl.) die; i.e., Matthew has transformed Mark to make the demons die. Thus Jesus "tortures" the demons "before the appointed time" by sending them to the torments of hell, and Matthew thus "deals in a bit of realized eschatology." This reconstruction is far from convincing.

1. There is no hint that the drowning of the pigs sends the demons to hell.

2. Mark also shifts from the singular—the herd rushing down the slope—to the plural—"were drowning." The only difference is that Matthew has omitted reference to the number "two thousand."

3. But if Matthew's plural verb cannot refer back to "two thousand," its most natural subject is the word "pigs," found in this same verse (32). The reason Matthew does not use a singular verb for died is because it would be awkward to speak of a herd's dying. Matthew has therefore preserved Mark's pattern—single verb followed by plural verb.

32–34 The question as to why Jesus would grant the demons their desire and let them destroy the herd of pigs (v.32), the livelihood of their owners, is part of larger questions as to why human beings are possessed or why disease, misfortune, or calamity overtake us—questions only to be answered within the context of a broad theodicy outside the scope of this commentary. But the context offers some hints. He who is master of nature (vv.23–27) is also its ultimate owner (vv.28–34; cf. Ps 50:10). The "appointed time" (v.29) for full destruction of the demons' power has not yet arrived. The pigs' stampede dramatically proved that the former demoniacs had indeed been freed (v.33). But in the light of vv.33–34, the loss of the herd became a way of exposing the real values of the people in the vicinity. They preferred pigs to persons, swine to the Savior.

This ending of the pericope bears significantly on its total meaning. If the story shows once more that Jesus' ministry was not restricted to the Jews but foreshadowed the mission to the Gentiles, it likewise shows that opposition to Jesus is not exclusively Jewish. To this extent it confirms earlier exegesis (see on 8:11–12) that showed that opponents in Matthew are not selected on the basis of race but according to their response to Jesus.

Notes

28 The textual evidence in all three synoptic Gospels, though highly complex, has been well summarized by Metzger (*Textual Commentary*, pp. 23–24). The three options are Gadara, Gerasa, and Gergesa. In Mark and Luke the textual evidence is strongest for Gerasa, probably in reference to a little village (modern Kersa or Koursi) on the eastern shore. However, there was a city of the Decapolis named Gerasa (modern Jerash) some thirty miles southeast of Galilee. Clearly that is geographically incompatible with v.32; so early copyists made emendations.

Gadara (modern Um Qeis), also a Decapolis city, was five miles southeast. Origen (*In Ioannes* 6.41) objected to both Gerasa (as commonly understood to refer to the city thirty miles off) and Gadara for similar reasons of distance. But Josephus (Life 42[9]) says Gadara had territory and villages on the border of the lake, and probably this included the little village of Gerasa. Indeed coins of Gadara sometimes display a ship (cf. HJP, 2:132–36). Gadara was thus the regional or toparchic capital (cf. Sherwin-White, p. 128, n. 3). The external evidence in Matthew favors Gadara: for some reason the name of the toparchic capital was preferred to Gerasa (which in Matthew enjoys only versional support).

Origen, rejecting Gerasa and Gadara, proposed Gergesa, but on entirely inadequate grounds, including doubtful etymology (cf. Metzger, above; Tj. Baarda, "Gadarenes, Gerasenes, Gergesenes, and the 'Diatessaron' Traditions," in Ellis and Wilcox, pp. 181–97). Gergesa could also be suggested by a very guttural "r" in Gerasa. Other variants doubtless resulted from later attempts at "correction" and from mutual assimilation (cf. further Lane, p. 181, n. 6, and Franz Annen, *Heil für die Heiden* [Frankfurt: Josef Knecht, 1976], pp. 201–4).

32 The phrase $\kappa\alpha\tau\grave{\alpha}$ $\tau o\tilde{v}$ $\kappa\rho\eta\mu\nu o\tilde{v}$ (*kata tou krēmnou*, "down the steep bank") is a very rare instance of this preposition plus genitive in a local sense and here means "down and over" (BDF, par. 225) or "down along" (Moule, *Idiom Book*, p. 60).

---

b. *Healing a paralytic and forgiving his sins*

9:1–8

> ¹Jesus stepped into a boat, crossed over and came to his own town. ²Some men brought to him a paralytic, lying on a mat. When Jesus saw their faith, he said to the paralytic, "Take heart, son; your sins are forgiven."
> ³At this, some of the teachers of the law said to themselves, "This fellow is blaspheming!"
> ⁴Knowing their thoughts, Jesus said, "Why do you entertain evil thoughts in your hearts? ⁵Which is easier: to say, 'Your sins are forgiven,' or to say, 'Get up and walk'? ⁶But so that you may know that the Son of Man has authority on earth to forgive sins. . . ." Then he said to the paralytic, "Get up, take your mat and go home." ⁷And the man got up and went home. ⁸When the crowd saw this, they were filled with awe; and they praised God, who had given such authority to men.

Again Matthew's account is shortened (cf. Mark 2:2–12; Luke 5:17–26), the entrance through the roof having been eliminated. The interrelationships among the Synoptics in this pericope are complex. It has been shown, as Bo Reicke says, that the various narrative elements "cannot be derived from any source that did not include the essentials of the quotation elements represented by three gospels together" ("The Synoptic Reports on the Healing of the Paralytic: Matt. 9:1–8 with Parallels," in Elliott, p. 325; though it is doubtful that Reicke has disproved the two-source hypothesis, as he seems to think).

The shortened opening does not change this from a "miracle story" to a "controversial story" (contra Held, in Bornkamm, *Tradition*, pp. 176f.). Heil ("Healing Miracles," pp. 276–78) has shown that the form-critical marks of a miracle story are retained. Still less is this a miracle story into which a controversy about forgiving sin has been inserted, sparked by the church's attempt to tie its own forgiving function to Jesus' ministry (so Bultmann, *Synoptic Tradition*, pp. 14–16). The pericope is exclusively christological and has nothing to do with the disciples. Form-critical categories are handled mechanically if taken a priori to require that no controversy triggered by the way Jesus performed a healing *could* have been passed on! Moreover the close connections between sin and sickness (see on v. 17) and this extension of Jesus' authority beyond healing, nature, and the demonic realm to the forgiveness of sins make the narrative internally coherent and contextually suitable.

1 It is unclear whether this verse ties in more closely with 8:28–34 or with 9:2–8. The problem is not just academic, for the preceding pericope is almost certainly chronologically later (cf. Mark 5:1–20) than this one (cf. Mark 2:2–12); and a break

more easily fits between 9:1 and 9:2 than between 8:34 and 9:1. Begged to leave (8:34), Jesus embarked in the boat he had so recently left and returned to "his own town," viz., Capernaum (4:13), on the western shore of the lake.

A larger problem concerning synoptic interrelationships now faces us. Matthew 9:14 and Luke 5:33 show that the questions about fasting sprang from the dinner Matthew sponsored. And 9:18 shows that the healing of Jairus's daughter and of the hemorrhaging woman immediately followed. Mark 5:21–23 and Luke 8:40–44 place the raising of Jairus's daughter after Jesus returned from Gadara (as in Matthew) but the healing of the paralytic (Mark 2:2–12; Luke 5:17–26) much earlier—even though Matthew places it after Gadara and seems to tie it to the pericopes that follow in his account.

Harmonization should be avoided where details are obscure, but refusal to attempt harmonization of documents treating the same events is methodologically irresponsible. Here a fairly straightforward solution is possible. There is a significant time lapse between Matthew's calling and the dinner he gives his friends. All three synoptists put these two personally related events side by side. But significantly no synoptist makes a temporal connection between the two. The following shows the arrangement.

Time A: before Gadara { healing of a paralytic / calling of Matthew [TIME LAPSE: Gadara incident and others]	All Synoptics put these two events together	Mark and Luke place these three together at Time A	Matthew places all four together at Time B
Time B: after Gadara { dinner given by Matthew / raising of Jairus's daughter			

Thus all the Synoptics put the raising of Jairus's daughter in the correct chronological order. Mark and Luke report the healing of the paralytic and the calling of Matthew at the earlier time, when they occurred, but then link to this Matthew's dinner—a topical arrangement. Matthew links all four together, placing them later, though there is a chronological break at vv. 1–2 (see above) and again between Matthew's call and Matthew's dinner. The first evangelist has introduced the first chronological break in order to preserve the topical arrangement of his presentation of Jesus' authority and the second break (vv. 9–10), along with Mark and Luke, because of the personal connection (Matthew's call and Matthew's dinner). This rather obvious solution is invalid only if Matthew's (and Luke's) sole source of information in this pericope is Mark. But despite some critics, this is most unlikely (cf. Introduction, sections 1–5).

2 Many (e.g., Weiss, Hill) insist that though in Mark and Luke the paralytic is lowered through a roof, here the imperfect *prosepheron* ("they were bringing," NASB) means the paralytic and his bearers met Jesus in the street. But the imperfect tense often adds color to action (cf. the imperfect even in Luke), and little is gained by manufacturing discrepancies.

Jesus "saw" *their* faith—presumably that of the paralytic and those carrying him—exemplified in their coming. But he spoke only to the paralytic. "Son" (*teknon*) is no more than an affectionate term from one's senior (cf. 1 John 2:1, 28 et al.). What Jesus went on to say implies a close link between sin and sickness (see on 8:17)—perhaps in this case a direct one (cf. John 5:14; 1 Cor 11:29–30). It implies that of the two, paralysis and sin, sin is the more basic problem. The best MSS read *aphientai* ("Your sins are forgiven"), not the perfect *apheontai* ("Your sins have been forgiven"): see Notes. The latter might imply that the man's sins were forgiven at some time in the past and now remain forgiven.

3 Some teachers of the law (see on 2:4; 8:18–22) muttered among themselves that Jesus was blaspheming. It is God alone who forgives sin (Isa 43:25; 44:22), since it is against him only that men commit sin (Ps 51:4). The verb *blasphēmeō* often means "slander"; and when something is said that slanders God, the modern meaning of "blaspheme" is not far away. Though among Jews in Jesus' day the precise definition of blasphemy was hotly disputed (cf. SBK, 1:1019f.), the consensus seemed to be that using the divine name was an essential element. Here the teachers of the law, in their whispered consultation, expanded blasphemy to include Jesus' claim to do something only God could do.

4 Jesus had seen the faith of the paralytic and his friends; now he saw the evil thoughts of some of the teachers of the law (cf. Notes). Such discernment may have been supernatural, though not necessarily so. In this situation it would not have been difficult to surmise what the teachers of the law were whispering about. Jesus' charge probed beyond their talk of blasphemy to what they were thinking in their hearts. And what they were thinking was untrue, unbelieving, and blind to what was being revealed before their eyes.

5–7 Jesus did not respond to his opponents' thoughts according to the skeptical view—viz., that to say "your sins are forgiven" is easier to say than "Get up and walk" (v.5). On the contrary, he responded according to the perspective of the teachers of the law—viz., that to say "Get up and walk" is easier since only God can forgive sins. Jesus claimed to do the more difficult thing. Thus v.6 is ironical—"All right, I'll also do the lesser deed." Yet if Jesus had blasphemed in pronouncing forgiveness, how could he now perform a miracle (cf. John 9:31)? But so that they might know that he had authority to forgive sin, he proceeded to the easier task. The healing therefore showed that Jesus truly had authority to forgive sins. To do this is the prerogative of the "Son of Man." This expression goes beyond self-reference and, seen in the light of the postresurrection period, surely indicates that the eschatological Judge had already come "on earth" (cf. "here" in 8:29) with the authority to forgive sin (cf. Hooker, *Son of Man*, pp. 81–93). This is the authority of Emmanuel, "God with us" (1:23), sent to "save his people from their sins" (1:21). Jesus did not finish the sentence: the broken syntax (BDF, par. 483) is followed by Jesus' word of power and his command to the paralytic to go home (*hypage*, "go," is here gentle as in 8:13, not rough as in 4:10). To sum up, the healing not only cured the paralytic (v.7), it also assured him that his sins were forgiven and refuted the charge of blasphemy.

8 The external evidence for "were afraid" is early and in three text types (Alexandrian, Western, Caesarean). Copyists, failing to see the profundity of the verb, softened it to "were amazed." NIV's "were filled with awe" implies fear but is too paraphrastic. Men *should* fear the one who has the authority to forgive sins. Indeed, they should fear whenever they are confronted by an open manifestation of God (cf. 17:6; 28:5, 10). Such fear breeds praise.

Matthew alone adds the clause "who had given such authority to men." Many argue that "to men" refers to the church and cite 16:19; 18:18 in support (e.g., Benoit, Held, Hill, Hummel). But this is unlikely. If "Son of Man" (v.6) refers to the eschatological Judge, then it is unlikely that this function is to be shared with the church, at least in the same way (cf. Colpe, TDNT, 8:405). The pericope has christological, not ecclesiastical, concerns, compatible with the prologue (1:21, 23; see on vv.5–7). The onlookers simply saw a man exercising the authority of God, but readers recognize him as "God with us" and eschatological "Son of Man." God's gracious reign has come "on earth" (v.6); the kingdom of David's Son, who came to save his people from their sins, has dawned.

Notes

2 The reasons the perfect displaced the present in many MSS are clear enough: the present in Greek is often durative, which here makes little sense ("your sins are being forgiven"); and there is assimilation to Luke 5:20, where the text is firm (Mark 2:5 has a similar difficulty). In any case, the Greek present can have a punctiliar force (cf. Burton, *Syntax*, p. 9; Turner, *Syntax*, p. 64).

4 "Seeing their thoughts," not "knowing their thoughts," is almost certainly the correct reading, not least because the change from the former to the latter is comprehensible, but the reverse is highly unlikely. But "seeing" is obviously metaphorical, a point recognized by KJV and NIV in their periphrastic rendering "knowing."

5. Calling Matthew

9:9

9As Jesus went on from there, he saw a man named Matthew sitting at the tax collector's booth. "Follow me," he told him, and Matthew got up and followed him.

9 The locale is probably the outskirts of Capernaum. Matthew was sitting "at the tax collector's booth," a customs and excise booth at the border between the territories of Philip and Herod Antipas. On attitudes toward tax collectors, see on 5:46 (cf. also SBK, 1:377–80). Having demonstrated his authority to forgive sins (vv.1–8), Jesus now called to himself a man whose occupation made him a pariah—a sinner and an associate of sinners (cf. 1 Tim 1:15).

The name "Matthew" may derive from the Hebrew behind "Mattaniah" (1 Chron 9:15), meaning "gift of God," or, in another etymology, from a word meaning "the faithful" (Heb. *'emet*). In Mark the name is "Levi" (though in Mark there are difficult textual variants), and the change to "Matthew" in the first Gospel has prompted much speculation. The most radical theory is that of R. Pesch ("Levi-Matthäus," ZNW 59 [1968]: 40–56), who says that the first evangelist purposely substituted a name from the apostolic band because he habitually uses "disciple" for the Twelve and therefore could not allow an outsider to stand. The evangelist then made a "sinner" out of him to represent the "sinners" among the apostles. "Matthew" in the first Gospel is thus reduced entirely to a redactional product. But

Pesch's understanding of "disciple" is questionable (see on 5:1–2; 8:18–22), and his skepticism is vast.

Since Jews not uncommonly had two or more names, the simple equation of Levi and Matthew is the most obvious course to take. Matthew may have been a Levite. Such a heritage would have assumed intimate acquaintance with Jewish tradition. Mark and Luke have "Matthew" in their lists of apostles (Mark 3:18; Luke 6:15; Pesch has to say Mark 3:18 is also redactional). See for another example of a prominent NT figure with two names the apostle Paul. Acts has both "Saul" and "Paul," but in his own writings Paul always refers to himself by the latter name.'So Mark and Luke use both "Levi" and "Matthew," but Matthew uses only the latter. (There is no evidence that either "Paul" or "Matthew" are Christian names, and the parallel is inexact because "Paul," unlike "Matthew," is a Gentile name.)

Gundry (*Use of OT*, pp. 181–83) suggests that Matthew's work as a tax collector assured his fluency in Aramaic and Greek and that his accuracy in keeping records fitted him for note taking and later writing his Gospel. Hill (*Matthew*), following Stendahl (Peake, p. 673j), thinks it unlikely that a person living on "the despised outskirts of Jewish life" could be responsible for this Gospel. But does it not also seem unlikely that "a son of thunder" should become the apostle of love, or that the arch-persecutor of the church should become its greatest missionary and theologian? If Matthew wrote 9:9 regarding his own call, it is significant that it is more self-deprecating than Luke's account, which says that Matthew "left everything" and followed Jesus.

6. *Eating with sinners*

9:10–13

> ¹⁰While Jesus was having dinner at Matthew's house, many tax collectors and "sinners" came and ate with him and his disciples. ¹¹When the Pharisees saw this, they asked his disciples, "Why does your teacher eat with tax collectors and 'sinners'?"
> ¹²On hearing this, Jesus said, "It is not the healthy who need a doctor, but the sick. ¹³But go and learn what this means: 'I desire mercy, not sacrifice.' For I have not come to call the righteous, but sinners."

On the chronological relation between v.9 and vv.10–13, see on 9:1. Matthew abbreviates the account of Jesus' eating with tax collectors and sinners, excluding descriptive elements that do not contribute to the confrontation, but adding an OT quotation (v.13).

10–11 For comment on the opening words *kai egeneto* ("and it came to pass"; NIV, "while"), see on 7:28–29. The Greek text does not mention "Matthew's" house, though v.9 implies it is Matthew's and both Mark and Luke specify it (so NIV). Jesus himself had said that even a tax collector has his friends (5:46), and Matthew's dinner substantiates this. "Sinners" may include common folk who did not share all the scruples of the Pharisees (cf. TDNT, 1:324–25); hence the quotation marks in NIV. But almost certainly it groups together those who broke Pharisaic Halakoth (rules of conduct)—harlots, tax collectors, and other disreputable people (cf. Hummel, pp. 22ff.). Though eating with them entailed dangers of ceremonial defilement, Jesus and his disciples did so. The Pharisees' question, put not to Jesus but to his disciples, was less a request for information than a charge; and contemptuously it lumped together "tax collectors and sinners" under one article (cf. 11:19; Luke 15:1-2 for the same attitude).

There can be little doubt that Jesus was known as a friend to tax collectors and sinners (Matt 11:19; cf. M. Völkel, "'Freund der Zöllner und Sünder,'" ZNW 69 [1978]: 1-10; and see note on 5:46).

12-13 These verses again connect Jesus' healing ministry with his "healing" of sinners (see on 8:17). The sick need a doctor (v.12), and Jesus healed them; likewise the sinful need mercy, forgiveness, restoration, and Jesus healed them (v.13). The Pharisees were not so healthy as they thought (cf. 7:1-5); more important they did not understand the purpose of Jesus' mission. Expecting a Messiah who would crush the sinful and support the righteous, they had little place for one who accepted and transformed the sinner and dismissed the "righteous" as hypocrites. Jesus explained his mission in terms reminiscent of 1:21. There is no suggestion here that he went to sinners because they gladly received him; rather, he went to them because they were sinners, just as a doctor goes to the sick because they are sick.

The quotation (v.13) is from Hosea 6:6 and is introduced by the rabbinic formula "go and learn," used of those who needed to study the text further. Use of the formula may be slightly sardonic: those who prided themselves in their knowledge of and conformity to Scripture needed to "go and learn" what it means. The quotation, possibly translated from the Hebrew by Matthew himself, is cast in Semitic antithesis: "not A but B" often means "B is of more basic importance than A."

The Hebrew word for "mercy" (*ḥeseḏ*) is close in meaning to "covenant love," which, according to Hosea, is more important than "sacrifice." Through Hosea, God said that the apostates of Hosea's day, though continuing the formal ritual of temple worship, had lost its center. As applied to the Pharisees by Jesus, therefore, the Hosea quotation was not simply telling them that they should be more sympathetic to outcasts and less concerned about ceremonial purity, but that they were aligned with the apostates of ancient Israel in that they too preserved the shell while losing the heart of the matter, as exemplified by their attitude to tax collectors and sinners (cf. France, *Jesus*, p. 70). Jesus' final statement (v.13b) therefore cannot mean that he viewed the Pharisees as righteous people who did not need him, who were already perfectly acceptable to God by virtue of their obedience to his laws so that their only fault was the exclusion of others (contra Hill, *Greek Words*, pp. 130f.). If the Pharisees were so righteous, the demand for righteousness surpassing that of the Pharisees and teachers of the law (5:20) would be incoherent.

On the other hand, it may not be exactly right to say that "righteous" is ironic here. The saying simply defines the essential nature of Jesus' messianic mission as he himself saw it. If pushed he would doubtless have affirmed the universal sinfulness of man (cf. 7:11). Therefore he is not dividing men into two groups but disavowing one image of what Messiah should be and do, replacing it with the correct one. His mission was characterized by grace, a pursuit of the lost, of sinners. The verb *kalesai* ("to call") means "to invite" (unlike Paul's usage, where the call is always efficacious). By implication those who do not see themselves in the light of Jesus' mission not only fail to grasp the purpose of his coming but exclude themselves from the kingdom's blessings.

If Matthew does not add "to repentance" after "sinners" (as Luke 5:32), it is not because he is disinterested in repentance (cf. 3:2; 4:17). Rather, the words are not in his principal source (Mark) and do not in any case contribute to his present theme.

Hosea 6:6 is also quoted in 12:7, again in a context challenging the Pharisees' legal scruples. Cope (*Matthew*, pp. 68–70) suggests that the verse reveals a contrast between the substantial demands of mercy and merely legal and ceremonial piety, a contrast traceable in the following pericopes (vv. 14–17, 18–26, 27–34, 35–38). But his evidence is slightly overdrawn. In 9:27–34, for instance, vv. 27–31 raise no overt hints of ceremonial defilement.

7. Fasting and the dawning of the messianic joy

9:14–17

> ¹⁴Then John's disciples came and asked him, "How is it that we and the Pharisees fast, but your disciples do not fast?"
>
> ¹⁵Jesus answered, "How can the guests of the bridegroom mourn while he is with them? The time will come when the bridegroom will be taken from them; then they will fast.
>
> ¹⁶"No one sews a patch of unshrunk cloth on an old garment, for the patch will pull away from the garment, making the tear worse. ¹⁷Neither do men pour new wine into old wineskins. If they do, the skins will burst, the wine will run out and the wineskins will be ruined. No, they pour new wine into new wineskins, and both are preserved."

14 Mark (2:18–22; cf. Luke 5:33–39) says that both the Pharisees and the disciples of John were fasting—probably on one of the regularly observed but voluntary fast days (see on 4:2; 6:16–18)—and that "some people" asked this question. Luke makes it the Pharisees, Matthew the disciples of John. On the face of it (see Luke), the setting is the same as for the previous pericope, and regarding fasting the disciples of John are in accord with the Pharisees. The Baptist himself showed a noble freedom from jealousy when Jesus' ministry began to supersede his own (cf. esp. John 3:26–31). But some of John's disciples felt differently now that he was in prison (4:12); and because they kept up their leader's asceticism (11:18), not heeding his strong witness to Jesus, they saw an occasion for criticism.

Most modern commentators believe that here Matthew is referring to the Baptist's followers who never accepted Jesus' supremacy and who by the end of the first century had developed their own sect. Doubtless Matthew would have cheerfully applied Jesus' response to them also. But there is no reason to deny that this incident happened during Jesus' ministry. Moreover, after the bridegroom was taken away (v. 15), Jesus' disciples often fasted (e.g., Acts 13:3; 14:23; 27:9), making it less likely that these Baptist sectarians would have leveled their charge after the Passion and Resurrection than before it. Just as the "questioners" (accusers?) had approached Jesus' disciples about his conduct (v. 11), so now questioners approached Jesus about his disciples' conduct.

15 For his response Jesus used three illustrations (Luke 5:39 adds a fourth), all given in the same order by the Synoptics. There seems little to be gained by supposing that the sayings were at one time separate.

The first illustration about the "guests of the bridegroom" (lit., "the sons of the brideschamber"; see on 5:9; 8:12) picks up a metaphor from the Baptist, who saw himself as the "best man" and Jesus as the groom (John 3:29). This similar metaphor would therefore be the more effective to this audience—Jesus is the groom and the disciples his "guests" who are so overjoyed at being with him that for them to fast is inappropriate.

In exonerating his disciples' eating, Jesus used messianic-eschatological terms. In the OT the bridegroom metaphor was repeatedly applied to God (Isa 54:5–6; 62:4–5; Hos 2:16–20); and Jews sometimes used it of marriage in connection with Messiah's coming or with the messianic banquet (cf. SBK, 1:500–518; and in the NT, cf. Matt 22:2; 25:1; 2 Cor 11:2; Eph 5:23–32; Rev 19:7, 9; 21:2). Thus Jesus' answer was implicitly christological: he himself is the messianic bridegroom, and the Messianic Age has dawned.

The objection is often made that the second part of Jesus' answer, regarding the disciples' mourning once the groom is taken (*aparthē*, "taken," may bear overtones of Isa 53:8 LXX) from them, is not authentic on two chief grounds.

1. Such an obvious reference to the Passion (and Ascension?) comes too early in Jesus' ministry. Some try to avoid this objection by supposing that Jesus was saying no more than that he like other men must die sometime. Neither the objection nor its proposed solution is relevant to one who has already revealed so formidable a messianic self-consciousness.

2. Matthew has allegorized the original parable—a sign of late accretion or adaptation. Yet this simplistic view of "parable" will not withstand scrutiny (cf. further on 13:3a). Above all the language is so cryptic that it is doubtful whether even Jesus' disciples grasped the messianic implications of these words till the early weeks of the postresurrection church.

16–17 Luke 5:36 labels these illustrations "parables." In general terms the first of this pair is clear enough: a piece of unshrunk cloth tightly sewed to old and well-shrunk cloth in order to repair a tear will cause a bigger tear (v.16). Admittedly the grammar is difficult (cf. Notes). The second (v.17) is also a "slice of life" in the ancient world. Skin bottles for carrying various fluids were made by killing the chosen animal, cutting off its head and feet, skinning the carcass, and sewing up the skin, fur side out, to seal off all orifices but one (usually the neck). The skin was tanned with special care to minimize disagreeable taste. In time the skin became hard and brittle. If new wine, still fermenting, were put into such an old skin, the buildup of fermenting gases would split the brittle container and ruin both bottle and wine. New wine was placed only in new wineskins still pliable and elastic enough to accommodate the pressure.

These illustrations show that the new situation introduced by Jesus could not simply be patched onto old Judaism or poured into the old wineskins of Judaism. New forms would have to accompany the kingdom Jesus was now inaugurating; to try to domesticate him and incorporate him into the matrix of established Jewish religion would only succeed in ruining both Judaism and Jesus' teaching.

Two extreme interpretations must be avoided.

1. Some, noticing that the words "and both are preserved" (v.17) are found only in Matthew, conclude that this first Gospel, unlike Mark, envisages the renewal and preservation of Judaism, not its abolition. This will not do: the "both" that are preserved refers to the new wine and the new wineskins, not the old wineskins. Jesus' teaching and the kingdom now dawning must be poured into new forms. Matthew makes it at least as clear as does Mark that the new wine can only be

preserved in new forms. Is it any surprise that Matthew includes explicit mention of the church (16:18; 18:17)?

2. Dispensationalists are inclined to make this wine so new that there is no connection whatever with what has come before. Walvoord (p. 70) cites Ironside: "He had not come to add something to the legal dispensation but to supersede it with that which was entirely new. . . . The new wine of grace was not to be poured into the skin-bottles of legality." So sharp an antithesis is suspect on three grounds: (1) the grace–legality disjunction is greatly exaggerated; (2) it is not very obviously a set of Matthean categories; and (3) Matthew, as we have seen, repeatedly connects the OT with his own message in terms of prophecy and fulfillment.

The two parables of vv.16–17 are frequently said to be independent sayings tacked on here, since they go beyond the question of fasting. That may be, but all three synoptists put them in the same place. Moreover they go beyond the question of fasting only to lay the groundwork for the coherence of Jesus' answer about fasting. The newness Jesus brings cannot be reduced to or contained by traditions of Jewish piety. The messianic bridegroom has come. These parables bring unavoidable and radical implications for the entire structure of Jewish religion as its leaders then conceived it. Scholars who understand the first Gospel to reflect a Jewish Christian community that preserves all the old forms of piety not only misinterpret 5:17–20 but do not adequately weigh this pericope.

Notes

16 The verb αἴρει (airei, "takes," "draws," or "pulls") is consistently transitive in the active voice (BAGD, s.v.), and therefore τὸ πλήρωμα αὐτοῦ (to plērōma autou, lit., "its fullness"; NIV, "patch") must be construed as the direct object, perhaps referring to the overlapping section of the patch. See the rendering of Michael G. Steinhauser ("The Patch of Unshrunk Cloth [Mt 9[16]]," ExpT 87 [1975–76]: 312f.): "No one puts a patch of unshrunk cloth to an old cloak; because the patch of unshrunk cloth draws the overlapping section of the unshrunk cloth from the cloak and the tear becomes worse."

8. A resurrection and more healings (9:18–34)

a. Raising a girl and healing a woman

9:18–26

[18]While he was saying this, a ruler came and knelt before him and said, "My daughter has just died. But come and put your hand on her, and she will live." [19]Jesus got up and went with him, and so did his disciples.

[20]Just then a woman who had been subject to bleeding for twelve years came up behind him and touched the edge of his cloak. [21]She said to herself, "If I only touch his cloak, I will be healed."

[22]Jesus turned and saw her. "Take heart, daughter," he said, "your faith has healed you." And the woman was healed from that moment.

[23]When Jesus entered the ruler's house and saw the flute players and the noisy crowd, [24]he said, "Go away. The girl is not dead but asleep." But they laughed at him. [25]After the crowd had been put outside, he went in and took the girl by the hand, and she got up. [26]News of this spread through all that region.

For the chronology, see on v.1. Matthew abbreviates Mark (5:21–43; cf. Luke 8:40–46) by almost one-third. Again, the three synoptists are very close in reporting the words of Jesus.

Gérard Rochais (*Les récits de résurrection des morts dans le Nouveau Testament* [Cambridge: University Press, 1980], pp. 88–99) reduces the point of Matthew's account to the importance of faith. Faith is indeed an important theme (v.22), but scarcely exclusive of others. While these are best discovered inductively, we may note that in vv. 18–34 Jesus performs three new kinds of miracles: raising the dead (the healing of the hemorrhaging woman is already an integral part of this account in the Markan source) and healing the blind and the dumb. The latter two appear in Matthew much earlier than in the closest parallels in Mark and Luke (see on vv. 27–31), because his topical concerns demand it. He includes at this point these final examples of spheres over which Jesus has authority because they figure in his defense to the disciples of John the Baptist (11:2–5): the blind receive sight, the lame walk, those who have leprosy are cured, the deaf hear (usually also associated with muteness), the dead are raised. Jesus' messianic credentials are thus being grouped together.

18–19 Matthew tightly links this narrative to the dinner in his house. Mark 5:21 provides another setting: while Jesus was by the lake, etc. This anomaly has called forth numerous explanations, mostly unsatisfactory. Some have postulated that Matthew here follows another source (a desperate expedient that does not explain why he chooses to contradict Mark); others that Matthew simplifies Mark in the interests of catechesis (How is catechesis helped by a different setting almost as long as the first?); others by supposing the dinner party in v.10 took place in a house by the lake (barely possible but artificial); others that vv.14–17 should be detached from the dinner (barely possible, but artificial in light of Luke 5:33).

The best solution accepts the connection between Matthew's dinner (vv.9–13), the discussion about fasting (vv.14–17), and this miracle (vv.18–26). But the NIV rendering of Mark 5:21–22 links Jesus by the lake with the approach of the synagogue ruler ("While he was by the lake, one of the synagogue rulers . . . "). The Greek does not suggest this; syntactically Jesus' presence by the lake terminates the thought of Mark 5:21: Jesus crossed back after the Gadara episode, a large crowd again gathered, and he was by the lake. Verse 22 then begins a new pericope without a necessary transition—which is exactly what Mark does elsewhere (e.g., 3:20, 31; 8:22; 10:46; 14:66). In some instances like this one (Mark 5:22; cf. 1:40), the precise division is ambiguous. But Mark's practice elsewhere encourages us to think this interpretation is right, and the NIV translation wrong.

Further, the words *kai idou* in Luke 8:41 should not be rendered "Just then" (NIV). This suggests that Jairus approached Jesus almost immediately on disembarking from the boat. In fact, *kai idou* in Luke very often either does not or cannot mean "just then" (e.g., Luke 5:18; 7:37, 9:30, 39 et al.) and is not so rendered by NIV. Though the words can fix a chronological connection, they may simply suggest a new or surprising development or even serve as a loose connective. There seems little merit in translating them so as to exclude the possibility of an obvious harmonization.

"A ruler" (cf. Notes) in the context of Capernaum almost certainly refers to a synagogue ruler (v.18), a point made explicit by Mark 5:22, which also tells us his name was Jairus. He must therefore have been a Jew and a man of considerable influence in the lives of the people. He "knelt before" Jesus: the verb here does not suggest "worship" (contra KJV) but deep courtesy, a pleading homage before someone in a position to grant a favor (see on 2:2; 8:2). His daughter "has just died": attempts to make *arti eteleutēsen* mean "is now dying" (NIV mg.) stem not from Greek syntax but from too simplistic a desire to harmonize this account with Mark and Luke. Better to recognize that Matthew, having eliminated the messengers as extraneous to his purposes, condenses "so as to present at the outset what was actually true before Jesus reached the house" (Broadus): such is Matthew's condensed style elsewhere (see on 8:5).

The synagogue ruler felt Jesus' touch had special efficacy, but his faith was not as great as that of the centurion who believed that Jesus could heal by his word (8:5–13). Jesus did not refuse him but responded to faith, small or great. He "got up" (v.19; the word *egeirō* most likely means, in this context, "rose from reclining at table" [cf. v.10]; see on harmonization problem, above) and "went with [*akoloutheō*, an evidence that this verb does not necessarily imply discipleship; see on 8:23] him."

20–21 The nature of the woman's hemorrhage (v.20) is uncertain; if, as seems probable, it was chronic bleeding from the womb, then she was perpetually unclean (cf. Lev 15:25–33). The regulation of such a woman's life was considered so important that the Mishnah devotes an entire tractate to the subject (*Zabim*) and gives some of the "remedies" for staunching the flow. Having heard of others who had been healed at Jesus' touch, this woman decided to touch even a tassel of Jesus' cloak (v.21). Moved in part by a superstitious view of Jesus, she struggled through the crowd, which, because of her "unclean" condition, she should have avoided.

The word *kraspedon* can mean either "edge" or "tassel." The former may be the meaning here (so NIV); but the latter is certainly the meaning in 23:5. Tassels (Heb. *ṣîṣit*) were sewn on the four corners of every Israelite's cloak (Num 15:37–41; Deut 22:12) as reminders to obey God's commands. While the tassels could easily become mere showpieces (23:5), Jesus himself, like any male Jew, doubtless wore them.

22 Though Matthew's account is again abbreviated, various explanations of this— e.g., short accounts are easier to memorize (Hill, *Matthew*), or Matthew eliminates magical elements (Hull, pp. 136f.)—are less convincing than the obvious one: viz., Matthew keeps only what is of most interest to him. The account is so short that it is not entirely clear whether Jesus turned and saw the woman before or after she touched him. The parallel accounts say the latter, and this may well be reflected in the perfect tense "your faith *has healed* you." The woman was healed on touching Jesus' cloak. He said that it was her faith that was effective, not the superstition mingled with it.

This seems better than the view that holds that Jesus first encouraged the woman ("Take heart, daughter") and then healed her without any reference to touching. Matthew 9:2; 14:27 are cited as parallels for this order. In fact, the three incidents differ somewhat; 9:2 according to the best variant says, in effect, "Take heart, for I now forgive you"; 9:22 says, "Take heart, for you have now been healed"; and 14:27 is quite different, since "Take heart" logically relates to "It is I," and the miracle of the stilling of the tempest is yet future. The final clauses of v.22 should therefore be interpreted to mean, not that the woman was healed from the "moment" Jesus spoke, but that she was healed from the *hōra* (lit., "hour") of this encounter with Jesus.

23–26 Flute players (v.23) were employed both on festive occasions (Rev 18:22) and at funerals. Matthew alone mentions them, not so much because he had special knowledge of Jewish funeral customs (cf. M *Ketuboth* 4:4, which required even a poor family to hire two flute players and one professional wailing woman), but out of personal recollection. Jesus was about to reverse funeral symbolism of the finality of death. The "noisy crowd" was made up of friends mourning, not in the hushed whispers characteristic of our Western funerals, but in loud outbursts of grief and wailing augmented by cries of hired mourners. Jesus' miracle not only brought a corpse to life (v.24) but hope to despair.

"Laughed" (*katagelaō*) occurs only here (v.24) and in the synoptic parallels. The crowd mocked Jesus, not just because he had said, "The girl is not dead but asleep," but even more because they thought that this great healer had arrived too late. Now he was going too far; carried away by his own success, he would try his skill on a corpse and make a fool of himself. In such a situation Jesus' words became, in retrospect, all the more profound. They not only denied that death—confronted by his power—was final, they also assumed that contrary to the Sadducean view (22:23) "sleep" better described the girl's condition. In the Bible "sleep" often denotes "death" but never "nonexistence" (cf. Dan 12:2; John 11:11; Acts 7:60; 1 Cor 15:6, 18; 1 Thess 4:13–15; 2 Peter 3:4).

The mocking crowd was ejected from the house (v.25). Matthew does not tell us, as Mark does, that the five witnesses remained; nor does he give us Jesus' words. But Matthew says that Jesus touched the corpse; and the body, far from defiling him, came to life. By itself the miracle did not prove Jesus to be more than a prophet or an apostle (cf. 1 Kings 17:17–24; 2 Kings 4:17–37; Acts 9:36–42). But prophets and apostles never claimed to be more than their office indicated. Jesus made vastly greater claims; so for Matthew the miracle showed that Jesus' authority as the Christ extended even over the dead.

Notes

18 Ἄρχων εἷς (*archōn heis*) is a relatively rare but not unknown way of saying "a ruler" or "a certain ruler," *heis*, (lit., "one") functioning more or less like the enclitic τις (*tis*, "a certain"; cf. Gr. 8:19). Interpretation is compounded by complex variants, probably generated not only by the rarity of the construction but the ambiguity of uncial texts: ΕΙΣΕΛΘΩΝ could be read εἷς ἐλθών (*heis elthōn*, lit., "one having come") or εἰσελθών (*eiselthōn*, lit., "having entered"), the latter presupposing the house of v.10. For a defense of the text behind NIV, cf. J. O'Callaghan, "La variante εισ/ελθων en Mt 9, 18," *Biblica* 62 (1981): 104–6.

20 "Tassel" or "edge" in Matthew and Luke makes this one of the most important "minor agreements" of Matthew and Luke against Mark, one that has generated many theories. Some take it with other "minor agreements" as sufficient evidence to defend the Griesbach hypothesis (Introduction, section 3); others postulate a shared source, a coincidence, a textual emendation, or (most recently) the influence of Mark 6:56 (J.T. Cummings, "The Tassel of His Cloak: Mark, Luke, Matthew—and Zechariah," in Livingstone, 2:47–61). However explained—and perhaps some theory of common information is best—it is scarcely enough to threaten the two-source hypothesis. Why Matthew should include such a descriptive detail when he eliminates so much is hard to say. Yet Matthew's narrative is not unpolished: he includes the piquant touch and occasional small detail, while eliminating characters and scenes not germane to his purpose.

---

b. Healing two blind men

9:27–31

> [27]As Jesus went on from there, two blind men followed him, calling out, "Have mercy on us, Son of David!"
> [28]When he had gone indoors, the blind men came to him, and he asked them, "Do you believe that I am able to do this?"
> "Yes, Lord," they replied.
> [29]Then he touched their eyes and said, "According to your faith will it be done to you"; [30]and their sight was restored. Jesus warned them sternly, "See that no one knows about this." [31]But they went out and spread the news about him all over that region.

This pericope is usually taken as a doublet of the Bartimaeus miracle (20:29–34; Mark 10:46–52; Luke 18:35–43). But close examination shows little verbal correspondence between the Synoptics; and such correspondence as exists is considerably less than that between two pericopes in Matthew telling of entirely different miracles (cf. Bornkamm, *Tradition*, pp. 219–20). Blindness was and still is common in the Mideast. Jesus performed many such miracles (see on 4:23; 8:16–17; 9:35). The most striking parallel is the cry "Have mercy on us, Son of David" (v.27). But this also occurs in 15:22 in a story having nothing to do with blindness; so the title "Son of David" may well have another explanation (see below). Certainly the point of 20:29–34 is quite different from this pericope. Here the focus is on Jesus' authority and the blind men's faith; there it is on the compassion of Jesus the King as he interrupts his journey to Jerusalem to respond to their cries. Moreover Matthew, we have repeatedly observed, condenses his narratives. Proposals that similar stories are doublets (a form of lengthening) must therefore be treated with suspicion. Likewise the supposition that Matthew has two blind men because Mark (his source) has two stories (8:22–26; 10:46–52), each describing the healing of one blind man, and that Matthew has simply added the number of the men and put them into one story is fanciful. Mark does have two stories of separate healings, one of which Matthew takes over (Mark 10:46–52; Matt 20:29–34). And Matthew and Mark each add another healing-of-the-blind miracle (Matt 9:27–31; Mark 8:22–26). This is scarcely surprising, in view of the prevalence of blindness and the extent of Jesus' healing ministry.

27–28 Apparently Jesus was returning from the ruler's house (v.23) either to his own house (4:13) or to that of Matthew (vv.10, 28—the article in Greek implies it was either his own dwelling or the one previously mentioned). We should probably envisage a large crowd after the dramatic raising of the ruler's daughter. Attached to the crowd were two blind men who had faith enough to follow him indoors.

This is the first time Jesus is called "Son of David" (v.27), and there can be no doubt that the blind men were confessing Jesus as Messiah (see on 1:1). They may have been physically blind, but they really "saw" better than many others—further evidence that Jesus came to those who needed a doctor (vv.12–13; see on 15:22). "The use of the Davidic title [cf. 15:22; 20:30; 21:9, 15; 22:42] in address to Jesus is less extraordinary than some think: in Palestine, in the time of Jesus, there was an intense Messianic expectation" (Hill, *Matthew*). The Messianic Age was to be characterized as a time when "the eyes of the blind [would be] opened and the ears of the deaf unstopped," when "the lame [would] leap like a deer, and the tongue of the dumb shout for joy" (Isa 35:5–6). If Jesus was really the Messiah, the blind reasoned, then he would have mercy on them; and they would have their sight. So their need drove them to faith. Perhaps this is what lies behind the fact in the Synoptics that "Son of David" is so often associated with the needy—those possessed by demons or, as here, in need of healing (cf. C. Burger, *Jesus als Davidssohn* [Göttingen: Vandenhoeck und Ruprecht, 1970]; Dennis C. Duling, "The Therapeutic Son of David: An Element in Matthew's Christological Apologetic," NTS 24 [1978]: 392–410).

Jesus did not deal with the blind men until they were indoors (v.28). This may have been to dampen messianic expectations (see on v.30) on a day marked by two highly public and dramatic miracles (v.26). It may also have been a device to increase their faith. The latter is suggested by his question (v.28), which accomplished two other things: (1) it revealed that their cries were not merely those of desperation only but of faith; and (2) it showed that their faith was directed not to God alone but to Jesus' person and to his power and authority. Their title for Jesus was therefore right; he is truly the messianic Son of David. Thus we return to the first reason for delaying the healing—its being done within the house prevented the excited crowd from witnessing an implicit christological claim.

29–31 Jesus' touching the blind men's eyes (v.29)—perhaps no more than a compassionate gesture to encourage faith—was not the sole means of this healing: it also depended on Jesus' authoritative word. "According to your faith" does not mean "in proportion to your faith" (so much faith, so much sight) but rather "since you believe, your request is granted"—cf. "your faith has healed you" (v.22). The miracle accomplished (v.30), Jesus "warned them sternly" to tell no one: *embrimaomai* ("I sternly warn") occurs only five times in the NT and always in connection with deep emotion (cf. Mark 1:43; 14:5; John 11:33, 38). This rather violent verb reveals Jesus' intense desire to avoid a falsely based and ill-conceived acclaim that would not only impede but also endanger his true mission (see on 8:4). But the men whose faith brought them to Christ for healing did not stay with him to learn obedience. So the news spread like wildfire throughout the region (cf. v.26).

Notes

27 Instead of the vocative υἱέ (*huie*, "son"), the text offers nominative υἱὸς Δαυίδ (*huios Dauid*, "son of David"). What is surprising is that the nominative noun in such a construction is anarthrous. This may well reflect Hebrew construction (cf. BDF, par. 147[3]).

c. Exorcising a dumb man

9:32–34

> [32]While they were going out, a man who was demon-possessed and could not talk was brought to Jesus. [33]And when the demon was driven out, the man who had been mute spoke. The crowd was amazed and said, "Nothing like this has ever been seen in Israel."
> [34]But the Pharisees said, "It is by the prince of demons that he drives out demons."

Again many see in these verses a "partial doublet," this time with 12:22–24; and again the verbal parallels are minimal. Hill (*Matthew*) says that 9:32–34 has been formed out of 12:22–24 "in order to complete the cases of miraculous healing presupposed in 11.5 and 10.1." But Matthew 4:24 shows that Jesus performed many exorcisms. Was Matthew so pressed for another example that he had to tell the same story twice? If so, why is the demon-possessed man in Matthew 12 both blind and mute and this one only mute? Moreover, if v.34 is genuine (see below), it is surely not surprising that the charge of being in league with Beelzebub (12:24) should begin on a private scale and take some time to explode into the open (12:24). In any case the charge is presupposed by 10:25.

32–33 The word *kōphos* ("could not talk") in classical, Hellenistic, and biblical Greek means "deaf" or "dumb" or "deaf mute"; the two ailments are commonly linked, especially if deafness is congenital. Perhaps the man here (v.32) was not only mute but a deaf mute. (On demon possession, see on 4:24, 8:28, 31.) The NT frequently attributes various diseases to demonic activity; but since the same ailment appears elsewhere without any suggestion of demonic activity (e.g., Mark 7:32–33), the frequent connection between the two is not based on primitive superstition but presupposes a real ability to distinguish between natural and demonic causes. The crowd's amazement (v.33) climaxes the earlier excitement (vv.26, 31). Nothing has ever been seen like this in Israel—and, by implication, if not among God's chosen people, then nowhere. But the same amazement ominously sets the stage for the Pharisees' cynical response (v.34).

34 This verse is missing from the Western textual tradition; and Allen, Klostermann, Zahn, and others follow suit, detecting an intrusion from 12:24. But the external evidence is strong; and the verse seems presupposed in 10:25. This is not the first intimation of direct opposition to Jesus in Matthew (vv.3, 11, 14, 24; cf. 5:10–12, 44); and even here the imperfect *elegon* (lit., "they were saying"; NIV, "said") may imply that the ferment was constantly in the background. But the tide of opposition, which later brought Jesus to the cross, now becomes an essential part of the background to the next discourse (cf. esp. 10:16–28).

9. Spreading the news of the kingdom (9:35–10:4)

a. Praying for workers

9:35–38

> [35]Jesus went through all the towns and villages, teaching in their synagogues, preaching the good news of the kingdom and healing every disease and sickness.

³⁶When he saw the crowds, he had compassion on them, because they were harassed and helpless, like sheep without a shepherd. ³⁷Then he said to his disciples, "The harvest is plentiful but the workers are few. ³⁸Ask the Lord of the harvest, therefore, to send out workers into his harvest field."

As 4:23–25 prepares for the first discourse (5–7), so vv.35–38 provide a report and summary that prepares for the second (10:5–42). A new note is added; not only are we told again of the extensiveness of Jesus' labors, but we now learn that the work was so great that many workers were needed. This leads to the commissioning of 10:1–4 and to the related discourse of 10:5–42.

Mark 6:6b has few affinities with this passage. Verse 35 is close to 4:23. Verse 36 is akin to Mark 6:34, and vv.37–38 to Luke 10:2 (cf. also John 4:35).

35 The setting is the same as in Mark 6:6b. For the exegesis, see on 4:23. The principal difference is the omission of any mention of Galilee, though doubtless that is the region in view. It is possible, as older commentaries suggest, that this represents a second circuit through Galilee; but in view of Matthew's highly topical arrangement, it is precarious to deduce so much from it. Verse 35 summarizes the heart of Jesus' Galilean ministry and prepares us for the new phase of mission via the Twelve. (On "their" synagogues, see also on 7:29 and 10:17.)

36 Like Yahweh in the OT (cf. Ezek 34), Jesus showed compassion on the shepherdless crowds and judgment on the false leaders. The "sheep" Jesus sees are "harassed" (not "fainted" [KJV], which has poor attestation), i.e., bullied, oppressed; and in the face of such problems, they are "helpless," unable to rescue themselves or escape their tormentors. The language of the verse is close to Numbers 27:17 (which could almost make Joshua a "type" of Jesus); but other parallels (e.g., 1 Kings 22:17; 2 Chron 18:16; Isa 53:6; Ezek 34:23–24; 37:24) remind us not only of the theme's rich background but also that the shepherd can refer either to God or to the Davidic Messiah God will send (cf. 2:6; 10:6, 16; 15:24; 25:31–46; 26:31).

37–38 The metaphor changed from sheep farming to harvest (v.37), as Jesus sought to awaken similar compassion in his disciples. Later on the harvest is the end of the age (13:49) and the judgment it brings—a common symbol (cf. Isa 17:11; Joel 3:13). Many commentators see this verse as a warning to Israel that judgment time is near. The word "plentiful" stands in the way of this interpretation; it makes sense only if here *therismos* does not mean "harvest-time" but "harvest-crop" (cf. BAGD, s.v.), as in Luke 10:2; John 4:35b. In that case the crop will be plentiful; many people will be ready to be "reaped" into the kingdom.

Jesus is speaking here to "his disciples," which many take to refer to the Twelve. More likely "his disciples" designates a larger group exhorted to ask (v.38) that the Lord of the harvest (possibly "Lord who is harvesting," if this is a verbal genitive; cf. G.H. Waterman, "The Greek 'Verbal Genitive,' " in Hawthorne, p. 292) will thrust laborers into his *therismou* (here in the sense "harvest field"). By contrast the Twelve are immediately commissioned as workers (10:1–4). This interpretation best fits 10:1: Jesus "called his twelve disciples to him." The clause is clumsy if they are the same as the "disciples" of 9:37–38 and natural only if they are part of the larger group.

b. Commissioning the Twelve

10:1–4

> ¹He called his twelve disciples to him and gave them authority to drive out evil spirits and to cure every kind of disease and sickness.
> ²These are the names of the twelve apostles: first, Simon (who is called Peter) and his brother Andrew; James son of Zebedee, and his brother John; ³Philip and Bartholomew; Thomas and Matthew the tax collector; James son of Alphaeus, and Thaddaeus; ⁴Simon the Zealot and Judas Iscariot, who betrayed him.

1 He whose word (chs. 5–7) and deed (chs. 8–9) were characterized by authority now delegates something of that authority to twelve men. This is the first time Matthew has explicitly mentioned the Twelve (cf. v.2; 11:1; 20:17; 26:14, 20, 47), who are introduced a little earlier in Mark (3:13–16). This commission appears to be the culmination of several previous steps (John 1:35–51; see on Matt 4:18–22). Indeed, Matthew's language suggests that the Twelve became a recognized group somewhat earlier. At the same time this commission was a stage in the training and preparation of those who, after Pentecost, would lead the earliest thrust of the fledgling church. Twelve were chosen, probably on an analogy to the twelve tribes of Israel (cf. also the council of twelve at Qumran, 1QS 8:1ff.), and they point to the eschatological renewal of the people of God (see on 19:28–30).

The authority the Twelve received enabled them to heal and drive out "evil [lit., 'unclean'] spirits"—spirits in rebellion against God, hostile to man, and capable of inflicting mental, moral, and physical harm, directly or indirectly. This is the first time in Matthew that demons are so described, and only again at 12:43 (but see on 8:16). "Every kind of disease and sickness" is exactly the expression in 4:23; 9:35. The authority granted the Twelve is in sharp contrast to the charismatic "gifts [pl.] of healing" at Corinth (1 Cor 12:9, 28), which apparently were individually more restricted in what diseases each could cure.

2–4 For the first and only time in Matthew, the Twelve are called "apostles." *Apostolos* ("apostle"), cognate with *apostellō* ("I send"), is not a technical term in the background literature. This largely accounts for the fact that as used in NT documents it has narrower and wider meanings (cf. DNTT, 1:126–37). Luke 6:13 explicitly affirms that Jesus himself called the Twelve "apostles"; and certainly Luke shows more interest in this question than the other three, partly in preparation for his work on the Acts of the Apostles. But in the NT the term can mean merely "messenger" (John 13:16) or refer to Jesus ("the apostle and high priest whom we confess," Heb 3:1) or elsewhere (esp. in Paul) denote "missionaries" or "representatives"—i.e., a group larger than the Twelve and Paul (Rom 16:7; 2 Cor 8:23). Nevertheless, the most natural reading of 1 Corinthians 9:1–5; 15:7; Galatians 1:17, 19 et al. is that even Paul could use the term in a narrow sense to refer to the Twelve plus himself (by special dispensation, 1 Cor 15:8–10).

Lists of the Twelve are found here and in three other places in the NT:

Matthew 10:2-4	Mark 3:16-19	Luke 6:13-16	Acts 1:13
Simon Peter	Simon Peter	Simon Peter	Simon Peter
Andrew	James	Andrew	John
James	John	James	James
John	Andrew	John	Andrew
Philip	Philip	Philip	Philip
Bartholomew	Bartholomew	Bartholomew	Thomas
Thomas	Matthew	Matthew	Bartholomew
Matthew	Thomas	Thomas	Matthew
James son of Alphaeus	James son of Alphaeus	James son of Alphaeus	James son of Alphaeus
Thaddaeus	Thaddaeus	Simon the Zealot	Simon the Zealot
Simon the Cananaean	Simon the Cananaean	Judas brother of James	Judas brother of James
Judas Iscariot	Judas Iscariot	Judas Iscariot	[Vacant]

Many significant things arise from comparing these lists.

1. Peter is always first, Judas Iscariot always last. Matthew uses "first" in connection with Peter; the word cannot mean he was the first convert (Andrew or perhaps John was) and probably does not simply mean "first on the list," which would be a trifling comment (cf. 1 Cor 12:28). More likely it means *primus inter pares* ("first among equals"; cf. further on 16:13-20).

2. The first four names of all four lists are those of two pairs of brothers whose call is mentioned first (cf. 4:18-22).

3. In each list there are three groups of four, each group headed by Peter, Philip (not to be confused with the evangelist), and James the son of Alphaeus respectively. But within each group the order varies (even from Luke to Acts!) except that Judas is always last. This suggests, if it does not prove, that the Twelve were organizationally divided into smaller groups, each with a leader.

4. The commission in Mark 6:7 sent the men out two by two; perhaps this accounts for the pairing in the Greek text of Matthew 10:2-4.

5. Some variations in order can be accounted for with a high degree of probability. For the first four names, Mark lists Peter, James, John, and appends Andrew, doubtless because the first three were an inner core privileged to witness the raising of Jairus's daughter and the Transfiguration and invited to be close to Jesus in his Gethsemane agony. Matthew preserves the order suggested by sibling relationships. He not only puts himself last in his group but mentions his less-than-savory past. Is this a sign of Christian humility?

6. Apparently Simon the Canaanite (Matt, Mark) is the same person as Simon the Zealot (Luke, Acts). If so, then apparently Thaddaeus is another name for Judas the brother of (or son of) James (see further below).

Not much is known concerning most of these men. For interesting but mostly incredible legends about them, see Hennecke (pp. 167-531).

Simon Peter. "Simon" is probably a contraction of "Simeon" (cf. Gen. 29:33). Natives of Bethsaida on Galilee (John 1:44), he and his brother Andrew were fishermen (Matt 4:18-20) and possibly disciples of John the Baptist before they became disciples of Jesus (John 1:35-42). Jesus gave Simon the name Cephas (in Aram.; "Peter" in Gr. [John 1:43]; see on 4:18). Impulsive and ardent, Peter's great strengths were his great weaknesses. New Testament evidence about him is abundant. Tracing Peter's movements after the Jerusalem Council (Acts 15) is very difficult.

Andrew. Peter's brother is not nearly so prominent in the NT. He appears again only in Mark 13:3; John 1:35–44; 6:8; 12:22, and in late and unreliable traditions. The Johannine evidence shows him to have been quietly committed to bringing others to Jesus.

James and John. James was probably the older (he almost always appears first). But as he became the first apostolic martyr (Acts 12:2), he never achieved his brother's prominence. The brothers were sons of Zebedee the fisherman, whose business was successful enough to employ others (Mark 1:20) while his wife was able to support Jesus' ministry (Matt 27:55–56; Luke 8:3). His wealth may help account for the family's link with the house of the high priest (John 18:15–16), as well as for the fact that he alone of the Twelve stood by the cross. The brothers' mother was probably Salome (cf. Matt 27:56; Mark 15:40; 16:1), and her motives were not unmixed (see on Matt 20:20–21). Perhaps the sons inherited something of her aggressive nature; whatever its source, the nickname "sons of thunder" (Mark 3:17; cf. also Mark 9:38–41; Luke 9:54–56) reveals something of their temperament. John may have been a disciple of John the Baptist (John 1:35–41). Of James we know nothing until Matthew 4:21–22. John was undoubtedly a special friend of Peter (Luke 22:8; John 18:15; 20:2–8; Acts 3:1–4:21; 8:14; Gal 2:9). Reasonably reliable tradition places him after the Fall of Jerusalem in Ephesus, where he ministered long and usefully into old age, taking a hand in the nurture of leaders like Polycarp, Papias, and Ignatius. Broadus's summary does not seem too fanciful: "[The] vaulting ambition which once aspired to be next to royalty in a worldly kingdom (20:20ff.], now seeks to overcome the world, to bear testimony to the truth, to purify the churches, and glorify God."

Philip. Like Peter and Andrew, Philip's home was Bethsaida (John 1:44); he too left the Baptist to follow Jesus. For incidents about him, see John 6:5–7; 12:21–22; 14:8–14. In the lists he invariably appears first in the second group of four. Polycrates, a second-century bishop, says Philip ministered in the Roman province of Asia and was buried at Hierapolis.

Bartholomew. The name means "son of Tolmai" or "son of Tholami" (cf. LXX Josh 15:14) or "son of Tholomaeus" (cf. Jos. Antiq. XX, 5[i.1]). Many have identified him with Nathanael on the grounds that (1) the latter is apparently associated with the Twelve (John 21:2; cf. 1:43–51), (2) Philip brought Nathanael to Jesus (John 1:43–46), and (3) Philip and Batholomew are always associated in the lists of apostles. The evidence is not strong; but if it is solid, we also know he came from Cana (John 21:2). He is remembered for Jesus' tribute to him (John 1:47).

Thomas. Also named "Didymus" (John 11:16; 21:2), which in Aramaic means "Twin," Thomas appears in Gospel narratives only in John 11:16; 14:5; 20:24–29. Known for his doubt, he should also be known for his courage (John 11:16) and his profound confession (John 20:28). Some traditions claim he went to India as a missionary and was martyred there; others place his later ministry in Persia.

Matthew. See on 9:9; Introduction, section 5.

James the son of Alphaeus. The extra phrase distinguishes him from James the son of Zebedee. If we assume (and this is highly likely) that this James is not the same as "James the brother" of Jesus (see on 13:55), we know almost nothing about him. Assuming Matthew = Levi (see on 9:9), then Matthew's father was also called Alphaeus (Mark 2:14); and if this is the same Alphaeus, then James and Matthew are another pair of brothers among the Twelve. Some have argued that Alphaeus is an alternative form of Cleophas (Clopas), which would mean that "James son of Alphaeus" is the same person as "James the younger" (Mark 15:40) and that his mother's name was Mary (Matt 27:56; Mark 15:40; 16:1; John 19:25). But such connections are by no means certain.

Thaddaeus. The textual variants are difficult. The longer ones (e.g., KJV, "Lebbaeus, whose surname was Thaddaeus") are almost certainly conflations. "Thaddaeus" has the support of early representatives from Alexandrian, Western, and Caesarean witnesses (cf. Metzger, *Textual Commentary*, p. 26). Through elimination he appears to be identified with (lit.) "Judas of James"—which could mean either "Judas son of James" or "Judas brother of James." The former is perhaps the more normal meaning; but the author of the Epistle of Jude designates himself as "Jude [Gr. *Ioudas*] . . . a brother of James" (Jude 1, where *adelphos* ["brother"] is actually used). If Jude is the apostolic "Judas of James," then the meaning of the latter expression is fixed. On the other hand, if canonical Jude is the half-brother of Jesus and full brother of Jesus' half-brother James (see on 13:55), then "Judas of James" most likely means "Judas son of James." "Thaddaeus" comes from a root roughly signifying "the beloved." Perhaps this apostle was called "Judas the beloved" = "Judas Thaddaeus," and "Thaddaeus" was progressively used to distinguish him from the other Judas in the apostolic band. Only John 14:22 provides us with information about him. Later traditions are worthless.

Simon the Zealot. Matthew and Mark have "Simon the Cananaean" (not "Canaanite," which would suggest a pagan Gentile; cf. the different Gr. word in 15:22). "Cananaean" (*qan'ân*) is the Aramaic form of "Zealot" specified in Luke–Acts. The Zealots were nationalists, strong upholders of Jewish traditions and religion; and some decades later they became a principal cause of the Jewish War in which Rome sacked Jerusalem. The Zealots were probably not so influential in Jesus' time. The nickname may reveal Simon's past political and religious associations; it also distinguishes him from Simon Peter.

Judas Iscariot. Judas's father is called "Simon Iscariot" in John 6:71; 13:26. Scholarly interest has spent enormous energy and much ingenuity on the name "Iscariot." Explanations include (1) "man of Kerioth" (there are two eligible villages of that name (cf. ZPEB, 3:785; IBD, 2:830); (2) transliteration of Latin *sicarius*, used to refer to a Zealot-like movement; (3) "man of Jericho," an explanation depending on a Greek corruption; (4) a transliteration of the Aramaic *šeqaryaᶜ* ("falsehood," "betrayal"; cf. C.C. Torrey, "The Name 'Iscariot,'" HTR 36 [1943]: 51–62), which could therefore become a nickname for Judas only after his ignominy and not at this point in his life; (5) "Judas the dyer," reflecting his occupation (cf. A. Ehrman, "Judas Iscariot and Abba Saqqara," JBL 97 [1978]: 572f.; Y. Arbeitman, "The Suffix of Iscariot," JBL 99 [1980]: 122–24); (6) as an adaptation of the last, "Judas the redhead" (Albright and Mann). The first and fifth seem most likely; the second is currently most popular. Judas was treasurer for the Twelve, but not an honest one

(John 12:6; 13:29; see also on 26:14–16; 27:3–10). Matthew and Mark add the damning indictment—"who betrayed him." Luke 6:16 labels him a traitor.

Notes

1 The construction ὥστε (hōste, "so that") plus an infinitive to indicate purpose is extraordinary (cf. BDF, par. 390[3]; Zerwick, par. 352) but cannot easily be taken any other way.

B. *Second Discourse: Mission and Martyrdom* (10:5–11:1)

1. *Setting*

10:5a

⁵These twelve Jesus sent out with the following instructions:

5 For a general introduction to the discourses and their problems, see comments at 5:1. On the face of it, this discourse is as tightly bracketed as the others (v.5a; 11:1), giving at least the impression that all the material of vv.5b–42 was delivered on one occasion. It is also peculiarly difficult. Two separate but related questions need careful attention before a judgment is formed.

The literary question. Roughly speaking, vv.5–15 have some parallels with Mark 6:8–11; Luke 9:3–5; 10:5–15. The last of these references, however, concerns the mission of the Seventy-two, not found in Matthew or Mark. Matthew 10:16a is close to Luke 10:3. But Matthew 10:17–25, concerning the disciples' persecution and their arraignment before tribunals, finds its closest parallel in the Olivet Discourse (Mark 13:9–13; Luke 21:12–19; cf. Matt 24:9–14). The final section (vv.26–42), setting out conditions for discipleship in more general terms, resembles material in Mark 9 and Luke 12:2–12. With the exception of only a few places (vv.5–6, 8, 16b), little in vv.5–42 is peculiar to the first Gospel, though admittedly some parallels are not as close as others.

The most common literary theory is that Matthew composed this address from segments of his two principal sources, Mark and Q. Those who reject Mark's priority and insist on Matthew's priority do not need Q and have an easier time defending the unity of this chapter. But Mark's priority still has best credentials (cf. Introduction, section 3), and so the problems remain. David Wenham ("The 'Q' Tradition") has followed Schürmann and Lambrecht in arguing that almost this entire discourse comes from various strands of the Q tradition (this does not necessarily mean Q is a single, written document). Mark's parallels are thereby judged secondary and condensations of earlier sources.

The historical and theological question. How do such source theories affect the context Matthew establishes? Here there is little agreement. F.W. Beare ("The Mission of the Disciples and the Mission Charge: Matthew 10 and Parallels," JBL 89 [1970]: 1–13) does not think there ever was a mission of the Twelve. The setting is a fabrication designed to enhance the discourse, itself an edited collection of sayings, few of them authentic. Many scholars, including conservative ones, suppose the discourse to be an amalgam of authentic material given on at least two separate occasions (Allen, Grosheide, Ridderbos). Tasker leaves the question open. R. Morosco ("Redaction Criticism and the Evangelical: Matthew 10 a Test Case," JETS 22 [1979]: 323–31) resurrects the old theory of B.W. Bacon, assuming not only five discourses in Matthew, but also their having been modeled on the five books of the Pentateuch (cf. Introduction, section 14). Morosco does not make clear, however, whether he thinks (1) that there is some historical commissioning of the Twelve to which a collage of material has been attached, (2) that a discourse was delivered on that occasion and this is an expanded adaptation of it, or (3) that the setting itself is fictitious.

Related to the historical question are several observations about the content of Matthew 10. In vv.5–16, all Jesus' instructions neatly fit the situation of the Twelve during Jesus' public ministry. This includes Jesus' prohibition of ministry to others than Jews (vv.5–6). But vv.17–22 clearly envisage a far more extensive ministry— even to kings and Gentiles. The persecution described does not fit the period of the first apostolic ministry but looks beyond it to times of major conflict long after Pentecost. As a result the great majority of modern commentators take this to be what Schuyler Brown describes as a literary means for Jesus to instruct "the Matthean community through the transparency of the twelve missionary disciples" ("The Mission to Israel in Matthew's Central Section," ZNW 69 [1978]: 73–90)— though, of course, many of the sayings are not thought to be dominical.

The historical and especially the literary issues are complex and intertwined, as is clear from the diversity of proposed solutions. The evidence can be weighed variously. Most solutions mask some unproved presuppositions and embrace a succession of judgments that could go another way.

The setting Matthew gives must be accepted. Although he arranges much of his material topically, uses loose time-connectives, condenses his sources and sometimes paraphrases them, there is no convincing evidence that Matthew *invents* settings. Nor will appeal to some elusive genre suffice. If Matthew is a coherent writer, such nonhistorical material must be reasonably and readily separable from his historical material, if the alleged "genre" was recognizable to the first readers. Verse 5a could scarcely be clearer: "These twelve Jesus sent out with the following instructions."

Since Luke records both the commission of the Twelve and that of the Seventy-two (9:1–6; 10:1–16), we must assume that these were separate events. But probably the Twelve were part of the Seventy-two; instructions given the latter were therefore given the former. Although v.5a is historically specific about the fact of Jesus' instructing the Twelve and commissioning them, it does not pinpoint the exact time in his ministry when this took place. We have already found that Matthew, in condensing the account of the raising of Jairus's daughter and omitting the messengers, effectively collapses the first approach of Jairus and the news from the messengers, with the result that the daughter is presented as dead a little earlier than in the synoptic parallels (see on 9:18–26). Similarly, if Jesus instructed the Twelve both at their own first commissioning and later as part of the commissioning of the Seventy-two, the omission of the latter might well be motive enough to combine elements of the two sets of instructions. Both v.5a and 11:1 would still be strictly true.

David Wenham ("The 'Q' Tradition") would go further: he notes that 11:1 is the only ending to a Matthean discourse that omits "these words" or "these parables" or the like and wonders whether the omission might be a hint that this second discourse, unlike the others, is meant to be taken as a Matthean collection of Jesus' sayings. Such an argument from silence seems a slender thread on which to hang so much, not least because, apart from the opening words *kai egeneto* (lit., "and it happened"—see on 7:28–29), the fivefold formula at the end of each discourse varies considerably. But it is difficult simply to discount the possibility; and the suggestion that Matthew has collapsed the two commissionings is not implausible, even if not demonstrable.

Careful study of vv.5–42 suggests that the discourse is more unified than often recognized. Many of the alleged discrepancies are artificial. There is no conflict, for instance, between the ready harvest of 9:37–38 and the resistance in 10:16–22 (contra Morosco, *Redaction Criticism*, p. 325). "The blood of the martyrs is the seed of the church" is a valid principle; and many great awakenings, including the Whitefield and Wesleyan revivals, have shown afresh that the harvest is most plentiful when the workers reap in the teeth of opposition. If Matthew omits the account of the Twelve's actual departure and return (kept in Mark 6:12–13; Luke 9:6, 10), it cannot mean that he does not know of the event or does not believe it happened; otherwise 10:1, 5; 11:1 are incoherent. Matthew is less interested in the details of many events he relates than in Jesus' words; but "less interested" does not mean "not interested," which seems to be the favorite disjunction of many redaction critics.

Certainly vv.17–23 go beyond the immediate mission of the Twelve, and in at least two ways the latter verses envisage a mission to the Gentiles, unlike vv.5b–6, and far severer opposition than anything the Twelve faced during Jesus' ministry. Yet these are not new themes; we have already found Jesus predicting severe persecution (5:10–12 et al.), seeing a time of prolonged witness to the "world" (5:13–14; 7:13–14) after his departure (9:15), and many Gentiles participating in the messianic banquet (8:11–12). Therefore it is surely not unnatural for Jesus to treat this commission of the Twelve as both an explicit short-term itinerary and a paradigm of the longer mission stretching into the years ahead. For the latter, the Twelve need further instruction beyond those needed for the immediate tour, which they must see as in part an exercise anticipating something more. In this sense the Twelve become a paradigm for other disciples in their post-Pentecost witness, a point Matthew understands (cf. 28:18–20); and in this sense he intends that Matthew 10 should also speak to his readers.

The very fact that Matthew includes both what is historically specific in the first, short-term commission (e.g., restriction to Jews, certain clothing) and what is historically relevant only to the post-Pentecost church strongly supports his material's authenticity. If he were simply addressing his own community, much of chapter 10 would be irrelevant. Attempts to get around this by envisaging a divided Matthean community of people for or against a Gentile mission (e.g., S. Brown, "The Two-fold Representation of the Mission in Matthew's Gospel," ST 31 [1977]: 21–32 are extremely speculative. Such a theory depends not only on a selective reading of the Gospels that judges inauthentic all evidence that refutes it, but also on an evangelist abysmally incapable of editing his sources into a coherent whole. Yet Schuyler Brown ("Matthean Community," p. 194) writes: "The fact that contradictory missionary mandates are placed on Jesus' lips is evidence enough that he himself took no position on this matter, one way or the other, and this is not surprising. Jesus took for granted that he and his disciples were sent to Israel."

The presuppositions here are (1) that Jesus did not envisage a racially mixed church and (2) that the Gospels must be read as church documents that do not distinguish between Jesus' day and the time of writing. The first point is repeatedly denied by all four Gospels; the second is called in question by explicit "before–after" passages (e.g., John 2:20–22) and themes or titles (see excursus at 8:20). Jesus says and does many things in the Gospels before the Cross and Resurrection that are fully comprehensible only after these events. The real contrast between vv.5–16 and vv.17–42 is salvation-historical. There is implicit recognition that the two situations are not the same, but the first prepares for the second. This distinction is ascribed to Jesus and thus confirms that he saw a continuing community that would grow under fire. Moreover there is evidence elsewhere that Jesus was prepared to discuss widely separate events within the same framework if those separate events are internally connected in some way (see on chs. 24–25).

If this second discourse is coherent, some account must be given of parallels scattered elsewhere in the Synoptics. Earlier discussion (see on chs. 5–7) is still relevant: Jesus was an itinerant preacher who said the same things many times in similar words; the evangelists rarely claim to present *ipsissima verba* but only *ipsissima vox* (see on 3:17); their discourses are very substantial condensations in line with their own interests; they do not hesitate to rearrange the order of presentation of some material within a discourse in order to highlight topical interests. But the sad fact is that there are few methodologically reliable tools for distinguishing between, say, two forms of one aphoristic saying, two reports of the same saying uttered on two occasions, or one report of one such saying often repeated in various forms but preserved in the tradition in one form (surely not problematic if only the *ipsissima vox* is usually what is at stake).

Suppose, for instance, that David Wenham ("The 'Q' Tradition") is essentially right, and most of vv.5–42 comes from Q, conceived as a variety of sources, oral and written, of Jesus' words: what historical conclusions does such a theory entail? The surprising answer is "Not much." For it is possible that some sayings of Jesus, repeated by him often and on diverse occasions, were jotted down in a sort of amalgam form encapsulating their substance and then used by the evangelists in different contexts and adapted accordingly. Those contexts may well include the historical settings in which the teaching was first uttered. That would be easy to believe if the apostle Matthew really did compose the first Gospel (cf. Introduction, section 5). Authorship does not necessarily affect the authority of any NT book. But it does affect the way the tradition descended and thereby limits the wildest form-critical speculation (cf. Introduction, section 2).

Although Wenham's Q hypothesis may be challenged at many points on the ground that his argument turns on debatable judgments, yet the chief point is that the notion of Q sources behind vv.5–42 does not itself preclude the authenticity or unity of this discourse. A dozen variations could be shown to produce the same equivocal result. Problems arise only when theories regarding the contributing factors (authors, sources, context, redaction, historical reconstruction of Jesus' life and of the early church) are so aligned as to produce a synthesis that quite unnecessarily contradicts the text or some part of it. This is extremely unfortunate when in fact the text is the only hard evidence we have.

It is not possible in small compass to demonstrate the many factors contributing to scholars' diverse decisions in each passage of the mission discourse and how such factors may, taking full account of the hard evidence, come together in a way justifying Matthew's presentation of this material as a discourse to the Twelve. While the following exposition focuses on the meaning of the text as it stands, a few hints are given as to how difficult source critical and historical problems may be most profitably probed.

2. The commission

10:5b–16

"Do not go among the Gentiles or enter any town of the Samaritans. [6]Go rather to the lost sheep of Israel. [7]As you go, preach this message: 'The kingdom of heaven is near.' [8]Heal the sick, raise the dead, cleanse those who have leprosy,[a] drive out demons. Freely you have received, freely give. [9]Do not take along any gold or silver or copper in your belts; [10]take no bag for the journey, or extra tunic, or sandals or a staff; for the worker is worth his keep.

[11]"Whatever town or village you enter, search for some worthy person there and stay at his house until you leave. [12]As you enter the home, give it your greeting. [13]If the home is deserving, let your peace rest on it; if it is not, let your peace return to you. [14]If anyone will not welcome you or listen to your words, shake the dust off your feet when you leave that home or town. [15]I tell you the truth, it will be more bearable for Sodom and Gomorrah on the day of judgment than for that town. [16]I am sending you out like sheep among wolves. Therefore be as shrewd as snakes and as innocent as doves."

5b–6 Jesus forbade the Twelve (v.5b) from taking "the road to the Gentiles" (cf. Notes)—presumably toward Tyre and Sidon in the north or the Decapolis in the east—and from visiting Samaritan towns in the south. They were to remain in Galilee, ministering to the people of Israel (v.6). Jews despised Samaritans, not only because they preserved a separate cult (cf. John 4:20), but also because they were a mixed race, made up partly of the poorest Jews who had been left in the land at the time of the Exile and partly of Gentile peoples transported into the territory and with whom the remaining Jews had intermingled, thereby succumbing to some syncretism (cf. 2 Kings 17:24–28; cf. ISBE, 4:2673–74). The Twelve were to restrict themselves to "the lost sheep of Israel." This designation does not refer to a certain segment of the Jews (so Stendahl, Peake, 683–84), since in the OT background (esp. Ezek 34; see on Matt 9:36; cf. Isa 53:6; Jer 50:6) the term refers to all the people (Hill, *Matthew*).

Why this restriction? In part it was probably because of pragmatic considerations. That Jesus felt it necessary to mention the Samaritans at all presupposes John 4. The disciples, happy in the exercise of their ability to perform miracles, might have been tempted to evangelize the Samaritans because they remembered Jesus' success there. Judging by Luke 9:52–56, however, the Twelve were still temperamentally ill-equipped to minister to Samaritans. And even after Pentecost, despite an explicit command from the risen Lord (Acts 1:8), the church moved only hesitantly toward the Samaritans (Acts 8).

The most important consideration, however, was not pragmatic but theological. Jesus stood at the nexus in salvation history where as a Jew and the Son of David he came in fulfillment of his people's history as their King and Redeemer. Yet his personal claims would offend so many of his own people that he would be rejected by all but a faithful remnant. Why increase their opposition by devoting time to Gentile ministry? His mission, as predicted, was worldwide in its ultimate aims (see on 1:1; 2:1; 3:9–10; 4:15–16; 5:13–16; 8:1–13; 10:18; 21:43; 24:14; 28:16–20); and all along he had warned that being a Jew was not enough. But his own people must not be excluded because premature offense could be taken at such broad perspectives. Therefore Jesus restricted his own ministry primarily (15:24), though not exclusively (8:1–13; 15:21–39), to Jews. He himself was sent as their Messiah. The messianic people of God developed out of the Jewish remnant and expanded to include Gentiles. The restriction of vv.5–6, therefore, depends on a particular understanding of salvation history (cf. Meier, *Law*, pp. 27–30), which ultimately goes back to Jesus. This Paul well understood: both salvation and judgment were for the Jew first, then for the Gentile (Rom 1:16); and this conviction governed his own early missionary efforts (e.g., Acts 13:5, 44–48; 14:1 et al.).

On modern theories of the significance of vv.5–6, see on v.5a.

7–8 The content of the disciples' message was very like that in 3:2; 4:17. "Repent" is not mentioned but is presupposed. The long-awaited kingdom was now "near" enough (see on 4:17) to be attested by miracles directed at demonism and malady. The "authority" in v.1 cannot be limited to the list of powers mentioned there, for here (v.8) two more are added: raising the dead (textually well attested, if not quite certain) and cleansing lepers (see on 9:18–26; 8:1–4, respectively).

Jesus expected the Twelve to be supported by those to whom they were to minister (cf. vv.9–13; 1 Cor 9:14), but they needed to understand that what they had received—the good news of the kingdom, Jesus' authority, and this commission—they had received "freely" (not "in large bounty"—though that was true—but gratis). Therefore it would have been mercenary to charge others (NEB: "You have received without cost; give without charge"; cf. *Didache* 11–13; *Pirke Aboth* 1:13). The danger of profiteering is still among us (cf. Micah 3:11).

9–10 The imperative *mē ktēsesthe* ("Do not take along," v.9) more likely means "Do not procure" (as in Acts 1:18; 8:20; 22:28). Even then the longer expression *mē ktēsesthe . . . eis* ("Do not procure . . . with a view to [filling your belts]") could mean either "Do not accept money [i.e., fill your moneybelt] for your ministry" or "Do not provide your belt with money when you start out." The parallel in Mark 6:9 obviously means the latter. Gold, silver, and copper refer either to money or to a supply of the metals that could be exchanged for goods or money.

Mark permits "taking" (*airō*) sandals and a staff (a walking stick) and forbids everything else (6:8); Matthew's account forbids "procuring" (*ktaomai*) even sandals or a walking stick (v.10). It may be that Mark's account clarifies what the disciples are permitted to bring, whereas Matthew's assumes that the disciples already have certain things (one cloak, sandals, a walking stick) and forbids them from "procuring" anything more. Two cloaks (cf. on 5:40) might seem too much but would be comforting if sleeping out. The disciples needed to learn the principle that "the worker is worth his keep" (cf. 1 Cor 9:14; 1 Tim 5:17–18) and to shun luxury while learning to rely on God's providence through the hospitality of those who would take them in overnight, thus obviating the need for a second cloak. See further discussion in the Notes.

What is clear is that the Twelve must travel unencumbered, relying on hospitality and God's providence. The details ensure that the instructions were for that mission alone (cf. Luke 22:35–38) and confirm Matthew's consciousness of the historicity of this part of the discourse.

11–15 To settle into the house of a "worthy" person (v.11) implies that the disciples were not to shop around for the most comfortable quarters. In this place "worthy" probably does not refer to a morally upright, honorable, or religious person but to one willing and able to receive an apostle of Jesus and the gospel of the kingdom (cf. discussion in Bonnard)—the opposite of "dogs" and "pigs" (7:6). As the disciples entered the house, they were to give it their "greeting." Luke (10:5) gives us the actual words: "Peace to this house." Neither Matthew nor Luke is introducing post-resurrection notions of šālôm ("peace"), even though later Christians would be reminded of the peace Jesus achieved for them (Luke 24:36; John 14:27 et al.). Instead the greeting prepares for v.13: "As you enter the home" (NIV; same word as "house" in v.12, probably with the meaning "household"), you are to give the normal greeting; but if the home turns out to be "unworthy" (as defined above), contrary to what you had been led to believe, then let your greeting of peace return to you (v.13); i.e., don't stay. The Twelve were emissaries of Jesus. Those who received them received him (cf. v.40). Their greeting was of real value because of their relationship to him. Loss of their greeting was loss of their presence and therefore loss of Jesus. Potiphar's household was blessed because of Joseph's presence (Gen 39:3–5). How much more those homes that harbored the apostles of the Messiah!

What was true for the home applied equally to the town (v.14). A pious Jew, on leaving Gentile territory, might remove from his feet and clothes all dust of the pagan land now being left behind (SBK, 1:571), thus dissociating himself from the pollution of those lands and the judgment in store for them. For the disciples to do this to Jewish homes and towns would be a symbolic way of saying that the emissaries of Messiah now view those places as pagan, polluted, and liable to judgment (cf. Acts 13:51; 18:6). The actions, while outrageously shocking, accord with Matthew 8:11–12; 11:20–24. Sodom and Gomorrah faced catastrophic destruction because of their sin (Gen 19) and became bywords of loathsome corruption (Isa 1:9; Matt 11:22–24; Luke 17:29; Rom 9:29; 2 Peter 2:6; Jude 7; cf. Jub 36:10). Although there is still worse to come for them on the Day of Judgment, there is yet more awful judgment for those who reject the word and the messengers of the Messiah (cf. Heb 2:1–3).

Once again the christological claim, though implicit, is unambiguous. As in 7:21–23, Jesus here insists that one's eternal destiny turns on relationship to him or even to his emissaries. At the same time, even in this early ministry, Jesus' apostles were to face the certainty of opposition—as did Jesus himself, rejected at Nazareth (13:53–58) and in Samaria (Luke 9:52–53), and not believed in the towns of Galilee (11:20–24). That early opposition pointed to the greater suffering still to come (vv.17ff.) and also aligned the disciples of Jesus with the prophets of old (5:10–12) and with Jesus himself (10:24–25). Thus the disciples began to learn that the advance of the kingdom was divisive (vv.34–35; cf. 2 Cor 2:15–16) and would meet with violent opposition (see on 11:11–12).

16 The first part of v.16 has a close parallel in Luke 10:3, part of the commission to the Seventy-two. Because it is short and aphoristic, it is impossible to be certain how many times Jesus said it. Here it links the preceding pericope with the following warnings about persecution. The verse goes as well with what succeeds as what precedes.

Jesus pictured his disciples, defenseless in themselves, located in a dangerous environment. This is where he himself was sending them. The shepherd in this metaphor sends his sheep into the wolf pack (cf. 7:15; John 10:12; Acts 20:29). Therefore they must be *phronimoi* ("shrewd") as serpents, which in several ancient Near Eastern cultures were proverbial for prudence. But prudence can easily degenerate into cheap cunning unless it goes with simplicity. The disciples must prove not only "shrewd" but *akeraioi* ("innocent"; used elsewhere in the NT only in Rom

16:19; Phil 2:15). Yet innocence becomes ignorance, even naiveté, unless combined with prudence.

The dove was not an established symbol. In Hosea 7:11 a dove is pictured as "easily deceived and senseless." In a late Midrash the serpent–dove contrast appears ("God saith to the Israelites: 'Towards me they are sincere as doves, but toward the Gentiles they are cunning as serpents'" [Cant.R.2:14]). Yet not only is this Midrash late, the contrast is not at all what Jesus had in mind. His followers were to be, not prudent toward outsiders and innocent toward God, but both prudent and innocent in their mission to outsiders. In this light the dove image becomes clear. Doves are retiring but not astute; they are easily ensnared by the fowler. So Jesus' disciples, in their mission as sheep among wolves, must be "shrewd," avoiding conflicts and attacks where possible; but they must also be "innocent," i.e., not so cautious, suspicious, and cunning that circumspection degenerates into fear or elusiveness. The balance is difficult, but not a little of Jesus' teaching combines such poles of meaning (see on 7:1–6).

Notes

---

5 The prohibition εἰς ὁδὸν ἐθνῶν μὴ ἀπέλθητε (eis hodon ethnōn mē apelthēte) means literally "Do not go away on the road of the Gentiles"—i.e., Do not go in the direction of (Aram. לְאֹרַח leʾōrah) the Gentiles; "Do not take the road to Gentile lands" (NEB).

9–10 Though the distinction between κτάομαι (ktaomai, "procure") and αἴρω (airō, "take") may work in Matthew and Mark, it fails in Luke, who uses airō (as in Mark) but forbids a staff in 9:3 and sandals in 10:4. This suggests to Marshall (Luke, pp. 352f.) that Matthew and Luke depend on Q as opposed to Mark. That is possible. But the fact that Luke's verb (airō) is the same as Mark's calls it in question. Many solutions have been proposed, none altogether convincing (cf. E. Power, "The Staff of the Apostles: A Problem in Gospel Harmony," Biblica 4 [1923]: 241–66; Lagrange; Schniewind; Lane, pp. 207f.). Perhaps the simplest is that Luke has not changed Mark but in both passages (Luke 9:3; 10:4) draws from Q, like Matthew; but in 9:3 Luke changes ktaomai ("I procure") to airō ("I take"), which has a semantic range large enough to mean the former, and in 10:4 changes ktaomai to βαστάζω (bastazō, "bear," "carry"), the latter perhaps suggesting carrying some luggage: no "purse" ("no money"), no "bag" (no "luggage"), and no "sandals" (none carried). This suggestion is supported by the fact that the two verbs in Luke and the one in Matthew are all imperatives, unlike Mark's subordinate construction and subjunctive mood. In other words Matthew and Luke agree not only on what is permitted but on the grammatical construction. Luke's only agreement with Mark is in one of his two verbs.

16 The pronoun ἐγώ (egō, "I") is probably not emphatic, as ἰδοὺ ἐγώ (idou egō, lit., "behold I") reflects a Semitic parallel that is unemphatic (cf. Turner, Syntax, p. 38).

---

3. Warnings of future sufferings (10:17–25)

a. The Spirit's help

10:17–20

[17]Be on your guard against men; they will hand you over to the local councils and flog you in their synagogues. [18]On my account you will be brought before governors and kings as witnesses to them and to the Gentiles. [19]But when they arrest

you, do not worry about what to say or how to say it. At that time you will be given what to say, [20]for it will not be you speaking, but the Spirit of your Father speaking through you.

There are parallels in vv. 17–25 both to 24:9, 13 and to Luke 6:40; 12:11–12; 21:12. Although it has often been affirmed, it is doubtful that Matthew has simply pulled back some material from the Olivet Discourse (see on 10:5a). But there may be substantial reliance on Q (cf. D. Wenham, "The 'Q' Tradition"). The language is demonstrably Palestinian. Even if Matthew applies some of these things to his own readers (cf. Hare, pp. 96–114), there is no reason to doubt the authenticity of these warnings. What this means is that Jesus envisaged an extended time of witness in the midst of persecution—in short, a witnessing and suffering church.

17 The *de* ("But," NIV) does not have adversative force. It merely connects this warning with the aphorism in v. 16, showing how it is to be applied. The men who will hand the disciples over must be Jews, as the context is the synagogue; and so the persecution here envisaged is Jewish persecution of Christians (unlike v. 18). The *synedria* ("local councils," pl. only here in the NT), which could be civic or synagogal, were charged with preserving the peace. That flogging is used for punishment, rather than the broader term "beating," implies that the opposition is not mob violence but the result of judicial action (Hare, p. 104). Moreover Jesus is envisaging a time before the absolute separation of church and synagogue has taken place, for synagogue floggings (cf. 23:34; Mark 13:9; Acts 22:19; cf. 2 Cor 11:24–25) were most easily inflicted on synagogue members. At a later period the worshipers would sometimes sing a psalm while the flogging took place. But there is no evidence this was practiced in NT times. In any case we are reminded of the slowness with which Jewish Christians withdrew from broader Jewish worship in the post-Pentecost period.

The reference to "their" synagogues is often interpreted as an anachronism, reflecting the church–synagogue polarity (see on 4:23; 7:29; 9:35; 11:1; 12:9; 13:54). Normally the word "their" is explicitly Matthean, but here Jesus uses it. This may suggest redactional phrasing. Significantly, however, the OT prophets in speaking for God commonly used "their" and "them" language when referring to apostate Israel. Here it is very likely that the OT background explains the usage. And because Matthew makes much of the failure of most Jews to receive their own Messiah, it is likely that the OT has affected his phrasing elsewhere. Certainly Christian readers, understanding themselves to be recipients of the revelation most Jews had refused, would see the "their" within this polarized context. Nevertheless the term itself is no proof of anachronism unless it was similarly anachronistic in its OT setting, which is absurd. Indeed, if this OT background is determinative, then both Jesus and Matthew self-consciously spoke of Israel from the perspective of a divine revelatory stance that warned Israel afresh against apostasy, a theme elsewhere made explicit (e.g., 8:11–12).

18 As the witness would extend at some future time beyond Galilee and the Jewish race, so also the opposition: "governors" (*hēgemonas*, rulers and magistrates at various levels) and "kings" make this clear. As in 8:4 and 24:14, the "witness" is not against people but to them; it becomes either the means by which they accept the truth or, when they reject it, a condemnation. The disciples would be harassed and persecuted, not on account of who they are but on account of who Christ is (see on 5:10–12). For his sake their witness would extend "to them and to the Gentiles"— probably not a reference "to Jews [or Jewish magistrates] and to the Gentiles," but "to governors and kings and to [other] Gentiles." Overlapping between the paired elements is not uncommon in such constructions (e.g., Mark 16:7; Gr. of Acts 5:29; 9:16; cf. Hare, pp. 108–9).

19–20 The translation of *paradidōmi* (lit., "I hand over," as in v.17) as "arrest" (v.19) is doubtful. The subject is ambiguous: "people," "opponents," or "Jewish leaders" could be "handing over" the disciples to the Gentile authorities. Later on this happened to Paul and other Christians, who at first witnessed to their faith with relative impunity under the Roman laws granting exemptions from emperor worship to Jews, but fell victim to increasing Roman wrath as the Jews progressively denied any link between themselves and Christians.

Confronting a high Roman official would be far more terrifying to Jewish believers than confronting a synagogue council. High officials, even when hated, were accorded far greater respect than in modern democracies; and they used professional orator-lawyers in legal matters (e.g., Tertullus, Acts 24:1). But if Jesus warned his disciples of dangers, he also promised them help: the Spirit would speak through them when the time came; so they should not fret about their response. This promise is neither a sop for lazy preachers nor equivalent to the promises given the Twelve in the farewell discourse (John 14–16) that the Spirit would recall to their memory all they had heard from Jesus (John 14:16, 26). It is a pledge to believers who have been brought before tribunals because of their witness. The promised assistance does not assume an absolute disjunction between "you" and the "Spirit" (v.20), for the underlying Semitic disjunction is rarely absolute (e.g., Gen 45:8; Exod 16:8; cf. Zerwick, par. 445). The history of Christian martyrs is studded with examples of the fulfillment of this promise.

Unlike Luke, Matthew does not often mention the Spirit. But from other passages in his Gospel, it is clear that he associates the Spirit with the kingdom's dramatic coming (3:11; 12:28, 31) and the church's witness (28:18–20). That same Spirit, "the Spirit of your Father," would provide Jesus' followers with the help they needed under persecution when facing hostile officials.

b. *Endurance*

10:21–23

> 21"Brother will betray brother to death, and a father his child; children will rebel against their parents and have them put to death. 22All men will hate you because of me, but he who stands firm to the end will be saved. 23When you are persecuted in one place, flee to another. I tell you the truth, you will not finish going through the cities of Israel before the Son of Man comes.

21–22 It is not enough for Jesus' disciples to be opposed by Jewish and Gentile officialdom; they will be hounded and betrayed by their own family members (v.21; see further vv.34–39). The theme of division between persons as a sign of the End is not unknown in Jewish apocalyptic literature (4 Ezra 5:9; Jub 23:19; 2 Baruch 70:3—though none of these refers explicitly to family divisions). Here the allusion is to Micah 7:6, quoted in vv.35–36. "All men" (v.22) does not mean "all men without exception," for then there would be no converts, but "all men without distinction" —all men irrespective of race, color, or creed. That the good news of the kingdom of God and his righteousness should elicit such intense and widespread hostility is a sad commentary on "all men." The hatred erupts, Jesus says, *dia to onoma mou* (lit., "on account of my name")—either because one bears the name "Christian" (cf. 1 Peter 4:14) or, less anachronistically and more likely, "on account of me" (see on 5:10–12).

The one who "stands firm"—the verb *hypomenō* does not signify active resistance so much as patient endurance (cf. LXX Dan 12:12; Mark 13:13; Rom 12:12; 1 Peter 2:20)—will be saved; but he must stand firm *eis telos* ("to the end"). Though this anarthrous expression could be taken adverbially to mean "without breaking down," it is far more likely purposely ambiguous to mean either "to the end of one's life" or, because of the frequent association of *telos* ("end") and cognates with the eschatological end, "to the end of the age." This is not to say that only martyrs will be saved; but if the opposition one of Jesus' disciples faces calls for the sacrifice of life itself, commitment to him must be so strong that the sacrifice is willingly made. Otherwise there is no salvation. Thus from earliest times Christians have been crucified, burned, impaled, drowned, starved, racked—for no other reason than that they belonged to him. As with martyrs among God's people before the coming of Christ, so now: the world was not worthy of them (Heb 11:38).

23 This verse is among the most difficult in the NT canon. The textual variants (cf. Metzger, *Textual Commentary*, p. 28) are complex but affect the main interpretive questions little.

1. Some have understood the coming of the Son of Man to refer to a coming of the historical Jesus in the wake of the mission of the Twelve as in the mission of the Seventy-two (Luke 10:1). The focus of attention has thus reverted back to the immediate commission (vv.5b–16). Jesus is telling the Twelve to "get a move on," because they will not have visited the cities of Israel before he "comes" to them— i.e., catches up with them. This view has been elegantly defended by J. Dupont ("'Vous n'aurez pas achevé les villes d'Israël...' [Mat. X[23]]," NovTest 2 [1958]: 228–44), who points out that elsewhere Matthew can bring the title "Son of Man" back (from 16:21 to 16:13) to a new location where it is equivalent to no more than a sonorous "I" (assuming his source is Mark 8:27, 31). Dupont suggests that in Matthew's source 10:23 was read after 10:5–6, which would confirm his interpretation. This view therefore turns in part on finding a source common to Matthew 10:23 and Luke 10:1—presumably a Q tradition—and this possibility has been strengthened somewhat by the source-critical arguments of H. Schürmann ("Zur Traditions- und Redaktionsgeschichte von Mt 10, 23," *Biblische Zeitschrift* 3 [1959]: 82–88) and David Wenham ("The 'Q' Tradition"), who try to show that v.23 springs from Q. The arguments are unconvincing. In Wenham's case they hinge on the assertion that v.23 is awkward because the literary parallel wth vv.19–20 is inexact (v.23 uses the verb "to persecute" instead of the verb "to hand over"). But it is not at all clear why Matthew should use the same verb: most Semitic parallelism depends on small verbal changes.

David Wenham ("The 'Q' Tradition") argues that v.23 "seems something of an afterthought in its present position following the climactic 'he who endures to the end shall be saved.'" But v.23 is anticlimactic only if the coming of the Son of Man refers exclusively to Jesus' follow-up ministry. If instead Jesus in v.22 is enjoining perseverance amid suffering witness, in clear reference to a post-Pentecost setting, then the persecution in v.23 should be similarly interpreted. The disciples' perseverance to the end does not mean withdrawal but moving on from city to city until the Son of Man comes. In this light v.23 is still difficult but certainly not anticlimactic. Indeed, this first interpretation fails to come to grips with two major hurdles. It fails to explain adequately why Matthew should move a comprehensible saying from a location following vv.5–6 (or even v.14) and place it here, where (we must implausibly suppose) the verse has nothing to do with its immediate context. Moreover, the geographical territory to be covered (see on 4:23–25) embraces enough towns and villages that, under this interpretation, the urgent call for haste seems inept. And Luke 10:1; the alleged parallel, does not speak of ministry to all the cities of Israel but only to the towns to which Jesus was about to go. Above all there is no evidence in any Gospel that the Twelve were actively persecuted during their first mission but only on occasion rebuffed (as in vv.11–15).

2. Some take "the Son of Man's coming" to refer to the public identification of Jesus as the Messiah, presumably at the Resurrection (Sabourin) or shortly after. Not only would this be an odd use of the expression, but the interpretation fails to show how the disciples were actually persecuted up to that time, or how there could be any urgency in such a deadline. Older commentators follow a similar line, exchanging the coming of the Spirit (John 14:23) for the Resurrection (e.g., Chrysostom, Calvin, Beza). But we have noted that the Spirit is not a major theme in Matthew (see on v.20); and in any case never in the NT is the Son of Man completely identified with him. A better modification of this view is offered by Stonehouse (*Witness of Matthew*, pp. 139f.) and Gaechter (*Matthäus*), who argue that this is the lesser inbreaking of the kingdom in the events succeeding Pentecost, the most probable meaning of 16:28 (below). But in v.23 this interpretation fails to account for the note of urgency. One might almost make a case for delaying witness until such an inbreaking.

3. Others take the verse to refer to the Second Coming, equivalent to 24:30; 25:31; 26:64. Although some would argue the point (see on Matt 24–25), the language of the Son of Man's coming most easily fits that interpretation. The problem then is the words "of Israel," so difficult in this interpretation that they are wrongly omitted by B (Alexandrian) and D (Western). Various expedients are appealed to in order to mitigate the problem: "Israel" is a symbol for the world or for the church, or there is some kind of double fulfillment (on the latter, cf. Hendriksen, who speaks of "prophetic foreshortening"; and A. Feuillet, "Les origines et la signification de Mt 10, 23b," CBQ 23 (1961): 197f.—though the article as a whole, pp. 182–90, supports 7 below). That "Israel" represents church or world is almost impossible in the context of Matthew's theology, and that there is some kind of double fulfillment is not much more than a surreptitious appeal for double incoherence: in the first fulfillment the difficulties of 1 remain, and in the second the problem words "of Israel" are still not explained. Whatever one thinks of multiple fulfillment in the Scriptures, this is not a clear instance of it. Bonnard sees a reference to Jesus' second coming in v.23b but sees no urgency. The verse simply insists on all the possibilities of witness given in Israel until the End and closely ties together Israel with that end (as in Rom 11:25). This view has its attractions. Nevertheless the note of urgency linking v.23a and v.23b cannot be disposed of so easily. Gundry has a similar view and also argues that the verse is redactional and therefore not authentic.

4. At the turn of the century, Schweitzer (pp. 358ff.) used this text to develop his "thoroughgoing eschatology." He argued that v.23b shows that Jesus believed the end of time would take place so soon that he did not expect to see the disciples return before the End arrived. Jesus was wrong, of course, and therefore had to readjust his own theology. This was the first "delay of the Parousia." Unfortunately Jesus was also wrong in expecting God to exonerate him before he died. Therefore the church was forced to adjust its theology to accommodate these errors; and only a few traces of Jesus' earliest teachings, like this passage, still peep unambiguously through the text. This view is well criticized by Kümmel (*Jesus' Promise*, pp. 61ff.).

5. A combination of the last two views is now espoused by several scholars (e.g., Fenton, Hill) who think v.23b refers to the Second Coming and that Jesus expected it within one generation or so (see also on 24:34; Hill specifies forty or fifty years). But there are so many hints of a much longer delay before the Second Coming (e.g., 13:24 33; 18:15 35; 19:28; 21:43; 23:32, 39 et al.; cf. Maier) that there seems little to be gained by this interpretation and much to be lost.

6. Dispensationalists are inclined to see v.23b as a reference to the Second Coming that "views the entire present church age as a parenthesis not taken into account in this prophecy" (Walvoord; cf. A.C. Gaebelein). Quite apart from the correctness or otherwise of the entire theological structure presupposed by this interpretation, it detaches v.23 from its context (if vv.16–22 refer to post-Pentecost *Christian* experience—so Walvoord) or else detaches vv.16–23 from their context (if the verses do not apply to any of Jesus' disciples but to believers living during the Tribulation after the church has been raptured away). There is no exegetical warrant for either detachment; and both would be incomprehensible, not only to Jesus' hearers, but also to the first readers of Matthew's Gospel.

7. The "coming of the Son of Man" here refers to his coming in judgment against the Jews, culminating in the sack of Jerusalem and the destruction of the temple (so France, *Jesus*, p. 140; Feuillet, "Les origines," pp. 182–98; Moule, *Birth*, p. 90; J.A.T. Robinson, *Jesus and His Coming* [London: SCM, 1957], pp. 80, 91–92; and others). Calvin thinks this interpretation farfetched, Hill that it is improbable. In fact a powerful case can be made for it. The coming of the Son of Man refers to the same event as the coming of the kingdom, even though the two expressions are conceptually complementary. Thus *the* coming of the Son of Man brings in the consummated kingdom (see on 24:30–31; 25:31). But the kingdom, as we have seen, comes in stages (see on 4:17; 12:28). In one sense Jesus was born a king (see on 2:2); in another he has all authority as a result of his passion and resurrection (28:18); and in yet another his kingdom awaits the end. Mingled with this theme of the coming of the kingdom are Jesus' repeated warnings to the Jews concerning the disaster they are courting by failing to recognize and receive him (cf. esp. Feuillet). In this he stands on the shoulders of the OT prophets; but his warnings are unique because he himself is the eschatological judge and because the messianic reign is now dawning in both blessing and wrath (8:11–12; 21:31–32).

Against this background the coming of the Son of Man in v.23 marks that stage in the coming of the kingdom in which the judgment repeatedly foretold falls on the Jews. With it the temple cultus disappears, and the new wine necessarily takes to new wineskins (see on 9:16–17). The age of the kingdom comes into its own, precisely because so many of the structured foreshadowings of the OT, bound up with the cultus and nation, now disappear (see on 5:17–48). The Son of Man comes.

Above all this interpretation makes contextual sense of v.23. The connection is not with v.22 alone but with vv.17–22, which picture the suffering witness of the church in the post-Pentecost period *during a time when many of Jesus' disciples are still bound up with the synagogue*. During that period, Jesus says in v.23, his disciples must not use the opposition to justify quitting or bravado. Far from it. When they face persecution, they must take it as no more than a signal for strategic withdrawal to the next city (W. Barclay, *The Gospel of Matthew*, 2 vols. [Philadelphia: Westminster, 1975], 1:378–80) where witness must continue, for the time is short. They will not have finished evangelizing the cities of Israel before the Son of Man comes in judgment on Israel.

Interpreted in this way the "Son of Man" saying of v.23 belongs to the eschatological category (see excursus on 8:20), but the eschatology is somewhat realized. The strength of this interpretation is sometimes diluted by applying it unchanged to 16:28; 24:31 (so France, *Jesus*). In fact there are important differences disallowing the view that all these texts refer to the Fall of Jerusalem in A.D. 70. Nevertheless they confirm the view that "the coming of the Son of Man" bears in Matthew the same rich semantic field as "the coming of the kingdom" (see on 6:10; 12:28).

c. Inspiration

10:24–25

> 24"A student is not above his teacher, nor a servant above his master. 25It is enough for the student to be like his teacher, and the servant like his master. If the head of the house has been called Beelzebub, how much more the members of his household!

24–25 The two brief analogies in vv.24–25a occur in various forms elsewhere in the NT (Luke 6:40; John 13:16; 15:20) and in Jewish literature (b *Berakoth* 58b); and like many good proverbs, they could be applied variously by capable preachers. Here Jesus forbids the disciples from being surprised when they suffer persecution. If they follow him, they should expect no less. The statement reveals something of Jesus' perception of the nature of his own ministry and of the way the "gospel of the kingdom" will advance in the world.

Those who deny the authenticity of vv.24–25a and other passages in which Jesus speaks implicitly of his sufferings do so not on literary evidence but on the basis of a priori decisions about what Jesus could and could not have known.

The insult "Beelzebub" (or, to preserve the best orthography, *Beelzeboul*) has an uncertain derivation. In the NT the term occurs only here and at 12:24, 27; Mark 3:22; Luke 11:15, 18–19. It may have come from OT Hebrew *ba'alzebûb* ("lord of flies"), a mocking takeoff of *ba'al zebûl* ("Prince Baal"), a pagan deity (2 Kings 1:2–3, 16). But in that case one wonders why the final syllable has been changed in NT Greek to *boul*. Other derivations include a mocking "lord of dung" and "lord of the heights" (heaven). One of the best suggestions is that of E.C.B. MacLaurin ("Beelzeboul," NovTest 20 [1978]: 156–60), who shows it may well be a straightforward translation of *oikodespotēs* ("head of the house," NIV). Beelzeboul is recognized in the NT as the prince of the demons and identified with Satan (12:24–27; Mark 3:22–26; Luke 11:18–19). Thus the real head of the house, Jesus, who heads the household of God, is being wilfully confused with the head of the house of demons. The charge is shockingly vile—the Messiah himself rejected as Satan! If so, why should his disciples expect less?

This verse has not been constructed by the evangelist out of bits from 12:22–32, as if the charge were leveled at Jesus only the once. On the contrary, 9:34 suggests that it was a frequent slur.

4. Prohibition of fear (10:26–31)

a. The emergence of truth

10:26–27

> 26"So do not be afraid of them. There is nothing concealed that will not be disclosed, or hidden that will not be made known. 27What I tell you in the dark, speak in the daylight; what is whispered in your ear, proclaim from the roofs.

Probably vv.26–27 are also transitional, like v.16. Consideration of how disciples must expect to face persecution and opprobrium makes it necessary to say something about how to handle fear (vv.26–31) and about the high standards of discipleship such a perspective presupposes. There are similar sayings elsewhere (cf. Luke 12:2–9; see also Mark 4:22; 8:38; Luke 9:26; 21:18). Yet there is no easy source pattern (cf. Hill); and most of the individual sayings are brief, easily memorized, and usable again and again.

26–27 "Them" refers to the persecutors (v.23). The connective *oun* ("So") may simply begin a new exhortation based on the preceding (Bonnard), or it may offer a tighter connection: in view of a master who suffers ahead of his disciples, *therefore* do not fear, etc. The truth must emerge; the gospel and its outworkings in the disciples may not now be visible to all, but nothing will remain hidden forever. And if the truth will emerge at the End, how wise to declare it fully and boldly now. Flat rooftops of Palestinian houses provided excellent places for speakers (cf. Jos. War II, 611 [xxi. 5]). In a sense the apostles were to have more of a public ministry than Jesus himself. He told them things in private, some of which they did not even understand till after the Resurrection (see excursus on 8:20; cf. John 14:26; 16:12–15). But they were to teach them fully and publicly.

b. The nonfinality of death

10:28

> 28Do not be afraid of those who kill the body but cannot kill the soul. Rather, be afraid of the One who can destroy both soul and body in hell.

28 The second reason for learning not to fear men emerges from the fact that the worst they can do does not match the worst God can do. Though Satan may have great power (6:13; 24:22), only God can destroy soul and body in hell. "The fear of the LORD is" therefore "the beginning of wisdom" (Prov 9:10); for if God be truly feared, none other need be. Fear of men proves to be a snare (Prov 29:25). The same thought is found in extracanonical Jewish literature (e.g., Wisd Sol 16:13–14; 2 Macc 6:26; 4 Macc 13:14–15).

For "hell," see on 5:22. The force of *psychē* ("soul") in the NT is closely related to *nepeš* ("soul") and *lēb* ("heart," "inner man") in the OT (for full discussion, cf. DNTT, 3:676–89). The thought is not so much of an ontological part utterly distinct from body as of the inner man destined for salvation or damnation (cf. 1 Peter 1:9; 2:11, 25; 4:19). Unavoidable in this context is the thought that hell is a place of torment for the whole person: there will be a resurrection of the unjust as well as of the just.

c. Continuing providence

10:29–31

> [29]Are not two sparrows sold for a penny? Yet not one of them will fall to the ground apart from the will of your Father. [30]And even the very hairs of your head are all numbered. [31]So don't be afraid; you are worth more than many sparrows.

29–31 The third reason for not being afraid is an a fortiori argument: If God's providence is so all embracing that not even a sparrow drops from the sky apart from the will of God, cannot that same God be trusted to extend his providence over Jesus' disciples? The sparrow was used for food by very poor people. Two might be sold for "a penny" (one-sixteenth of a denarius, which was about a day's wage; cf. Deiss LAE, pp. 272–75). "Your Father" adds a piquant touch: this God of all providence is the disciples' Father. God's sovereignty is not limited only to life-and-death issues; even the hairs of our heads are counted. Jesus' third argument against fear is thus the very opposite of what is commonly advanced. People say that God cares about the big things but not about little details. But Jesus says that God's sovereignty over the tiniest detail should give us confidence that he also superintends the larger matters.

5. Characteristics of discipleship (10:32–39)

a. Acknowledging Jesus

10:32–33

> [32]"Whoever acknowledges me before men, I will also acknowledge him before my Father in heaven. [33]But whoever disowns me before men, I will disown him before my Father in heaven.

32–33 Many assume that Matthew here edits Mark 8:38, which was addressed to a crowd (cf. also Luke 12:8–9). But Mark's words have a structure that has led to much of the debate over the "Son of Man" question.

> Whoever confesses me . . .
> The Son of Man will confess . . .
> Whoever disowns (or is ashamed of) me . . .
> The Son of Man will disown (or be ashamed of) . . . .

This ABAB parallelism has induced many, especially since Bultmann (*Synoptic Tradition*, pp. 112, 128), to argue that the historical Jesus distinguished the Son of Man from himself (cf. excursus on 8:20), and that Matthew's editing, by eliminating the "Son of Man" elements and substituting the first person personal pronoun, has identified Jesus with the Son of Man. The explanation of Hooker (*Son of Man*, pp. 120–21, 189) is generally satisfying. The "I" clauses in Mark picture Jesus speaking to those thinking of following him in his earthly life; the "Son of Man" clauses picture Jesus in the future, and at this point some of his claims are still veiled. It is difficult to see how Jesus could have proclaimed another Son of Man and still have left room for himself. Elsewhere he explicitly identifies the two (Mark 14:61–62). But we may take Hooker's argument one step further. Obviously vv. 32–33 are not addressed to indiscriminate crowds but to the Twelve. The reason for the clarity of Matthew's form of the saying may therefore turn, not on a development in the church's theology, but on the distinction in the audience. This was one of the things Jesus said clearly to his disciples in secret and which they would one day shout from the housetops (v. 27).

Though addressed to the Twelve (vv. 1–5), like much of vv. 17–42, this saying looks beyond the apostles to disciples at large. The point is made clear by "Whoever" (v. 32). A necessary criterion for being a disciple of Jesus is to acknowledge him publicly (cf. Rom 1:16; 10:9). This will vary in boldness, fluency, wisdom, sensitivity, and frequency from believer to believer (cf. Calvin); but consistently to disown Christ (same verb as in 26:69–75) is to be disowned by Christ. Jesus now speaks not of "your Father" (as in v. 29) but of "my Father." In view is his special filial relationship with the Father, by which the final destiny of all humanity depends solely on his word (see on 7:21–23; cf. 25:12). The christological implications of Jesus' words are unavoidable. "Jesus makes the entire position of men in the world to come, whether for weal or woe, to depend upon their relationship to and attitude toward him in this present world. Is this a claim which any mere man might have made? Do we not encounter here essentially the exclusiveness of Acts 4:12?" (Stonehouse, *Origins*, p. 190).

Notes

---

32 The rather strange Greek ὁμολογεῖν ἐν ἐμοί (*homologein en emoi*, "to acknowledge me") is perfectly natural Aramaic (but not Heb.); cf. Moulton, *Accidence*, p. 463; Moule, *Idiom Book*, p. 183.

---

b. *Recognizing the gospel*

10:34–36

34"Do not suppose that I have come to bring peace to the earth. I did not come to bring peace, but a sword. 35For I have come to turn

" 'a man against his father,
a daughter against her mother,
a daughter-in-law against her mother-in-law—
36 a man's enemies will be the members of his
own household.'

34–36 As many Jews in Jesus' day thought the coming of Messiah would bring them political peace and material prosperity, so today many in the church think that Jesus' presence will bring them a kind of tranquility. But Jesus insisted that his mission entailed strife and division (v.34). Prince of Peace though he is (see on 5:9), the world will so violently reject him and his reign that men and women will divide over him (vv.35–36); cf. Luke 12:49–53; cf. Neil, pp. 157–60). Before the consummation of the kingdom, even the peace Jesus bequeaths his disciples will have its setting in the midst of a hostile world (John 14:27; 16:33; cf. James 4:4).

The repeated statement "I have come" shows Jesus' christological and eschatological awareness (contra Arens, pp. 63–90 who uses the same evidence to argue that such elements must be church creations). Earlier he warned his disciples of the world's hatred of his followers, a hatred extending even to close relatives (vv.21–22); now he ties this perspective to an OT analogy (Mic 7:6; on the text form, cf. Stendahl, *School*, pp. 90f.; Gundry, *Use of OT*, pp. 78f.). Micah describes the sinfulness and rebellion in the days of King Ahaz; but insofar as Jesus' disciples by following him align themselves with the prophets (5:10–12), then the situation in Micah's time points to the greater division at Messiah's coming. Many critics think these verses apply solely to Christians in Matthew's day, and doubtless they caused Matthew's readers to think of their own sufferings. But some older commentators (e.g., Plumptre) wonder whether the Twelve, even during Jesus' earthly ministry, did not face some opposition from family and friends—as did Jesus himself (13:53–58; John 7:3–5). Even today the situation has not greatly eased. In the "liberal" West people who have become Christians have occasionally been disowned and disinherited by their families and have lost their jobs. And under totalitarian regimes of the right or the left there has been and still is untold suffering for Christ—witness Christians in the Gulag Archipelago.

c. *Preferring Jesus*

10:37–39

37"Anyone who loves his father or mother more than me is not worthy of me; anyone who loves his son or daughter more than me is not worthy of me; 38and anyone who does not take his cross and follow me is not worthy of me. 39Whoever finds his life will lose it, and whoever loses his life for my sake will find it.

37–39 The absolutism of the Semitic idiom (Luke 14:26) is rightly interpreted by Matthew: a man must love (for comments on this verb, see on 5:43) his wife, family, friends, and even his enemies; but he must love Jesus supremely (v.37). Again the saying is either that of the Messiah or of a maniac. The rabbinic parallels of the master–disciple relationship (cf. M *Baba Metzia* 2:11) are not very close; though they place the master above the father, they allow the disciple's personal interest to stand above his allegiance to his master. Jesus demanded death to self (vv.38–39). "Taking one's cross" does not mean putting up with some awkward or tragic situation in one's life but painfully dying to self. In that sense every disciple of Jesus bears the same cross. After Jesus' death and resurrection, the emotional impact of these sayings must have been greatly heightened; but even before those events, the reference to Crucifixion would vividly call to mind the shame and pain of such a sacrifice. For "worthy," see on v.11.

The appeal is not to gloom but to discipleship. There is a strong paradox here. Those who lose their *psychē* ("soul," "life"—see on vv.28–30), whether in actual martyrdom or disciplined self-denial, will "find" it in the age to come. Those who "find" it now (the expression in classical Greek means "to win or preserve" life) by living for themselves and refusing to submit to the demands of Christian discipleship lose it in the age to come (cf. 16:25; Mark 8:35; Luke 9:24; 17:33).

6. Encouragement: response to the disciples and to Jesus

10:40–42

> 40"He who receives you receives me, and he who receives me receives the one who sent me. 41Anyone who receives a prophet because he is a prophet will receive a prophet's reward, and anyone who receives a righteous man because he is a righteous man will receive a righteous man's reward. 42And if anyone gives even a cup of cold water to one of these little ones because he is my disciple, I tell you the truth, he will certainly not lose his reward."

The foregoing teaching about what it means to be a disciple of Jesus has its darker side. This final section of the discourse is more encouraging—it reverts again to the ultimate tie between the treatment of Jesus and that of his followers (see on vv.24–25); it turns our eyes to the future (see on v.28) and shows us that God is indebted to no one.

40–42 It is commonly understood in the NT that a man's agent must be received as the man himself (v.40; cf. Luke 10:16; John 12:44–45; 13:20; Acts 9:4). And as this section closes the discourse that opens with instructions to the Twelve, many interpret "prophet" and "righteous man" (v.41) as alternative designations of the apostles in v.40, and v.42 as an extension to all disciples (e.g., Bonnard; Allen; Manson, *Sayings*, p. 183). By contrast David Hill ("Δίκαιοι as a Quasi-Technical Term," NTS 11 [1964–65]: 296–303; cf. also Cothenet) has advanced another interpretation. He suggests that both "prophets" and "righteous men" refer to distinguishable classes within Christianity. "Prophets" are distinguishable from "apostles," and "righteous men" refers to some other distinguishable group of teachers (cf. also 13:17; 23:29; and on 7:15–23). Hill further suggests (*Matthew*) that v.42, derived from Mark 9:41, is given this setting "to suggest that travelling and persecuted missionaries [the "little ones"] are dependent on the hospitality and help of non-Christians." E. Schweizer ("Observance of the Law and Charismatic Activity in Matthew," NTS 16 [1969–70]: 213–30) says the colocation of "prophet" and "righteous man" in v.41 means that Matthew urges his community to imitate the ideal of a charismatic ("prophet") still bound by the law as interpreted by Jesus ("righteous man"). E. Käsemann (*New Testament Questions of Today* [London: SCM, 1969], pp. 90–91) sees in "prophets" the leaders of Matthew's community and in "righteous men" the general body of believers.

A better synthesis is possible. As the discourse, viewed as a whole, moves from the Twelve to all believers, so also does its conclusion. Verse 40 probably refers primarily to the apostles, and vv.41–42 move through "prophets" and "righteous men" down to "these little ones"—viz., the least in the kingdom, seen as persecuted witnesses in the latter part of the discourse. The order "descends" only according to prominence. But the classes mentioned are not mutually exclusive, since "these little ones" surely includes the apostles, prophets, and righteous men; they are all "little ones" because they are all targets of the world's enmity. To give a cup of cold, freshly drawn water, the least courtesy demands, to the least disciple just because he is a disciple does not go unrewarded. Thus the "little ones" are not portrayed as a special class of "travelling missionaries" (contra Hill, *Matthew*) but as disciples. "Prophets" are referred to, not because Christian prophets are in view, but because this is an already accepted category for God's spokesmen and for those with whom Jesus' followers are aligned (5:10–12).

"Righteous men" is more difficult. But in two of the three passages where the term occurs in connection with "prophets" (13:17; 23:29), it must refer to righteous men of earlier generations—OT and perhaps Maccabean figures, not Christian contemporaries of Matthew, and not traveling teachers. It seems best to take the term here from the same perspective. None of Hill's evidence points unambiguously to a class of teachers known as "righteous men." Most of his DSS evidence (1QS 3:20, 22; 5:2, 9; 9:14; 1QSa 1:2, 24; 2:3) clearly demonstrates that the sectarians perceived themselves as "the righteous" over against other men. Moreover it is far from certain that Daniel 12:3 refers to a part of the people of God with a special assignment to teach righteousness: even there it is easy to detect a reference to all of God's people. After all, "righteousness" is a category already used in Matthew to describe all of Jesus' disciples (5:20).

Some scholars have been too eager to read anachronisms into the text and detect special groups on the basis of slender evidence. In reality v.40, though very general, applies in the first instance to the Twelve; v.41 repeats the aphorism twice more using OT categories familiar to Jesus but extending the application from prophets to all of God's righteous people. Verse 42 groups the previous aphorisms together to make it quite clear that the sole reason for rewarding those who treat Jesus' disciples well is not because they are prophets or righteous people—they are in fact but "little ones"—but because they are Jesus' disciples. The prophet's reward and the righteous man's reward are therefore not disparate but kingdom rewards (see on 5:12) that are the fruit of discipleship. To receive a prophet because he is a prophet (as in 1 Kings 17:9–24; 2 Kings 4:8–37) presupposes, in the context of v.40, that he is Christ's prophet—so also for the "righteous man." Thus the person who receives a prophet receives Christ, his word, his ways, and his gospel, and expresses solidarity with the people of God, these little ones, by receiving them for Jesus' sake (cf. 2 John 10–11; 3 John 8). No such person will lose his reward. While the applications to Matthew's churches, as to our own, are many, the text itself does not venture so far.

Notes

41–42 The expression εἰς ὄνομα προφήτου (*eis onoma prophētou*, "because he is a prophet"), with its parallels, is an instance of the causal use of *eis* (cf. Zerwick, pars. 98, 106; contra M.J. Harris, DNTT, 3:1187). Some hold this is important in understanding Matthew's baptismal formula, but see on 28:18–20.

7. Transitional conclusion: expanding ministry

11:1

¹After Jesus had finished instructing his twelve disciples, he went on from there to teach and preach in the towns of Galilee.

1 For the significance of the formulas that end Jesus' discourses, see on 7:28–29. This one omits "these things" or the like (see on 10:5a). Unlike Mark 6:30; Luke 9:10, there is no mention of the return of the Twelve, since their early successes are of less concern to Matthew than is Jesus' teaching. Attention returns to Jesus' ministry, for he did not send out the apostles in order to relieve himself of work but in order to expand the proclamation of the kingdom (9:35–10:4).

Notes

1 The pronoun αὐτῶν (autōn, "their," NIV mg.) is exceptionally awkward here. It cannot refer to the apostles but to the Galileans, not mentioned in the context. Nor can this easily be taken as an anachronistic distinction between church and synagogue. Most likely it is an instance of pronominal sense-construction not uncommon in then contemporary secular Greek and found throughout the NT (cf. Turner, *Insights*, pp. 149–50). If so, it is especially important not to be hasty in reading church–synagogue anachronisms into other similar passages (see on 4:23; 7:29; 9:35; 10:17).

IV. Teaching and Preaching the Gospel of the Kingdom: Rising Opposition (11:2–13:53)

A. *Narrative* (11:2–12:50)

1. *Jesus and John the Baptist* (11:2–19)

a. *John's question and Jesus' response*

11:2–6

> ²When John heard in prison what Christ was doing, he sent his disciples ³to ask him, "Are you the one who was to come, or should we expect someone else?"
> ⁴Jesus replied, "Go back and report to John what you hear and see: ⁵The blind receive sight, the lame walk, those who have leprosy are cured, the deaf hear, the dead are raised, and the good news is preached to the poor. ⁶Blessed is the man who does not fall away on account of me."

Matthew 12–13 depends in large part on Mark 2:23–3:12; 3:20–4:34. Before this comes 11:2–30, most of which is paralleled in various parts of Luke. Thematically the three chapters (11–13) are held together by the rising tide of disappointment in and opposition to the kingdom of God that was resulting from Jesus' ministry. He was not turning out to be the kind of Messiah the people had expected. Even John the Baptist had doubts (vv.2–19), and the Galilean cities that were sites of most of Jesus' miracles hardened themselves in unbelief (vv.20–24). The nature of Jesus' person and ministry were "hidden" (an important word) from the wise, despite the most open and compassionate of invitations (vv.28–30). Conflicts with Jewish leaders began to intensify (12:1–45), while people still misunderstood the most basic elements of Jesus' teaching and authority (12:46–50). But does this mean that he had been checkmated or that the kingdom had not come after all? Matthew 13 is the answer—the kingdom of God was continuing its advance even though it was often contested and ignored.

Matthew 11:2–19 is closely paralleled by Luke 7:18–35. Occasional divergences are noted below (see esp. on v.19).

2–3 According to Josephus (Antiq. XVIII, 119[v.2]), Herod imprisoned John the Baptist in the fortress of Machaerus, east of the Dead Sea. The bare fact is recorded in Matthew 4:12, the circumstances in 14:3–5. Apparently John had been in prison during Jesus' extensive Galilean ministry, perhaps as long as a year. The one to whom he had pointed, the one who would come in blessing and judgment (3:11–12), had brought healing to many but, it would seem, judgment to none—not even to those who had immorally and unlawfully confined the Baptist in a cruel prison, doubtless made the more unbearable for its contrast with his accustomed freedom (cf. Luke 1:80).

John heard "what Christ was doing" (v.2). The clause hides two subtle points. First, the use of (lit.) "the Christ" is peculiar, for at this stage in Jesus' ministry there was but little thoughtful ascription of this title to Jesus; and Matthew normally avoids it. Some have thought that at this point Matthew was somewhat careless about consistency in his narrative. Precisely the opposite is the case. The entire Gospel is written from the perspective of faith. The very first verse affirms Jesus as the Messiah, and the prologue (chs. 1–2) seeks to prove it. So at this point Matthew somewhat unusually refers to Jesus as "the Christ" in order to remind his readers who it was that John the Baptist was doubting. Though John doubted, from Matthew's perspective the time for doubt had passed. Far from being an anachronism, this use of "the Christ" is Matthew's own designation of Jesus. Indeed, Matthew's fidelity is attested by the way he distinguishes between his own understanding and insight, drawn from his postresurrection perspective, and the gradual development of that understanding historically, including the Baptist's doubts.

The second point is that *ta erga tou Christou* (lit., "the works of Christ"; NIV, "what Christ was doing") is suitably vague to embrace a triple allusion, not only to Jesus' miracles (chs. 8–9), but also to his teaching (5–7) and growing mission (10).

As a result of these reports, John sent a pointed question "by" (reading *dia* as in RSV, not *duo* ["two"] as in KJV) his disciples. This use of "disciples" shows that the term is a nontechnical one for "Christians" or "the Twelve" in Matthew (see on 5:1–6; 9:37). The objection, probably first raised by D.F. Strauss (*The Life of Jesus Critically Examined* [1846; reprint ed., London: SCM, 1973], pp. 219–30, esp. p. 229), that John was in no position to send messengers presumes to know more about security arrangements at Machaerus than we do—the more so since the Gospels show that Herod himself was ambivalent toward the prophet (Mark 6:17–26). John's question was whether Jesus was *ho erchomenos* ("the coming one," v.3), exactly the same expression ascribed to John at 3:11 (cf. also 21:9; 23:39; John 6:14; 11:27; Heb 10:37). The expression is not a common messianic title in intertestamental literature. It probably was drawn from such passages as Psalm 118:26; Isaiah 59:20. The description of the actions of "the coming one" in 3:11 nullifies the old theory (Schweitzer) that the Baptist merely expected Elijah *redivivus* ("come to life again") to follow him. John was asking Jesus whether he was the Messiah.

The question at first glance seems so out of character for what we know of the Baptist that many of the Fathers and Reformers, and even Bengel, suggest that John asked it, not for his own sake, but for the sake of his followers. Not a shred of exegetical evidence supports this view. Not only may the Baptist have become demoralized, like his namesake Elijah, but the Baptist had preached in terms of imminent blessing and judgment. By contrast Jesus was preaching in veiled fulfillment terms and bringing much blessing but no real judgment (cf. Dunn, *Jesus*, pp. 55–62), and as a result the Baptist was having second thoughts.

4–6 Jesus' answer briefly summarized his own miracles and preaching, but in the language of Isaiah 35:5–6; 61:1, with possible further allusions to 26:19; 29:18–19. At one level the answer was straightforward: Isaiah 61:1 is an explicit messianic passage, and Isaiah 35:5–6, though it has no messianic figure, describes the return of God's people to Zion with accompanying blessings (e.g., restoration of sight). Jesus definitely claimed that these messianic visions were being fulfilled in the miracles he was performing and that his preaching the Good News to the poor (see on 5:3) was as explicit a fulfillment of the messianic promises of Isaiah 61:1–2 as Luke 4:17–21. The powers of darkness were being undermined; the kingdom was advancing (cf. v.12).

But there is a second, more subtle level to Jesus' response. All four of the Isaiah passages refer to judgment in their immediate context: e.g., "your God will come . . . with vengeance; with divine retribution" (35:4); "the day of vengeance of our God" (Isa 61:2). Thus Jesus was allusively responding to the Baptist's question: the blessings promised for the end time have broken out and prove it is here, even though the judgments are delayed (cf. Jeremias, *Promise*, p. 46; Dunn, *Jesus*, p. 60). Verse 6, which may include an allusion to Isaiah 8:13–14 (in which case Jesus is set in the place of Yahweh: see on 11:10), is then a gentle warning, applicable both to John and his disciples: Blessed (see on 5:3) is the "man who does not fall away" (for this verb, see on 5:29) on account of Jesus, i.e., who does not find in him and his ministry an obstacle to belief and therefore reject him. The miracles themselves were not irrefutable proof of who Jesus was (cf. Mark 8:11–12 and parallels); faith was still required to read the evidence against the background of Scripture and to hear in Jesus' claim the ring of truth. But the beatitude in this form assumes the questioner has begun well and now must avoid stumbling. It is therefore an implicit challenge to reexamine one's presuppositions about what the Messiah should be and do in the light of Jesus and his fulfillment of Scripture and to bring one's understanding and faith into line with him.

b. *Jesus' testimony to John* (11:7–19)

1) *John in redemptive history*

11:7–15

> ⁷As John's disciples were leaving, Jesus began to speak to the crowd about John: "What did you go out into the desert to see? A reed swayed by the wind? ⁸If not, what did you go out to see? A man dressed in fine clothes? No, those who wear fine clothes are in kings' palaces. ⁹Then what did you go out to see? A prophet? Yes, I tell you, and more than a prophet. ¹⁰This is the one about whom it is written:
>
>> " 'I will send my messenger ahead of you,
>> who will prepare your way before you.'ᵈ
>
> ¹¹I tell you the truth: Among those born of women there has not risen anyone greater than John the Baptist; yet he who is least in the kingdom of heaven is

greater than he. ¹²From the days of John the Baptist until now, the kingdom of heaven has been forcefully advancing, and forceful men lay hold of it. ¹³For all the Prophets and the Law prophesied until John. ¹⁴And if you are willing to accept it, he is the Elijah who was to come. ¹⁵He who has ears, let him hear.

John had often borne witness to Jesus; now Jesus bears witness to John. But, as we will see, the effect is to point back to himself as the sole figure who brings in the kingdom. Historically it was almost inevitable for Jesus to define the position of John the Baptist with respect to himself. Most scholars doubt he did so consecutively as set forth here. Nevertheless the passage holds together well, and there is little literary or historical evidence to suggest that this is a composite of words spoken on other occasions. The parallel in Luke 7:24–35 preserves the same themes and movement. It omits Matthew 11:12–13 and adds Luke 7:29–30. The extra verses in Matthew are usually said to derive from Mark 9:11–13. But the two passages are linguistically and thematically rather distinct, and it is easy to imagine that Jesus had to take some position on John more than once and very definitely so for his disciples. Moreover the tone of this passage reflects no personal conflict between John and Jesus. And this, contrary to much recent discussion, is typical of the NT witness of the relationship between the two men (cf. esp. J.A.T. Robinson, *Twelve*, pp. 28–52).

7–8 "Began" (v.7) does not imply that Jesus commences his remarks while the Baptist's disciples were leaving and completed them only after they had gone (Broadus); as in v.20, it means that he took the opportunity to speak to the crowd about John. The rhetorical questions are a gently ironic way of eliminating obviously false answers in order to give the truth in vv.10–11. "A reed [probably a collective singular referring to cane grass, found in abundance along the Jordan] swayed by the wind" suggests a fickle person, tossed about in his judgment by the winds of public opinion or private misfortune (Lucian uses a similar metaphor, BAGD, p. 398). Certainly the people did not go out to witness such an ordinary spectacle. Nor did they go out into the desert to find a man dressed "in fine clothes" (v.8). "Fine" (*malakos*), used elsewhere in the NT only at Luke 7:25 and 1 Corinthians 6:9, connotes "softness" or even "effeminacy" and may be ironic. Contrast the rugged garb the prophet actually wore (see on 3:4–6). Those who are "in kings' palaces" is a sly cut at the man who was keeping John in prison.

It appears, then, that Jesus spoke in this way to disarm suspicion among the people that John's question (v.3) might betray signs of fickleness (v.7) or undisciplined weakness (v.8). Not so, responds Jesus; the man the people went out to see was neither unstable nor faithless. His question arose not from personal weakness or failure but from misunderstanding about the nature of the Messiah, owing to John's place in salvation history (see on v.11). Hence Jesus addressed the crowd, not to defend himself following the Baptist's question, but to defend the Baptist.

9–11 What the people had flocked to the desert to see was a prophet (v.9), since it was commonly agreed that a true prophet had not appeared for centuries but only the *baṭ-ḳôl* (lit., "daughter of a voice"; see on 3:17). Small wonder there was such excitement. Jesus confirms the crowd's judgment but goes beyond it—John was not only a prophet but more than a prophet. In what respect? In this: Not only was he, like other OT prophets, a direct spokesman for God to call the nation to repentance, but he himself was also the subject of prophecy—the one who, according to Scripture, would announce the Day of Yahweh (v. 10).

The form of the quotation shows influence from Exodus 23:20 (LXX) in the first clause (cf. Gundry, *Use of OT*, pp. 11f.). Yet there is no doubt that the primary passage being cited is Malachi 3:1. The messenger in Malachi 3:1 (Elijah in Mal 4:5–6) prepares the way for the great and dreadful Day of Yahweh. The form of the text, adding "ahead of you" (probably by using Exod 23:20) in the first line, changing "before me" to "before you" in the second line, and adding "your," has the effect of making Yahweh address Messiah. On any reading of Malachi 3:1 (on which see France, *Jesus*, pp. 91f., n. 31), Yahweh does not address Messiah; but inasmuch as the messenger prepares the way for Yahweh (Mal 4:5–6), with whom Jesus is constantly identified in the NT (see on 2:6; and esp. 3:3), this periphrastic rendering makes Jesus' identity unambiguous (cf. France, *Jesus*, p. 155). Even if Malachi 3:1 had been exactly quoted, the flow of the argument in Matthew demands that if John the Baptist is the prophesied Elijah who prepares the way for Yahweh (3:3; cf. Luke 1:76) or for the Day of Yahweh (Mal 4:5–6), and John the Baptist is Jesus' forerunner, then Jesus himself is the manifestation of Yahweh and brings in the eschatological Day of Yahweh.

Hill (*Matthew*) comments: "It is probable that the quotation has been inserted by the evangelist; it breaks the logical connection between verses 9 and 11, and anticipates the mysterious announcement in verse 14." It seems difficult to have it both ways: if the quotation anticipates v. 14, then it must be left in place unless v. 14 is also judged inauthentic. More important, v. 10, far from breaking them up, ties v. 9 and v. 11 together. By citing Malachi, Jesus (v. 10) has shown in what way John the Baptist is greater than a prophet: he is greater in that he alone of all the prophets was the forerunner who prepared the way for Yahweh-Jesus and personally pointed him out. While the OT prophets doubtless contributed to the corpus of revelation that pointed to Messiah, they did not serve as immediate forerunners. This is what makes John greater than a prophet (v. 9)—indeed the greatest born of women (v. 11; i.e., the greatest human being; cf. Job 14:1).

Thus far the argument flows coherently. But who is the "least in the kingdom of heaven," and how is he greater than John the Baptist? Many have found this comparison so difficult that some fanciful suggestions have been made. McNeile holds the kingdom to be entirely future: the least in the kingdom will *then* be greater than John *now* is. But will not John also be in the kingdom then? And how will this contribute to the argument? Others argue that *ho mikroteros* means not "the least" but "the younger," the "lesser" in a purely temporal sense. In this view it refers to Jesus: Jesus, though lesser through being younger, is greater than John the Baptist (so Chrysostom; Augustine; cf. Fenton; BDF par. 61 [2]; O. Cullmann, "Ὁ ὀπίσω μου ἐρχόμενος," *Coniectanea Neotestamentica* 11 [1947]: 30; Zerwick, par. 149; M. Brunec, "De Legàtioni Ioannis Baptistae (Mt 11:2–24)," *Verbum Domini* 35 [1957]: 262–70). This implies that John the Baptist is himself, according to Matthew, in the kingdom—a conclusion widely defended, largely on the grounds of comparing the ministries of John and Jesus (e.g., 3:2; 4:17; so, for instance, Walter Wink, *John the Baptist in the Gospel Tradition* [Cambridge: University Press, 1968], pp. 33–35).

It must be admitted, however, that *ho mikroteros* is made to mean "the younger" chiefly because v. 11 is so difficult. In view of the fact that a comparison establishing

John as greater than the prophets immediately precedes this text, it is most natural to take *ho mikroteros* as meaning "the least" in the kingdom. This entails the view that John the Baptist was not himself in the kingdom. Parallels between John's and Jesus' preaching are readily explained (see on 4:17), and v.12 can best be taken that way as well (see below).

In what way, then, is the least in the kingdom greater than John the Baptist? The answer must not be in terms of mere privilege—viz., the least are greater because they live to see the kingdom actually inaugurated—but in terms of the greatness already established for John. He was the greatest of the prophets because he pointed most unambiguously to Jesus. Nevertheless even the least in the kingdom is greater yet because, living after the crucial revelatory and eschatological events have occurred, he or she points to Jesus still more unambiguously than John the Baptist. This interpretation entirely suits the context and accomplishes three things.

1. It continues a defense of John by showing that his question (v.3), which springs neither from fickleness nor weakness (vv. 7–8), does not make him forfeit his primacy among the prophets because of his being the forerunner of Jesus (vv.9–10), but that the question owes its origin to his still-veiled place in the redemptive history now unfolding.

2. By contrast it continues the theme of discipleship whose essential function is to acknowledge Jesus before people (10:32–33) and establishes that function as the disciples' essential greatness. Even the least in the kingdom points to Jesus Christ more clearly than all his predecessors, not excluding John. For they either live through the tumultuous events of the ministry, Passion, and beyond, after which things are much clearer; or they enter the kingdom after these events, with the same clear understanding. Thus the ground is being laid for the Great Commission: clear witness to Christ before men is not only a requirement of the kingdom (10:32–33) and a command of the resurrected Lord (28:18–20) but the true greatness of the disciple (11:11).

3. At the same time, by explaining John's greatness and his place in salvation history, this verse points back to the preeminence of Jesus himself.

12 This enigmatic saying has called forth a host of interpretations. These depend on several alternatives related to several exegetical turning points that can be combined variously. A complete list of the possibilities (for bibliography, see Chilton, *God in Strength*, pp. 203ff.) must be passed over in favor of an interpretation that does justice both to the context and to the language. The turning points are three.

1. "From the days of John the Baptist until now." As already pointed out (vv.10–11), most commentators understand "until" in v.13 to be an exclusive usage, putting John within the kingdom (though most scholars hold that Luke 16:16 is an inclusive usage of "until"). Indeed, John P. Meier ("John the Baptist in Matthew's Gospel," *JBL* 99 [1980]: 383–405) makes it the crux of his interpretation of Matthew's treatment of the Baptist. The phrase "from the days of John the Baptist" is almost certainly a Semitic way of saying "from the time of the activity of John the Baptist" (cf. Jeremias, *NT Theology*, pp. 46f.). John's ministry provides the *terminus a quo*, the phrase "until now" the *terminus ad quem*. But many argue that "until now" means "up until" Matthew's time of writing, not "up until" Jesus' time of speaking (e.g., Cope, *Matthew*, pp. 75f.; Albright and Mann). This interpretation is rendered plausible (Albright and Mann) because the rest of the verse seems to picture violent

men ransacking the kingdom (see discussion below); and this certainly did not happen in the short time between the Baptist's death and this saying by Jesus during his earthly ministry.

A better synthesis emerges by taking the text strictly. The idiom "from . . ." in Matthew *includes* the following term (cf. 1:17; 2:16; 23:35; 27:45; Schweizer). But the entire expression "from the days of John the Baptist" does not say that John inaugurates the kingdom but only that during his time of ministry it was inaugurated and (or) attacked. The expression does not even assume John's death; it only assumes that the crucial period of his ministry during which the kingdom was inaugurated lies in the past. Now that kingdom has begun, in however preliminary a way, with Jesus' preaching and powerful works during "the days of John the Baptist." Thus there is no reason why the Prophets and the Law should not prophesy "until John" in an inclusive sense (v.13)—an interpretation that not only agrees with Luke 16:16 but goes best with Matthew 11:9-11.

Whether the kingdom has been "forcefully advancing" (NIV) or attacked (see below), this has been going on from its inception under Jesus' ministry during the days of John the Baptist (there had to be temporal overlap if the forerunner was to prepare his way and point him out) "until now"—viz., till this point in Jesus' ministry. This does not mean that the activity (whether of forceful advance or of being attacked) stops at that point, any more than the same expression in John 2:10 (the only other place it occurs in the NT) means that everybody at the wedding instantly stopped drinking the best wine. The continuation is not the focus of interest.

2. "The kingdom of heaven has been forcefully advancing." The crux of the problem is the verb *biazetai* ("has been forcefully advancing"). The form is either middle or passive. If the former, the NIV rendering, or something like it, is right; if the latter, it means that the kingdom is being attacked (in a negative sense) or is being forcefully advanced (by God?) (cf. TDNT, 1:610f.). In Greek sources relevant to the NT, *biazetai* is considerably more common in the deponent middle than in the active or passive voices (in the NT the verb is found only here and in Luke 16:16); and this supports the NIV rendering of the clause (cf. BAGD, pp. 140–41; DNTT, 3:711–12) as Ridderbos, NEB (mg.), Hendriksen, Chilton, and others do. But many object to this rendering on one of two grounds: (1) it brings a notion of "force" to the kingdom contrary to the Gospels' emphases; and (2) it deals poorly with the last clause of the text, since *biastēs* really must not be rendered "forceful man" (in a positive sense) but "violent man" (see discussion, below). The first objection is insubstantial. The kingdom has come with holy power and magnificent energy that has been pushing back the frontiers of darkness. This is especially manifest in Jesus' miracles and ties in with Jesus' response to the Baptist (v.5). Some kind of compulsion even of people is presupposed elsewhere (Luke 14:23). Moreover the force implied by the middle deponent verb is not always violent or cruel (cf. BAGD). The second objection is important and brings us to the third part of the verse.

3. "And forceful men lay hold of it." Hendriksen, for instance, thinks the cognate noun *biastēs* ("forceful man") finds its meaning now established by the considerations discussed above for the meaning of the verb *biazetai* ("has been forcefully advancing"). The kingdom is making great strides; now is the time for courageous souls, forceful people, to take hold of it. This is no challenge for the timorous or fainthearted. This interpretation is possible but not convincing. The noun *biastēs* is rare in Greek literature (only here in the NT), but where it occurs it always has the negative connotations of violence and rapacity. Moreover the verb *harpazousin* ("lay

hold of"), a fairly common verb, almost always has the same evil connotations (a rare exception is Acts 8:39). For these reasons most commentators see a reference to violent men and then read the verb in the preceding clause as a passive: "the kingdom of heaven is suffering violence and violent men are seizing it"—so, more or less, KJV, NASB, Wey, NEB (text), Hill, Gaechter, Maier, Hobbs, E. Moore ("Βιάζω, ἁρπάζω and Cognates in Josephus," NTS 21 [1975]: 519–43), C. Spicq (*Notes de lexicographie néo-testamentaire*, 2 vols. [Göttingen: Vandenhoeck und Ruprecht, 1978], s.v.), and many others. There are many conflicting views about who the violent men are—Zealots, Pharisees, evil spirits and their human hosts, Herod Antipas, Jewish antagonists in general. But the thrust is the same in any case.

Not satisfied with this, others have made suggestions, none convincing. The kingdom of heaven "has been taken by storm and eager men are forcing their way into it" (offered by Ph and Wms and defended by McNeile) is a rendering that combines the unlikelihood of a passive verb with the unlikelihood of a positive-connotative noun. James Swetnam, in a review of Spicq (*Biblica* 61 [1980]: 440–42), wants the verse to mean that from the time of John the kingdom has been suffering violence (passive verb) *of interpretation*; and those who are of like-minded violence—i.e., who understand the kingdom in the same way—are the ones who snatch it away. To the weaknesses of the last suggestion, this one adds an unparalleled meaning ("to suffer violence of interpretation") to the verb.

The best solution is to take the verb in its most likely voice, middle deponent, and the noun and verb of the last clause with their normal evil connotations: viz., from the time of John the Baptist (as explained above) until now, the kingdom of heaven has been forcefully advancing; and violent or rapacious men have been trying (conative present) to plunder it—so Pamment (pp. 227f.), though she then makes the rendering nearly incoherent by saying the kingdom of heaven is exclusively future (see also on 5:3). Furthermore, the verbs in the last two clauses are both in the present tense. If they are rendered as presents in English, the syntax is wrong: "From the time of John until now the kingdom is forcefully advancing, and violent men are pillaging it." But that acceptable Greek syntax calls in question Pamment's views on the futurity of the kingdom of heaven and sets up the picture of a tremendous, violent struggle being waged even as Jesus speaks. Certainly "Jesus considers his ministry to be a time when the Kingdom can be attacked as being present" (Hill, *Matthew*; cf. Kümmel, *Jesus' Promise*, pp. 121ff.).

If this is a form of antanclasis (a figure of speech in which the same word is repeated in a different or even contradictory sense), based in this instance not on exactly the same word but on a cognate, the verse admirably suits the context. The argument up to v.11 has established John the Baptist's greatness, grounded in his ministry of preparing for and pointing out Christ; and it has anticipated the witness of those in the kingdom who are even greater than John because the least of them testifies to Christ yet more clearly. Now, Jesus goes on to say, from the days of the Baptist—i.e., from the beginning of Jesus' ministry—the kingdom has been forcefully advancing (the point also made in Luke 16:16). But it has not swept all opposition away, as John expected (see on vv.2–4).

Simultaneous with the kingdom's advance have been the attacks of violent men on it. That is the very point John could not grasp. Now Jesus expressly affirms it. The statement is general because it does not refer to just one kind of opposition. It includes Herod's imprisonment of John (cf. J.A.T. Robinson, *Twelve*, pp. 44–45), the attacks by Jewish leaders now intensifying (9:34; 12:22–24), the materialism that craved a political Messiah and the prosperity he would bring but not his righteousness (11:20–24). Already Jesus has warned his disciples of persecution and suffering (10:16–42); the opposition was rising and would get worse. Meanwhile, not the aggressive zealots will find rest for their souls, but the weary, the burdened, the children to whom the Father has revealed the truth (vv.25–30). The last-mentioned passage is the death-knell of those who think the *biastai* are "forceful men" (in a positive sense): that is exactly what the chapter, taken as a whole, rules out. Instead, we are hearing the sound of divine grace, a note that becomes a symphony later in this Gospel.

If this interpretation is sound, there seems little reason either for thinking that v.12 is out of place or for seeing in it the later creation of the church.

13 In view of the preceding, "until John" means up to and including John. The Baptist belongs to the last stage of the divine economy before the inauguration of the kingdom (as in Luke 16:16). Sigal ("Halakah," pp. 68f.) mishandles this verse because he treats it as if the Prophets and the Law must prophesy about John rather than until John. Some of what the OT says about John has been set out in v.10; here the point is to set out the redemptive-historical turning point that has brought about the transformation of perspectives explained in vv.11–12. The two anomalies in the verse are (1) "the Prophets" precedes "the Law," an unusual order (cf. 5:17; 7:12), and (2) both "Prophets" and "Law" prophesy—and both anomalies serve the same purpose: a powerful way of saying that the entire OT has a prophetic function, a function it maintained up until, and including, John the Baptist.

In the twin settings of Matthew's "fulfillment" theme (see on 2:15; 5:17–20) and the role of John the Baptist (11:10), it is understood that now, after John the Baptist, that which Prophets and Law prophesied has come to pass—the kingdom has dawned and Messiah has come. This establishes the primary function of the OT in Matthew's Gospel: it points to Jesus and the kingdom. This confirms our interpretation of 5:17–20. The *gar* ("For") therefore ties v.13, not to v.11, but to v.12 (confirming v.12 as an integral part of the argument). Verse 13 further explains that "from the days of John the Baptist"—i.e., from the beginning of Jesus' ministry—the kingdom has been forcefully advancing. The Prophets and the Law prophesied until then and, implicitly, prophesied of this new era. And from that time on, the fulfillment of the prophecy, the kingdom itself, has been forcefully advancing.

14–15 The argument returns to vv.9–10, stating explicitly what Jesus said there: John the Baptist was the prophesied "Elijah" (v.14). This locates his place and function in the history of redemption and affirms again that what Jesus was doing was eschatological—he was bringing in the Day of Yahweh. The clause "if you are willing to accept it" does not cast doubt on the truth of the identification; but, like v.15, it acknowledges how difficult it was to grasp it, especially before the Cross and the Resurrection. For if the people had truly understood, they would necessarily have seen Jesus' place in salvation history as the fulfillment of OT hopes and prophecy. That is why the sonorous formula of v.15 is added (cf. 13:9, 43; 24:15; Rev 2:7, 11 et al.): the identification of John with prophesied Elijah has messianic implications that "those with ears" would hear. The formula is both a metaphorical description of and a challenge to spiritual sensitivity to the claims of the gospel.

Notes

8 Here and in v.9, ἀλλά (*alla*, "but") is used after a rhetorical question, with the answer implied but suppressed. In other words the Greek conjunction here adopts the force of Aramaic אֶלָּא (*'ellā'*, "if not"). But this meaning of *alla* is also a feature of classical Greek; and NIV, following McNeile, translates it "if not."

9 The meaning of τί (*ti*) affects punctuation: if "what," read τί ἐξήλθατε ἰδεῖν; προφήτην (*ti exēlthate idein; prophētēn*) as "What did you go out to see? A prophet?" if "why," read "Why did you go out to see a prophet?" The problem is compounded by an important variant that reverses the last two Greek words and makes impossible the former punctuation. But the textual evidence is strongest for the order given above, and the parallel use of *ti* in vv.7–8 likewise favors "what." It is doubtful whether Gospel of Thomas 78, which prefers "why," is authentic.

12 Obviously related to the interpretation of this verse is the interpretation of the parallel in Luke 16:16. The clause "the good news of the kingdom of God is being preached" is an acceptable parallel to Matthew's "the kingdom of heaven has been forcefully advancing" and eliminates the perplexing verb βιάζεται (*biazetai*, "is forcefully advancing"). The problem lies in the last clause of Luke 16:16: καὶ πᾶς εἰς αὐτὴν βιάζεται (*kai pas eis autēn biazetai*), which might mean (1) "and everyone is forced into it" or (2), more plausibly, "and everyone is forcing his way into it" (NIV). The latter might be taken in a positive sense, in which case it is not parallel to Matt 11:12 as we have interpreted it (above); or in a negative sense dealing with opponents manifesting hostile intent, in which case the clause is parallel to Matt 11:12 as we have interpreted it, but the verb is being used in a different sense than in Matthew, where the negative part of the verse depends only on the cognate noun, not the verb. The question remains a very difficult one (cf. discussion in Marshall, *Luke*, pp. 626–30).

14 It is difficult to know why, according to John 1:21, the Baptist should deny that he was Elijah. Modern scholarship for the most part assumes independent and mutually contradictory traditions about the Baptist that reached the separate evangelists, who passed them on without recognizing the problem. But other suggestions include (1) John denied he was Elijah because his questioners expected a literal fulfillment—if he had answered in the affirmative, they would therefore have heard an untruth—and (2) John the Baptist saw himself as the voice of one crying in the wilderness (cf. John 1:23) but did not himself recognize that he was also fulfilling the Malachi prophecy. The second alternative may have support from Matt 11:7–15; for according to it, John's knowledge did not extend to the nuanced dimensions of Christian "already–not yet" eschatology, and he may well have been in the dark on other points.

---

2) *The unsatisfied generation*

11:16–19

[16]"To what can I compare this generation? They are like children sitting in the marketplaces and calling out to others:

[17]" 'We played the flute for you,
    and you did not dance;
we sang a dirge,
    and you did not mourn.'

[18]For John came neither eating nor drinking, and they say, 'He has a demon.' [19]The Son of Man came eating and drinking, and they say, 'Here is a glutton and a drunkard, a friend of tax collectors and "sinners." ' But wisdom is proved right by her actions."

16-17 See the close parallel in Luke 7:31-35. "Comparison" stands at the heart of Jesus' parables (see on 13:24). Here Jesus uses an analogy to show his view of "this generation" (v.16), a designation recurring in Matthew 12:41-42, 45; 23:36; 24:34 (cf. 12:39; 16:4; 17:17) and used of Jesus' generation in connection with their general rejection of himself as Messiah. This identification of "this generation" is confirmed here by the next pericope (vv.20-24). "It cannot but be noted that the Lord, *nihil humani a se alienum putans* ['judging nothing human to be without interest to himself'], as he took notice of the rending of mended garments (9:16), and the domestic concerns of the children in their beds (Luke 11:7), so also observes the children's play in the market place, and finds in everything the material for the analogies of his wise teaching" (Stier). There are either two kinds of games (v.17), a wedding game and a funeral game, or, less likely, two cries within one game; but the children cannot be satisfied with either.

18-19 "For" shows that Jesus now gives the reason the behavior of "this generation" suggests the comparison he has drawn. John the Baptist lived ascetically, "neither eating nor drinking" (v.18), i.e., neither indulging in dinner parties (cf. 3:4) nor drinking alcohol (cf. Luke 1:15). Although he drew crowds (vv.7-8) and many were willing to enjoy his light for a time (John 5:35), yet the people as a whole rejected him, even charging him with demon possession. Jesus came eating and drinking (9:10-11; Luke 15:1-2; cf. John 2:1-11) and was charged with gluttony, drunkenness, and bad associations (v.19; cf. Prov 23:20). Like disgruntled children, "this generation" found it easier to whine their criticisms and voice their discontent than to "play the game." Jesus says in effect: "But all you do is to give orders and criticize. For you the Baptist is a madman because he fasts, while you want to make merry; me you reproach because I eat with publicans, while you insist on strict separation from sinners. You hate the preaching of repentance, and you hate the proclamation of the Gospel. So you play your childish game with God's messengers while Rome burns!" (Jeremias, *Parables*, pp. 161-62).

But the criticism runs at a still deeper level. If they had understood John, they would have understood Jesus, and vice versa; the thought has links with vv.7-15 (Bonnard).

Here Jesus uses "Son of Man" not only as a self-reference but as a veiled messianic allusion (see on 8:20). For tax collectors and sinners, see on 5:46.

The closing proverb has provoked much debate because Luke has "all her children" and Matthew "her actions." This proved so difficult that copyists in many MSS assimilated Matthew to Luke, where the text is relatively firm (cf. Metzger, *Textual Criticism*, p. 30; and esp. O. Linton, "The Parable of the Children's Game," NTS 22 [1975-76]: 165-71). But the problem cannot be so easily evaded. Aramaic reconstructions are not convincing.

Luke's form is probably original. It is commonly interpreted to mean that the claims of widsom are proved true by all her children—all who accept the message of widsom's envoys, John and Jesus (cf. Luke 7:29-30; some do accept it: cf. Marshall, *Luke*, pp. 303f.). Why the change to "actions" in Matthew? Suggs (pp. 36-58) argues that the proverb should not be read as the conclusion to the immediately preceding parable but to vv.2-18 and notes the use of *erga* ("actions") in v.2 (NIV, "what Christ was doing"). On this basis he argues that the proverb in Matthew reflects Son-of-Man "wisdom" christology: Wisdom is proved right by her actions, and those actions are the actions of Christ (vv.2–5). Jesus is therefore widsom incarnate (similarly, but more cautiously, David R. Catchpole, "Tradition History," in Marshall, *NT Interpretation*, pp. 167–71; Dunn, *Christology*, pp. 197f.; and many others).

Certainly wisdom, already personified in the OT (e.g., Job 28; Prov 1; 8) and developed in Jewish tradition into a quasi-personal hypostasis in heaven, an agent who (or which) expresses the mind of God (cf. TDNT, 7:465–526; F. Christ, *Jesus Sophia* [Zürich: Zwingli, 1970], pp. 13–60, 156–63), sometimes serves in the NT as a vehicle for christology. Yet here wisdom is best understood in its more traditional association with God. God's wisdom is vindicated by her (wisdom's) actions. The wisdom-christology theory must be rejected here. The theme of chapter 11 is not christology but the place of John the Baptist (and therefore of Jesus) in salvation history. The addition of such a christology in v.19b adds little to the argument, and Suggs's detailed reasons for defending this view entail reconstructions of church history fundamentally questionable on other grounds.

The proverb should be read in the light of the preceding parable: God's wisdom has been vindicated (*edikaiōthē*; NIV, "is proved right"—but the aorist, contra Jeremias [*Parables*, p. 162, n. 42] and Turner [*Syntax*, p. 73], should not be taken as gnomic in this highly specific context) by her actions—i.e., by the lifestyles of both John and Jesus, referred to in the previous verses. Wisdom in the OT is much concerned with right living. John and Jesus have both been criticized and rejected for the way they live. But wisdom, preeminently concerned about right living, has been vindicated by her actions: their respective lifestyles are both acknowledged as hers (for questions of authenticity, cf. TDNT, 8:431–32).

A similar approach best interprets Luke. The phrase "all her children" does not refer to all those who accept John and Jesus as wisdom's envoys: vv.29–30 do not picture the masses accepting them but, unlike the Pharisees and other leaders, merely hearing them gladly. The parable follows in which "this generation" is denounced for not truly understanding and participating. Wisdom's "children" are therefore John and Jesus, not the crowds. "All her children" does not militate against this, because the form is proverbial and meant to include all God's messengers, even those so radically different as John and Jesus. The two forms of the saying are therefore not very far apart. Luke focuses on the lifestyles of John and Jesus as wisdom's children, thus concentrating on their persons; Matthew on their actions. Not only is this interpretation coherent and contextually suitable, but it wraps up the preceding section in which Jesus has been exonerating the Baptist by explaining his role in redemptive history and simultaneously castigating the people for their spiritual dullness.

Notes

16 KJV's "friends" is explained by minor textual support for ἑταίροις (*hetairois*, "friends") instead of ἑτέροις (*heterois*, "others").

19 Several have argued (most recently Linton ["Children's Game," pp. 177f.], following Wellhausen) that the preposition ἀπό (*apo*; "by," NIV) could be rendered "over against," reflecting מִן קֳדָם (*min qᵉdām*). In that case "children" is required; i.e., wisdom is proved right over against her children—the Pharisees and others who think they are right. But it is doubtful whether Greek readers would naturally think of *apo* in this way, and such a meaning is nonsensical in Matthew.

---

2. The condemned and the accepted (11:20–30)

a. The condemned: woes on unrepentant cities

11:20–24

> 20Then Jesus began to denounce the cities in which most of his miracles had been performed, because they did not repent. 21"Woe to you, Korazin! Woe to you, Bethsaida! If the miracles that were performed in you had been performed in Tyre and Sidon, they would have repented long ago in sackcloth and ashes. 22But I tell you, it will be more bearable for Tyre and Sidon on the day of judgment than for you. 23And you, Capernaum, will you be lifted up to the skies? No, you will go down to the depths. If the miracles that were performed in you had been performed in Sodom, it would have remained to this day. 24But I tell you that it will be more bearable for Sodom on the day of judgment than for you."

See Luke 10:12–15, in the context of the commission to the Seventy-two. The structure of the two passages is not close, the language moderately so. There is no particular reason to think that Matthew 11:20–24 is the original: "then" is a loose expression in this Gospel (see on 3:13) and "began" (see on v.7) not much tighter. Luke's context is not clearly original; the second person in 10:13–15 may argue against it (but see on v.24, below). But there is no way to rule out the possibility Jesus uttered these "woes" repeatedly as warnings.

The denunciation in the last pericope (vv.16–19) now becomes sharper. Structurally there are two series of warnings, each with the same sequence of warning (vv.21a, 23a), explanation (vv.21b, 23b), and comparison (vv.22, 24) (cf. Joseph A. Comber, "The Composition and Literary Characteristics of Matt 11:20–24," CBQ 39 [1977]: 497–504).

20 The verb *oneidizein* ("to denounce"), used only here and in 5:11; 27:44 in Matthew, is a strong verb, conveying indignation along with either insults (as in 5:11) or justifiable reproach (as here; cf. BAGD, s.v.). The expression *hai pleistai dynameis autou* (lit., "his very many miracles," elative superlative; cf. Turner, *Insights*, p. 34; id., *Syntax*, p. 31) is rightly rendered "most of his miracles." Jesus did not denounce these cities for vicious opposition but because, despite the fact that most of his miracles took place there—miracles that attested his messianic mission (vv.5–6)—they had not repented (see on 3:2; 4:17). The many miracles again remind us of the extent of Jesus' ministry (cf. 4:23; 8:16; 9:35; John 20:30; 21:25) and of the depth of responsibility imposed on those with more light. "Every hearer of the New Testament is either much happier (v.11), or much more wretched than them of old time" (Beng.)—those who lived before Christ.

21–22 *Ouai* can mean doom or solemn warning ("woe") or pity ("alas"); both are mingled here (v.21). Warnings have been given before; now woes are pronounced. Korazin is mentioned in the NT only here and in Luke 10:13. Its ruins may probably be identified with Kirbet Keraze, about two miles northwest of Capernaum. The Bethsaida in question was probably the home of Andrew, Peter, and Philip (John 1:44; 12:21) on the west side of Galilee, not Bethsaida Julius on the northeast shores near the Jordan inlet. Tyre and Sidon were large Phoenician cities on the Mediterranean, not far away, and often denounced by OT prophets for their Baal worship (Isa 23; Ezek 26–28; Joel 3:4; Amos 1:9–10; Zech 9:2–4). "Sackcloth" is a rough fabric made from the short hairs of camels and usually worn next to the skin to express grief or sorrow (2 Sam 3:31; 1 Kings 21:27; 2 Kings 6:30; Joel 1:8; Jonah 3:5–8). Ashes were added in cases of deep emotion (cf. Job 42:6; Dan 9:3), whether one put them on the head (2 Sam 13:19; Lam 2:10), sat in them (Jonah 3:6), lay on them (Esth 4:3), or even rolled in them (Jer 6:26; Mic 1:10). For "But I tell you" (v.22), properly "Indeed I tell you" (here and in v.24), see on 26:64.

Three large theological propositions are presupposed by Jesus' insistence that on the Day of Judgment (see on 10:15; cf. 12:36; Acts 17:31; 2 Peter 2:9; 3:7; 1 John 4:17; Jude 6), when he will judge (7:22; 25:34), things will go worse for the cities that have received so much light than for the pagan cities. The first is that the Judge has contingent knowledge: he knows what Tyre and Sidon would have done under such-and-such circumstances. The second is that God does not owe revelation to anyone, or else there is injustice in withholding it. The third is that punishment on the Day of Judgment takes into account opportunity. There are degrees of felicity in paradise and degrees of torment in hell (12:41; 23:13; cf. Luke 12:47–48), a point Paul well understood (Rom 1:20–2:16). The implications for Western, English-speaking Christendom today are sobering.

23–24 For Capernaum, see on 4:13. The city was not only Jesus' base (4:13), but he performed many specific miracles there (8:5–17; 9:2–8, 18–33; Mark 1:23–28; John 4:46–54). For the difficult textual variants, see Metzger (*Textual Commentary*, pp. 30f.) and France (*Jesus*, p. 243): the question, kept in the NIV (v.23), is probably right. Whether "go down" (conforming to Isa 14:15) or "will be brought down" (conforming to Luke 10:15) is correct, the thrust is clear; and the allusion to Isaiah 14:15 is unmistakable. The favored city of Capernaum, like self-exalting Babylon, will be brought down to Hades (see on 5:22). The OT passage is a taunt against the wicked and arrogant city, personified in its king; and Capernaum is lumped together with Babylon, which all Jews regarded as the epitome of evil (cf. Rev 17:5). The heaven–hades contrast can be metaphorical for exaltation–humiliation or the like (cf. Job 11:8; Ps 139:8; Amos 9:2; Rom 10:6–7). But in view of the surrounding references to "day of judgment," Hades must be given more sinister overtones. Similarly, though Sodom (Gen 19) was proverbial for wickedness (cf. Ezek 16:48), it will be easier on the Day of Judgment for "the land of Sodom" (so Gr., recalling that several cities were involved in the sin and the destruction) than for Capernaum (see on vv.21–22).

In the words "I tell you" (v.22), "you" is plural, probably implying the crowd (v.7), since the singular "you" is used for the city (vv.23–24, Gr.). This means that using the second person to address the cities is no more than a rhetorical device of Jesus' preaching.

b. *The accepted* (11:25–30)

1) *Because of the revelation of the Father*

11:25–26

> ²⁵At that time Jesus said, "I praise you, Father, Lord of heaven and earth, because you have hidden these things from the wise and learned, and revealed them to little children. ²⁶Yes, Father, for this was your good pleasure.

If vv.20–24 describe the condemned, vv.25–30 describe the accepted. Verses 25–30 can be broken into three parts: vv.25–26, 27, 28–30. The first two are paralleled by Luke 10:21–22. The unity of the three parts and the authenticity of each has been hotly debated. Contrary to earlier opinion (esp. E. Norden, *Agnostos Theos* [Stuttgart: Teubner, 1913]), the language is not that of Hellenistic mysticism (Norden proposed Ecclus 51 as the closest parallel, following Strauss) but is thoroughly Semitic (cf. W.D. Davies, " 'Knowledge' in the Dead Sea Scrolls and Matthew 11:25–30," *Christian Origins and Judaism* [London: Darton, Longman and Todd, 1962], pp. 119–44; Manson, *Sayings*, p. 79; Jeremias, *NT Theology*, pp. 24, 57f.), which means that the provenance is Palestinian. Further aspects of the authenticity question are discussed below (see esp. A.M. Hunter, *Gospel and Apostle* [London: SCM, 1975], pp. 60–67). Jesus' prayer builds on his rejection (vv.16–24) while still recognizing his mission (cf. 10:5–42).

25 The Greek *en ekeinō tō kairō* ("At that time") is a loose connective in Matthew (cf. 12:1; 14:1), loosely historical (it was about that time) and tightly thematic (this pericope must be read in terms of the preceding denunciation). Luke 10:21 has Jesus saying these words "at that hour" (*en autē tē hōra;* NIV, "At that time") when the Seventy-two joyfully returned from their mission, an event Matthew does not record. Luke's connective relates to the success of the mission; Matthew's assumes that there has been some success (God has revealed these things to little children) but draws a sharper antithesis between the recipients of such revelation and the "wise and learned" who, like the inhabitants of the cities just denounced, understand nothing.

While *exomologoumai soi* ("I praise you") can be used in the sense of "I confess my sins" (cf. 3:6), the basic meaning is acknowledgment. Sins truly acknowledged are sins confessed. When this verb is used with respect to God, the person praying "acknowledges" who God is, the propriety of his ways, and the excellence of his character. At that point acknowledgment is scarcely distinguishable from praise (as in Rom 14:11; 15:9; Phil 2:11; cf. LXX of Ps 6:6; 7:18; 17:50 et al.).

Here Jesus addresses God as "Father" and "Lord of heaven and earth" (cf. Ecclus 51:10; Tobit 7:18). These are particularly appropriate titles, because the former indicates Jesus' sense of sonship (see on 6:9) and prepares for v.27, while the latter recognizes God's sovereignty over the universe and prepares for vv.25–26. God is sovereign, free to conceal or reveal as he wills. God has revealed "these things"—the significance of Jesus' miracles (cf. vv.20–24), the Messianic Age unfolding largely unnoticed, the content of Jesus' teaching—to *nēpiois* ("little children," "childlike disciples," "simple ones"; Jeremias, *NT Theology*, p. 111; see further on 18:1–5; cf. John 7:48–49; 1 Cor 1:26–29; 3:18); and he has hidden them from the "wise and learned."

Many restrict the "wise and learned" to the Pharisees and teachers of the law, but the context implies something broader. Jesus has just finished pronouncing woes on "this generation" (v. 16) and denouncing entire cities (vv. 20–24). These are "the wise and learned" (better: "the wise and understanding") from whom the real significance of Jesus' ministry is concealed. The point of interest is not their education, any more than the point of interest in the "little children" is their age or size. The contrast is between those who are self-sufficient and deem themselves wise and those who are dependent and love to be taught.

For revealing the riches of the good news of the kingdom to the one and hiding it from the other, Jesus uttered his praise to his Father. Zerwick (par. 452) argues that though the construction formally puts God's concealing and his revealing on the same level, in reality it masks a Semitic construction (cf. Rom 6:17, which reads, literally, "But thanks be to God that you were servants of sin, you obeyed from the heart the form of teaching with which you were entrusted."). But this example does not greatly help here; for even when rendered concessively ("I praise you . . . because, *though* you have hidden these things from the wise and learned, you have revealed them to little children"), God remains the one who reveals and conceals.

Yet we must not think that God's concealing and revealing are symmetrical activities arbitrarily exercised toward neutral human beings who are both innocent and helpless in the face of the divine decree. God is dealing with a race of sinners (cf. 1:21; 7:11) whom he owes nothing. Thus to conceal "these things" is not an act of injustice but of judgment—the very judgment John the Baptist was looking for and failed to find in Jesus (see on 11:2–6). The astonishing thing about God's activity is not that God acts in both mercy and judgment but who the recipients of that mercy and judgment are: those who pride themselves in understanding divine things are judged, those who understand nothing are taught. The predestination pattern is the counterpoint of grace.

26 Far from bemoaning or finding fault with his Father's revealing and concealing, Jesus delighted in it. The conjunction *hoti* is best understood as "because" or "for" (NIV): I thank you *because* this was your good pleasure; and that is what Jesus "acknowledges" or "praises." Whatever pleases his Father pleases him. "It is often in a person's prayers that his truest thoughts about himself come to the surface. For this reason the thanksgiving of Jesus here recorded is one of the most precious pieces of spiritual autobiography found in the Synoptic Gospels" (Tasker). Jesus' balance mirrored the balance of Scripture: he could simultaneously denounce the cities that did not repent and praise the God who does not reveal; for God's sovereignty in election is not mitigated by man's stubbornness and sin, while man's responsibility is in no way diminished by God's "good pleasure" that sovereignly reveals and conceals (cf. Carson, *Divine Sovereignty*, pp. 205ff.).

Notes

25 The Greek has ἀποκριθεὶς ὁ Ἰησοῦς εἶπεν (apokritheis ho Iēsous eipen, "Jesus answered and said"), not just ὁ Ἰησοῦς εἶπεν (ho Iēsous eipen, "Jesus said," NIV); similarly 12:38; 17:4; 26:63 (mg.); 28:5, where there is no "question" to "answer." This simply reflects Hebrew idiom (Zerwick, par. 366).

2) *Because of the agency of the Son*

11:27

> 27"All things have been committed to me by my Father. No one knows the Son except the Father, and no one knows the Father except the Son and those to whom the Son chooses to reveal him.

27 Despite contrary opinions, the arguments for the authenticity of this saying are very strong. Long rejected because it was thought to reflect Johannine theology, which was judged to be the product of late Hellenization, this verse has by and large gained the recognition of scholarship that the "knowledge" categories here are Jewish and the structure of the verse Semitic (cf. Jeremias, *Prayers*, pp. 45ff.). Dunn (*Christology*, pp. 199–200) has shown that the closest parallels to v.27 are in the election language of the OT, a strong argument for the unity of vv.25–27.

Hill (*Matthew*) denies the authenticity of the saying but candidly admits, "The greatest barrier to the acceptance of the genuineness of the verse is the supposition that Jesus could not have made such an absolute claim for himself." This turns in part on the observation that, apart from the fourth Gospel, the absolute expression "the Son" is exceedingly rare. But significantly it does occur twice more in Matthew, at 24:36 (cf. Mark 13:32) and 28:19 (elsewhere, cf. 1 Cor 15:28; Heb 1:8). Jeremias (*Prayers*) argues that Jesus' habit of addressing God as "Father" could well have contributed to such a self-understanding on the part of Jesus; but even he thinks v.27 should be understood generically: "Just as only a father really knows his son, so only a son really knows his father" (p. 50). But even if he is right, in a context where (1) Jesus has just addressed God as "Father" (vv.25–26), (2) makes himself a son in an exclusive sense, (3) with the sole power to mediate knowledge of God, one must conclude that the "generic" statement Jeremias finds could *only* be applied to Jesus, and that in such a way as to make his sonship exclusive.

Past interpreters often said that "the Son" is never used in pre-Christian sources as a title for the Messiah. With the discovery of 4QFlor 10–14, citing 2 Samuel 7:14 and applying to "the Branch" of David the words "I will be his Father and he shall be my Son," this judgment must be reconsidered. Though it may not be a direct messianic title, it was certainly used to refer to an apocalyptic figure who was the son of a king, presumably David and thus picks up OT uses of "Son" (cf. Ps 2; see on 2:15; 3:17; 16:13–16; cf. Fitzmyer, *Wandering Aramaen*, pp. 102–7; M. Hengel, *The Son of God* [Philadelphia: Fortress, 1976]; Guthrie, *NT Theology*, 301ff.). As with "Son of Man" (see excursus on 8:20), so with "Son of God": it appears that Jesus used a designation not firmly defined and open to several interpretations as part of his gradual self-disclosure, a revelation that could be fully grasped only after the Cross and the Resurrection. Thus for Matthew there is no doubt of what Jesus is saying, because Matthew's "Son" or "Son of God" categories must be seen against the backdrop, not only of the prologue, but also of 3:17.

The latter passage raises a still more basic point. Cannot Jesus himself be thought to originate some things? Was the church so rich in imagination and Jesus so imaginatively poor that all new developments in titles and theology must be ascribed only to the church? If 3:17 is historical, why should not Jesus think of himself as the Son in 11:27? Is it necessary to conclude, with Hill, that 11:27 cannot be authentic because it sounds like the authority of the postresurrection Jesus in 28:18?

And if the two do sound alike, why should we not therefore conclude that there is more continuity between the earthly ministry of Jesus and the resurrected Lord than most scholars are prepared to admit?

Verse 27 is a christological claim of prime importance, fitting easily into the context. After declaring that the Father gives true understanding of "these things" to "little children" (vv.25-26), Jesus now adds that he is the exclusive agent of that revelation. "All things" may have reference not to "all authority" (as in 28:18) but to "all divine knowledge," all knowledge of "these things" (in v.25). But because the Son has not only knowledge but the authority to choose those to whom he will reveal God, probably "all things" includes authority. The reciprocal knowledge of Son and Father where the Father is God presupposes a special sonship indeed. And this unique mutual knowledge guarantees that the revelation the Son gives is true. Not least astonishing about this reciprocity is the clause "No one knows the Son except the Father." Even if it is rendered in Jeremias's way (above), in this exclusivistic context it makes a claim no mere mortal could honestly make. There is a self-enclosed world of Father and Son that is opened to others only by the revelation provided by the Son. "It is one thing to know by equality of nature, and another by the condescension of him who reveals" (Jerome, cited in Broadus). This revelation is not only factual (the Son reveals "these things") but personal (the Son reveals "him"—the Father).

The Son reveals the Father to those whom he, from time to time, wills (present subjunctive: cf. Turner, *Syntax*, p. 107). Just as the Son praises the Father for revealing and concealing according to his good pleasure (v.26), so the Father has authorized the Son to reveal or not according to his will. The text places enormous emphasis on Jesus' person and authority. The thought is closely echoed both in John (3:35; 8:19; 10:15; 14:9; 16:15) and in the Synoptics (Matt 13:11; Mark 4:11—Jesus makes known the secrets of the kingdom; cf. Matt 10:37-39; 11:25; Luke 10:23-24; ch. 15 et al.). What is made clear in this passage is that sonship and messiahship are not quite the same. "Sonship precedes messiahship and is in fact the ground for the messianic mission" (Ladd, *NT Theology*, pp. 165-67, esp. p. 167).

3) *Because of the Son's gentle invitation*

11:28-30

> 28"Come to me, all you who are weary and burdened, and I will give you rest. 29Take my yoke upon you and learn from me, for I am gentle and humble in heart, and you will find rest for your souls. 30For my yoke is easy and my burden is light."

These verses are only in Matthew. Jesus is the one who alone reveals the Father (v.27). Jesus it is who invites, not "the wise and learned" (v.25), but "the weary and burdened" (v.28). The Son reveals the Father, not to gratify learned curiosity or to reinforce the self-sufficiency of the arrogant, but to bring "the little children" (v.25) to know the Father (v.27), to introduce the weary to eschatological rest (v.28)—or, as the angel once said to Joseph, so that Jesus Messiah might save his people from their sins (1:21).

Partly because these verses have some links with Ecclesiasticus 51:23-27, where wisdom invites men to her yoke, several have argued that Matthew here identifies Jesus with hypostasized wisdom (e.g., Zumstein, pp. 140ff.; Dunn, *Christology*, pp.

200f.). But the contrasts between Ecclesiasticus 51 and this passage are more impressive than the similarities. In the former, Sirach is in fact inviting men to take on the yoke of studying Torah as the means of gaining acceptance and rest; in the latter, Jesus offers eschatological rest, not to the scholar who studies Torah, but to the weary. Jesus' teaching must be adopted, not Torah; and this stands, as the next pericopes show (12:1–8, 9–14), in welcome relief to legalistic understanding of the OT.

28 The "me" is grammatically unemphatic but in the wake of v.27 extremely important. Jesus invites the "weary" (the participle suggests those who have become weary through heavy struggling or toil) and the "burdened" (the passive side of weariness, overloaded like beasts of burden) to come to him; and he (not the Father) will give them rest. There is an echo of Jeremiah 31:25, where Yahweh refreshes his people through the new covenant.

While there is no need to restrict the "burdens," it is impossible not to be reminded of the "heavy loads" the Pharisees put on men's shoulders (23:4; cf. 12:1–14; cf. Schlatter; Klostermann; M. Maher, " 'Take my yoke upon you' [Matt.xi.29]," NTS 22 [1976]: 97–103). The "rest" (cf. use of cognate term in Heb 3–4) is eschatological (cf. Rev 6:11; 14:13) but also a present reality.

29–30 The "yoke" (v.29), put on animals for pulling heavy loads, is a metaphor for the discipline of discipleship. If Jesus is not offering the yoke of the law (*Pirke Aboth* 3:6; cf. Ecclus 51:26), neither is he offering freedom from all constraints. The "yoke" is Jesus' yoke, not the yoke of the law; discipleship must be *to him*. In view of v.27, "learn from me" cannot mean "imitate me" or "learn from my experience" (contra Stauffer, TDNT, 2:348f.) but "learn from the revelation that I alone impart" (cf. Schmid).

The marvelous feature of this invitation is that out of his overwhelming authority (v.27) Jesus encourages the burdened to come to him because he is "gentle and humble in heart." Matthew stresses Jesus' gentleness (18:1–10; 19:13–15). Apparently the theme is connected with the messianic servant language (Isa 42:2–3; 53:1–2; cf. Zech 9:9, cited in Matt 21:5) that recurs in 12:15–21. Authoritative revealer that he is, Jesus approaches us with a true servant's gentleness. For the present his messianic reign must not be understood as exclusively royal. On "rest," see v.28; but here the words "and you will find rest for your souls" are directly quoted from Jeremiah 6:16 (MT, not LXX). The entire verse is steeped in OT language (cf. Gundry, *Use of OT*, p. 136); but if this is intended to be not just an allusion but a fulfillment passage, then Jesus is saying that "the ancient paths" and "the good way" (Jer 6:16) lie in taking on his yoke because he is the one to whom the OT Scriptures point. That yoke is "easy" (good, comfortable) and his burden is light (v.30). The "rest" he promises is not only for the world to come but also for this one as well.

The implicit contrast between Jesus' yoke and that of others is not between antinomianism and legalism, for in a deep sense his demands (5:21–48) are far more radical than theirs; nor between salvation by law and salvation by grace (contra Bornkamm, *Tradition* p. 148, n. 2); nor between harsh attitudes among Jewish teachers of the law and Jesus' humane and humble approach (Klostermann). No, the contrast is between the burden of submission to the OT in terms of Pharisaic regulation and the relief of coming under Jesus' tutelage as under the authority of gentle

Revealer to whom the OT, the ancient paths, truly pointed (cf. H.D. Betz, "The Logion of the Easy Yoke and of Rest [Matt 11:28–30]," JBL 86 [1967]: 10–24).

3. Sabbath conflicts (12:1–14)

a. Picking heads of grain

12:1–8

> [1]At that time Jesus went through the grainfields on the Sabbath. His disciples were hungry and began to pick some heads of grain and eat them. [2]When the Pharisees saw this, they said to him, "Look! Your disciples are doing what is unlawful on the Sabbath."
>
> [3]He answered, "Haven't you read what David did when he and his companions were hungry? [4]He entered the house of God, and he and his companions ate the consecrated bread—which was not lawful for them to do, but only for the priests. [5]Or haven't you read in the Law that on the Sabbath the priests in the temple desecrate the day and yet are innocent? [6]I tell you that one greater than the temple is here. [7]If you had known what these words mean, 'I desire mercy, not sacrifice,' you would not have condemned the innocent. [8]For the Son of Man is Lord of the Sabbath."

Opposition to Jesus had already surfaced (9:3, 11, 14, 34; 10:25; 11:19). Now it erupts in a concrete issue that generates enough hatred to lead Jesus' enemies to contemplate murder (v.14).

Matthew now picks up the narrative from Mark 2:23 (cf. Mark 2:23–28; Luke 6:1–5) at the point where he had left the source as far back as Matthew 9:18. Only here does he speak of conflicts over the Sabbath (though cf. 13:54–58; 24:20).

The Jewish rules of conduct about Sabbath were extremely detailed; and it was wryly admitted that "the rules about the Sabbath . . . are as mountains hanging by a hair, for [teaching of] Scripture [thereon] is scanty and the rules many" (M *Hagigah* 1:8). Yet for many Jews of Jesus' day the Sabbath was a joyful festival, a sign of the covenant, a reminder of divine creation in six days, and, provided the rules were obeyed, a means of gaining merit for Israel (Mek Exod 20:16; 23:15; 26:13; b *Shabbath* 10b). At many points there were diverse interpretations; and though the Pharisees were strict, the Qumran covenanters were stricter yet (CD 10:14–11:8). (For detailed study and bibliography of vv.1–14 in the context of the canonical question of the relation between Sabbath and Lord's Day, cf. Carson, "Sabbath.")

1 "At that time" need not mean the same day as the events of chapter 11 but "at about that time" (see on 3:1; 11:25; cf. 13:1). Here it introduces an *example* of burdensome Pharisaic regulation (arising out of 11:28–30) along with the theme of rising opposition to Jesus that ties much of this section (11:2–13:53) together.

Various explanations for what Jesus' disciples (presumably the Twelve) did have been advanced. Some scholars have noted that only Matthew mentions their hunger and have suggested that they ate the grain out of necessity (Kilpatrick, p. 116; Willy Rordorf, *Sunday*, tr. A.A.K Graham [London: SCM, 1968]). But there is no necessity unless one has not eaten for days. The reference to hunger is simply part of the story: why else would the disciples pick a little grain? Samuele Bacchiocchi's suggestion (*From Sabbath to Sunday* [Rome: Pontifical Gregorian University Press, 1977], p. 50) that Jesus' rebuke (v.7) implies that the Pharisees should have taken Jesus and his disciples home for lunch after the synagogue service instead of criticizing them for picking heads of grain is fanciful.

Manson (*Sayings*, p. 190) remarks that Jesus and his disciples were going from place to place on missionary work and so invests their act with kingdom significance. But why, then, were they not charged with exceeding a Sabbath day's journey (about eleven hundred meters; cf. M *Sotah* 5:3)? And what were the Pharisees doing there? The scene is reminiscent of a Sabbath afternoon stroll within the permitted distance. P.K. Jewett (*The Lord's Day* [Grand Rapids: Eerdmans, 1971], p. 37) suggests the disciples were making a path for Jesus, an idea based on Mark's "began to make their way." This will not do in Matthew and wrongly interprets Mark. A path cannot be made merely by picking heads of grain. At the time fields were not separated by fences but by landmark stones (cf. Deut 19:14). Paths went right across fields or closely skirted them, the grain being sown to the field's very edge and sometimes beyond (cf. 13:4); and the right to pluck grain casually (though not necessarily on the Sabbath) was established by Deuteronomy 23:25.

2 The Pharisees' charge that the disciples were breaking the law was based, not on their picking grain in someone else's field, but on the fact that picking grain—i.e., "reaping" (cf. j. *Shabbath* 7.2,9.c)—was one of thirty-nine kinds of work forbidden on the Sabbath (M *Shabbath* 7:2) under prevailing Halakah. Though exceptions to these were granted in the case of temple service and where life was at stake, neither exception applied here. Sigal ("Halakah," p. 160) argues that not all authorities prohibited what the disciples were doing; but M *Shabbath* 10:2, to which he refers, does not deal with casually picking grain in an open field and so is in any case irrelevant. At a much later period, the Gemara expressly permits picking grain by hand and eating it on the Sabbath but merely forbids the use of a tool (b *Shabbath* 128a, b; cf. Bonnard). But this refinement is much later and may even owe something to Christian influence.

3–4 The use of counterquestion and appeal to Scripture was common, though not exclusively so, in rabbinic debates (cf. v.5; 19:4; 21:16, 42; 22:31). The account to which Jesus refers is from the "former prophets," as the Jews called these books (1 Sam 21:1–6). (On the regulations regarding the consecrated bread [lit., "bread of the presentation"], see Exod 25:30; Lev 24:5–9.)

The "house of God" that David entered was the tabernacle (cf. Exod 23:19; Judg 18:31; 1 Sam 1:7, 24; 3:15; 2 Sam 12:20; Ps 5:7), at that time at Nob, just south of Jerusalem. Both David and his companions ate what should only have been eaten by the priests and did so after lying to the priest about their mission. It is possible that this event took place on a Sabbath, since 1 Samuel 21:5–6 sounds as if the consecrated bread had just been changed. Many Jews understood the text that way (cf. SBK, 1:618f.; TDNT, 7:22). But Jesus makes nothing of David's deceit nor depends on any supposition regarding the day on which it occurred. If it was on a Sabbath, others than the priests should not have eaten that bread; and if it was not a Sabbath, the bread should not have been changed, let alone eaten by nonpriests.

The argument takes a common rabbinical form (cf. Sigal, "Halakah," pp. 162f.): viz; the juxtaposition of two apparently contradictory statements from Scripture in order to draw a Halakic conclusion (a conclusion regarding regulations for conduct). On the one hand, David ate; on the other, it was unlawful for him to do so. Jesus' point is not simply that rules admit of exceptions but that the Scriptures themselves do not condemn David for his action; therefore the rigidity of the Pharisees' interpretation of the law is not in accord with Scripture itself (cf. Cranfield, *Mark*, pp. 11f.; Lane, *Mark*, p. 117). The point is not "The Sabbath is delivered unto you, you are not delivered unto the Sabbath" (Mek Exod 26:13; cf. 2 Macc 5:19) but that the Pharisees' approach to the OT was wrong and could not explain the incident of David.

How, then, does this apply to Jesus and his disciples? They were not desperate and famished, unlike David and his men. It is not even clear how they were breaking any OT law, where commandments about the Sabbath were aimed primarily at regular work. The disciples were not farmers trying to do some illicit work, but they were itinerant preachers casually picking some heads of grain. Indeed, apart from Halakic interpretations, it is not at all obvious that any commandment of Scripture was being broken. It seems, then, that Jesus used the David incident not merely to question the Pharisees' view of the Sabbath, for the David incident was not directly relevant. Rather he was questioning their approach to the law itself.

There is more. In the incident to which Jesus referred, regulations (even of the written law) were set aside for David "and his companions." Is there not therefore a case for setting aside regulations (which had no clear base in the written law) for Jesus and those with him (so Hooker, *Son of Man*, pp. 97f.)? This analogy holds good only if Jesus is at least as special as David, and it is to this conclusion that the argument builds in the following verses.

5-6 Jesus' second appeal, preserved only in Matthew (doubtless because it was of interest to his Jewish-Christian readers), is from Torah in the narrow sense of Pentateuch (cf. Num 28:9-10). Formally speaking the Levitical priests "broke" the Sabbath every week (v.5), since the right worship of God in the temple required them to do some work (changing the consecrated bread [Lev 24:8] and offering the doubled burnt offering [Num 28:9-10]). In reality, of course, the priests were guiltless; the law that established the Sabbath also established the right of the priests, formally speaking, to "break" it (for a similar argument, cf. John 7:21-23).

But how does this apply to Jesus and his disciples? The form of the argument is *qal wahômer* (lit., "the light and the weighty," an *a fortiori* argument [see on 5:25-30]), a recognized procedure for establishing a Halakic regulation (Daube, *New Testament*, pp. 67ff.). But this is valid only if the "one greater than the temple" (v.6) is truly greater. The "one greater" is neuter (the masculine variant is poorly attested) as in vv.41-42—i.e., "something greater" (NIV mg.). The neuter, however, can refer to persons when some quality is being stressed rather than the individual per se (Turner, *Syntax*, p. 21).

So the question remains, Who or what is greater than the temple? B. Gerhardsson ("Sacrificial Service and Atonement in the Gospel of Matthew," *Reconciliation and Hope*, ed. R. Banks [Exeter: Paternoster, 1974], p. 28), followed by David Hill ("On the Use and Meaning of Hosea vi.6 in Matthew's Gospel," NTS 24 [1978]: 115), argues that this refers to the service or worship of God in which Jesus was engaged. This is greater than the service of the temple performed by the priests. But Jesus and his disciples were not really "engaged" in such service while plucking heads of grain, the way the priests were engaged in worship on the Sabbath. Moreover the comparison in the text is not with the service of the temple but with the temple itself.

Others have argued that what is greater than the temple is the love command

(Sigal, "Halakah," pp. 163–66; cf. D.M. Cohn-Sherbok, "An Analysis of Jesus' Arguments Concerning the Plucking of Grain on the Sabbath," *Journal for the Study of the New Testament* 2 [1979]: 31–41; cf. Sand, pp. 43–45), finding support for this in the plea for mercy in v.7. But the supremacy of the love command has not yet been introduced (cf. 22:34–40). More importantly the argument neglects the sequential–eschatological "is here." This refutes Sigal's insistence that Jesus is answering purely on the level of dispute over Halakah. Instead, he is insisting that a new and greater development–thing–person has arrived at this point in history, something not there before. And the reference to "mercy" (v.7) is open to a better interpretation.

There are still other suggestions. But the most likely is that the "something greater" is either Jesus himself (Bornkamm, *Tradition*, p. 35; Georges Gander, *L'Evangile de l'Englise: Commentaire de l'Evangile selon Matthieu* [Aix-en-Provence: Faculté Libre de Théologie Protestante, 1967]) or the kingdom (Lohmeyer, *Matthäus*). And in fact the two merge into one. If the kingdom, it is the kingdom Jesus is inaugurating; if Jesus, it is not only Jesus as a man but as Messiah, Son of David (vv.3–4), Son of Man (v.8), the one who ushers in the Messianic Age. Yet "Jesus" is perhaps marginally more plausible, not only because of the christological connections just alluded to, but also because of the parallel drawn by Jesus himself between his own body and the temple (26:61; cf. John 2:20–21).

Jesus' argument, then, provides an instance from the law itself in which the Sabbath restrictions were superseded by the priests because their cultic responsibilities took precedence: the temple, as it were, was greater than the Sabbath. But now, Jesus claims, "something" greater than the temple is here. And that, too, takes precedence over the Sabbath. This solution is entirely consistent with what we have perceived to be Jesus' attitude to the law in this Gospel. The law points to him and finds its fulfillment in him (see on 5:17–48). Not only, then, have the Pharisees mishandled the law by their Halakah (vv.3–4), but they have failed to perceive who Jesus is. The authority of the temple laws shielded the priests from guilt; the authority of Jesus shields his disciples from guilt. It is not a matter of comparing Jesus' action with the action of the priests; nor is it likely that Jesus is suggesting that all his disciples are priests (contra Lohmeyer). "Rather, it is a question of *contrasting* [new emphasis] His authority with the authority of priests" (Carson, "Sabbath," p. 67).

7–8 Again (cf. v.3) Jesus rebuked the Pharisees for their failure to understand the Scriptures (cf. John 5:39), and this time (v.7) he quoted Hosea 6:6 as he had once before (see on 9:13). The relevance of this quotation from the "latter prophets" depends on the Pharisees' attitude to the law being as worthy of condemnation as the attitude of those who relied superficially and hypocritically on mere ritual in Hosea's day. Jesus claims, in effect, that the Pharisees had not really grasped the significance of the law, and this was demonstrated by their Halakah. The accusers stand accused; the disciples are explicitly declared "innocent." Their innocence was not (contra Rordorf) established on their being hungry but on the ground that something greater than the temple was present. In other words the Son of Man is Lord of the Sabbath. Whether "For" (v.8) relates to v.6 or v.7 is unclear and of little consequence. If the former, it sums up Messiah's supremacy over the temple; if the latter, it does the same but also serves as explicit ground for the innocence of the disciples.

Some have argued that "Son of Man" here has corporate significance: the community of Jesus' disciples together is "Lord" of the Sabbath (e.g., T.W. Manson, "The Son of Man in Daniel, Enoch and the Gospels," BJRL 32 [1949–50]: 191). But this is based on a disputed understanding of "Son of Man" (see excursus on 8:20) and on a misunderstood connection with Mark 2:27 (on which cf. Carson, "Sabbath," pp. 62–65). In all three Synoptics the Son of Man is David's son, Jesus the Messiah (Hill). But the title is ambiguous enough that few would grasp the point till after the Resurrection, at which time few could miss it. The claim (v.8) is implicitly messianic, a claim that goes beyond the mere right to tamper with Halakah. It places the Son of Man in a position to handle the Sabbath law any way he wills, or to supersede it in the same way that the temple requirements superseded the normal Sabbath restrictions (cf. Hooker, *Son of Man*, pp. 100ff.).

Notes

4 Moule (*Idiom Book*, p. 27) points out that ὃ οὐκ ἐξὸν ἦν αὐτῷ φαγεῖν (*ho ouk exon ēn autō phagein*, "which was not lawful for him to eat") is a mixed construction: the relative pronoun *ho*, which refers to the eating of the bread in the preceding clause, seems to serve simultaneously as subject of *ouk exon ēn* and object of *phagein*. Moule suggests the clause is being treated as if it had begun with ἀλλά (*alla*, "but") or καίπερ (*kaiper*, "although").

The reading ἔφαγεν (*ephagen*, "he ate") has very strong attestation but is rejected by Metzger (*Textual Commentary*, p. 31) and UBS 3d ed. in favor of ἔφαγον (*ephagon*, "they ate"), supported only by ℵ B and one miniscule, on the grounds that it represents the nonparallel reading (cf. Mark 2:26; Luke 6:4). But the change may have gone the other way, in order to make it unambiguous that not only David but all his men ate—a fact clearly relevant to Jesus and his disciples. "He ate and his companions" is an acceptable but ambiguous way of saying in Greek "he and his companions ate."

b. *Healing a man with a shriveled hand*

12:9–14

⁹Going on from that place, he went into their synagogue, ¹⁰and a man with a shriveled hand was there. Looking for a reason to accuse Jesus, they asked him, "Is it lawful to heal on the Sabbath?"

¹¹He said to them, "If any of you has a sheep and it falls into a pit on the Sabbath, will you not take hold of it and lift it out? ¹²How much more valuable is a man than a sheep! Therefore it is lawful to do good on the Sabbath."

¹³Then he said to the man, "Stretch out your hand." So he stretched it out and it was completely restored, just as sound as the other. ¹⁴But the Pharisees went out and plotted how they might kill Jesus.

Luke (6:6–11) specifies that this event took place on another Sabbath (cf. Mark 3:1–6). Unlike the previous pericope, Jesus does not refer to Scripture. This time it is *his* activity that is in question, not that of his disciples; and his argument, at first glance a stinging *ad hominem*, holds deeper implications.

The first-century Jews discussed at length what was permitted in caring for the sick on the Sabbath (e.g., M *Eduyoth* 2:5; M *Shabbath* 6:3; Mek Exod 22:2; 23:13). Jesus' attitude was more fundamental: it is lawful to do good on the Sabbath.

9-10 "Going on from that place" (v.9) is a Matthean connective to move the action from the field to the synagogue without reference to time. Regarding "their" synagogue, see on 10:17; 11:1. All three synoptists make plain the malice in the Pharisees' watching (Mark) and question (Matthew). In Mark and Luke, Jesus precipitates the action by calling forward the man with the shriveled hand; in Matthew that is omitted.

The form of the Pharisees' question in Matthew (v.10) is general. The customary Jewish ruling was that healing was permitted on the Sabbath when life was in danger (cf. M *Yoma* 8:6; Mek Exod 22:2; 23:13), which of course did not apply here. Even so, what rabbinic discussion had in view was medical help by family members or professionals, not miraculous healings. But Jesus did not reply on that level.

11-13 For the third time in this Gospel, Jesus' argument depends on a contrast between animals and men (cf. 6:26; 10:31) and presupposes the greater value of human beings based on their special creation: man alone was made in the image of God (Gen 1-2). This particular argument occurs only in Matthew; but a similar analogy is drawn in Luke 13:15; 14:5. In all three instances Jesus assumed that the Pharisees would lift an animal out of a pit on the Sabbath—though the most that was allowed at Qumran was to do something that would enable the animal to help itself (CD 11:13-14). Sigal ("Halakah," pp. 169f.), in support of his too rigid theory that the Pharisees are to be identified as *perushim* (see Introduction, section 11.f), is reduced to thinking that *probaton hen* (v.11) should be taken literally to mean "one sheep," viz., the last one. But the expression probably means no more than "a sheep" (see on 8:19).

Jesus' argument is again *qal waḥomer* (see on vv.5-6): If a sheep, how much more a man (v.12)? Neither the sheep in the pit nor the man in Jesus' presence is in mortal danger. The question is simply one of doing good. This does not mean Jesus is saying that failure to do good is itself an evil thing (e.g., Klostermann; Cranfield, *Mark*, p. 120). Jesus is talking about what is "lawful," not what is required; and if it were absolutely true that failure to do good is *always* evil, there would be no possibility of any rest at all. Jesus' rhetorical question therefore has a narrower focus: Was the Sabbath a day for maleficent activity—like their evil intentions in questioning him—or for beneficent action, like the healing about to be done?

The healing (v.13), like that in 9:1-8, comes after the shocking word (in all three Synoptics) and therefore serves to confirm that word. The miracle itself says nothing of the cripple's faith, since the focus is not on him but on the Pharisees. Yet in light of the preceding interchange, it also confirms Jesus' claim to lordship over the Sabbath, as his healing in 9:1-8 confirmed his authority to forgive sins.

14 A great deal has been made of the fact that Matthew omits mention of the Herodians (Mark 3:6), as if that proves that the point of reference is now after A.D. 70, when the Herodians no longer existed and the sole opponents were the Pharisees (e.g., Hummel, pp. 12ff.; Hill, *Matthew*). But giving reasons for *omissions* in Matthew is extremely hazardous (see on 8:1-4). And in this instance it is noteworthy that Matthew mentions the Herodians in 22:16 and refers often to the Sadducees.

Sigal ("Halakah," p. 175) wants *apolesōsin* ("destroy") to mean, not "kill," but "put under the synagogue ban," because no Pharisee would consider executing another Jew merely over a Halakic dispute. While he is correct in the latter supposition, the point is that these Sabbath confrontations are *not* mere disputes over Halakah. They have to do with Jesus' fundamental messianic claims, a point vigorously denied by Sigal, who generally assigns passages like v.8 to later Christian theology and reduces the remainder to purely Halakic categories. But it is very doubtful (contra Sigal) that Jesus tolerated the oral tradition implicit in much Jewish Halakah (cf. Jeremias, *NT Theology*, pp. 208–11). Moreover the Sabbath-controversy pericopes cohere as they stand: this first mention of a plot to kill Jesus springs not from disputes over the legality of various Sabbath activities but over Jesus' authority. The Sabbath conflicts are not the cause of the plotting but its occasion. Therefore Sabbath disputes were not mentioned at Jesus' trials; in themselves they were never as much an issue as Jesus' claim to be Sabbath's Lord.

4. *Jesus the prophesied Servant*

12:15–21

> [15] Aware of this, Jesus withdrew from that place. Many followed him, and he healed all their sick, [16] warning them not to tell who he was. [17] This was to fulfill what was spoken through the prophet Isaiah:
>
> > [18] "Here is my servant whom I have chosen,
> > the one I love, in whom I delight;
> > I will put my Spirit on him,
> > and he will proclaim justice to the nations.
> > [19] He will not quarrel or cry out;
> > no one will hear his voice in the streets.
> > [20] A bruised reed he will not break,
> > and a smoldering wick he will not snuff out,
> > till he leads justice to victory.
> > [21] In his name the nations will put their hope."

Verses 15–16 constitute a brief summary of Mark 3:7–12, omitting, among other things, a "Son of God" title. To this summary Matthew adds a fulfillment passage, citing Isaiah 42:1–4. Thus he interprets Jesus' healing ministry, not so much in terms of "Son of God" or even royal "Son of David" christology, but in terms of Yahweh's Suffering Servant (see also on 8:17). This section simultaneously contrasts the hatred of the Pharisees (v.14) with Jesus' tranquility (v.19) and gentleness (v.20) and prepares the way for themes in the rest of the chapter (discussed below).

15–17 Jesus often withdrew when opposition became intense (cf. 4:12; 14:13; 15:21; 16:5); at least that was his custom until the appointed hour arrived (26:45; cf. John 7:8). This practice becomes for his disciples an example of moving from place to place (10:23). Thus his extensive ministry continued (cf. 4:23; 8:16; 9:35). Warnings to those healed to keep silence increased for the same reasons as before and with as little effect (cf. 8:4; 9:30). But Jesus' conduct under these pressures, Matthew perceives, was nothing less than the fulfillment of the Scriptures. Though the Pharisees might plot to kill him (v.14), he would not quarrel or cry out (v.19). Despite all Matthew has done to show Jesus to be the messianic Son of David and unique Son of God, he wants to separate himself from exclusively royal and militaristic interpretations of Messiah's role. He knows that the ministry of Jesus Messiah must also be understood as the fulfillment of the prophecies of the Suffering Servant.

18–21 This quotation (Isa 42:1–4), the longest in Matthew, is remarkable for its text form. The changes have been variously assigned to Matthew's "school" (Stendahl, *School*, pp. 107ff.), to a developing Christian apologetic (Lindars, *Apologetic*, pp. 147-52), to the evangelist's redactional interests (Hill, *Matthew*). Certainly there is a mixed text-character here (for details, cf. Gundry, *Use of OT*, pp. 110-16), and the reason for each change is not easy to discern.

The noun *pais* ("servant," v. 18) can also mean "son," though the Hebrew is unambiguously "servant." Cope (*Matthew*, pp. 44f.), in line with his generally plausible view that this quotation anticipates the major themes of the rest of Matthew 12, suggests that Matthew exploits the Son–Servant ambiguity to anticipate vv. 46-50—his disciples are brothers and sisters, but he is the unique Son of the Father. This seems tenuous, for elsewhere in Matthew God is the Father of the disciples (e.g., 6:9, 26; 10:29) as well as of Jesus (though in a somewhat different sense). The link between this quotation and vv. 46-50 is on a different level, a christological one: viz., Jesus cannot be understood in terms of the normal family relationships that bind humanity. He is God's chosen Servant, the one on whom God has poured out his Spirit with a specific mission in view. Therefore his disciples, not his family, must be reckoned closest to him.

The words "whom I have chosen" (Heb. "whom I uphold") may have been borrowed by Matthew from the second line of Isaiah 42:1, or from Isaiah 43:10; 44:1 (thus making the quotation composite); and "the one I love" carries overtones of Matthew 3:17; 17:5, because love and election are closely connected. God's "delight" in his servant and the mention of the Spirit God puts on him to a special degree (cf. John 3:34) remind us of both Jesus' baptism and his transfiguration (3:16-17; 17:5), where Jesus was called God's Son. Yet far from subsuming Jesus' servant role under his sonship (Kingsbury), Matthew omits Mark's mention of "Son of God" (Mark 3:11) and here makes the servant motif preeminent (cf. Hill, "Son and Servant," pp. 4-12).

This "servant" will proclaim "justice" to the nations: neither the Hebrew *mišpaṭ* nor Greek *krisis* easily suggests "the true faith" (JB). But the suggestion is not entirely without merit, since what is in view is "justice"—i.e., righteousness broadly conceived as the self-revelation of God's character for the good of the nations (cf. Isa 51:4), yet at the same time calling them to account. Concern for the Gentiles thus emerges again (cf. 1:1; 2:1-12; 3:9; 4:15-16; 8:5-13 et al.) in anticipation of the Great Commission (28:18-20).

But even within this chapter, the twin themes of Spirit and Gentiles are programmatic (Cope, *Matthew*, pp. 32ff.; Hill, "Son and Servant," pp. 10f.). God has poured out his Spirit on his Servant; so the exorcisms he performs by the Spirit constitute proof of the kingdom's inauguration (v. 28). Therefore blasphemy against that Spirit cannot be forgiven (see on v. 32). Moreover the pericope about the sign of Jonah (vv. 38-41) returns to the theme of the place of the Gentiles in the merciful salvation of God and warns "this wicked generation" (v. 45) once more.

The servant "will not quarrel or cry out" or raise his voice in the streets (v. 19). The picture is not one of utter silence (else how could he "proclaim" justice [v. 18]? cf. John 7:37) but of gentleness and humility (11:29), of quiet withdrawal (see on vv. 15-17) and a presentation of his messiahship that is neither arrogant nor brash.

The first two lines of v. 20 are very close to both LXX and MT. The double metaphor breathes compassion: the servant does not advance his ministry with such callousness to the weak that he breaks the bruised reed or snuffs out the smoldering wick (smoldering either because it is poorly trimmed or low on oil). This may include reference to Jesus' attitude to the sick (v.15). But the last clause of v.20 ("till he leads justice to victory"), apparently a paraphrase of Isaiah 42:3 ("in faithfulness he will bring forth justice") and Isaiah 42:4 ("till he establishes justice on earth") under influence of Habakkuk 1:4 (cf. Gundry, *Use of OT*, pp. 114f.), suggests something more—namely that he brings eschatological salvation to the "harassed and helpless" (9:36), the "weary and burdened" (11:28).

"Leads" is a trifle weak for *ekbalē:* though the verb can have a wide semantic range, it requires something like "thrusts forth" in this context (used elsewhere in this chapter in vv.24, 26, 27 [*bis*], 28, 35 [*bis*]). What is pictured is a ministry so gentle and compassionate that the weak are not trampled on and crushed till justice, the full righteousness of God, triumphs. And for such a Messiah most Jews were little prepared (cf. Pss Sol 17:21). Small wonder that the Gentiles put their hope in his name (v.21; cf. Isa 11:10; Rom 15:12). The Hebrew reads literally "the coastlands wait for his laws," but the word "coastlands" often signifies Gentiles (*ethnē;* NIV, "nations"); and "will put their hope" is idiomatic for "look forward to" or "expect."

"Name" follows the LXX, even though MT has "law" (*torāh*, "teaching"). In view of the mixed text-character, which testifies to Matthew's ability and willingness to use the MT or to set it aside (unless, with Gundry [*Use of OT*, pp. 115f.], we postulate that LXX here renders a lost Hebrew original), this must be thought strange if certain recent reconstructions of the importance of the law in Matthew are correct (cf. Introduction, section 11.c). However, if, as we have maintained, the law in this Gospel serves primarily to point to Jesus, then it is not surprising that Matthew prefers the LXX term. For "in his name," see on 5:10-12.

5. Confrontation with the Pharisees (12:22-37)

a. The setting and accusation

12:22-24

> [22]Then they brought him a demon-possessed man who was blind and mute, and Jesus healed him, so that he could both talk and see. [23]All the people were astonished and said, "Could this be the Son of David?"
> [24]But when the Pharisees heard this, they said, "It is only by Beelzebub, the prince of demons, that this fellow drives out demons."

For a convenient summary of the parallels, see Albright and Mann. The analogous incident in 9:32-34 is not a doublet but a sample of the same outrageous charge that is raised in v.24.

22 The *tote* ("then") is very loose (see on 2:7; 11:20), and probably this event took place a good deal later (compare Mark and Luke). NIV sounds as if the man suffered from three distinct ailments; the Greek, very condensed, puts blind and mute (*kō-phos*, as in 9:32) in opposition to "demon-possessed," suggesting the latter is the cause of the other two. The healing itself is told with admirable brevity, for it is not so much the miracle itself that captures the attention of the synoptists as the confrontation that follows.

23-24 The acute astonishment of the crowd (the verb *existanto*, "were astonished," is used only here in Matthew, though it is common in Mark and Luke) prompted the question (v.23). Its form in Greek suggests the crowds were none too sure: "This couldn't be the Son of David, could it?" The question does not ask whether Jesus is a magician of the kind attributed by popular superstition to David's son Solomon (contra Loren L. Fisher, "'Can This Be the Son of David?'" *Jesus and the Historian*, ed. F.T. Trotter [Philadelphia: Westminster, 1968], pp. 82–97) but whether Jesus is the Messiah (see on 1:1; 9:27; 15:22). The Messiah was expected to perform miracles (cf. v.38); so the exorcism-healing stood in Jesus' favor. But perhaps his reticence, his nonregal sayings, and his servant ministry engendered doubt. Matthew's readers can see the connection between the Suffering Servant (vv.18–21) and the Son of David (vv.22–23), but those who witnessed Jesus' ministry could not view it in the light of the Resurrection.

On "Beelzebub" (v.24), see on 10:25.

b. *Jesus' reply* (12:25-37)

1) *The divided kingdom*

12:25-28

> 25Jesus knew their thoughts and said to them, "Every kingdom divided against itself will be ruined, and every city or household divided against itself will not stand. 26If Satan drives out Satan, he is divided against himself. How then can his kingdom stand? 27And if I drive out demons by Beelzebub, by whom do your people drive them out? So then, they will be your judges. 28But if I drive out demons by the Spirit of God, then the kingdom of God has come upon you.

While the structure of vv.25–37 is parallel to that of Mark 3:23–30, Matthew's length is surprising. Some but not all of Matthew's "response" section is closer to Luke than to Mark. Most likely Matthew used both Mark and a "Q" source for this narrative. Part of Jesus' response in Matthew is scattered in Luke (cf. Luke 6:43–45; 11:17–23; 12:10), prompting some to think this passage to be a composite of a number of independent sayings. That is possible; the transitions are loose, and, unlike the five major discourses, the end of the response is not decisive. But it is also possible that one of the two Lukan parallels (Luke 6:43–45) has been placed elsewhere for topical reasons and that the other (12:10) is simply a report of a similar saying. At any rate the argument in Matthew 12:25–37 is unified and coherent.

25–26 Jesus "knew their thoughts" (v.25; cf. 9:4). The narrative is condensed (cf. Mark 3:20, 23), and the "house" is not mentioned. The argument is clear: any kingdom, city, or household that develops internal strife will destroy itself. The same holds true for Satan's *basileia* ("kingdom," v.26), his exercise of authority among his minions (cf. H. Kruse, "Das Reich Satans," *Biblica* 58 [1977]: 29–61). "For the prince of the demons to cast out his subjects would be virtually casting out himself, since they were doing his work" (Broadus).

27 Whether the words *hoi huioi hymōn* (lit., "your sons") mean no more than "your people" (the Jews) or those instructed by the Pharisees (cf. 22:15–16; 23:9–15) is uncertain. Jesus' argument is ad hominem: he is saying "your sons" cast out demons on occasion (a not uncommon practice linked to some bizarre notions; cf. Jos. Antiq. VIII, 45–48[ii.5]; id., Wars VII, 185[vi.3]; Tobit 8:2–3; Justin Martyr *Dialogue* 85;

cf. Acts 19:13), and I do this so powerfully that great damage is done to Satan's kingdom. So if I who do so much damage to his kingdom by my exorcisms perform them by Satan's power, by whom do your sons drive out demons?

28 Luke 11:20 has "the finger of God" instead of "the Spirit of God." Possibly the latter is original (cf. Dunn, *Jesus*, pp. 44–46), but the matter is of little consequence since they both refer to the same thing (cf. Exod 8:19; Deut 9:10; Ps 8:3). Matthew's phrase makes a clearer connection with 12:18 (Isa 42:1) and a more specific contrast with Beelzebub (cf. Gundry, *Matthew*). Only here and in Matthew 19:24; 21:31, 43 does Matthew have "kingdom of God" instead of "kingdom of heaven" (see on 3:2); and this may reflect his source, common to Luke (though elsewhere, when following a source, Matthew changes to "kingdom of heaven" except at 19:24), or he may use "kingdom of God" stylistically to go with "Spirit of God." What is certain is that Jesus knows that his exorcisms, performed by the Spirit of God, prove that the kingdom age has already dawned.

Of course this also implies that Jesus is King Messiah without explicitly affirming it. Dunn (*Jesus*, pp. 46–49) rightly emphasizes the realized eschatology but over-states his Spirit christology when he adds, "The eschatological kingdom was present for Jesus only because the eschatological Spirit was present in and through him. In other words, it was not so much a case of 'Where *I* am there is the kingdom,' as, 'Where the *Spirit* is there is the kingdom' " (emphasis his).

Four considerations argue strongly against this view.

1. Dunn has introduced a disjunction alien to the text ("only because the eschato-logical Spirit was present," he says) and maintains the disjunction by interpreting Jesus' messianic claims in non-Spirit dress as anachronistic. Jesus knew *both* that he was unique, the promised Messiah, *and* that the eschatological Spirit was on him.

2. If Jesus' self-recognition turned exclusively on his ability to exorcise demons by the Spirit's power, then on what basis could he deny similar self-recognition to the "your people" (v.27) who also drove out demons? In other words, Spirit-prompted phenomena were not sufficient in themselves for Jesus' self-understand-ing, especially in the light of his own warnings in this respect (cf. 7:21–23).

3. Dunn has too quickly turned this pericope into a question of Jesus' self-under-standing ("The eschatological kingdom was present for Jesus," he says), whereas on the face of it Jesus is arguing, not to convince himself, but manifestly to convince the Pharisees that the kingdom had come on them.

4. In his Gospel's structure Matthew is less interested in Jesus' self-understand-ing than in his apologetics and fulfillment of OT prophecies (see the reference to "Spirit" in v.18).

Notes

26 The first clause is an excellent instance of a "real" condition, εἰ (*ei*, "if ") plus the indica-tive, in which the "reality" need not be admitted by the speaker but only assumed for the sake of argument (cf. RHG, p. 1008; Zerwick, par. 306).

2) *The strong man's house*

12:29

> [29]"Or again, how can anyone enter a strong man's house and carry off his possessions unless he first ties up the strong man? Then he can rob his house.

29 The opening *ē* (lit., "or"; cf. 7:9; 12:5; 20:15) here means "Or look at it another way." Some Jewish expectation looked forward to the binding of Satan in the Messianic Age (As Moses 10:1; cf. Rev 20:2); and under this metaphor Jesus is the one who ties up the strong man (Satan) and carries off his "possessions" (*ta skeuē;* "vessels" preserves the metaphor of the house and has no relation to [demonic] possession except metaphorically). The argument has thus advanced: if Jesus' exorcisms cannot be attributed to Satan (vv.25–26), then they reflect authority greater than that of Satan. By this greater power Jesus is binding "the strong man" and plundering his "house." So the kingdom of heaven is forcefully advancing (see on 11:12).

3) *Blasphemy against the Spirit*

12:30–32

> [30]"He who is not with me is against me, and he who does not gather with me scatters. [31]And so I tell you, every sin and blasphemy will be forgiven men, but the blasphemy against the Spirit will not be forgiven. [32]Anyone who speaks a word against the Son of Man will be forgiven, but anyone who speaks against the Holy Spirit will not be forgiven, either in this age or in the age to come.

30 Here several of Jesus' sayings are aphoristic. Their relation to the pericope is internal, not grammatical; and the relation to what precedes goes back to the tradition itself and cannot be ascribed to Matthew (cf. Luke 11:23).

The general thrust of v.30 is straightforward: in our relationship to Jesus there can be no neutrality. As to some issues and persons, neutrality is possible and may even be wise. But in the great struggle (vv.25–29), neutrality is impossible. The claims of the kingdom and the demands of Jesus are so exclusivistic that to be indifferent or apathetic to him is to be on the side of those who do not confess that he is the Messiah who brings in the kingdom of God (cf. 11:16–24). Jesus' claim implies a high christology, which is underlined by the harvest figure in v.30b (cf. 3:12; 6:26; John 4:36). Jesus is the one who will harvest in the last days, a function the OT regularly assigns to God. Hill (*Matthew*) objects to the authenticity of the setting of this saying on the grounds that an affirmation about the impossibility of neutrality with respect to Jesus "is hardly likely to have been addressed to implacable opponents such as the Pharisees." But crowds were also present (v.23). And this form of statement could serve as both a rebuke to the Pharisees and a warning to the questioning crowd (v.23) that failure to follow Jesus wholeheartedly is as dangerous as outright opposition.

The inverted saying—"whoever is not against us is for us" (Mark 9:40; Luke 9:50) —and this one "are not contradictory if the one was spoken to the indifferent about themselves and the other to the disciples about someone else" (McNeile).

31–32 "And so"—*dia touto* (lit., "on account of this")—ties the statements about blasphemy against the Spirit (v.31) to the preceding verse. But the transition cannot easily be readily grasped till vv.31–32 are understood. Introduced by the solemn "I tell you" (see on 5:18), these statements constitute a pair, one from Mark (v.31 = Mark 3:28), one from Q (v.32 = Luke 12:10, in a different context; cf. comment, above). "Blasphemy" is extreme slander (see on 9:3), equivalent to "speaking against" (cf. v.32). Blasphemy against God was viewed by Jews with utmost gravity (26:65); but here Jesus makes a sharp distinction between blasphemy against the Son of Man, which is forgivable, and blasphemy against the Spirit, which is not.

His statement is remarkable because one of the glories of the biblical faith is the great emphasis Scripture lays on the graciousness and wideness of God's forgiveness (e.g., Pss 65:3; 86:5; 130:3–4; Isa 1:18; Mic 7:19; 1 John 1:7). A common interpretation of vv.31–32 is that they originated with a Christian prophet speaking for the exalted Jesus and are here read back into the life of the earthly Jesus. The blasphemy against the Son of Man is rejection of him by nonbelievers, and this is clearly forgivable when a person becomes a Christian. But blasphemy against the Holy Spirit is committed by a Christian (Christians after Pentecost would understand that only believers enjoy the Spirit) and is equivalent either to apostasy or to rejection of a Christian prophet's inspired message. For this there is no forgiveness (so Stendahl, Peake, 684q; and in a highly structured scheme, M.E. Boring, "The Unforgivable Sin Logion Mark III 28–29/Matt XII 31–32/Luke XII 10: Formal Analysis and History of the Tradition," NovTest 18 [1976]: 258–79).

But there is strong and consistent evidence that the writers of the NT did *not* read words of Christian prophets back into the life of the historical Jesus (cf. esp. Bonnard; J.D.G. Dunn, "Prophetic 'I'-Sayings and the Jesus Tradition: The Importance of Testing Prophetic Utterances within Early Christianity," NTS 24 [1978]: 175–98). It is highly unlikely that "Son of Man" would be used as an object of blasphemy without some qualifications about "Son of Man" (i.e., as "earthly Jesus only," etc.), which do not appear until Origen. Moreover this does not explain what these sayings are doing in their Gospel contexts (esp. Mark and Matthew).

The views of many older conservative scholars are also unhelpful. Broadus, for instance, ties blasphemy against the Holy Spirit to the "age of miracles" when the Spirit's power could be directly perceived—and rejected. But apart from the question of whether miracles take place now, Jesus elsewhere warned that miracles are not *necessarily* the criterion of true discipleship (7:21–23), i.e., they do not *necessarily* reveal the Spirit's presence and power.

Among the many other interpretations of this difficult incident, the best treats it in its setting during Jesus' life. The Pharisees have been attributing to Satan the work of the Spirit and have been doing so, as Jesus makes plain, in such a way as to reveal that they speak, not out of ignorance or unbelief, but out of a "conscious disputing of the indisputable" (the phrase is from G.C. Berkouwer, *Sin* [Grand Rapids: Eerdmans, 1971], p. 340; cf. pp. 323–53, to which this exposition is indebted).

The distinction between blasphemy against the Son of Man and blasphemy against the Spirit is not that the Son of Man is less important than the Spirit, or that the first sin is prebaptismal and the second postbaptismal, still less that the first is against the Son of Man and the second rejects the authority of Christian prophets. Instead, within the context of the larger argument the first sin is rejection of the truth of the gospel (but there may be repentance and forgiveness for that), whereas the second sin is rejection of the same truth in full awareness that that is exactly what one is doing—thoughtfully, willfully, and self-consciously rejecting the work of the Spirit even though there can be no other explanation of Jesus' exorcisms than that. For such a sin there is no forgiveness, "either in this age or the age to come" (cf. 13:22; 25:46)—a dramatic way of saying "never" (as in Mark 3:29).

If this interpretation is correct, the distinction between Son of Man and Spirit is relatively incidental. After all, blasphemy against the Spirit is also a rejection of Jesus' own claims: the christological implications of the sin are not diminished but increased in moving from "blasphemy against the Son of Man" to "blasphemy against the Spirit." This provides a clue for understanding how the unforgivable sin of which Jesus here speaks compares with the sins referred to in Hebrews 6:4–6; 10:26-31; and possibly 1 John 5:16. In each instance there is self-conscious perception of where the truth lies and the light shines—and a willful turning away from it. This is very different from Paul's persecution of the church (1 Cor 15:9), which was not unforgivable (1 Tim 1:13).

C.K. Barrett (*The Holy Spirit and the Gospel Tradition* [London: SPCK, 1966], pp. 106–7) discusses this matter wisely, except for his assumption that the sin is committed within the church and "because it denies the root and spring of the Church's life, cannot rediscover the forgiveness by which the sinner first entered the community of the forgiven." But the biblical texts are more subtle than that. The author of Hebrews says, with a surprising combination of tenses, "We have come [perfect] to share in Christ if we hold firmly [aorist subjunctive] to the end the confidence we had at first" (Heb 3:14). In other words our past participation in the blessings of the gospel is valid only if we continue in it. John presupposes the same thing—that those who leave the church show that they never really belonged in it (1 John 2:19; 2 John 9). Even Hebrews 6:4–6; 10:26-31 shows how much of the truth may be grasped, how much of the life of the age to come may be sampled, without coming to the place from which there is no turning back (cf. Philip E. Hughes, *A Commentary on the Epistle to the Hebrews* [Grand Rapids: Eerdmans, 1977], in loc.). This is apostasy, and it involves a break with what one has formally adhered to.

The universal witness of the NT is that apostasy if persisted in not only damns but shows that salvation was never real in the first place. The NT reveals how close one may come to the kingdom—tasting, touching, perceiving, understanding. And it also shows that to come this far and reject the truth is unforgivable. So it is here. Jesus charges that those who perceive that his ministry is empowered by the Spirit and then, for whatever reason—whether spite, jealousy, or arrogance—ascribe it to Satan, have put themselves beyond the pale. For them there is no forgiveness, and that is the verdict of the one who has authority to forgive sins (9:5-8).

The significance of the transitional words "And so" now becomes plain. Neutrality to Jesus is actually opposition to him (v.30); and therefore Jesus gives this warning regarding those who blaspheme against the Spirit, since the self-professedly neutral person may not recognize the inherent danger of his position.

4) Nature and fruit

12:33-37

> 33"Make a tree good and its fruit will be good, or make a tree bad and its fruit will be bad, for a tree is recognized by its fruit. 34You brood of vipers, how can you who are evil say anything good? For out of the overflow of the heart the mouth speaks. 35The good man brings good things out of the good stored up in him, and the evil man brings evil things out of the evil stored up in him. 36But I tell you that

men will have to give account on the day of judgment for every careless word they have spoken. ³⁷For by your words you will be acquitted, and by your words you will be condemned."

This section has no parallel in Mark, but it fits well into Matthew. A similar metaphor occurs in 7:16-19; but there the point is that Jesus' disciples must test character by conduct, whereas here it is that conduct, especially speech, reveals character. Therefore the only remedy is a radical change of heart. Parts of vv.33-34 are also reflected in Luke 6:43-45.

33 It is possible to construe the expression "make a tree good . . . bad" to mean "suppose a tree is good . . . bad." But in that case the word "and" fits badly, and the final "for" clause relates poorly to what precedes. Jesus is rather telling his hearers to make the tree good or bad, knowing that its fruit will be correspondingly good or bad, because a tree is recognized by its fruit (cf. Ecclus 27:6). To speculate on the means—pruning, grafting, watering, fertilizing—is to go beyond the metaphor.

34-35 Then Jesus drives the point home. "You brood of vipers" (v.34; see on 3:7; 23:33) was most likely addressed to the Pharisees in the crowd (cf. vv.23-24), though this is not certain (cf. 7:11). Verse 35 makes a tight connection with v.33: what a person truly is determines what he says and does. Out of the *perisseuma* ("overflow," v.34—what remains, the excess) the "mouth speaks." *Perisseuma* is used in the NT only here and in Mark 8:8; Luke 6:45; 2 Corinthians 8:14 (*bis*) of the heart, the center of human personality (see on 5:8). It is the mouth that reveals what is in the heart. How, then, can those who are evil say anything good? What is needed is a change of heart.

36-37 These two verses occur only in Matthew. That Jesus describes the evil of the "brood of vipers" in terms of their hearts or natures does not thereby excuse them. Far from it! A person will be held accountable on the Day of Judgment for "every careless word" (v.36). The Greek *argos* ("careless") does not refer here to "unfounded" words (JB) but to words that might be thought "insignificant" (Stendahl, Peake) except for their revealing what is in the heart. Jesus is saying that every spoken word reflects the heart's overflow and is known to God. Therefore words are of critical importance (cf. Eph 5:3-4, 12; Col 3:17; James 1:19; 3:1-12).

The change to the second person (v.37) implies that the saying may be proverbial. Here it heightens the warning that what one says about Jesus and his miracles reveals what one is and that he will be judged accordingly. Jesus' authority in saying this is staggering. It is not he who is being assessed when men ask, "Could this be the Son of David?" (v.23), or utter blasphemies (v.24); it is they who are being assessed, and by their words they will be judged.

Notes

36 The syntax is difficult. If πᾶν ῥῆμα ἀργόν (pan rhēma argon, "every careless word") is construed as nominative, there is an awkward anacolouthon (. . . περὶ αὐτοῦ λόγον [peri *autou logon*, lit., "concerning his (or its) word"]; cf. 13:19); but this may be accusative by attraction to the relative ὅ (*ho*, "which").

---

c. Continued confrontation (12:38-42)

1) Request for a sign

12:38

> 38Then some of the Pharisees and teachers of the law said to him, "Teacher, we want to see a miraculous sign from you."

38 One might take *apekrithēsan* ("answered"; NIV, "said") as meaning that the Pharisees and teachers of the law were continuing the controversy. That is possible, and the parallel in Luke 11:29-32 is sufficiently detached from its context to permit this interpretation. But *apekrithēsan* does not always have its full strength in Matthew (see on 11:25); so it seems best not to insist on the continuance of the controversy.

In 9:11 Matthew mentions only Pharisees, whereas the parallel in Mark 2:16 has Pharisees and teachers of the law. On that basis many say Matthew has pruned the expression because in his day, unlike the days of Jesus' ministry, only the Pharisees, understood to represent the rabbis (cf. Introduction, section 11.f), constituted any real opposition. Here, however, the roles are reversed: Mark (8:11) has "Pharisees"; Matthew (12:38) mentions "Pharisees and teachers of the law." Such changes are of little use in establishing Matthew's life-setting.

The Jewish leaders phrased their question respectfully ("Teacher"; see on 8:19) and asked for a "sign" (*sēmeion*), not just for another miracle. Jesus had already done many miracles. Old Testament and intertestamental Jewish literature shed light on the request (cf. K.H. Rengstorf, TDNT, 7:208-21, 225-29; F.J. Helfmeyer, TDOT, 1:167-88; and 1 Sam 2:30-33; 1 Kings 20:1-14; Isa 7:10-25; b *Sanhedrin* 98a; b *Baba Metzia* 59b; cf. O. Linton, "The Demand for a Sign from Heaven [Mk.8,11-12 and Parallels]," ST 19 [1965]: esp. 123ff.). A "sign" was usually some miraculous token to be fulfilled quickly, or at once, to confirm a prophecy. The Jews were not asking for just another miracle, since they had already persuaded themselves that at least some of those Jesus had performed were of demonic agency (12:24); they were asking for a "sign" performed on command to remove what seemed to them to be the ambiguity of Jesus' miracles. (In John "sign" is not so much something people ask for as the evangelist's standard label for what the synoptists call "powers" or "wonders." The "signs" Jesus performs under John's pen bear implicit and explicit symbolic weight.)

2) The sign of Jonah

12:39-42

> 39He answered, "A wicked and adulterous generation asks for a miraculous sign! But none will be given it except the sign of the prophet Jonah. 40For as Jonah was three days and three nights in the belly of a huge fish, so the Son of Man will be three days and three nights in the heart of the earth. 41The men of Nineveh will stand up at the judgment with this generation and condemn it; for they repented at the preaching of Jonah, and now one greater than Jonah is here.

⁴²The Queen of the South will rise at the judgment with this generation and condemn it; for she came from the ends of the earth to listen to Solomon's wisdom, and now one greater than Solomon is here.

39-40 The Pharisees and teachers of the law did not, in Jesus' view, stand alone: they represented this "wicked and adulterous generation" (v.39; cf. 11:16–24). "Adultery" was frequently used by OT prophets to describe the spiritual prostitution and wanton apostasy of Israel (Isa 50:1; 57:3; Jer 3:8; 13:27; 31:32; Ezek 16:15, 32, 35–42; Hos 2:1–7; 3:1 et al.). Here Jesus applies it to his contemporaries as did his brother James later on (James 4:4). Israel had largely abandoned her idolatry and syncretism after the Exile. But now Jesus insists that she was still adulterous in heart. In the past God had graciously granted "signs" to strengthen the faith of the timid (e.g., Abraham [Gen 15]; Gideon [Judg 6:17–24]; Joshua [Josh 10]). Here, however, Jesus says that signs are denied "this wicked and adulterous generation," because they are never to be performed on demand or as a sop to unbelief (cf. 1 Cor 1:22).

In Mark 8:11–12, Jesus refuses to give any sign; but in Matthew and Luke (Q) the sign of Jonah is expected. This has led many to conclude that the reference to Jonah is an unauthentic, late addition (Stendahl, Peake; G. Schmitt, "Das Zeichen Jona," ZNW [1978]: 123–29, suggests that the addition was made in the seventh decade A.D. through the influence of *Lives of the Prophets*). On the other hand, Taylor (*Mark*, p. 363), quoted by Hill (*Matthew*), suggests Mark has abbreviated the original in the interests of his messianic-secret theme so as to produce a flat refusal to provide a sign. But the difference between Mark and the other two synoptists may be more subtle. Rightly understood the sign, which is the exception in Matthew and Luke, is not a sign at all as Jesus' opponents understood the word. It becomes a sign only for those with eyes to see. In that sense there is no exception: Jesus offers no miraculous token on demand. That is Mark's point, a point not contradicted by the "exception" the other synoptists record.

But what is "the sign of Jonah"? This question is tied to the absence of 12:40 from the parallel in Luke and its being regarded as a late addition. The argument, it is said, must therefore run from 12:39 to 12:41; and the sign of Jonah must be his preaching of repentance, a ministry in which Jesus has likewise been engaged. Verse 40 is, then, a late typological addition.

Nevertheless a good case can be made for the authenticity of v.40 (cf. especially France, *Jesus*, pp. 80–82). Luke does not simply "drop out" Matthew 12:40. Rather, following the reference to the "sign of Jonah," Luke writes (11:30): "For as Jonah was a sign to the Ninevites, so also will the Son of Man be to this generation." He then includes the visit of the queen of the South before returning to the men of Nineveh, who will rise up and condemn Jesus' contemporaries (cf. Matt 12:41). In other words Luke, for whom Jonah's preaching is not a sign, does not support the alleged continuity between Matthew 12:39 and 12:41. If this is correct, then either Matthew 12:40 is an enlargement of an original but cryptic Luke 11:30, or else Luke 11:30 is an effort to veil the specificity of an original Matthew 12:40. The latter view is more credible, for Luke has an obvious reason for making the saying more cryptic —viz., the reference to three days and three nights, so readily understood in Matthew's Jewish environment (see below), would be problematic to Luke's readers who would see a conflict with the length of time Jesus was actually in the tomb. The same concern doubtless accounts for Justin Martyr's quoting (*Dialogue* 107:1) Matthew 12:39 and saying that Jesus was speaking cryptically of the Resurrection, though Justin does not actually quote v.40.

The rejection of v.40 is tied to the interpretation of the "sign of Jonah." If v.40 is removed, the "sign" is most likely the preaching. But this is intrinsically unlikely: in both Matthew and Luke the sign is future to Jesus' utterance (Matt 12:39; Luke 11:30), which suits Jesus' death and resurrection but not his preaching. Verse 40 therefore becomes an integral part of Matthew's pericope. And the contention of R.A. Edwards (*The Sign of Jonah* [London: SCM, 1971], pp. 25ff.), that the sayings of this pericope are in the form of a new *Gattung*, a Christian invention after Jesus' time, has been disproved by lists of much older examples of the same form (cf. Daryl Schmidt, "The LXX Gattung 'Prophetic Correlative,'" JBL 96 [1977]: 517–22).

In "the sign of Jonah," then, "of Jonah" must be construed as an epexegetic genitive (Zerwick, par. 45; Turner, *Syntax*, p. 214). It is the sign that Jonah himself was, not the sign given him or presented by him. This interpretation commonly accepts the view that the Ninevites learned what had happened to Jonah and how he got to their city. Jonah himself thus served as a "sign" to the Ninevites, for he appeared to them as one who had been delivered from certain death (cf. J. Jeremias, TDNT, 3:409; Eugene H. Merrill, "The Sign of Jonah," JETS 23 [1980]: 23–30). As Jonah was three days and three nights in the belly of the fish, so the Son of Man— seen here in his suffering role (see on 8:20)—will be three days and three nights in the "heart [perhaps an echo of Jonah 2:3; cf. Ps 46:2] of the earth"—a reference to Jesus' burial, not his descent into Hades. That is to say, Jesus' preaching will be attested by a deliverance like Jonah's only still greater; therefore there will be greater condemnation for those who reject the significance of Jonah's deliverance.

Some scholars perceive the strength of the argument for the authenticity of this pericope but interpret v.40 as if it were referring to the "sign" of the coming Son of Man (24:30), or to Jesus' vague awareness that he must die sometime, or that Jesus by his suffering will carry the truth of God to the Gentiles as Jonah did. But this overlooks the connection between Jonah and Jesus established by the text. Grant the authenticity of v.40, and the only legitimate conclusion is that Jesus knew long in advance about his death, burial, and resurrection, and saw his life moving toward that climax; and the christological implications must not be avoided.

Jonah spent "three days and three nights" in the fish (Jonah 1:17). But if the normal sequence of Passion Week is correct (see on 26:17–30), Jesus was in the tomb only about thirty-six hours. Since they included parts of three days, by Jewish reckoning Jesus was buried "three days" or, to put it another way, he rose "on the third day" (16:21). But this does not cover more than two nights. Some advocate a Wednesday crucifixion date (see on 26:17); but though that allows for "three days and three nights," it runs into difficulty with "on the third day." In rabbinical thought a day and a night make an *ōnāh*, and a part of an *ōnāh* is as the whole (cf. SBK, 1:649, for references; cf. further 1 Sam 30:12–13; 2 Chron 10:5, 12; Esth 4:16; 5:1). Thus according to Jewish tradition, "three days and three nights" need mean no more than "three days" or the combination of any part of three separate days.

41 The first point of comparison between Jonah and Jesus is that they were both delivered from death—a deliverance that attested the trustworthiness of their preaching. The second point of comparison is the different responses of the hearers. The men of Nineveh repented. But even though "something [neuter, as in 11:19;

12:6; NIV, 'one'] greater than Jonah is here"—the reference is to Jesus, not his deliverance, because the comparison is with Jonah, not his deliverance—the people of Jesus' day—"this generation" (cf. v.39)—did not repent. Therefore men of Nineveh (the nouns are anarthrous) "will stand up with" this generation at the final judgment—i.e., they will rise to bear witness against them (see on 11:20-24; and on the Semitic legal idiom, cf. Mark 14:57; Black, *Aramaic Approach*, p. 134). Thus Jesus' "sign" does not meet the Jews' demand for a special token (see on v.38). Yet it is the only one he will provide. For his own followers, his authority will be grounded in his death and resurrection. And as for those who do not believe, they will only prove themselves more wicked than the Ninevites.

42 Jonah and Solomon are linked in other Jewish literature (cf. D. Correns, "Jona und Salomo," in Haubeck and Bachmann, pp. 86-94). The nature of the link—Jonah and the queen with "this generation" rising at the Judgment—strongly supports the view that for Jesus, Jonah was a historical person. The queen of the South (the Arabian peninsula, which for the Jews was "at the ends of the earth"; cf. Jer 6:20; Joel 3:8, NASB) was the queen of Sheba (1 Kings 10:1-13), who came to Jerusalem because of reports of Solomon's wisdom. But Jesus is "something greater" (see on v.41) than Solomon; Jesus is the Messiah, who will introduce the promised eschatological age. Therefore the queen of Sheba will rise at the Judgment to join the Ninevites in condemning the unbelieving generation of Jesus' time.

Notes

---

41 The phrase εἰς τὸ κήρυγμα Ἰωνᾶ (*eis to kērygma Iōna*, "at the preaching of Jonah") cannot be final but establishes the ground for the Ninevites' repentance. On this rather rare use of *eis*, cf. Turner, *Syntax*, p. 255; Zerwick, par. 106; BDF, par. 207(1). See note on 10:41.

---

d. *The return of the evil spirit*

12:43-45

> [43]"When an evil spirit comes out of a man, it goes through arid places seeking rest and does not find it. [44]Then it says, 'I will return to the house I left.' When it arrives, it finds the house unoccupied, swept clean and put in order. [45]Then it goes and takes with it seven other spirits more wicked than itself, and they go in and live there. And the final condition of that man is worse than the first. That is how it will be with this wicked generation."

The parallel in Luke 11:24-26 is, as here, tied to the Beelzebub controversy, though the preceding verse is different (Luke 11:23 = Matt 12:30). Though many think Luke applies the parable to the individual and Matthew to the nation, this contrast is too facile. Luke omits (according to the best texts) the connective *de* ("and" or "but"). This suggests an independent saying that fits the movement of the chapter but is not meant to be tied too tightly to the verse preceding it. The warning in both Matthew and Luke is not (contra Marshall, *Luke*, p. 479) aimed at "those who exorcise demons without giving a positive substitute to their patients." In both Matthew (12:27) and Luke (11:19) the comparison Jesus draws between himself and other exorcists is not meant to prove his superiority but to show that even Jewish exorcists achieve some success in their work by virtue, not of Beelzebub, but of God's power.

This story about the unclean spirit who after being driven out returns with seven wicked spirits goes beyond Jesus' comparison; for Luke (11:21-22) has shown Jesus' authority in binding Satan, and Matthew (12:38-42) has insisted that Jesus is greater than Jonah and Solomon. In other words, in both Gospels this pericope is set in a milieu of veiled messianic claims. The point here and in Luke is that those who through the kingdom power of God experience exorcisms must beware of neutrality toward Jesus the Messiah, for neutrality opens the door to seven demons worse than the one driven out. Commitment to Jesus is essential. Thus the pericope supports Luke 11:23, which, like Matthew 12:30, rules out neutrality.

Against the broader background in Matthew of the Beelzebub controversy and the sign of Jonah, in sweeping out the house and ridding it of its demons, Jesus has been testifying to the presence of the kingdom (12:28). Yet many of that "wicked and adulterous generation" are so neutral toward him they require signs (12:38) and fail to see that one greater than Jonah and Solomon has come. Luke 11:23 does not mean that Matthew 12:43-45 and Luke 11:24-26 refer to individual demon possession in contrast to the national rejection of Jesus Messiah portrayed in Matthew; on the contrary, both evangelists deal with the same issue, the extreme danger of being neutral toward Jesus (see further on v.45).

43 When an evil spirit (see on 8:28; 10:1) leaves a man (lit., "the man," but the article presents a typical case), it goes "through arid places" in search of rest. This conforms to the view that demons have an affinity for such places (Tobit 8:3; cf. Rev 18:2). Ultimately, however, they seek another body in order to do even more harm.

44 Verse 43 implies the possibility of repossession. While v.44 may be theoretically interpreted as a universal fact of experience, that would make Jesus' exorcisms an invitation to catastrophe. So it is better to take the language of the text as a Semitic paratactic conditional protasis to v.45 (i.e., "If the demon on his arrival finds the house unoccupied, etc."; cf. H.S. Nyberg, "Zum grammatischen Verständnis von Matth.12,44f.," *Coniectanea Neotestamentica* 13 [1949]: 1-11; Jeremias, *Parables*, pp. 197f.) or to take the details of the story as representing a dangerous contingency (Beyer, 1:281-86).

45 Though the seven evil spirits may have been harder to drive out than just one (cf. Mark 5:9; 9:29), the text only mentions their greater wickedness. The man from whom the demon had been driven out is now in a far worse condition than before. Jesus' final statement in this pericope—"That is how it will be with this wicked generation" (omitted by Luke)—does not change the point of the story from one of demon possession to the nation's failure to recognize Jesus, for both Matthew and Luke understand the story to demand recognition of Jesus Messiah. But what Matthew adds (1) closes off the main part of the pericope by referring again to "this wicked generation" (cf. 12:39)—a common but overlooked Matthean device (see on 15:20)—and (2) makes the warning less cryptic than Luke (cf. v.40; Luke 11:30).

Though Luke knows the danger into which the Jews' rejection of Jesus (Luke 21:20–24) will place them, this is not for him, as it is for Matthew, a major theme.

6. Doing the Father's will

12:46–50

> 46While Jesus was still talking to the crowd, his mother and brothers stood outside, wanting to speak to him. 47Someone told him, "Your mother and brothers are standing outside, wanting to speak to you."
> 48He replied to him, "Who is my mother, and who are my brothers?" 49Pointing to his disciples, he said, "Here are my mother and my brothers. 50For whoever does the will of my Father in heaven is my brother and sister and mother."

Here Matthew basically follows Mark 3:31–35 (cf. Luke 8:19–21; John 7:3–5), though he omits the background in Mark 3:20–21. As a result these verses are not so much a confrontation between Jesus and his family as a statement about what it really means to be a disciple of Jesus and to be totally committed to him. The way for us to be as close to Jesus as his nearest and dearest is to do the will of his Father.

46–47 The obvious implication is that Jesus is inside the house (cf. Mark 3:20, 31). Though v.47 is omitted in many MSS, probably by homoeoteleuton (words, clauses, or sentences with similar endings being dropped by oversight: both v.46 and v.47 end in *lalēsai* ["to speak"]), it was likely in the original text and clearly helps the sense of the pericope. While the verse might represent assimilation to Mark 3:32, this would not explain *tō legonti autō* ("to the one who had spoken to him," omitted from v.48 in NIV), which presupposes v.47.

The most natural way to understand "brothers" (v.46) is that the term refers to sons of Mary and Joseph and thus to brothers of Jesus on his mother's side. To support the dogma of Mary's perpetual virginity, a notion foreign to the NT and to the earliest church fathers, Roman Catholic scholars have suggested that "brothers" refers either to Joseph's sons by an earlier marriage or to sons of Mary's sister, who had the same name (cf. Lagrange; McHugh, pp. 200ff.). Certainly "brothers" can have a wider meaning than male relatives (Acts 22:1). Yet it is very doubtful whether such a meaning is valid here for it raises insuperable problems. For instance, if "brothers" refers to Joseph's sons by an earlier marriage, not Jesus but Joseph's firstborn would have been legal heir to David's throne. The second theory —that "brothers" refers to sons of a sister of Mary also named "Mary"—faces the unlikelihood of two sisters having the same name. All things considered, the attempts to extend the meaning of "brothers" in this pericope, despite McHugh's best efforts, are nothing less than farfetched exegesis in support of a dogma that originated much later than the NT (see on 1:25; Luke 2:7; cf. Broadus on 13:55–56).

48–50 Jesus' searching question (v.48) and its remarkable answer (vv.49–50) in no way diminish his mother and brothers but simply give the priority to his Father and doing his will. "For, had He not entered into earthly kinship solely for the sake of the higher spiritual relationship which He was about to found . . . ? Thus, it was not that Christ set lightly by His Mother, but that He confounded not the means with the end" (LTJM, 1:577). Henceforth the disciples are the only "family" Jesus recognizes.

The metaphorical nature of v.49 is shown by the "ands" (v.50): "my brother and sister [Jesus had physical sisters; cf. 13:56] and mother" instead of ". . . or . . . or." We do not make ourselves Jesus' close relatives by doing the will of his heavenly Father. Rather, doing the Father's will *identifies* us as his mother and sisters and brothers (cf. 7:21). The doing of that will turns on obedience to Jesus and his teaching, according to Matthew, for it was Jesus who preeminently revealed the will of the Father (cf. 11:27). This means that Jesus' words in this pericope are full of christological implications, but they also establish the basic importance of the community now beginning to form around him, God's chosen Servant who, despite rising opposition, will lead justice to victory (12:18, 20).